MW00810416

Volume One of Andrew Greenwell's English translation of Denis the Carthusian's *Commentary on the Psalms* is a remarkable achievement, offering wide access to a text of great importance. Denis' erudition, insight and originality, as well as his refined ability to keep various interlocutors in view are robustly displayed. Readers will find his attention to the relationship between the letter of history and the spiritual senses particularly engaging. The wealth of helpful notes in this edition will help us all gain a deeper appreciation for the workings of one of the late medieval world's most respected voices. A translator has to share something of the spirit of the original author, and this translation is the work of one who certainly does.

—✠ MOST REV. DANIEL E. FLORES, Bishop of Brownsville, TX

In this impeccably well-done translation from Latin of the beautiful commentary on Psalms 1–25 of Denis the Carthusian, Andrew Greenwell has demonstrated that he is precisely the kind of layman Pope St. John Paul II called for in his 1988 post-synodal apostolic exhortation to the lay faithful. He is in love with the Lord Jesus Christ and totally given over to the service of His Mystical Body, the Church. I highly recommend this beautiful work. I am deeply grateful to Andrew for offering it to all of us as a resource.

—DEACON KEITH FOURNIER, J.D., M.T.S., M.Phil., Dean of Catholic Identity Director of Deacon Formation General Counsel Catholic, Diocese of Tyler, Texas

Greenwell's welcome translation of Denis the Carthusian's first major work is a gift to those who seek primarily to understand the Psalms in the context of revelation and faith above the narrower priorities of modern academia. Denis' richly Christological exposition of each psalm, applying the four senses of scripture, is witness to Carthusian life faithfully and fruitfully lived.

—FR. HUGH SOMERVILLE KNAPMAN, OSB, Monk of Douai; author of *Ecumenism of Blood: Heavenly Hope for Earthly Communion*

We can find no better prayers than the ones God Himself has given us. The Psalms are the heart of Holy Scripture, the summary of all its treasures, the daily bread of Christ's faithful. The mysteries contained in the Psalms are simple, and yet so sublime, that we need a guide to open up the Scriptures to us. Denis the Carthusian, a fine connoisseur of the Psalms, is an exemplary guide. This English translation is a remarkable accomplishment, for which we are all indebted to Andrew Greenwell.

—DOM PIUS MARY NOONAN, OSB, Notre Dame Priory, Tasmania

Now here is a treasure that those who take their *lectio divina* seriously appreciate beyond telling: Denis the Carthusian's commentary on the Psalms — no less!

—ABBOT PHILIP ANDERSON, OSB, Clear Creek Abbey

# BEATUS VIR

D.DIONYSIVS CARTHVSIEÑ
DOCTOR EXTATICVS.

BENEDIC
TVS DEVS
IN SECVIA

# BEATUS VIR

DENIS THE CARTHUSIAN

## COMMENTARY
### *on the*
### DAVIDIC
# *Psalms*

## VOLUME I
## [PSALMS 1-25]

*Which are most learnedly explained, to the degree able,
in their multiple senses, namely* LITERAL, ALLEGORICAL,
TROPOLOGICAL, *&* ANAGOGICAL, *with nothing except
the most sound Scriptures of both Testaments.*

*Translation & Introduction by*
ANDREW M. GREENWELL

AROUCA
PRESS

Arouca Press
PO Box 55003
Bridgeport PO
Waterloo, ON N2J3G0
Canada
www.aroucapress.com
Send inquiries to info@aroucapress.com


Book and cover design by
Michael Schrauzer

## DEDICATION

*To my children,*
*Elizabeth Grace, Mary Abigail, and Christopher Michael*

*Ecce haereditas Domini, filii; merces, fructus ventris.*
*Sicut sagittae in manu potentis, ita filii excussorum.*
*Beatus vir qui implevit desiderium suum ex ipsis:*
*non confundetur cum loquetur inimics suis in porta.*
— Psalm 126:3–5

*Quas tibi, Deus meus, voces dedi, cum legerem psalmos David, cantica fidelia, sonos pietatis excludentes turgidum spiritum.... Quas tibi voces dabam in Psalmis illis et quomodo in te inflammabar ex eis et accendebar eos recitare, si possem, toto orbe terrarum adversus typhum generis humani! Et tamen toto orbe cantantur, et non est qui se abscondat a calore tuo.*

—St. Augustine, *Confessions*, IX, 4, 8.

# CONTENTS

*Abbreviations* . . . . . . . . . . . . . . . . . . . . . . . . . . . . . xii

*An Introduction to the Life, Times, & Works*
  *of Denis the Carthusian* . . . . . . . . . . . . . . . . . . . . . . xiii

*Bibliography & Further Reading* . . . . . . . . . . . . . . . . . . . .xviii

*Introduction to Denis the Carthusian's*
  *Commentary on the Psalms* . . . . . . . . . . . . . . . . . . . . xix

*Acknowledgments* . . . . . . . . . . . . . . . . . . . . . . . . . xxxviii

COMMENTARY ON THE DAVIDIC PSALMS . . . . . . . . . . . . . . 1

PSALM 1 . . . . . . . . . . . . . . . . . . . . . . . . . . . . . . . . 25

PSALM 2 . . . . . . . . . . . . . . . . . . . . . . . . . . . . . . . . 45

PSALM 3 . . . . . . . . . . . . . . . . . . . . . . . . . . . . . . . . 59

PSALM 4 . . . . . . . . . . . . . . . . . . . . . . . . . . . . . . . . 73

PSALM 5 . . . . . . . . . . . . . . . . . . . . . . . . . . . . . . . . 87

PSALM 6 . . . . . . . . . . . . . . . . . . . . . . . . . . . . . . . . 97

PSALM 7 . . . . . . . . . . . . . . . . . . . . . . . . . . . . . . . . 121

PSALM 8 . . . . . . . . . . . . . . . . . . . . . . . . . . . . . . . . 137

PSALM 9 . . . . . . . . . . . . . . . . . . . . . . . . . . . . . . . . 163

PSALM 10 . . . . . . . . . . . . . . . . . . . . . . . . . . . . . . . . 177

PSALM 11 . . . . . . . . . . . . . . . . . . . . . . . . . . . . . . . . 185

PSALM 12 . . . . . . . . . . . . . . . . . . . . . . . . . . . . . . . . 193

PSALM 13 . . . . . . . . . . . . . . . . . . . . . . . . . . . . . . . . 209

PSALM 14 . . . . . . . . . . . . . . . . . . . . . . . . . . . . . . . . 217

PSALM 15 . . . . . . . . . . . . . . . . . . . . . . . . . . . . . . . . 235

PSALM 16 . . . . . . . . . . . . . . . . . . . . . . . . . . . . . . . . 255

PSALM 17 . . . . . . . . . . . . . . . . . . . . . . . . . . . . . . . . 309

PSALM 18 . . . . . . . . . . . . . . . . . . . . . . . . . . . . . . . . 323

PSALM 19 . . . . . . . . . . . . . . . . . . . . . . . . . . . . . . . . 333

PSALM 20 . . . . . . . . . . . . . . . . . . . . . . . . . . . . . . . . 349

PSALM 21 . . . . . . . . . . . . . . . . . . . . . . . . . . . . . . . . 389

PSALM 22 . . . . . . . . . . . . . . . . . . . . . . . . . . . . . . . . 401

PSALM 23 . . . . . . . . . . . . . . . . . . . . . . . . . . . . . . . . 411

PSALM 24 . . . . . . . . . . . . . . . . . . . . . . . . . . . . . . . . 427

PSALM 25 . . . . . . . . . . . . . . . . . . . . . . . . . . . . . . . . 453

# ABBREVIATIONS

DS  Heinrich Denziger, *Enchiridion Symbolorum Definitionum et Declarationum de Rebus Fidei et Morum* (*Compendium of Creeds, Definitions, and Déclarations on Matters of Faith and Morals*) (P. Hünerman, ed.) (Robert Fastiggi and Anne Englund Nash, eds., Eng. ed.) (43rd ed.) (San Francisco: Ignatius Press 2012).

PG  *Patrologiae cursus completus. Series Graeca.* Ed. J.-P. Migne. Paris: Migne, 1857–1886.

PL  *Patrologiae cursus completus. Series Latina.* Ed. J.-P. Migne. Paris: Migne, 1844–1864.

ST  St. Thomas Aquinas, *Summa Theologiae* (corpusthomisticum.org)

CCC  Catechism of the Catholic Church

# AN INTRODUCTION
*to the*
# LIFE, TIMES & WORKS
OF
# Denis the Carthusian

### ELIZABETH G. G. SNELLER

ENIS DE LEEUWIS WAS BORN IN THE VIL-
lage of Rijkel in 1402 A.D. Rijkel is a quaint village in the County
of Hesbaye, in what is modern day Belgium. Hesbaye, commonly called
Hasbania in medieval Latin, is nestled amongst an undulation of hillocks
near the Maas River in Limburg province. Denis would have spent his
youth surrounded by the idyllic Flemish countryside. Sint-Truiden, the
abbey and oppidum city, was but a short distance away. At a very young
age, Denis possessed great discipline, a naturally pious spirit, and an
unslakable thirst for knowledge. Denis attended day school at Sint-Truiden where he showed great enthusiasm and an above par aptitude in
his studies. In 1415, he began attending the abbey boarding school at
Zwolle in the Dutch province of Overijssel. The school at Zwolle was
immensely prestigious at the time, attracting promising young minds
from across Germany and the Low Countries. While at Zwolle, Denis
began his philosophical studies and had his first contacts with Modern
Devotion (*devotio moderna*), and became deeply drawn to monastic life.
At this time, he perfected his Latin and began to develop his unique
writing style. In 1417, Denis returned home after the death of his teacher
John Cele; however, his stay was to be brief.

By the age of eighteen, Denis had found his vocation. He felt a strong
affinity to the Carthusian order and he applied for admission at the monastery at Roermond. He was denied entry due to his age — ordinarily, one
had to be twenty years old to be admitted to the Carthusian order, and
Denis was two years shy of that age. The prior at Roermond, however, did
not want Denis to lose hope; he strongly advised Denis to enroll at the
University of Cologne and further his education until he was old enough
to be admitted to Roermond. Denis followed that advice, and, in the two

years that followed, Denis immersed himself in the study of theology and philosophy. At Cologne, Denis began his study in the *via Thomae*, and Thomas Aquinas would remain his *Doctor ordinarius* throughout his life,[1] even though Denis would come to oppose some of Aquinas's foremost views, as early as 1430.[2] This later divergence from a strict Thomistic Scholasticism follows the path taken by many of the Albertist thinkers, led principally by Heymerich van de Velde,[3] who dominated the faculty University of Cologne at the time of Denis's academic pursuits there.[4]

In 1423 or 1424, Denis matriculated with a Master of Arts[5] from Cologne. He entered the charterhouse at Roermond with great haste and devoted himself to the way of the Carthusians — a life of quiet, thoughtful devotion in an effort, by grace, to develop as deep an understanding and love of God that one can hope to achieve through contemplation and prayer. Denis would partake in the night Office, Mass, and occasional recreation with his brothers, but the rest of his time was dedicated to "contemplation and action."[6] He divided his days into strict halves. The first half was to be spent in solitary prayer. The second half belonged to writing and study. Denis's strict adherence to this rigid schedule is possibly why he was the most prolific writer of the Middle Ages; he produced an estimated four times as many works as that most inexhaustible Doctor of the Church, Saint Augustine.[7] He reserved only three hours for nightly rest.

1   Kent Emery, Jr., "Cognitive Theory and the Relation Between the Scholastic and Mystical Modes of Theology: Why Denys the Carthusian Outlawed Durandus of Saint-Pourçain," *Crossing Boundaries at Medieval Universities* (Leiden: Brill, 2011), 145–171. (ed. Spencer E. Young).

2   *Ibid.* In this article, Emery gives a brief sketch of Denis's life, peers, and studies at Cologne before delving deeply into his later stances. It is interesting to note that [Denys] "incepted under the Master Guillelmus de Breda, with whom many years later he would engage in a bitter dispute about simony."

3   Alessandro Palazzo, "Denis the Carthusian," *Encyclopedia of Medieval Philosophy: Philosophy Between 500 and 1500* (London: Springer, 2011), 258–60. (ed., Henrik Lagerlund).

4   Emery Jr., "Cognitive Theory," 145–46.

5   *Ibid.* Emery notes that Denis did not study theology at Cologne in the traditional sense, due to both his quick entry into Roermond and the habit of the secular masters at Cologne to teach philosophy via the *Summae* and commentaries on 13th century thinkers such as Thomas and Albert, in the *viae antiquae*.

6   Terrence O'Reilly, Introduction in *The Spiritual Writings of Denis the Carthusian* (Dublin: Four Courts Press, 2005), ix–xiv. (trans., Íde Ní Riain).

7   Kent Emery, Jr., "At the Outer Limits of Authenticity: Denys the Carthusian's Critique of Duns Scotus and His Followers," *Philosophy and Theology in the Long Middle Ages: A Tribute to Stephen F. Brown* (Leiden: Brill, 2011), 641–71. (eds., Kent Emery, Russell Friedman, Andreas Speer).

Despite the eremitic nature of the Carthusian *Statutes* which govern their way of life, Denis was not as isolated from his fellow man as it might initially seem. He engaged in spirited correspondence with many of his contemporaries, particularly Nicolas of Cusa of the Cologne School,[8] to whom he dedicated some of his writings.[9] He was an avid, keen participant in doctrinal disputes that were sparking fiery discourse across the late medieval academic world. Denis embodied all of the spiritual concepts of the 15th century in both his many works and in his personal life, including scholastic philosophies, mysticism, the Modern Devotion, monastic theology, and *sermones ad saeculares*.[10] Due to the great breadth of topics broached by the busy Denis, one might rightfully dub him "the last omnicompetent theologian"[11] He was often asked for his opinion on a great variety of topics by both secular and ecclesiastical authorities. He was thus acutely aware of the maladies, both social and spiritual, that beleaguered the late medieval world. His advice exhibits a fundamental conservatism and an expressed and profound hope for a return to a more pious time, therefore staying true to the motto of Denis's Carthusian Order: *Stat crux dum volvitur orbis*.[12]

Denis composed over one hundred and fifty works during his life. He drew his inspiration from Aristotle, the Vulgate, Thomas Aquinas, Henry of Ghent, Albert the Great, and the 15th century Albertists.[13] His body of work is driven by his three great enthusiasms: sacred Scripture, Thomas Aquinas, and Dionysius the Pseudo-Areopagite.[14] He created a three-tiered order of wisdom that helped him to organize his writings: 'natural wisdom naturally acquired,' 'supernatural wisdom naturally acquired,' and 'supernatural wisdom supernaturally bestowed.'[15]

---

8  Andrea Fiamma, "Nicholas of Cusa and the So-called Cologne School of the 13th and 14th Centuries," *Archives d'histoire doctrinale et littéraire du Moyen Âge*, 2017/1 (Volume 84), 91–128. See this for further reading on Cusanus and his relationship to the Cologne School.

9  Palazzo, 258.

10  Kent Emery, Jr., "Monastic, scholastic and mystical theologies from the later Middle Ages," *Variorum collected studies* (London: Ashgate, 1996), 561

11  Denys Turner, "Why Did Denys the Carthusian Write Sermones ad Saeculares?" Medieval Monastic Preaching (Leiden: Brill, 1998), 20 (ed., Carolyn Muessig).

12  "The Cross is steady as the world turns."

13  Palazzo, 258.

14  O'Reilly, x.

15  Kent Emery, Jr., "The Matter and Order of Philosophy According to Denys the Carthusian," *Was ist Philosophie im Mittelalter? Akten des X. Internationalen Kongresses für Mittelalterliche Philosophie der Société Internationale pour l'Etude de la Philosophie Médiévale, 25. bis 30. August 1997 in Erfurt* (Miscellanea Mediaevalia 26

*De Lumine Christianae Theoriae* was his first and most sweeping opus—a work where "he managed to deftly address all of the vital topics of his day displaying a complete mastery of the doctrines of all the major ancient, Arabic, and Jewish philosophers."[16] Denis composed commentaries on the works of Peter Lombard, Boethius, his favorite, the Pseudo-Dionysius, and John Climacus. He wrote over nine hundred sermons. His commentary on the Vulgate, which began with his *Commentary on the Psalms*, earned papal praise, while his many treaties, such as his *Summa Fidei Orthodoxæ* and *Compendium Theologicum*, cemented his reputation as a theologian. His most applauded philosophical treatises include *De Ente et Essentia, Compendium Philosophicum, De Venustate Mundi et Pulchritudine Dei.* The most recent compilation of his massive body of work, published between 1896 and 1935, spans forty-three hefty volumes in quarto. His last work was *De Meditatione,* which was completed in 1469.

This remarkable learning and even more remarkable output was achieved within the silence of Denis's Charterhouse, save the precious few excursions he made outside of its walls. This unusual activity, however, lead to some conflict with the cenobitic community of Roermond, some of which viewed these intellectual efforts with suspicion. An example of this is an inquiry put forth by the Carthusians in 1446 into Denis's activities, and we know of this because of Denis's own response to the complaints made against him.[17] It seems that some of his brothers doubted the seemliness of his extraordinary devotion to writing, scholarship, and discourse with secular and private persons, and so demanded Denis elucidate and defend these activities as consonant with his Carthusian vocation. It seemed to some within his order that his extreme prolificacy had to be incompatible with the demands of the Carthusian *Statutes.* In response, Denis maintained that his writing is a necessary work of tremendous piety and discipline. He insisted that this activity actually bolstered his ability to adhere to the stillness of spirit, silence of voice, and seclusion of body required of him.[18] It may also be that the small Charterhouse could ill afford the great expense of the materials Denis required for his academic and literary pursuits.[19]

---

(Berlin-New York: De Gruyter, 1998), 668 (eds., Jan A. Aertsen and Andreas Speer).

16   Palazzo, 259.

17   Denys the Carthusian, *Protestatio ad Superiorem Suum,* in *Opera omnia,* Tome I, lxxi–lxxii.

18   *Protestatio,* lxxii. "Fecit etiam libentius me manere in solitudine."

19   Denys Turner, "Why Did Denys the Carthusian Write Sermones ad Saeculares?" (Leiden: Brill 1998), 22 (ed., Carolyn Muessig).

In August of 1451, it is believed that he and his peer Nicolas of Cusa embarked on a mission of Papal Legation across the Low Countries and into the Rhineland. Their mission was one of religious renewal and reform, crucial in those times teetering on the brink of the Renaissance.[20] They also cried for a crusade against the ever-encroaching Turks led by Mehmet the Conqueror, to whom Constantinople would tumble a mere two short year later. Denis's world was one of great religious crisis, and Denis's dogged adherence to tradition was reflective of the efforts to address the tumult and upheaval occurring in the medieval Church. He left Roermond again in 1465 for a brief sojourn to the Charterhouse at Vught—he had been assigned to aid in its foundation and increase. His health, once happily robust, began its slow decline. The last years of his life he was wracked with chronic pain, the stone, and sporadic paralysis amongst other corporal ailments. He offered up his suffering to God with a stoicism and quiet serenity and resolve. He died in 1471 at the age of 69.

For centuries after his death, Denis's writings were crucial reading for those who were serious students of philosophy and theology. In the century following his death, a common phrase uttered across academic circles was "He who read Denis, leaves nothing unread."[21] Although a case could clearly be made for his official beatification, none has yet come to fruition. Popularly, he has posthumously been awarded the title of "Doctor Ecstaticus," the Ecstatic Doctor, due to the ecstasies he experienced as a young monk. It is rumored that his writing fingers are incorrupt and that his skull emitted a pleasant aroma upon his exhumation in 1608.

20 O'Reilly, xi–xii.
21 *Qui Dionysium legit, nihil non legit.*

# BIBLIOGRAPHY
# &
# FURTHER READING

## PRIMARY SOURCES

Doctor Ecstaticus D. Dionysius Cartusianus, *Opera omnia, cura et labore monachorum ordinis Cartusiensis*, 43 vols, Montreuil/Tournai/Parkminster: Typis Cartusiae S. M. de Pratis, 1896–1935.

## SECONDARY SOURCES

Emery Jr., "At the Outer Limits of Authenticity: Denys the Carthusian's Critique of Duns Scotus and His Followers." In *Philosophy and Theology in the Long Middle Ages: A Tribute to Stephen F. Brown*. Edited by Kent Emery, Russell Friedman, Andreas Speer. 641–671. Leiden: Brill, 2011.

Emery, Kent Jr., "Cognitive Theory and the Relation Between the Scholastic and Mystical Modes of Theology: Why Denys the Carthusian Outlawed Durandus of Saint-Pourçain." In *Crossing Boundaries at Medieval Universities*. Edited by Spencer E. Young. 145–171. Leiden: Brill, 2011.

Emery, Kent Jr., *Monastic, scholastic and mystical theologies from the later Middle Ages*, Variorum collected studies. 561. London: Ashgate, 1996.

Emery, Kent Jr., "The Matter and Order of Philosophy According to Denys the Carthusian." In *Was ist Philosophie im Mittelalter? Akten des X. Internationalen Kongresses für Mittelalterliche Philosophie der Société Internationale pour l'Etude de la Philosophie Médiévale, 25. bis 30. August 1997 in Erfurt*. (Miscellanea Mediaevalia 26) Edited by Jan A. Aertsen and Andreas Speer. 667–679. Berlin-New York: De Gruyter, 1998.

Fiamma, Andrea, "Nicholas of Cusa and the So-called Cologne School of the 13th and 14th Centuries." In *Archives d'histoire doctrinale et littéraire du Moyen Âge*, 2017/1 (Volume 84), 91-128.

Palazzo, Alessandro. "Denis the Carthusian." In *Encyclopedia of Medieval Philosophy: Philosophy Between 500 and 1500*. Edited by Henrik Lagerlund. 258–260. London: Springer, 2011.

Turner, Denys. "Why Did Denys the Carthusian Write *Sermones ad Saeculares?*" In *Medieval Monastic Preaching*. Edited by Carolyn Muessig. 19–36. Leiden: Brill, 1998.

# INTRODUCTION
## *to*
# DENIS THE CARTHUSIAN'S
# *Commentary on the Psalms*

### THE PSALMS

*Divino afflatu compositos Psalmos, quorum est in sacris litteris collectio, inde ab Ecclesiae exordiis non modo mirifice valuisse constat ad fovendam fidelium pietatem, qui offerebant hostiam laudis semper Deo, id est, fructum labiorum confitentium nomini eius.*[22]

— Pope St. Pius X

HEY DO NOT THINK OF THE PSALMS," Anthony Esolen wrote wistfully about moderns in his *The Hundredfold: Songs for the Lord*.[23] I suppose it is too much to ask *moderns* to think of the Psalms, though we may have a reasonable hope that they would; but *we* Christians certainly ought to *think* of the Psalms. Indeed, we must do even more than *think* of the Psalms; we must *invest* ourselves in them. If Christians do not *invest* in the Psalms—and I mean invest in its etymological sense of clothing ourselves (*investire*) with them, habituating ourselves in them, internalizing them—we are the most pitiable of men. And then, after doing all we can to *internalize* them, we must *externalize* them, for as St. John Paul II noted in his encyclical *Veritatis splendor*: "In the Psalms we are able to find the sense of praise, gratitude, and veneration the chosen people are commanded to adopt towards God's law, together with an exhortation to know it, meditate upon it, and translate it into life."[24]

If the Parable of the Talents has any eschatological purchase, those of us among the faithful who neglect the Psalter may face the ire of

---

22 Pope St. Pius X, *Divino afflatu*. "The collection of Psalms, composed under divine inspiration, and found collected in sacred Scripture, has, from the very beginnings of the Church, shown a wonderful power of fomenting devotion among the Christian faithful, who offered a sacrifice of praise always to God, that is, the fruit of lips confessing his name."

23 Anthony M. Esolen, *The Hundredfold: Songs for the Lord* (San Francisco: Ignatius Press, 2019).

24 John Paul II, *Veritatis Splendor*, 44.

the divine and most benevolent Master. For our Lord left us with the treasure of the Psalter which many of us have treated with malfeasance. While we perhaps are not guilty of burying the Psalter in a field to preserve it out of fear — for very few of us moderns seem to fear the Lord — we ought not for all that pat ourselves on the back. For we may instead be in the even worse state of casually laying  150 Psalms aside — each one worth, in a spiritual sense, substantially more than a talent — on a shelf or a coffee table out of a lukewarm ambivalence.

The Church teaches that the Eucharist, the Sacrifice of the Mass, is the "summit of the Christian life."[25] And this is so. Yet for there to be a summit, there must be a base; like castles, there are no "summits in the air." The base, then, of that summit that is the Eucharist and the Mass is the Psalter, which comes to us in a most usable, ordered form in the *Divine Office*, the official, public prayer of the Church. This foundational aspect of the Psalter is why the "book of Psalms has ever been one main portion of the devotions of the Christian Church, in public and in private, since that Church was." [26]

The centrality of the Psalms in guiding and giving structure to the Christian *conversatio* or manner of life is unassailable. The frequency by which the Psalms are uttered by our mouths and, more importantly, how deeply imbedded they are in our hearts — how often we think of them and act upon them — is a measure of the health, at least by a Christian metric, of one's personal and communal spiritual life. In a work erroneously attributed to St. John Chrysostom (and so dubbed written by Pseudo-Chrysostom), the state of a healthy society requires the Psalms of David to be "first, middle, and last" in our interior and external life. Καὶ πρῶτος καὶ μέσος καὶ τελευταῖος: *et primus et medius et postremus*. The Psalms ought to be our companions during our vigils, at our deaths, in our monasteries and convents and hermitages, true, but even among young maidens twisting the threads of the warp in plying the woof.[27] In a word: everywhere. The Psalter should be heard, to paraphrase and adapt St. Teresa of Avila, among the pots and pans.

St. Benedict of course knew this: contrary to moderns, he thought deeply about the Psalms. And, since *operatio sequitur esse*, action follows upon being, Benedict structured his famous Rule — it is nothing other than a written Constitution of how one ought to be, and therefore to

---

25  CCC § 1324 (quoting VII, LG, ii).
26  John Henry Newman, Sermon 18, *Sermons Bearing on Subjects of the Day* (New York: Longmans, Green & Co. 1898), 256.
27  PG 64, 12–13.

live — to assure that all 150 Psalms were prayed by his monks every week.[28]

Informed and fueled by the Psalms, the impetus of the Holy Spirit, and his famous rule, St. Benedict — and those thousands upon thousands of Benedictines who came after him — served as messengers of peace, effectors of union, masters of civil culture, and heralds of the Christian religion and monastic life in the West. In short, the Psalter helped order both private and public life in the European Continent, and this marvelous accomplishment earned St. Benedict the title of Patron of Europe.[29] If Faith is Europe, and Europe is the Faith, as Hilaire Belloc succinctly put it,[30] it is in very large part because of the Psalms. Without the Psalms there is no Christendom.

The Psalms, of course, are a Christian patrimony that came to us from the Jews. While the Law was stripped of its judicial and ceremonial precepts as the Old Covenant was replaced by the New Law of the Gospel, the Psalms slid easily without any accommodation from one dispensation to another not only without diminution, but with an increase. So as St. John Henry Newman observed: "if there be one thing more than another Jewish in our received form of religion, it is the use of the Psalter."[31] This most Jewish patrimony was in a way plundered from the Jews, sort of like the Jews plundered the Egyptians of their treasures centuries earlier to worship God in the wilderness. And this spiritual plunder was naturally and organically transplanted from Jerusalem to Christian soil, not unlike the Malbec grape went from France to Argentina.

Now, since we have brought up the topic of wine, we might recall that Jesus taught that no one ought to put new wine into old wineskins; otherwise, the new wine will burst them. New wine must be put into new wineskins the Divine Vintner says; thereby, both are preserved (Luke 5:37). Yet Jesus also said that no one drinking old wine wants the new. For, "the old is better" (Luke 5:38).

What do new wine and old wineskins have to do with the Psalms? Well, this: the Psalms are both *old* wine *and new* wine. In their old sense, their literal sense, they deal with David and such things as his trials with Saul, his sorrow in losing his friend Jonathan. They deal with his repentance for sins brought on by his lust for Bathsheba, including the murder of Uriah, and his battle against the Philistines and Israel's other enemies. They involve the historical recollection of God's favor in the Exodus

---

28  *Reg. Ben.* xviii.
29  Paul VI, *Pacius Nuntius*, AAS 56 (1964), 965–967 (Oct. 24, 1964).
30  Hilaire Belloc, *Europe and the Faith* (New York: Paulist Press 1921), viii.
31  Newman, *op. cit.*, 231.

from Egypt, and the sorrows of the Babylonian captivity. They refer to the blood of temple worship, with the sacrifice of goats and bulls, and turtledoves and bread, and even with swallows flying in and out of temple heights. In his *Explanation of the Psalms*, St. Robert Bellarmine calls the Psalms a "compendium and summation" of Jewish sacred history, of the Law, and of the Prophets. All these, Bellarmine says, are comprehended "entirely by the Psalms of David in a most concise manner."[32] This is the old wine, what we might call the old Psalms, the *Psalmi veteres*.

But for the Christian, the Psalms also — and preeminently — spoke of something *new*: Jesus Christ, the Messiah King, the Lord who said to his Lord, sit at my right hand, the Priest forever according to the order of Melchisedech.[33] In a manner of speaking, all the Apostles and the early disciples of Jesus were like St. Paul. The scales had to fall from their eyes, and by grace and faith in the teachings and deeds of Jesus, and by the inspiration of the Holy Spirit, they understood the Psalms *anew*. By the grace of God and the "instinct" of the Holy Spirit, they *saw* the *sensus plenior*, the deeper Christological message, within the Psalms. To switch senses, they heard Christ's *voice* in the Psalms. And, to switch senses again, relished in this Christological way, the Psalms retained the taste of the *old wine*, the taste of which they had enjoyed from their youth. But from this new Messianic point of view the Psalms were also *new wine*. The Psalms thus (to change sense yet again) had gained an entirely different spiritual *bouquet*. The best wine had been saved until the last, when the Apostles had the "sober intoxication" or "drunken soberness" of the Spirit. By being born again, that is, by being made *anew*,[34] they also became *new* wineskins which could readily hold this *new* wine without bursting. As St. Paul says, "if then any be in Christ a new creature, the old things are passed away, behold *all things are made new*."[35] And this, presumably, included the Psalms. As St. John Henry Newman observed, this Christological meaning of the Psalms is not "occasional or faint." Rather "it must run through it; it must be strong, definite, and real."[36] The Psalms, Newman says, may and should be made "to breathe of Christ."[37] "We ought," Denis the Carthusian agrees, "as much as possible refer" the Psalms "to Christ."[38]

---

32  Roberti Bellarmini, *Explanatio in Psalmos* (Lugduni: Antonium Beaujollin 1690), praef.
33  Ps. 109(110):1, 4.
34  John 3:3, 7.
35  2 Cor. 5:17.
36  Newman, *op. cit.*, 257.
37  *Ibid.*, 258.
38  Article XXI (Psalm 5:1).

The Church hears voices in the Psalms the Jew did not hear. Indeed, what marvelous voices! Augustine was later to identify these voices in his own commentary on the Psalms, the famous *Enarrationes in Psalmos*. As it turned out, there are many voices in the Psalms other than merely the voice of David. There is the *vox de Christo*, the voice about Christ. There is the *vox Christi*, the voice of Christ. There is the *vox ad Christum*, the voice to Christ. There is, moreover, a double voice, a voice where the head and the body, the *totus Christus*, join. There is thus the *vox de Ecclesia* in the Psalms, the voice about the Church, and the *vox Ecclesiae*, the voice of the Church, which has incorporated the Psalms into her liturgy — the Mass and the Divine Office. So in Christ, the *Psalmi veteres* — though no jot or tittle was changed — became the *Psalmi novi*. The Psalms were then both old and new and fitted for new men made new by the new Adam.

## THE COMMENTARIES

*Proportionable to the excellence of the Psalms,*
*has been the number of their expositors.*
— George Horne[39]

The Church has always recognized the importance of the Psalms. Indeed, the Psalms already season the Gospels with salt and they pepper St. Paul's epistles. And it was not long after that that homilies and commentaries were written on some or all of them by learned and holy men.[40] Some of the better known of these works that have come down to us include Eusebius, Bishop of Caesarea's *Commentary on the Psalms*, St. Hilary's *Homilies on the Psalms* and *Tractates on the Psalms*, St. Basil's *Homilies on the Psalms*, St. Gregory of Nyssa's *On the Inscriptions of the Psalms*, St. John Chrysostom's *Commentary on the Psalms*, St. Ambrose and his *Exposition on the Psalms*, St. Jerome — who of course translated the Psalms from the Greek and then again from the Hebrew into Latin — also wrote small commentaries, the *Commentarioli* and his *Tractates* on the Psalms, St. Augustine's *Expositions on the Psalms*, and Cassiodorus's *Exposition on the Psalms*.

---

39 George Horne, *A Commentary on the Book of Psalms* (London: Longman & Co., 1856), vi.

40 Some of the Commentaries are actually aggregations of homilies. Some, like Cassiodorus's *Commentary* is a commentary strictly so called. Some, like Augustine's *Expositions on the Psalms* are a combination of both. St. Augustine's *Expositions on the Psalms* has the dignity of being "the only collection of expositions on the entire Psalter from any of the fathers of the western church." Susan Gillingham, *Psalms Through the Centuries* (Malden, MA: Blackwell Publishing 2008), 38.

After the fall of the Roman Empire there was a sort of lull on Com-mentaries — though the Psalms were never forgotten; indeed, they were quietly building the foundation for medieval Europe, a foundation that would ultimately blossom into the high middle ages. Nevertheless, the light on the commentaries never fully extinguished, as Venerable Bede, St. Alcuin, and Remigius wrote some works on the Psalms, though nothing as comprehensive as St. Augustine's *Enarrationes in Psalmos*.

After this temporary respite, however, commentaries on the Psalms began to be penned again. For example, we have the commentaries or other works on the Psalms by Bruno, Bishop of Wurzburg, Bruno of Segni, Euthymius Zigabenus, Gergohus the Great, St. Albert the Great, St. Thomas Aquinas, Ludolph the Carthusian, and Michael Ayguan. And then sometime after them came Denis the Carthusian. There are, of course, others after Denis the Carthusian authored his *Commentary*, for example St. Robert Bellarmine's whose work we quoted earlier. But let us now focus on the Carthusian.

# THE COMMENTARY
## OF DENIS THE CARTHUSIAN

*This exquisitely beautiful writer excels him-self in his commentary on the Psalms.*
—John Mason Neale[41]

### GENERAL SCHEMA

LTHOUGH DENIS WAS TO AUTHOR COMMEN-taries on all the books of Scripture, his *Commentary on the Psalms* was his first venture into this genre. Denis started his commentarial journey in 1434 with his *Commentary on the Psalms*,[42] seeing them as the fulcrum as it were, or perhaps better, the *corpus callosum*—that thick, connective, communicative Scriptural tissue—between the Old and New Testaments.

The general scheme of the *Commentary* is not particularly innova-tive. After an introduction where Denis outlines the different kinds of prophets and grades of prophecies, Denis addresses where David and his

41  John Mason Neale & R. F. Littledale, *A Commentary on the Psalms from Prim-itive and Medieval Writers* (London: Joseph Masters & Co. 1884), 82. (4th ed.).
42  Denis states in Article XLIII (Psalm 17:42) of his *Commentary* that it has been 1434 years from the birth of the Lord.

prophecies in the Psalms fit in. Denis concludes that, *from a Christological* perspective, David is the greatest of prophets, exceeding in this area even Moses. He then introduces the four ways of looking at Scripture—literal, allegorical, tropological, and anagogical—and the seven rules of interpretation that were first summarized by Tyconius and adopted by St. Augustine. With respect to these patristic and medieval tools that have fallen into desuetude, we might recall the words of Pope Benedict XVI:

> Today it has been rediscovered that [the patristic and medieval interpretation of the four senses: the literal or historical, the allegorical or Christological, the tropological or moral, and the anagogical, which orients a person to eternal life] are dimensions of the one meaning of Sacred Scripture and that it is right to interpret Sacred Scripture by seeking the four dimensions of its words.[43]

Denis then launches into the question of (the Davidic) authorship of the Psalms and their compilation by Esdras, following which he describes the various Latin translations. He closes his introduction with a description of the spiritual virtue of the Psalms, the manner of praying or singing them, and his intentions in writing the *Commentary*.

The basic pattern Denis uses in proceeding through the Psalms is likewise customary. Denis's general scheme is to address the Psalms, Psalm by Psalm, in one or more articles. He then goes through the Psalm verse-by-verse, phrase by phrase, even word by word, parsing it where it needs to be parsed. He does this by viewing the Psalms through his up to four interpretive lenses: literal, allegorical, tropological, and anagogical. Now, Denis's view of the literal sense is broader than one might first think, in particular when it comes to the Messianic Psalms, which though literally about David they are, in Denis's view, also *literally* about Christ. While Denis does not ignore the *Sitz in Leben* of the author—which he attributes most likely to being David—he operates on the principal that the thing signified is more interesting than the thing signifying. And since David is a type of Christ, Denis looks at some Psalms as literally dealing with Christ, in which case they do not refer to Christ by means of allegory but directly to Christ through David. In applying the various lenses to the Psalms, however, Denis is flexible. In some Psalms he devotes one or more articles to each interpretative mode. In

---

43 Benedict XVI, General Audience, Feb. 10, 2010, http://www.vatican.va/content/ benedict-xvi/en/audiences/2010/documents/hf_ben-xvi_aud_20100210.html.

others he foregoes one or more of the interpretations as not applicable. Some Psalms he treats in one article, in which case he devotes, where needed, subsections under that article for different modes of interpretation. After all applicable interpretations are exhausted, he closes with an exhortation or peroration to his fellow readers (or chanters) of the Psalms. He rounds up his conclusion with a short little prayer which draws upon the Psalm and his commentary on it, and which acts as a sort of graceful *codetta* before advancing to the next Psalm.

In the main, Denis the Carthusian's *Commentary on the Psalms* then fits nicely into the commentarial tradition that preceded it. And yet it does not. There are some features of Denis's *Commentary* that make it unique or at least notable. The first might be called the *ecstatic* nature of the *Commentary*. The second might be characterized as its heavy, almost exclusive, reliance on what can be called the *analogy of Scripture* as a means for interpreting the Psalms. The third is its decidedly *Thomistic* nature. Next, we would be remiss if we did not point out Denis's conviction that the Psalms reveal to us the *mind of Christ*. Finally, there are frequently times that Denis gives moral direction or practical advice as to developing the virtues, both theological and moral, both infused and acquired, and the gifts of the Holy Spirit. He also stresses the use of the Psalms in the quest to advance in perfection as we seek to put on Christ and to die to self. They school us in the manner of living — the *conversatio* — that is part of the easy and light yoke of Christ, the *imitatio Christi*, the imitation of Christ, and the *sequela Christi*, the following of Christ.

## ECSTATIC NATURE

With Denis, we are moved to look at the Psalms from an entirely different register than we might be used to. Perhaps one stark way of exhibiting the difference is to compare and contrast a couple modern commentaries' treatment of Ps. 17(18):2, *Diligam te, Domine, fortitudo mea,* "I will love you, O Lord, my strength," with Denis the Carthusian's treatment of it.

First let us turn to the commentary in the *Navarre Bible:*

> 18:1-2. Both here and at the end of the psalm (vv. 46-49) we
> find God being proclaimed as an all-powerful protector — a
> "rock," "fortress", "shield" etc.[44]

---

44  *Navarre Bible: The Psalms and the Song of Solomon* (New York: Scepter Publishers, 2003), 79. The *Navarre Bible* then resorts to St. Augustine's *Commentary* on Ps. 17(18):3, thereby entirely skipping 17(18):2.

There is nothing about love here. It is even worse if we turn to the *Jerome Biblical Commentary*. After commenting on the "archaisms and Ugaritic allusions" in this Psalm (as if the knowledge of "archaisms and Ugaritic allusions" will do anything to help us arrive at the love of God), the sum total of its commentary on the meaning of *Diligam te, Domine, fortitudo mea*, "I will love you, O Lord, my strength" is this: Structure: 2-4, hymnic introduction.[45]

What sort of insouciance sluffs off the words of such longing, a prayer to the God of the Universe and the Redeemer of mankind — "I will love you, O Lord, my strength" — by demoting it as a mere "hymnic introduction"? This is on the verge of blasphemy by omission.

Now compare these succinct, matter-of-fact, banal expositions to Denis's treatment of it in his *Commentary*:

> Giving thanks to God in this manner for this spiritual liberation, Christ says: 17{18}[2] *Diligam te, Domine; I will love you, O Lord*. And the beginning of this Psalm is something fittingly applied to Christ as man, and to the Church, and indeed any true member of the faithful. Therefore he says: *I will love you, O Lord*, that is, I shall always love you, sometimes because of your immense goodness, for which you are loveable beyond any measure; sometimes because of the benefits that you have conveyed to me; sometimes because of the promises you have prepared for me. Indeed, love is the first and greatest gift, and in it all gifts are given gratuitously. Consequently, we are not able to repay God for his benefits — indeed we are unable to repay any benefactor whatsoever — with anything greater or more dignified than love. For Christ as God, loves the Father with a love simply infinite; but as man, he loves God with a greater love than all the elect put together. But every single one of us is obligated more ardently to love God the more benefits he has received from him. And this verse can be understood as a kind of prayer, in this sense: *I will love you, O Lord*, that is, grant that I may love you, O Lord. *Fortitudo mea, my strength*, that is, cause of all my fortitude, without whom I am able to do nothing.

45  Raymond E. Brown, ed., *St. Jerome Biblical Commentary* Eaglewood Cliffs, NJ: Prentice-Hall 1968), 578.

The Anglican John Mason Neale[46] stumbled upon Denis the Carthusian while working on his own extensive Commentary on the Psalms, and he recognized quality when he saw it. "This exquisitely beautiful writer," he says, "excels himself in his commentary on the Psalms." He calls him "one of the most original" of all the many commentators he had surveyed.[47]   One of the original aspects of Denis's *Commentary* is precisely this ecstatic character. It is for this reason that he has been popularly ascribed the title of *Doctor Ecstaticus*, the Ecstatic Doctor. Denis's *Commentary* was written by a man in love with God to be read by men in love with God or men desiring to be in love with God. It was not made for men interested in "Ugaritic allusions."

The ecstatic nature shows itself from time to time in the *Commentary* when Denis shifts into a mode where he is praying to God, so that the *Commentary* changes or shifts from a third person *doctoral* or didactive mode, to a second person *rogational* or prayer-like mode. In his *rogational* (second person) mode, it is as if he is explaining or elaborating upon or praying the Psalm to God, sublime and blessed, in the form of a prayer. An instance of this is in his commentary on Psalm 17:29:

> 17{18}[29] *Quoniam tu illuminas lucernam meam; for you light my lamp*, that is, [you light] my reason, which is the ruler and lord of all my acts, for reason directs the will and the other powers; *Domine, O Lord*, Jesus Christ, who is *the true light*, enlightening *every man that comes into this world.* (John 1:9) And he enlightens me not only with a natural light, but also the light of grace. And because this is so, *Deus meus, illumine tenebras meas; O my God, enlighten my darkness*, that is, all of the darkness in the recesses of my interior, which, because of their great imperfection and the obscurity of vices in them, are called darkness, in the manner that very virtuous and erudite men are called light. And so, O Lord Christ, *enlighten my darkness*, that is, expel from my soul the blindness of ignorance, the overshadowing of passions, and the stains of all sins: since it is fitting for me, since *when I sit in darkness, the Lord is my light . . . he will bring me forth into the light, I shall behold his justice.* (Micah 7, 8b, 9b).

---

46   The Anglican clergyman John Mason Neale (1818–1866) was influenced by the Oxford Movement, of which John Henry Newman was a leader, and so he had an ear for things Catholic.

47   Neal, *op. cit.*, 82.

## ANALOGIA SCRIPTURAE

Neale praises Denis because it "is wonderful that so voluminous an author should have been, in this exposition, so little indebted to other commentators."[48] Indeed, this was the very intent of the Carthusian who sought, as is touted in the title to the *Commentary*, to explain the Psalms, "to the degree able...with nothing except the most sound Scriptures of both Testaments." Denis, then, uses a sort of *analogia scripturae* — using Scripture to explain Scripture[49] — something which would warm Pope Benedict XVI's heart.[50] Denis reaches to other Scriptures to explain the Psalms, and he does this beautifully, with marvelous virtuosity, deftly yet humbly, and with none of the pretentiousness of an esthete. In handling each Psalm, it is as if the Psalm is the warp and all other Scripture supplies the woof which Denis, in the loom of his mind, uses to weave a wonderful commentarial tapestry. As Denis plainly put it, "no one is able to expound perfectly on David except the Holy Spirit who spoke to David,"[51] and this is what justifies his method.

As an example, we might look at a short excerpt explaining Psalm 1:1, all four sentences contain Scripture, either the Psalm verse being explained or another Scripture to explain, confirm, or give examples of it:

> What else is it to say *Blessed is the man who has not walked in the counsel of the ungodly* (Ps. 1:1) except blessed is the man who remains in the counsel of the godly, as much taking counsel of all right things as it is consenting to the right counsel of others? For this reason, it states in the Proverbs of Solomon: *There is safety where there is much counsel.* (Prov. 11:14) And Tobias instructing his son said: *Seek counsel always of a wise man.* (Tob. 4:19) Further, what is

---

48  *Ibid.*

49  This principle is expressed through various phrases such as *Scriptura ex Scriptura explicandam esse* and *Scriptura sacra sui ipsius interpres.* Though Retzke says that this phrase is used by St. Thomas Aquinas, it certainly is not found in his writings *in haec verba.* James T. Bretzke, S. J., *Consecrated Phrases: A Latin Theological Dictionary* (Collegeville, MN: The Liturgical Press, 2003), 12, 127. Still, it is consistent with St. Thomas's method.

50  Joseph Ratzinger (Benedict XVI), "Biblical Interpretation in Crisis," 1988 Erasmus Lecture, https://www.firstthings.com/web-exclusives/2008/04/biblical-interpretation-in-crisis.

51  Article VII.

the opposite of *Blessed is the man who has not walked in the counsel of the ungodly* (Ps. 1:1) other than unhappy or miserable is the man who walks in the counsel of the ungodly, or who counsels evil, or who conforms himself to evil counsel? Here, the most holy Isaiah confessed speaking on behalf of God: *Woe to you, apostate children . . . that you would take counsel, and not of me: and would begin a web, and not by my spirit.* (Is. 30:1).[52]

Even the dour Puritans divines, implicitly conceding their value, begrudgingly acknowledged Denis's *Commentaries*, and so, for example, Thomas Watson (*ca.* 1620–1686) quotes Denis verbatim without acknowledgment, Nathaniel Culverwell (*ca.* 1619–1651) calls him "the Carthusian," and Cotton Mather (1663–1728) just plain "Carthusian."[53]

## THOMISTIC NATURE

While superlatively Scriptural, the *Commentary* also relies heavily on the guiding hand of the Common Doctor of the Church, St. Thomas Aquinas. Proof of this can be found in the multiple references, both acknowledged and unacknowledged, to St. Thomas's *Summa Theologiae* and some of his other works. And so, besides being Scripturally rich, the *Commentary* is also marvelously Thomist. The reader will see the influence of St. Thomas and his *Summa* all throughout the *Commentary*, though, as explained above, it is a Thomism in an ecstatic register. Pseudo-Dionysius is also authoritative, though less so than St. Thomas. On occasion, a St. Augustine, St. Anselm, and other Fathers and commentators make cameo appearances. Aristotle, "the Philosopher," is there as an authority as to what human reason can contribute, but the Stagirite is definitely in the role of a handmaiden, or, perhaps better, a manservant. Nevertheless, without question the overwhelming protagonist in this *Commentary* is Scripture and the sacred writers. From Genesis to Revelation, it is sacred Writ that is used by Denis to expound the Psalms and to articulate their meaning.

---

52  Article VIII.
53  Thomas Watson, *A Body of Practical Divinity in a Series of Sermons on the Shorter Catechism* (Aberdeen: 1838), 568. Nathaniel Culverwell, *An Elegant and Learned Discourse of the Light of Nature,* (Oxford: Henry Dymock Bookseller 1669), 70. Cotton Mather, "The Life of Mr. Nathanael Rogers," *Magnalia Christi Americana* (Hartford: Silas Andrus and Son 1855), 415.

## THE MIND OF CHRIST

The Apostle Paul enjoins us: "For let this mind be in you, which was also in Christ Jesus."[54] As part of our obligation to fulfill this injunction, we must turn to the Psalms. After all, Jesus prayed the Psalms,[55] and, as Denis sees it, many of them in fact represent the *vox Christi*, and, by extension, the *sensus Christi*, the mind of Christ.

"For who has known the mind of the Lord, that we may instruct him? But we have the mind of Christ." 1 Cor. 2:16. The Psalms contain the mind of Christ. Particularly in the Messianic Psalms, which Denis characterizes as literally pertaining to Christ (with David being a sign or type of the Lord), and those Psalms which Denis allegorically applies to Christ, Denis seeks to enter into the mind of the Lord so that he might understand the relationship between the Father and the Son, or the relationship between the Head and the Mystical Body. An example of this is Denis's *Commentary* to Psalm 15:4:

> I, Christ, *non congregabo, will not gather together* either by myself or through the Apostles *conventicula eorum de san-guinibus, their meetings for blood offerings*, that is, the gatherings or meetings of those who are *for blood offerings*: that is, men of blood or the iniquitous I will not gather together into the Church of the elect: not that I absolutely will not gather them together, since I came to *save that which was lost* (Luke 19:10); but I will not gather them together according to their malice, and to the extent they are evil, it is clear to see that such will remain [lost] as they were. But I will convert the impious: and they who were evil, will be good; and they who were carnal and diabolical, will be divine and holy. For which reason, it follows: *nec memor ero nominum eourum per labia mea; nor will be mindful of their names by my lips*: that is, I will not call those kind with the name by which they were called before: pagans, blind, unbelievers, unlearned, cast away; after their conversion to me, they will be called Christians, enlightened, faithful, teachers of the Gentiles, and chief of the peoples.[56]

---

54  Phil. 2:5.
55  CCC § 2586.
56  Article XXXVIII (Psalm 15:4).

## CHRISTIAN PRAXIS

Denis also injects into his *Commentary*, where pertinent, matters relating to the moral spiritual life. An example of this is his discussion in commenting on Psalm 7:6 ("Let the enemy pursue my soul, and take it, and tread down my life on the earth, and bring down my glory to the dust") of the three grades of patience, and what is the minimal level for salvation, yet what should be sought in our effort at perfection:

> [T]here are three grades of patience. The first is to suffer with equanimity that punishment occasioned by the committed fault. The second is to undergo an occasioned unjust punishment without sorrow. The third is not only to tolerate the occasioned [unjust punishment] with joy, but also to return good for evil. Of these grades of patience, the first is the lowest, and it is necessary for salvation; and it is that of which the Savior said, *In your patience you shall possess your souls* (Luke 21:19). The second grade is higher; it is the one asserted by Peter in his first epistle, *For this is thankworthy, if for conscience towards God, a man endure sorrows, suffering wrongfully* (1 Pet. 2:19). But the third grade is the highest, which to imitate is a thing of Christian perfection.[57]

## CONCLUSION

In his book *The Essence of the Bible*, Paul Claudel wrote: "Let us read the Holy Writ, but let us read it as did the Fathers who showed us the best way of profiting by it; let us read it kneeling! Let us read it, not critically with the foolish curiosity that leads only to vanity, but with the eagerness of a famished heart!"[58] With respect to the Psalms, one of the better ways to follow Paul Claudel's advice is to read, reflect upon, and pray under the guidance of the Carthusian's *Commentary*, and pray with Denis incessantly and without interruption to *Deum unum ac trinum, sublimem et benedictum*, to the God one and three, sublime and blessed.

---

57  Article XXV (Psalm 7:6).
58  Paul Claudel, *The Essence of the Bible* (New York: Philosophical Library 1957), 31.

## A NOTE ON TRANSLATION & DEVICES

*[F]or in the very nature of the case, translation has been*
*an essential to the maintenance of religion among men.*
— Hilaire Belloc[59]

Hilaire Belloc has observed that translation is a "function of religion, for in the very nature of the case, translation has been an essential to the maintenance of religion among men."[60] That necessity has only become more urgent as knowledge of Latin by Catholics has lagged, even foundered, following changes in emphasis in Western education and the deemphasis of Latin among the Catholic clergy and in our Liturgy following the Second Vatican Council. This effectively has shut out many from the patrimony of the Church not unlike Atatürk's reforms in Turkey, where he enforced a Latin-script alphabet upon the citizens, replacing the Turko-Arabic script that had been used for almost a millennia, shut out future generations from their heritage. It is very difficult to argue a "hermeneutic of continuity" when the mass of people do not have access — because of the language barrier — to that with which you are supposed to be in continuity. We suffer, in Belloc's words, from "a singular disunion within that which is and must be essentially *one*."[61] In a sense, this inability to access the past has only exacerbated the problem raised by Belloc of the possibility that we should "fall dumb," and or that the "lantern be extinguished."[62] Thus, the religious function of translation would appear more essential now than ever before.

Denis has been called the last of the Scholastics, and in a way all the various scholastic streams, most especially the Thomistic, have emptied out into the Dionysian reservoir from which we ought to be able to draw. "You shall draw waters with joy out of the Savior's fountains."[63] The Dionysian reservoir is, in a way, a pristine, limpid reservoir. It is untainted by the paganism of the Renaissance. It is untouched by the polemics of the Protestant revolt and the Catholic Counter-Reformation. It is unpolluted by the novel theories of the *philosophes* of the Enlightenment. The epistemological turn of Descartes is unknown to it. Theological liberalism, the bane of St. John Henry Newman, is absent from it. Modernism tinges

59 Hilaire Belloc, "On Translation," *The Bible Translator* (London: United Bible Societies, 1959), 84.

60 *Ibid.*, 84

61 *Ibid.*, 85.

62 *Ibid.*, 84.

63 Is. 12:3.

it utterly nowhere. It is free of the theological and moral dissent which has plagued and dissipated and mollified and enervated Catholicism since Vatican II. In lawyer talk, we might say that the *Commentary on the Psalms* by Denis the Carthusian represents the last peaceable *status quo.*

With Denis, moreover, we are not forced to "squander" our "time on trivialities" of all the exegetical static of the historico-critical method, which sometimes interposes itself, as so much noise, between the Scriptures and the reader so as to render them sterile or even boring.[64] Whatever the merits of those methods in any particular case, it is as if we pay an intellectual tithe to the mint, and anise, and cumin of the historico-critical method, and yet entirely neglect the weightier meaning of Scripture.[65] We know about Q and JEDP and other academic conceits, but we have lost track of the one thing necessary, the *unum necessarium,* the *Deus sublimis et benedictus,* the God sublime and blessed, whom Denis the Carthusian yearned for, longed for, like a deer panting after water, and whom we address with the prayer, *Diligam te, Domine,* "I will love you, O Lord."

True, a modern academic might raise all sorts of philosophical, theological, exegetical, and philological issues with Denis's *Commentary* and run circles all around him in his areas of expertise, but that academic, however erudite he may be, will not ever hold a candle to Denis the Carthusian *as a Catholic doctor.* If one wants to learn about the Psalms and about the God who wrote them, and one has a choice between the *Jerome Biblical Commentary* edited by Fr. Raymond Brown and the *Commentary on the Psalms* by Denis the Carthusian, a wise man — though perhaps not the academic — would chose the latter.

But one cannot draw the waters from Denis the Carthusian if one does not know Latin. Hence the need to translate this *Commentary* which has never been translated into English since it was written in the 1430s. I will confess that I am neither a Latinist, nor a theologian, nor a medievalist, which might put me at an impossible disadvantage if this translation was a scholarly or academic work. But this translation is not intended to be an academic, critical work. The translation, though I have endeavored to be as faithful as I can to Denis's Latin, is not principally intended for the scholar; it is intended for people not unlike me, persons Denis calls "any member of the Catholic faithful," who may desire to be exposed to some of the riches of our Catholic patrimony

---

64  Ratzinger, *op. cit.*
65  *Cf.* Matt. 23:23.

but confront an insuperable language barrier. It is not scholarship that has driven my labors; it is love, love for our Lord Jesus, love for the Catholic Faith, love for the Psalms, love for Denis to make him better known to my English-speaking contemporaries. Sadly, there are not many translators of Denis the Carthusian who have taken the task of translating his works into English. Yet I can make mine the words of another non-academician who translated a few of his other works, Sister Íde Ní Riain, RSCH — may she rest in peace: "This translation makes no claim to be either a critical edition or a work of scholarship. It is simply a work of love."[66]

Of course, that I have defined my target audience as the Catholic faithful does not well define my audience, as this audience is rather an amorphous group. I cannot be assured that the reader will have a working knowledge much less a full knowledge of Latin, or theology, or scholasticism, or even of Catholic faith and morals. So in addition to the translation, I have added copious footnotes to explain certain Scholastic concepts and terms, or Catholic doctrinal issues, or Latin phrases which may not be familiar to the ordinary reader. I have also tried to locate the non-Scriptural sources that Denis sometimes mentions off-hand (while the express citations to Scripture are ample in the Latin text, the express citations to other sources are rare). Where I, at best an amateur Thomist *in via*, was astute enough to recognize the silent hand of St. Thomas, I tried to add citations to the *Summa* or some of St. Thomas's other works for reference or further reading. On occasion, the reason behind a citation to Scripture by Denis is not immediately apparent, and some sort of explanation is required. In such cases, where possible, I have elaborated in footnotes what Denis commented with respect to that Scripture in his other Scriptural Commentaries. My thinking behind all this was that unless the reader has a pretty good working knowledge of Catholic theology and scholastic terminology, in particular that of St. Thomas and the scholastics, and Denis's thoughts on Scriptures other than the Psalms, he or she might need some guidance or elaboration. In fact, if the reader persists through the whole *Commentary*, he or she will receive a full course of the Catholic Faith and a partial jaunt through St. Thomas's various works. It is as if a Catholic catechism and the *Summa* are embedded in the *Commentary*. This was not the intent or plan of Denis, of course, but the fact is that Scripture, Catholicism — the Catholic faith and morals —, and the

---

66  Denis the Carthusian, *Spiritual Writings* (Portland: Four Courts Press 2005), xix.

teachings of St. Thomas, *were connatural to him*. Denis is one that can be trusted *sentire cum Ecclesia*, to think with the mind of the Church in its Thomistic expression.

In offering the reader the aids of footnotes, I have tried to negotiate between the shoals of being overly academic and pedantic, on the one hand, and the opposite bank of treating the reader as a simpleton, on the other. Those notes that pertain to doctrine or try to explain the text are predicated by "E. N." Those that pertain more to issues with Latin are predicated by "L." Unless otherwise noted, the scriptural citations all come from the original Latin text. The footnotes' numbering begin anew with each Psalm; thus, when a footnote refers to another in the text its number is given after indicating whether it is found in the Preface or a Psalm. Thus a reference to P-46 means footnote 46 in the Preface, 2-31 means footnote 31 in Psalm 2, and so forth.

With respect to translating the many verses of Scripture quoted by Denis, I have resorted largely to the Douay-Rheims Challoner, since it so closely follows the Latin scripture upon which Denis relies and I suppose it to be somewhat familiar to the reader;[67] however, I have modernized the verbs and pronouns to conform to contemporary English usage so that there is no stark discontinuity between the Scripture and the Commentary. In some cases — particularly where Denis's Latin text departs from the Sixto-Clementine text upon which the Douay Rheims is based, or where the word selected by the Douay Rheims to translate the Latin is dated or does not quite conform to Denis's argument, I have departed from it. Where I have done so, I have tried to make a note of it. I have also tried to modernize or standardize the names of places and persons (*e.g.*, replacing Lebanon for Libanus and Elijah for Elias). Where Denis appears to be quoting a scripture exactly or near-exactly, the text is in italics. Where Denis appears to be referring to Scripture obliquely or through paraphrase, it is not italicized. References to the Psalm verses in the footnotes will be through the numbering of the Septuagint/Vulgate, and not based upon the numbering of Masoretic text. Also, although not in the Latin text, I have marked the scriptural quotations (where they are partial quotations of a verse) with an a or a b to give the reader guidance in the event he wants to look up the verse in the Scriptures. Thus John 11:2b, would mean somewhere in the latter half of John 11:2.

---

67 The Vulgate was not standardized during the time of Denis, and there were variants of it. The Douay-Rheims is based upon the Sixto-Clementine recension promulgated in 1562. Denis wrote approximately 130 years earlier.

In his *Pensées*, Joseph Joubert (1754–1824) wrote: "It is not my periods that I polish, but my ideas."[68] That is *a fortiori* true of Denis. A feature of his writing is the length of his sentences and a rather loose methodology of punctuation. To fit the discursive Carthusian's sentence into pithy English sentences, however, is an impossible task, sort of like making legato into staccato. It would be ruinous besides, and cruel, not unlike putting a straightjacket on an angel, if such a thing were possible. Though on occasion I felt forced to do so by sheer need, such instances are rare. In general, I have allowed the Dionysian sentence the degree of freedom it had in the priory in Roermond. It is just something we have to live with.

In undertaking all this effort, I am sure, depending upon the reader, some will think I failed. I may have failed in translation. I may have failed in English expression. I may have failed to understand Denis. I may have failed to explain something well. There are hundreds of thousands of decisions made during the translation of this large a *Commentary*. In a project of this size, some failure is quite likely. Even Homer nods; and I am not Homer. *Errare humanum est.* In any event, any errors are mine and can be attributed solely to me. However that may be, I might invoke here the sentiments of the author of the second book of Maccabees who felt similar trepidation at what he had been called to do: "If I have done well, . . . it is what I desired: but if not so perfectly, it must be pardoned me."[69] I trust the reader will remember our Lord's injunction to forgive seventy times seven.[70] And as a final fail-safe, I might take recourse to St. Augustine's prayer in his *De Trinitate*:

> *Domine Deus une, Deus Trinitas, quaecumque dixi in his libris de tuo agnoscant et tui; si qua de meo, et tu ignosce, et tui. Amen.*[71]

> O Lord, one God, God the Trinity, whatever I have said in this book that is of you, may those who are yours acknowledge; if anything of my own, may it be pardoned both by you and by those who are yours. Amen.

---

68  Joseph Joubert, *Pensées of Jourbet* (London: Macmillan & Co. 1877), 5 (trans., Henry Atwell).

69  2 Macc. 15:39.

70  Matt. 18:21–22.

71  *De Trinitate*, 15.28.51, PL 42, 1098.

## ACKNOWLEDGMENTS

*Gratias ago Deo meo semper pro vobis in gra-*
*tia Dei, quae data est vobis in Christo Iesu.*

— 1 Cor. 1:4

"No man is an island, entire of itself; every man is a piece of the continent, a part of the main," are John Donne's words. This is also true of anyone engaged in a translation and its publication. I thank first of all my wife, Betsy, who tolerated my long absences on weekends while I was engaged on this seemingly endless project. I thank my daughter Leelee for agreeing to write a biographical sketch on Denis (whose name I pronounce ˈdɛnɪs, but she insists on calling by the French pronunciation, dəˈni). I thank my legal assistant Cindi who helped proof the manuscript, often doing so during her time off. I thank Dr. Peter Kwasniewski for his role as intermediary in getting the fruit of my labor published. I thank those who have agreed to provide recommendations for my work, Bishop Daniel Flores of Brownsville, Texas, Deacon Keith Fournier of Tyler, Texas, Dom Hugh Knapman, OSB, Douai Abbey, Dom Pius Mary Noonan, OSB, Notre Dame Priory, and Abbot Philip Anderson, Clear Creek Abbey. I also want to thank Alex Barbas and Arouca Press for agreeing to take on this project and making Denis's *Commentary on the Psalms* available to the English-speaking public at large for the first time ever. Five hundred and ninety years was too long a time for Denis the Carthusian's *Commentary on the Psalms* to be translated into English. Above all, I want to thank God, *Deum, sublimem et benedictum*, who led me to Denis the Carthusian, and who has blessed me through him. My prayer is that the Carthusian will at long last come out the silence of his cloisters and bless English-speaking Catholics and persuade them and aid them to make the Psalms a centerpiece of their lives so that perhaps once again the Psalms can be first, middle, and last for us all. As Denis instructs, we are given the opportunity to enjoy "a certain soliloquy with God that is particularly so much more sweet, affective, ardent, and sincere the more the soul knows and tastes more deeply and clearly the power and sense of the Psalms." No reasonable man, no reasonable woman, ought to pass this oppor-tunity up.

# COMMENTARY
## *on the*
# DAVIDIC
# *Psalms*

## PART I
## [PSALMS 1–25]

### PREFACE

*David the son of Jesse said: The man to whom it was appointed concerning the Christ of the God of Jacob, the excellent psalmist of Israel said: The spirit of the Lord has spoken by me and his word by my tongue.* 2 Sam. 23:1, 2.

IN THE MANNER THAT THE ONLY-BEGOTTEN of God the Father, our Lord Jesus Christ, chose to become incarnate and be born from the particular seed of David[1] (whence also he is in a particular fashion called the branch or son of David),[2] so the Holy Spirit excellently filled the soul of the most blessed David with prophetic light, and he illustrated in a special way the mysteries of Christ; and David—recognizing the promised goodness of God—returned great thanks to God, and these he resplendently published to the whole world.

Considering this prophetic grace was given to him so eminently by divine inspiration, the words which I now introduced [*i.e.,* 2 Sam. 23:1, 2], in which he speaks of himself as much as another,[3] resound in the mind with thanksgiving and joy: *David, the son of Jesse,* he said; *the man appointed concerning the Christ of the God of Jacob,* that is, to whom was specially given the promise of the Christ of God, that is, the Savior of

---

1  Rom. 1:3.
2  Jer. 23:5; 33:15.
3  E. N. David speaks both of himself and of the Christ.

I

the world who comes forth from his seed. For this is what he says of the other: *of the fruit of your womb I will set upon your throne.*[4] And indeed this fruit or this son of David is he of whom the archangel Gabriel told the Virgin Mother: *The Lord God shall give unto him the throne of David his father; and he shall reign in the house of Jacob forever.*[5] And it is he of whom Isaiah predicted: *He shall sit upon the throne of David, and upon his kingdom.*[6] So one is able to ask how this is fulfilled in Christ, especially since he responded to Pilate: *My kingdom is not of this world.*[7] When also another might object: *The foxes have holes, and the birds of the air nests: but the Son of Man has nowhere to lay his head.*[8] And also when the people sought him out to make him king, he fled and he hid himself.[9] These words in the introduction, therefore, are not testimony of a proposed temporal dominion, a new earthly kingdom; rather, they testify to a spiritual ruler and an eternal princedom which now reigns by grace in the house of Jacob and the seat of David,[10] that is, in the Church militant and the hearts of the elect; and in the future age it will reign without end by glory.

With merit, therefore, David, who so clearly foretold of Christ, is called *the excellent psalmist of Israel,* that is, the most distinguished psalmist of the people, faithfully contemplating God. To which is also added, *the Spirit of the Lord spoke through me,* and this accords with that which Christ told his disciples, *It is not you that speak, but the Spirit of your Father that speaks in you.*[11]

Finally, prior to all the many things that are hinted at in these introductory words, this above all else is to be given attention: how beautiful and clear the Persons of the Trinity are expressed in them. And also touched upon is the Person of the Son with the name of *Christ;* and the true Person of the Holy Spirit referred to as the *Spirit;* the Person of the Father is expressed with the name *of God* as well as the name *Lord.* For Christ, is called Christ and the Son of God, since he is born from God the eternal Father, in the manner written in Scripture: *from the womb before the day star I begot you.*[12] But the Holy Spirit, is called

---

4  Ps. 131:11b.
5  Luke 1:32.
6  Is. 9:7.
7  John 18:36a.
8  Matt. 8:20.
9  *Cf.* John 6:15.
10  Luke 1:32b.
11  Matt. 10:20.
12  Ps. 109:3b.

the Spirit of God and of the Lord, in that proceeding by spiration from God, that is the Father and the Son, which are one God, by which — as from one eternal principle — the Holy Spirit flows.

# ARTICLE I

## WHAT A PROPHET IS, AND OF THEIR GRADES, AND WHICH PROPHETS ARE OF GREATER DIGNITY

ROPHECY PRINCIPALLY PERTAINS TO THE intellect. For prophecy is the supernatural knowledge of the future arrived at by divine inspiration. For indeed, prophets assert that which the revealing God has made known to them but which is hidden from others and which is to take place some distance in the future. It is for this reason that the Book of Samuel says: *For he that is now called a prophet, in time past was called a seer.*[13] And Samuel said to Saul: *I am the seer.*[14]

Moreover, prophecy is recognized as pertaining to the graces freely given (*gratias gratis datas*), such as the working of miracles, the interpretation of speech, and the discernment of spirits. For such and similar graces are common to both the good and the wicked. Truly, the graces freely given are distributed and are ordained to the utility of others, in the manner that the Apostle told the Corinthians: *And the manifestation of the Spirit is given to every man unto profit.*[15] To the extent, therefore, that the knowledge of a prophet is ordained towards this — so that others may know — prophecy thus secondarily pertains to speaking; and hence, the name Prophet is an accepted title for him who was mentioned in the preface. But because prophecy is about things that exceed natural reason, and it cannot be proved by natural reason, consequently the third thing that pertains to prophecy is the working of miracles, a confirmation of that which is prophetically announced. And in this manner is to understood what is written in Ecclesiastes: *Elijah ... did not fear the prince ... and after death his body prophesied,*[16] because after he was dead he raised the dead.[17] By this it was manifest that he was a true prophet.

---

13 1 Sam. 9:9.
14 1 Sam. 9:19.
15 1 Cor. 12:7.
16 Ecclus. 48:13, 14.
17 E. N. The prophet Elijah's bones raised the dead. *See* 2 Kings 13:21.

And Scripture says something similar about the bones of Joseph.[18]

Further, in the manner the natural light of the agent intellect is the principle of all possible natural knowledge of the intellect, so the supernatural and divine light is the principle of prophetic knowledge. For that reason, just as the possible knowledge of the natural intellect extends to all things (or can contain all things)[19] that, by the natural light of the agent intellect, are able to be discovered and known, so prophetic knowledge is occupied with all things which, by supernatural or divine light, are able to be revealed and known. Now, by divine light all things surely are able to be made manifest, that is, divine and human things, created and uncreated things, spiritual and bodily things, things of nature and things pertaining to morals. Whence prophecy extends to all these things. For there is sometimes even prophetic revelation which pertains to the majesty or the excellence of God, as when Isaiah said, speaking of himself: *I saw the Lord sitting upon a throne high and elevated,*[20] and that he heard the Seraphim crying "Holy" three times,[21] which serves as a revelation of the most blessed Trinity. And it was shown to the prophet Daniel *thousands of thousands ministered to God, and ten thousand times a hundred thousand stood before him.*[22] The seeing of spirits of heaven is without doubt prophetic revelation. Prophecy also contains those things which concern instructions to the morals of men, such as: *Deal your bread to the hungry.*[23] Also Micah the prophet: *I will show you, O man, what is good, and what the Lord requires of you: Verily, to do judgment, and to love mercy, and to walk solicitous with your God.*[24]

As much as some things exceed our natural reason and are further distant from our understanding, so also prophecies concern things that exceed and surpass our own reason, as do pure future contingencies, such as the acts of man are. For that reason, prophecy most properly appertains to the knowledge of future events. And in this manner Cassiodorus defined prophecy when he said: Prophecy is the divine inspiration or revelation announcing the outcome of events with immoveable truth.[25] And so similarly does Gregory in his work on Ezechiel say

---

18  Ecclus. 49, 17–18.
19  L. *omnium capax.*
20  Is. 6:1.
21  Is. 6:3.
22  Dan. 7:10.
23  Is. 58:7.
24  Micah 6:8.
25  E. N. Denis misquotes Cassiodorus (*ca.* 485–*ca.* 585 A. D.) slightly. Denis says : *Prophetia est inspiratio seu revelatio divina, rerum eventus immobili denutians*

that prophecy is so called because it foreannounces the future; so that when it is manifest in the past or [comes to be] in the future, it loses the character of its name.[26]

Moreover, there are many grades of prophecy, of which the lowest is that when the Holy Spirit moves someone from an interior inspiration to do an exterior work, such as is frequently written in the books of Judges, for the Spirit of the Lord rushed into Jephthah or Samson,[27] out of which they were induced to exercise certain exterior works. The second and higher grade of prophecy is when someone by the illumination of the Holy Spirit understands or perceives something in a supernatural way, as in the manner that Solomon possessed it, because the Lord gave him manifold wisdom and prudence beyond measure, so that *he disputed about trees from the cedar that is in Lebanon, unto the hyssop that comes out of the wall: and he discoursed of beasts, and of fowls, and of creeping things, and of fishes.*[28] For we find such things plainly scattered among the gentiles and the philosophers. Whence this second grade does not attain in the perfect measure of prophecy, since it does not relate to supernatural truths. Nevertheless, some things were revealed to Solomon which wholly exceeded the limits of natural reason, especially in the Song of Songs, and because of this knowledge, Solomon is truly and properly called a Prophet.

Therefore, the third grade of prophetic knowledge is when through imaginative[29] visions some supernatural truth is revealed, such as the manner that Daniel saw the Ancient of Days, that is, the eternal God, under similarity of images of things, as we read in the Book of Daniel: *I beheld until thrones were placed, and the Ancient of Days sat: his garment was white as snow, and the hair of his head like clean wool.*[30] This kind of true prophecy has many degrees, according to that which the holy Doctor

---

*veritate*. Cassiodorus states: *Prophetia est aspiratio divina quae eventus rerum aut per facta aut per dicta quorumdam immobili veritate pronuntiat.* "Prophecy is the divine breath which pronounces the outcome of events either through acts or by words of certain men with immovable truth." *Exp. Psalm.*, I, PL 70, 12.

26 E. N. The reference is to Pope St. Gregory's homily on Ezechiel (I, 1, 1): *Quia cum ideo prophetia dicta sit quod futura praedicat, quando de praeterito vel praesenti loquitur, rationem sui nominis amittit.* "For since, therefore, it is called prophecy, which predicts the future, when it talks of the past or the present, it loses the reason for its name." PL 76, 786. *See also* ST IIaIIae, q. 171, art. 3, s. c.

27 Judges 11:29; 14:6; 15:14. E. N. Jephthah was inspired to make a vow to the Lord, Samson to tear a lion into pieces, and to attack the Philistines with the jawbone of an ass.

28 1 Kings. 4:29, 33.

29 E. N. Meaning not a figment of the imagination, but composed of mental images.

30 Dan. 7:9.

[Thomas Aquinas] says in the second part of the second part [of the *Summa Theologiae*].[31] The first distinction rests in the difference of visions in dreams or while awake. Sometimes prophetic revelations are imparted in dreams, as it is written: *By a dream in a vision by night, . . . then he opens the ears of men.*[32] Yet sometimes he imparts prophecy in visions while awake, which is the manner we read about in the Book of Daniel.[33] And this degree [of prophecy] is of greater dignity than the first, because the strength of prophetic light is greater when the soul is awake and occupied with sensible things and is raised to supernatural things, than when the soul is asleep and is raised to supernatural things, being that things of the sense are already absent from it. The second distinction he makes in prophecy rests upon the difference of imaginative and sensible signs by which the mind of the Prophet is raised to the intellectual knowledge of supernatural truth. For to the degree signs of this kind were more expressive, the more sublime was the prophecy. Therefore, since, according to Augustine, words have the first and highest place among the various signs, it follows that the prophecy of him who hears words as if spoken — whether while awake or while asleep — is a higher prophecy than that of him who merely is shown a certain thing or similitudes signifying other things, as in the manner that the seven ears of corn shown to Pharaoh prefigured seven years of plenty,[34] and the boiling caldron shown to Jeremiah represented the city of Jerusalem on fire.[35] The third degree of prophecy which is above this is derived from access to the cause of prophetic knowledge. For it is a higher degree of prophecy in that it does not only perceive the spoken word, but also sees him who is speaking, such as when many different angels — who (as Dionysius [the Areopagite][36] attests) oversee and inspire prophetic revelations — appeared to the prophets Zacharias and Daniel.[37] And the fourth degree of prophecy is weighed from the condition of the one appearing or teaching [to the prophet]. For the prophecy is inferior if he who is seen appears in the person of a man than if he appears in the person of an angel. The

---

31  *ST,* IIaIIae, q. 174, art. 3, co.
32  Job. 33:15.
33  Daniel 10.
34  Gen. 41:26.
35  Jer. 1:13 *et seq.*
36  E. N. Pseudo-Dionysius (thought at one time to be biblical Dionysius the Areopagite mentioned in Acts 17:34) now generally believed to be a Christian Neoplatonist of the 5th or 6th century. As an authority, he is highly relied upon by St. Thomas Aquinas and by Denis.
37  Zach. 1; Dan. 7.

highest measure is if he appears in the person of God, in the manner that Micah[38] said: *I saw the Lord sitting on his throne, and all the army of heaven standing by him on the right hand and on the left.*[39]

Finally, the highest and most dignified degree of prophecy is when one is shown intelligible ad supernatural truth without imaginative vision, as for instance by anagogical and intellectual illumination. And such a mode exceeds the instruction (*rationem*) of the very words of prophecy, as Thomas [Aquinas] affirms.[40] Whence, this mode may better be said to be a third kind (*genus*) of prophesying, rather than a degree of prophecy. For one sees included in the very instruction of [the words of] prophecy a certain obscurity, such as [one sees] in the instruction of the faith. For these reasons, neither prophecy nor faith is ordered to them who comprehend,[41] that is to say, the blessed [in heaven]. But to be able to receive the instruction of prophecy proper, the mind of the Prophet must be led to intellectual knowledge as through an imaginative vision, as if it were through a medium. This is what some assert. And therefore according to this, the grades of prophecy are distinguished based upon imaginative vision.

# ARTICLE II

## ON THE KINDS OF PROPHECY, AND HOW
## PROPHECY IS INFALLIBLY FULFILLED

S THE MOST GLORIOUS PRINCE OF THE Apostles [Peter] summed up in his second epistle, *prophecy came not by the will of man at any time: but the holy men of God spoke, inspired by the Holy Spirit.*[42] For the object of prophecy is supernatural truth, which consists precisely in knowledge of divine things; and it transcends natural reason. The Divine knowledge truly knows both the future and all that which may be the subject of prophecy, that is, [the future] itself or [the objects of prophecy] themselves, as undoubtedly they are to be

---

38  E. N. Also known as Micheas.

39  1 King. 22:19.

40  *ST,* IIaIIae, q. 174, art. 3, co.

41  L. *comprehensores,* those who see (comprehend) directly in heaven, as distinguished from those still on earth, the *viatores* who only knew through senses or mediatively. *See* footnote 1-46 and Article IX (Psalm 1:3).

42  2 Pet. 1:21.

done by God. Secondly, he knows them in their immediate and proper causes, that is according to their relation to them. But the acquisition of prophetic knowledge is a certain expression or imprint outflowing from the divine knowledge and infused in the prophets.

To the degree, therefore, that the blessed and holy God knows things in the first way, prophecy of predestination[43] is received, which of necessity must always be fulfilled. But to the degree things are known in the second way, prophecy of threat,[44] which is not always fulfilled, except perchance by secret knowledge, as the destruction of Nineveh[45] or the death of Ezechiel.[46] In such prophecy is announced something according to the relation of a cause to its effect. And this relation is able to be impeded by other and stronger supervenient causes, especially when it pleases the divine will, which is the first cause of all things. And consequently such prophecy is not always fulfilled, such as happens in prophecy of promise,[47] as occurred with what was openly revealed to Jeremiah. For the Lord said to him: I will suddenly speak against a nation, and against a kingdom, to root out, and to pull down, and to destroy it. *If that nation against which I have spoken shall repent of their evil, I also will repent.*[48] And this clearly pertains to prophecy of threat. But a prophecy of promise immediately is added: *And I will suddenly speak of a nation and of a kingdom, to build up and plant it. If it shall do evil in my sight . . . I will repent of the good that I have spoken to do unto it.*[49] Whence, these kinds of prophetic announcements must always be so understood [as predicting the future], unless one places some sort of impediment, that is, something meritorious or unmeritorious of men, or some similar cause. Hence Gregory says that God does not change his counsel, though he may change his judgment.[50] And there is also another species of prophecy, which is called prophecy of

---

43  L. *prophetia praedestinationis.*
44  L. *prophetia comminationis.* Comminatory prophecy, that is, prophecy of denunciation containing a threat rather than prophecy of foreknowledge must be considered to be conditional.
45  Jonah 3:4.
46  Is. 38:1.
47  L. *prophetia promissionis.*
48  Jer. 18, 7–8.
49  Jer. 18:9–10.
50  L. *Deus non mutat consilium, quamvis mutet sententiam.* The reference is to Pope St. Gregory's *Moralia in Iob*, XVI, 22, 10: *Omnipotens enim Deus etsi plerumque mutat sententiam, consilium nunquam.* "For Almighty God, even though he often changes his judgment, he never changes his counsel." PL 75, 1127.

foreknowledge,[51] which is of things of the future which God foreknows, according as they are carried out by our will, and this is of both good and bad things.[52]

Four, therefore, are the species of prophecy; and yet the Gloss in the beginning of the book of Psalms, proposes only two species of prophecy, that is prophecy of foreknowledge and prophecy of threat. But the prophecy of promise can be understood to be comprehended by, and reduced to, the prophecy of threat. And also the prophecy of predestination can be contained as part of the prophecy of foreknowledge. For foreknowledge contains the notion as much of the elect as of the reprobate. Whence, the Apostle at times uses the word foreknowledge with regard to the good, in the manner [he uses it] in the book of Romans when speaking of God, when he says: *Whom he foreknew, he also predestined to be made conformable to the image of his Son.*[53] But because the notion of the elect proper has the name predestination, it may generally be included in foreknowledge, which also includes bad things, so foreknowledge is said of the evil and the reprobate. The aforementioned Gloss also says that the prophecy of foreknowledge is always fulfilled.

# ARTICLE III

## WHY DAVID WAS THE MOST EXCELLENT
## OF THE PROPHETS

ENIS [THE AREOPAGITE], IN THE FIRST chapter of his *Celestial Hierarchy*, touches upon the two ways by which the minds of holy theologians and Prophets are infused with prophetic revelations. For sometimes supernatural and prophetical truth is demonstrated through sensible signs; and sometimes truly only by the elevation of the mind in pure divine contemplation, without the covering of sensory form, or without the similitude of imaginative species. The first of these revelations is called symbolic because a symbol is a collection of sensible forms that demonstrate something invisible. And the second is named anagogic. For anagogy is the pure ascent of the mind unto divine things.

---

51  L. *prophetia praescientiae.*
52  E. N. By which he implies that the prophecy of predestination only involves good
     things, but the prophecy of foreknowledge may involve both good and bad things.
53  Rom. 8:29a.

Consequently, according to Augustine, the manifestation of prophetic form is caused or is accomplished in three manners. For some [prophecy] is accomplished only through imaginative vision, without any intellectual revelation, such as when Nebuchadnezzar saw a great statute;[54] and when Balthazar his son saw the fingers of a hand;[55] and in Pharaoh, who saw seven cattle and seven ox and seven ears of corn;[56] and of these, none was a prophet. For prophecy requires first a manifestation of some sort of revelation; second, [it requires] the reception [of divine communication] for the purpose of a truth. That is why it is written in Daniel: *There is need of understanding in a vision.*[57] Thus Joseph and Daniel, who understood and expressed the imaginative visions referred to, were Prophets. Sometimes in prophetic revelations imaginative vision and intellectual perception are simultaneously poured out, and this is the manner in which all the twelve Prophets whose books we have prophesied. But sometimes prophecy is poured out only according to intellectual enlightenment, and this manner of prophesying is more pure and more excellent. In this manner David is to have prophesied about all things. Whence the Gloss[58] in the beginning of the Psalms asserts that other Prophets prophesied through the various images of things and under the cover of words, such as through dreams, and words, and acts. But only David, by being impelled by the Holy Spirit without any exterior support, poured forth his prophecy.

Prophecy is of four modes: First, by acts, such as the ark of Noah signified the Church,[59] or the iron pan placed between Ezekiel and Jerusalem signified the devastation of the City of Jerusalem.[60] Second, prophecy occurs by words or sayings, such as when it was said to Abraham: *And in your seed shall all the nations of the earth be blessed.*[61] The third mode is by vision, as when Moses saw the burning bush that

---

54  Dan. 2:31.
55  Dan. 5:5.
56  Gen. 41:2, 5.
57  Dan. 10:1.
58  E. N. This is a reference to the *Glossa Ordinaria*, which is a medieval Latin commentary on the Bible. *See* PL 113, 842. "Many are the kinds that this grace is given," by the works of men, by births which signify the future, by speaking angels, by visions, by dreams, by clouds and voices in the heavens, but David prophesied "in none of these ways, but celestial aspirations internally brought out, the Spirit in him speaking." *David autem nullo horum, sed coelesti aspiratione intus eductus, Spiritus in eo loquente.*
59  Gen.6:14.
60  Ez. 4:3.
61  Gen. 22:18.

was not consumed.[62] The fourth mode is through dreams. In addition, there is a certain kind of prophecy of the past,[63] as when to Moses through prophetic revelation was made known the creation of the world. Whence it is said that [the words] *In the beginning God created heaven, and earth*[64] is prophecy. Another kind is the prophecy of the present,[65] such as when the Holy Spirit knows and reveals something that another person is thinking. And thus Elizabeth prophesied of the Incarnation of Christ in her presence as she said: *Whence is this to me, that the mother of my Lord should come to me?*[66] Nevertheless, as it has been said, in the strict sense prophecy is about nothing other than the future. And because the gift of prophecy belongs to the graces freely given,[67] and not to sanctifying grace,[68] therefore the spirit of prophecy also may be possessed by evil men when they speak, as occurred with Balaam who, although he was a soothsayer and magician and was evil, yet he nevertheless prophesied beautifully in the manner that is contained in the Book of Numbers.[69]

There is therefore the question whether David is the greatest prophet. And that he is more sublime than the other Prophets who had imaginative or bodily visions has been addressed above. But of this subject matter the chief question is whether he is a greater prophet than Moses.

And St. Thomas attends to this very question,[70] and he attests to a resolution, that, all things considered, and strictly speaking, Moses excelled in the gift of prophecy compared to David, although either David or others, with respect to certain things, might be able to exceed Moses, because it is seen that some have spoken more fully of the mystery of Christ, as did David, or because they performed greater miracles, such as Joshua at whose command the sun and the moon stood still in the sky for the expanse of a day.[71] But truly Moses — absolutely speaking — is the highest Prophet, and this is established because in his prophesying he saw in a unique way a vision as imaginative as it was intellectual, and also a proclamation of revealed truth, and an exhibition of miracles.

62 Ex. 3:2.
63 L. *prophetia de praeterito.*
64 Gen. 1:1.
65 L. *prophetia de praesenti.*
66 Luke 1:43.
67 L. *gratia gratis data.* Gratuitous grace.
68 L. *gratia gratum faciens.* Grace making one pleasing [to God].
69 Num. 24:5, *et seq.*
70 *ST,* IIaIIae, q. 174, art. 4, co.
71 Joshua 10:12–13.

Moses excelled in all these things. First, with respect to intellectual vision: because, according to Augustine, in this life he saw God in essence, as Paul did while in rapture,[72] as Augustine acknowledges in his twelfth book of his *The Literal Meaning of Genesis*,[73] and in the book *On Seeing God*.[74] Whence in the book of Numbers it is said of Moses: *Plainly, and not by riddles and figures does he see the Lord*.[75] Second, Moses excelled all others with regard to his imaginative visions, which he had almost at his pleasure, not only hearing and while dreaming, but also seeing angels speaking among themselves, and while awake. And thus it is said in Exodus that the Lord spoke to him — that is, the angel of the Lord — face to face, as a man is accustomed to talk to his friend.[76] Third, Moses excelled with respect to his prophetic announcements because he spoke to the entire people, placing before them the Law. Fourth, Moses excelled with respect to the exhibition of miracles, because he accomplished many great miracles before the wicked and before all people.

But Nicholas of Lyra[77] contradicts this answer, especially in this regard: that Thomas [Aquinas] prefers Moses to David in the gift of prophecy, because he [Moses] saw in the present life God in essence, [but Nicholas argues that to the opposite] in that such a vision does not pertain to prophecy. However, the conclusion of Thomas [Aquinas] remains fitting. For although this vision [of Moses] does not directly pertain to prophecy, yet to the extent that it is a miraculous activity, it [the vision] is asserted to pertain (*pertinere asseritur*) to it [prophecy], and so it is also deemed to pertain (*pertinere censetur*) to it. Whence in Deuteronomy it is written: *There arose no more a prophet in Israel like unto Moses, whom the Lord knew face to face, in all the signs and wonders, which he sent by him, to do in the land of Egypt*.[78]

That David, therefore, is called the most excellent of Prophets may be understood to this extent: that he prophesied most excellently and clearly of the mysteries of Christ.

---

72  2 Cor. 12:2–4.

73  *De Genesi ad Litteram Libri Duodecim.*

74  *Epistola CXLVII ad Paulinam de videndo Deum.*

75  Num. 12:8.

76  Ex. 33:11.

77  E. N. Nicholas of Lyra (*ca.* 1270–1349 A. D.) was a Franciscan theologian who wrote commentary on Scripture, his major work being *Postillae perpetuae in universam Sanctam Scripturam.*

78  Deut. 34:10–11a.

# ARTICLE IV

## ON THE FOUR EXPLANATIONS OF SACRED SCRIPTURE, AND THE SEVEN VERY USEFUL RULES TO UNDERSTAND SACRED SCRIPTURE

EARLY ALL OF SACRED SCRIPTURE, OR ITS theological doctrine, is marvelously veiled under certain figures and similitudes, so that the truth is hidden to unworthy and depraved men, but it stands out to truly studious and pious men on account of their good exertions. And also [the truth is veiled] because, according to Dionysius [the Areopagite],[79] it is impossible for us to make known to others the divine light unless it be covered by a variety of sacred anagogical veils. Whence the Damascene[80] says: It behooves us men existing under the weight of the flesh to know that it is not possible to know divine and immaterial things, unless we were to use the means of images and forms of similar nature. And Augustine says: Knowledge of the properties of natural things unlocks for us the secrets of sacred Scripture. Hence, it happens that sacred Scripture expresses itself in many ways because not only do names signify things, but also one thing may signify another. For the things themselves are connected to the divine knowledge, as the words are to one who reveals, because *He spoke, and they were made.*[81] Therefore, most sacred theology does not only concern itself with the signification of words, but also with the [underlying] properties of things.

In addition, there are four ways that sacred Scripture may be understood; namely, literally or historically, and spiritually or mystically. But mystical knowledge is three-fold, namely, it is allegorical, tropological or moral, and anagogical. For history teaches us that which occurred, allegory that which is to be believed, tropology that which is to be done, and anagogy that which is to be expected. History is the narration of things done (*res gestae*). And in fact the historical or literal sense is the foundation or basis of the other knowledge, and from it alone is to be found the valid grounds for proofs of the faith, as Augustine asserted in his epistle against Vincent the Donatist.[82] The allegorical sense is when

---

79  For Dionysius the Areopagite, *see* footnote P-36.

80  E. N. St. John of Damascus (*ca.* 675-749), a Father and Doctor of the Church, known in particular for his Exposition of the Orthodox Faith (*De Fide Orthodoxa*) and his vigorous defense of images (icons).

81  Ps. 148:5.

82  E. N. Epistle 93 to Vincent, Donatist Bishop of Cartenna.

that which is said or done by any person is understood to pertain to Christ or his Mystical Body, or when that which was observed regarding the Synagogue is referred to the Church. For all these things occurred to them in figure, and they are written for our instruction.[83] Now the tropological sense is when that which is written or told about Christ or the saints is applied and set forth for our moral formation. And the anagogical sense is when those things that have occurred in time lead to the contemplation of eternal things, and when those things which pertain to the Church militant are referred to the Church triumphant.

To show these senses, it is customary to use as an example the word Jerusalem; but because it is common and known almost by all, I omit it;[84] and I will put in its place an example of a phrase in all its meanings.[85] For that which is written of manna is — according to the literal [or historical] sense that is set forth — about that food which God rained upon the sons of Israel in the desert.[86] Allegorically, it exhibits the most superlatively worthy Sacrament of the Body and Blood of Christ, for manna was a figure of the Sacrament of the Altar. And tropologically, it expresses the spiritual nutrition of charity and grace with which God interiorly feeds, consoles, and strengthen his daily faithful servants in this present exile. Anagogically, it reveals that most happy feast of the blessed in heaven where, by a most blessed enjoyment, the superessential God is the food of the blessed. Whence it is written: *Blessed is he who shall eat bread in the kingdom of God.*[87] And again: *They shall be inebriated with the plenty of your house; and you shall make them drink of the torrent of your pleasure.*[88]

Furthermore, seven are the rules that Augustine, Bede, and Haymo[89] refer as having been posited by Tyconius[90] by which all ambiguities of

---

83   *Cf.* 1 Cor. 10:11; Rom. 15:4.
84   *E. N. E.g.*, Cassian, Conference XIV, 8: "[T]he one Jerusalem can be understood in four different ways, in the historical sense as the city of the Jews, in allegory as the Church of Christ, in anagoge as the heavenly city of God 'which is mother to us all' (Gal. 4:26), in the tropological sense as the human soul, which under this name, is frequently criticized or blamed by the Lord." John Cassian, *Conferences* (New York: Paulist Press 1985), 160 (Colum Luibheid, trans.).
85   L. *in integra oratione.*
86   Ex. 16:4 *et seq.*
87   Luke 14:15.
88   Ps. 35:9.
89   *E. N.* Probably Haymo (or Haimo) of Halberstadt (*ca.* 778–853 A. D.), a Benedictine monk, pupils of St. Alcuin, and well-known for his Scriptural commentaries, but possibly also Haymo of Faversham (d. 1244), a Franciscan friar, and a theologian and liturgist. He became general of that order, elected to that position in 1240.
90   *E. N.* Tyconius (also Ticonius or Tychonius) (*fl.* 370–390 A. D.) was an African Donatist who wrote the book, the *Seven Rules* (*De Septem Regulis*). *See Tyconius:*

opposing passages [in Scripture] are to be explained or resolved. For with these rules of the sacred Scriptures a series [of words] is changed, and its explanation is altered.

*The first rule*[91] is that sometimes language, under one and unvarying voice, is made to refer to Christ and to his Mystical Body, and so a series of words is made to transition from one [referent] into the other, even though it may come from the same series. In such instances it must be considered, therefore, whether it possibly refers to one thing or the other. Christ in turn may say something in the person of his members, as if saying it of himself, as in this instance here: *Why have You forsaken me? Far from my salvation . . .*[92] And again: *For I was hungry, and you gave me not to eat.*[93] And yet again: *Saul, Saul, why do you persecute me?*[94]

*The second rule*[95] is that holy Scripture at times speaks simultaneously of the Mystical Body of Christ as including those who truly pertain to Christ, and the Mystical Body as those who are such only by name, so that they are false, as when it is said: *When he slew them, then they sought him: and they returned, and came to him early in the morning.*[96] For in such expression Scripture appears to speak of one and the same thing, yet it also may speak of other things. For some were slain, but others who were seeking God returned.

*The third rule*[97] is that sacred Scripture, sometimes in the same voice, indicates literally something happening at the time, and from this the Spirit

---

*The Book of Rules* (Atlanta: Scholars Press, 1989) (trans. William S. Babcock). These were crafted *ut quis prophetiae immensam silvam perambulans his regulis quodam modo lucis tramitibus deductus ab errore defendatur,* "so that he who ambles about the immense forest of prophecy, led in the path by these rules of light, may be preserved from error."

91  E. N. The first rule — *de Domine et corpore eius, of the Lord and his body* — is meant to distinguish when a verse of Scripture refers to Christ and when it refers to his Mystical Body, the Church, a transference that can even occur mid-sentence. Generally, reason can be used to distinguish between the referents; but in difficult passages, recourse must be had to special interpretative grace.

92  Ps. 21:2.

93  Matt. 25:42.

94  Acts 9:4.

95  E. N. The second rule — *de Domine corpore bipertito, of the Lord's bipartite body* — considers the fact that in the Mystical Body, the Church, the wheat grows with the tares (Matt. 13:24-30), and so the rule is used to distinguish when a Scriptural passage refers to the "left" (sinister) side or "right" side of the Church, or moves from the "left" to the "right" or the "right" to the "left," as Tyconius puts it.

96  Ps. 75:34.

97  E. N. The third rule — *de promissis et lege, of the promises and the law* — relates to the relationship between the dispensation of the law and the dispensation of grace, as the law and grace are linked in Christ.

reveals to us something else for another time. Such occurs in the ceremonial precepts of the Old Law, which if interpreted in the literal sense [today] are deadly, but at the time of the law they were intended usefully to be observed. Whence the Apostle says: *The letter kills, but the spirit quickens.*[98]

*The fourth rule*[99] is that the divine Scripture sometimes, as if under the same voice or in similar sentences, transitions from genus to species, from whole to part, and conversely. And such manner of speaking is in the Prophets to a greatest degree general, as when — under the threats made to a particular people or a kingdom — the Prophets intend to announce that which is generally true for all in the future. Such is seen when Isaiah warns Babylon or Tyre, intending to similar warnings to all those who similarly do evil in their communities. Whence also Christ in the Gospel says: *And what I say to you, I say to all.*[100]

*The fifth rule*[101] is when Scripture refers to the whole through a part, or part through the whole, as when it speaks of the three days of the Lord's sepulture.[102] These kinds of expression are understood as synecdoches. And to this manner of expression are also referred all the defects or excesses of numbers and of times, as when past tense is used for future tense, or something less than the whole number; and then also when a time is to be accounted as nothing.

*The sixth rule*[103] is of recapitulation or anticipation, as when Scripture returns to that which occurred before, insofar as it might attach something, or conveniently might repeat it. In this manner, after Scripture in Genesis commemorates the sons of Noah divided by language and peoples, there is added: And the one people were also of one tongue,

---

98  2 Cor. 3:6b.

99  E. N. The fourth rule — *de specie et genere, of the particular and the general* — attempts to deal with the breadth given to certain words and their extension, or reach, or use; and it also addresses the use of signs or types in Scripture.

100  Mark 13:37.

101  E. N. The fifth rule — *de temporibus, of times* — addresses the Scriptural use of time, recognizing that days and years sometimes mean something more than literal days and years, allows for Biblical numerology, and recognizes the difference between *chronos* (χρόνος) and *kairos* (καιρός). "One day with the Lord is as a thousand years, and a thousand years as one day." 2 Pet. 3:8.

102  E. N. Denis refers to the fact that Jesus was dead not for three full days and nights (three 24-hour periods), but for part of Friday (which ended, under Jewish usage, at sundown), all of Saturday, rising from the grave on Sunday dawn, and yet under Scriptural usage it can be said to be "three days."

103  E. N. The sixth rule — *de recapitulatione, on recapitulation* — allows for a reasoned achronicity in Scripture, so that the present can refer to the past, the past to the present, the present and the past to the eschatological future and vice versa.

which in any case was before the predicted division.[104] In the same manner, after the fact something is narrated before it by anticipation. Such passages, therefore, are made true or explained by such rule.

*The seventh rule*[105] is of the devil and his body, as when they [bodies] are falsely ascribed to the devils, and vice versa. This occurs in Isaiah where we encounter words said of Lucifer, who is the chief of all evildoers, under the person of the king of Babylon.[106] Whence it is read: *How have you fallen from heaven, O Lucifer, who did rise in the morning?*[107] Similarly in Ezechiel, under the person of the king of Tyre, we find words referring to the devil.[108] And Christ in the Gospel said of Judas the betrayer: *One of you is a devil.*[109]

These are to be retained in the memory for the purpose of future understanding.

# ARTICLE V

## ON THE TITLE, AND THE AUTHOR, AND THE
## VARIOUS TRANSLATIONS OF THE BOOK OF PSALMS

NOW LET US LOOK AT THE TITLE OF THE book of Psalms. Under the circumstances, its title might be said to be such: *Beginning of the Book of Hymns, or of Soliloquies of the Prophet of Christ.*[110] This title is truly suggested in diverse ways by Catholic teachers. It is also something in which all are agreed and all address first [when they speak of the book of Psalms]. This book is accordingly called a *Book of Hymns* because a hymn is the praise of God with song. But song is the exaltation of the mind taken up by the eternal good, breaking

---

104 *Cf.* Gen. 11:1, 6.

105 E. N. The seventh rule — *de diabolo et eius corpore, on the Devil and his body* — is the demonic analogue to the second rule, but it concerns the devil, and his "body," or his followers.

106 Is. 14:4 *et seq.*

107 Is. 14:12a.

108 Ez. 28:12 *et seq.*

109 John 6:71.

110 E. N. *See* St. Thomas Aquinas's introduction (*proemium*) to his unfinished *Commentary on the Psalms*, from which Denis draws upon for this section, where he entitles the Psalms as: *Incipit Liber Hymnorum, seu Soliloquiorum Propheta David de Christo*, The Beginning of the Book of Hymns or Soliloquies of the Prophet David of Christ.

forth into voice. Because also this book teaches us to praise God with exultation abiding even into eternity, not only with the heart, but also with the voice, so it is fittingly called a *Book of Hymns*. But these hymns are written in Hebrew meter, which was difficult to translate. Also added to the title are the words *or of Soliloquies*, and this because David solely by the inspiration of the Holy Spirit, and intellectual revelation, without any external support, produced the Psalms; and thus as between him and the Holy Spirit, they may be seen as if they were a kind of soliloquy. Or also [they may be called soliloquies] because this book principally speaks of and addresses only Christ. Or again also [they may be called soliloquies] because a devoted soul proclaiming the Psalms enjoys a certain soliloquy with God that is particularly so much more sweet, affective, ardent, and sincere the more the soul knows and tastes more deeply and clearly the power and sense of the Psalms. And the title also contains the words *of the Prophet*. For indeed all are agreed in this, that all the Psalms are written under divine inspiration and so are in some way part of the prophetic genre. But whether strictly speaking one, or determined to be many, of this there exists various opinions, as will be discussed below. And the title follows with *Of Christ*. For behold here is the matter or subject of the book of Psalms. For it is about Christ, and not by any means only of the person of Christ, but of the whole Christ, that is of him and that which pertains to him, indeed of the Bridegroom and Bride, or the Head and the Mystical Body. For sometimes it speaks of the Head, that is of Christ himself according to himself; sometimes it speaks of his Body, that is the Church. Sometimes it pertains to Christ according to both senses. And finally, it may deal with Christ according to himself in three ways. First, according to his divinity, as in this place: *This day have I begotten you.*[111] Second, with respect to his humanity, as here: *I am a worm.*[112] Third, transumptively,[113] as when Christ is used in the voice of the members, as here: *O God, you know my foolishness.*[114]

Now we consider the manner in which the teachers vary in expounding about this title.[115] First, therefore, they dispute in that which says *Beginning of the Book*. For some say that the books of the Psalms are five in number because there are five distinctions that are to be found

---

111 Ps. 2:7b.
112 Ps. 22:7a.
113 L. *transumptive*, metaphorically, or transferred from one thing to another.
114 Ps. 68:6a.
115 E. N. Namely, *Beginning of the Book of Hymns, or of Soliloquies of the Prophet of Christ.*

in this book by the words *Amen, amen.*[116] But others assert that it is in any event one book because within it is said the following: *In the head of the book it is written of me.*[117] And in the Acts of the Apostles it is said: *For it is written in the book of Psalms.*[118] It does not say "in the books," but *in the book.* Nevertheless it seems, absent better judgment, that both positions can be legitimated, so that we may say that it is one book in total, and many partial books, in the manner that the book of Kings is called one, but it is also divided into four parts.[119] And the book of the Prophets is said to be one, and it can be divided in twelve partial books, especially since the prophet Nahum, whose prophecies are utterly most brief, in the beginning of his prophecies he says: *The book of the vision of Nahum.*[120]

Second, they disagree regarding the part of the title that says *of the Prophet,* that is, with respect to the author of the Psalms. For some affirm that all the Psalms were composed by David, namely, Augustine, Cassiodorus, the Glossator,[121] and many others. But others hold the opposite, for example, Jerome, Hilary, Chrysostom, and who are followed by Nicolaus of Lyra, asserting with Hebrew teachers who affirm the authors of the Psalms to be many. Which of these positions is more true, I am not able to discern with certainty.

Yet, as Gregory says in his first book *Moralia in Job,* it is largely futile to inquire who might be the author of the Book of Job, when it is most certain that the principal author of that book is declared to be the Holy Spirit. So also in the same manner it appears futile to scrutinize out of curiosity, or to make much of the dispute, as to whether David alone authored the Psalms; this is so since it assuredly is plain that all the Psalms were written through revelation of the Holy Spirit. Nevertheless, I am of the opinion that the more probable and more true [position] is that David alone is the author of the book of Psalms. Indeed, any other [opinion] does not appear to be true, since all the Psalms were revealed and written by the anagogical revelation of the Holy Spirit, that is without any exterior support of imaginative forms, or of bodily species and of sensible signs. And it is certain that it would not be able to be

---

116  E. N. The ending of the five books are identified by the words, Amen, amen, which terminate Psalms 40:14, 71:19, 88:53, 105:48, with 150:5 ending with Alleluia.
117  Ps. 39:8b.
118  Acts. 1:20a.
119  E. N. 1-4 Kings, also divided in 1-2 Samuel, and 1-2 Kings.
120  Nahum 1:1.
121  E. N. The person who compiled the *Glossa Ordinaria,* of which they were several. On the *Glossa Ordinaria* see footnote P-58.

said of David that he was the most excellent of the prophets unless he prophesied with anagogic and not symbolic revelations. Moreover, that which is from God is thus ordered.[122] Since, therefore, as nearly all are in agreement, Esdras, as a result of the Holy Spirit revealing and disposing, assembled the Psalms, and gathered them all into one book, it does not seem fitting to mix confusedly and in such a disordered fashion arrange the Psalms of so many diverse authors or prophets, putting now one, and at this time another Psalm, as if this book might be a kind of spiritual commonplace book,[123] or as if it were a certain kind of collection of diverse sayings. And [if this were so, that David did not author all the Psalms,] it would seem a marvel why the Psalms of David were not compiled into a special book by itself, since it is certain that the largest part of the Psalms was written by him, especially since when it came to the preservation of the other prophets such a form was found adequate. For however much possible the prophecies of the twelve prophets could have been collected into one book, the writings of each of them was nevertheless also able to be given its own book, and each one of the prophets was allotted a special and partial book, notwithstanding the fact that some of them agreed in many matters, and some are very brief. Nevertheless, if David alone did not write the Psalms, then certainly such a combination of Psalms would not be able to be labeled anything but disordered, or confused, and not made with a certain or clear order. Because I am unable to discover these things [in the Psalms] in the manner that I have stated, I submit that it is more probable [that David wrote all the Psalms], although I do not affirm anything determinatively.

One should keep in mind that St. Jerome translated the book of Psalms three times. First, according to the interpretation of the Septuagint, which is called the Roman Psalter because it was used by the Church of St. Peter. Second, at the insistence of Paul and Eustochius he authored another translation, not much different from the first translation, though closer to the Hebrew; and it is called the Gallic Psalter, because Pope Damasus, at the entreaty of Jerome, caused it to be sung in the Gallican Church; and this translation is also more common among the Latins. Third, he translated the book entirely from Hebrew, and the instance of a certain holy bishop named Sophronius, who frequently disputed with the Jews. Whence, he needed a text that was in all respects

---

122  *Cf.* Rom. 13:1b.

123  L. *rapiarius.* These were personal books into which prayers and devotional exercises were copied.

similar to the Psalter that was written in Hebrew, for it alone would be accepted by the Jews.

The true intention of the Book of Psalms is to unfold the mystery of Christ, and thus to raise up, reform, and bless in the new man Christ the fallen and deformed human race in the old Adam.

# ARTICLE VI

## ON THE POWER OF THE PSALMS, AND ON THE MODES OF PRAYING AND SINGING THEM

ECAUSE PSALMODY IS A CERTAIN SOLILO-quy of the Holy Spirit with the pious and devout soul, it is fitting that no man is able truly and experientially to know the power of the Psalms unless he sings the words of the most sacred palms with a pure and stable and free soul, turning to God with a clean and fixed mind, adverting with undivided attention the sense of the words, just as if he was forming and pronouncing them out of his own affection. For this (as Basil says) is to pray the psalms wisely, so that with intellectual sweetness and internal relish we ourselves might utter, with all reverence and custody of heart, the words of the Holy Spirit before the countenance of God, who truly is present everywhere, thinking about and recollecting what is written: *The meditation of my heart always in your sight.*[124] And again: *As the Lord lives...in whose sight I stand.*[125] And also what is in Jeremiah: *Cursed be he that does the work of the Lord carelessly.*[126] For the Holy Spirit, who is burning unharming fire[127] and most ardent charity, draws forth the most affectionate words from the Psalms, and describes all manner of men with fitting words. At one time putting forth those words which are received by the perfect, and these are songs out of the great fervor of charity. At other times putting forth words which concern the repentant and imperfect. Indeed, he has set forth a fitting canticle for every virtuous affection. For sometimes he sets forth those said in the person of Christ; sometimes those said in the person of the

---

124  Ps. 18:15.

125  1 Kings 17:1; 2 Kings 3:14.

126  Jer. 48:10 (*E. N.* Denis replaces the word *fraudulenter* (deceitfully) in the Vulgate with *negligenter* (negligently).

127  *E. N.* This would appear to be a reference to the revelation of the Lord to Moses in the burning bush, which the flames did not consume. Ex. 3:2.

Church; sometimes those in the person of sinners and penitents, sometimes those in the person efficaciously advancing [in the spiritual life]; sometimes those in the person of the perfect and the fervently diligent; sometimes those in the person of the just and zealous with the justice of God; sometimes those in the person of one giving thanks. Whence, he who desires to sing or read the Psalms with perfect devotion necessarily needs to conform his affections to the sentiment of the Psalms, and must adopt a resemblance to all the previously mentioned persons, according to what is required by the purpose of the Psalm. And so Denis [the Areopagite] says in the third chapter of the *Celestial Hierarchy* that in their mode of divine praise, the Psalms include and contain all that which is contained in sacred Writ.

Consequently, it is a very true statement that no mortal is able either to conceive with the mind or to express with words the power of the Psalms. For they teach the eradication of all vices, the adoption of all virtues, and the fullness of all perfection; they illuminate faith, they strengthen hope, they inflame charity, they instruct in humility, they especially commend meekness, and instruct patience and the other virtues, they powerfully delight the mind of the devoted reciter of Psalms, they take away all vices and the sorrows of a lifetime. And rejoicing in the continual chanting of the Psalms leads the wretched in this age into the heavenly and angelic life. And he who does so feels disgust at carnal delights, vehemently abhors vain and unfruitful words, secular rumors, and the wasting of time, is happy to separate from human conversation and endeavors to converse with God, and is adorned unceasingly with all the splendor of grace. Above all, the most inflaming and affective prayers, and the most joyful acts of thanksgiving, the most humble confession of sins, the most excellent praise of God, the commendation of all good, the detestation of all evil, and the most excellent and most sublime raising of the mind are contained in the Psalms. And so within the Psalms are contained the torment of the impious, the reward and joy of the elect, the rudiments for the beginning, the perfection of the proficient, the fullness of the perfect, the life of him who is active, and the observations of the contemplative.

With respect to the manner of singing the Psalms, what can be more apt than to say that which the most devout and most agreeable Bernard teaches?[128] I admonish—he says—you, most beloved brothers,

---

128  E. N. St. Bernard of Clairvaux (A. D. 1090–1153), Cistercian monk and mystic, also considered a Doctor of the Church (*Doctor Mellifluus*). This particular reference is to Sermon 47 on the *Song of Songs*.

strenuously to take part in the divine praises, as reverently and also with the same alacrity as serving the Lord, not reluctantly, not languidly, not listlessly, not sparing of voice, not cutting short words in the middle, not skipping over the whole, not with weak or slurred voice, sounding like a woman's nasal stammering; but in a manly fashion, as is worthy, bring forth resounding and affective voices of the Holy Spirit, thinking of nothing other than what you are singing. For the Holy Spirit is not pleased if you are neglectful with respect to that which you offer him. Surely, as Basil says,[129] God is to be prayed to and praised, not with a wandering soul which roams about here and there, but he ought to be adored solicitously, with a God-fearing spirit. And before prayer, the soul ought to prepare itself[130]—casting aside various and impertinent occupations, taking leave of anything impressing itself interiorly, and beginning with great seriousness—lest a small error in the beginning grow during the process and become a huge one at its end.

But to pray and to recite the Psalms in this manner, requires much, and demands a holy manner of life, so that before prayer a man so ought to have possession of himself, and to strive towards God, to examine carefully his perceptions, and to taste the powers of the divine words however much as is possible through the grace of God during that time of prayer and praise, with an interior stability of mind and ardent affection. For it behooves one above all to avoid aggravating sorrow, to hold as hateful dissipating levity, inordinate fear, immoderate anxiety, and all uncontrolled concupiscence, and to expel irrational passion from the soul; and to the extent we are more able to suspend our souls from all powers of inferior operations, and to detach ourselves more from the memory and love of the senses, to that extent we will be able to intend and to be open to the divine offices and holy prayers so as to say them with more affection, sweetness, and salubriousness. For *God is Spirit, and they that adore Him must adore Him in spirit.*[131]

Finally, all curiosity, all dissoluteness, all discord are to be greatly avoided in chant; and we ought to strive to be occupied with nothing else other than the Most High when busy with the highest of all works,

---

129  St. Basil of Caesarea (330–379 A. D.), Bishop of Caesarea who wrote many theological and polemical works, avidly supporting the Nicene statement of faith and battling against the Arians. St. Basil is also considered to be the father of Eastern monasticism. He is a Doctor of the Church, one of the four great Greek Fathers.

130  Ecclus. 18:23.

131  John 4:24.

while spiritually exulting him, opting to see, to hear, and to prize him alone, directing ourselves always to the senses of the words and to God more than with the chant or the mode of chanting, thinking of that saying of Blessed Augustine: While it happens to befall to me that I am moved more by the song than that which is sung, I profess to have committed something worthy of fault, and then I chose not to hear the singer.[132] Let us endeavor, therefore, that we may consider with our minds that which comes forth from our mouths. And if a man is of such learning so that he is unable to understand the holy Scriptures, and thus is not able to consider the sense of the Psalms with his mind, or [if he is able to understand] that which is sung only in its superficial and historical sense, such a man is seen to be included with those of no or little devotion, as is stated: *For the sparrow has found herself a house, and the turtle-dove a nest for herself where she may lay her young ones.*[133] Then we ought to study so that we might raise our mind with heartfelt affection to God, thinking us to stand before the presence of God, and to render service to the highest Lord and Judge of all. And thus considering the divine majesty or any other divine attribute, we will be able to stand before God with great devotion.

# ARTICLE VII

## ON THE INTENTION AND THE FORM OF
## PROCEEDING OF THIS PRESENT WORK

ESPITE THE FACT THAT SACRED SCRIPTURE already is seen to have been fully expounded by holy and great and orthodox teachers, especially the book of Psalms, and no one is able to expound perfectly on David except the Holy Spirit who spoke to David that he might abundantly enlighten, teach, and perfect his soul; nevertheless, ardently putting confidence in the goodness of God, I will undertake that which by any means exceeds my own strength, namely to expound in one way or another the Psalter, with hope of that reward which Wisdom promises, saying: *They that explain me shall have life everlasting.*[134] And again: *They that instruct many to justice, are as stars*

---

132  E. N. This is a reference to St. Augustine's *Confessions* X, 33.
133  Ps. 83:4.
134  Ecclus. 24:31.

*for all eternity.*[135] And this is to be understood to befit them whose life
or manner of living is in accord to their teaching. *But to the sinner God
has said: Why do you declare my justices?*[136] Indeed, as Blessed Thomas
says regarding the fourth book of the *Sentences*,[137] he who does not do
that which he teaches to others, assumes the burden of the very thing
he teaches, and sins mortally. This is so because to the extent he is
able, he hollows out the very intention of the Scriptures. Further, he
whose life is suitable to teaching is surely awarded gold, and even if he
never preaches to the people with his mouth, but expounds the sacred
Scripture, or composes books on theology, he speaks for the edification
of all of those who read them.

But lest anyone should think this work altogether superfluous, I
intend to expound on the book of Psalms in a certain special manner:
it is special, as it agrees with the sayings of the Saints, and not in the
sense of what I believe. I intend, therefore, to explain the Psalms according to the many understandings, according as the Lord may grant, that is
to expound the text literally, allegorically, tropologically, and anagogically,
to the degree that the text itself permits, and to the extent it is possible
for me, undertaking expositions of these texts now more, now less, as
the subject matter may require. Finally, in the manner that my Superior has enjoined upon me, I propose to avoid a colorful style, difficult
manners of expression, and impertinent subtilities, and to proceed in a
plain and simple fashion.

And that I may be able to proceed worthily and fruitfully, to the honor
of the most blessed and superlatively glorious honor of the Trinity, the
utility of all the readers and hearers, with all my heart I pray to and
invoke the abundant and incessant goodness of the Holy Spirit, for as
the book of Job has it: *There is a spirit in men, and the inspiration of
the Almighty gives understanding.*[138] For Christ speaking to his disciples
of the Holy Spirit said: *The Paraclete, the Holy Spirit, whom the Father
will send in my name, he will teach you all things, and bring all things to
your mind, whatsoever I shall have said to you.*[139]

---

135  Dan. 12:3b.
136  Ps. 49:16a.
137  *Super Sent.*, lib. 4 d. 19 q. 2 a. 2.
138  Job 32:8.
139  John 14:26.

# *Psalm 1*

## ARTICLE VIII

ON THE FIRST (THAT IS, LITERAL)
EXPOSITION OF THE FIRST PSALM:
*BEATUS VIR QUI NO ABIIT, &c.*
*BLESSED THE MAN WHO HAS NOT WALKED, &c.*

SDRAS, THAT SWIFT SCRIBE, WHO WAS
lifted up also with the prophetic spirit,[1] is said to have restored
the canonical books of the Old Testament burned by the Babylonians,
with the Holy Spirit revealing, first of all the Pentateuch, that is, the five
books of Moses which he discovered with the Samaritans. He restored,
therefore, the Psalms, and here he placed the first Psalm in the book of
Psalms as a kind of preface or prologue, as is popularly said. Whence
this Psalm is not designated with a title, since this Psalm is as it were
a title to the book that follows because it contains the summary and
material of the entire book, and it addresses generally that which in the
whole book of Psalms is addressed particularly.

---

1[1] *Blessed is the man who has not walked in the counsel of the ungodly,*
*nor stood in the way of sinners, nor sat in the chair of pestilence.*

*Beatus vir qui non abiit in consilio impiorum, et in via peccatorum*
*non stetit, et in cathedra pestilentiae non sedit.*

And so this Psalm is able to be understood literally of any virtuous
man. And that which follows regarding the ungodly and of their vanity
and their torments may be said of all evil men. Therefore, the author of
the present Psalm says:   1[1] *Beatus vir qui non abiit in consilio impio-*
*rum. Blessed is the man who has not walked in the counsel of the ungodly.*
Counsel is an act of prudence. And as prudence is of two kinds — namely,
true prudence and false prudence — so it is with counsel: some is true,
and some is false. True counsel pertains to those who diligently inquire
which are the ways and means that pertain to happiness. But false is that

---

1  E. N. See the books of 1 Esdras (Esdras) and 2 Esdras (Nehemiah). Esdras is
   also known as Ezra.

counsel of those who think of the ways of evil desire which lead to evil effect. And so it is said: *Blessed the man who has not walked in the counsel of the ungodly.* Someone can walk in the counsel of the ungodly in two ways. First, by giving evil counsel to others. Secondly, by consenting and acquiescing to perverse counsel. Therefore, *Blessed is the man who has not walked,* that is, has not withdrawn from God, into the *counsel of the ungodly,* by that which considers something evil or false, or acquiesces in the false counsel of others. For he who counsels others in evil is the cause and source of all the evil which is done as a result of his perverse counsel. And man departs or recedes from God in the counsel of the ungodly. This [departing or receding from God] is not said in terms of physical place — for God is everywhere, and penetrates all things, and is everywhere equally and immediately, according to Denis [the Areopagite] — but [it is said] in terms of dissimilarity. This is so because, by the counsel of the ungodly, a man makes himself dissimilar to God, who is just and hates the counsel of the iniquitous; and those departing in the counsel of the ungodly separate [themselves] from grace, and their mere presence detracts from godliness. For nothing will separate us from God except that by which we separate and distance ourselves from him. And truly nothing separates us from the Lord God except our own vices, such as Isaiah testified to, saying: Your sins have divided your God and you.[2] And nothing unites us and holds us fast to God except our virtues, which cast away our sins. And thus Isaiah again says: This is all the fruit, that it might remove your iniquity.[3]

Finally, what else is it to say *Blessed is the man who has not walked in the counsel of the ungodly* except blessed is the man who remains in the counsel of the godly, both giving counsel to others of right things and consenting to the right counsel of others? For this reason, it states in the Proverbs of Solomon: *There is safety where there is much counsel.*[4] And Tobias instructing his son said: *Seek counsel always of a wise man.*[5] Further, what is the opposite of *Blessed is the man who has not walked in the counsel of the ungodly* other than unhappy or miserable is the man who walks in the counsel of the ungodly, or who counsels

---

2  Cf. Is. 59:2a. *But your iniquities have divided between you and your God, and your sins have hid his face from you that he should not hear.*
3  Cf. Is. 27:9a. *Therefore upon this shall the iniquity of the house of Jacob be forgiven: and this is all the fruit, that the sin thereof should be taken away, when he shall have made all the stones of the altar.*
4  Prov. 11:14b.
5  Tob. 4:19.

evil, or who conforms himself to evil counsel? Here, the most holy
Isaiah confessed speaking on behalf of God: *Woe to you, apostate chil-*
*dren . . . that you would take counsel, and not of me: and would begin a*
*web, and not by my spirit.*[6]

A man is blessed in two ways, that is, in hope (*in spe*) and in reality
(*in re*). But a certain blessed man may be said to be blessed in hope in
two ways: first, according to his remote dispositions or potentially, in
the manner that we call the children of good nature blessed; and second,
with respect to the closeness to that disposition or habitually, as the
Savior says: *Blessed are the clean of heart: for they shall see God.*[7] In turn,
the blessed in reality is he who already enjoys God perfectly. Therefore,
blessedness in hope corresponds to those on earth (*viator*), and of this
we will now speak.

By that also which is said, *Blessed is the man,* we do not intend to
exclude a woman. For the word man in this place is meant not with
regard to the property of sex, but by reason with respect to virtue, which
neither is elevated by prosperity, nor is diminished by adversity, for it
is not like a reed shaken by the wind, but it is fixed in the Lord and
it advances along the royal way. This virtue existed in the noble Joshua
who did not turn to the right or left from the law of Moses.[8] But to
exist in this manner in regards to a man also is assuredly also found
with a woman who is of the same nature, as it was in her of whom
Solomon said: *Who shall find a valiant woman?*[9] And again: *She has*
*girded her loins with strength.*[10] And is this not the manner in which the
word man is said regarding the Virgin mother, of whom the Lord to the
devil under the name of the serpent said, *I will put enmities between you*
*and . . . she shall crush your head?*[11] And of course certain virile females
figuratively preceded this virile Woman: as that most holy Esther, who
never rejoiced in her regal decorousness and excellence with incomparable
temporal goods.[12] And also in that most strong Judith, who disposed
of the most cruel Holofernes in such a manly fashion.[13]

*Et in via peccatorum non stetit. Nor stood in the way of sinners.* A vicious
activity comes from evil counsel. An activity, however, is called a way

---

6  Is. 30:1.
7  Matt. 5:8.
8  Joshua 1:7.
9  Prov. 31:10a.
10  Prov. 31:17a.
11  Gen. 3:15.
12  Esther 14:18. *E. N.* In that she rejoiced, rather, only in the God of Abraham.
13  Judith 13:10.

because by it one arrives to an end. For good activity leads to eternal happiness, and evil activity to sempiternal misery. Blessed, therefore, are those who do not stand in the way of sinners, those who do not remain in iniquitous activity, nor acquiesce in evil activity, who neither glory when doing evil, nor *rejoice in most wicked things.*[14] Of this way, Solomon says: *There is a way which seems just to a man: but the ends thereof lead to death.*[15] And again: *The way of the wicked is darksome: they know not where they fall.*[16] On the contrary, of the way of the Lord it is written: *her ways are beautiful ways, and all her paths are peaceable.*[17]

*Et in cathedra pestilentiae non sedit. Nor sat in the chair of pestilence.* Pestilence is an infectious disease. And a chair is the seat of a doctor or a judge. Whence, to sit in a chair of pestilence is to corrupt or scandalize others with false doctrine or bad example, and to be a stumbling block to one's brothers. And the Savior makes manifest how damnable this is when he said: *He that shall scandalize one of these little ones that believe in me, it were better for him that a millstone should be hanged about his neck, and that he should be drowned in the depth of the sea.*[18] And also: *Woe to that man by whom scandal comes.*[19] Whence also the Apostle: *Let us not therefore judge one another any more. But judge this rather, that you put not a stumbling block or a scandal in your brother's way.*[20] In any case he who neither by word nor deed furnishes an occasion of sin to others does not sit in the chair of pestilence, and such a person is with merit called blessed.

Now threefold is the sin that is addressed in this first verse, and which it is urged to avoid; and that is the sin of iniquitous thoughts, the sin of unjust actions, and the sin of perverse instruction. And the first sin is adjoined with the word *Walk,* which indicates movement. The second is adjoined with the word *Stand*; and the third [with the word] *Sit*; and both of these [latter words] indicate repose. But greater it is to rest or remain sitting than standing. This is so because he who sins only by thought is easily able to retract it, but he who proceeds in deed finds it more difficult to turn back. But he who is already habituated in evil and poisons others is only corrected with greatest difficulty.

14  Prov. 2:14.
15  Prov. 14:12.
16  Prov. 4:19.
17  Prov. 3:17. E. N. I have placed masculine pronouns when referring to the Lord in lieu of the feminine which refer to Wisdom, in Latin, *sapientia,* a feminine noun. In Latin *eius* can be either feminine or masculine.
18  Matt. 18:6.
19  Matt. 18:7b.
20  Rom. 14:13.

1[2] *But his will is in the law of the Lord, and on his law he shall
meditate day and night.*

*Sed in lege Domini voluntas eius, et in lege eius meditabitur die
ac nocte.*

And thus because it is not sufficient not to do evil, but it behooves
one also to do good, as the Savior has attested, saying: *Every tree that
brings not forth good fruit, shall be cut down, and shall be cast into the
fire;*[21] for which reason, having stated what evil to avoid, in the verse
which follows it states that good which pertains to the blessed man. It
says, therefore: 1[2] *Sed in lege Domini voluntas eius. But his will is in
the law of the Lord,* that is, the desire of his heart and all the affection of
his mind tends to this, so that the law of God may be fulfilled, and so
that he might govern all his life according to the will of the most high
God. For we ought to temper our lives spontaneously and promptly by
the divine commandments, and not by compulsion or reluctantly; and we
ought completely to fulfill them more out of filial love than out of servile
fear, so that we are able to say to God: *Lord, all my desire is before you.*[22]
St. Paul also exhorts this, saying: *that you may prove what is the good, and
the acceptable, and the perfect will of God.*[23] And again: *For you have not
received the spirit of bondage again in fear; but you have received the spirit
of adoption of sons, whereby we cry: Abba (Father).*[24] Hence also David
says: *And you my son Solomon, know the God of your father, and serve him
with a perfect heart and a willing mind.*[25] But because self-will is blind,
and moved with self-love, and follows only its own impulses, it lacks the
direction of reason, since a reasonable service is to be rendered to God.[26]

Therefore, such a reasonable direction and examination is to conduct
the blessed man; it is consequently stated, while under such guidance, *et
in lege eius meditabitur die ac nocte, and on his law he shall meditate day
and night,* examining that which is pleasing to God, that which displeases
him, that which he has enjoined, that which he has prohibited, the way
a man may more quickly be able to accomplish it, how many are the
benefits God shows to men, how many are the goods he promises in
the future, how great is the blindness of the ingrate, and how severe the

---

21 Matt.3:10; 7:19.
22 Ps. 37:10a.
23 Rom. 12:2b.
24 Rom. 8:15.
25 1 Chr. 28:9a.
26 *Cf.* Rom. 12:1. *I beseech you therefore, brethren, by the mercy of God, that you
present your bodies a living sacrifice, holy, pleasing unto God, your reasonable service.*

torments of the reprobate. To contemplate these and such similar things faithfully is to meditate on the law of the Lord.

But in what manner is a man able to meditate on the law of the Lord day and night? Doesn't he have to turn to sleep, and doesn't he need to have time for the other necessities of this life so full of misery? And to this we respond that a just man ought to meditate on the law of the Lord day and night does not mean to be able to have actual memory of the divine law, or without ceasing to think of divine things during the expanse of every single hour, or at single moment; but rather it means that he does so at every proper and opportune time. For it is a natural expression to say that someone always does something when one means that he ought not to overlook to do that which he ought to, in the manner that we say: "This man always writes," "This man always frequents the church." It is in this sense that the Apostle says: *Pray without ceasing.*[27] And Moses says: *These words which I command you this day, shall be in your heart, and you shall tell them to your children, and you shall meditate upon them sitting in your house, and walking on your journey, sleeping and rising.*[28] In a different way, one is also able to say that someone can be said to pray and to mediate in two ways. The first way: because he is actually [in the midst of] exercising such things. In the second way: because he acts and lives in accordance with such acts. And so he who governs his entire life according to the tenor of the divine precepts incessantly night and day mediates on the law of the Lord and prays, in the manner that the Apostle teaches: *All whatsoever you do in word or in work,* he says, *do all in the name of the Lord Jesus Christ.*[29]

---

> 1[3]  *And he shall be like a tree which is planted near the running waters, which shall bring forth its fruit, in due season. And his leaf shall not fall off: and all whatsoever he shall do shall prosper.*
>
> *Et erit tamquam lignum quod plantatum est secus decursus aquarum, quod fructum suum dabit in tempore suo: et folium eius non defluet; et omnia quaecumque faciet prosperabuntur.*

Further, because it is natural for us to be led to the knowledge of spiritual things by their similarity to sensible things, consequently in the verses that follow, the sacred Scripture compares the justice of a blessed

---

27  1 Thess. 5:17.
28  Deut. 6:6–7.
29  Col. 3:17.

man to a tree planted beside water. Or it compares a blessed and just man in this manner, by reason of justice, so that virtue of justice which is a spiritual good is the formal cause of this comparison. Therefore, this is stated: **1[3]** *Et erit tamquam lignum quod plantatum est secus decursus aquarum, quod fructum suum dabit in tempore suo. And he shall be like a tree which is planted near the running waters, which shall bring forth its fruit, in due season.* A tree planted beside running waters or flowing waters flowers at the suitable time, and produces fruit, because its root attracts nutrient, that is, moisture, from the flowing waters. Whence in the Gospel, Christ says that the seed as soon *as it was sprung up withered because it had no moisture.*[30] The virtuous man is like this [which is expressed in the Psalm]. Because he places his confidence in God, and adheres to him, remaining in Christ as a branch to a vine, therefore he shares in the dew of the grace of God and the moisture of the life of the Holy Spirit, progressing *from virtue to virtue,*[31] and growing in charity from day to day.

*Et propterea folium eius non defluet. And* therefore *his leaf shall not fall off*: that is, his speech does not fall from the rectitude of the divine law because he fulfills that [injunction] of the Apostle: *Let your speech be always in grace seasoned with salt,*[32] that is, decorated with discretion. For he is not insolent in his speech, but *he refrains his lips.*[33] *Et omnia quaecumque faciet prosperabuntur. And all whatsoever he shall do shall prosper.* For we know this (as the apostle attests) because *to them that love God, all things work together unto good.*[34] All things that make a man blessed and just in the manner aforesaid will cause prosperity, that is, all their acts will advance them to true beatitude or eternal life. He will both more cautiously raise himself against, be more guarded about, and be more humbly sorrowful regarding the evil things that he may perchance commit from time to time in conjunction with the good he does. And indeed he will also more ardently love, for, as the Savior attests, he who loves much is forgiven much.[35] For which reason the Apostle says: *where sin abounded, grace did more abound.*[36] Whence also it is said of the man who is one of the elect: *When he shall fall he shall not be bruised, for the Lord puts his hand under him.*[37]

---

30  Luke 8:6.
31  Ps. 83:8b.
32  Col. 4:6.
33  Prov. 10:19.
34  Rom. 8:28a.
35  *Cf.* Luke 7:47.
36  Rom. 5:20.
37  Ps. 36:24.

1[4] *Not so the wicked, not so: but like the dust, which the wind drives from the face of the earth.*

*Non sic impii, non sic; sed tamquam pulvis quem proiicit ventus a facie terrae.*

But we might consider that the word is compared to a leaf and works to fruit. For just as the flower of a tree is useless and worthless when it does not result in any fruit, so also a beautiful word, or even a great or decorous exposition of words, is vain so long as life is inconsistent with such words. It is for this reason that the Lord cursed the fig tree that had foliage but did not have fruit.[38]   1[4] *Non sic impii, non sic. Not so the wicked, not so;* that is, things are not for the ungodly as was previously said for the just. For they are not possibly able to be compared to a tree planted beside running waters, but rather with a desiccated tree or a sterile palm, and a body separated from its head. For they do not have the roots of their heart fixed upon God, nor are they united to Christ by grace, nor are they leaning upon a stable foundation. For this reason, they are compared to dust, as the verse continues. *Sed tamquam pulvis quem proiicit ventus a facie terrae. But like the dust, which the wind drives from the face of the earth.* That is, such ungodly men are tossed about by the wind like dust. For as dust is always borne by the wind, so the ungodly are moved by various of their passions, and they depart from right reason. They do not adhere to God with a stable mind, but they withdraw themselves from divine love because of the love of temporal things, placing the creature in front of the Creator. But the consequence of this is explained in the verse that follows.

---

1[5] *Therefore the wicked shall not rise again in judgment: nor sinners in the council of the just.*

*Ideo non resurgent impii in iudicio, neque peccatores in concilio iustorum.*

1[5] *Ideo non resurgent impii in iudicio; therefore the wicked shall not rise again in judgment.* This verse is able to be understood in two ways. First, with respect to the judgment of discernment (*iudicio discretionis*)[39] that just

---

38  Mark 11:13–14.

39  E. N. In this concept of the judgment of discretion, Denis appears to be seizing upon the Pauline notion that, if we judge ourselves now, we may be able to avoid the judgment of condemnation at the end of time. *See* 1 Cor. 11:31 ("But if we judge ourselves, we should not be judged"). As Augustine stated it (using

and truly penitent men undergo daily, in which they examine themselves, and examine their conscience, and seek to discover, adjudge, reprove, condemn, lament, and overcome all the vices that are in them, as it is written: *Let us search our ways, and seek, and return to the Lord. Let us lift up our hearts with our hands to God in the heavens.*[40] The Apostle says this about this salutary judgment: *But if we would judge ourselves, we should not be judged.*[41] And judging themselves in this manner, they bear adversities with equanimity, saying to such: *As for us therefore let us not revenge ourselves for these things which we suffer. But esteeming these very punishments to be less than our sins deserve, let us believe that these scourges of the Lord, with which like servants we are chastised, have happened for our amendment, and not for our destruction.*[42] Second, it may be understood as referring to the future final judgment (*futuro extremo iudicio*), in which the ungodly shall not rise again unto the blessed immortality and felicitous change, but unto greater judgment. For (as the Apostle says) *We shall all rise again: but we shall not all be changed.*[43] But the first meaning appears to have greater concordance with the words that follow. For the following is added [to the verse]: *Neque peccatores in consilio iustorum,* nor sinners in the counsel of the just. The counsel of the just is so that [men] might correct and bewail their past sins, and then they might come forth guarding against future anxieties and fears. Sinners do not conform to this counsel, and hence — not acquiescing in the counsel of the just, nor doing fruits worthy of penance[44] — they do not rise from their vices in the counsel of the just.

---

1[6] *For the Lord knows the way of the just: and the way of the wicked shall perish.*

*Quoniam novit Dominus viam iustorum; et iter impiorum peribit.*

1[6] *Quoniam novit Dominus viam iustorum; for the Lord knows the way of the just,* that is, because God both knows and approves the way — that is the manner or the way of the just — therefore the ungodly separate themselves from the good according to the manner previously

---

1 Cor. 11:31 as authority): *a se ipso iudicatus, non iudicetur a Domino;* if we judge ourselves now, and confess that sin, then we will not be judged by God for that sin in the final judgment. *Sermon* 351, 4, 7.

40 Lam. 3:40–41.

41 1 Cor. 11:31.

42 Judith 8:26–27.

43 1 Cor. 15:51

44 *Cf.* Matt. 3:8.

stated, and the works of the ungodly do not prosper, that is, they do not lead to true beatitude, nor do they share in a happy end. And hence follows: *et iter impiorum peribit, and the way of the wicked shall perish,* that is, their life, action, and delights are destroyed, because after their temporal delights they will have eternal sorrow. Whence, in the last day, when they realize they have erred, and have repented too late, they shall say: *We have erred from the way of truth, . . . we wearied ourselves in the way of iniquity and destruction.*[45]

# ARTICLE IX

## EXPOSITION OF THE SAME FIRST PSALM ACCORDING TO THE ALLEGORICAL KNOWLEDGE, THAT IS, OF CHRIST

AS HAS BEEN PREVIOUSLY STATED, SACRED Scripture expresses itself allegorically where what is written in the Law or the Prophets or the Psalms is a revelation of Christ. It is understood [in such a case] that these Scriptures do not expound on Christ in their literal sense. Therefore, this Psalm, which literally addresses the just man and the ungodly in general, may be understood fittingly to reveal much of Christ allegorically.

> 1[1]  *Blessed is the man who has not walked in the counsel of the ungodly, nor stood in the way of sinners, nor sat in the chair of pestilence.*
>
> *Beatus vir qui non abiit in consilio impiorum, et in via peccatorum non stetit, et in cathedra pestilentiae non sedit.*

For he [the Psalmist] says:    1[1] *Beatus vir, Blessed be the man,* that is, Christ, who at the first instant of his conception in the Virgin Mother was a perfect and blessed man,[46] perfect not by reason of his age, but on

---

45  Wis. 5:6a, 7a.

46  E. N. By saying that Christ was "blessed" here and generally elsewhere, Denis is saying that our Lord, also in his human nature, enjoyed the beatific vision so that — contrary to an ordinary human being (who walks *in via* by faith) — the Lord was both a wayfarer (*in via*) and also enjoyed the vision of God (was a *comprehensor*). Pope Pius XII praises the effect of this beatific vision of Christ in his encyclical *Mystici Corporis Christi,* 75: "But the knowledge and love of our Divine Redeemer, of which we were the object from the first moment of His Incarnation,

account of the plenitude of grace, and the eminent virtue, and perfection of wisdom; in all of these things, the soul of Christ is perfectly created; these needed no perfection either by habituation or by exercise. Thus it is written: *The Lord will create a new thing upon the earth: a woman shall compass a man,*[47] that is, the chosen Virgin shall have in her womb a child in age, but a man in perfection. For Christ was blessed from the beginning of his conception in his mother, in accordance with the most perfect enjoyments of Divinity, and his most clear and most beatific vision; for so clear, and so blessed did the soul of Christ see from the first instant of its creation, [that it was no different than] in the manner he is even now. For never did he make any progress essentially in the privilege of the blessed.[48] For the human nature of Christ, from the beginning of its creation, was united personally with the Word or by means of the hypostatic union, that is, it subsisted in that same Being personally in which the Only-Begotten of God eternally subsists, since it was assumed by the uncreated Being of the Son of God. It is very clear, therefore, that the soul of Christ from its inception was granted the beatific vision of God, as the Damascene attests and also Thomas [Aquinas].[49] For it is something less for the blessed to contemplate God than it is to be united to his person. So, therefore, Christ is the blessed man.[50] And the word

---

exceed all that the human intellect can hope to grasp. For hardly was he conceived in the womb of the Mother of God, when he began to enjoy the Beatific Vision, and in that vision all the members of his Mystical Body were continually and unceasingly present to him, and he embraced them with his redeeming love. O marvelous condescension of divine love for us! O inestimable dispensation of boundless charity! In the crib, on the Cross, in the unending glory of the Father, Christ has all the members of the Church present before him and united to him in a much clearer and more loving manner than that of a mother who clasps her child to her breast, or than that with which a man knows and loves himself."

47 Jer. 31:22. *E. N.* The reference to Jeremiah by Denis departs from the Sixto-Clementine Vulgate slightly. Instead of *femina circumdabit virum,* Denis has, *mulier circumdabit virum.*

48 *E. N.* St. Thomas Aquinas distinguishes between essential beatitude and accidental beatitude, and consequently also essential rewards and accidental rewards. This distinction is found in passing in numerous parts of his *Summa Theologiae.* Essential beatitude is the possession or immediate vision of God. Accidental beatitude is that joy in any created good that is superadded to the essential beatitude, including the joy in the communion of saints, in good deeds done on earth, in the special aureoles or halos given to virgins, doctors, or martyrs, in the resurrection of the body and the joy in the glorified body, and so forth. Since Jesus had the beatific vision from the first moment of his conception (*i.e.,* he was in possession of essential beatitude), he could not have possibly advanced in essential beatitude.

49 Damasc. Lib. III; Thom. 3, q. 10. [*E. N.* This is a footnote in the Latin text]

50 *E. N.* The implicit argument in these two cryptic sentences is that if Christ

man is used because he was never deficient in any way in true fortitude, but in all things he conducted himself most virtuously.

So blessed is that man, that is to say, Christ, *qui non abiit in consilio impiorum, who has not walked in the counsel of the ungodly*; for he did not consent in the least to the greatest temptations of the tempter or give any consideration to adoring him,[51] nor did he favor the evil counsel of the Scribes and Pharisees; but was most full of [good] counsel—which is one of the seven gifts of the Holy Spirit.[52] *Et in via peccatorum non stetit. Nor stood in the way of sinners*, because he was most immune from any kind of sin. For he did not assume any detracting defects [of human nature],[53] but only those relating to nature or to its punishment, as are hunger, thirst, fear, suffering, and death. *Et in cathedra pestilentiae non sedit. Nor sat in the chair of pestilence.* For he never exhibited a bad example, nor did he advance any perverse teaching; and, although the Jews were frequently scandalized by his words and his acts, such scandals were nothing other than [a reflection of] their own wickedness and infirmity.[54] Again, the life of Christ was the exemplar of all holiness and perfection; and all his actions are for our instruction, as he himself said: *I am the light of the world; he who follows me, walks not in darkness.*[55] And so Christ brought to the world the most salvific doctrine, and he joined thereto the precepts of the law and of evangelical counsel, which wholly contain the fullness of perfection. For he did not come to destroy the law, but to fulfill it.[56]

We should touch upon these three things by which Christ is distinguished from the first parent. For Adam walked in the counsel of the ungodly when he consented to the serpent at the instigation of Eve. And he stood in the way of sinners since he ate the fruit from the forbidden tree. And he sat in the chair of pestilence since he excused his own sin, and he sought to throw the blame upon the woman, indeed, even in a way upon the Creator: *The woman, he said, whom you gave me to be my companion, gave me of the tree, and I did eat.*[57] It is openly clear that none of this was found in Christ.

---

enjoyed the grace of union (a greater grace), then he clearly would have enjoyed the lesser grace (the beatific vision). *In maiori includitur minus.*

51  Matt. 4:6-7; 9-10.
52  Is. 11:2.
53  E. N. Defects that detracted or reduced Christ's human perfection.
54  Matt. 15:12.
55  John 8:12.
56  Cf. Matt. 5:17.
57  Gen. 3:12.

1[2]  *But his will is in the law of the Lord, and on his law he shall*
      *meditate day and night.*

      *Sed in lege Domini voluntas eius, et in lege eius meditabitur die*
      *ac nocte.*

1[2] *Sed in lege Domini voluntas eius. But his will is in the law of the Lord.*
This is fittingly said in a singular and most perfect way of Christ. For he
alone perfectly fulfilled the precept of divine charity in this life, even much
more perfectly than all the other blessed [angels and saints] in heaven
themselves were able to fulfill. For in all his acts he always conducted
himself with all his heart, with all his mind, and with all his strength, and
with all his soul directed to God, contemplating, loving, honoring him,
and in all things obeying him, in the manner that he himself speaking of
the Father attests to in the Gospel: *For I do always the things that please*
*him.*[58] And again: *I seek not my own glory, but I honor my Father.*[59] And
therefore as he neared the Passion, he said to the Father: *Not as I will, but*
*as you will.*[60] And this [following of the will of God with perfect love]
only Christ as man fulfilled in this life perfectly and actually: *Et in lege*
*eius meditabitur die ac nocte; and on his law he shall meditate day and night,*
that is, at all times and in every moment. For the intellectual operations
of Christ were unable to be interrupted by sleep or any exterior act, or
through any appetite of the senses, or by any other thing whatsoever. But
all that was in him was most completely ordered, and always that which
was lower was at the service of the higher and moved by its command.
And so the soul of Christ meditated on divine things without any interruption. For those things which are, which were, and which will be, and
especially that which pertains to the mystery of human redemption, he
knew and always actually saw in the Word, even as he does now.[61]

------

1[3]  *And he shall be like a tree which is planted near the running waters,*
      *which shall bring forth its fruit, in due season. And his leaf shall*
      *not fall off: and all whatsoever he shall do shall prosper.*

      *Et erit tamquam lignum quod plantatum est secus decursus aqua-*
      *rum, quod fructum suum dabit in tempore suo: et folium eius non*
      *defluet; et omnia quaecumque faciet prosperabuntur.*

------

58  John 8:29.
59  John 8:50a, 49b.
60  Matt. 26:39b.
61  E. N. It is manifest that Denis rejects any notion of any ignorance of the intellect
    or weakness of the will whatsoever in Christ.

**1[3]** *Et erit tamquam lignum quod plantatum est secus decursus aquarum, quod fructum suum dabit in tempore suo. And he shall be like a tree which is planted near the running waters, which shall bring forth its fruit, in due season.* This describes the fecundity as well as the usefulness of Christ by a comparison to a tree which is planted near running waters. For such tree brings forth flowers in its time, and produces fruit, and thus is delightfully looked upon, usefully eaten, and becomingly possessed. So Christ, who is *beautiful above the sons of men,*[62] and *on whom the angels desire to look,*[63] is delightful to him who sincerely contemplates him, spiritually useful to him who eats him, and most becomingly and good to him who possesses him through charity and grace. In the manner also that a highly-yielding tree produces fruit copiously and refreshes many, so does Christ bring much fruit, since by his most precious Blood he redeemed the human race, and produced so many individual fruits, that is, the many souls of the elect he saved by his death. Whence, enduring the Passion, and himself carrying the Cross, he himself was compared to a green tree during that time when he said to the weeping women: *Weep not over me; but weep for yourselves, and for your children.... For if in the green wood they do these things, what shall be done in the dry?*[64]

One is able to expand upon this [reference to a tree in the Psalm] as the tree of life planted in Paradise, which on that account Christ is compared to, because as man may always have lived had he been able to eat of the tree, so he who eats Christ worthily will not die in eternity.[65] By the tree [referred to in this Psalm] one is able also to understand that wisdom, of which Solomon speaks, for *she is a tree of life* for all those who understand her.[66] Truly Christ is the Wisdom of God the Father.[67] The Wisdom planted near running waters is the only-begotten Son of God, truly incarnate, who might be compared to flowing waters in that he lived among sinful men without sin. According to this sense, therefore, the Incarnation of the Word of God is intimated; and this sense is, as it were, said not only as similarity [or analogy], but also expresses the [direct] truth, because in this way Christ himself is the very tree that is planted near the flowing waters.

---

62  Ps. 44:3a.

63  1 Pet. 1:12b.

64  Luke 23:28b, 31.

65  *Cf.* John 6:52.

66  Prov. 3:18.

67  1 Cor. 1:24b.

*Et folium eius non defluet; and his leaf shall not fall off*, because the words of Christ, both in preaching and in prayer, were not empty, nor did they perish, nor [were they] brought to nothing, but they brought fruit in the heart of the elect; and they [his words] will be confirmed in the end, in the manner that he himself said: *Heaven and earth shall pass, but my words shall not pass.*[68] *Et omnia quaecumque faciet prosperabuntur. And all whatsoever he shall do shall prosper.* All the works of Christ were meritorious; indeed, whatever he thought, said, and did, to the extent he was a wayfarer (*viator*), was productive of merit. It follows from this that he always actually merited. But because he as man, having that humanity united to the Word, was also a most perfect beholder of God in heaven (*comprehensor*), as it regards the superior part of the soul, consequently he himself did not essentially merit a reward, nor did he in any way whatsoever make progress.[69] Nevertheless, his whole life essentially gained the rewards of merit, because all that he thought, said, or did proceeded out of the most excellent fervor of divine charity. For whom, therefore, did he essentially merit a reward but for his members or his Mystical Body, which is the Church? For us, therefore, the whole life of Christ was meritorious. And thus all things whatsoever that Christ did are profitable, that is, they succeed in obtaining eternal life for the predestined, those upon whom the merits of Christ are applied through the sacraments of the Church, and through faith and charity, and who work together with it toward their eternal happiness. This is what the Lord says through Isaiah: *The word of justice which shall go forth from my mouth: it shall not return to me void, but it shall do whatsoever I please, and shall prosper in the things for which I sent it.*[70]

---

**1[4]** *Not so the wicked, not so: but like the dust, which the wind drives from the face of the earth.*

*Non sic impii, non sic; sed tamquam pulvis quem proiicit ventus a facie terrae.*

Following this, Scripture addresses those who are not in union with Christ or who do not imitate his ways. For it says: **1[4]** *Non sic impii, non sic. Not so the wicked, not so.* None of the Saints is able to equal

---

68 Matt. 24:35.
69 For the difference between the *viator* and *comprehensor see* footnotes P-41 and 1-46 and Article IX (Psalm 1:3); for the distinction between essential beatitude and reward and accidental beatitude and reward, *see* footnote 1-48.
70 Is. 55:11.

Christ, yet they are similar to him. For Christ, to the extent that he is God, exceeds all things infinitely in every perfection; but as man he is also greater, and is more worthy, and is dearer to God than the whole entirety of the elect — of angels as well as men. *For God does not give the Spirit by measure* to Christ the man.[71] Therefore, the good faithful, those who faithfully follow Christ the King, [do so] in the manner that is written, *He that says he abides in him, ought himself also to walk, even as he walked.*[72] Such good faithful — who, not departing into the counsel of the ungodly, nor standing in the way of sinners, nor sitting in the seat of pestilence, but their will is in the law of the Lord — Christ in a certain manner assimilates. But for the ungodly it is not so. For these are in no way similar to Christ, a similitude of virtue and grace, and they are not loved by him according to present justice with a love of grace-filled charity, since similarity is the cause of love; indeed he hates them with a perfect hate.[73] To whom this applies is immediately clear. *Sed tamquam pulvis quem proiicit ventus a facie terrae. But like the dust, which the wind drives from the face of the earth.* For in the manner that wind drives dust from its place, so the word of Christ drives the ungodly from the surface of the earth, from the congregation of the just, from the society of the Saints, when he separates the sheep from the goats,[74] when he purges his floor, when he gathers the wheat into his barn, and burns the chaff with unquenchable fire,[75] when it will be said to those who are at his left those most bitter words, *Go you cursed into everlasting fire.*[76]

---

**1[5]** *Therefore the wicked shall not rise again in judgment: nor sinners in the council of the just.*

*Ideo non resurgent impii in iudicio, neque peccatores in concilio iustorum.*

**1[5]** *Ideo non resurgent impii in iudicio; therefore the wicked shall not rise again in judgment,* because those that are divided from Christ, and are lacking in all grace, do not arise in judgment. This is able to be so

---

71 John 3:34b.
72 1 John 2:6.
73 *Cf.* Ps. 138:22. *I have hated them with a perfect hatred: and they are become enemies to me.*
74 Matt. 25:33.
75 Luke 3:17.
76 Matt. 25:41.

understood of the judgment of discretion (*iudicio discretionis*), by which the good judge themselves, (and of which the Prophet states, *I will show you, O man, what is good, and what the Lord requires of you: Verily, to do judgment;*[77] and Job, *Let us choose to us judgment, and let us see among ourselves what is the best;*[78] and, *Can he be healed who loves not judgment?*[79]), of the judgment of remuneration of the blessed, which is explained in the article immediately above. *Neque peccatores in consilio iustorum* resurgent. *Nor sinners in the council of the just* rise again. By council is properly meant the questioning through reason of what one has done and what has been omitted. Therefore, the council of the just is, whether they love God above all things, they reverently serve him, they grow daily in his charity and grace, and whether they worthily repent of all the evil they have perpetrated. In those that are in the council of the ungodly, [such questionings] do not arise, but they remain in the dregs of vices and sordid passions. They do not hear Paul crying out: *Rise you who sleep, and arise from the dead.*[80] And again: *Mind the things that are above.*[81]

---

1[6]  For the Lord knows the way of the just: and the way of the wicked shall perish.

Quoniam novit Dominus viam iustorum; et iter impiorum peribit.

1[6] *Quoniam novit Dominus viam iustorum; for the Lord knows the way of the just*, that is, they have the truth who now know difference between the ungodly and the just as has just been stated; for the Lord Jesus Christ, who is the King of kings and the Lord of lords,[82] the Judge of the living and the dead,[83] knows the way of the just, that is, he receives the works of the good, of those whose very hairs on their head are numbered.[84] *Et iter impiorum peribit; and the way of the wicked shall perish*. For they do not attain their last end, which is the blessed God.

---

77  Micah 6:8.
78  Job 34:4.
79  Job 34:17.
80  Eph. 5:14. *E. N.* The verse continues: *and Christ shall enlighten you.*
81  Col. 3:2. *E. N.* The verse continues: *not the things that are upon the earth.*
82  Rev. 19:16.
83  Heb. 12:23.
84  Luke 12:7.

# ARTICLE X

## EXPOSITION OF THE SAME FIRST PSALM
## ACCORDING TO ITS TROPOLOGICAL SENSE

ECALLING (AS IT WAS EXPLAINED BEFORE), the tropological or moral sense of Scripture is when that which is written or stated of Christ or of sacred things is applied to a knowledge regarding moral matters. For all things that were written of Christ our Head, were written for our edification. They are not written only of Christ, but also with a view of his saints, that they may be led to imitate him, as Augustine observes. And so sacred Scripture is most usefully understood tropologically to the extent that, recalling or expounding sacred Scripture, we praise Christ and the saints, and we transfer so as to inform ourselves that which is written of them; and thus [through this means] knowing our imperfections, we might take pains for our spiritual health, and studiously strive to imitate their perfection which we praise.

---

1[1]   *Blessed is the man who has not walked in the counsel of the ungodly, nor stood in the way of sinners, nor sat in the chair of pestilence.*

*Beatus vir qui non abiit in consilio impiorum, et in via peccatorum non stetit, et in cathedra pestilentiae non sedit.*

Yet the tropological exposition of this Psalm does not differ from the first or the literal exposition, for this Psalm instructs nothing other than that which that literal exposition teaches ought to be done. And so the [tropological] sense is entirely the same [as the literal or allegorical sense], but it refers to something else. Whence, according to this sense, that is, the tropological sense, Scripture says:   1[1] *Beatus vir qui non abiit in consilio impiorum. Blessed is the man who has not walked in the counsel of the ungodly*: so that certainly it exhorts and teaches all the faithful not to acquiesce in wicked counsel, and not stand in the ways of sinners doing evil, and not sit in the seat of pestilence by setting bad examples or introducing false doctrines. So that the more he follows what is read, to that extent he devoutly converts and brings spiritual doctrine to his soul. And from that which it says, recites, or reports as pertaining to the torment or abandonment of the ungodly, he is able to conceive a holy fear, so as not to suffer similar things. Or, seeing such as are preserved by the merciful God, [to conceive] an act of grace and a kindling of love; or, if it regards those evils with which the [ungodly] are tortured and abandoned with a healthy sorrow, to consider to find the way out. And that which it says or reports which pertains to the perfection and blessedness of the just is able to enkindle [in the reader] imitation, and to strengthen [him] in hope.

Therefore, according to this sense it speaks to the devout, or the penitent, or any other person [in this manner]: *Blessed is the man who has not walked in the counsel of the ungodly*: this instructing that one resolve not to assent to any evil counsel, and repent of any perverse counsel in which he may have acquiesced, and that he speak to God so that in all things he may be directed to discovery of, and consenting to, wholesome counsel, as Tobias teaches: *Bless God at all times: and desire of him to direct your ways, and that all your counsels may abide in him.*[85] For we are in need to be illumined and directed by the Holy Spirit's gift of counsel so that we do not depart in the counsel of the ungodly, in the manner that the Wise man says: *Who among men is he that can know the counsel of God? Or who can think what the will of God is, except you, O Lord, give wisdom, and send your Holy Spirit from above.*[86]

---

1[2] *But his will is in the law of the Lord, and on his law he shall meditate day and night.*

*Sed in lege Domini voluntas eius, et in lege eius meditabitur die ac nocte.*

In this manner a man ought to form his affection in everything single thing that follows, according to the demands of each one of those words; as it says, *et in via peccatorum non stetit, nor stood in the way of sinners*, he might consider in all things not to sin, and to feel sorrow for all past evil actions. And since it says, *et in cathedra pestilentiae non sedit, nor sat in the chair of pestilence*, he might propose not to corrupt anyone, not to scandalize anyone, that he may not destroy a soul for which Christ found worthy to die.[87] In a similar manner, when it says, 1[2] *Sed in lege Domini voluntas eius, but his will is in the law of the Lord*, he ought studiously to reject any wandering away, to detach himself from his affection from transitory things, and to arouse that every desire of his be towards the observation of the divine law. And so that he may carry this

---

85  Tobit 4:20.
86  Wis. 9:13, 17.
87  *Cf.* Rom. 14:15.

out, that he might turn to the good, and that he may endeavor to do with
all his strength that which follows, *et in lege eius meditabitur die ac nocte,
and on his law he shall meditate day and night.* And by this meaning that
he might spurn with his mind all unfruitful and evil occupations, and
he might labor to fill his heart with godly meditations, in the manner
that the Lord says: *Take away the evil of your devices from my eyes.*[88]

---

1[3]   *And he shall be like a tree which is planted near the running waters,
which shall bring forth its fruit, in due season. And his leaf shall
not fall off: and all whatsoever he shall do shall prosper.*

*Et erit tamquam lignum quod plantatum est secus decursus aqua-
rum, quod fructum suum dabit in tempore suo: et folium eius non
defluet; et omnia quaecumque faciet prosperabuntur.*

Moreover, since the Psalm says,   1[3] *Et erit tamquam lignum quod
plantatum est secus decursus aquarum, and he shall be like a tree which is
planted near the running waters,* he might pray, and desire with all his
heart, that he might be a good tree which bears good fruit. [He should
thus pray and desire that] by living well he might thereby edify others
by word and example. [And he should also ask] that he might instruct
others not so much by speaking as by acting in conformity with that
which was said by the Savior: *So let your light shine before men, that they
may see your good works, and glorify your Father who is in heaven.*[89] But
when it says, *et folium eius non defluet, and his leaf shall not fall off,* it
proposes that one always possess modesty and caution when speaking.
And when is added *et omnia quaecumque faciet, prosperabuntur, and all
whatsoever he shall do shall prosper,* he should desire to be numbered
among that group of which the Apostle says: *We know that to them that
love God, all things work together unto good.*[90]

---

1[4]   *Not so the wicked, not so: but like the dust, which the wind drives
from the face of the earth.*

*Non sic impii, non sic; sed tamquam pulvis quem proiicit ventus
a facie terrae.*

But from this it follows,   1[4] *Non sic impii, non sic, not so the wicked,*

---

88   Isaiah 1:16.
89   Matt. 5:16.
90   Rom. 8:28.

*not so*, to take great care not to occupy oneself with that which is written about the wicked; but rather [occupying himself] with the judgment of discretion (*iudicio discretionis*) he may lift himself from sin, and might endeavor to remain in the counsel of the just.

# ARTICLE XI

## EXPOSITION OF THE SAME FIRST PSALM
## ACCORDING TO ANAGOGICAL KNOWLEDGE

NAGOGICALLY, THE PSALM ABOVE IS EVI-
dently explicable as dealing with the *comprehensor* or the blessed in heaven,[91] so that we might know from the exposition of this Psalm, what we might hope of it for ourselves.

1[1]   *Blessed is the man who has not walked in the counsel of the ungodly,*
       *nor stood in the way of sinners, nor sat in the chair of pestilence.*

       *Beatus vir qui non abiit in consilio impiorum, et in via peccatorum*
       *non stetit, et in cathedra pestilentiae non sedit.*

1[2]   *But his will is in the law of the Lord, and on his law he shall*
       *meditate day and night.*

       *Sed in lege Domini voluntas eius, et in lege eius meditabitur die*
       *ac nocte.*

Therefore, Scripture says:1[1] *Beatus vir qui non abiit in consilio imp-*
*iorum*, Blessed is the man who has not walked in the counsel of the ungodly. Man, in this place, refers not to [the male] sex, but is intended to refer to the vigorous of heart: and so the holy angels are able to be called men [in this sense] because of all the divine works in which they most powerfully and forcefully exert themselves. Whence it is said of the angels: *Behold two men stood by them.*[92] And [Pope St.] Gregory [the Great] said: The angel is a rational animal, not because he is of a material or sensitive nature, but because of intellectual perfection. Yet the holy angels do not walk in the counsel of the ungodly, because they did not consent to the counsel of

---

91  For the difference between the *viator* (wayfarer) and the *comprehensor* (blessed in heaven enjoying the vision of God), *see* footnotes P-41 and 1-46 and Denis's own discussion in Article IX (Psalm 1:3).

92  Acts 1:10.

Lucifer and the fallen angels. So also none of the humans who attain the beatific vision walk in the counsel of the ungodly, in the sense of permanently remaining in it, but from this life they depart disposed in a good way.

Accordingly, 1[1] *Beatus vir, Blessed is the man,* means all of the elect, by virtue of power, human or angel, already enjoying happily God, *qui non abiit in consilio impiorum, who has not walked in the counsel of the ungodly,* of those who have been hurled down [from heaven to hell], that is of the perverse angels or men. *Et in via peccatorum non stetit, and have not stood in the way of sinners,* that is, he has not sinned with Lucifer and the others rebelling against God, inflating themselves with pride, or temerariously and presumptuously campaigning against the Creator. *Et in cathedra pestilentiae non sedit, and in the chair of pestilence he does not sit,* that is, he does not lead others to sin, in the manner that Lucifer and the corruptors of their neighbors. 1[2] *Sed in lege Domini voluntas eius, but his will is in the law of the Lord.* This most fully accords with all the blessed in heaven, because they fulfill most perfectly the precept of the love of God, and with all their affection are turned to God, and adhere to him always and inavertibly (*inavertibiliter*).[93] *Et in lege eius, and in His law,* that is, in loving and doing the precept of both loving and doing that is set forth before them from God: in this law do they meditate *die ac nocte, night and day,* that is, aeviternally[94] — which includes all time — those contemplating attentively in an incessant manner so as to reverently assist and promptly obey God, and keep all his ordinances.

---

1[3] *And he shall be like a tree which is planted near the running waters, which shall bring forth its fruit, in due season. And his leaf shall not fall off: and all whatsoever he shall do shall prosper.*

*Et erit tamquam lignum quod plantatum est secus decursus aquarum, quod fructum suum dabit in tempore suo: et folium eius non defluet; et omnia quaecumque faciet prosperabuntur.*

1[3] *Et erit tanquam lignum,* etc., *And he shall be like a tree,* etc. All the blessed already enjoying God are very well compared to a tree planted beside running waters, because it is inebriated with the torrent of divine pleasure:[95] and so it brings the most abundant fruit, which unceasingly

---

93  L. *inavertibiliter*: so affixed that it cannot be averted, deflected, or moved.

94  E. N. Something aeviternal has a beginning in time, but has no end going forward, so is eternal from the point of its beginning. This is distinguishable from God who has no beginning and no end, and so is eternal.

95  *Cf.* Ps. 35:9.

occupies the most holy acts, and is never disengaged or unfruitful, but it eternally remains in continual contemplation and love of the Godhead. *Et folium eius non defluet, and his leaf shall not fall off,* that is, the praise which honors God never ceases. *Et omnia quaecumque faciet, prosberabuntur, and all whatsoever he shall do shall prosper,* that is, they are ordained infallibly to the divine honor; and no adversity whatsoever is able to impair it, but they are joined to God in perpetual security.

---

1[4]  *Not so the wicked, not so: but like the dust, which the wind drives from the face of the earth.*

*Non sic impii, non sic; sed tamquam pulvis quem proiicit ventus a facie terrae.*

1[4] *Non sic impii, non sic, not so the wicked, not so:* that is, the apostate angels and unjust men *are not so,* that is, they are not blessed as is now said of the angels and holy men. *Sed, but,* they are *tanquam pulvis quem proiicit ventus a facie terra, like the dust, which the wind drives from the face of the earth.* For the evil angels immediately upon sinning were hurled down from heaven, as the Savior says in the Gospel: *I saw Satan like lightning fall from heaven.*[96] And Isaiah: *How are you fallen from heaven, O Lucifer, who did rise in the morning?*[97]   1[5] *Ideo non resurgunt impii in iudicio, therefore the wicked shall not rise again in judgment.* For the demons do not repent, but they are obstinate in evil, just as are also all those who are damned. Therefore, they do not rise again from their evil will in a judgment of discretion, taking stock of themselves and correcting themselves.   [6] *Quoniam novit Dominus viam iustorum, for the Lord knows the way of the just.* For all the acts of the blessed in heaven are always most pleasing and fully acceptable to God. *Et iter impiorum peribit, and the way of the wicked shall perish.* Again, the way of the fallen angels was the desire of ascending immoderately toward the similitude of God. But this way, or such an arrogant pride, shall perish, for they will not be able to acquire in any manner that which they desired to obtain.

Additionally, we hope peradventure to obtain for ourselves this blessedness of the elect in heaven, if we do that which they did, at least to the extent which it is possible for us to do, that is to say, not turning to the counsel of the ungodly, not standing in the way of sinners, and not sitting in the seat of pestilence.

---

96  Luke 10:18.
97  Isa. 14:12a.

# PRAYER

GOD, AUTHOR OF ALL GOOD THINGS, fill us, we beseech you, with your grace so that our will may always be directed to your law: and that with such inspiration from you, we might so meditate upon it day and night, that we may merit thereby to take possession of the fruits of eternal felicity.

*Auctor omnium bonorum Deus, reple nos, quaesumus, gratia tua, ut voluntas nostra dirigatur semper in lege tua: quatenus te inspirante, die ac nocte in ea sic meditemur, ut fructum aeternae felicitatis percipere mereamur.*

# Psalm 2

## ARTICLE XII

### LITERAL EXPOSITION OF THE SECOND PSALM:
### *QUARE FREMUERUNT GENTES, &c.*
### *WHY HAVE THE GENTILES RAGED, &c.*

HE TITLE OF THE PSALM NOW BEING expounded is this: *the Psalm of David*. One should consider (as St. Jerome says) that the book of Psalms is like a large house, having many cellars and chambers, and every such room has its own key and its own entrance. But the doorway of this whole house is the first Psalm, whose key is the Holy Spirit. The other Psalms being as it were separate and distinct rooms have their own keys, that is, their own appropriate signs. For as each house has its key, and each inn its own sign, so are the titles of the Psalms to each Psalm, for by them is given the entrance to the understanding of the Psalm.

To continue, the title of this present Psalm may be explained variously, just as this Psalm can be expounded in different manners. For certain persons explain it literally as referring to the Jewish people upon returning from the Babylonian captivity. But others hold that it relates to David himself, asserting that David wrote this Psalm in praise of God after his victory over the Philistines, whom he defeated when they rose up against him when they heard that he was anointed as king of the whole people of Israel. But in whatever manner this Psalm can be taken and explained, whether in this sense or another, one particular interpretation is nevertheless improper. For that verse which is found later, *the Lord has said to me, You are my Son, this day I have begotten you*, can properly refer neither to the Jewish people nor to David at the same time, most particularly if it is subtly explained in its most profound sense, as is evident. Therefore, if what Nicholas of Lyra reports is true,[1] none of the Jewish teachers expound this Psalm in this manner. For he reports that Rabbi Solomon, the greatest modern doctor of the Jews, testifies and states about this Psalm: Our elders expound this Psalm as dealing with the reign of the Messiah or Christ, but because of heretics

---

1  E. N. On Nicholas of Lyra, *see* footnote P-77.

51

this should be explained as dealing with David. He calls heretics those Jews who converted to the faith of Christ. Whence it is apparent that this Psalm is said to expound upon David only to avoid the arguments that the converted Jews took for granted regarding this Psalm as proof of the Christian faith. Nevertheless, whatever is said of this issue, it is not becoming nor licit to any Christian expounding upon this Psalm to expound it in any manner except as referring to the Christ. For the fourth chapter of Acts and the first chapter of Hebrews bring forward this Psalm as probative of the Christian faith.[2] Proof of the faith through sacred Scripture is not strong when interpreted in its mystical sense, as it is when examined in its literal sense, as St. Augustine affirms in his epistle against Vincentius the Donatist.[3]

And so, this Psalm, expounding literally of Christ, means its afore-mentioned title is able to be understood in this way: *The Psalm*, that, is this reflection, which is called a Psalm because it exhorts to good acts, is attributed to *David*, that is, the Christ. For David, brave in battle and of desirable aspect may be interpreted:[4] and this most prominently is fitting of Christ, when he stands firmly as the Lord of power,[5] who overcomes the prince of this world,[6] and is beautiful above the sons of men.[7]

------

2[1]  *Why have the Gentiles raged, and the people devised vain things?*

*Quare fremuerunt gentes, et populi meditati sunt inania?*

2[2]  *The kings of the earth stood up, and the princes met together, against the Lord and against his Christ.*

*Astiterunt reges terrae, et principes convenerunt in unum adversus Dominum, et adversus Christum eius.*

Therefore, holy David, foreknowing by the revelation of the Holy Spirit of the impiety of the evil men that would persecute and kill Christ, as if wondering at their malice, says:  2[1] *Quare fremuerunt gentes? Why have the Gentiles raged?* that is, why have the Gentiles, why were the Roman soldiers, why were the ministers Herod and Pilate irrationally malignant as if wild animals or beasts, and why were they so moved

------

2  Acts 4:25, 26; Heb. 1:5.
3  *E. N. See* footnote P-82.
4  *E. N.* These are the standard interpretations given to the name of David.
5  *Cf.* Ps. 23:10.
6  *Cf.* John 12:31.
7  Ps. 44:3.

against the Son of God? *Et populi, and the people,* that is the sons of Israel, to whom in a special way Christ had been sent, *meditati sunt inania, devised vain things,* since they *have devised counsels which they have not been able to establish?*[8] For they desired to extirpate the name of the Lord Jesus, slaying him as if he were a seducer and impious, in the manner that is written of him: *Let us put wood on his bread, and cut him off from the land of the living.*[9] But of this the very opposite was the result, because after the death of Christ, his name was known everywhere, and the faith he established is diffused throughout the whole world. Whence also before the Passion he said: *I, if I be lifted up from the earth, will draw all things to myself.*[10]   **2**[**2**] *Astiterunt reges terrae, et principes convenerunt in unum adversus Dominum, et adversus Christum eius. The kings of the earth stood up, and the princes met together, against the Lord and against his Christ.* Who are these kings if not that Herod who desired to destroy Jesus, while the latter was still a small infant,[11] and that Herod who with his armed men spurned him, and dressed him with a white robe to mock him, and delivered him over to Pilate?[12] And who are these princes, unless it be Annas and Caiaphas and Pilate?[13] It is these who stood up and met together against the Lord, that is, God the Father, and against his Christ, that is, his only begotten and beloved Son. As an aside, it is said that the two Herods[14] stood up against Christ: not that they stood against him at the same time (since the first Herod had died by the time of the Passion), but because both were equally moved with malice and through disbelief against Christ.

---

**2**[**3**]  *Let us break their bonds asunder: and let us cast away their yoke from us.*

*Dirumpamus vincula eorum, et proiiciamus a nobis iugum ipsorum.*

---

8  Ps. 20:12.
9  Jer. 11:19. *E. N.* The verse continues: *and let his name be remembered no more.* Traditionally, in reference to Christ, this verse of Jeremiah has been understood as meaning "let us put the cross on his body." See, e.g., Lactantius, *Divine Institutes* (4.18), PL 6, 568, or Tertullian, *Against Marcion*, IV, 11, PL 2, 492.
10  John 12:32.
11  Matt. 2:16.
12  Luke 23:11.
13  John 11:47 *et seq.*
14  *E. N.* The "Herods" are Herod "the Great" (ruled 37–4 B. C.), who sought out the Christ child to kill him, and Herod Antipas (ruled 4.B. C.–A. D. 39) who imprisoned and executed St. John the Baptist and cooperated with Pontius Pilate to put Jesus to death.

Consequently, the words which follow are said of the kings and princes:    2[3] *Dirumpamus vincula eorum; let us break their bonds asunder*, that is, in killing Christ, and condemning his doctrine, let us destroy the law and religion of the Father and the Son. This they said, not that they acknowledged Jesus to be the Son of God with a knowledge that was certain and steadfast, or because they regarded one who killed Jesus to be resisting God: for *if they had known it, they never would have crucified the Lord of glory;*[15] but they also put to death Jesus as a blasphemer and seducer,[16] judging themselves to be doing a service to God.[17] To be sure, this ignorance of theirs did not excuse them in any way, because their malice is what blinded them,[18] and they affirmatively willed not to believe in his divine miracles. In what other manner, therefore, is it said of these ungodly men, *let us break their bonds asunder*, except because he whom they killed with such impiety truly was the Son of God, he whom if one rejects also rejects the Father? For he who does not honor the Son, does not honor the Father who sent him.[19] Well also by the word *bonds* is understood the law of God or religion, because by the law sins are restrained and restricted, so that the reins of sin are not relaxed. Religion (*religio*) is so named from unbinding (*religando*) or binding up (*ligando*), since it unbinds (*religat*) from the world, and binds (*ligat*) him to the divine service. *Et proiiciamus a nobis iugum ipsorum, and let us cast away their yoke from us*, that is, let us not obey the precepts of God the Father and Christ. For the aforementioned kings and princes did not wish to assent to the doctrines of Christ.

---

2[4] *He that dwells in heaven shall laugh at them: and the Lord shall deride them.*

*Qui habitat in caelis irridebit eos, et Dominus subsannabit eos.*

2[4] *Qui habitat in caelis irridebit eos. He who dwells in heaven shall laugh at them.* Here is set forth the wages or the deserts of those evil men that have been mentioned. He who dwells in the heaven shall laugh at them: that is, God, the just judge, who dwells in the most pure and holy heart, raising his Son from death on the third day, will exhibit to them the derision they are worthy of. He also shall laugh at them in the day

---

15   1 Cor. 2:8.
16   Matt. 9:3; 27:63.
17   John 16:2.
18   Wis. 2:21.
19   John 5:23.

of final judgment. *Et Dominus subsannabit eos; and the Lord shall deride them.* It is the manner of sacred Scripture, according to St. Augustine, to repeat the same thing with other words so that it may make known the truth more clearly, and those hearing it or reading it may attend to it more. This is what is being done here. For that which has been said before — *He who dwells in the heaven shall laugh at them* — is now repeated by saying, *And the Lord shall deride them*: demonstrating to them as being most worthy of the greatest contempt, since he will have turned back their malignity upon their head,[20] and he will have caused all their effects to turn exactly to the contrary of their machinations. Whence the book of Wisdom says of the ungodly: *I also will laugh in your destruction, and will mock when that shall come to you which you feared.*[21] It describes God as laughing and deriding, but not through corporal movement or the manner of flesh, but by a sort of similitude of operation, or by reason of effect; that is, because he inflicts upon such person punishment as if he were a laugher or a derider.

---

2[5]  *Then shall he speak to them in his anger, and trouble them in his rage.*

*Tunc loquetur ad eos in ira sua, et in furore suo conturbabit eos.*

2[5] *Tunc*, then, that is to say, when he shall laugh at them, *loquetur ad eos in ira sua*, he shall speak to them in his anger. This will occur in the day of the great and final judgment, when the entire Trinity will adjudge authoritatively, and Christ as man [will adjudge] ministerially and executively. Then, through Christ who will carry out the sentence, the whole Trinity will utter the judgment upon those who have been rejected: *Go you cursed, into everlasting fire.*[22] One is also able to explain these words as referring to those labeled evil and reprobate by the Apostles and holy preachers, through whom the Lord speaks in his anger, when openly he causes the word of God to be preached to the reprobate, but inwardly he does not open their hearts nor does he touch their affections; but he hardens them, casting them off in their guilt, and rendering them obstinate. In this manner the unbelieving Jews are spoken of by the holy Apostles. *Et in furore suo conturbabit eos, and he shall confound them in his rage.* This we see fulfilled in the Jews following the death of Christ, for

---

20  Cf. Ps. 7:17. *His sorrow shall be turned on his own head: and his iniquity shall come down upon his crown.*

21  Prov. 1:26.

22  Matt. 25:41.

from the time of their destruction by Titus and Vespasian,[23] they have been ejected from the promised land, and they have been oppressed by many hardships. And also in the day of the universal judgment, he will confound them when they shall be cast off into fire, where (as Job says) *the shadow of death and no order, but eternal horror dwells.*[24]

---

**2[6]** *But I am appointed king by him over Sion his holy mountain, preaching his commandment.*

*Ego autem constitutus sum rex ab eo super Sion, montem sanctum eius, praedicans praeceptum eius.*

Consequently, the Prophet [David] introduces the words of Christ, saying of them the following:    **2[6]** *Ego autem, But I*: as if saying, they shall perish this way, *but I constitutus sum rex ab eo, am appointed king by him.* Inasmuch as he is God, Christ has full authority over all creatures. But [in this Psalm] he does not, in this manner, constitute himself king over anything, since he, with the Father and the Holy Spirit, is one and the same Creator of all things, and Lord, Judge, and King; but [this Psalm refers to his being appointed King, stating that] inasmuch as he is man, all power in heaven and earth is given him, as Matthew has written.[25] So also he is constituted King by him, that is to say God the Father, indeed by all the most exceedingly blessed Trinity, whose works are indivisible. *Super Sion, montem sanctum eius, over Sion his holy mountain,* that is, over his people Israel, especially they who believe in him: which is said to be a mountain, because of the sublimity of the law and the grace of the elect. Indeed, all the Prophets call the Messiah the King of Israel. Or by Sion, the meaning of which might be interpreted as observation (*speculatio*), can be understood to be the Church militant, that is, the Christian people contemplating Christ and his law, and by faith and grace raised above all other peoples, as a mountain is elevated above the surrounding parts of the earth. *Praedicans praeceptum eius; preaching his commandments,* that is, teaching the evangelical law, first by myself,[26] and thereafter through the Apostles full of the Holy Spirit. In this verse, the human nature of

---

23  *E. N.* Vespasian (9–79 A. D.) and Titus (39–81 A. D.). The Roman emperors responsible for destroying Jerusalem and its Temple (70 A. D.) during the First Jewish-Roman War.

24  Job. 10:22.

25  *Cf.* Matt. 28:18b.

26  *E. N.* The commentary on the Psalm goes back to first person, which, given Denis's exegesis, means Christ is speaking in first person in this sentence.

Christ is touched upon; the verses which follow handle his divine nature and his eternal generation, when it is said:

---

**2[7]** *The Lord has said to me: You are my son, this day have I begotten you.*

*Dominus dixit ad me : Filius meus es tu; ego hodie genui te.*

**2[7]** *Dominus,* the Lord, that is to say, God the Father, *dixit ad me,* has said to me, namely, Jesus Christ: *Filius meus es tu. You are my Son.* As the Gospel relates, this was said by the Father to the Son at the Baptism and Transfiguration of Christ.[27] And it is said of Christ the Son of God, not through an adoption by grace as it is with other holy men, but [he is called] Son by the identity of nature, or the unity of essence: because he is begotten from eternity from the substance of the Father. And thus there is added: *Ego hodie genui te, this day have I begotten you,* that is, in the day of eternity, in which there is no before and after, new or old, change or *shadow of alteration,*[28] but this day is precisely and identically eternity, which is the simultaneous and perfect possession of endless life *(interminabilis vitae tota simul perfecta posessio).*[29] This eternity embraces all time, and all by which the difference of time is signified by us, all that is included when we say God was, God is, and God will be. By convention we also designate by the present tense that which contains itself in the manner of repose and of fixity. Therefore, the Prophet [David] desiring to insinuate accurately the eternal generation of Christ, used the present tense, saying: *This day have I begotten you,* which words are those of the Father to the Son. For whatever the Father does and knows, this the Son says: and he says generating *(generando),*[30] because generating gives to the Son the divine Essence, which in giving, he gives [with such generation] knowledge of all Truth, since the divine Essence is itself *Wisdom* of which *there is no number.*[31]

---

**2[8]** *Ask of me, and I will give you the Gentiles for your inheritance, and the utmost parts of the earth for your possession.*

*Postula a me, et dabo tibi gentes haereditatem tuam, et possessionem tuam terminos terrae.*

---

27  Matt. 3:17; 17:5.
28  James 1:17b.
29  E. N. A reference to Boethius's *Consolation of Philosophy,* V, 6.
30  E. N. Generating in the sense of being begotten.
31  Ps. 146:5b.

**2[8]** *Postula a me, et dabo tibi gentes haereditatem tuam; ask of me, and I will give you the Gentiles for your inheritance.* These are the words of the Father to Christ the man, which are not befitting for the Father to ask [the Son] according as he [the Son] is God.[32] God the Father, therefore, says to the Incarnate Son: O Son, ask it from me, and I will give you the Gentiles. This Christ frequently did, when he prayed for the salvation of the world;[33] and his Passion was the most efficacious request, for through it he merited for himself the dominion over the Church militant. *And I will give you the Gentiles for your inheritance.* The Father fulfilled this promise when through the preaching of Christ and his Apostles and their successors the Gentiles converted to Christ; and so the Gentiles, who beforehand were possessed by demons, were made the possession of Christ. And they, who at one time belonged to the prince of the world, were made his inheritance. *Et possessionem tuam terminos terrae; and the utmost parts of the earth for your possession*: that is, I will give to you not only one province, one tongue (*linguam*),[34] or one kingdom, but *the utmost parts of the earth*, that is, I will subject the world to the very ends of its boundaries to your law.[35] For indeed, the doctrine of the Apostles has spread forth over the entire earth. Whence, it is said in a later Psalm: *And he shall rule from sea to sea, and from the river unto the ends of the earth.*[36] Regarding this regal dignity of Christ and the subjection of the world, Daniel says: The Ancient of Days, that is the eternal God, *gave him power, and glory, and a kingdom: and all peoples, tribes and tongues shall serve him.*[37]

---

**2[9]** *You shall rule them with a rod of iron, and shall break them in pieces like a potter's vessel.*

*Reges eos in virga ferrea, et tamquam vas figuli confringes eos.*

**2[9]** *Reges eos in virga ferrea. You shall rule them with a rod of iron.* Christ rules the Church with a rod of iron, that is, in constant and

---

32  E. N. Because, as God, the Son can say by nature and not through any sort of request or prayer founded upon grace, even the grace of union, "all things that the Father has are mine." John 16:15.

33  John 17:1–25.

34  E. N. The word "tongue" is used to refer to an ethno-linguistic division, *e.g.*, as when Churchill wrote the history of the "English-speaking peoples."

35  *Cf.* Ps. 18:5. *Their sound has gone forth into all the earth: and their words unto the ends of the world.*

36  Ps. 71:8.

37  Dan. 7:14.

unchanging equity. For the Christian law and Christian doctrine, by which the Christian faithful are ruled by Christ through his vicars and prelates, may be compared to a rod of iron on account of the rigor of justice; for all manner of evil howsoever small is in some manner pro-hibited and condemned. *Et tamquam vas figuli confringes eos; and shall break them in pieces like a potter's vessel*: not in any case crushing nature or destroying natural existence, but by extirpating vice, correcting morals, and shattering their self-will.

---

2[10]  *And now, O you kings, understand: receive instruction, you that judge the earth.*

*Et nunc, reges, intelligite; erudimini, qui iudicatis terram.*

2[10] *Et nunc, reges, intelligite; and now, O you kings, understand.* Here is placed the guardianship of the doctrine of salvation, indeed of all things. *And now*, that is, according to what has been said of the gover-nance of Christ, *kings*, that is all of the vicars of Christ, you who preside over his people, indeed each thing which ought to be ruled, ruling your-selves according to the rule of reason, understand both words and what is being declared. *Erudimini, qui iudicatis terram. Receive instruction, you who judge the earth*, that is, studiously busy yourself with my guidance, you who judge the inhabitants of the earth.

---

2[11]  *Serve you the Lord with fear: and rejoice unto him with trembling.*

*Servite Domino in timore, et exsultate ei cum tremore.*

2[11] *Servite Domino in timore; serve the Lord with fear*, so that you may be both fearful and solicitous, and so in a manner worthy you may rule your subjects and reverently walk before God, seduced neither by pride or vain security, nor negligently doing those things for which there are binding precepts for you to follow. And so therefore it is written: *Unless you hold yourself diligently in the fear of the Lord, your house shall quickly be overthrown.*[38] *For the fear of God drives out sin.*[39] *Et exsultate ei cum tremore; and rejoice unto him with trembling*: that is, O kings of the earth and all men, exult in him, that is, rejoice in the praise of God: rejoice, I say, in the exercise of the divine worship, in the praise of God, in all his service, and especially in contemplation and in love of

38  Ecclus. 27:4.
39  Ecclus. 1:27.

him. And do this, with fear, that is, with great and reverential fear. Let not your exultation be followed by any dissolution or lack of custody of heart, and so spiritual enjoyment turn into carnal pleasure. In whatever manner one falls into this [dissolution or failure to guard the heart], those things which began by means of the spirit, are finished by means of the flesh.[40] In this [verse of the Psalm and its use of the word fear], however, we should understand not servile fear, but initial or filial fear.[41]

2[12] *Embrace discipline, lest at any time the Lord be angry, and you perish from the just way.*

*Apprehendite disciplinam, nequando irascatur Dominus, et pereatis de via iusta.*

2[12] *Apprehendite disciplinam;* embrace discipline, that is, freely embrace brotherly instruction, charitable reproof, and the scourges of God, and with equanimity bear adversity; *nequando irascatur Dominus, lest at any time the Lord be angry,* as a result of your negligence or impatience; *et pereatis de via iusta, and you perish from the just way:* for when God is angered with the sinner, he then abandons him; but when man is abandoned by God, and deprived of his grace, he straightway perishes, falls, and departs from the just way, that is, from the obedient observation of the precepts and from all meritorious actions.

2[13] *When his wrath shall be kindled in a short time, blessed are all they that trust in him.*

*Cum exarserit in brevi ira eius, beati omnes qui confidunt in eo.*

2[13] *Cum exarserit in brevi ira eius; when his wrath shall be kindled in a short time,* that is, when the anger of God is furiously inflamed, as especially it will be at Judgment Day; then *beati omnes qui confidunt in eo, blessed are all they that trust in him,* that is, all who in some way hope in the Lord will then come unto blessedness. [The Psalm says] *in a short time* because the final judgment will not last even one day; or [it can mean] *in a short time* because we do not know either the day or the hour[42] that we shall depart from this present life, when — at the same time — we shall

---

40  Cf. Gal. 3:3. *Are you so foolish, that, whereas you began in the Spirit, you would now be made perfect by the flesh?*

41  *E. N. See ST,* IIaIIae, q. 19, art. 2. Initial fear *(timor initialis)* is that fear between servile fear and filial fear and so shares characteristics of both.

42  Matt. 25:13.

be justly judged, when every person will receive in accordance with his works[43] at that very instant when the soul leaves the body.

# ARTICLE XIII

## TROPOLOGICAL EXPOSITION OF
## THE SAME SECOND PSALM

**A**ND NOW, TROPOLOGICALLY EXPLAINING this Psalm, when it says, *Why have the Gentiles raged*, these words refer to any and all Christians, imitators of the cruciform steps (*vestigia cruciformiter imitantis*) of Christ, who desire to suffer with Christ, until that time when in the time hereafter he may reign with him.

2[**1**]  *Why have the Gentiles raged, and the people devised vain things?*

*Quare fremuerunt gentes, et populi meditati sunt inania?*

2[**2**]  *The kings of the earth stood up, and the princes met together, against the Lord and against his Christ.*

*Astiterunt reges terrae, et principes convenerunt in unum adversus Dominum, et adversus Christum eius.*

Therefore, perturbed at the fact of righteous men persecuted by evil men, any true believer, says:   2[**1**] *Quare fremuerunt gentes, why have the Gentiles raged*, that is, unbelieving men, the Turks,[44] pagans, Jews, and heretics? *Et populi, and the people*, that is, bad Christians, lovers of the world, and those wise in ways of the flesh, *meditati sunt inania; they have devised vain things?*   2[**2**] *Adstiterunt reges terrae. The kings of the earth stood up.* That is, unbelieving emperors and other kings, persecutors, and tyrants; *et principes; and the princes*, that is, all other remaining judges, and also those princes who are Christian only in name, *convenerunt in unum, met together as one*, that is, they conceived the same malice, and they have come to agreement in the same counsel, *adversus Dominum, against the Lord*, that is, against Almighty God, *et adversus Christum eius, and against his Christ*, that is, against any Christian man, anointed with sacred chrism or spiritually anointed and full with the grace of the

---

43  Rom. 2:6; 1 Cor. 3:8.
44  *E. N.* Understood generically as referring to Muslims, followers of Islam.

Holy Spirit. For he who rises up against the servants of God, rises up against God, in the manner that Christ attested to: As you did it to the least of one of mine, you have done it to me.[45] And to Paul while still persecuting: *Why do you persecute me?*[46]

---

**2[3]** *Let us break their bonds asunder: and let us cast away their yoke from us.*

*Dirumpamus vincula eorum, et proiiciamus a nobis iugum ipsorum.*

**2[3]** *Dirumpamus vincula eorum.* Let us break their bonds asunder, that is, let us destroy the laws and religion of the Christians, as was expounded upon in the previous article. For the unbelieving persecutors intended these things, as did Nero, Domitian, Diocletian.[47] *Et proiiciamus a nobis iugum ipsorum.* And let us cast away their yoke from us. These are the words of Christians that are living evil lives, who have confessed to having the faith, but who spurn the works of faith, and persecute the devoted ones. These say: *Let us cast away from us their yoke,* that is, let us thrust back from us the preaching, warnings, and reprobation of those who preach contrary to our own wills, who warn us about the eternal scourges and punishments of God, and judge our lives as unjust and wicked: that is, those teaching the word or manifesting the word, spurning the world and all its honors, and desires, and glory, and parents, and kindred, and wives, and country, relinquishing all for the sake of Christ.[48]

---

**2[4]** *He that dwells in heaven shall laugh at them: and the Lord shall deride them.*

*Qui habitat in caelis irridebit eos, et Dominus subsannabit eos.*

**2[5]** *Then shall he speak to them in his anger, and trouble them in his rage.*

*Tunc loquetur ad eos in ira sua, et in furore suo conturbabit eos.*

**2[4]** *Qui habitat in caelis, he who dwells in heaven,* that is, Christ who sits at the right hand of the Father, *irridebit eos, shall laugh at them,* that is, all those evil men mentioned hereinbefore: *et Dominus, and the Lord,* that is, the entire superlatively happy Trinity, who is one God and also

---

45  *Cf.* Matt. 25:40.
46  Acts 9:4.
47  Nero (A. D. 37–68), Domitian (A. D. 51–96), and Diocletian (A. D. 244–311) were among the Roman emperors who persecuted Christians and the early Church.
48  *Cf.* Matt. 19:29.

one Lord, *subsannabit eos, shall deride them,* and this because Christ, who
in his nature as a man, will carry out his judgment against the unjust
from the commission [given to him as man] by the entire Trinity,[49] in
the manner that is contained in the Gospel of St. John: the Father *has
given all judgment to the Son.*[50]    **2[5]** *Tunc, then,* that is, in the day of
Judgment, when the previously mentioned laughter shall take place, then,
I say, Christ *loquetur ad eos, he shall speak to them,* that is the unjust
and the persecutors of the good, *in ira sua, in his anger,* saying: Go, *you
cursed, into everlasting fire.*[51] *Et in furore suo conturbabit eos, and trouble
them in his rage,* making them to be swallowed by the earth and shut
up in the prison of hell with the demons.

---

**2[6]**  But I am appointed king by him over Sion his holy mountain,
        preaching his commandment.

        *Ego autem constitutus sum rex ab eo super Sion, montem sanctum
        eius, praedicans praeceptum eius.*

**2[6]** *Ego autem constitutus sum rex ab eo super Sion. But I am appointed
king by him over Sion.* In this [verse] most fittingly is encompassed good
prelates and holy bishops, and the great faithful preachers. For of these,
any one of them can say: *Ego autem, But I am,* etc. as he might have
said: they so perish, but I *constitutus sum rex, am appointed king,* that is a
prelate, rector, or doctor, *ab eo, by him,* that is, by Christ as his vicar, *super
Sion montem sanctum eius, over Sion his holy mountain,* that is, over the
Christian people overseen by God, *praedicans praeceptum eius, preaching
his commandment,* that is, teaching to preserve the commandments of
Christ. One is able also to interpret this verse as applying to any one of
the faithful: for any one of the faithful is constituted a king, that is, the
lord of his own acts, over Sion his holy mountain, namely, over himself.
For the temple of God, which you are, is holy, as the Apostle says.[52] For
whoever disdains the things of the earth and seeks the things of heaven
is able to be called Sion and the holy mountain of the Lord, because he
fastens the affections of his mind toward the sublime, and is raised up
into God. But it is also said a man is king over himself because he does
things freely, and that he ought to live under the direction of reason and

---

49  *Cf.* Matt. 25:41 *et seq.*
50  John 5:22b.
51  Matt. 25:41.
52  *Cf.* 1 Cor. 3:17. *But if any man violate the temple of God, him shall God destroy.
    For the temple of God is holy, which you are.*

should govern himself justly. Whence in Ecclesiasticus: *God made man…,
and left him in the hand of his own counsel.*[53] So also does any man preach
the precepts of God when he informs and excites himself, his heart always
coming back to, and reflecting upon, the testimony of sacred Scripture.

---

2[7] *The Lord has said to me: You are my son, this day have I begotten you.*

*Dominus dixit ad me : Filius meus es tu; ego hodie genui te.*

2[7] *Dominus dixit ad me: Filius meus es tu, etc. The Lord has said to
me: You are my Son, etc.* This is what the Apostle said: *The Spirit himself
gives testimony to our spirit, that we are the sons of God.*[54] The Lord says
to any one of his devotees by an internal inspiration: You are my son;
this day have I begotten you, that is, in the day that I caused you to
be reborn in the Baptismal fount. Indeed, whenever he infuses into us
charity and the grace of the Holy Spirit, then God spiritually regenerates
us, giving us a spiritual, divine, and heavenly existence.

---

2[8] *Ask of me, and I will give you the Gentiles for your inheritance,
and the utmost parts of the earth for your possession.*

*Postula a me, et dabo tibi gentes haereditatem tuam, et possessionem
tuam terminos terrae.*

2[9] *You shall rule them with a rod of iron, and shall break them in
pieces like a potter's vessel.*

*Reges eos in virga ferrea, et tamquam vas figuli confringes eos.*

2[8] *Postula a me, et dabo tibi gentes haereditatem tuam. Ask of me, and
I will give you the Gentiles for your inheritance.* Inheritance is the name
given to that which is used by someone for his pleasure, converting it to
his own advantage. In such a manner just and holy men possess men as
an inheritance, that is, because by turning a group of people that are in
sin they obtain the advantage of their enjoyment. For whichever people
does this are converted to be just, and this to their own advantage, and
thus all works together unto their good.[55] And so, if they are honored
and praised by the ungodly, they are not raised up, but from this they
are worthy to be humiliated. But if they are despised and are troubled
by the ungodly, they are not oppressed, but through patience they remain

---

53  Ecclus. 15:14.
54  Rom. 8:16.
55  *Cf.* Rom. 8:28.

unmoved. *Et possessionem tuam terminus terra; and the utmost part of the earth for your possession*: that is, I the Lord will give to you the ends of the earth so that you might possess them. Whence the Apostle: *as having nothing*, he says, *possessing all things.*[56] For the just have as much of the earth as they desire, if they faithfully ask for it in the manner that the Savior said: *Seek first the reign of God, and his justice, and all these things shall be added unto you.*[57] And the Lord gives good prelates to the people as their inheritance, as often as they possess them in good governance.    **2[9]** And thus all prelates and Christian faithful, worthy vicars of Christ, rule those in their charge *in virga ferrea, by a rod of iron*, that is, with steadfast justice, and righteous instruction; and he breaks them *tamquam vas figuli, like a potter's vessel* for he makes them bridle their unruly desires (*concupiscentias*), to correct their morals, and to subdue themselves.

---

**2[10]**  *And now, O you kings, understand: receive instruction, you that judge the earth.*

*Et nunc, reges, intelligite; erudimini, qui iudicatis terram.*

**2[10]** *Et nunc, reges, intelligite. And now, O you kings, understand.* This and that which follows elaborates something which is superior. This good admonition is set forth to the rulers as being opportune before all other things. For the prelates are greatly in need of a continuous fear of good, indeed, even a great trembling, so that they are not negligent in what they do, lest they delight in ruling, and through their preoccupation with external matters they become empty within.

And so in this manner we are taught morally from this Psalm not to be disheartened in adversity, nor to become vanquished by the persecutions of the wicked, but — taking into consideration the vengeance of the divine justice and the eternal damnation of the ungodly — we manly strive to follow the steps of our Head, or of Christ: *who having joy set before him, endured the cross, despising the shame;*[58] who also exclaimed to his faithful, *If any man will come after me, let him deny himself, and take up his cross daily, and follow me.*[59] Also from that which is said — *The Lord has said to me: You are my son, this day have I begotten you* — we are taught and we are admonished to consider the eminence of the grace

---

56  2 Cor. 6:13b.
57  Matt. 6:33.
58  Heb. 12:2.
59  Luke 9:23.

of God and the magnitude of the benefits which are gathered together for us, so that we might be grateful to God, ardent in his love, and so might be made more full with greater gifts from the Lord. For he that has, will be given, that is, he who is thankful to God, and glories not in himself, as there is nothing that he has not received from the Lord alone; but he who does not have this [attitude], that is, the ingrate, that which he is seen to have shall be taken from him.[60]

# ARTICLE XIV

## WHY THIS PSALM IS NOT EXPOUNDED ALLEGORICALLY, ALTHOUGH IT CAN BE EXPOUNDED ANAGOGICALLY

ROM THAT WHICH HAS BEEN POINTED out—that this Psalm literally speaks of Christ—it is certain that the Psalm is not to be explained allegorically. For Scripture is explained allegorically when that which is literally written of another is understood to be said of Christ. So, if a Psalm of David or another speaks of another subject, let us say for example the Jews, then we are able to explain it allegorically to refer to Christ.

2[1]  *Why have the Gentiles raged, and the people devised vain things?*

*Quare fremuerunt gentes, et populi meditati sunt inania?*

2[2]  *The kings of the earth stood up, and the princes met together, against the Lord and against his Christ.*

*Astiterunt reges terrae, et principes convenerunt in unum adversus Dominum, et adversus Christum eius.*

2[3]  *Let us break their bonds asunder: and let us cast away their yoke from us.*

*Dirumpamus vincula eorum, et proiiciamus a nobis iugum ipsorum.*

2[4]  *He that dwells in heaven shall laugh at them: and the Lord shall deride them.*

*Qui habitat in caelis irridebit eos, et Dominus subsannabit eos.*

---

60  Matt. 13:12; 25:29; 1 Cor. 1:31.

**2[1-4]** But the Psalm is suitable to be explained anagogically, so that from where says, *Quare fremuerunt gentes, Why have the Gentiles raged,* up and through where it says, *Qui habitat in caelis, he who dwells in heaven,* are words that may be referred to any one of the blessed in heaven, for these things are said against them to make known the enormity of the sins which they who now enjoy God amassed against God and his Christ when they were in this life. And this utterance is also fitting especially to the holy martyrs who, conforming themselves to the divine justice, opted for the vengeance of the ungodly, and in arriving to this they said thus: *Why have they raged, etc.* Whence it is written: *Under the altar of God, the saints cried, Lord, revenge our blood;*[61] and earlier: *the just shall rejoice when he shall see the revenge.*[62] Meanwhile, the blessed in heaven, as though consoling themselves of the delay in the divine judgment, say to themselves: *He who dwells in heaven shall laugh at them.*

---

**2[6]**  *But I am appointed king by him over Sion his holy mountain, preaching his commandment.*

*Ego autem constitutus sum rex ab eo super Sion, montem sanctum eius, praedicans praeceptum eius.*

**2[7]**  *The Lord has said to me: You are my son, this day have I begotten you.*

*Dominus dixit ad me : Filius meus es tu; ego hodie genui te.*

**2[8]**  *Ask of me, and I will give you the Gentiles for your inheritance, and the utmost parts of the earth for your possession.*

*Postula a me, et dabo tibi gentes haereditatem tuam, et possessionem tuam terminos terrae.*

**2[9]**  *You shall rule them with a rod of iron, and shall break them in pieces like a potter's vessel.*

*Reges eos in virga ferrea, et tamquam vas figuli confringes eos.*

**2[6]**[63] Only someone already enjoying God is able to say: *Ego autem constitutus sum rex ab eo super Sion mentem sanctum eius.* But I am appointed king by him over Sion his holy mountain: that is, in the empyrean heaven I received the crown of victory and the regal diadem for having

---

61  Rev. 6:9, 10.
62  Ps. 57:11.
63  Denis skips Psalm 2:5.

endured the tribulations and labors in the world; *praedicans, preaching,* that is, extolling and praising, *praeceptum eius, his commandment,* that is to say of the [commandment of the] Lord, because he is just, and because by fulfilling it one acquires the possession of happiness.    **2[7]** *Dominus dixit ad me: Filius meus es tu. The Lord has said to me: You are my son.* Those along the way (*viatores*) are called sons of God as a result of the grace of adoption and the imperfect likeness [they have to God]; but well are those in heaven (*in patria*) called sons of God on the grounds that they enjoy the glory of the fruit of beatitude and a perfect likeness, because they see God as he is.[64] Accordingly, of any of the blessed it is most optimally fitting to say: *The Lord has said to me: You are my son,* because you are perfectly conjoined and assimilated to me. *Ego hodie, I this day,* that is, in the day that I blessed you with my vision, *genui te, I have begotten you.* For then [at one's particular judgment] from him who is on the way (*de viator*) both imperfect and miserable, God will make a beholder (*comprehensorem*), both perfect and happy.[65]    **2[8]** *Postula a me, et dabo tibi gentes hereditatem, etc. Ask of me, and I will give you the Gentiles for your inheritance, etc.* The Lord says this to the blessed when they live in time according to the knowledge we have touched upon in the preceding interpretation. Or now this is said of them because the saints in heaven have for themselves as subjects the peoples of this world, in the manner that we read in the Book of Wisdom: *They shall judge justly nations, and rule over people.*[66]    **2[9]** *Reges eos in virga ferrea. He shall rule them with a rod of iron.* Certain it is that wayfarers (*viatores*) are ruled by the holy angels with a rod of iron, that is with a just and strong direction. And the souls of the blessed rule us, by praying for us. *Et tanquam vas figuli confringes eos. And you shall break them in pieces like a potter's vessel.* These words refer to the saints who will judge with Christ, because they together with Christ will shatter and destroy the ungodly from having any spiritual, blessed, and glorious existence.

---

64  "The 'uncreated grace' whereby we are justified, because it consists primarily in God's personal self-communication, relates us to each of the divine persons. As Son, Christ communicates to his members the filial and servant character of his own existence. Because we are mystically identified with the second person of the Holy Trinity we become, in the memorable phrase of Emile Mersch, 'sons in the Son' (*filii in Filio*)." Avery Cardinal Dulles, S. J., "Justification in Contemporary Catholic Theology," *Justification by Faith* (Minneapolis: Augsburg 1985), 260–61.

65  For the difference between the *viator* (wayfarer) and the *comprehensor* (blessed in heaven enjoying the vision of God), *see* footnotes P-41 and 1-46 and Denis's own discussion in Article IX (Psalm 1:3).

66  Wis. 3:8.

2[10]  *And now, O you kings, understand: receive instruction, you that judge the earth.*

*Et nunc, reges, intelligite; erudimini, qui iudicatis terram.*

2[10]-[13] Next are the words that follow: *Et nunc, reges, intelligite, and now, O kings, understand,* these are the words of the Church triumphant to the Church militant even until the end of time. For the angels who are *administrating spirits,*[67] exhort men on behalf of God and all the blessed, and they protect them [the faithful members of the Church militant] before they do others, speaking to them through mental inspirations, which are hidden interior locutions: *And now, O kings, understand.* And these words express that which has been [already] explained [earlier].

Accordingly, from the anagogical exposition of this Psalm, we are taught to contemplate the glory of the blessed in heaven, that is, what great happiness has been assigned them, and what great prize they have received for the temporal and relatively small troubles of the present life. And from this contemplation, we ought to be enkindled to obtain such happiness, and on account of their love, vigorously follow the example, life, morals, and the tribulations of the blessed, until such time that we are happily joined in their fellowship after this present exile.

# PRAYER

MERCIFUL AND MOST KIND GOD, WHO everywhere protects and defends those who are servants to you, grant to us faithfully to live in Christ your Son, perpetually to serve him in fear, and to exult him with trembling, so that seized with the instruction of justice, and remaining steadfast in it, we may ultimately be blessed in perpetuity.

*Miserator et piissime Deus, qui tibi famulantes ubique tueris
et defendis, dona nobis in Christo Filio tuo fideliter
vivere, eique iugiter servire in timore et exsultare
cum tremore: ut apprehensa iustitiae
disciplina, in ea persistentes beati in
perpetuum existamus.*

---

67  Heb. 1:14a.

# Psalm 3

## ARTICLE XV

3[1] *The Psalm of David when he fled from the face of his son Absalom.*

*Psalmus David, cum fugeret a facie Absalom filii sui.*

THIS IS THE TITLE OF THIS PSALM:  3[1] *Psalmus David, cum fugeret a facie Absalom, filli sui. The Psalm of David when he fled from the face of his son, Absalom.* For certain, this Psalm from a literal standpoint relates to David, and so the title does not present any difficulty. For he who knows the Scriptures will see that it relates to how Absalom, who was desirous of attaining the kingship [of Israel], wished to kill his holy father, David,[1] so that by his death he might reign; and with the army all assembled, he wished to besiege Jerusalem. Hearing of this, David with his household fled; and, at length, his army defeated and put to flight the army of Absalom. And Joab, head of the militia, slew Absalom while the latter hung from an oak tree. During this persecution, therefore, David wrote this Psalm, which literally is to be understood as relating to him, and yet it may also pertain just as truly and efficaciously to Christ.

---

3[2] *Why, O Lord, are they multiplied that afflict me? Many are they who rise up against me.*

*Domine, quid multiplicati sunt qui tribulant me? Multi insurgunt adversum me.*

3[3] *Many say to my soul: There is no salvation for him in his God.*

*Multi dicunt animae meae: Non est salus ipsi in Deo eius.*

Speaking therefore about himself to God:   3[2] *Domine,* inquit, *quid multiplicati sunt qui tribulant me? Lord,* he says, *why are they multiplied that afflict me?* That is, on what grounds? It is as if he is saying: There is

---

1  2 Kings 15–18.

71

no reasonable cause [against me], but a powerful conspiracy. For however much David sinned — committing adultery and murder, because he knew Bathsheba, and arranging to order her husband Uriah to be killed — yet he also ardently repented of it; and also as punishment for such sins, the Lord permitted him to be persecuted so; but those who persecuted him were unjustly motivated, they adjudged him to be entirely rejected by God.    3[3] *Multi dicunt animae meae, many say to my soul,* that is, many are speaking of my soul: *Non est salus ipsi in Deo eius. There is no salvation for him in his God.* That is, [the enemies were taking the position in justification of their aims that] he was entirely cursed and reproved because of his enormous sins, that is to say, his homicide and adultery. Whence Ahithophel and many others persuaded the people that God had rejected David, and therefore they persecuted him [believing themselves to be] without sin, and supported and adhered to Absalom.

---

>   3[4]  *But you, O Lord are my protector, my glory, and the lifter up of my head.*
>
>   *Tu autem Domine, susceptor meus es, gloria mea, et exaltans caput meum.*
>
>   3[5]  *I have cried to the Lord with my voice: and he has heard me from his holy hill.*
>
>   *Voce mea ad Dominum clamavi; et exaudivit me de monte sancto suo.*

3[4] *Tu autem Domine, susceptor meus es. But you, O Lord are my protector.* These are the words of David, who is trying to console himself, speaking lovingly and rejoicingly to God, as if saying: "They have so given up on me; but you, O Lord, are the protector of my soul," that is, you are my forgiver, receiving my penance, and hearing my prayers; *gloria mea, my glory,* that is, the object and the cause of my grace, because in you alone I glory,[2] and with this grace of holy glory you fill me. And so there follows: *ex exaltans caput meum, and the lifter of my head,* that is, raising up my mind towards you, and giving confidence of raising my eyes towards you. For that reason,    3[5] *Voce mea ad Dominum clamavi, I have cried to the Lord with my voice,* pleading to be set free from the evil of punishment and guilt (*poenae et culpae*), and committing myself totally to his will. And this not in vain, for it continues: *et exaudivit me de montem sancto suo, and he has heard me from his holy hill,* that is, from the sublime throne of his dominion, or from his surpassing and highest mercy.

---

2  *Cf.* 2 Cor. 10:17.

3[6]  *I have slept and taken my rest: and I have risen up, because the Lord has protected me.*

*Ego dormivi, et soporatus sum; et exsurrexi, quia Dominus suscepit me.*

3[7]  *I will not fear thousands of the people, surrounding me: arise, O Lord; save me, O my God.*

*Non timebo millia populi circumdantis me. Exsurge, Domine; salvum me fac, Deus meus.*

3[6] *Ego dormivi, et soporatus sum, I have slept and taken my rest.* Viewed literally, sleep has the power to mitigate sorrow, as if it were a bath. David, therefore, by sleeping made provisions for the lightening of his sorrow, as far as natural causes, both of sleep and from the infusion of divine consolation. For that reason, he said: *et exsurrexi, quia Dominus suscepit me, and I have risen up, because the Lord has protected me,* that is, by his grace and mercy he has joined himself to me, and has strengthened my heart in him. Whence there is joined to it:   3[7] *Non timebo millia populi circumdantis me, I will not fear thousands of the people surrounding me,* that is, I will stand in fearful awe of none of the multitude rising up against me; and so that I might firmly persevere in this fortitude of soul, *exsurge, Domine, arise O Lord,* not arising from a place, but rendering aid and having you in the manner of arising; *salvum me fac, Deus meus, save me, O my God.*

---

3[8]  *For you have struck all them who are my adversaries without cause: you have broken the teeth of sinners.*

*Quoniam tu percussisti omnes adversantes mihi sine causa; dentes peccatorum contrivisti.*

3[8] *Quoniam tu percussisti omnes adversantes mihi sine causa, for you have struck all of them who are my adversaries without cause.* Here we return to cause, not to that cause which has been spoken of, but to the cause which follows: for David does not therefore pray to God to be saved, because God slew all the adversaries himself, for the prayer followed that prosecution. But because the Lord defeated the adversaries of David that favored Absalom, either by frightening them, or wounding them, or slaying them; therefore, he broke the teeth of sinners, that is, he shut the mouths of those who spoke against David and repressed their evil words. Therefore, he adds thereunto: *dentes peccatorum contrivisit, you have broken the teeth of sinners.*

3[9] *Salvation is of the Lord: and your blessing is upon your people.*

*Domini est salus; et super populum tuum benedictio tua.*

3[9] Truly, because all this victory of David was arranged and put together by God, therefore he adds: *Domini est salus, salvation is of the Lord*, that is, the liberation from the adversaries was attributable to God, and to him it is rightly ascribed. Consequently, David changes the person, through means of a literary device which is called metaplasm;[3] and speaking to the Lord, he says: *et super populum tuum, and upon your people*, that is, upon they who stood by me, *benedictio tua, your blessing*, that is, the combination of your gifts, protection and redemption: because the army of David, though small as it was in comparison to the army of Absalom, nevertheless prevailed with the help of God.

# ARTICLE XVI

## ALLEGORICAL EXPOSITION OF THE SAME THIRD PSALM

3[1] *The psalm of David when he fled from the face of his son Absalom.*

*Psalmus David, cum fugeret a facie Absalom filii sui.*

THE CATHOLIC TEACHERS AUGUSTINE AND Cassiodorus and others expound the words of this Psalm as dealing with Christ; but that which literally deals with David, they understand as allegorically dealing with Christ. For whatever may be declared by the Psalm may fittingly be explained as relating to Christ. So also the title is explained mystically. For David (as has been shown) by reason of interpretation is a figure of Christ. But Absalom, whose name is interpreted as peace of the father (*pax patris*), is a type of the traitor Judas, of which it is said in a later Psalm, *For even the man of peace, in whom I trusted;*[4] and also in the Gospel, where Christ said that the sons of the bridegroom cannot fast as long as the bridegroom is with them,[5] the other disciples were called sons of Christ or sons of the bridegroom.

---

3   *E. N. metaplasmus.* Alteration of regular verbal, grammatical, or rhetorical form, by addition, omission, or transposition for the purpose of some literary effect. In this case, the movement is from third person [he, the Lord] to second person [you/your people].

4   Ps. 40:10.

5   *Cf.* Matt. 9:15.

The title    3[1] *Psalmus David, cum fugeret a facie Absalon filii sui, the Psalm of David when he fled from the face of his son, Absalom,* may be understood in the sense: the Psalm speaking of Christ, when he fled from the intention of Judas, the erstwhile disciple of his. For it is then that Christ abandoned the heart of Judas, when, *after the morsel, Satan entered into him.*[6]

---

3[2]    *Why, O Lord, are they multiplied that afflict me? Many are they who rise up against me.*

*Domine, quid multiplicati sunt qui tribulant me? Multi insurgunt adversum me.*

3[3]    *Many say to my soul: There is no salvation for him in his God.*

*Multi dicunt animae meae : Non est salus ipsi in Deo eius.*

In this way, therefore, Christ by speaking to God the Father, or, more precisely, to the most eminent holy Trinity, or assuredly Christ as man speaking to himself as God:    3[2] *Domine, O Lord,* he says, that is — O Father God, or O God triune and simple, who is Lord of all, or Word and Son of God, who assumed into your personality my humble state — *quid, why,* that is, how did I merit that, *multiplicati sunt qui tribulant me, many are they who rise against me,* that is, who seek to kill me, and rail against me, and seek to injure me? It is as if he said, [I merited it] "not at all," for Christ did not sin in any way so as to merit that he suffer.[7]    3[3] *Multi insurgent adversum me. Many are they who rise up against me,* those, that is to say, who oppress me, namely the Pharisees and the Scribes, together with the high priest and the people. *Multi dicunt animae mae: Non est salus ipsi in Deo eius. Many say to my soul: there is no salvation for him in his God.* These that are referred to here are the previously identified Jews, who regarded Christ to be a blasphemer, a glutton, one possessed by demons, and insane, as is often expressed in the Gospels.[8]

---

3[4]    *But you, O Lord are my protector, my glory, and the lifter up of my head.*

*Tu autem Domine, susceptor meus es, gloria mea, et exaltans caput meum.*

---

6 John 13:27.
7 E. N. In other words, it is a negative rhetorical question.
8 Mark 2:7; Matt. 11:19; John 10:20.

**3[4]** *Tu autem, Domine, susceptor meus es. But you, O Lord, are my protector*: that is, you, the Word and Only-Begotten of God according to divine nature, are my protector with respect to the human nature. For Christ as God protected and assumed the human nature in the unity of a person. *Gloria mea, my glory*, that is, the object of my beatitude, because the glory of the humanity of Christ consists in the union and vision of the Godhead itself. Whence there follows: *et exaltans caput meum, and the lifter up of my head*, that is, the elevating of my created, or human, understanding, to the clear and blessed vision of the essence of the Godhead, which Christ as man, saw from the first instant of his conception in the Virgin Mother, as has been stated [earlier in this work]. Or this [as an alternative explanation]: *Tu autem, Domine, susceptor meus es. But you, O Lord, are my protector*: that is, you God the Father, or the entire Trinity, are my protector, that is, you are he who hearkens and preserves me, from whose love and good pleasure I neither wish nor am able to separate myself. *Gloria mea, my glory*, that is, the cause and reason for all of my joy; *et exaltans caput meum; and the lifter up of my head*, that is, honoring and glorifying me in signs and in virtues, by which it is possible for men to know me to be truly the Christ and your Son, indeed even the true God. And thus by the word *head* is able to be understood are referring to Christ's divinity: for the head of Christ is God, according to the Apostle.[9] And this God the Father or God the Trinity exalted, when by the Spirit he revealed to men that Christ was God and man,[10] not one in nature, but one in person. Whence Christ says: *Glorify you me, O Father, with yourself, with the glory which I had, before the world* was made:[11] not that Christ ever parted with the glory that he had before the world was created, but he prayed this way so that the certain knowledge he had might be known to men. Whence it says also: *Father, the hour is come, glorify your Son, that your Son may glorify you;*[12] and where is this to be accomplished unless it be in the heart of men?

---

**3[5]**  *I have cried to the Lord with my voice: and he has heard me from his holy hill.*

*Voce mea ad Dominum clamavi; et exaudivit me de monte sancto suo.*

**3[5]** *Voce mea ad Dominum clamavi. I have cried to the Lord with my voice.* According to the testimony of the Evangelists, Christ would

---

9   1 Cor. 11:3b.
10   Matt. 3:16, 17.
11   John 17:5.
12   John 17:1.

stay up the whole night in prayer to God,[13] and at the approach of the Passion, he prayed three times to the Father,[14] and did so not in vain because it states further, *et exaudivit me de monte sancto suo, and he has heard me from his holy hill*, that is, from his highest dwelling place, or from his sublime justice. For a later Psalm has this to say: *Your justice is as the mountains of God.*[15] Therefore from this justice, God heard Christ, because — divine justice dictating — it was becoming for Christ to be heard in all his prayers to God, as he was most obedient in all things to that God. For God fulfilled that prayer which Jesus poured out before the Passion saying: *Let this chalice pass from me.*[16] For he did not pray absolutely to be freed from the Passion. But this is what he ultimately desired and prayed for: that he might fulfill the will of the Father, saying: *not my will, but yours.*[17] This is the reason why the Apostle said to the Hebrews regarding Christ: *He was heard for his reverence.*[18] Also, Christ said to the Father: *I give you thanks that you have heard me; and I knew that you hear me always.*[19]

3[6]   *I have slept and taken my rest: and I have risen up, because the Lord has protected me.*

*Ego dormivi, et soporatus sum; et exsurrexi, quia Dominus suscepit me.*

Consequently, Christ spoke of his Passion, Burial, and Resurrection, saying:   3[6] *Ego dormivi, I have slept*, the sleep of death on the Cross; *et soporatus sum, and taken my rest*, three days and nights laying in the tomb. For the death of the saints is called sleep because they are raised up by God unto an immortal life. And the burial of Christ is well called sleep because he rose again so quickly (namely in three days). Whence it follows, *et exsurrexi, and I have risen up*, from the enclosure of the sepulcher, as he came forth from the enclosure of the Virgin's womb; *quia Dominus suscepit me, because the Lord has protected me*, that is, he has brought be back from the number of the dead.

---

13  Luke 6:12.
14  Matt. 26:39–44.
15  Ps. 35:7a.
16  Matt. 26:39.
17  Luke 22:42.
18  Heb. 5:7.
19  John 11:41, 42.

**3[7]** *I will not fear thousands of the people, surrounding me: arise, O Lord; save me, O my God.*

*Non timebo millia populi circumdantis me. Exsurge, Domine; salvum me fac, Deus meus.*

**3[7]** *Non timebo millia populi circumdantis me.* I will not fear thousands of people surrounding me. These may be the words of Christ after the Resurrection, because rising from the dead, *he dies now no more,*[20] for he rose up immortal. And therefore as to the rest of the verse *I will not fear thousands of people,* that is, however many great a multitude desire to resist me or surround me — not that after the Resurrection those adverse to Christ would be strong enough to surround and overcome him, because neither did he engage with the ungodly after death, nor did he appear to the unjust, but [he appeared only] to the *witnesses preordained by God;*[21] and therefore it is said, *I will not fear a thousand people surrounding me* (for he did not fear them after the Passion), because he rose again impassible.[22] Now, these words are also able to be understood as referring to Christ before the Passion. For however much natural fear he allowed admittance when as the Passion approached and when he began to sorrow, and to be despondent, to be struck with fear, and to become weary, and when his sweat became as drops of blood dripping onto the ground;[23] he nevertheless rose to prayer, and undaunted he faced the crowd of the wicked men and said: *Whom do you seek?*[24] And so it says, *I will not fear thousands of the people surrounding me;* and so that I might not be afraid, I pray, O Lord,[25] *exsurge,* arise, come to my rescue; *salvum me fac, Deus meus, save me, O my God,* from death, not deserting me to the sepulcher, nor abandoning my soul in hell, but bringing me back to heaven.

---

**3[8]** *For you have struck all them who are my adversaries without cause: you have broken the teeth of sinners.*

*Quoniam tu percussisti omnes adversantes mihi sine causa; dentes peccatorum contrivisti.*

---

20  Rom. 6:9.
21  Acts 10:41.
22  E. N. Impassibility is the quality or characteristics of not being able to suffer.
23  Matt. 25:17; Mark 14:33; Luke 22:44.
24  John 18:4, 7.
25  E. N. Here, Denis uses the first person as if Christ was praying in this way or intending the Psalm to be understood in this way.

3[8] *Quoniam tu percussisti omnes adversantes mihi sine causa. For you have struck all them who are my adversaries without cause.* Often with the Prophets, the past or present time is used to refer to the future; and this method we see implemented here. Because *you have struck,* should be interpreted to mean "because you will strike," *all of them who are my adversaries without cause,* that is, my persecutors and crucifiers, and the incredulous Jews, who are struck with eternal punishment, and their posterity who are captive even in the present, driven away, those expelled, and the many involved in misery, that is, except those who have repented. *Dentes peccatorum contrivisti, you have broken the teeth of sinners,* that is, the blasphemies, mockeries, and contradictions of those who in life and death and after death ridiculed me and disparaged me you will grind down, displaying their falsehood, and deservedly tormenting them with punishment. *Domini est salus, salvation is of the Lord,* that is, my salvation from the hands of the wicked is from God; *et super populum tuum, and upon your people,* that is, upon those who believe in me, and are following in my steps, *benedictio tua, your blessing,* that is, the assortment of your graces, O Lord Father. For these are the words of Christ to God.

# ARTICLE VII

## TROPOLOGICAL EXPLANATION OF
## THE SAME THIRD PSALM.

3[1] *The psalm of David when he fled from the face of his son Absalom.*
*Psalmus David, cum fugeret a facie Absalom filii sui.*

ESIDES [THE LITERAL AND ALLEGORICAL understandings discussed above,] this Psalm can be understood as relating to any just man or the whole Church militant. [We can do so] to the extent that we may accept as moral instruction those things which are written of the highest just man and the Saint of Saints,[26] our

---

26  L. *Sanctus Sanctorum,* Saint of Saints. "[I]n the case of Christ's constitutive anointing we are talking about an anointing of His whole being and thereby not only is he anointed a priest, but also His flesh is anointed to be the priest's vestment, the sacrifice (*cf.* the typological admixture of oil to the food offering, Lev. 2:1 ff.), the altar, the sanctuary, and the living Ark of the Covenant, generally to be the Holy one and the Holy of Holies in each and every respect, so that

Lord Jesus Christ. And we are instructed thereby as to what it is we ought to be doing, if we undergo those sorts of things which occurred to the ancient holy men and to the Son of God. For in David is contained not only a figure of Christ, but also of any just man as well as the Church, because the Church by virtue of its spouse, Jesus Christ, and any Christian faithful, is David, that is, being strong of hand and the having the aspect of desirability.[27] But Absalom is a type of the world, and of those who persecute and tempt the just. Whence, according to tropology, the sense of the title of this Psalm is    3[1] *Psalmus David, cum fugerit a facie Absalon filii sui, the Psalm of David when he fled from the face of his son, Absalom*, that is, the song of the Church and any of the just, since they, by a good manner of living, draw apart from the counsel of the unclean and the ungodly who are sons of the Church in potency, and not in act: in name, and not in reality.[28]

---

3[2]  *Why, O Lord, are they multiplied that afflict me? Many are they who rise up against me.*

*Domine, quid multiplicati sunt qui tribulant me? Multi insurgunt adversum me.*

3[3]  *Many say to my soul: There is no salvation for him in his God.*

*Multi dicunt animae meae: Non est salus ipsi in Deo eius.*

It speaks therefore of the Church, as it speaks also of any rational creature, struck, pressed upon, and wearied by various temptations, myriad tribulations, and miseries.    3[2] *Domine, O Lord*, that is, O adored eternal and almighty God, or O Lord, that is, O Jesus Christ; *quid multiplicati sunt qui tribulant me? Why are they multiplied that afflict me?* That is to say, the world, the flesh, and the devil, because these three

---

he is simply the *Sanctus sanctorum* [Saint of saints] precisely because he is also the *Sanctum sanctorum* [Holy of Holies]. Matthias Joseph Scheeben, *Handbook of Catholic Dogmatics* § 384 (Steubenville: Emmaus Academic 2020).

27  E. N. Again, these are classic etymologies associated with the name "David": "strong of hand" and "desirable of aspect."

28  E. N. These are Aristotelian/Thomistic principles used to explain change in being. They are correlative so that an act is the act of a potency, and the potency is the potency to some act. Here, members of the Church that are not in a state of sanctifying grace or those outside of the Church altogether (such as pagans and Jews) are members of the Body of Christ, the Church, only potentially (in potency). Those Catholic "in name only," and "not in reality," are nominal Catholics who do not participate in the life of the Church; they are in mortal sin, and are thus lacking in sanctifying grace and a formed faith.

are the enemies of the just man. *Multi insurgunt adversum me, many are they who rise up against me,* namely, worldly men, carnal desires, and the powers of the air:[29] for these disturb and trouble the just.   **3[3]** *Multi dicunt, many say,* that is, sow by word and deed, *animae meae: Non est salus ipsi in Deo eius; to my soul, There is no salvation for him in his God.* The worldly and ungodly adjudge the life of the just to be madness, and *their end is without honor;*[30] and for that reason they hold them *in derision and for a parable of reproach.*[31]

---

**3[4]** *But you, O Lord are my protector, my glory, and the lifter up of my head.*

*Tu autem Domine, susceptor meus es, gloria mea, et exaltans caput meum.*

**3[5]** *I have cried to the Lord with my voice: and he has heard me from his holy hill.*

*Voce mea ad Dominum clamavi; et exaudivit me de monte sancto suo.*

Thereafter follows a most sweet word, and one that is of greatest consolation: which word anyone finding himself in tribulation and temptation may say to God with loving trust.   **3[4]** *Tu autem, Domine, susceptor meus es, but you, O lord, are my protector,* to whom in adversity I find refuge and succor; *gloria mea, my glory,* to whom in all grief I am made happy and am relieved; *et exaltans caput meum, and the lifter up of my head,* that is, rescuing my soul from all dejection. Whence it is written: *As we know not what to do, we can only turn our eyes to you.*[32]   **3[5]** *Voce mea ad Dominum clamavi, I have cried to the Lord with my voice.* By this verse all the faithful are taught that at time of tribulation this is what must be done. For [the faithful Christian] ought with his voice to cry — that is, ardently and with deep feeling of heart to cry — to the Lord: and then the Lord will hear him, so that declaring that which is here revealed, he says, *et exaudivit me de monte sancto suo, and he has heard me from his holy hill.* But it behooves one to pray perseveringly, indeed, *without ceasing.*[33]

---

29  E. N. *aeries potestates,* aerial powers. *Cf.* Eph. 2:2. A reference to demonic powers.
30  Wis. 5:4.
31  Wis. 5:3b.
32  2 Chr. 12b.
33  1 Thess. 5:17.

3[6]  *I have slept and taken my rest: and I have risen up, because the
Lord has protected me.*

*Ego dormivi, et soporatus sum; et exsurrexi, quia Dominus sus-
cepit me.*

3[7]  *I will not fear thousands of the people, surrounding me: arise, O
Lord; save me, O my God.*

*Non timebo millia populi circumdantis me. Exsurge, Domine; sal-
vum me fac, Deus meus.*

3[6] *Ego*, I, that is to say the Church or any just man, *dormivi, have
slept,* that is, I have been oppressed by tribulations, so that *my soul
is weary of my life,*[34] and because of that weariness, I have slept;[35] *et
soporatus sum, and have taken my rest,* by the time one has persevered
in such anxiety; *et exsurrexi, and I have risen up,* that is, I have received
consolation, and I have prevailed, not by my own strength or merits, but
*quia Dominus suscepit me, because the Lord has protected me,* that is, his
mercy has embraced me and has granted admittance to my prayers. Or it
may be interpreted thus: *Ego dormivi, I have slept,* that is, I was prostrate
in sin and was cast down; *et soporatus sum, and taken my rest,* that is, I
remained in the delight of sins, and because of indolence I have ceased
from doing good works. Of the sinner, the Apostle exclaims: *Arise, you
who sleep.*[36] And Solomon: *How long will you sleep, O sluggard?*[37] For
he who does not contemplate heavenly things, who does not hear the
word of God, who does not exercise himself in some sense in spiritual
activity sleeps. *Et exsurrexi, quia Dominus suscepit me, and I have risen
up because the Lord has protected me,* that is, I have ceased from vice, and
began to live justly, because the Lord is merciful to me, surpassing in
indulgence and grace. Whence it says thereafter:    3[7] *Non timebo millia
populi circumdantis me, I will not fear thousands of the people surrounding
me,* that is, I will not stand in awe of mob of adversaries. For the heart
firm in God has nothing to fear but God, because if he fears men at all,
he does so only on account of God. For *the just, bold as a lion, shall be
without dread.*[38] And, *He that fears man, shall quickly fall:*[39] But because

---

34  Job 10:1a.
35  *Cf.* Ps. 118:28. *My soul has slumbered through heaviness: strengthen you me in
your words.*
36  Eph. 5:14.
37  Prov. 6:9.
38  Prov. 28:1b.
39  Prov. 29:25a.

he does not have any fortitude whatsoever in himself, therefore is added: *Exsurge, Domine, salvum me fac, Deus meus. Arise, O Lord, save me, O my God.* For it is fitting that God begins, continues, and completes the good in us; and so unceasingly ought we to cry out to him.

3[8] *For you have struck all them who are my adversaries without cause: you have broken the teeth of sinners.*

*Quoniam tu percussisti omnes adversantes mihi sine causa; dentes peccatorum contrivisti.*

3[8] *Quoniam tu percussisti omnes adversantes mihi sine causa. For you have struck all them who are my adversaries without cause.* In the Gospel, Christ says to his disciples: *Have confidence, I have overcome the world.*[40] For he has overcome the prince of this world. So, therefore, the Church and any one that is devoted to Christ is able to say: *For you have struck,* that is, you have overcome and condemned, *all them who are my adversaries without cause,* that is, the world, or worldly men and demons, who oppose me endeavoring to avert me from all good, and to entangle me in vices. *Dentes peccatorum contrivisti. You have broken the teeth of sinners.* That is, you have crushed underfoot the words or the mouths of those who defame the life of the good, and tear to pieces their honorable reputation, at least by proscribing such actions. This verse can also be interpreted differently by accepting the past tense for the future tense, in the manner of prophetic speech. *Quoniam tu percussisti, for you have struck,* that is, you, O Lord Jesus Christ, judge of all, you have slain in the day of judgment, *omnes adversantes mihi sine causa, all them who are my adversaries without cause,* that is, those who in an unjust manner vexed and troubled me: and then *dentes peccatorum, the teeth of sinners,* that is, the words of the detractors or the envious, *contrivisti, you have broken,* that is, you will grind down, you will beat back, you will condemn.[41]

Therefore, he who is battered by temptations and tribulations might sing this Psalm, and if he sings it attentively, he certainly will experience a great alleviation, and he will be aware of that which truly and salubriously James in his epistle counsels: *Is any of you sad? Let him pray. Is he cheerful in mind? Let him sing.*[42]

---

40 John 16:33.
41 Denis does not address Psalm 3:9.
42 James 5:13.

# PRAYER

B Y OUR VOICE TO YOU, O LORD OUR GOD, crying out in prayer, hear us from your holy mountain: arise in our aid, so that through your assistance we may obtain salvation and eternal blessing.

*Voce nostra ad te, Domine Deus noster, oration clamantes,*
*exaudi nos de monte sancto tuo: exsurge in adiutorium*
*Nostrum, ut tua opitulatione salute et aeternam*
*benedictionem consequamur.*

# Psalm 4

## ARTICLE XVIII

### EXPOSITION OF THE FOURTH PSALM:
### *CUM INVOCAREM, &c.*
### *WHEN I CALLED UPON HIM, &c.*

4[1]  *Unto the end, in verses. A psalm for David.*

   *In finem, in carminibus. Psalmus David.*

HE NEXT PSALM IS ONE THAT HAS THE TITLE: 4[1] *In finem, psalmus cantici David. Unto the end, a Psalm for David*: that is, this reflection, which exhorts [the reader] to the performance of good works, is a musical Psalm, that is, it includes spiritual jubilation, and makes us rejoice in the eternal good. *David*, that is, the Psalm was authored by him; *in the end*, that is, directing us towards Christ, who is the Alpha and Omega,[1] the beginning and the end, of all things. For the word *end* can mean two things. Namely, it can mean the consumption of something, as we may say about a candle fully consumed by its flame, "The candle is at an end." And there is an *end* of consummation or perfection, as we might assert about a home already completed, "The home is at an end." And it is in this second manner that Christ is the end of all things, for he is our consummate perfection and our happiness. This Psalm contains within it, therefore, a spiritual doctrine or moral instruction, an enkindling of hope and internal joy.

---

4[2]  *When I called upon him, the God of my justice heard me: when I was in distress, you have enlarged me. Have mercy on me: and hear my prayer.*

   *Cum invocarem exaudivit me Deus iustitiae meae, in tribulatione dilatasti mihi. Miserere mei, et exaudi orationem meam.*

In this manner, the Prophet [David] speaks in the person of the Church or in the person of any just man:   4[2] *Cum invocarem exaudivit me Deus iustitiae meae, When I called upon him, the God of my justice heard*

---

1  Rev. 1:8; 21:6; 22:13.

*me*: that is, when I have internally asked God, when out of an internal affection I have cried out to him, during such times when I might have prayed with the whole mind occupied in regarding God; *I called upon the God of my justice*, that is, he from whom I have all that is good, from whom I have all the justice I practice. And in this the Prophet [David] instructs us, so we might reach out to God in all our anxieties and in a most intimate way. But by the verses *the God of my justice heard me* which he adds, he kindles and confirms our hope, so that we might confidently invoke him, as if he were saying: "In whatever manner I might call upon God, he hears me, and so also he will hear you, if purely, perseveringly, and without any hesitation you might seek to pray, not as a result of your own justice, but confident in the mercies of God." *In tribulatione dilatasti mihi, when I was in distress, you have enlarged me*: that is, in affliction of my spirit, or in the infirmity of my body, I am interiorly consoled, given true patience by which I joyfully endure and with equanimity bear all manner of adversities, so that in him my heart is enlarged by mental and holy joy. For by sorrow the heart is narrowed and restrained, but by joy it is enlarged and widened. Whence the Apostle exhilarated by the memory of his disciples wrote: *our heart is enlarged.*[2] True, because man must always be in fear and take care as long as he remains in the present exile, and so he should not see himself securely in possession of the grace and consolation from God. But rather he should always be troubled by the danger of the future, in the manner that is written: *Blessed is the man that is always fearful.*[3] And therefore the Psalm continues: *Miserere mei, have mercy on me*, having sympathy for me that I might not fall in future danger, and that I might not lose the grace that I have received, and that I may not find myself being ungrateful to you. *Et exaudi orationem meam, and hear my prayer*. By this the affection is enkindled, and as it were warmed, desiring that God may have mercy on him.

---

4[3]    *O you sons of men, how long will you be dull of heart? Why do you love vanity, and seek after lying?*

*Filii hominum, usquequo gravi corde? Ut quid diligitis vanitatem, et quaeritis mendacium?*

In addition, because fraternal charity demands that man desire to communicate to his neighbor the divine grace imparted to him, praying,

---

2   2 Cor. 6:11b.
3   Prov. 28:14a.

teaching, or living by example, so in the first of his epistles, the most glorious prince of the apostolic order [Peter] exhorts: *As every man has received grace, ministering the same one to another, as good stewards of the manifold grace of God.*[4] And consequently, the Church or any just man, after his heart is filled by prayer before God, turns toward others to instruct them, and says: **4[3]** *Filii hominum, O sons of men.* In Hebrew, it reads: O Sons of Adam. For Adam with the Hebrews is not only a proper name, but also an appellation designating that which is man. And so, *O sons of men,* O sons of Adam, of sons of the first parents, who bear the earthly image and not the heavenly one,[5] that is, who imitate the prevarication of Adam, and not the obedience of Christ, *Usquequo gravi corde? How long will you be dull of heart?* That is, how long will you have a downward heart? How much longer will you immerse yourself in the affection of transitory things, not following those things that are above you? *Ut quid diligitis vanitatem, why do you love vanity,* that is, these most vain things of the temporal order? Which, while you love them more than you do God, are the most vain things, things which divert the mind from its greatest good, and which involve you in the most vile consolations. *Et quaeritis mendacium, and you seek after lying,* mutually deceiving yourselves? Or [another way of understanding it is], Why do you seek after lying things, that is, goods of the senses and delights of the flesh? These promise to the lover a certain satisfaction and happiness, but they fail in fulfilling that promise, because desire does not find rest in them; indeed, the love and delight of fleshly things entangle you in many miseries, anxieties, sadness, and evils.

---

> **4[4]** *Know you also that the Lord has made his holy one wonderful: the Lord will hear me when I shall cry unto him.*
>
> *Et scitote quoniam mirificavit Dominus sanctum suum; Dominus exaudiet me cum clamavero ad eum.*

Consequently, Scripture proposes the consideration that, to be entitled to merit, sinners must turn away from earthly things, and arouse [a sense of] their [need to be in] subjection to God. **4[4]** *Et scitote, And know,* that is, wisely think, *quoniam mirificavit Dominus sanctum suum; that the Lord has made his holy one wonderful,* that is, that he marvelously adorned and exalted his holy one, that is, anyone who perfectly and purely

---

4  1 Pet. 4:10.
5  *Cf.* 1 Cor. 15:49.

governs himself, or by excellent grace in the present, or by glory already in heaven, or by the divine marvel by which God extends to men which—if accepted—is for him the life of the saints. Or [it may be interpreted] thus: *Know that the Lord,* that is, God the Father, *has made his holy one,* that is, Jesus Christ, who in the Gospel of Mark is called *the Holy one of God,*[6] whom he magnified before his birth, by preaching through the Prophets that he was soon to be born, and at his birth, drawing him out from the enclosed womb of the Virgin, and after his birth, because his angels announced his birth to the shepherds;[7] and in the desert, when he was among the beasts, and the angels ministered to him;[8] and also in death, by the supernatural eclipse of the sun;[9] and after death, by the Resurrection, Ascension, and sending of the Holy Spirit. *Dominus exaudiet me, cum clamavero ad eum. The Lord will hear me when I shall cry out to him.* This is a word of good hope which is born out of the love of God. For he who loves God, firmly hopes, and God will not deny to him any of those things that incline to true salvation. And also in this word the hope held out to us is the hope of attaining the grace of the Lord, by which we are made holy, and by which are glorified by him.

---

4[5]  *Be angry, and sin not: the things you say in your hearts, be sorry for them upon your beds.*

*Irascimini, et nolite peccare; quae dicitis in cordibus vestris, in cubilibus vestris compungimini.*

4[5] *Irascimini, et nolite peccare. Be angry, and sin not.* This certain anger (*ira*) proceeds out of the zeal of justice, one following reason and willingly assumed, as far as by it man may accomplish more strongly a virtuous work. For this anger (*ira*) is good, unless it possibly becomes excessively heated or inflamed, or demands [from a situation or from another person] a greater punishment than is merited by a wrong. Therefore, it is of this anger that one is exhorted: *Be angry,* that is, against vice, against the devil, against your negligences; and do not sin, that is, do not permit that the passion of anger so grows as to disturb reason or strives for immoderate vengeance. And therefore this anger (*ira*) is different than the anger which is vicious, which cuts off reason, and frequently resists it, and whose motives are also primarily venial: and so

---

6  Mark 1:24.
7  *Cf.* Luke 2:9, 12.
8  Matt. 4:1, 11; Mark 1:13.
9  Luke 23:44, 45.

by anger (*ira*) one is to understand what is being said by, *be angry*. And this is said, then, not for the purpose of exhorting that we might become enraged, but by exhibiting assistance and counsel, so we may know that which occurs to us when the movement of anger grows. And so is added to this, *and sin not*, that is, restrain anger, so that it is not known to others by word or gestures, or certainly that it does not proceed to deeds. And the following words plainly unfold all this. *Quae dicitis in cordibus vestris, the things you say in your hearts*, that is, [the things] you think within your soul, *in cubilibus vestris compungimini, be sorry for them upon your beds*, that is, in the silence of your minds do penance of the sin of your thoughts, do not consent to illicit suggestions. For hearts might be likened to being the beds of deliberations.

---

4[6] *Offer up the sacrifice of justice, and trust in the Lord: many say, Who shows us good things?*

*Sacrificate sacrificium iustitiae, et sperate in Domino. Multi dicunt: Quis ostendit nobis bona?*

But because it is just not sufficient to abstain from vice, therefore the following is added:   4[6] *Sacrificate sacrificium iustitiae, offer up the sacrifice of justice.* That which is offered to God is called sacrifice. But external sacrifice is a sign of the interior sacrifice, which the spirit itself offers to God by holy devotion, true charity, and a deepest humility, ascribing to God oneself and all of one's own goods, and devoting to his veneration whatever one is, is able to be, and whatever one does. And so, *offer up the sacrifice of justice*, that is, employ all of your interior and exterior works to the honor of God. And so that they may be pleasing to God, occupy yourself fully to pass your life with others in a praiseworthy manner and to live justly. But because from such laudable manner of living someone may possibly extol himself, and to glory and to trust in his own merit, therefore is added: *et sperate in Domino, and trust in the Lord*: not in your justice, but in his mercy, from whom is all of our sufficiency.[10] *For they, not knowing the justice of God, and willing to establish their own, have not submitted themselves to the justice of God.*[11]

*Multi dicunt: Quis ostendit nobis bona? Many say: Who shows us good things?* This is the question of evil men, who either negate the providence of God or do not consider that there is another life after this one. Of

---

10 *Cf.* 2 Cor. 3:5.
11 Rom. 10:3.

which kinds of persons, Malachi said: *Your words have* prevailed *over me, says the Lord.... Vain is he who serves God.*[12] And what kind of an advantage is there, [they ask,] because if we keep his precepts, we walk sorrowful before God? And these things they say: *Who shows us good things?* that is, *Who knows if the spirit of the children of Adam ascend upward,*[13] and whether there is a life in which each one will be recompensed justly? And this word can be represented in another manner. For many, namely philosophers of the Academy,[14] asserted that it was not possible for men to know anything with certainty, whence they harbored doubt as to all things, and they spoke only in terms of opinions. Of these sorts, therefore, the Prophet [David] said: *Who shows us good things?* that is, what makes us able to know the truth with certainty? And to this question the Prophet responds:

4[7]   *The light of your countenance O Lord, is signed upon us: you have given gladness in my heart.*

*Signatum est super nos lumen vultus tui, Domine: dedisti laetitiam in corde meo.*

4[7] *Signatum est super nos lumen vultus tui, Domine.* The light of your countenance, O Lord, is signed upon us: that is, impressed upon our soul is a certain participation of the light of your countenance, which is the divine intellect; and in the bright clarity of this light we are shown good things, that is, we intellectually see the immortality of our soul, divine providence, the just recompense for all; and in it we recognize with certitude the truth of things. But this light *signed upon us* may, in a certain manner, be said of the natural light of the human intellect by which philosophers are able to understand truthfully many things regarding the things we have spoken about;[15] But these things are better understood through the supernatural light, namely faith and the splendor of the grace of God, reforming in us the image of the blessed Trinity, or the gift of wisdom and knowledge. *Dedisti laetitiam in corde meo; you have*

---

12   Mal. 3:13, 14a. E. N. Denis has *praevaluerunt* (prevailed); the Sixto-Clementine Vulgate has *invaluerunt* (grew powerful).

13   Eccl. 3:21a.

14   E. N. The philosophical school established by Plato circa 387 B. C. in Athens.

15   E. N., In other words about the existence of God, his providence, and final judgment. These are called the *praeambula fidei*, the preambles of the faith, and they can be known by the natural light of reason. DS 3002-03 (Vatican I). See *also* Ralph McInerny, *Praeambula Fide: Thomism and the God of the Philosophers* (Washington, DC: CUA Press, 2006).

*given gladness in my heart*: that is, O Lord, from the fact that I know
the light of your countenance to be signed over me, I spiritually rejoice,
and with great vehemence do I exult: and especially I ascribe to you
that joy, not wanting to appear ungrateful.

4[8] *By the fruit of their corn, their wine and oil, they are multiplied.*

*A fructu frumenti, vini, et olei sui, multiplicati sunt.*

4[8] *A fructu frumenti, vini et olei sui; by the fruit of their corn, their
wine and oil,* that is, out of the abundance of temporal things, *multiplicati sunt, they are multiplied,* that is, from that one highest thing which
alone is necessary,[16] many men are adverse, miserably wandering about
and distracted. Who are these men? None others but those of whom
it has already been said, *Many say, who shows us good things?* That is,
worldly men, men darkened by the riches of the world and the delights
of the flesh; they who in no manner affix their heart unto God simply,
but are rather preoccupied with perishable goods. Of these, Hosea says:
*Their heart is divided: now they shall perish.*[17] And the apostle Judas in
his epistle: *These are they, who separate themselves, sensual men, having
not the Spirit.*[18] Notwithstanding these men, there is a certain corn and
a certain wine from which good fruit is to be multiplied, that is, to be
augmented with fruitfulness and in number. Of which Zacharias says:
*What is the good thing* of the Lord, and *what is his beautiful thing, but the
corn of the elect, and wine springing forth virgins?*[19] This cannot be better
explained, except as referring to the Sacrament of the Body and Blood
of Christ. Similarly, something like this is said of oil in a later Psalm:
*You have anointed my head with oil.*[20] But these are not corn, wine, and
oil of those of whom now Scripture is referring to [that is those worldly
men], but of the elect, and therefore it adds, *their (sui).*[21]

4[9] *In peace in the selfsame I will sleep, and I will rest.*

*In pace in idipsum dormiam, et requiescam.*

---

16 *Cf.* Luke 10:42.
17 Hosea 10:2.
18 Jude 19.
19 Zach. 9:17.
20 Ps. 22:5a.
21 E. N. That is, the genitive pronoun sui, "their," makes it clear that the corn and
the oil are the ordinary products of the earth produced by the toil of worldly
men, not the spiritual corn and oil of those marked by the light of the Lord.

**4[10]**  *For you, O Lord, singularly have settled me in hope*

*Quoniam tu, Domine, singulariter in spe constituisti me.*

These men, therefore, so multiplied as has already been said,[22] are unstable, unsettled, distracted; but I (says the Church or any just man),  **4[9]** *In pace in id ipsum dormiam et requiescam; in peace and in the selfsame I will sleep, and I will rest.* Peace refers to that tranquility of good order, or the cessation from disorder (*perturbatione*): as when the flesh obeys the spirit, sensuality obeys reason, and reason obeys God. But in itself, peace is God sublime and blessed, *with whom there is no change, nor shadow of alteration,*[23] for he exists always and invariably to the same extent perfect, to the same extent blessed, and to the same extent glorious. And thus, *In pace,* in peace, that is, in true tranquility of mind and in stable ordering, *in id ipsum,* in the selfsame, that is, in the eternal God who is always the same, *dormiam,* I will sleep, that is, I will cease from exterior occupations, from the handling of sensible things, *et requiescam, and I will rest,* that is, I will take repose delightfully in the taste of the divine sweetness, in the contemplation of the divine goodness, in the ardor of divine love, now, indeed, inchoately through grace, but in the future consummately through glory. And this because, O Lord God, I dare to say,  **4[10]** *Quoniam tu, Domine, singulariter in spe constituisti me, because you, O Lord, singularly have settled me in hope.* Indeed, although there is no cause for despair in the present life, but God is able to give to all men hope to arrive to that which no eye has seen, *nor ear heard,*[24] yet God settles just men *singularly in hope,* because through the reception of the present gift the expectation of the future is certain to them. Also, what else is this divine consolation in the present time of trial, but for the security and pledge of the future felicity, and a certain pre-taste of the heavenly joy? The just man, therefore, considering the collective benefits of God himself, and by the contemplation of the divine goods, and seizing with his soul a special and great confidence in God, securely and lovingly may speak to the Most High: *Because you, O Lord, singularly have settled me in hope.*

---

22  E. N. These are the many scoffers mentioned in verse 6.

23  James 1:17b.

24  1 Cor. 2:9a.

# ARTICLE XIX

### IN WHAT MANNER THIS FOURTH PSALM
### IS ABLE TO BE VARIOUSLY EXPLAINED;
### AND ESPECIALLY OF ITS EXPLANATION
### IN THE PERSON OF CHRIST.

4[4] *Know you also that the Lord has made his holy one wonderful:
the Lord will hear me when I shall cry unto him.*

*Et scitote quoniam mirificavit Dominus sanctum suum; Dominus
exaudiet me cum clamavero ad eum.*

ECAUSE INDEED THIS PSALM HAS ALREADY
been explained [tropologically] from the literal sense as being of
the Church herself and any just man, it is certain that it literally can be
explained as having to do with David, who is the author of this Psalm,
because he himself is numbered among the Saints, and he himself truly
was often heard by God while he called upon him. And in David's
tribulations the Lord brought to him great patience, so that it expanded
his heart, because he learned in spirit that very thing that afterwards
the Apostle would manifestly teach, *that the sufferings of this time are
not worthy to be compared with the glory to come.*[25] And that also which
follows,   4[4] *Et scitote quoniam mirificavit Dominus sanctum suum, and
know you also that the Lord has made his holy one wonderful,* is literally
true of David. For he was marvelously and vigorously preserved and
saved by God from the hand of Saul, and from any dangers, and various
persecutions;[26] and he killed a lion and a bear, in the manner written in
the Book of Kings;[27] and he was filled with the spirit of prophecy, and
he saw the angel of the Lord persecuting the people of Israel.[28]

---

4[2] *When I called upon him, the God of my justice heard me: when
I was in distress, you have enlarged me. Have mercy on me: and
hear my prayer.*

*Cum invocarem exaudivit me Deus iustitiae meae, in tribulatione
dilatasti mihi. Miserere mei, et exaudi orationem meam.*

---

25  Rom. 8:18.
26  1 Kings chps. 18, 23, *etc.*
27  1 Kings 17:34–36.
28  2 Kings 24:17; 1 Chr. 21:16.

Moreover, according to this literal understanding of David or the Synagogue, this Psalm was able to be interpreted tropologically to relate to any just man or the Church; but because now this Psalm is explained as pertaining to the Church or any just man, there is no other need for another explanation. But it must carefully pondered by anyone devoutly reading this Psalm that he intently direct the words to himself, and so he might undertake to adopt a manner of living so that this Psalm can truly be understood as referring to his own person. That, at any rate, would happen if he always is accustomed to pray, if in all situations and in necessity he confidently resorts to God, as the only Savior, the most faithful helper, and the singular hope. For then, he not only will believe himself frequently to be heard by God, but he will also experientially sense it; and so with a great act of thanksgiving he will sing:    4[2] *Cum invocarem, exaudivit me Deus iustitiae meae, when I called upon him, the God of my justice heard me.* On top of that, the Lord will fill him with so much grace that he will not only endure with joy the difficult things and troublesome things with which he is confronted, but he will always be ready to prefer the more burdensome things for the love of God and for the cleansing of his sins. And this is truly to be *enlarged in distress*: to have the soul ready for more difficult things, following the example of the holy David, who, while he was fleeing Absalom, said: If I find *grace in the sight of the Lord, he will bring me again*; but *if he shall say to me: You please me not, I am ready, let him do that which is good before him,*[29] that is, he might drive me from my kingdom, and, if it pleases him, have me killed.

This Psalm can be especially well explained as referring to Christ, and such an interpretation would be allegorical if it is drawn from that which literally refers to David. Nevertheless, of no other person is it able to be interpreted [with as much justification] as it is of Christ, following solely a literal interpretation. Christ, therefore, by reason of his assumed nature, or the Prophet [David] speaking in the person of Christ says: *When I have called upon him, the God of my justice heard me,* that is, God, one and three, or the very Word and Son of God, who has assumed my humanity. For as already was said above, Christ always was heard by God *for his reverence.*[30] *In tribulatione dilatasti mihi, when I was in distress, you have enlarged me.* This most perfectly coincides with Christ, because — throughout all the persecution and suffering that he endured from the time of his nativity even unto the time of his death on

29  2 Kings 15, 25, 26.
30  Heb. 5:7b.

the Cross—he was never inordinately sorrowful; but all things he most
agreeably and with greatest desire endured for the sake of the salvation
of the world, always ready to accept something more difficult if it might
please the Father. Again, it fittingly applies to Christ because, in all his
adversities and punishments, he enjoyed the joy of the beatific fruition,[31]
and so God spiritually enlarged and gladdened his mind. Christ also
prayed to God himself to have mercy, not for the remission of his own
guilt, but either for the guilty [members] of the Church, or for his body,
which was to be resurrected and glorified from death.

**4[4]** *Et scitote quoniam mirificavit Dominus sanctum suum. Know also
that the Lord has made his holy one wonderful.* The manner in which this
applies to Christ is handled in the earlier explanation. But it should be
added that the blessed and holy God made wonderful throughout the
entire world his Son, giving the Apostles and all the most holy ministers
of Christ the grace of miracles, the spirit of prophecy, kinds of tongues,
an excellence of life, and the extirpation of idolatry.[32] And in this way,
he does not cease to cause wonder regarding his beloved Son, and to
glorify faith in him through great prodigies, adjoining the seal of his
testimony to the Gospel of Christ.

---

**4[5]** *Be angry, and sin not: the things you say in your hearts, be sorry
for them upon your beds.*

*Irascimini, et nolite peccare; quae dicitis in cordibus vestris, in
cubilibus vestris compungimini.*

**4[5]** *Irascimini, et nolite peccare. Be angry, and sin not.* This is the word
of Christ to the unbelieving Jews, as if he were saying: "If there arises
in you a certain movement of anger against me, when you hear me say
that I am the Christ, the judge of the world, and the Son of God,[33] you
who see me subject to the weakness and mortality of the flesh; do not
sin, that is, do not consent, do not blaspheme, do not be incredulous,
because such things that you see me do, such things no other has the
power to do. For my works which I delivered up to my Father, have
given testimony of me."[34]

---

31 E. N. Denis speaks of the joy of the beatific fruition (*gaudium beatificae fruitionis*),
   a reference to Christ's beatific vision even while on earth, so that Christ was
   both a *viator* as well as a *comprehensor.*
32 *Cf.* Mark 16:17, 18.
33 *Cf.* Matt. 26:64.
34 *Cf.* John 5:36a.

**4[6]** *Offer up the sacrifice of justice, and trust in the Lord: many say, Who shows us good things?*

*Sacrificate sacrificium iustitiae, et sperate in Domino. Multi dicunt: Quis ostendit nobis bona?*

**4[6]** *Sacrificate sacrificium iustitiae. Offer up the sacrifice of justice.* This is the word of the Lord, of the Savior, to the orthodox Church,[35] indeed to all who after the promulgation of the Gospel desire to be saved, as if to be saying: "Cease from the sacrifices of the old law, which are not able to remove sin, nor are they able to perfect those who draw near, because they do not contain grace, but they only are a figure of it."[36] Whence Isaiah says: *He that sacrifices an ox, is as if he slew a man: he that kills a sheep in sacrifice, as if he should brain a dog.*[37] "Cease from these sacrifices, therefore, in the time of the new law, and *offer up the sacrifice of justice,* that is, the Sacrament of the Altar, which is the end and the consummation and the truth of all the sacrifices of the law. Offer up, I say, this sacrifice, that is offer yourself to God, either celebrating, or being present at its celebration."

---

**4[8]** *By the fruit of their corn, their wine and oil, they are multiplied.*

*A fructu frumenti, vini, et olei sui, multiplicati sunt.*

**4[8]**[38] *A fructu frumenti, vini et olei sui, multiplicati sunt. By the fruit of their corn, their wine, and their oil, they are multiplied.* As much as this was interpreted as applying to evil men, as related above, so also is it able to be construed to apply to the good. This is how St. Thomas in his hymn for the feast of Corpus Christi also understands it, where from these words the following antiphon is crafted: *A fructu frumenti et vini et olei multiplicati fideles in pace Christi requiescunt.*[39] *From the fruit of corn and wine and oil the faithful are multiplied and rest in the peace of Christ.* This, therefore, is its sense: The faithful *are multiplied,* in both faith and merit, *from the fruit of corn, and wine,* that is, from the effect of the grace of

---

35  E. N. This is a reference to the Catholic Church, *i.e.,* the "orthodox" Church in the sense of the "rightly-believing" Church. The word orthodox stems from the Greek ὀρθόδοξος (*orthodoxos*), a combination of ὀρθός (*orthos*), "straight or right," and δόξα (*doxa*) "opinion."
36  Cf. Heb. 10:1-4, 11.
37  Is. 66:3.
38  Denis skips verse 7 of Psalm 4.
39  E. N. The antiphon in the second Nocturn of Matins for the Feast of Corpus Christi in the Roman Breviary does not mention oil: *A fructu frumenti et vini multiplicati fideles in pace Christi requiescunt.*

both the Body and the Blood of Christ, *and his oil*, that as from the fruit of spiritual consolation, which they obtain by Eucharistic communion.

---

4[9]  *In peace in the selfsame I will sleep, and I will rest.*

*In pace in idipsum dormiam, et requiescam.*

4[10]  *For you, O Lord, singularly have settled me in hope*

*Quoniam tu, Domine, singulariter in spe constituisti me.*

4[9] *In pace in idispsum, dormiam, et requiescam. In peace in the selfsame, I will sleep, and I will rest.* Christ affirms this of his death and burial. For he slept on the Cross, and rested in a sepulchral monument, for at no time was the tranquility of the interior of his mind violently shaken, or confounded, or diminished, but in all distress that belonged to his punishment he was constant, solid, and remained immovably in God. And therefore this verse may be interpreted in a different manner. For the soul of Christ always saw the face of God the Father, because it was not a wayfarer (*viatrix non erat*): and so from the first moment of his creation, he was in the highest and most tranquil peace; and he slept in God from all distraction and any turning away, and from all restlessness he immovably rested in him.   4[10] *Quoniam tu, Domine, singulariter in spe constituisti me. For you, O Lord, singularly have settled me in hope.* These words are of Christ, as man, to God. For Christ, because he did not exist as a pure wayfarer (*purus viator*), therefore he had neither faith, nor hope, as hope is a theological virtue having God as its immediate object, since as we say, hope is the expectation of future blessedness. But never was blessedness something future or something absent from the soul of Christ. But as hope is a certain expectation of a future good, so Christ in this manner had hope. For he expected to rise again from the dead, and to be glorified in the body. To such expectations he said to the Father: *In peace, I will sleep, etc.* because you, O Lord, *singularly in hope*, namely of the resurrection and the glorification, *you have settled me*. For as much as all the faithful have hope of rising again and being glorified in the last day, Christ also as man was settled in hope of rising again and being glorified in a singular way, because he hoped on the third day to rise again in an impassible and glorious body.[40]

Other things which are not now set forth, are plainly seen from what has been said in the preceding explanations.

---

40  Matt. 16:21, 20:19; Mark 9:30; Luke 9:22; 18:33.

# PRAYER

————————————

RANT, WE BESEECH YOU, O ALMIGHTY
God, the joy of your Spirit in our hearts, so that offering up
the sacrifice of justice, and continually placing our hope in you, at
the instant of the end of life we may sleep in the peace of Christ,
and forever rest in his kingdom.

————————————

*Da, quaesumus omnipotens Deus, laetitiam Spiritus tui in
corde nostro: ut sacrificantes sacrificium iustitiam, ac
iugiter in te sperantes, instante termino vitae,
in pace Christi dormiamus, et in eius
regno perenniter requiescamus.*

# Psalm 5

## ARTICLE XX

### EXPLANATION OF THE FIFTH PSALM:
### *VERBA MEA AURIBUS PERCIPE, DOMINE, &c.*
### *GIVE EAR, O LORD, TO MY WORDS, &c.*

5[1] *Unto the end, for her that obtains the inheritance. A psalm of David.*

*In finem, pro ea quae haereditatem consequitur. Psalmus David.*

THE TITLE OF THIS PSALM IS: 5[1] *IN FINEM, pro ea quae haereditatem consequitur. Unto the end, for her that obtains the inheritance.* In Genesis one reads how Abraham had two wives: one of them, namely Sara, with her son Isaac, remained at home, and obtained the inheritance; the other, namely Hagar, was driven away with her son.[1] It is possible to explain this Psalm literally in reference to this history, so that this Psalm is written in reference to Sara and her son; and many more things are more fittingly exposited from the thing signified [by the literal or historical figures of Sara and Hagar], namely, of the Church, which is signified by Sara, the Synagogue, which is signified by Hagar, driven away and rejected.[2] The sense is therefore: this Psalm directs us *in finem, unto the end,* that is, in Christ or in the heavenly inheritance or eternal life, and it is *pro ea, by her,* that is to say, the Church, *quae consequitur hereditatem, that obtains the inheritance,* that is, God or the enjoyment of God. For God is called our inheritance because he sustains and surrounds us, and we are described as the inheritance of God for he cares for us and rules us, and with his Blood redeems us.

---

5[2] *Give ear, O Lord, to my words, understand my cry.*

*Verba mea auribus percipe, Domine; intellige clamorem meum.*

5[3] *Hearken to the voice of my prayer, O my King and my God.*

*Intende voci orationis meae, rex meus et Deus meus.*

The Prophet [David] speaking in the person of the Church, praying

---

1 Gen. 21:1–14.
2 Gal. 4:22–31.

99

for himself and her members, first puts forward a prayer and says: 5[2] *Verba mea auribus percipe, Domine: intellige clamorem meum.* Give ear, O Lord, to my words, understand my cry. 5[3] *Intende voci orationis meae.* Hearken to the voice of my prayer. Three explanations are expressed by this affection of the heart, seeing that the desire of the heart burns with more interior intensity the more frequently it has expressed the words. For the more the words of the heart are repeated to express the affection, to that degree the affection of the heart is more amply inflamed, and so prayer more quickly obtains its effect. Whence, the manner of Scripture is this: that in those things which regard the affection, the same thing is often repeated, with the purpose that the affection might be ignited. It is also possible among these explanations to assign a distinction, so that what is being said is: *Give ear, O Lord, to my words*, that is, my vocal prayers; and *understand my cry*, that is, the affection of my heart. For by clamor or cry the Holy Scripture understands a spiritual clamor or cry. The ears of the Lord are his wisdom and his kindness. By wisdom he surely knows and perceives all things. Through his kindness he gives the gifts (*dona*) of nature, and the bestowals (*munera*) of grace, abundantly giving to all men, not casting out reproach.[3] And he says to God, *understand my cry*: not as if it is not possible that God is unable to understand anything, for *all things are naked and open to his eyes*,[4] but *understand*, that is, through your approval recognize, with your attention take heed, and by your wisdom render aid. *Rex meus*, my King, by reason of governance, *et Deus meus*, and my God, by reason of creation. But since God is King and God of all things, why is *my King and my God* said, unless on account of a special providence, which he provides to his elect, and directs them in the paths of eternal life, preserving them from evil and rescuing them from danger? Thus it says: *My God*, because I attend to you especially, I cleave to you alone, I commit myself entirely to you. This cannot be said to those *whose god is their belly*,[5] or gold, or any another such thing.

———————

5[4] *For to you will I pray: O Lord, in the morning you shall hear my voice. Quoniam ad te orabo, Domine, mane exaudies vocem meam.*

5[5] *In the morning I will stand before you, and will see: because you are not a God that wills iniquity. Mane astabo tibi, et videbo quoniam non Deus volens iniquitatem tu es.*

———————

3  *Cf.* James 1:5.
4  Heb. 4:13.
5  Phil. 3:19.

**5[4]** *Quoniam ad te orabo, Domine, mane exaudies vocem meam, For to you will I pray, O Lord, in the morning you shall hear my voice*: that is, because I will pray, O Lord, to you, directing my affection to you, or striving and taking delight in you so that I might possess you in the heavenly homeland (*in patria*) in eternity. Or [we can understand it thus] *to you*, that is directing my prayers and my honor and glory to your name. For this reason will I pray to you, that on this account *in the morning you shall hear my voice*, that is, quickly and in haste. Or [alternatively], *in the morning*, that is, when you pour out the light of your mercy over me. Or [in the further alternative], *in the morning*, that is, at the beginning of any good works. And before my prayer is finished, you will hear me: for as is testified through Isaiah: *I will hear*, he says, *as they are yet speaking, I will hear.*[6] *In the morning you shall hear*, not with presumption, but with hope, and calling forth for mercy. **5[5]** *Mane, in the morning*, that is, since Christ, who is the sun of justice and the splendor of the eternal light,[7] having enlightened my soul seated in darkness, and having cast out from me the blindness of ignorance and the obscurity of vice; *adstabo tibi, I will stand before you*, offering to you my heart ready with great affection to serve and obey. *Et videbo, and I will see*, that is, I will contemplate in splendor and I will know with certainty, *quoniam non Deus volens iniquitatem tu es, because you are not a God that wills iniquity*: indeed all iniquity and all impurity are faults that are displeasing to you, and you do not will them effectively, but permissively.[8]

---

**5[6]** *Neither shall the wicked dwell near you: nor shall the unjust abide before your eyes.*

*Neque habitabit iuxta te malignus, neque permanebunt iniusti ante oculos tuos.*

**5[6]** *Neque habitabit iuxte te malignus. Neither shall the wicked dwell near you*: that is, the wicked man, namely, he who desires to harm others, will not be joined with you, nor, if close by, will he be able to hinder you. It is not that he will be separated from you — you who are everywhere and penetrate all things[9] — by the distance of space; but because the

---

6 Is. 65:24b

7 Wis. 7:26a; *Cf.* Heb. 1:3.

8 E. N. This refers to the well-known distinction between God's effective will (*voluntas effectiva*) and his permissive will (*voluntas permissiva*).

9 E. N. Denis shifts, as he frequently does, to speak directly to God using the second person.

dissimilitude of sin he withdraws from you, holy and just God; nor will he be joined to you, by grace in the present time, nor by glory in the future. As it is written in Scripture, *Take the wicked man away, so that he may not see the glory of God.*[10] *Neque permanebunt iniusti ante oculos tuos,* nor shall *the unjust abide before your eyes,* that is, before the presence of your majesty, before the sight of your mercy. Or thus [is a possible construction]: *the unjust shall not abide before your eyes,* that is, they are not known by you through the knowledge of approbation (*approbationis notitiam*).[11] Whence it is said in a later Psalm: *Let them be blotted out of the book of the living.*[12] And in another place: *I know you not.*[13] For the eyes of God is his intellect.

---

**5[7]** *You hate all the workers of iniquity: You will destroy all that speak a lie. The bloody and the deceitful man the Lord will abhor.*

*Odisti omnes qui operantur iniquitatem; perdes omnes qui loquuntur mendacium. Virum sanguinum et dolosum abominabitur Dominus.*

**5[7]** *Odisti omnes qui operantur iniquitatem. You hate all the workers of iniquity.* Hate, to the extent that it is a passion of the soul, is not to be found in God, except transumptively (*transumptive*),[14] that is, in a certain manner similar to [the way] anger [is predicated of him]. But to the extent it is [understood as] the will's detestation of the willing of evil, in this manner can it correspond to God: and so God hates evildoers because he removes them and casts them off of him. For he hates them, not on account of their nature, but because of their fault. Whence the wise man said: *You love all things that are, and hate none of the things which you have made.*[15] And nevertheless in that same book we have: *To God the wicked and his wickedness are hateful*[16] *Perdes omnes qui loquuntur mendacium, you will destroy all those whose speak a lie,* that is, you will

---

10  Is. 26:10 (LXX). E. N. This (LXX) is a reference to the Latin translation of the Greek Septuagint, which is itself a translation of the Hebrew.

11  E. N. Scholastic theologians distinguished between various kinds of knowledge in God, including the *notitia visionis* (the knowledge of vision) and the more restrictive knowledge of approval or approbation (*notitia approbrationis*). God is said to have no knowledge of the evil doers in this restrictive sense of knowledge of approbation.

12  Ps. 68:29a.

13  Matt. 25:12; Luke.13, 25, 27.

14  E. N. Transumptively, meaning a transfer or substitution of terms (taking the emotion of anger from man and transferring it to God): metaphorically.

15  Wis. 11:25.

16  Wis. 14:9.

condemn eternally liars, unless they repent. For as it is written in the book of Wisdom: *The mouth that lies, kills the soul.*[17] They who are aware of a pernicious lie, who engage in it with the intention of deceiving or of harming, and then proceed to it with malice, these are contrary to God and in mortal sin, since God is himself truth. Likewise [to be regarded] is an officious lie, that is, a lie said for some sort of self-preservation or convenience. And so is a jocose lie, that proceeds out of levity, and is said for the reason of amusement. But these two latter sorts of lies are not mortal, but venial. *Virum sanguinum, the bloody man,* is the murderer, in reality or with hate (*re vel affectum*), according to John.[18] *The bloody man, et dolosum, and deceitful,* that is, the double-tongued, dissimulators, false teachers, and hypocrites, *abominabitur Dominus, the Lord will abhor,* despising them, and expelling them from the fellowship of the elect.

---

**5[8]** *But as for me in the multitude of your mercy, I will come into your house; I will worship towards your holy temple, in your fear.*

*Ego autem in multitudine misericordiae tuae introibo in domum tuam; adorabo ad templum sanctum tuum in timore tuo.*

Therefore, the Church or any particular just man turning towards God says the words:   **5[8]** *Ego autem in multitudine misericordiae tuae, But I in the multitude of your mercy,* that is, supply [your grace O Lord] so that I might be delivered from the aforesaid sins and punishments, that I may persevere in your grace, and I may round out my life with a blessed end. And this is the word of good hope, or so it can be understood by means of prayer. *Introibo in domum tuam, I will come into your house,* that is, in the heavenly Jerusalem or the Church triumphant after this present life of exile, so that I may build around me the walls of Jerusalem, within which I truly will enter every day by affection, desiring *to be dissolved and to be with Christ.*[19] *Adorabo ad templum sanctum tuum, I will worship towards your holy temple,* that is, in all my prayers and adoration I will direct my intentions, and I will affix my desire to the heavenly city, so that I might be deserving to come to it. But *I will worship,* not lacking in reverent fear and with a wandering mind, but *I will worship in timore tuo, in your fear:* because it is becoming to worship you, Lord of highest majesty, with great reverence and exceptional custody of heart

---

17  Wis. 1:11.
18  1 John 3:15a.
19  Phil. 1:23b.

**5[9]** *Conduct me, O Lord, in your justice: because of my enemies, direct my way in your sight.*

*Domine, deduc me in iustitia tua: propter inimicos meos dirige in conspectu tuo viam meam.*

Finally, in order that I may be led finally to the previously-mentioned blessedness, I pray now,    **5[9]** *Domine, O Lord, deduc me in iustitia tua, conduct me in your justice,* that is, give me the grace of walking in the right way that arrives at you, so that I might obey by all means your precepts, and that I might conform in all holy words to your law. Lead me so that I might not go astray — that the passions and vice do not becloud the intellect — and I fall in the presence of my enemies: but be to me my guide, making known to me through the illumination of your Holy Spirit in what manner I might walk with caution, that I might make progress from virtue to virtue, and end the course of my life in happiness. *Propter inimicos meos dirige in conspectus meo viam tuam, because of my enemies direct your way in my sight:*[20] that is, because you see me, O Lord God, in the midst of snares already put in place, and [because you see] my enemies — which are the flesh, the world, and the powers of the air[21] — everywhere encompassing me, for that very reason *direct,* that is, place, and set forth with clarity in memory, *in my sight,* that is, within the consideration of my intellect, *your way,* that is, the law of your commandments, never to forget those things which you have commanded me, and which are acceptable to you.

---

**5[10]** *For there is no truth in their mouth; their heart is vain.*

*Quoniam non est in ore eorum veritas; cor eorum vanum est.*

**5[11]** *Their throat is an open sepulcher: they dealt deceitfully with their tongues: judge them, O God. Let them fall from their devices: according to the multitude of their wickedness cast them out: for they have provoked you, O Lord.*

*Sepulchrum patens est guttur eorum; linguis suis dolose agebant, iudica illos, Deus. Decidant a cogitationibus suis; secundum multitudinem impietatum eorum expelle eos, quoniam irritaverunt te, Domine.*

---

20  E. N. The text replaces *tuo* with *meo* and *meam* with *tuam.* So that it reads *Propter inimicos meos dirige in conspectu meo viam tuam* (because of my enemies, direct your way in my sight) instead of *Propter inimicos meos dirige in conspectu tuo viam meam* (because of my enemies, direct my way in your sight).

21  E. N. For "powers of the air," *see* footnote 3-29.

**5[10]** *Quoniam non est in ore eorum, for there is not in their mouth,* that is to say [in the mouths] of my enemies, *veritas, truth,* but rather deceit. *Cor eorum vanum est, their heart is vain,* that is, it is opposed to the highest good, to the incommutable God, to the eternal truth, and has turned to fleeting and vain things. **5[11]** *Sepulcrum patens est guttur eorum, for their throat is an open sepulcher,* that is, it is similar to an open grave into which man easily falls, and in which he is quickly corrupted. Such a throat evil men have in themselves, for from them proceed deadly and pestiferous words; and their speech causes persons to fall, and corrupts the innocent and the simple, unless God makes provision to protect against it. *Linquis suis dolose agebant, they dealt deceitfully with their tongues,* proposing evil under the guise of the good, so that they may more effectually beguile.

*Iudica illos Deos. Judge them, O God.* This the Prophet [David] or any just man says, not wanting vengeance, but announcing beforehand the truth, or conforming himself to the divine justice. And so, *Judge them, O God,* that is, justly condemn them within your justice. *Decidant a cogitationibus suis, let them fall from their devices:* that is, that they may not obtain that which they strive to obtain, but apprehend the shrewd with their own shrewdness: *Dissemblers and crafty men prove the wrath of God,*[22] in the manner that Job states it. *Secundum multitudinem impietatum eorum expelle eos, according to the multitude of their wickedness cast them out:* that is, according to the gravity of their sins, cast them from you into just torments, so that as much as they glorified themselves in evil, so might they receive in torments.[23] *Quoniam irritaverunt te, Domine, for they have provoked you, O Lord,* that is, they have provoked you to anger and indignation — not that the invariable and most tranquil God may be truly angered, or may be made bitter, or may be provoked, as Jeremiah says: *Do they provoke me to anger, says the Lord? Is it not themselves, to the confusion of their countenance?*[24] God is therefore said to be provoked to anger and irritation on account of the similarity of operation, because something similar to anger occurs when he terribly torments the ungodly. And in this word — *irritaverunt, they have provoked* — it is pointed out what an enormity it is to offend God, and how fearful a thing it is *to fall into the hands of the living God.*[25]

---

22 Job 36:13.
23 *Cf.* Rev. 18:7.
24 Jer. 7:19.
25 Heb. 10:31.

5[12] *But let all them be glad that hope in you: they shall rejoice forever, and you shall dwell in them. And all they that love your name shall glory in you.*

*Et laetentur omnes qui sperant in te; in aeternum exsultabunt, et habitabis in eis. Et gloriabuntur in te omnes qui diligunt nomen tuum.*

5[13] *For you will bless the just. O Lord, you have crowned us, as with a shield of your good will.*

*Quoniam tu benedices iusto. Domine, ut scuto bonae voluntatis tuae coronasti nos.*

5[12] *Et laetentur omnes qui sperant in te, but let them all be glad that hope in you,* that is, let them who place their entire hope in your mercy exult in their interior and do so with holy rejoicing. *In aeternum exsultabunt, they shall rejoice forever:* because now they are consoled by you in time, as they at length will reign in eternity with you; *et habitabis in eis, and you shall dwell in them* through charity and grace. *For the temple of God is holy, which you are,*[26] said the Apostle. *If anyone love me, he will keep my word, and my Father will love him, and we will come to him, and will make our abode with him.*[27]

*Et gloriabuntur in te omnes qui diligunt nomen tuum. And all they that love your name shall glory in you.* The love (*caritas*) of God is not capable of being idle, but always, to the degree it is able, it manifests itself in both interior and exterior acts. For the acts of charity are: to will good to the beloved, to rejoice in his perfection, and to wish for him happiness. Therefore, he who truly loves God, rejoices greatly in his most immense perfection, and he with all his heart rejoices in his happiness: and such glorying is most divine, and most pleasing to God, and of highest merit. Therefore, O Lord, those loving you, *shall glory in you,* 5[13] *quoniam tu benedices, for you will bless,* that is, you will confer grace, and you will give copious gifts *iusto, to the just:* indeed you, in whose contemplation is found the full plenitude of joy, will show your face to them, as is said in a later Psalm, *You shall fill me with joy with your countenance.*[28] Whence in the Gospel: *He that loves me, shall be loved of my Father: and I will love him, and will manifest myself to him.*[29]

---

26  1 Cor. 3:17b.
27  John 14:23.
28  Ps. 15:11a.
29  John 14:21b.

*Domine, ut scuto bonae voluntatis tuae coronasti nos, O Lord, you have crowned us, as with a shield of your good will*: that is, O Lord, you have crowned us, that is, you have made us a kind of king and priest,[30] giving us the power to become sons of God,[31] and to triumph over the adversaries, adorning us with the various gifts of the Holy Spirit, subjecting all things under our feet.[32] In this manner does he crown us, expanding upon it, since he adds: *As with a shield of good will*, that is, with the armor of your most kind mercy. It is as if he were saying: In such manner *have you crowned us*, that is, every part of us you have adorned with your grace and have raised us toward the sublime, as if we might be in a certain manner a shield that provides both cover and protection: indeed, with a shield of your good will, that is, your will that is both good and kind, which is for us as a shield, *you have crowned us*, anticipating by grace, preserving with mercy, and promising beatitude through its consummation.

# ARTICLE XXI

## IN WHAT MANNER THIS FIFTH PSALM ESPECIALLY AND FITTINGLY CAN BE EXPOUNDED OF CHRIST

5[1] *Unto the end, for her that obtains the inheritance. A psalm of David.*

*In finem, pro ea quae haereditatem consequitur. Psalmus David.*

GAIN, SINCE THE TITLE OF THE BOOK OF Psalms may be said to be such—*Here begins the book of the Hymns of the Prophet of Christ*—we ought as much as possible refer to Christ in this most holy book. It is possible, therefore, not only to interpret this Psalm fittingly of Christ, but also its title, so that the sense of its title is: 5[1] *In finem, pro ea quae consequitur hereditatem, unto the end, for her that obtains the inheritance*, that is, this Psalm directs us to the end,

---

30  *Cf.* 1 Pet. 2:9. *E. N.* Denis refers to the general character of all the baptized. "The Christian faithful are those who, inasmuch as they have been incorporated in Christ through Baptism, have been constituted as the people of God; for this reason, since they have become sharers in Christ's priestly, prophetic, and royal office in their own manner, they are called to exercise the mission which God has entrusted to the Church to fulfill in the world, in accord with the condition proper to each one." CCC § 871.

31  *Cf.* John 1:12.

32  *Cf.* Ps. 8:8.

that is, eternal felicity, and it is for it that we pursue the inheritance. That is to say, this Psalm addresses the human nature of Christ, which is united by a hypostatic union to the Word of God, so that so specially and so eminently he has obtained the inheritance, that is, the fullness of all gifts from the Godhead and the most happy enjoyment of God, so that through it he leads the entirety of the human race to the blessed life: for *of his fulness we all have received, and grace for grace,*[33] as John says.

---

**5[2]**  *Give ear, O Lord, to my words, understand my cry.*

*Verba mea auribus percipe, Domine; intellige clamorem meum.*

Christ by reason of praying in his human nature says to the Father, or to the entire Trinity, or to himself, according as he is God:  **5[2]** *Verba mean auribus percipe, Domine. Give ear, O Lord to my words.* What else are these words which Christ prays God to hear, but those prayers which he pours forth for his members, that is, for us? Of which [words from Christ in his human nature to God] we read in the Gospel of John: *I pray not for the world, but for them whom you have given me.*[34] *I pray not that you should take them out of the world, but that you should keep them from evil.*[35] And again: *Holy Father, keep them in your name whom you have given me; that they may be one, as we also are.*[36] And in another place to Peter: *I have prayed for you, that your faith does not fail.*[37] *I have prayed,* he says, *for you,* that is, for the whole Church. Whence, to return [back to John] he says to the Father: And not for these, that is to say the Apostles, *only do I pray, but for them also who through their word shall believe in me, that they may be one, as you, Father, are in me, and I in you, so that . . . they may be made perfect in one.*[38] In addition he adds: *Intellige clamorem meum, understand my cry.* What is this cry of the Son of God which he desires to understand from the Father? It is nothing other than the prayers which he sent forth while hanging on the Cross, when he said, *Father, forgive them, for they know not what they do;*[39] and again, when he cried in a loud voice and said, *Father, into your*

---

33  John 1:16.
34  John 17:9.
35  John 17:15.
36  John 17:11b.
37  Luke 22:32.
38  John 17:20, 21, 23.
39  Luke 23:34.

*hands I commend my spirit:*[40] and turning again to John, when he said, *I thirst,*[41] that is, I desire the salvation of men.

5[3] *Hearken to the voice of my prayer, O my King and my God.*

*Intende voci orationis meae, rex meus et Deus meus.*

5[3] *Intende voci orationis meae, Rex meus, Hearken to the voice of my prayer, O my King:* the King, indeed, of all things, but especially my King, for you have so led me, your Incarnate Son, who never sinned, who never departed from the right way, who never had any imperfection within me; *et Deus meus, and my God:* God, indeed, of all things, but singularly my God, for I alone, inasmuch as I am man, loved, honored, and venerated you more than all intellectual creatures put together.

5[4] *For to you will I pray: O Lord, in the morning you shall hear my voice.*

*Quoniam ad te orabo, Domine, mane exaudies vocem meam.*

5[5] *In the morning I will stand before you, and will see: because you are not a God that wills iniquity.*

*Mane astabo tibi, et videbo quoniam non Deus volens iniquitatem tu es.*

5[6] *Neither shall the wicked dwell near you: nor shall the unjust abide before your eyes.*

*Neque habitabit iuxta te malignus, neque permanebunt iniusti ante oculos tuos.*

5[4] *Quoniam ad te orabo, Domine. For to you will I pray, O Lord.* This fits Christ, because when the Devil said to him: *All these will I give you, if falling down you will adore me,* he responded: *Begone, Satan: for it is written, The Lord your God shall you adore, and him only shall you serve.*[42] *Mane exaudies vocem meam, in the morning you shall hear my voice,* that is, speedily. For in what way could the heavenly Father deny to his most beloved Son, in whom he was well pleased?[43]　5[5] *Mane astabo tibi, et videbo, quoniam non Deus volens iniquitatem tu es. In the morning I will stand before you, and will see: because you are not a God that wills iniquity.*

40　Luke 23:46.
41　John 19:28b.
42　Matt. 4:9, 10.
43　Matt. 3:17; 17, 5.

*In the morning,* that is, first of all and before all other preoccupations; *I will stand before you,* just as it is written, *Seek you therefore first the kingdom of God, and his justice.*[44] This is particularly fittingly said of Christ, because he was appointed by God to be judge of the just and of the impious.[45] And thus he stands near God judging as a result of his commission, and being united in heart with his highest justice, always in full accord with his will: and so he sees, that is, he clearly recognizes, because God who is judge by his authority does not will iniquity.    **5[6]** *Neque habitabit iuxta te malignus,* etc. *Neither shall the wicked dwell near you,* etc. And since this is so, therefore, O Father God, I will judge in the manner that I know to be in accord with your sentiments, separating the good from the evil, and I will gather together the good in the palace of your glory, but the evil I will hurl down to the eternal fire.[46]

---

**5[8]**  *But as for me in the multitude of your mercy, I will come into your house; I will worship towards your holy temple, in your fear.*

*Ego autem in multitudine misericordiae tuae introibo in domum tuam; adorabo ad templum sanctum tuum in timore tuo.*

**5[8]**[47] *Ego autem in multitudine misericordiae tuae, But as for me in the multitude of your mercy:* that is, I your Son, as man, anticipate your great and your many mercies: for only by divine condescension and mercy is my humanity united to your Word, filled with all grace, without any previous merit (*sine praeviis meritis*) preserved from all fault, and complete in all good. In this merit, therefore I say myself to be *in the multitude of your mercy. Introibo in domum tuam, I will come into your house,* that is to say, in the day of the Ascension, when I will return to the heavenly home. Or [this meaning may be given it], *In your house,* that is, in your consecrated temple in Jerusalem, in which Christ preached and did miracles, and from which he cast out all the sellers and buyers saying, *My house shall be called the house of prayer.*[48] For in this temple in which the Lord Christ entered into, the prophet Haggai so predicted: *The desired of all nations shall come, and I will fill this house with glory,* says the Lord.[49] And Christ adored in the fear of the Lord in this temple: for

---

44  Matt. 6:33a.
45  *Cf.* Acts 10:42.
46  *Cf.* Matt. 25:32, 33, 44.
47  Denis skips verse 7 here.
48  Matt. 21:12, 13.
49  Haggai 2:8.

he was filled *with the spirit of the fear of the Lord*, according to th
of Isaiah.[50] Even now, the apostle says this of Christ already
before the right had of the Father, because he *makes intercession f*

5[9] *Conduct me, O Lord, in your justice: because of my enemies, direct
my way in your sight.*

*Domine, deduc me in iustitia tua: propter inimicos meos dirige in
conspectu tuo viam meam.*

5[9] *Domine, deduc me in iustitia tua. Conduct me, O Lord, in your justice.* Christ makes this prayer for his mystical body, which is the Church.
For he did not pray to be guided in the way of God, because he was
confirmed in the good, and he was unable to obtain merit for himself
or to perfect himself because he had a perfect and complete knowledge
of God (*quoniam comprehensor fuit perfectus*). Yet nevertheless he still
prayed for himself, namely for the glorification of his body, and such
similar things.

The rest of this Psalm is clear from what has been said in the preceding explanations.

### THE MORAL SENSE

5[2] *Give ear, O Lord, to my words, understand my cry.*

*Verba mea auribus percipe, Domine; intellige clamorem meum.*

BUT HOW THIS PSALM MAY BE EXPLAINED MOR-
ally is already satisfactorily explained, and there is no difficulty pertaining
to it. Truly, we are instructed by this Psalm in the same proportion as
we pray it with great attention. For in what manner are we able to say
to God,   5[2] *Verba mea auribus percipe, Domine, Give ear, O Lord, to
my words,* if we are not aware with the ears of the heart to whom it is
we are speaking? And how do we say to him, *Intellige clamorem meum,
understand my cry,* if we do not mentally, but only vocally, cry out to
him? Who, therefore, harbors the impression that God attends to the
voice of our prayers if we were to pray verbally with an inattentive and
wandering heart? And so it is written: *Before prayer prepare your soul: and
be not as a man that tempts God.*[52] For this Psalm teaches us diligently

---

50 Is. 11:3a.
51 Rom. 8:34b.
52 Ecclus. 18:23.

to think about how enormous and damnable it is not to obey God, and to engage rightly in communications with him, because God has hate for the wicked,[53] and he eternally separates them from himself,[54] consigning them to eternal torment. Finally, we are taught to hope in God, to rejoice in hope, to love in joy, and to rest in love.

# PRAYER

OUR KING AND GOD, LEAD US IN YOUR justice because of our enemies, and direct our life before your presence, so that crowned by you with the shield of your good will, you may rejoice in us and dwell in us eternally.

*Rex et Deus noster, deduc nos in iustitia tua propter inimicos nostros, et dirige in conspectu tuo viam nostram: ut in nobis scuto bonae voluntatis tuae coronates, in aeternum exsultes et habites.*

---

53  *Cf.* Wis. 14:9.
54  *Cf.* Matt. 25:41.

# Psalm 6

## ARTICLE XXII

### EXPLANATION OF THE SIXTH PSALM:
*DOMINE, NE IN FURORE, &c.*
*O LORD, NOT IN YOUR INDIGNATION, &c.*

6[1] *Unto the end, in verses, a Psalm for David, for the octave.*

*In finem, in carminibus. Psalmus David. Pro octava.*

NOW THINGS HAVE ALREADY BEEN WRITTEN about the title to this Psalm:[1]   6[1] *In finem, psalmus David, pro octava. Unto the end, a Psalm of David, for the octave.* The sense of this is: This Psalm is composed by the holy David, and it directs us to the end or to Christ, who is the end of our pilgrimage. *For the octave,* that is, it is written and edited in fear of the final (*extremi*) judgment, which will occur in the last day, which is called *the octave,* because it follows after the time of this age, which is unfurled in seven days. Briefly, words are a sign of that [concept] which dwells in the mind. Whence, in accordance with the diverse affections of the soul so also there are formed diverse words in prayers and praises. For on occasion the soul is afflicted by a violent fear, at times with ardent love, at times with unusual delights, and at times with immoderate sorrow: and, according to this, speech varies exteriorly. It is also obvious that words more full of feeling proceed from more ardent affections.

---

6[2] *O Lord, rebuke me not in your indignation, nor chastise me in your wrath.*

*Domine, ne in furore tuo arguas me, neque in ira tua corripias me.*

Therefore, the faithful and fearful soul believing itself wanting, and, taking into consideration the strictures of the future judgment, is thoroughly frightened, and, endeavoring within the time he has to appease his Judge, he pours fourth these kinds of prayers:   6[2] *Domine, O Lord,* he says, *ne in furore tuo arguas me, rebuke me not in your indignation:* that is, O Lord, do not so abandon me in this present life to impenitence,

---

1 *See* Article XVIII (Psalm 4:1).

without amendment, unpunished, so that in the day of judgment *you might rebuke me in your indignation*, that is, according to the most strict zeal of your justice, when the time of penance no longer subsists, and mercy for the miserable is no longer had, but the fullest justice will be applied. And therefore it is then that you will appear — in particular to the reprobate — as furious or indignant through the strictness or severity of your examination, and the harshness of your torments; and this effect of your justice is called furor or indignation. But in the manner that grace provides the means for the bewailing of sin, the avoiding of dangers, and the doing of virtuous works, *rebuke me not in your indignation*. For you will not judge twice for the same thing.[2] *Neque in ira tua corripias me, nor chastise me in your wrath*: that is, *do not* in this manner permit me to neglect the time of indulgence, [this time] of penance, so that, in the hour of my particular judgment, when, namely, my soul departs from the body and is presented before your tribunal, you *chastise me in your wrath*, that is, in the severity of the divine justice, condemning my soul to hell, until it is reunited to the body in the last day, and together with it will share in a double punishment. For the judgment is to be double, that is to say, universal, which will be at the end of time, when all men will be judged together. The other judgment is the particular judgment, where, at the time of death, the soul is judged singly. But the universal judgment is more terrible than the particular judgment because in it the soul and body both are damned, and the judge will then appear much more terrible. And many other things there will be before those who face that most horrible judgment, such as the burning world,[3] the gaping infernal regions, accusing demons, nearby-standing angels, and [in such environment] to be accused, to be rejected, to be confounded, to be damned before all angels, men, and demons: for they will make known the sins of everyone to everyone, so that all will recognize the judgment to be most just. Hence, *indignation (furor)*, which denotes something more than wrath *(ira)*, pertains to the universal judgment; but wrath *(ira)* to the particular judgment.

There can also be derived another explanation from what is here said, that being this: *Domine, ne in furore tuo arguas me, O Lord, rebuke me not in your indignation*, that is, do not condemn me in eternity, *neque in ira tua corripias me, nor chastise me in your* wrath, do not torment me in purgatory; but now [while in this life] purge me daily, paternally correcting, sweetly inflaming me with your holy love, for *charity covers a multitude of*

---

2  *Cf.* Nahum 1:9.
3  E. N. A reference to the final conflagration. *See ST,* IIIa Supp., q. 74.

*sins,*[4] and deal with me according to your mildness. For that reason, holy Job prayed: *Suffer me, therefore, that I may lament my sorrow a little before I go, and return no more, to a land that is dark and covered with the mist of death.*[5] Additionally, Jeremiah, not able to bear the furor of the future judgment while considering it, prayed thus: *Correct (corripe) me, O Lord, but yet with judgment: and not in fury (furore), lest you bring me to nothing.*[6]

---

6[3]  *Have mercy on me, O Lord, for I am weak: heal me, O Lord, for my bones are troubled.*

*Miserere mei, Domine, quoniam infirmus sum; sana me, Domine, quoniam conturbata sunt ossa mea.*

A sinner, therefore, who is truly penitent, and who is not able to perceive any means [within himself] of responding to and satisfying himself to God, will pray, and will say that which follows:  6[3] *Miserere mei, Domine, Have mercy on me, O Lord,* sharing in the suffering of my misery, that is, by means of you having compassion, that is, by your delivering me from all anxiety and need; *quoniam infirmus sum, for I am weak,* for I am capable of nothing in and of myself, but all my sufficiency comes from you,[7] is dependent upon your grace, and flows out of your mercy. *I am weak,* I am unable *to answer him one for a thousand;*[8] I am unable, indeed I cannot even chose, to put up resistance before your countenance: and so *sana me, Domine, heal me, O Lord,* that is, from the sins which are the wounds of my soul, cleanse me and deliver me, and not only their fault (*culpam*), but also mitigating the punishments (*poenam*); *quoniam conturbata sunt ossa mea, for my bones are troubled,* that is, the powers of my soul are shaken and disturbed. For adversities, passions, and vices frequently impede and defile acts of virtue, and by this means they debilitate the virtuous habits. And hence, because of the admixture of our imperfections with our acts of virtue, *all our justices* [are] *as the rag of a menstruous woman.*[9] Hence, to remove the impediments to our virtue, we need the gifts of the Holy Spirit, which are distinguishable from the virtues, and provide aid to them.

---

4  1 Pet. 4:8b.
5  Job 10:20b–21.
6  Jer. 10:24.
7  *Cf.* 2 Cor. 3:5.
8  Job 9:3b. *E. N.* In other words, we cannot sufficiently answer for one of our sins, much less for the thousands of which we are guilty.
9  Is. 64:6.

**6[4]** *And my soul is troubled exceedingly: but you, O Lord, how long?*

*Et anima mea turbata est valde; sed tu, Domine, usquequo?*

**6[4]** *Et anima mea turbata est valde, and my soul is troubled exceedingly*, that is to say, by the recollection of past evils, by the consideration of future punishments, by the contemplation of divine justice, and on account of the difficulty of arriving to true perfection, which it so vehemently desires. *Sed tu, Domine, usquequo? But you, O Lord, how long?* That is, how long will you leave me in such tribulation? How long should I be in understanding that you will not come to my help, and not imparting the desired fulness of grace?

---

**6[5]** *Turn to me, O Lord, and deliver my soul: O save me for your mercy's sake.*

*Convertere, Domine, et eripe animam meam; salvum me fac propter misericordiam tuam.*

**6[5]** *Convertere, Domine, turn to me, O Lord*, that is, turn me toward you; or *turn*, so that as a result of the grace having been withdrawn on account of my sins you turned away from me, by the infusion of grace you might return to me; *turn* from vengeance to indulgence, from the rigor of justice to the sweetness of clemency. *Et eripe animam meam, and deliver my soul*, from all danger, from unfruitfulness and tediousness in making headway in good, and from existing disorder. *Salvum me fac, O save me*, now by grace and in the future by glory: and this not as a result of my justice, but *propter misericordiam tuam, for your mercy's sake*. For I know, O Lord, what you through holy Ezechiel stated: *It is not for your sake that I will do this*,[10] said the Lord, *be it known to you*,[11] but for my holy name's sake.[12]

---

**6[6]** *For there is no one in death, that is mindful of you: and who shall confess to you in hell?*

*Quoniam non est in morte qui memor sit tui; in inferno autem quis confitebitur tibi?*

**6[6]** *Quoniam non est in morte qui memor sit tui, For there is no one in death that is mindful of you*: that is, you are not mindful in remembering

---

10  Ez. 36:22a.
11  Ez. 36:32a.
12  Ez. 36:22a.

merit to one existing in mortal sin; and therefore I request that your grace fill me, so that my works might be meritorious.[13] Or [an alternative way of understanding it is], *there is no one in death, that is mindful of your memory of salvation;* and this truly is said of those who have died without charity and grace. For those who are in purgatory, are in the memory of God: the others [those in hell] do not hope to be freed from punishment. *In inferno autem quis confitebitur tibi? In hell, who shall confess to you?* It is as if he says [by an implied answer], "No one," because neither the confession of the divine praises nor the confession of any individual guilt is found in hell. And indeed, this is consistent with what Solomon says: *Whatsoever your hand is able to do, do it earnestly: for neither work, nor reason, nor wisdom, nor knowledge shall be in hell, to where you are hastening.*[14]

Up to this point, the most blessed David in his own person speaks of the truly repentant man, he elaborates upon the manner a man repenting from sin prays to the heavenly Judge. Now, he additionally teaches, by his own example, what the person repenting ought to do, so that not only by word, but also by deed he might reconcile himself to God. For he says:

------

6[7] *I have labored in my groanings, every night I will wash my bed: I will water my couch with my tears.*

*Laboravi in gemitu meo; lavabo per singulas noctes lectum meum; lacrimis meis stratum meum rigabo.*

6[7] *Laboravi in gemitu meo, I have labored in my groanings:* that is, I am interiorly contrite of my sins, although I do not omit the exterior acts of penance and the works of satisfaction, but weeping, abstaining, persisting in holy vigils I prostrate myself. For sin, because of the delight that is attached to it, is made up for by the [good] work to which there is adjoined a certain affliction. Also, this which is said — *I labored in my groanings* — can be understood here to refer to the interior effort, for

------

13  E. N. God does not "remember" the previous merits of a man in mortal sin; however, these previous merits are "remembered" upon the sinner regaining the state of grace. "All merit is lost when mortal sin is committed. When grace is recovered, it is the consentient opinion of theologians that the former merit is restored. They infer this from the text 'For God is not unjust, that He should forget your work and the love which you have shown in His name' (Hebr. VI, 10). If merit were not restored, the loss would not be wholly repaired, yet the sin is certainly wholly forgiven; which seems to be inconsistent." Charles Coppens, S. J., *The Catholic Religion* (St. Louis, MO: B Herder 1917), 215.

14  Eccl. 9:10.

indeed the interior effort exceeds the exterior effort, just as the interior pain exceeds the exterior pain. In this way, therefore, *I have labored in my groanings*, that is, in interior sadness of heart have I labored, interiorly meditating, scorning myself, and mentally entreating God. For, as Agathon the Anchorite said,[15] there is not a work as great as praying intently to God. For most laborious is it for the heart daily to serve in fullness because of the fragility and instability of the human soul.

*Lavabo per singulas noctes lectum meum. Every night I will wash my bed.* He who desires to fulfill these words literally might show true penance. Yet this should be seen as impossible to fulfill literally, if it is reasonably understood, so that it has this sense: *Every night I have washed*, that is, at some time of each night, *my bed*, that is a certain part of the bed, this in that by the abundance of tears is meant not so much my external condition, but also the part of the bed next to the face that is dampened. For a man must place himself in bed as if in a tomb, and reflect upon his sins, and death, and the divine judgment; and in this express himself to God, and to wash his face and his bed with holy tears, and therefore there is added, *lacrimis meis stratum meum rigabo, I will water my couch with tears*: and this follows the same explanation as has been stated. By the term *night* we can also understand as sins; and by *bed*, the conscience or evil desires; and by *couch*, evil customs. So that it read in this sense: *I will wash*, or I will clean, *every night*, that is, by singular vices,[16] lamenting for each memory of their occurrence, and even more for how often, *my bed*, that is my conscience, casting away those for which I have remorse of conscience; or, *my bed*, that is, evil desires, in which as if prostrate in bed I have laid down in or have been at rest with. For this I will wash, for this punishing myself, removing this from the rest of me. *My couch*, that is evil custom, *I will water with my tears*, that is, I will greatly bewail, I will not cease until I shall have extirpated it completely, and I shall acquire the habit of the opposing virtue, which, assuredly requires a great and long labor.

---

15  E. N. The reference is to St. Agathon the Anchorite, also known as Abba Agathon, an Egyptian monk that died around 435 A. D. Asked by his fellow monks what virtue required the most effort, Abba Agathon answered: "[T]here is no greater labor than that of prayer to God. For every time a man wants to pray, his enemies, the demons, want to prevent him, for they know that it is only by turning him from prayer that they can hinder his journey. Whatever good work a man undertakes, if he perseveres in it, he will attain rest. But prayer is warfare to the last breath." *The Sayings of the Desert Fathers (Apothegmata Patrum)*, No. 9 (trans. Sister Benedicta Ward) (Kalamazoo, Cistercian Publications, Inc. 1984).

16  E. N. In other words, in an *examen* of conscience, vice by vice, sin by sin.

6[8]  *My eye is troubled through indignation: I have grown old among
all my enemies.*

*Turbatus est a furore oculus meus; inveteravi inter omnes inimicos
meos.*

6[8]  *Turbatus est a furore oculos meus, My eye is troubled through indignation*: that is, the consideration of my mind is troubled, it is shaken or
terrified, *from indignation*, that is, from the distress of the judgment of
God, or because of the weighty vengeance of divine justice. Or this [is
an alternative explanation]: *My eye is troubled through indignation*, that
is, my intellect is made disquiet and uneasy *through indignation*, that
is, from the furious anger (*ira*) or indignation (*indignatione*), which I
conceive to be against me on account of the enormity of my sin. Surely,
passions, even if they are good and willingly assumed, have the tendency
yet in some way to disturb reason.[17] *Inveteravi, I have grown old*, that
is, I have become old in soul, and near its end,[18] sordid lying down
in vices, and am far from spiritual youth, which is the reformation of
the mind by grace; and this, *inter omnes inimicos meos, amongst all my
enemies*, that is, among all they who endeavor to divert me from the
highest good, which are the world, the devil, vice, and the disordered
desires of the flesh. Amongst those *I have grown old*, consenting to their
suggestions and conforming myself to their works. I have not attained
that which the divine Apostle exhorted: Strip *the old man with his deeds*,
and put on *the new, who is renewed* from day to day *unto knowledge of
him who created him.*[19]

---

6[9]  *Depart from me, all you workers of iniquity: for the Lord has
heard the voice of my weeping.*

*Discedite a me omnes qui operamini iniquitatem, quoniam exaudivit
Dominus vocem fletus mei.*

Now, therefore, I desire to obey him who says, *Let us therefore cast
off the works of darkness;*[20] and therefore 6[9][21] *Discedite a me, depart
from me*, that is, do not lead me unto sinning; *depart* from the counsel,
resemblance, life, and affections of *omnes qui operamini iniquitatem, all*

---

17  *ST,* IaIIae, q. 22 *ff.*
18  *Cf.* Heb. 8:13.
19  Col. 3:9, 10.
20  Rom. 13:12b.
21  Denis skips Psalm 6:8 in this Article.

*who work iniquity*, who do not wish to do penance with me. For I do not will to consent to your counsel, I do not will to be similar to you, I do not will to imitate either your life or your affections. And this, therefore, *quoniam exaudivit Dominus vocem fletus mei; because the Lord has heard the voice of my weeping*, that is, the interior affection, from which the voice and tears spring forth, and on account of which they declare themselves to be heard. For not clamor, but love,[22] not the tears of the eyes, but contrition of the heart penetrates the heavens and enter into the ears of God.

---

6[10]  *The Lord has heard my supplication: the Lord has received my prayer.*

*Exaudivit Dominus deprecationem meam; Dominus orationem meam suscepit.*

Lastly, this hearing of his is twice repeated, so as to express how gracious God is, and how delightful it is to be in the Lord on account of his benefits. For he says:   6[10] *Exaudivit Dominus deprecationem meam, the Lord has heard my supplication*, granting indulgence; *Dominus orationem meam suscepit, the Lord has received my prayer*, showing us grace. For no one is released from mortal sin unless he is at the same time filled with sanctifying grace (*gratia gratum faciens*).

---

6[11]  *Let all my enemies be ashamed, and be very much troubled: let them be turned back, and be ashamed very speedily.*

*Erubescant, et conturbentur vehementer omnes inimici mei; convertantur, et erubescant valde velociter.*

But because the soul is pious and loving, it wishes and prays for others that they receive the same grace that it knows has been given to it by God, and, for that reason praying for true repentance for others,   6[11] *Erubescant, let them be ashamed*, he says, that is, let them be ashamed of their evil guilt, *et conturbentur vehementer, and be very much troubled*, and may they be troubled, by that by which I am troubled, that is, being awakened toward the good, *omnes inimici mei, all my enemies*, that is, they who hate me, because they desire to turn me away from God; but

---

22 *Non clamor, sed amor.* This suggests a short poem, which is found in various forms, generally ascribed to the Franciscan, Thomas of Celano. *Non clamor, sed amor / non vox, sed votum / non cordula, sed cor / psallit in aure Dei.* Not clamor, but love / not the voice, but devotion / not the string, but the heart / sings in the ear of God.

I love them who have the capacity to be blessed on account of the good of nature; and I would not love those also who are my friends, unless I also prayed for them. *Convertantur, let them be turned back* from vain and transitory things to the true and immutable good, *et erubescant, and let them be ashamed.* The repetition of the word is an indication of affection. *Let them be ashamed,* therefore, *valde velociter, very speedily,* because there is danger in procrastination. Whence it is written: *Delay not to be converted to the Lord, and defer it not from day to day,*[23] *and say not: the mercy of the Lord is great,*[24] *for his wrath shall come on a sudden, and in the time of vengeance he will destroy you.*[25]

Finally, it is certain that this Psalm literally can be referred to David, because he was not only a sinner and a penitent, but he also committed a great sin, and as a result he is the hope and exemplar of all penitents, in most efficaciously doing penance, most fully obtaining mercy, and most excellently acquiring grace. It is believed also that he frequently literally fulfilled that which is said: *I have labored in my groanings, every night I will wash my bed.* If, therefore, it is understood in such a manner to refer to David, then allegorically it can be interpreted as applying to any efficacious penitent, and so it can be explained in this manner. But because these explanations do not differ, except that one teaches that which is a fact, and the other that which ought to be done, therefore this one exposition suffices.

This Psalm is also the first Psalm among the Penitential Psalms,[26] all of which are scrutinized, and understood, and read with great diligence, because in them there is a sort of book and mirror to teach the sinner to look upon himself, to reflect upon the enormity of his sins, to be terrified of the divine judgment, so that he might pour out most devoutly, with the most amount of feeling, indeed most efficacious prayers to God, which quickly deserve to be heard, if they are also founded upon the taste of heart (*gustu cordis*) and heartfelt contrition. Consider, therefore, O sinner and penitent, holy David; labor with him in the groaning of your heart; do not give yourself any rest, until you reconcile yourself to your Judge; wash your bed every night, in the manner that Jeremiah desired, *Let my eyes shed down tears night and*

---

23  Ecclus. 5:8.
24  Ecclus. 5:6a.
25  Ecclus. 5:9.
26  E. N. The Seven Penitential Psalms are Psalms 6, 31, 37, 50, 101, 129, and 142. On his deathbed, St. Augustine requested that these psalms be inscribed on the walls in his bed chamber so that he could recite them as he approached death.

day, and let them not cease.[27] Whence also holy Job said: *Before I eat I sigh: and as overflowing waters, so is my roaring.*[28] He does not clean and adorn the most white sheets [of his bed] from the careless washing with dirty waters, but rather purges and bedecks his rational soul with the profusion of penitential tears.

# PRAYER

ALMIGHTY GOD, WE SUPPLIANTLY implore your most kind clemency, that you do not in your indignation rebuke, nor in your wrath chastise, us who by unremitting deviations from your commandments offend you, but convert and also rescue our souls from eternal damnation, and save us because of your mercy.

*Piissimam clementiam tuam, omnipotens Deus, suppliciter imploramus: ut qui assiduis excessibus te offendimus, non in furore tuo arguas, neque in ira tua corripias; sed converte et ab aeterna damnatione eripe animas nostras, et salvos nos fac propter misericordiam tuam.*

---

27  Jer. 14:17.
28  Job. 3:24.

# Psalm 7

## ARTICLE XXIII

### LITERAL EXPLANATION OF THE SEVENTH PSALM:
### *DOMINE DEUS MEUS, IN TE SPERAVI*
### O LORD, MY GOD, IN YOU HAVE I PUT MY TRUST

7[1] *The psalm of David which he sung to the Lord for the words of Chusi the son of Iemini.*

*Psalmus David, quem cantavit Domino pro verbis Chusi, filii Iemini.*

**B**EFORE THIS PSALM IS PLACED THIS TITLE: 7[1] *Psalmus David, quem cantavit Domino pro verbis Chusi, filii Iemini. The Psalm of David which he sung to the Lord for the words of Chusi, the son of Gemini.* This title may be explained in a variety of ways based upon the fact that this Psalm can be explained in diverse ways. According to the literal understanding of this Psalm, the meaning of the title is easy. For one reads in the book of Kings the manner in which David, fleeing the persecution of Absalom, sent back his friend Chusi to Absalom in order that he might explore his plans, and that he might directly make known these to King David; and this was done.[1] And so, it was on the occasion of the words which Chusi related to David, that the holy David proclaimed this Psalm. It is more fittingly explained as referring to the thing signified, than the signifying figure; it can also be explained of the act itself and signifying [act]. Hence, it is thus first explained, but exceedingly briefly and cursorily, because such [historical] exposition is less fruitful or sweet, and insufficiently agreeable and pleasing, to the more devout brothers.[2]

---

1  2 Kings 15: 14, 16, 32–26; 17:7-21.

2  E. N. In other words, the signifying figure or act will be first addressed, and then the signified figure or act. The latter is more fruitful and sweet. As the illustrious Abbot of St. Denis Suger (1081-1151 A. D.), had inscribed on an altar panel in his monastery, *significata magis significante placent*, the things that are signified are more pleasing than the thing which signifies. *Oeuvres Complètes de Suger* (Paris 1867), 193.

7[2]  *O Lord my God, in you have I put my trust: save me from all
them that persecute me, and deliver me.*

*Domine Deus meus, in te speravi; salvum me fac ex omnibus
persequentibus me, et libera me.*

7[3]  *Lest at any time he seize upon my soul like a lion, while there is
no one to redeem me, nor to save.*

*Nequando rapiat ut leo animam meam, dum non est qui redimat,
neque qui salvum faciat.*

David, therefore, desired to be freed from the ambush which Absalom
through the counsel of Ahithophel prepared,[3] and thus he prayed:    7[2]
*Domine Deus meus, in te speravi. O Lord, my God, in you I put my trust:*
and so in this manner I am found worthy to be heard, because I know
that you do not forsake those who hope in you,[4] on account of which I
trustingly take refuge in and prevail upon you; *salvum me fac ex omnibus
persequentibus me, et libera me, save me from all them that persecute me, and
deliver me:*    7[3] *Nequando, Lest,* that is, neither at one or another time, my
enemy *rapiat . . . animam meam, seize upon my soul,* that is, extinguish my
life, *ut leo, like a lion,* which animal customarily kills: nay, I say, he so seizes
and carries off so quickly, *dum non est qui redimat, neque qui salvum faciat,
while there is no one to redeem me, nor to save,* that is, because there is no
one that can redeem me or save me unless it be you who redeems and saves.

---

7[4]  *O Lord my God, if I have done this thing, if there be iniquity in
my hands,*

*Domine Deus meus, si feci istud, si est iniquitas in manibus meis,*

7[5]  *If I have rendered to them that repaid me evils, let me deservedly
fall empty before my enemies.*

*Si reddidi retribuentibus mihi mala, decidam merito ab inimicis
meis inanis.*

7[6]  *Let the enemy pursue my soul, and take it, and tread down my
life on the earth, and bring down my glory to the dust.*

*Persequatur inimicus animam meam, et comprehendat; et conculcet
in terra vitam meam, et gloriam meam in pulverem deducat.*

---

3  2 Kings 17:1–4.
4  Cf. Judith 13:17. *Praise you the Lord our God, who has not forsaken them that hope
in him.*

Consequently, seeing that his adversaries pressed upon him, and they asserting themselves justly to be pursuing him, David excuses himself from the sin in the manner that in the exposition of the third Psalm is fully explained.[5] He says:     7[4] *Domine Deus meus, si feci istud, O Lord my God, if I have done this thing,* that is, if I have been the cause of that which is being imposed upon me, and *si est iniquitas in manibus meis, and if there be iniquity in my hands,* of which I am not already contrite,     7[5] *si reddidi retribuentibus mihi mala, if I have rendered to them that repaid me evils,* that is, if I have rendered evil for evil: If, I say, any of that is in me, *decidam merito, let me deservedly fall,* that is, justly fall and be overcome, *ab inimicis meis inanis, empty before my enemies,* that is, without success and empty of grace. For David gave orders to preserve and not to kill young Absalom, and he did good to Saul and his rivals[6] And then this [sentiment] is more clearly stated by that which follows:     7[6] *Persequatur inimicus* meus, *Let my enemy pursue,* that is to say, Absalom, and all of those who adhered to him, *animam meam, et comprehendat, my soul, and take it,* that is, extinguish my very self, or my bodily life, and capture or destroy me; *et conculcet in terra vitam meam, and tread down my life on the earth,* extinguishing from it its most innermost part, *et gloriam meam in pulverem deducat; and bring down my glory to the dust,* that is, to take away the regal power from me.

---

7[7]   *Rise up, O Lord, in your anger: and be exalted in the borders of my enemies. And arise, O Lord my God, in the precept which you have commanded:*

*Exsurge, Domine, in ira tua; et exaltare in finibus inimicorum meorum; et exsurge, Domine Deus meus, in praecepto quod mandasti:*

7[8]   *And a congregation of people shall surround you. And for their sakes return you on high.*

*Et synagoga populorum circumdabit te: et propter hanc in altum regredere.*

But because it was not so, there follows:     7[7] *Exsurge, Domine, Rise up, O Lord,* with your assistance, *in ira tua, in your anger* fighting for me, justly attacking the ungodly in the present, that they not perish eternally; *et exaltare in finibus inimicorum meorum, and be you exalted in the borders of my enemies,* that is, triumph and prevail in the place and

---

5 Article XV (Psalm 3:2).
6 2 Sam. 18:5; 1 Sam. 24:4–8, 12 and elsewhere.

the land of those that are averse to me, giving me victory against them, that they may desist from ruling over the land over which they had obtained dominion by violence. *Et exsurge, and arise,* that is, appear in action and in justice, *Domine Deus meus, in praecepto quod mandasti, O Lord my God, in the precept which you have commanded:* that is, by the precept of your law show the ungodliness of my adversaries. For the law instructs that sons should honor their parents,[7] and subject themselves to the king; and against this Absalom and those who favored him acted, seeking to expel David from his kingdom.    7[8] *Et synagoga populorum, and a congregation of people,* that is, the congregation of the good and the faithful, *circumdabit te, shall surround you,* that is, will flock together from all parts to you, adhering to you, and approving of your justice. *Et propter hanc, and for their sakes,* that is, for the salvation and the ordering (*informationem*) of the congregation or your people, *in altum regredere, return on high,* that is, declare the majesty of your justice, driving out the ungodly and the proud, but raising up the humble and the godly. Or [it could be seen this way], *return,* that is, return on high, that is, in the height of your glory, so that the evil men whom you permitted for a time to reign, now you will justly constrain, and they will no longer preside and will be more heavily condemned.

---

7[9]  The Lord judges the people. Judge me, O Lord, according to my justice, and according to my innocence in me.

*Dominus iudicat populos. Iudica me, Domine, secundum iustitiam meam, et secundum innocentiam meam super me.*

7[10]  The wickedness of sinners shall be brought to naught: and you shalt direct the just: the searcher of hearts and reins is God.

*Consumetur nequitia peccatorum; et diriges iustum, scrutans corda et renes, Deus.*

7[9] *Dominus iudicat, the Lord judges,* that is, he discerns, and he justly repays, *populos, the people,* rendering to each man according to his works.[8] *Iudica me, Domine, secundum iustitiam meam, Judge me, O Lord, according to my justice,* that is, according to the requirements of my merits, *et secundum innocentiam meam super me, and according to my innocence in me:* that is, compensate me according to my abstinence from evil, doing to me as I have done to my neighbor, seeing that as I have not inflicted

---

7  Ex. 20:12.
8  *Cf.* Rom. 2:6; 1 Cor. 3:8.

injury upon them, so neither will you inflict injury upon me. This is the
word of perfect men; and blessed is he who in fullness of conscience is
able to say this of himself to God who is knowing of all things.   7[10]
*Consumetur, it shall be brought to naught,* that is, he will accept the end,
*nequitia peccatorum, the wickedness of sinners,* lest they add sins to their
sins, treasuring up to themselves wrath in the day of wrath;[9] *et diriges
iustum, and you shall direct the just,* that is, you will guide the just in
the right way, and you will make perfect the just, *scrutans corda et renes,
Deus, the searcher of hearts and reins*[10] *is God,* that is, accurately and
intimately seeing thoughts, and weighing the desires and delights.

---

7[11]  *Just is my help from the Lord: who saves the upright of heart.*

  *Iustum adiutorium meum a Domino, qui salvos facit rectos corde.*

7[12]  *God is a just judge, strong and patient: is he angry every day?*

  *Deus iudex iustus, fortis, et patiens; numquid irascitur per singulos dies?*

7[11] *Iustum adiutorium meum a Domino, qui salvos facit rectos corde.
Just is my help from the Lord, who saves the upright of heart.* Because it was
said above, *if there be iniquity in my hands,* etc., and *Judge me according
to my justice,* therefore it follows that it is justly meritorious to ask to be
helped by the Lord, whose property it is to save those of right or just
heart.   7[12] *Deus iudex, God is judge,* infallible in all things, *iustus, just,*
with him *there is no respect of persons,*[11] *fortis, strong,* whose judgment
nobody is able to resist, *et patiens, and patient,* that is long-suffering in
forbearance; *numquid irascitur, is he angry,* that is, he takes vengeance
and justly repays, *per singulos dies, every day,* that is, as quickly as the evil
deserve? It is as if saying: "No"; but continually and with equanimity
he tolerates the ungodly, so that they may be converted.

---

9 *Cf.* Rom. 2:5.
10 L. *renes,* literally, the kidneys and (except where the actual organ is intended,
   *e.g.,* Ex. 29:13; Lev. 3:4) translated in the Douay Rheims by the English cognate
   *reins* (*compare* the English word *renal*). The Latin *renes* is a translation of the
   Hebrew כְּלָיוֹת (*kelayoth*), which means kidneys. In addition to referring to the
   actual organs, the kidneys or reins—used frequently in conjunction with reference to the "heart"—are used metaphorically to refer to the emotional seat of
   man, the "inward parts" (*e.g.,* Ps. 139:13 Prov. 23:16), the seat of man's character
   (*e.g.,* Ps. 12:2; 16:7), his conscience (*e.g.,* Ps. 7:9; 26:2; Jer. 17:10), the source of
   his strength (*e.g.,* Job 40:7; 2 Sam. 20:8).
11 Rom. 2:11.

7[**13**]  *Except you will be converted, he will brandish his sword: he has bent his bow and made it ready.*

*Nisi conversi fueritis, gladium suum vibrabit; arcum suum tetendit, et paravit illum.*

7[**14**]  *And in it he has prepared the instruments of death, he has made ready his arrows for them that burn.*

*Et in eo paravit vasa mortis, sagittas suas ardentibus effecit.*

Nevertheless, O ungodly, so that the delay of the wrath of God might not render you indolent, or full of dread, or untroubled, therefore I say to you:    7[**13**] *Nisi conversi fueritis, except you will be converted* to saving repentance, *gladium suum vibrabit, he will brandish his sword,* that is, he will carry out his vindicating and manifest punishment, especially in the future, that is, in the universal judgment, when all flesh will see Christ the Judge.[12] *Arcum suum tetendit, he has bent his bow,* that is, he has threatened a hidden vengeance to the ungodly, because he removes his grace and paternal correction, which is a hidden and dreadful punishment of divine justice; *et paravit illum, and made it ready,* that is to say, the bow is readied to deliver arrows, that is, deadly and eternal condemnations to the ingrate and the hardened.    7[**14**] *Et in eo, and in it,* namely in his bow, *paravit vasa mortis, he has prepared the instruments of death,* that is, in the outpouring of his death-dealing punishments of his vengeance, indeed, even eternal torments. *Sagittas suas, his arrows,* that is, the infliction of punishments, *ardentibus effecit, he has made ready for them that burn,* that is, he has prepared to let loose upon those in the heat of illicit desires.

---

7[**15**]  *Behold he has been in labor with injustice; he has conceived sorrow, and brought forth iniquity.*

*Ecce parturiit iniustitiam; concepit dolorem, et peperit iniquitatem.*

7[**16**]  *He has opened a pit and dug it; and he is fallen into the hole he made.*

*Lacum aperuit, et effodit eum; et incidit in foveam quam fecit.*

7[**15**] *Ecce parturiit iustitiam. Behold he has been in labor with justice.* That is, the ungodly man through the devil's suggestion has acted against the divine precept; *concepit dolorem, he has conceived sorrow,* that is, a disordered affection and evil intention: for the disordered affection is itself

---

12  Job 19:26; Matt. 25: 31 *et seq.*

its own punishment;[13] *et peperit iniquitatem, and brought forth iniquity,*
that is, it has led to the effect that the soul intended.   7[**16**] *Lacum
aperuit, he has opened a pit,* that is, not only has he sinned as to himself,
but he has also presented to others an occasion of sin; *he has opened a
pit,* that is, a bad example or he has administered false counsel to his
neighbor; *et effodit eum, and he has dug it,* that is, this pit, to the extent
that it was in him, led those outside of him to evil deeds; or *he has dug it,*
that is, he has implanted it deeply in the hearts of others; or *he has dug it,*
he has industriously and penetratingly thought regarding how he might
open this pit to others and lead others into it; *et incidit in foveam quam
fecit, and he is fallen into the hole he made,* that is, he himself has fallen
into the fraud or the evil or the pit which he prepared for others. Each
and every iniquitous act redounds upon its own author, and he firstly
and principally harms himself; indeed, while he might desire to deceive
others, he himself is duped by a demon; and while he prepares others
the evil of punishment or temporal harm, he falls into the evil of guilt
and eternal punishments. This was fulfilled in Absalom, who led others
to the persecution of his father and to death;[14] but he fell into the trap
which he had made, for he turned in flight and was caught by the snare
of the tree, and at length was transpierced with three lances by Joab.[15]

7[**17**]  *His sorrow shall be turned on his own head: and his iniquity shall
come down upon his crown.*

*Convertetur dolor eius in caput eius, et in verticem ipsius iniquitas
eius descendet.*

7[**17**] *Convertetur dolor eius in caput eius. His sorrow shall be turned
on his own head,* that is, the evil of the ungodly man returns back to
him, and is added to his account, and harms him, and embeds in the
conscience the worm of his vices; *et in verticem ipsius, and upon his crown,*
that is, in his intellect, which is the highest power of the soul, *iniquitas
eius descendet, his iniquity shall come down upon,* or will with increase
redound back to him. This, he says, not as a result of desiring it, but
by means of prophesying, or certainly desiring that, by being punished

13  *Animus enim inordinatus sibi ipsi est poena.* Cf. St. Augustine, *Confessions,* I, 12,
19: *Iussisti enim et sic est, ut poena sua sibi sit omnis inordinatus animus.* "For
you commanded and it is so: that every disordered affection should be its own
punishment."
14  2 Sam. 19:10-12.
15  2 Sam. 18:7-15.

by God in time, the ungodly man may not be tormented eternally.[16]

---

7[18]    *I will give glory to the Lord according to his justice: and will sing to the name of the Lord the most high.*

*Confitebor Domino secundum iustitiam eius, et psallam nomini Domini altissimi.*

7[18]    *Confitebor Domino, I will give glory to the Lord,* through the confession of praise, that is, I will praise the Lord, and I will sing him praises, *secundum iustitiam eius, according to his justice,* that is, in proportion that his justice declares him most worthy of all praise, he who renders to every man in the manner which he deserves;[17] *et psallam nomini Domini altissimi, and I will sing to the name of the Lord most high,* that is, to the Lord himself, whose name *is above all names:*[18] for he takes the name for the name he is named, and not through the voice of him saying the name (*pro nomine nominato, non pro voce nominante*).[19]

---

# ARTICLE XXIV

## ALLEGORICAL EXPLANATION OF THIS SEVENTH PSALM

7[1]    *The psalm of David which he sung to the Lord for the words of Chusi the son of Iemini.*

*Psalmus David, quem cantavit Domino pro verbis Chusi, filii Iemini.*

**I**N ADDITION, ACCORDING TO THE ALLEGOR-ical explanation of this Psalm, which namely expounds upon Christ, it is fitting to disclose the mystical title of this Psalm. For by David is understood Christ; by Absalom, the Jewish people persecuting Christ.

---

16  E. N. That chastised and punished by God during this life might cause him to repent, turn to God, and so result in his salvation.

17  Rom. 2:6; 1 Cor. 3:8.

18  Phil 2:9.

19  E. N. We do not name God; rather God names himself in revelation. "The name ... is concerned to make the thing nameable, that is, 'invocable,' to establish a relation to it. . . . When God names himself after the self-understanding of faith, he is ... making himself nameable; he is handing himself over to men in such a way that he can be called upon by them. And by doing this he enters into coexistence with them; he puts himself within their reach; his is 'there' for them." Joseph Ratzinger, *Introduction to Christianity* (San Francisco: Ignatius 2004), 91–92.

By Achitophel, which is interpreted as the downfall of a brother, is understood as Judas, who betrayed Christ,[20] who deigned to call himself the brother of men.[21] By Chusi, which is interpreted as silence, is understood the mystery of human redemption, justly hidden from the Jews, but mercifully revealed to the Gentiles, namely, the Incarnation of the Son of God, and his Passion and Resurrection. By Jemini, which is interpreted as favorable (*dexter*), is understood God the Father, who acted favorably and in a well-disposed fashion to the Gentiles, enlightening their hearts so that they might recognize the mysteries of Christ. That is, therefore, the sense of the title:    7[1] *In finem,*[22] *psalmus David,* that is, this Psalm directing us to the end, that is, to God and eternal life, is attributed to David, that is, it treats of Christ, in whose person David here is speaking; *quem cantavit Domino, which he sung to the Lord,* that is, to the glory of the Father, *pro verbis Chusi, for the words of Chusi,* that is, for the revelation of the secret, namely, for the manifestation of the Incarnation: Chusi, I say, *filii Jemini, the son of Jemini,* that is, for the revelation of the secret revealed by God the Father, who by revealing this was for us Jemini, that is, favorably and propitiously.

7[2]    *O Lord my God, in you have I put my trust: save me from all them that persecute me, and deliver me.*

*Domine Deus meus, in te speravi; salvum me fac ex omnibus persequentibus me, et libera me.*

Therefore construing this Psalm as pertaining to Christ, Christ says to God the Father or to the entire supremely blessed Trinity:    7[2] *Domine Deus meus, in te speravi, O Lord my God, in you have I put my trust.* Christ insofar as he is man, is the servant of God, in the manner that it is pronounced: *Behold my servant shall understand, he shall be exalted, and extolled, and shall be exceeding high.*[23] And so, *O Lord,* whose precepts, as man, I always obey; *my God,* who created me, to the extent that I accepted the form of a servant: as the Lord says through Isaiah: *I the Lord have created him;*[24] whom I singularly I worship, most ardently love, incessantly contemplate, and to whom I always unalterably adhere; *in you I have put my trust,* not as do the other wayfarers (*viatores*), that

20 Mat. 26:47–50.
21 Matt. 12:49, 50; Mark 3:34, 35, *etc.*
22 *E. N.* This appears to be in error, since Psalm 7:1 does not begin with these words.
23 Is. 52:13.
24 Is. 45:8b.

is through hope (*spem*) which is a theological virtue,[25] but by a certain trust (*fiduciam*) by which I desire to be freed by you from the evil of punishment, and to be glorified in body; *save me*, by the glory of the Resurrection, and through the preservation from punishment which the Jews sought to inflict on me before the preordained hour of the Passion had come. And so, therefore *save me from those who persecute me*, that is to say, from the princes of the priests, the Pharisees and the Scribes: not so that I might not be killed by them, but that you might advance my Resurrection, and in three days you might raise me up again; *and deliver me* from all distress of this present life. For this Christ desired in the manner that is declared in the Gospel: *O incredulous generation, how long shall I be with you? How long shall I suffer you?*[26] But although Christ most certainly foreknew that he would be relieved in such a manner, he nevertheless prayed for salvation in this way, because he knew that it was thus preordained by God, so that by prayer he might acquire it.

———————

7[3]    *Lest at any time he seize upon my soul like a lion, while there is no one to redeem me, nor to save.*

*Nequando rapiat ut leo animam meam, dum non est qui redimat, neque qui salvum faciat.*

7[3] *Nequando rapiat ut leo animam meam*, lest at any time he seize upon my soul like a lion, that is, that my enemy not altogether destroy my bodily life, protecting the body in the enclosure of the tomb, separated from the soul for a time, as long as three days; and thus the faith of the believers might perish. Now Christ desired to reunite the soul to the body quickly, because his bodily life was most desirable and most noble on account of its personal union with the Word. Or it might be understood thus: *lest like a lion*, that is the devil who is as it were a lion, *seize my soul*, holding it in hell,[27] as was the case with other saints. Whence, the Passion being imminent, Christ told his disciples: *For the prince of this world is coming, and in me he has not anything.*[28] That he not *seize upon my soul*, I say, *dum non est qui redimat, neque qui salvum faciat, while there is no one to redeem me, nor to save me*: because no one else is able to redeem me, and to save me by resurrecting me from the dead but you.

———————

25  *ST* IIaIIae, q. 17, art. 5.
26  Mark. 9:18.
27  *E. N.* This is a reference not to the hell of the damned, but the hell or limbo of the fathers, the *limbus patrum*, such as referred to by the Apostle's Creed.
28  John 14:30b.

7[4]  *O Lord my God, if I have done this thing, if there be iniquity in my hands,*

*Domine Deus meus, si feci istud, si est iniquitas in manibus meis,*

7[5]  *If I have rendered to them that repaid me evils, let me deservedly fall empty before my enemies.*

*Si reddidi retribuentibus mihi mala, decidam merito ab inimicis meis inanis.*

7[6]  *Let the enemy pursue my soul, and take it, and tread down my life on the earth, and bring down my glory to the dust.*

*Persequatur inimicus animam meam, et comprehendat; et conculcet in terra vitam meam, et gloriam meam in pulverem deducat.*

Consequently, Christ exhibits his immunity from all sin, saying:   7[4] *Domine Deus meus, si feci istud, O Lord my God, if I have done this thing,* that is, if I have committed that which the Jews sought to apply to me, saying: *Behold a man that is a glutton and a wine drinker,*[29] *he is mad,*[30] *he casts out devils by Beelzebub, the prince of devils.*[31] *Si est iniquitas in manibus meis, if there be iniquity in my hands:* in the same manner they said before Pilate: *We have found this man perverting our nation, and forbidding to give tribute to Caesar, and saying that he is Christ the king.*[32]   7[5] *Si reddidi retributentibus mihi mala, if I have rendered to them that repaid me evils.* Christ not only did not return evil for evil, but he returned good for evil, teaching, praying, performing miracles, so that he might convert unbelievers to have faith. Indeed, even hanging on the Cross, he prayed for the most ungodly deicides: *Father, forgive them, for they know not what they do.*[33] For this reason, according to the Prophet, Christ said to his Father: *Shall evil be rendered for good, because they have dug a pit for my soul? Remember that I have stood in your sight, to speak good for them, and to turn away thy indignation from them.*[34]

*Decidam merito ab inimicis meis inanis, Let me deservedly fall empty before my enemies:* that is, if at this or some other time, I have given such occasion then let me justly be struck down by my adversaries, as if empty of grace. For he who commits a fault suffers deservedly the punishment

---

29  Matt. 11:19.
30  John 10:20.
31  Luke 11:15.
32  Luke 23:2.
33  Luke 23:34.
34  Jer. 18:20.

[due it]. And a man ought more to desire to submit to bodily death than to commit the smallest venial sin.[35] And therefore he says:    7[6] *Persequatur inimicus animam meam et comprehendat, Let the enemy pursue my soul, and take it*: that is, if I am defiled by any of the aforementioned evil, then let the enemy, that is the Jew or any other unbeliever, pursue me, seek to kill me, and let him take my soul, that is, let him carry out his will in me; *et conculcet in terra vitam meam, and let him tread down my life on the earth*, that is, let him disdain, vilify, and suppress my deeds, as if both unjust and worldly; *et gloriam meam in pulverem deducat, and let him bring down my glory to the dust*, that is, let him reject, banish, and utterly extinguish the honor and excellent reputation of my name, exposing me not to be the Christ, but a false prophet.

———————

7[7]    *Rise up, O Lord, in your anger: and be exalted in the borders of my enemies. And arise, O Lord my God, in the precept which you have commanded:*

*Exsurge, Domine, in ira tua; et exaltare in finibus inimicorum meo-rum; et exsurge, Domine Deus meus, in praecepto quod mandasti:*

After this, Christ prays for the conversion of the unbelievers, for the spread of the faith and the defeat of its adversaries.    7[7] *Exsurge, Domine, in ira tua, Rise up, O Lord, in your anger*: that is, because, O Lord, I have steadfastly borne persecution and death without sin for your honor and the salvation of the world; and therefore *arise*, that is, from repose proceed to act, *in your anger*, that is, in just judgment, or in your tranquil justice, strictly judging all things; *et exaltare, and be you exalted*, that is, rule and reign by faith and worship, *in finibus inimicorum meorum, in the borders of my enemies*, that is in the Gentile lands, or in the hearts of the unbelievers, converting them to the purity of the Christian faith, in the manner that you earlier promised to do: *I will give you the Gentiles for your inheritance, and the utmost parts of the earth for your possession.*[36] Or, *be you exalted* in the *borders of my enemies*, that is, in all in the possession of the devils, who living evilly are as if

———————

35    E. N. "The Catholic Church holds it better for the sun and moon to drop from heaven, for the earth to fail, and for all the many millions on it to die of starvation in extremest agony, as far as temporal affliction goes, than that one soul, I will not say, should be lost, but should commit one single venial sin, should tell one willful untruth, or should steal one poor farthing without excuse." St. John Henry Newman, *Apologia Pro Vita Sua* (London: Longmans, Green, Reader, and Dyer 1875), 247.

36    *See* Ps. 2:8.

they possess them as their own. The boundary or end, therefore, *of my enemies*, that you make subject to me the hearts blinded by demons and possessed by them in a miserable servitude, and subdue to your allegiance all those who previously spurned you and were disobedient to you, and that, believing through me, they might worship and honor you.

*Et exsurge, Domine Deus meus, in praecepto quod mandasti,* and *arise, O Lord my God in the precept which you have commanded*: that is, as you by the law ordered all to do, so act you.[37] For you commanded that honor and glory be dispensed to the just and the innocent, but that punishment and confusion be meted out to the ungodly and the persecutors. In this *precept*, therefore, *arise*, acting in accordance with this established course: raising me up, the Christ, your only Son, put to death though blameless, revealing me to men by the preaching of the Apostles, and lifting the hearts of the believers; but damning, dispersing, and forsaking the obstinate Jews. And this is chiefly said as a prediction rather than as an imprecation.

----

   7[8] *And a congregation of people shall surround you. And for their sakes return you on high.*

   *Et synagoga populorum circumdabit te: et propter hanc in altum regredere.*

   7[8] *Et synagoga populorum circumdabit te,* and *a congregation of people shall surround you*: that is, if you were to be exalted in the stated manner, and my name would be made known to all men, then certainly the *congregation of people*, that is, the congregation of the true Israelites and all of the elect, *shall surround you*, adhering to you by charity and through sincere worship. But because God is immense, it can be asked in what manner his people are able to surround him. And we respond that men surround God, not that they enclose or encircle God, but because by a loving soul and a most pure heart they lovingly embrace with the arms of their holy love, in the manner that the spouse of the only-begotten incarnate Son of God says in the Song of Songs: *Who shall give you to me for my brother, . . . that I may find you without, and kiss you, and . . . will take hold of you?*[38] Or the people is said to surround God because in the manner of surrounding someone they have him, while from all parts they turn to him and they attach themselves

----

37  E. N. In other words, act consistent with your command.
38  Songs 8:1a, 2a.

to him as if encircling. *Et propter hanc, and for their sakes*, that is, on account of the salvation of the elect, *in altum regredere, return you on high*, that is, magnify yourself, and make known that you alone ought to be adored, you who in a certain manner belittled yourself when you permitted idolatry and sin to become powerful.

---

7[9]    *The Lord judges the people. Judge me, O Lord, according to my justice, and according to my innocence in me.*

   *Dominus iudicat populos. Iudica me, Domine, secundum iustitiam meam, et secundum innocentiam meam super me.*

7[10]   *The wickedness of sinners shall be brought to naught: and you shall direct the just: the searcher of hearts and reins is God.*

   *Consumetur nequitia peccatorum; et diriges iustum, scrutans corda et renes, Deus.*

7[9] *Dominus iudicat populos, the Lord judges the people*, scrutinizing them, separating them, and rewarding them. *Iudica me, Domine, secundum iustitiam meam, et secundum innocentiam meam super me. Judge me, O Lord, according to my justice, and according to my innocence in me.* This only Christ can becomingly say in its highest and most optimum manner, since he lived out his life most purely, free from all stain of sin. He, therefore, says in the utmost security: *Judge me, O Lord*, that is, discern my cause, and rescue me from the ungodly; and restore me *according to my justice*, that is according to the dignity and merits of my life, seeing that I always honored you, and thus may you honor and glorify me, as you said through Samuel: *whosoever shall glorify me, him will I glorify: but they that despise me, shall be despised.*[39] *And according to my innocence in me*: that is, as I transgressed not at all, but exceeded the remedy required to obtain eternal beatitude for the entire human race; and the wickedness of the ungodly will not prevail over me.    7[10] *Consumetur nequitia peccatorum, the wickedness of sinners shall be brought to naught*, that is, the malice of the Jews and of my persecutors shall be ended, and it will be punished with just punishment. *Et diriges iustum, and you shall direct the just*, that is, you will guide me, the Saint of Saints,[40] to yourself in the Ascension, and you will place me to your right: precisely in the manner that it has been fulfilled.

---

39  1 Sam. 2:30b.
40  On "Saint of Saints" as a name for Christ, *see* footnote 3-26.

7[11] *Just is my help from the Lord: who saves the upright of heart.*

*Iustum adiutorium meum a Domino, qui salvos facit rectos corde.*

7[12] *God is a just judge, strong and patient: is he angry every day?*

*Deus iudex iustus, fortis, et patiens; numquid irascitur per singulos dies?*

7[11] *Iustum adiutorium meum a Domino, Just is my help from the Lord:* because in all things I sought the honor of the Father, and it is just to be aided by him.     7[12] *Deus iudex,* God the judge, by his authority and through his interior scrutiny, *iustus, fortis,* just, strong, indeed almighty, *et patiens, and patient:* [this refers] not that patience which is a moral virtue, that breaks and orders the passion of sorrow, in the manner that meekness does anger; but [rather it refers to] patience according to the long-suffering postponement of punishment. *Numquid irascitur per singulos dies? Is he angry every day?* That is, will he take vengeance unexpectedly and immediately for the crucifiers and the killers and the adversaries of Christ his beloved Son? It is as if he says: "No"; but he expected the conversion of the Jews a long time after the Passion of Christ. And this the Holy Spirit says through the prophet, so as to confute the error or—perhaps better—the blindness of the Jews. For they spoke among themselves: If this is the Christ, the elect of God, then surely he will save him from our hands, and he will not give leave to have him killed: for which reason we test him by torture to see whether he is the Son of God. And this is beautifully intimated in the book of Wisdom.[41] For against such persons, therefore, it says: *Is God angry every day?* That is, will he deliver the just man, and vindicate his injuries?

---

7[13] *Except you will be converted, he will brandish his sword: he has bent his bow and made it ready.*

*Nisi conversi fueritis, gladium suum vibrabit; arcum suum tetendit, et paravit illum.*

7[14] *And in it he has prepared the instruments of death, he has made ready his arrows for them that burn.*

*Et in eo paravit vasa mortis, sagittas suas ardentibus effecit.*

---

41  Wis. 2:17–19: *Let us see then if his words be true, and let us prove what shall happen to him, and we shall know what his end shall be. For if he be the true son of God, he will defend him, and will deliver him from the hands of his enemies. Let us examine him by outrages and tortures, that we may know his meekness and try his patience.*

But, O Jew, let not the long-suffering patience of God be for you the occasion for greater damnation: because 7[13] *Nisi conversi fueritis, except you will be converted* to Christ whom you have denied, and suspended on wood (*in ligno*), God, *the judge, gladium suum vibrabit: arcum suum tetendit, et paravit illum, will brandish his sword: he has bent his bow, and made it ready.* This is commonly accepted to refer to the destruction and devastation fulfilled by Vespasian and Titus. For the sword and bow of Vespasian and Titus,[42] are said to be the sword and bow of God, because by divine ordination they came to persecute the Jews. Whence, in Ezechiel, the Lord calls the sword of the King of Babylon his sword.[43] 7[14] *Et in eo, and in it,* that is to say, in his bow, the Lord *paravit vasa mortis, he has prepared the instrument of death*; and what are the instruments of death he soon insinuates: *sagittas suas ardentibus effecit, he has made ready his arrows for them that burn.* For arrows express the instruments of death, for causally they contain death, and quickly are they able to inflict it. God has prepared these arrows of death, or he has prepared them that burn, that is, the Jews furiously raging against Christ.

---

7[15]   *Behold he has been in labor with injustice; he has conceived sorrow, and brought forth iniquity.*

   *Ecce parturiit iniustitiam; concepit dolorem, et peperit iniquitatem.*

7[16]   *He has opened a pit and dug it; and he is fallen into the hole he made.*

   *Lacum aperuit, et effodit eum; et incidit in foveam quam fecit.*

7[17]   *His sorrow shall be turned on his own head: and his iniquity shall come down upon his crown.*

   *Convertetur dolor eius in caput eius, et in verticem ipsius iniquitas eius descendet.*

7[15] *Ecce parturiit, behold, he has been in labor* the people of the Jews *iniustitiam, with injustice* calumniating the works of Christ, and attributing it to the devil;[44] *concepit dolorem, he conceived in sorrow*: because they were sorrowful on account of the glory of the miracles of Christ, and that because of this many believed in him. Whence also

---

42  E. N. Vespasian (9–79 A. D.) and Titus (39–81 A. D.). The Roman emperors responsible for destroying Jerusalem and its Temple (70 A. D.) during the First Jewish-Roman War.

43  Eze. 21:3–5; 30:24, 25; 32:10, 11. E. N. In a similar way, Atilla the Hun was called the *flagellum Dei*, the scourge of God.

44  Luke 11:15.

they thought to kill Lazarus who had been raised by Christ, because many believed in Christ on account of him being raised from death.[45] *Et peperit iniquitatem, and he brought forth iniquity*: that is, the Hebrew people from the pain that they conceived against Christ, burst forth to that most grave iniquity that killed the only-begotten Son with the most desecrated and most sacrilegious hands.  7[16] *Lacum aperuit, they opened a pit*, that is they planned the convenient time of destroying Christ, or prepared the snare of death, *et effodit eum, and dug it*, darkly taking counsel of the way the name and memory of Jesus might be utterly extinguished; *et incidit in foveam quam fecit, and he is fallen into the hole he made*, because by killing Christ, they merited to be killed, to be destroyed, and to be diminished, as in fact we see occurred.  7[17] *Convertetur dolor eius in caput eius, his sorrow shall be turned on his own head*: because that which the Jewish people thought to do to Christ, he suffered; *et in verticem ipsius iniquitas eius descendet, and his iniquity shall come down upon his crown*; that is, the sin of the Jews who denied and killed Christ and exclaimed, *His blood be upon us and our children*.[46] It is a prophecy that has been fulfilled. *Shall come down*, I say, that is, will redound and will return in *his crown*, that is, in the understanding of these people: so that their hearts are deeply darkened, and determined in evil; and from this malice they do not recede, except at the end of time, when there will be one shepherd and one fold.[47]

---

7[18]  *I will give glory to the Lord according to his justice: and will sing to the name of the Lord the most high.*

*Confitebor Domino secundum iustitiam eius, et psallam nomini Domini altissimi.*

7[18] *Confitebor Domino secundum iustitiam eius. I will give glory to the Lord according to his justice.* These are words of thanksgiving of the most-high Christ to God for all those things previously stated. *I will give glory*, he says, *to the Lord*, that is, to God the Father or to the entire Trinity, *according to his justice*, by which he exalted me, freed me, and raised me again, and destroyed the incredulous: *et psallam nomini Domini altissimi, and I will sing to the name of the Lord most high*, that is, I will say praises to the triune and most simple God.

---

45  John 12:10, 11.
46  Matt. 27:25b.
47  *Cf.* John 10:16b.

# ARTICLE XXV

## TROPOLOGICAL EXPLANATION OF THIS SEVENTH PSALM

7[1]  *The psalm of David which he sung to the Lord for the words of Chusi the son of Iemini.*

*Psalmus David, quem cantavit Domino pro verbis Chusi, filii Iemini.*

HE SENSE OF THE TITLE OF THIS PSALM above, according to a tropological exposition, is thus:    7[1] *In finem,*[48] *psalmus David, in the end, the Psalm of David,* that is, this Psalm is directing us to the end, that is in Christ, is attributed to David, that is, the faithful person, which is a revelation of the mystery of Christ: *quem, which* Psalm that faithful person *cantavit Domino, sung to the Lord,* that is to the praise of God, *pro verbis Chusi, for the words of Chusi,* that is, for the manifesting of the high silence, which Christ contended with against the Jews, hiding his mystery in his Passion.

---

7[2]  *O Lord my God, in you have I put my trust: save me from all them that persecute me, and deliver me.*

*Domine Deus meus, in te speravi; salvum me fac ex omnibus persequentibus me, et libera me.*

7[3]  *Lest at any time he seize upon my soul like a lion, while there is no one to redeem me, nor to save.*

*Nequando rapiat ut leo animam meam, dum non est qui redimat, neque qui salvum faciat.*

The faithful man, therefore, desiring to entreat God, first alleges merit, saying:    7[2] *Domine Deus meus, in te speravi, O Lord my God, in you have I put my trust:* doing this so that through such an introduction he might attract the attention of the ears of the divine mercy, and that he conceive in himself a greater confidence of being heard. For by hoping in the Lord he is found worthy to be heard by him. And so, *Domine, O Lord,* of all things; *Deus meus, my God,* because of a singular affection and fervor of heart in you, *in te speravi, in you have I put my trust.*  For *cursed be the man that trusts in man, and makes flesh his arm.*[49] Conse-

---

48  *See* footnote 7-22.
49  Jer. 17:5.

quently, I will hope in you, because you alone are able to save me. But, see to it, O slave of God, that these things truly befit you; see to it that he who is Lord of all things, and is in particular your God, so that with total and pure and integrated soul you might adhere to him, that you might cast off far away from you all affections that separate you from the love of the highest good: because *one thing is necessary.*[50] Blessed is the man who is able in to speak to God in this fashion: *My God.* This is not so of all men, but only if one looks to the perfect. For the most holy and most divine Dionysius [the Areopagite][51] in his books writes: *God, and if I may say so, my.*[52] He did not dare absolutely to say, *My God:* which, however, he could say most truly, because ignited by the love of God, he was marvelously on fire like a red-hot iron or a glowing coal.

*Salvum me fac ex omnibus persequentibus me, save me from all them that persecute me,* so that I may not be vanquished by the temptations of the devil, nor be stained by the enticements of the flesh, nor seduced by the world; *et libera me, and deliver me* from the bonds of sin, and from the evil yet to come.     7[3] *Nequando rapiat, lest at any time he seize,* he, the persecutor and enemy, *ut leo animam meam, upon my soul like a lion,* drawing my soul to consent to sin, or causing it to fall in another manner. Whence in the first epistle of Peter we are taught: *Be sober and watch: because your adversary the devil, as a roaring lion, goes about seeking whom he may devour. Whom you must resist, strong in faith.*[53]

---

7[4]  *O Lord my God, if I have done this thing, if there be iniquity in my hands,*

   *Domine Deus meus, si feci istud, si est iniquitas in manibus meis,*

7[5]  *If I have rendered to them that repaid me evils, let me deservedly fall empty before my enemies.*

   *Si reddidi retribuentibus mihi mala, decidam merito ab inimicis meis inanis.*

7[4] *Domine Deus meus, se feci istud, O Lord my God, if I have done this thing* that follows, namely, *si est iniquitas in manibus meis, if there be iniquity in my hands,* that is in my deeds and in my words: not that I have never sinned, or that I am immune from all sin (for *if we say*

---

50  Luke 10:42a.
51  For Dionysius the Areopagite, *see* footnote P-36.
52  L. *Deus, et si fas est dicere, meus.*
53  1 Pet. 5:8, 9a.

*that we have no sin, we deceive ourselves;*[54] and *no one is clean from stain, though his life be but one day upon earth*[55]); and therefore I say, there is no iniquity in my hands, because I do not intend to harm anyone, and you, O Lord, I purpose faithfully to obey, and I sorrow for my past sins: and so I believe myself pure from all mortal sin, especially with regard to that which follows.   7[5] *Si reddidi retribuentibus mihi mala, if I have rendered to them that repaid me evils,* that is, if I have avenged myself, if I have not been kindly indulgent with my neighbor, if I have not fulfilled that commanded by the Apostle: *Be not overcome by evil, but overcome evil by good;*[56] *decidam merito ab inimicis meis inanis, let me deservedly fall empty before my enemies,* that is, then deservedly will my adversaries prevail over me. For if iniquity is found in my hands, that is, consent to sinning, the resolution of causing harm, and if I have avenged myself, then I do not deserve to be heard by you: and so destitute of works and of your grace, from the outset I will fall and will be deficient. But that which is said, *let me deservedly fall empty before my enemies, etc.* and, *let the enemy pursue, etc.*[57] is not said by way of imprecation or by desire, but by making known the truth.

---

7[6]   *Let the enemy pursue my soul, and take it, and tread down my life on the earth, and bring down my glory to the dust.*

*Persequatur inimicus animam meam, et comprehendat; et conculcet in terra vitam meam, et gloriam meam in pulverem deducat.*

If, I say, *I have rendered to them that repaid me evils,*   7[6] *persequatur inimicus animam meam, et comprehendat, let the enemy pursue my soul, and take it*: that is, because then by all means I have deserved to suffer this persecution. *Let the enemy,* that is the tempter, that is to say, the devil or the world or the fomes or tinder of sin (*fomes peccati*), *pursue my soul,* trying to induce it to fault; *and take it,* that is, to hold it captive in the law of sin; *et conculcet in terra vitam meam, and tread down my life on the earth,* that is, that it may subject the affection of my soul to temporal and worldly things, and that it my attach my actions to lowly and vile things. And this in the manner that Jeremiah said to the Lord: *they that depart from you, shall be written in the earth;*[58] *et gloriam meam*

---

54  1 John 1:8a.
55  Job 14:4 (antiq. vers.)
56  Rom. 12:21.
57  E. N. This refers to the beginning of Ps. 7:5, discussed in the next paragraph.
58  Jer. 17:13.

*in pulverem deducat, and bring down my glory to the dust,* that is, the intellectual portion of my soul, by which I am separated from the brute beasts and [by which] I am ordered with the image of the most high Trinity, may be so darkened that I might consider myself as if irrational, and compare myself to a senseless beast of burden.

From this all is taught and commended to us the virtue of patience, that we might not do harm to or desire to harm anyone, not demanding any vengeance, not entertaining the zeal of bitterness regarding anyone, but rather forgiving from the heart; because in no other manner are we able to be heard by the Lord; but we must lay bare and uncover all the traps of our enemies, in the manner that the sage states: *He who seeks to revenge himself, shall find vengeance from the Lord. Man to man reserves anger, and does he seek remedy of God? He has no mercy on a man like himself . . .* and *who shall obtain pardon for his sins?*[59] And there are three grades of patience. The first is to suffer with equanimity that punishment occasioned by the committed fault. The second is to undergo an occasioned unjust punishment without sorrow. The third is not only to tolerate the occasioned [unjust punishment] with joy, but also to return good for evil. Of these grades of patience, the first is the lowest, and it is necessary for salvation; and it is that of which the Savior said, *In your patience you shall possess your souls.*[60] The second grade is higher; it is the one asserted by Peter in his first epistle, *For this is thankworthy, if for conscience towards God, a man endure sorrows, suffering wrongfully.*[61] But the third grade is the highest, which to imitate is a thing of Christian perfection.

---

7[7]  *Rise up, O Lord, in your anger: and be exalted in the borders of my enemies. And arise, O Lord my God, in the precept which you have commanded:*

*Exsurge, Domine, in ira tua; et exaltare in finibus inimicorum meorum; et exsurge, Domine Deus meus, in praecepto quod mandasti:*

7[8]  *And a congregation of people shall surround you. And for their sakes return you on high.*

*Et synagoga populorum circumdabit te: et propter hanc in altum regredere.*

---

59  Ecclus. 23:1a, 3, 4a, 5b.
60  Luke 21:19.
61  1 Pet. 2:19.

After this, the faithful person prays for the Resurrection of Christ, by which is revealed his hidden divinity. And this is able to be the prayer of the ancient saints, saying:    7[7] *Exsurge, Domine, Rise up, O Lord*, O Christ and Messiah King, from death, *in ira tua, in your anger*, justly forsaking the obstinate and the unbelieving, and mercifully calling the faithful elect; *et exaltare in finibus inimicorum meorum, and be you exalted in the borders of my enemies.* This statement has been sufficiently explained in the prior article. But it is able to be explained otherwise in this place: *Rise up, O Lord*, that is, save me, and make me to rise up from the torpor of sloth, and from all vice; and *be you exalted in the borders of my enemies*, that is, by charity and faith reign and inhabit my body and all my members, in which thrive the law of sin,[62] and in the strength of my soul, in which even more amply dominates the infection or tinder (*fomes*) of original sin. And these powers are the concupiscible and irascible appetites, the reason, and the will, in which are to be found the four wounds of the soul: for in the concupiscible appetite is concupiscence; in the irascible appetite, weakness; in the reason, ignorance; and in the will, malice. In this, therefore, O Lord, *be you exalted* and reign, expelling vice, subjecting the body to the spirit, adorning the natural powers with the virtues, so that they might not be outside the *borders of my enemies*, that is, that they may not be otherwise ruled by the devil and vice.

*Et exsurge, Domine Deus meus, and arise, O Lord my God*, hearing and helping me, *in praecepto quod mandasti, in the precept which you have commanded*, that is, giving the power to follow and to implement the precepts by which you have commanded us to abstain from carnal desires,[63] and live our lives *soberly, justly, and godly.*[64]    7[8] *Et synagoga populorum circumdabit te, and a congregation of people shall surround you*: that is, if you were to give me that grace to live in a holy manner, surely many would be edified by my example and would be converted to you: and so a congregation of people will flock to you praying for grace, and you would give them that same kind of life that you gave me. And so following this: *et propter hanc, and for their sakes*, that is the salvation of the congregation or the faithful people, *in altum regredere, return you on high*, that is, in the highest part of my soul rule and preside, directing all my works so as to accord with the dominion (*imperium*) of divine law and right reason.

---

62  *Cf.* Rom. 7:23.
63  *Cf.* 1 Pet. 2:11b.
64  Tit. 2:12.

7[9] *The Lord judges the people. Judge me, O Lord, according to my justice, and according to my innocence in me.*

*Dominus iudicat populos. Iudica me, Domine, secundum iustitiam meam, et secundum innocentiam meam super me.*

7[10] *The wickedness of sinners shall be brought to naught: and you shall direct the just: the searcher of hearts and reins is God.*

*Consumetur nequitia peccatorum; et diriges iustum, scrutans corda et renes, Deus.*

7[9] *Iudica me, Domine, secundum iustitiam meam. Judge me, O Lord, according to my justice.* This is the prayer of the perfect man, who is not puffed up with his perfection, but thankful to the Lord, knowing his merits to be the gifts of God; and his good is recalled not to his own praise, but to the honor of the Creator. And so he says: *Iudica me, Domine, Judge me, O Lord*, that is, discern and separate me from the society of evil men, that I might not take part in them by act or by desire. For however much I might live with them in terms of locale, nevertheless in the future life I will be separated from them by place and glory, *according to my justice*, by the good that I have done, *et secundum innocentiam meam, and according to my innocence*, by the evil from which I turned away.  7[10] *Consumetur nequitia peccatorum, the wickedness of sinners shall be brought to naught*, that is it will not last a long time, but all persecution and temptation of evil which oppresses the just will receive its end. For brief are all those things which afflict us in any manner,[65] but eternal are the joys wherein the just take rest; and eternal are the torments where the ungodly remain. *Et diriges iustum, and you shall direct the just*: that is, you will put in order their thoughts, affections, words and deeds, and you will guide them rightly to you, who are the ultimate end of all things. And the rest of the Psalm which remains may be explained as it was explained earlier.

But attend to yourself, O brother, since you sing or read this Psalm, that your mouth does not condemn you, namely if there is iniquity, that is, an evil will, or an impenitent heart, in your hands, that is, in the practical use of your powers; and that you do not will to do evil to do those who have done evil, but desire to return good for evil. And forgive if you have anything against anyone, that also the heavenly Father might forgive you. For as we know, patience is of greatest necessity: and who does not have it, will never or at least rarely be at rest.

65 *Cf.* Rom. 8:18.

# PRAYER

O LORD OUR GOD, IN WHOM WE HOPE, deliver your faithful from all visible enemies persecuting them, that receiving from you secure protection, we might continually sing without fear your blessed name.

*Domine Deus noster, in quem speramus, libera fideles tuos ex omnibus se persequentibus inimicis visbilibus, ut te protectore securitate accepta, sine timore iugiter psallamus nomini tuo benedicto.*

# Psalm 8

## ARTICLE XXVI

### EXPOSITION OF THE EIGHTH PSALM:
### DOMINE, DOMINUS NOSTER, QUAM ADMIRABILE, &c.
### O LORD, OUR LORD, HOW ADMIRABLE, &c.

8[1]  Unto the end, for the presses: a Psalm of David.

In finem, pro torcularibus. Psalmus David.

THE SENSE OF THE TITLE OF THIS PSALM above, according to a tropological exposition, is thus:  8[1] In finem, pro torcularibus, psalmus David. Unto the end, for the presses, a Psalm of David: that is, this Psalm is composed by David, in other words, directing us in Christ, written and produced for the presses, that is, for the congregation of the faithful, who during the present time are squeezed by many tribulations as if by certain presses, to the end of being purged from vice.

---

8[2]  O Lord our Lord, how admirable is your name in the whole earth! For your magnificence is elevated above the heavens.

Domine, Dominus noster, quam admirabile est nomen tuum in universa terra! Quoniam elevata est magnificentia tua super caelos.

The prophet is therefore speaking to God in the person of the Church militant, or in any particular one of the faithful imitating the way of Christ, saying  8[2] Domine, O Lord through a universal presiding over all things, Dominus noster, our Lord through special providence, which directs us to eternal life, removing impediments to salvation, for which reason to you alone, as the true God, we singularly [...], quam admirabile est nomen tuum in universa terra! How admirable is your name in the whole earth! That is, how imperviously incomprehensible, and excellent and magnificent you are ineffable, to the men spread over the entire orb of the earth! God [...] holy, in himself entirely invisible, above all essence (supress [...] and utterly unknown to all human minds and wayfarers: be [...]

is held to inhabit inaccessible light[1] and said to Moses, man does not see me, and live.[2]

Moreover, we get to know him to the extent we are able to know him through his effects. But the effects of God are twofold, namely natural and supernatural. And the more sublime and more incomprehensible the effects of God are, the more God is proved from their contemplation to appear more magnificent. For the supernatural effects, which pertain to the mysteries of grace, are more sublime and much more incomprehensible than the natural effects which are observed from the law and order of nature: and yet still in both God is worthy of admiration. But in the supernatural things he is more admirably displayed. Therefore, the blessed God always and everywhere has been sublime and admirable in regard to his natural effects; and from their observation all men are always able to know God, the incomprehensible creator. But by means of supernatural effects, God was especially admirable in the land of the Hebrews at the time of the Mosaic law: as it says in a later Psalm: *In Judea God is known: his name is great in Israel.*[3] But during the time of grace and the evangelical law, God is made admirable not only in land, namely, Judaea,[4] but indeed in the entire earth, wherever the Gospel of the Kingdom of God is preached: because God, through his servants, has performed great miracles in all the ends of the earth, and he has displayed to all men the hidden and secret things of his wisdom through the preaching of the Apostles revealing the mystery of the Incarnation, Passion, Resurrection, and Ascension of Christ, and the other marvelous testimonies of the Christian law and faith, and from all of which the mightily admirable and thoroughly inscrutable name of the Lord is made known to all the ⸻ of the world, in the manner the Apostle stated: *O the depth ⸻ of the wisdom and of the knowledge of God! How incompreh⸻ ⸻dgments, and how unsearchable his ways!*[5]

⸻rit, therefore, the supernatural works of God in ⸻Christ that would be manifest to the whole world, ⸻the most blessed David said *O Lord, our Lord, how ⸻me in the whole earth!* And although this can be said to ⸻s it is of any divine Person, it can especially be referred ⸻hence he suggests immediately thereafter the reason for

⸻ :16.
1  Cf. ⸻
3  Cf⸻
4  Ma⸻
5  Ro⸻

this admirableness: *Quoniam elevata est magnificentia tua, for your magnificence is elevated*: that is, you yourself, who are great and magnificent, are exalted *super caelos, above the heavens*: in the manner the Apostles says, *He that descended is the same also that ascended above all the heavens, that he might fill all things.*[6] For from this that Christ ascended and is seated with God the Father, his name has been made admirable in all the earth, because it was then that he sent the Holy Spirit, and the Apostles began to preach for he it is *who was appointed by God, to be judge of the living and of the dead.*[7] Therefore, Christ according to both of his natures is admirable, although most maximally according to his divine nature; but the elevation also applies to him by reason of his human nature.

---

8[3] *Out of the mouth of infants and of sucklings you have perfected praise, because of your enemies, that you may destroy the enemy and the avenger.*

*Ex ore infantium et lactentium perfecisti laudem propter inimicos tuos, ut destruas inimicum et ultorem.*

8[3] *Ex ore infantium et lactentium perfecisti laudem propter inimicos tuos. Out of the mouth of infants and sucklings you have perfected praise, because of your enemies.* This cannot be better explained than by literal reference to that praise which in the day of Palms the children of the Hebrews encountering Christ exclaimed: *Hosanna to the son of David: Blessed is he that comes in the name of the Lord,*[8] *the king of Israel.*[9] For Christ responded to the indignant princes of the priests, who were displeased at him being praised that way: *Have you never read: Out of the mouth of infants and of sucklings you have perfected praise?*[10] It is as if he had said: "You who are the teachers in Israel should have recognized this verse deservedly to have been prophesied of me, and now being fulfilled in me."

And therefore the Church says to Christ: *out of the mouth of infants and sucklings*, that is, out of the mouth of children and simple men: who are said to be *infants* because they are illiterate; and *sucklings*, because they are innocent, in the manner that the Apostle says, *Do not become children in sense: but in malice be children*;[11] *perfecisti*, you have perfected,

---

6 Eph. 4:10.
7 Acts 10:42.
8 Matt. 21:9b.
9 John 12:13b.
10 Matt. 21:16.
11 1 Cor. 14:20.

O Christ, *laudem, praise*, because by the inspiration of the Holy Spirit who proceeds from you, you instructed the hearts of the aforesaid children, so that they might so praise you; *propter inimicos tuos, because of your enemies*, that is, because confounding the unbelievers just as the Apostle stated, that *the weak things of the world God has chosen, that he may confound the strong;*[12] *ut destruas, that you might destroy*, that is, at the present time you might remove from grace, and in the future repulse from glory, *inimicum, the enemy*, that is, the people of the Jews that opposed you, *et ultorum, and the avenger*, that is, the same people persecuting you, who killed you as though you were a blasphemer and a man unfaithful to the law, and so they saw themselves as vindicating the injury done to God by acting against you. Whence, other translations have [in place of avenger] the word defender (*defensorem*). For the Jews excused themselves from sin in regard to the killing of Christ, defending themselves by the law, which they said was not observed by Jesus. For they said: *This man is not of God, who keeps not the sabbath.*[13]

This part is also able to be explained in another way, so that it has this sense: *out of mouth of infants and sucklings*, that is, from the preaching and doctrine of the Apostles, who are called infants and sucklings, not by reason of their age, but as a result of comparing them to the peculiar quality of children, just as the Savior says: *Unless you be converted, and become as little children, you shall not enter into the kingdom of heaven.*[14] And the Apostle: *As newborn babes, desire the rational milk without guile.*[15] *Perfecisti, you have perfected*, O Lord, *laudem, praise*, that is, you have promulgated the evangelical law, in which is contained your praise; *ut destruas, that you may destroy*, that is, confound and reprove, *inimicum, the enemy*, that is, every philosopher of this world, extolling himself, and laughing at the simplicity of faith, *et ultorem, and the avenger*, that is, every tyrant and persecutor of the faithful. And due to this fact — that all the world was converted by these illiterate, ineloquent, few, and simple men to such an incomprehensible and exceedingly marvelous faith of Christ — [16] it is evident proof that this faith is from God; because unless God had been operating supernaturally through these men, in no manner would the world have been able to be converted. Thus it confounded the inane loquacity of the philosophers, and the furious rage of the tyrant, and so such were left behind and rejected;

12  1 Cor. 1:27b.
13  John 9:16a.
14  Matt. 18:3.
15  1 Pet. 2:2.
16  *Cf.* 1 Cor. 1:17 *et seq.*

and the illiterate and simple were elected by God, and were moved up to such a height of grace, in the manner that in a later Psalm is said of the Apostles: *For the strong gods of the earth are exceedingly exalted.* [17]

---

8[4]  *For I will behold your heavens, the works of your fingers: the moon and the stars which you have founded.*

*Quoniam videbo caelos tuos, opera digitorum tuorum, lunam et stellas quae tu fundasti.*

8[5]  *What is man that you are mindful of him? Or the son of man that you visit him?*

*Quid est homo, quod memor es eius? Aut filius hominis, quoniam visitas eum?*

8[4] *Quoniam videbo caelos tuus. For I will behold your heavens.* This can be explained in two ways, namely spiritually or mystically; and so it refers to that which was stated before it, for it is now ascribed to their cause, so that is understood in this sense: *O Lord, our Lord, how admirable is your name in the whole earth!* And *out of the mouth of infants and sucklings you have perfected praise*: and therefore this I say, and I know, *for I will behold*, that is, I will spiritually contemplate and will consider *your heavens*, that is, the holy Apostles, in whom you inhabit as in heaven, *opera digitorum tuorum, the works of your fingers*, that is, the creatures of your wisdom, which you distinguished in the most orderly way, giving different gifts of graces. And not only do I see these heavens, but also I consider *lunam, the moon*, that is, the Church militant, receiving all its light from Christ, the Sun of Justice, *et stellas, quae tu fundasti, and the stars which you have founded*, that is, orthodox men, faithful to the highest level, or the holy Doctors, who instruct others with their word, life, and wisdom, of which Daniel says, *they that instruct many to justice, as stars for all eternity.* [18] These stars you, O God, *have founded*, that is, by the Holy Spirit you have instructed, and you have fixed most strongly in the faith, as the stars are affixed in the heavenly orb.

This part can also be explained literally, and so it refers to that which follows, as in this sense: *For I will behold your heavens*, that is, from that which I behold (and I know the heavens to be yours, that is, created by you), and *I behold the moon and stars, which you have founded*, that is, you have fashioned them from nothing to be something stable and

---

17  Ps. 46:10.
18  Dan. 12:3b.

incorruptible, in the manner that is written, *The Lord by wisdom has founded the earth, has established the heavens by prudence.*[19] From this, I say, *I behold* these, because I turn towards and I say, O Lord:    8[5] *Quid est homo quod memor es eius? What is man that you are mindful of him?* That is, it is from the fact that I know the heavens, the moon, and the stars to be your works it stands out clearly that man is a thing so vile and so slight, especially in comparison to you, that it is a marvel that *you are mindful* of man, rescuing him by mercy and grace. *Aut, or* what is *filius hominis, the son of man,* that is, Christ, according to the fact that he is man and a creature in a certain manner, *quoniam visitas eum, that you visit him,* assuming his human nature to the personal union of your divine nature? For this was done, O Lord, not by previous merit (*merita praevia*) of the man Christ, but only by your uncreated grace.

Again, this and what follows can be understood to refer to Christ literally, hence it follows that the Apostle by this scripture shows the excellence of Christ to be above that of the angels. For he says: *For God has not subjected unto angels the world;*[20] *but we see Jesus, who was made a little lower than the angels, for the suffering of death, crowned with glory and honor.*[21] But an argument from the authority of Scripture is not strong unless it is in accordance with a literal understanding, as has explained above.

---

8[6]    *You have made him a little less than the angels, you have crowned him with glory and honor:*

*Minuisti eum paulo minus ab angelis; gloria et honore coronasti eum:*

8[6] *Minuisti, You have a little less,* O Lord God, *eum, him,* that is to say, Christ as man, *paulo minus ab angelis, a little less than the angels,* that is, in a certain manner you have made him inferior to the angels, obviously in that he was made passible and mortal. *Gloria et honore coronasti eum. You have crowned him with glory and honor.* Glory is a brilliant knowledge with praise (*clara cum laude notitia*);[22] but true honor

---

19  Prov. 3:19.
20  Heb. 2:5a.
21  Heb. 2:9a.
22  E. N. This is a reference to St. Augustine's definition of glory (*Contr. Max. Haer. Ar. Ep.*, II, 13, 2) adopted by St. Thomas Aquinas (though attributed by him to St. Ambrose): *Gloria est clara notitia cum laude,* which has been variously translated as a "clear recognition with praise," "a brilliant celebrity with praise," See *ST,* IaIIae, q. 2, art. 3, co. Josef Pieper expounds this phrase as "'fame,' as being publicly taken notice of and recognized by God himself." Josef Pieper, *Faith, Hope, Love* (San Francisco: Ignatius Press 1997).

is showing of reverence as a sign of virtue (*exhibitio reverentiae in signum virtutis*).[23] Therefore, God *crowned*, that is, fully and in multiple ways adorned Christ in glory in order that he might reveal to men his majesty, giving them a brilliant knowledge of Christ; he *crowned* him also with honor, in that he led all the elect to venerate him. And thus he *crowned* Christ with honor and glory, because according to the merit of his obedience, Passion, and Death, he raised him from the dead, glorified him in body, exalted him above all the heavens, and placed him at his right hand. And this is what the Apostle said: Christ became for us *obedient unto death . . . for which cause God also has exalted him, and has given him a name which is above all names, so that in the name of Jesus every knee should bow, of those that are in heaven, on earth, and under the earth.*[24]

---

8[7]   *And have set him over the works of your hands.*

*Et constituisti eum super opera manuum tuarum.*

8[8]   *You have subjected all things under his feet, all sheep and oxen: moreover the beasts also of the fields:*

*Omnia subiecisti sub pedibus eius, oves et boves universas, insuper et pecora campi.*

8[7] *Et constituisti eum super opera manuum tuarum. And you have set him over the works of your hands.* And so God *set him over the works* of his *hands*, for he placed him before and preferred him above all other creatures. For Christ as man also purifies, illumines, and perfects the highest of the angels, according to Denis [the Areopagite]; *and of his fulness we all have received.*[25] And this he manifests more clearly, saying:   8[8] *Omnia subiecisti sub pedibus eius, you have subjected all things under his feet:* that is, not only have you visited upon Christ according as man the things previously stated, but also *you have subjected all things under his feet,* that is, you made subject to the power of Christ insofar as he is man the whole universe, visible and invisible, rational and non-rational, intellectual and anything else remaining. For all things which Christ as God created are subjected to him as man by God the Father or the entire Trinity. As he said after his Resurrection: *All power is given to me in heaven and in earth.*[26] Indeed from the first moment of his Incarnation,

---

23   E. N. This definition is Aristotelian through St. Thomas. See *ST*, IIaIIae, q. 103, art. 1.
24   Phil. 2:8a, 9–10.
25   John 1:16.
26   Matt. 28:18b.

all things were subject to him according to his union with the Word; but after the Resurrection, this subjection began to be known more fully when in the name of Christ great and many miracles began to be done.

---

8[9] *The birds of the air, and the fishes of the sea, that pass through the paths of the sea.*

*Volucres caeli, et pisces maris qui perambulant semitas maris.*

Consequently, that which was said generally, is given more specificity: *Oves et boves universas, insuper et pecora campi,* 8[9] *volucres caeli, et pisces maris, qui perambulant semitas maris. All sheep and oxen: moreover the beasts also of the fields,* 8[9] *the birds of the air, and the fishes of the sea, that pass through the paths of the sea.* That, it seems to some, ought not to be taken literally. But although it can be interpreted to harmonize with a mystical meaning, it is also can literally refer to beasts, which are said to be subject to Christ, not only as the rest of men are, but because they obey him in those things which transcend the natural law and the order of things, namely in miraculous effects. Whence Christ said to his Apostles: *And these signs shall follow them that believe: In my name they shall cast out devils: they shall speak with new tongues, they shall take up serpents; and if they shall drink any deadly thing, it shall not hurt them.*[27] And many of the Saints, acting in the power of Christ, supernaturally made animals submit in this manner.

Expositing it truly mystically, by *sheep* we understand the good faithful, of whom the Lord spoke when he said to Peter, *Feed my sheep.*[28] By *oxen* we understand teachers (*doctores*) teachers, who cultivate and make fertile the divine words in the hearts of the believers. By *beasts of the fields* we understand the delicate and fleshly, which, like animals, graze themselves. By *birds of the air* we comprehend the proud and those boasting of themselves; or also of the contemplatives, whose *conversation is in heaven.*[29] For by *beasts* one is able to comprehend the good Christians, who following Christ are able to say: *For your sake we are put to death all the day long. We are accounted as sheep for the slaughter.*[30] And by *fish of the sea* we understand, they who wander about and are driven here and there with worldly things: for these *pass through the paths of the sea,* that is, this age, of which in a later Psalm is said, *So is*

---

27 Mark 16:17-18a.
28 John 21:17b.
29 Phil. 3:20.
30 Rom. 8:36.

*this great sea, which stretches wide its arms.*[31] For all these kinds of men are subject to Christ, because he is able to save those whom he wishes, and he will with power and justice judge all men and every single man. And because for a time the reprobate are joined in the Church with the elect, and by faith they are subject to Christ, some of the evil are also converted to him through charity and the purity of life, as the Apostle testifies to, for *Christ came into this world to save sinners.*[32]

8[10]   *O Lord our Lord, how admirable is your name in all the earth!*

*Domine, Dominus noster, quam admirabile est nomen tuum in universa terra!*

Finally, inflamed by the consideration of these marvels, and spiritually exhilarated, the holy Prophet [David] repeats in this Psalm the beginning exordium, saying:   8[10] *Domine, Dominus noster, quam admirabile est nomen tuum in universa terra! O Lord, our Lord, how admirable is your name in all the earth!*

In this Psalm, therefore, is most evidently declared by the holy David the dual nature of Christ, namely the divine and human, and of the unity of person, as also was done in the second Psalm, and as he does often in those that follow below.

Because this Psalm is suitable for the praise of the Godhead, and for the recollection of his benefits, it ought to be always brought forth with enormous joy of heart and great fervor of charity, as we might rejoice in the Lord our God, and we might show him thanks for his benefits.

## MORAL INTERPRETATION

8[5]   *What is man that you are mindful of him? Or the son of man that you visit him?*

*Quid est homo, quod memor es eius? Aut filius hominis, quoniam visitas eum?*

8[6]   *You have made him a little less than the angels, you have crowned him with glory and honor:*

*Minuisti eum paulo minus ab angelis; gloria et honore coronasti eum:*

---

31  Ps. 103:25a.

32  1 Tim. 1:15 (E. N. the Sixto-Clementine Vulgate has "Christ Jesus").

**8[7]** *And have set him over the works of your hands.*

*Et constituisti eum super opera manuum tuarum.*

Morally, on the other hand, we can expound this Psalm, from that part where it states, *Who is man*, as understanding it to refer to any man, so that it has this sense:    **8[5]** *Quid est homo quod memor es eius, what is man that you are mindful of him?* assuming that it refers to human nature. *Aut filius hominis*, *or the son of man*, that is, anyone of the race of Adam, *quoniam visitas eum, that you visit him*, not only spiritually by the infusion of grace, but also bodily after the Incarnation moving about among men? This is in the manner that Baruch says: He who made the stars, *this is our God, . . . and afterwards he was seen upon earth, and conversed with men.*[33] Or [we can understand it thus], *you visit him* through the apparitions of angels, by the oracles of the prophets, by the preaching of the Apostles, by the operation of signs.    **8[6]** *Minuisti eum paulo minus ab angelis, you have made him a little less than the angels*: that is, you have so exceedingly raised men by these benefits that have been mentioned, so it would appear as if made the equivalent (*parificatus*) of angels, and but a small distance from their dignity. And this he clearly establishes by saying, *gloria et honore coronasti eum, you have crowned him with glory and honor*, that is, you have made him spectacular and honorable in the minds of the angels. And this because God so visited and benefited men, that the holy angels ascribe them worthy of glory and honor, and most diligently they watch over them, and most reverentially minister to them. Or [alternatively], *you have crowned him with glory and honor*, that is, you have adorned their soul with the image of the Holy Trinity: on account of which they are more sublime and more excellent than all irrational creatures. And hence is added:    **8[7]** *Et constituisti eum super omnia opera manuum tuarum*, and you have set him over all *the works of your hands*. For all elements and compounds God created for us, and he ordained them to our utility, necessity, and use.

---

**8[8]** *You have subjected all things under his feet, all sheep and oxen: moreover the beasts also of the fields:*

*Omnia subiecisti sub pedibus eius, oves et boves universas, insuper et pecora campi.*

**8[8]** *Omnia subiecisti sub pedibus eius, you have subjected all things under his feet*: not simply all things, but all things which are subordinate

---

33  *Cf.* Baruch 3:35b, 36a, 38.

to them, *oves et boves universas*, etc., *all sheep and oxen*, etc. Not that all these obey entirely man at will, and never inflict harm upon him; but because man naturally is of greater dignity than them, for he is created in the image and likeness of God. Moreover, we are even able to say that the angels and heavenly bodies are in a certain manner subject to man, in that they minister to him. For of the angels the Apostle [Paul] said that they are all *ministering spirits, sent to minister for* the elect.[34] And of the orbits of the heavens and the plans and the stars, Moses said: *Lest lifting your eyes up to heaven, you see the sun and the moon, and all the stars of heaven, and being deceived by error you adore and serve them, which the Lord your God created for the service of all the nations, that are under heaven.*[35]

Whether this part of the Psalm is interpreted of Christ, or of any man, it always declares that error of the Manichaeans[36] who say that those things that are corruptible or corporal in nature were not created by the God of light; this is the error also of certain philosophers, who posit that these variable and irrational things are not subject to divine providence: and of which persons it is stated in the Book of Job: *Do you not think that God is higher than heaven,*[37] *and that he does not consider our things, and he walks about the poles of heaven?*[38] From this which is stated above is destroyed the opinion of the Pythagoreans,[39] which said that it was a sacrilege to kill and eat brute animals.

---

34 Heb. 1:14a. *E. N.* Denis believed St. Paul to be author of the epistle to the Hebrews. This was the traditional majority view, though there was some controversy to it. St. Jerome, for example, in his letter to Dardanus, the prefect of Gaul, writes: "the epistle which is inscribed to the Hebrews (*ad Hebraeos*) is received not only by the churches of the east, but by all past church writers of the Greek tongue as the apostle Paul's, but many allow as legitimate [opinion] as it being either by Barnabas or Clement. It is of not of great interest whose it is, since it is the work of a churchman and daily is celebrated in the reading of the churches." PL 22, 1103. For this reason, St. Jerome placed *Hebrews* at the end of what he thought were St. Paul's unquestionable works.

35 Deut. 4:19.

36 *E. N.* The Manicheans were the followers of the Persian religious leader known as Mani (*ca.* 216–275/77 A. D.), who taught a dualistic cosmology, and posited two equal principles or gods, a good god of spirit and an evil god that created matter. The material world was thus thought as opposed to good.

37 Job 22:12a.

38 Job 22:14b.

39 Originating in the 6th century B. C., Pythagoreanism — founded upon the teachings of the philosopher Pythagoras (*ca.* 570–490 B. C.), emphasized the incorporeal over the corporeal. Its followers abstained from eating flesh.

# ARTICLE XXVII

## ANALOGICAL EXPOSITION OF THIS EIGHTH PSALM

8[2]    *O Lord our Lord, how admirable is your name in the whole earth! For your magnificence is elevated above the heavens.*

*Domine, Dominus noster, quam admirabile est nomen tuum in universa terra! Quoniam elevata est magnificentia tua super caelos.*

RIEFLY, THIS PSALM, UNDERSTOOD ANA-gogically, may be expounded to be about the Church triumphant or about anyone of the blessed in heaven. The Church triumphant (which consists of the society of angels and men), therefore, always contemplating the face of the Holy Trinity, though it does not have the ability to comprehend him perfectly, says:    8[2] *Domine, O Lord* of all things through your omnipotence, *Dominus noster, our Lord,* through the blessed enjoyment and consummate glory, *quam admirabilem est nomen tuum, how admirable is your name,* that is, how incomprehensible, *in universa terra, in the whole earth,* that is, in all of the regions of the living, in all the land of the living, in the minds of all the heavenly citizens! For only God can comprehend himself perfectly, and so is added: *Quoniam elevata est magnificentia tua, for your magnificence is elevated,* that is, the sublimeness of your majesty is elevated, *super caelos, above the heavens,* that is, above all the capacity and knowledge of the heavenly intellects. For since God, blessed and holy, is truly immense, he infinitely transcends the capacity of all created and finite intellects. And therefore, the saints in heaven, although they see God as he is, that is to say by sight, all the same they do not know God in such a clear and plain fashion as he is able to know himself. It is for this reason that the Psalm says: *Your magnificence is elevated* not by reason of movement or of place, since he is unmovable and is not fixed in any place, but through dignity and incomprehensibility.

8[3]    *Out of the mouth of infants and of sucklings you have perfected praise, because of your enemies, that you may destroy the enemy and the avenger.*

*Ex ore infantium et lactentium perfecisti laudem propter inimicos tuos, ut destruas inimicum et ultorem.*

**8[3]** *Ex ore infantium et lactentium perfecisti laudem. Out of the mouth of infants and sucklings you have perfected praise.* This the blessed in heaven are able to say literally to the glory of God, of the souls of the Holy Innocents slain by Herod, indeed of the spirits of all the elect children who have died before the age of reason, who at the time of the natural law were saved by the faith of the parents, and during the time of the written law by circumcision, and during the time of the law of grace by baptism. *Out of their mouths,* that is, in their minds, God in heaven brings to perfection their praise, because he makes it so that they unceasingly are able to praise him. *Propter inimicos tuos, because of your enemies* confounding them, namely as you confound Lucifer and his angels, when they see the souls of children to be lifted up on high to the glory from which they were cast down; *ut destruas inimicum, that you may destroy the enemy,* that is, that first apostate, the adversary of the human race, *et ultorem, and the avenger,* that is, the same person, who is called the avenger, because he seduced the first parents and he, with his surrounding attendants, never ceases to tempt the human race.

And this Psalm can also be explained as referring to all the Saints in heaven, because however great they are in wisdom and greatness, yet in comparison to the immense wisdom and infinite power of the Creator, they are as *infants and sucklings.* Whence from their humility, and out of the reverence of God they say to God of themselves: *From the mouths of infants and sucklings,* that is, from the minds of humble angels and men, *perfecisti laudem tuam, you have perfected* your *praise,* revealing to them your essence, which — they beholding — they always praise you, *propter inimicus tuus, because of your enemies,* that is, so that you might reject the proud angels and all sons of pride, *ut destruas, so that you may destroy,* that is, that you might deprive from the longed-for end, and you might eternally condemn, *inimicum et ultorum, the enemy and the avenger,* that is, the powers of the air which wrestle continually against us.[40]

---

8[4] *For I will behold your heavens, the works of your fingers: the moon and the stars which you have founded.*

Quoniam videbo caelos tuos, opera digitorum tuorum, lunam et stellas quae tu fundasti.

Next the Church triumphant or any one of the blessed says to God:     8[4] *Quoniam videbo caelos tuos, opera digitorum tuorum,* for I

---

40 *Cf.* Eph. 6:12.

*will behold your heavens, the works of your fingers*, that is, all the angelic
orders and blessed souls in which you dwell by fully enjoyed charity and
glory; and I will see *lunam, the moon*, that is, the humanity of Christ,
which is united with the Son of justice, the Word or Son of God, *et
stellas, and the stars*, that is, also the highest of the blessed, who, having
the resemblance of stars above all others, irradiate from the fullness
of infused divine light and so shine upon the others; *quae tu fundasti,
which you have founded*, that is, that you have confirmed eternally in
your beatific vision.

---

8[5]   *What is man that you are mindful of him? Or the son of man
that you visit him?*

*Quid est homo, quod memor es eius? Aut filius hominis, quoniam
visitas eum?*

8[6]   *You have made him a little less than the angels, you have crowned
him with glory and honor:*

*Minuisti eum paulo minus ab angelis; gloria et honore coronasti eum:*

8[7]   *And have set him over the works of your hands.*

*Et constituisti eum super opera manuum tuarum.*

8[8]   *You have subjected all things under his feet, all sheep and oxen:
moreover the beasts also of the fields:*

*Omnia subiecisti sub pedibus eius, oves et boves universas, insuper
et pecora campi.*

And because this is so, O Lord God,    8[5] *Quid est homo quod memor
es eius, what is man that you are mindful of him*, converting him to you,
and leading him to eternal beatitude? *Aut filius hominis, quoniam visitas
eum, or the son of man, that you visit him*, not only by grace during his
time of wayfaring, but also by glory in heaven?    8[6] *Minuisti eum
paulo minus ab angelis, you have made him a little less than the angels:*
which may be said in that by nature he is inferior to the angels, though
he is similar in the supernatural. For it is promised and given to me
to enjoy a similar beatitude with the angels, as the Savior says, that
they *shall be as the angels of God.*[41] *Gloria et honore*, that is with great
joy and in great excellence, *coronasti eum, you have crowned him*, given
to him angelic felicity;    8[7] *et constituisti eum super opera manuum*

---

41  Matt. 22:30b; Mark 12:25.

*tuarum, and you have set him over the works of your hands:* for,   **8[8]**
*omnia subiecisti sub pedibus eius, for you have subjected all things under his
feet.* This most especially refers to Christ the man, because he is exalted
above all angelic hierarchies; and all angels minister to him at his will.
And the rest of the Psalm that remains is satisfactorily expounded by
the earlier expositions.

# PRAYER

HROUGH YOUR ADMIRABLE NAME
extended by the Apostles throughout all the earth, O Lord
Jesus Christ, perfect the praise of your victory in us, who are the
work of your hands, so that, the enemy brought to ruin, we might
be crowned in perpetual triumph of glory and honor.

*Per admirabile nomen tuum in universa terra, Domine Iesu
Christe, per Apostolos propagatum, perfice laudem
victoriae tuae in nobis, qui sumus opera digitorum
tuorum: ut destructo inimico, perpetuo
gloriae et honoris coronemur triumpho.*

# *Psalm 9*

## ARTICLE XXVIII

### EXPOSITION OF THE NINTH PSALM:
### *CONFITEBOR TIBI, DOMINE.*
### *I WILL GIVE PRAISE TO YOU, O LORD.*

9[1]  *Unto the end, for the hidden things of the Son. A psalm for David. In finem, pro occultis filii. Psalmus David.*

HE TITLE OF THIS PSALM IS:  9[1] *IN FINEM, pro occultis filii, psalmus David, unto the end, for the hidden things of the son, a psalm for David*: that is, this Psalm is directing us in Christ; it was created and written by David for *the hidden things of the Son*, that is, the double judgment of Christ, which is to us hidden, because his judgments are incomprehensible.[1] The first is the judgment of discretion, by which someone is called by mercy, but another is relinquished to justice. The second is also the judgment of examination and retribution, which will occur at the end of time, which, although it will be open and visible, yet the day and time are hidden.[2] This is, therefore, what the Prophet speaks of in this Psalm, speaking in the person of the Church, or in the person of an individual of the faithful: of the dual judgment of Christ, of his judiciary power, and also of the many benefits conferred upon him, and of the evil and damnation of the Antichrist.

---

9[2]  *I will give praise to you, O Lord, with my whole heart: I will relate all your wonders.*

*Confitebor tibi, Domine, in toto corde meo; narrabo omnia mirabilia tua.*

Therefore it says:  9[2] *Confitebor tibi, Domine, in toto corde meo, I will give praise to you, O Lord, with my whole heart*, that is, I will praise you with a complete and sincere affection, as one totally adhering to you, and drawing myself away from all vain things; or *with my whole*

---

1  *Cf.* Rom. 11:33.
2  *Cf.* Matt. 24:36.

*heart*, that is with reason and will, so that my confession of praise will proceed out of wisdom and charity. Of course, a man whose heart has no part attached to fleeting things, or inclined to unprofitable things, but is totally recollected in God confesses and praises the Lord with his whole heart. *Narrabo, I will relate*, that is, I will do all things to your praise, *omnia mirabilia tua, all your wonders*. It seems that this is contrary to that which is said in Ecclesiasticus: *There are many things hidden from us that are greater than these: for we have seen but a few of his works.*[3] And in the book of Job: *Lo, these things are said in part of his ways: and seeing we have heard scarce a little drop of his word, who shall be able to behold the thunder of his greatness?*[4] But also in the Gospel of John the Scripture says: *Many other signs also did Jesus ... which are not written in this book,*[5] *which, if they were written every one, the world itself, I think, would not be able to contain the books that should be written.*[6] In short, what kind of man knows all the wonders which the almighty and boundless God unceasingly performs in heaven, and on earth, and even in unto the abysses [of hell]? The sense, therefore, is this: *I will relate all your wonders*, that is, all your mighty works that are written about in your law or were revealed by you to me. And this is contained in Ecclesiasticus: *Has not the Lord made the saints to declare all his wonderful works, which the Lord Almighty* steadfast in his glory *has firmly settled?*[7]

---

**9**[3]  *I will be glad and rejoice in you: I will sing to your name, O you Most High.*

*Laetabor et exsultabo in te; psallam nomini tuo, Altissime.*

**9**[3] *Laetabor, I will be glad*, with mental joy, *et exsultabo, I will rejoice*, with external gladness which proceeds from interior joy, *in te, in you*, O Lord, not in carnal or vile things; *psallam, I will sing*, that is, I will declare your praise by good works, *nomini tuo, to your name*, that is, to you yourself, *Altissime, O you Most High*, to whom no thing is similar; or, *most high* adverbially, that is, in a most excellent manner, namely exhibiting to you the worship of latria, or the adoration that is proper to you alone.[8] Attend,

---

3  Ecclus. 24:36.
4  Job 26:14.
5  John 20:30.
6  John 21:25.
7  Ecclus. 42:17. E. N. The Sixto-Clementine Vulgate has the verb *stabiliri* (to be established), whereas Denis has the adjective *stabilis* (established).
8  E. N. Denis is saying that the term *Altissime* (*Most High*) may be understood

therefore, to the words of this law, so that you comport yourself to God in accordance with their tenor, confessing him not with an inconstant and unbecoming soul, one other than pleasing to God.

———————

9[4] *When my enemy shall be turned back: they shall be weakened and perish before your face.*

*In convertendo inimicum meum retrorsum; infirmabuntur, et peribunt a facie tua.*

9[4] *In convertendo inimicum meum retrorsum, When my enemy shall be turned back*: that is, when, O Lord, you have converted my enemy, that is, any kind of adversary to my salvation, so as to turn him back, subduing him, and giving me the virtue so that I might resist him; then *infirmabuntur, they shall be weakened*, that is, they will be debilitated, *et peribunt, and will perish*, that is, fall away, *a facie tua, before your face*, that is, from the presence of your grace by which I am able to resist and prevail over him. At first it says *enemy* in an indeterminate manner, stating it singularly but meaning it in a plural manner; therefore, he adjoins to it *they shall be weakened*, where he expresses in a plural manner that which he had previously denominated in singular manner.[9] Looked at morally, anyone tempted by the devil, the flesh, or the world can cry out this verse to God, so as if to say: I without doubt, of my own power, am unable to resist this adversary, but you, O Lord, turning my enemies back will make them fall away. *For if God be for us, who is against us?*[10] This verse is able especially to be considered the word of the Church to Christ, so as to be understood in this sense: *When my enemy shall be turned back*, that is, at the time that you overcame by the merits of your Passion the devil, then also *they shall be weakened*, that is, all my adversaries are weakened. Or [this verse might be understood anagogically in this way], when in the final judgment you will condemn them, then they will perish entirely from your face, because they will go to the eternal fire.

———————

nounally, referring to God, or adverbially, referring to the description of the praise sung to him by us.

9  E. N. Denis observes that the noun *inimicum* (enemy) is singular, whereas the verb *infirmabuntur* (they shall be weakened) is plural; thus, there is a lack of agreement between the singular noun and the plural verb. Denis overcomes this lack of agreement by noting that the noun is used indeterminately and so should be understood in a plural sense, though it is in a singular form.

10  Rom. 8:31.

9[5]  *For you have maintained my judgment and my cause: you have
sat on the throne, who judge justice.*

*Quoniam fecisti iudicium meum et causam meam; sedisti super
thronum, qui iudicas iustitiam.*

9[5] *Quoniam fecisti iudicium meum, for you have maintained my judgment,* that is, you have decreed through your justice between me and
between my adversaries, approving me and disapproving them: for God
performs this judgment every day; *et causam meam fecisti, and* you have
maintained *my cause,* judging in my favor, and commending the reasons
for what I am being judged. God also does this through the Prophets
and the Apostles; and daily does he do this through the ministers of
the Church or the prelates, whose task it is to praise the good and to
reprove the impious. Or thus [can this verse be understood]: *For you
have maintained my judgment,* that is, you have sustained the judgment
of death that I deserved, when it was decreed by Pilate that you be
crucified; and this you patiently endured for my sins, for which reason
the verse continues, *and* you have maintained *my cause,* that is, you have
submitted to the punishment due my fault, by which I was deserving of
death. And then this word—*you have maintained (fecisti)*—is employed
as a passive verb.[11] And this [verse] may also be understood to refer the
examination and recompense of the last judgment, so as to be understood in this sense: *Because you have maintained (fecisti),* that is you will
maintain *(facies),* my judgment in the last day, when you will separate
the Church of the elect from the body of the ungodly by [distinguishing
their] condition and reward: and then also you will maintain *my cause,*
approving my justice.

*Sedisti super thronum, qui iudicas iustitiam. You have sat on the throne
who judges justice.* The uncircumscribable and incorporeal God is specially declared to sit upon a throne, that is, above the angels of the order
of Thrones,[12] who are the lowest order in the first heavenly hierarchy,
because by them he determines his justice, and they are intimately ready
to receive God in themselves. Whence, to abide in them, and to preside

---

11  E. N. The verb *fecisti* is in the second person singular, perfect in tense, indicative
   in mood, and active in voice. Denis notes, however, that though in the active
   voice, it is interpreted as a passive in voice, so that "you maintained" or "you made"
   *(fecisti)* is interpreted as "you have maintained" or "you were made" *(factus es).*

12  E. N. One of the nine choirs of angels as found in Scripture (*cf.* Gal. 3:26–28;
   Matt. 22:24–33; Eph. 1:21–23; Col. 1:16) and in the schema of Pseudo-Dionysius
   (*On the Celestial Hierarchy*) are: Seraphim, Cherubim, Thrones, Dominions,
   Virtues, Powers, Principalities, Archangels, and Angels.

over them is what is meant by stating to sit on them. Thus it says, *you have sat*, indeed and you always sit upon the Thrones, that is, upon any one of the angels of that order. And one is also able to understand by Thrones the judicial power of Christ, so that it reads in this sense: *You have sat, O* Christ, *on the throne*, that is, you are remaining quiet and in restraint of your power of adjudicating, because you have been appointed judge of all things,[13] and you judge with tranquility.[14] For we are accustomed to say this sort of thing of someone: "He sits there for three years," that is, he was and he remained there for that length of time. *Who judges justice*, that is, you strictly examine it, and it is a true and pure justice; and if there is any injustice that inheres in it, you will punish it. Hence, according to this strict justice, Peter in his Epistle says: *And if the just man shall scarcely be saved, where shall the ungodly and the sinner appear?*[15] Or [this verse might be interpreted to mean], *you judge justice*, separating injustice from justice, and justly recompensing.

---

9[6]   *You have rebuked the Gentiles, and the wicked one has perished: you have blotted out their name for ever and ever.*

*Increpasti gentes, et periit impius: nomen eorum delesti in aeternum, et in saeculum saeculi.*

9[6] *Increpasti gentes, you have rebuked the Gentiles*, through the Prophets, by you yourself, and through your holy Apostles making known their sin; *et periit impius, and the wicked one has perished*: that is, the sinner has converted toward his amendment, and so *he has perished*, not through the corruption of nature, but by the expulsion of fault, in the manner that is written in Proverbs: *Turn the wicked, and they shall not be.*[16] Or [the verse could be understood], *the wicked one has perished*, that is, the devil is ejected from the hearts of the repentant, as the Savior has said: *Now is the judgment of the world: now shall the prince of this world be cast out.*[17] *Nomen eorum, their name*, that is, the people who have been rebuked, and who finally have turned to Christ, *delesti in aeternum, et in saeculum saeculi, you have blotted for ever and ever*, because they who in times past were admonished and were idolaters, unbelievers, and sons of devils, after the conversion to Christ, became and are called Christians, that is, sons of

---

13   *Cf.* Acts 10:14.
14   Wis. 12:18a.
15   1 Pet. 4:18.
16   Prov. 12:7a.
17   John 12:31.

God. — Or [another interpretation is] thus: *You have rebuked the Gentiles,* that is, the obstinate and rebellious you have justly damned. For correction is sometimes received by the evildoer, as it was in the Book of Zacharias: *The Lord rebuke you, O Satan.*[18] *And the wicked one has perished,* that is from being spiritual and from the existence of grace straightaway fell and was cut down. And therefore, O Lord, *their name you have blotted for ever and ever.* From where? Nowhere other than from the book of life and from the number of those who have obtained mercy.

---

9[7]    *The swords of the enemy have failed unto the end: and their cities you have destroyed. Their memory has perished with a noise.*

*Inimici defecerunt frameae in finem, et civitates eorum destruxisti. Periit memoria eorum cum sonitu.*

9[8]    *But the Lord remains forever. He has prepared his throne in judgment.*

*Et Dominus in aeternum permanet. Paravit in iudicio thronum suum.*

9[9]    *And he shall judge the world in equity, he shall judge the people in justice.*

*Et ipse iudicabit orbem terrae in aequitate, iudicabit populos in iustitia.*

9[7] *Inimici defecerunt frameae in finem.* The swords of the enemy have failed unto the end. By sword (*frameas*), which is a sword (*gladius*) that is double-edged, is understood the manifold cunning of the devil, which tempts and overcomes men. *Swords,* therefore, that is, deceptions and snares, *of the enemy,* that is, of the devil, *have failed unto the end,* that is, they have eternally perished, by the price of the Blood, and the merits of the death, of Christ, *vis-à-vis* the elect. *Et civitates eorum, and their cities,* that is, the hearts and the bodies of the ungodly, in which at one time reigned and was inhabited by the devil, as when in cities are in possession [of an enemy], *destruxisti, you have destroyed,* by abandoning the obstinate and saving the penitent, and in this way you have destroyed the obstinate from being in a state of grace, but the penitent from being in a state of fault. *Periit memoria eorum cum sonitu. Their memory has perished with a noise.* That is, the evil and those destitute of the grace of God have been consigned to oblivion with respect to God, according to he who says, *I know you not:*[19] for they are not known by approval of, nor have they

---

18   Zach. 3:2a.
19   Luke 13:27a.

acquired any regard from, the divine mercy. When the trumpet sounds, that is, quickly and as immediately handed over to oblivion: because at that very hour that a man sins mortally, he merits to be forsaken by God; and if he dies in a state of mortal sin, he quickly is given up to sempiternal oblivion, and all of his justices which he might have done, the Lord shall forget.[20]   **9[8]** *Et Dominus in aeternum permanet. But the Lord remains forever.* For he subsists without change and is eternal.

*Paravit in iudicio thronum suum. He has prepared his throne in judgment.* That is, Jesus Christ, the Judge and Lord of all, ordained his judicial power to judging, so that nothing whatsoever remains unexamined or unrecompensed.   **9[9]** *Et ipse iudicabit orbem terrae, and he shall judge the world,* that is, all the inhabitants of the earth, *in aequitate, in equity,* that is rendering to each person in accordance with his works; *iudicabit populos in iustitia, he shall judge the people in justice,*[21] exhibiting that which he has stated, to *the whole world (orbem terrae).* The Lord, therefore, shall judge the people in justice: for *God is not a respecter of persons, but in every nation, he that fears him, and works justice, is acceptable to him.*[22]

---

**9[10]**   *And the Lord is become a refuge for the poor: a helper in due time in tribulation.*

*Et factus est Dominus refugium pauperi; adiutor in opportunitatibus, in tribulatione.*

**9[10]** *Et factus est Dominus refugium pauperi,* and the Lord is become a refuge for the poor; that is, Christ who in death of each individual [and their particular judgment] and at the Last Judgment is a just albeit frightful judge, though now in the interim of this life he has become our refuge, that is our advocate, in the manner that John in his Epistle attests to: *We have an advocate with the Father,* he says, *Jesus Christ the just, and he is the propitiation for our sins.*[23] For he showed to the Father his kindredship to us *(latus),*[24] and even his wounds, indeed, our very nature which he assumed on our behalf: and so he intercedes for us as if he we are his

---

20   Cf. Ez. 18:24b.
21   E. N. Denis leaves off the second verb *iudicabit* (he shall judge).
22   Acts 10:34b–35.
23   1 John 2:1b–2a.
24   L. The word *latus* literally is "side," but to translate it so in this context appears too restrictive. It can also refer poetically (synecdochally) to the body as whole, but also to kindredship, even friendship (someone at your side) *See* Freund and Andrews, *Latin-English Lexicon* (New York: Harper & Brothers 1851) (s.v. "latus").

brothers, as Haymo notes.[25] Or [it might be understood in this manner], *the Lord*, that is, God triune and simple, *is become a refuge for the poor*, that is, the contrite and humble, as Isaias says: *But to whom shall I have respect, but to him that is poor and little, and of a contrite spirit, and that trembles at my words?*[26] For the poor man is he who does not trust in his own strength, nor glory in himself on account of his own merits, nor is he inordinately concerned with earthly riches, but he is content having food and something wherewith he may be covered.[27]

The manner in which the Lord is the *refuge of the poor* follows: *adiutor in opportunitatbis, in tribulatione*, a helper in due time, in tribulation. For the Lord has become our *helper in due time*, [that is, to our advantage,] namely, conferring grace and those things which are necessary for salvation, and keeping men safe, and not that a man may be raised up to [temporal] prosperity, but that he may be restored to grace; and the Lord has become a *helper in tribulation*, giving patience in adversity, and delivering us from evil. For we are in need of the help of God in both prosperity and adversity, in whatever extent and whatever place we might be travelling in the royal way, according to that which is written: *In the day of good things be not unmindful of evils: and in the day of evils be not unmindful of good things.*[28]

---

**9[11]**  *And let them trust in you who know your name: for you have not forsaken them that seek you, O Lord.*

*Et sperent in te qui noverunt nomen tuum, quoniam non dereliquisti quaerentes te, Domine.*

**9[11]**  *Et, and*, because it is for this reason just given, O Lord, *sperent in te qui noverunt nomen tuum*, let them trust in you who know your name, that is, those who out of internal inspiration, or the instruction of Scripture, or through their own contemplation recognize how good, sweet, faithful and merciful the Lord is, just as Jeremiah in his Lamentations testified to: *The Lord is good to them that hope in him, to the soul that seeks him;*[29] *quoniam non dereliquisti quaerentes te, Domine*, for you have not forsaken them that seek you, O Lord, if only they might knock persistently and faithfully, seeking him without becoming weary, saying

---

25  *See* footnote P-89.
26  Is. 66:2b.
27  *Cf.* 1 Tim. 6:8.
28  Ecclus. 11:27.
29  Lam. 3:25.

with holy Job: *Although he should kill me, I will trust in him.*[30] The
Lord should be awaited, therefore, patiently and with the most certain
fidelity, in accordance to that which Isaiah exhorts: *the Lord is the God
of judgment: blessed are all they that wait for him.*[31]

9[12]  *Sing you to the Lord, who dwells in Sion: declare his ways among
the Gentiles.*

*Psallite Domino qui habitat in Sion; annuntiate inter gentes studia eius.*

Because, therefore, the Lord is so good, for that reason   9[12] *Psallite, Sing* all of you, living rightly and always giving thanks, *Domino qui
habitat in Sion, to the Lord who dwells in Sion,* that is, in the Saints
and in spiritual contemplatives, in both the Church triumphant and
the Church militant. *And,* O Sion, that is, spiritual men, who are now
walking by faith, not by sight,[32] *annuntiate inter gentes, declare among
the Gentiles,* that is, preach to all, *studia eius, his ways,* that is, virtuous
works and the benefits of God furnished to the human race. This verse
can also refer in a special sense to the Apostles and the first preachers
of the Gospel, so that it is understood in this sense: *Declare among the
Gentiles his ways,* that is, preach the evangelical law to the Gentiles, and
do not be afraid of doing this, because it will not be purposeless to do
this, but your work shall be your reward. And therefore it adds:

9[13]  *For requiring their blood he has remembered them: he has not
forgotten the cry of the poor.*

*Quoniam requirens sanguinem eorum recordatus est; non est oblitus
clamorem pauperum.*

9[13] *Quoniam requirens sanguinem eorum recordatus est; for requiring
their blood he has remembered them:* that is, the Lord *requiring the blood*
of the announcing to the Gentiles *his ways,*[33] *has remembered,* how much,
namely, the announcers of his ways have exerted themselves and have
done for him, how much they have endured in the cause of justice from

30 Job 13:15a.
31 Is. 30:18b.
32 *Cf.* 2 Cor. 5:7.
33 E. N. In other words, requiring the preaching of the Gospel to the Gentiles
in the great commission: *teach all nations; baptizing them in the name of the
Father, and of the Son, and of the Holy Ghost. Teaching them to observe all things
whatsoever I have commanded you.* Matt. 28:19–20a.

their persecutors and tyrants: because this is recalled: he requires *their blood*, that is, he will vindicate the persecution and death which they have unjustly endured, afflicting the ungodly. The Lord *non est oblitus, has not forgotten*, that is, the preaching, praise, humble prayers: for in his time he will bestow upon them copious mercy, although at times it may appear as if he has forgotten, because he delays for a long time, and permits his saints to suffer tribulation.

9[14]  *Have mercy on me, O Lord: see my humiliation which I suffer from my enemies.*

*Miserere mei, Domine: vide humilitatem meam de inimicis meis.*

9[15]  *You that lift me up from the gates of death, that I may declare all your praises in the gates of the daughter of Sion.*

*Qui exaltas me de portis mortis, ut annuntiem omnes laudationes tuas in portis filiae Sion.*

After these things, it explains what this cry of the poor is, which also the prayer of each individual spurning the vanities of the world.  9[14] *Miserere mei, Domine, have mercy on me, O Lord*, rendering me aid; *vide humilitatem meam, see my humiliation*, that is, consider the oppression and punishment which I suffer, *de inimicis meis, from my enemies*, that is, from the persecutors and tyrants. And this I pray, not that you might condemn them in eternity, but so that you might increase grace in me, and strengthen my fortitude and patience.  9[15] *Qui exaltas me de portis mortis, you who lift me up from the gates of death*, that is, you, who through the Passion and the Blood of Christ, your Son, deliver me from eternal death, or from mortal sins, which are the broad and wide way by which many go down to eternal punishment,[34] which is eternal death. And thus, O Lord, *you lift me up from the gates of death, ut annuntiem, that I might declare*, that is, that, teaching others, I might recall in thanksgiving and might rousingly sing, *omnes laudationes tuas, all your praises*, that words pertinent to your praise, *in portis filiae Sion, in the gates of the daughter of Sion*, that is, in faith, hope, and charity, by which one goes to the Kingdom of God, just as if going through the *gates of the daughter of Sion*, that is, in that Church militant, or in the sight of the faithful. For we must lead others to the praise of God, preaching, teaching, or living in an exemplary manner, according as it

---

34  *Cf.* Matt. 7:13.

may be demanded by each person's vocation, just as the Savior says: *So let your light shine before men, that they may see your good works, and glorify your Father who is in heaven.*[35]

---

**9[16]** *I will rejoice in your salvation: the Gentiles have stuck fast in the destruction which they have prepared. Their foot has been taken in the very snare which they hid.*

*Exultabo in salutari tuo. Infixae sunt gentes in interitu quem fecerunt; in laqueo isto quem absconderunt comprehensus est pes eorum.*

**9[16]** *Exultabo in salutari tuo, I will rejoice in your salvation,* that is, in the beatitude which is promised to me by you, in which I now rejoice by hope, but which in a little while I will enjoy it in reality; or, *I will rejoice in your salvation,* that is, in the salvation set out by you for me; or, *in your salvation,* that is, in Christ your Son, who (Simeon attesting) is *your salvation, which you have prepared before the face of all peoples.*[36] In this *salvation I will rejoice,* contemplate his benefits gathered together for me, and expecting his promise, stored up and ready for me.

*Infixae sunt gentes in interitu quem fecerunt. The Gentiles have stuck fast in the destruction which they have prepared.* This is what in the seventh Psalm was spoken of: *he is fallen into the hole he made.*[37] And so *the Gentiles* and those living in impious ways, *have stuck fast,* that is, they are immersed and are captured, *in the destruction which they have prepared,* that is, in the death by which they have carried out against holy men. For many tyrants, on account of death afflicted to the saints, also in the present life miserably perish, as in found in many [historical] chronicles. *In laqueo isto quem absconderunt, in the very snare which they hid,* that is in the evil that they had hiddenly prepared for others, *comprehensus est pes eorum, their foot has been taken in,* that is, justly are they punished for their affections, for the evil that they have prepared for others, they also having suffered in the present: as Aman who was hung on a gibbet which he had prepared for Mordechai.[38] And if in the present time he does not effect such retribution, still without doubt it will be more terrible in the future; and then *in the snare which they hid,* their foot will be taken in, for their deceit and malice, will be poured out upon their head, especially in the day of judgment. For which reason it continues:

---

35 Matt. 5:16.
36 Luke 2:30–31.
37 Ps. 7:16.
38 Esther 7:10.

**9[17]** *The Lord shall be known when he executes judgments: the sinner has been caught in the works of his own hands.*

*Cognoscetur Dominus iudicia faciens; in operibus manuum suarum comprehensus est peccator.*

**9[18]** *The wicked shall be turned into hell, all the nations that forget God.*

*Convertantur peccatores in infernum, omnes gentes quae obliviscuntur Deum.*

**9[19]** *For the poor man shall not be forgotten to the end: the patience of the poor shall not perish forever.*

*Quoniam non in finem oblivio erit pauperis; patientia pauperum non peribit in finem.*

**9[17]** *Cognoscetur Dominus iudicia faciens*, *The Lord shall be known when he executes judgments*: for in the future *all flesh shall see the salvation of our God*,[39] and then Christ will appear clearly;[40] and it will be made known to all men that he is doing justice, and justly judging all men. *In operibus manuum suarum comprehensus est peccator*, *the sinner has been caught in the works of his own hands*: for their works follow them.[41] And therefore he whom the Lord has found to have fallen into sin, he will lay hold of him and damn him. **9[18]** *Convertantur peccatores in infernum*, *the wicked shall be turned into hell*: that is in the day of judgment all who are obstinate in evil will be thrust into hell: those, that is, of whom the Psalm adds, *omnes gentes quae obliviscuntur Deum*, *all the nations that forget God*, that is, who expel God from their memory, not contemplating him nor loving him, but holding him in disdain or not keeping his commandments. **9[19]** *Quoniam non in finem oblivion erit pauperis*, *for the poor man shall not be forgotten to the end*: that is, the faithful and humble man, however much he may seem to be abandoned by God in time, yet finally *the just shall be in everlasting remembrance*,[42] because in the day of judgment he will be saved in eternity. *Patientia pauperum non peribit in finem*, *the patience of the poor shall not perish forever*, that is, he will not lack his due reward, but he will be granted eternal happiness.

---

39  Luke 3:6.
40  *Cf.* Luke 21:27.
41  Rev. 14:13b.
42  Ps. 111:7a.

**9[20]** *Arise, O Lord, let not man be strengthened: let the Gentiles judged in your sight.*

*Exsurge, Domine; non confortetur homo: iudicentur gentes in conspectu tuo.*

In what follows the Church speaks to Christ of the casting away of the Antichrist. **9[20]** *Exsurge, Domine, Arise, O Lord.* O Christ, O Judge, during the times of the Antichrist, *arise*, rendering aid to the faithful and hastily preparing for judgment: because such will be his persecution, that unless those days were shortened, *no flesh would be saved.*[43] *Non confortetur homo, let not man be strengthened*, that is, let not the Antichrist prevail against the Church: [the Antichrist,] who will be the worst man, and to the point even that the human condition would not be able to support worse evil than his. *Iudicentur gentes in conspectus tuo, let the Gentiles be judged in your sight*: that is, all the followers and promoters of the Antichrist who adhere to him to the end, will be judged by a judgment of rejection by you in the final judgment.

---

**9[21]** *Appoint, O Lord, a lawgiver over them: that the Gentiles may know themselves to be but men.*

*Constitue, Domine, legislatorem super eos, ut sciant gentes quoniam homines sunt.*

During this time, or before the final judgment which will immediately follow after the persecution of the Antichrist, as is clear in the Gospel,[44] **9[21]** *Constitue . . . legislatorem, Appoint . . . a lawgiver*, that is, the Antichrist, who promulgates the full law aimed at the blasphemy of Christ, *super eos, over them*, that is, over the unjust people deceived by him. It should be noted, however, that the evil of punishment is effectively from God: as is said by Amos the prophet: *Shall there be evil in a city, which the Lord has not done?*[45] But the evil of fault is from God permissively and indirectly, because he does not impede it: in the manner that the Lord is said to have hardened the heart of the Pharaoh,[46] and to strengthen the heart of Sehon the king of the Amorites,[47] and Og, the king of Basan.[48]

---

43  *Cf.* Matt. 24:1; Matt. 24:2a.
44  Matt. 24:29.
45  Amos 3:6b.
46  Ex. 9;12.
47  Deut. 2:30.
48  Num. 21:33.

In the same manner the Lord is said to constitute the Antichrist over the people, because he permits this to happen because of their sins. Whence of the Antichrist the Apostle speaks: *And then that wicked one shall be revealed, he says, . . . whose coming is according to the working of Satan, in all power, and signs, and lying wonders, and in all seduction to iniquity to them who perish, because they receive not the love of truth, that they may be saved; and therefore God shall send them the operation of error, to believe lying.*[49] *Sciant,* that they may know, that is, that through the experience of being punished they may recognize, *gentes, the Gentiles,* those believing in the Antichrist, *quoniam homines sunt, that they are just men* seduced by vanity, not sons of God as they suppose themselves to be; for they regarded the Antichrist to be the true Christ, and by believing in him they thought themselves to be sons of God. But, O just Lord, judge them, who in the present life do not wish to adhere to the true Christ, that they might recognize that they have erred, even in the punishments of hell.

---

**9[22]{10[1]}**  *Why, O Lord, have you retired afar off? Why do you slight us in our wants, in the time of trouble?*

*Ut quid, Domine, recessisti longe, despicis in opportunitatibus, in tribulatione?*

**9[22]{10[1]}**[50] *Ut quid, Domine, recessisti longe? Why, O Lord, have you retired far off?* This the Church says to Christ, designating the most ferocious rage of the persecution of the Antichrist. Indeed, so extreme will the severity be of that persecution, that it will seem that God in some manner has abandoned his own. For how great will that persecution be while the pious martyr will offer his body to be punished and the impious persecutor performs marvels before the eyes of those suffering? Indeed, the Church then, it is believed, will not be able to perform miracles, unless by the strength of Elijah and Enoch or a few others. The Church therefore says with astonishment: *Why, O Lord, have you retired far off?* That is, you will so hold and so absent yourself for a long time. *Despicis, slight us,* that is, you hold yourself out in the manner of one despising, *in opportunitatibus, in our wants,* that is, in the necessities of the Christians, *in tribulatio, in the time of trouble,* as they undergo that most bitter persecution: because you permit those

---

49  2 Thess. 2:8a, 9–10.

50  E. N. Here the number of the Psalms and verses depart depending upon whether the Vulgate/Septuagint is used or the Masoretic text. The numbering of the Masoretic text will be indicated within braces, *i.e.,* {}.

to be handed over to the hands of the ungodly, and to undergo such burdensome tribulations, such great tribulations as never before have been, nor exist now, nor will in the future ever be; and because of this, it will appear as if you disregard the prayers of the faithful.

---

**9[23]{10[2]}** *Whilst the wicked man is proud, the poor is set on fire: they are caught in the counsels which they devise.*

> *Dum superbit impius, incenditur pauper: comprehenduntur in consiliis quibus cogitant.*

**9[23]{10[2]}** *Dum superbit impius,* while the wicked man is proud, that is the Antichrist, who will call himself the Son of God, and according to the Apostle, *is lifted up above all that is called God:*[51] while, I say, the man of sin, the son of perdition will be so proud, *incenditur pauper, the poor is set on fire,* that is, then the Christian people, who then will be very poor and will be held in contempt, will be struck down with various punishments. For by fire Scripture customarily signifies all kinds of punishments. It is also able to be accepted in a literal manner, because the Antichrist will burn with fire many of the Christians. *Comprehenduntur in consiliis quibus cogitant, they are caught in the counsels which they devise:* that is, the Antichrist and his ministers *are caught* and are taken captive or tormented *in the counsels which they devise* by Christ: because that which they devise to do to the Christians, that Christ will do to them; because as the divine Apostle attests, *Jesus shall kill with the spirit of his mouth.*[52] And Isaiah also predicts this: *with the breath of his lips,* he says, *he shall slay the wicked,*[53] that is, the Antichrist.

---

**9[24]{10[3]}** *For the sinner is praised in the desires of his soul: and the unjust man is blessed.*

> *Quoniam laudatur peccator in desideriis animae suae, et iniquus benedicitur.*

Next, it sets forth the cause confirming the Antichrist in his error: **9[24]{10[3]}** *Quoniam laudatur peccator in desideriis animae sua, for the sinner is praised in the desires of his soul:* that is, the Antichrist who is the head of all evil men, will be praised by his followers in all

---

51  2 Thess. 2:4.
52  2 Thess. 2:8.
53  Is. 11:4b.

his affections and deeds. For his desire is that the faith of Jesus Christ be everywhere eradicated, in order that he himself may be believed to be the Christ: in this desire, he also will be praised by his followers. *Et iniquus, and the unjust man,* that is the Antichrist, the teacher of impiety, *benedicitur, is blessed,* that he is blessed by his worshippers as if a god.

---

9[25]{10[4]}    *The sinner has provoked the Lord according to the multitude of his wrath he will not seek him.*

*Exacerbavit Dominum peccator, secundum multitudinem irae suae, non quaeret.*

9[26]{10[5]}    *God is not before his eyes: his ways are filthy at all times. Your judgments are removed from his sight: he shall rule over all his enemies.*

*Non est Deus in conspectu eius, inquinatae sunt viae illius in omni tempore. Auferuntur iudicia tua a facie eius; omnium inimicorum suorum dominabitur.*

9[27]{10[6]}    *For he has said in his heart: I shall not be moved from generation to generation, and shall be without evil.*

*Dixit enim in corde suo: Non movebor a generatione in generationem, sine malo.*

9[25]{10[4]} *Exacerbavit, he has provoked,* that is, he [the Antichrist] has greatly offended, *Dominum, the Lord,* Jesus; *peccator, the sinner,* that is the Antichrist, *secundum multitudinem irae suae, according to the multitude of his wrath,* that is, according to the exigency of his many sins, which will merit the anger of God, *non quaeret, he will not seek,* penance, that is, because he will be obstinate in his evil.    9[26]{10[5]} *Non est Deus in conspectus eius, God is not before his eyes:* that is, the Antichrist will not himself consider the punishment from God prepared for him or imminent, nor will he fear God; but in the manner that the prophet Daniel prophesied, he shall speak *against every god,* and *against the God of gods.*[54] *Inquinatae sunt viae illius, his ways are filthy:* that is, the works of the Antichrist are vicious, *in omni tempore, at all times,* that is from the first moment where he begins to use reason: indeed all his life will be sin. For Lucifer, the Devil, will descend to him while he is in the womb of his mother, and will direct him in all things.

---

54  Dan. 11:36.

*Auferuntur iudicia tua a facie eius, your judgments are removed from his sight*: because he will be blind as to so many things because of his pride, so that he will not regard himself adjudged by God; and with intrepid and astonishing blindness he will regard himself to be the true Christ, because he will see himself to succeed at all that he does by will, and not to be judged by God in any way in anything. However, he will not be excused from sin, because he will not be possessed by the devil, in the manner of the possessed or the insane: but he will be fully possessed of reason, and would he so wish to direct himself to it, he would see himself to err. The divine *judgments* are therefore *removed from his sight*, that is, from the consideration of his intellect. *Omnium inimicorum suorum dominabitur, he shall rule over all his enemies*, that is, *he will rule over all* those unwilling to obey him, because he will kill them; or they will flee and hide themselves from him. Whence we read in the book of Daniel: *I beheld, and lo, that horn made war against the saints, and prevailed over them.*[55]  **9[27]{10[6]}** *Dixit enim in corde suo, for he has said in his heart*, that is, he thought upon that which follows: *Non movebor a generatione in generationem, I shall not be moved from generation to generation*, that is, I shall not be deprived from this power and reign and glory, *from generation to generation*, that is, at no time, or during some duration where generations are able to succeed each other: because as long as it lasts, he will not believe his reign to be subject to coming to an end. For the judgments of God *are removed from his sight*, the consequence of which is that he will not estimate himself as being overcome by anyone, but that he will [figure that he will] perdure in perpetuity. *Sine malo, without evil*. This refers to the pronoun "I," understood in this sense: "I am without evil," that is, I, living and reigning without any impediment and punishment, *shall not be moved*, etc.

---

**9[28]{10[7]}**  *His mouth is full of cursing, and of bitterness, and of deceit: under his tongue are labor and sorrow.*

> *Cuius maledictione os plenum est, et amaritudine, et dolo; sub lingua eius labor et dolor.*

**9[28]{10[7]}** *Cuius maledictione os plenum est, his mouth is full of cursing*, that is, of blasphemies against Christ, *et amaritudine, and of bitterness*, that is, with threatening severity, because those not obedient to him he will threaten with death; *et dolo, and deceit*, for many he will deceive

---

55 Dan. 7:21.

with blandishments; or *deceit*, that is, cunning and fallacious assertions and explanations of sacred Scripture. For he will select the scriptures of the Old Testament for himself; and so he will explain them, so that they appear as being fulfilled in him, and by this means he will regard himself to be the Christ; indeed, by this many will regard him to be the Christ. *Sub lingua eius labor et dolor, under his tongue are labor and sorrow*: because with his mind he will conduct himself and with his mouth he shall speak, is how he brings servile labor and deadly sorrow to holy men, not only by himself, but by his collaborators. Whence it follows:

---

9[29]{10[8]} *He sits in ambush with the rich in private places, that he may kill the innocent.*

> *Sedet in insidiis cum divitibus in occultis, ut interficiat innocentem.*

**9[29]{10[8]}** *Sedet in insidiis, He sits in ambush*, that is, he sits lying in wait, in the hidden manner of thieves, devising ways of inflicting harm, *cum divitibus, with the rich*, that is, with his ministers, whom he will make rich, in order that he may draw many to himself, *in occultis, in private places*, that is, deceiving in hidden ways. For he will have a great appearance, one by which he will deceive the world; and it will then be very difficult to distinguish between truth and falsity, and between good and evil. For he will deceive the world in various ways, namely, by the performance of miracles, by his constructions of Scripture, by his simulation of holiness, by his false happiness, and by the innumerable multitude of those following him. He sits also in the manner foretold *in ambush, ut interficiat innocentem, that he may kill the innocent*, that is, the pious and charitable Christian people.

---

9[30]{10[9]} *His eyes are upon the poor man: He lies in wait in secret like a lion in his den. He lies in ambush that he may catch the poor man: to catch the poor, while he draws him to him.*

> *Oculi eius in pauperem respiciunt; insidiatur in abscondito, quasi leo in spelunca sua. Insidiatur ut rapiat pauperem; rapere pauperem dum attrahit eum.*

**9[30]{10[9]}** *Oculi eius, his eyes*, both of the heart as well as those of the body, *in pauperum, upon the poor man*, that is, upon the Christian faithful, *respiciunt, rest upon*: in order either to seduce them through attraction, or to kill those resisting him; *insidiatur in abscondito, he lies* *in wait in secret,* that is, hiddenly devising traps, *quasi leo in spelunca, like a lion in his den.* Of course, the lion in his den lying in wait for the gentle animals is savage and strong: and so the Antichrist will be severe, prevailing over godly men. *Insidiatur ut rapiat pauperem, he lies in ambush that he may catch the poor man,* that is to say, that he might attack the Christian, trusting not in himself, but in the Lord; and *he lies in ambush rapere pauperem dum attrahit eum, to catch the poor while he draws him to him.* This can be explained in two ways. The first is this: *To lie in ambush to catch the poor man,* that is, that he may destroy him spiritually, depriving from the faith and the grace of Christ, while he attracts him, that is, while he leads and draws him to his law. The second is this: *To lie in ambush to catch the poor,* in order that he might destroy him bodily while he drags him into torture.

---

9[31]{10[10]} *In his net he will bring him down, he will crouch and fall, when he shall have power over the poor.*

> *In laqueo suo humiliabit eum; inclinabit se, et cadet cum dominatus fuerit pauperum.*

9[31]{10[10]} *In laqueo suo, in his net,* that is, in his deceptions and deceits, *humiliabit eum, he will bring him down,* that is, he will oppress and afflict the poor and the faithful. For the persecution of the Antichrist will not only be violent, as is the persecution of tyrants, not only deceitful, as is that of the heretics; but it will be both violent on account of the secular power, and deceitful on account of the apparent holiness of life and the performance of signs. Whence of the Antichrist is written: *He had two horns, like a lamb,*[56] and he spoke as a dragon.

*Inclinabit se, et cadet cum dominatus fuerit pauperum, he will crouch and fall, when he shall have power over the poor:* that is, the Antichrist after he does all these things will then bow down by necessary compulsion, that is, he will humble himself not through true humility, but in a forced manner he will lay down the pride of his soul, in the manner that Antiochus (a figure of the Antichrist) did, who because he labored under great pain, said, not from true repentance, but from having to endure punishment: *It is just to be subject to God, and that a mortal man should not equal himself to God.*[57] *And he will fall,* that is, he will

---

56 Rev. 13:11b.
57 2 Macc. 9:12b. E. N. The death of Antiochus IV Epiphanes (*ca.* 215 B. C.–164 B. C.) is chronicled in 2 Macc. 9:5-13. His repentance came too late and was not based upon proper motive.

be struck down by Christ, *when he shall have power over the poor,* that is, over the Christians. He will dominate the poor or the Church militant, persecuting and oppressing it for three-and-a-half years, as we know from the prophet Daniel: *They shall be delivered into his hand until a time, and times, and half a time.*[58] For the Hebrews by the word "time" understand a year; by the word "times," they understand two years; and by the words "half a time" they understand half a year. And this is what is said about the Antichrist and his followers: *The holy city they shall tread under foot two and forty months,*[59] that is, they will oppress the Church militant three-and-a-half years. For forty-two months makes three-and-a-half years. Whence, again in Revelation it says: *And there was given to him a mouth speaking great things, and blasphemies: and power was given to him to do two and forty months.*[60] Therefore, after this time, the persecution of the Antichrist will cease, since just as it will be most severe, so it will be most brief. For as the Savior attests, it is *for the sake of the elect those days shall be shortened.*[61]

---

**9[32]{10[11]}** *For he has said in his heart: God has forgotten, he has turned away his face not to see to the end.*

*Dixit enim in corde suo: Oblitus est Deus; avertit faciem suam, ne videat in finem.*

Then follows the cause of the demise of the Antichrist:  **9[32]** **{10[11]}** *Dixit enim in corde suo: Oblitus est Deus, For he has said in his heart: God has forgotten,* that is, he does not pay heed to my works so as he might judge them; *avertis faciem suam, he has turned away his face,* that is, his consideration, *ne videat in finem, not to see to the end,* that is, he will never condemn me. This the Antichrist says in his heart, or since because of the blindness of his heart he will believe this to be so, or because he will live in such a manner, so he will not regard God to be the judge of men. But it should not be suggested that he will openly say these words; indeed, he will say God is the judge of all men, even as he shall see himself to be the Son of God and the universal judge. But whether this is said as referring to the soul's judgment, as some propose, or as others suggest under the form of the good he may have defrauded, there is no certainty.

---

58  Dan. 7:25b.
59  Rev. 11:2b.
60  Rev. 13:5.
61  Matt. 24:22b.

**9[33]{10[12]}** *Arise, O Lord God, let your hand be exalted: forget not the poor.*

*Exsurge, Domine Deus, exaltetur manus tua; ne obliviscaris pauperum.*

**9[34]{10[13]}** *Wherefore has the wicked provoked God? For he has said in his heart: He will not require it.*

*Propter quid irritavit impius Deum? Dixit enim in corde suo: Non requiret.*

**9[33]{10[12]}** *Exsurge, Domine Deus. Arise, O Lord God.* This is the prayer of the Church, which prays for the final defeat of the Antichrist, and the full deliverance of the faithful. *Arise, O Lord God,* who for a time delaying and not hearing, as if you appeared asleep; but now, *arise,* helping, and in the manner of having you at our side; *et exaltetur manus tua, and let your hand be exalted,* that is, let your power be made manifest, slaying and damning the Antichrist; *ne obliviscaris pauperum, forget not the poor,* that is, withdraw for a long time the protection and help of our mercy from your people. **9[34]{10[13]}** *Propter quid, wherefore,* that is, the fruit or the utility, *irritavit, has he provoked,* that is, has offended, *impius, the wicked,* that is to say, the Antichrist [will scoff], *Deum, God? Dixit enim in corde suo: Non requiret. For he has said in his heart: He will not require it.* That is, God will not demand from me the reason for my acts, nor will he take revenge for the blood of the Christians which I slay.

---

**9[35]{10[14]}** *You see it, for you consider labor and sorrow: that you may deliver them into your hands. To you is the poor man left: you will be a helper to the orphan.*

*Vides, quoniam tu laborem et dolorem consideras, ut tradas eos in manus tuas. Tibi derelictus est pauper; orphano tu eris adiutor.*

Besides, the Church turns itself towards God. **9[35]{10[14]}** *Vides, You see it:* that is, that which the Antichrist says is false, to have turned away your face, that you might not see in the end: indeed, you see, for *all things are naked and open to your eyes;*[62] and this is clear from the fact, *quoniam tu laborem et dolorem consideras, for you consider labor and sorrow,* that is, you diligently attend to labor and sorrow, which

---

62 Heb. 14:13b.

184 DENIS THE CARTHUSIAN : Commentary on the Psalms : Volume 1

your saints patiently endured from the Antichrist and his followers; *ut tradas eos in manus tuas, that you may deliver them into your hands*, that is, so that you may accept and give thanks for the labors and sorrows of the saints, giving to them eternal rest and perpetual joy. Or [it may be understood in this fashion], *that you may deliver them*, that is the Antichrist and his followers, *in your hands*, that is, in the power of your justice, inasmuch as you eternally will condemn them.

*Tibi, to you*, O Lord, *derelictus est pauper, is the poor man left*, that is, the Christian people, for there is no other who might fight for them except for you, Lord God, especially during the time of the Antichrist; *orphano, to the orphan*, that is, to the forsaken people, who other than you have no one to give them consolation, and it is as if not having a helping father or a consoling mother: in this manner will be the Christian people during the time of the Antichrist; *tu eris adiutor, you will be a helper*, for you will redeem them, you will not abandon your elect in the end.

———————

**9[36]{10[15]}** *Break the arm of the sinner and of the malignant: his sin shall be sought, and shall not be found.*

> *Contere brachium peccatoris et maligni; quaeretur peccatum illius, et non invenietur.*

**9[36]{10[15]}** *Contere, break*, that is, reduce to nothing, *brachium peccatoris et maligni, the arm of the sinner and the malignant*, that is the power of the Antichrist: who, according to the prediction of Daniel, only so long will he crush the saints of the most High, until it will be taken away.[63] *Quaeretur peccatum illius, et non invenietur. His sin shall be sought, and shall not be found*: that is, delight and glory and malice of the Antichrist will be so destroyed, as if it never existed. Or [it may be understood] thus: *His sin shall be sought, and it shall not be found*: because after the death of the Antichrist, certain of his obstinate ministers will persist in their malice, and they will seek [to continue] the sin of their slain ruler, desiring to taste of the delights and to live falsely in the manner that he did; but their sin will not arrive at this. Christ attests: *For when they shall say, peace and security, then shall sudden destruction come upon them.*[64]

———————

63 *Cf.* Dan. 7:25, 26.
64 1 Thess. 4:3; *Cf.* Luke 21:34, 35.

**9[37]{10[16]}** *The Lord shall reign to eternity, yea, for ever and ever: you Gentiles shall perish from his land.*

> *Dominus regnabit in aeternum, et in saeculum saeculi; peribitis, gentes, de terra illius.*

**9[38]{10[17]}** *The Lord has heard the desire of the poor: your ear has heard the preparation of their heart.*

> *Desiderium pauperum exaudivit Dominus; praeparationem cordis eorum audivit auris tua.*

**9[39]{10[18]}** *To judge for the fatherless and for the humble, that man may no more presume to magnify himself upon earth.*

> *Iudicare pupillo et humili, ut non apponat ultra magnificare se homo super terram.*

**9[37]{10[16]}** *Dominus, the Lord,* that is, Jesus of Nazareth, who is the true Christ and the Creator of all things, and the Lord, *regnabit in aeternum et in saeculum saeculi, shall reign to eternity, yea, for ever and ever,* because *of his kingdom there shall be no end;*[65] nor also the Catholic faith, by which he reigns in this age, while in the world never failing totally, even in the time of the Antichrist when it will diminish more than before. *Peribitis gentes, you Gentiles shall perish,* that is, the ungodly, you who adhere to the Antichrist, and you who do not repent, *de terra illius, from his land,* that is, from the region of the living, because they will be expelled from the kingdom of heaven: indeed, they will perish from this inferior and rudimentary earth, for they will be cast down into hell; and this, therefore, because **9[38]{10[17]}** *Desiderium pauperum, the desire of the poor,* that is, the prayers of the faithful, *exaudivit Dominus; praeparationem cordis eorum, the Lord has heard; the preparation of their heart,* that is, the promptitude by which they in adversity faithfully adhere to you, *auris tua, your ear,* O Lord, *audivit, has heard,* that is, your wisdom received and rewarded. **9[39]{10[18]}** *Iudicare pupillo et humili, to judge for the fatherless and for the humble,* that is, you carry out such a kind and manner of just judgment, that from all that you may judge, you will recognize and render just: as it is said in a subsequent Psalm, *that you may be justified in your words, and may overcome when you are judged;*[66] *for the fatherless and for the humble,* that is, to the salvation and glory of the fatherless and the humble, namely,

65 Luke 1:33.
66 Ps. 50:6.

that judging you might save the fatherless and the humble, that is, each person spurning this earth and regarding themselves as nothing; *ut non apponat ultra magnificare se homo super terram, that man may no more presume to magnify himself upon the earth*, that is, so that at the end he might deal harshly with the pride of the Antichrist, that finally he may never venture to wish to dominate someone else.

## OTHER SHORT EXPOSITION

9[23]{10[2]}   *Whilst the wicked man is proud, the poor is set on fire: they are caught in the counsels which they devise.*

*Dum superbit impius, incenditur pauper: comprehenduntur in consiliis quibus cogitant.*

9[24]{10[3]}   *For the sinner is praised in the desires of his soul: and the unjust man is blessed.*

*Quoniam laudatur peccator in desideriis animae suae, et iniquus benedicitur.*

Finally, having undertaken [to expound upon] this Psalm, which literally expounded is about the Antichrist, it may be explained morally as referring to his members, namely, to the persecutors of the Church, and to all other unjust men: to whom either all or many of those things already said can be applied to them, such as   9[23]{10[2]} *While the wicked man is proud, the poor is set on fire*; and   9[24]{10[3]} *For the sinner is praised in the desires of his soul*; and almost all others. Also, those things that have been explained about the Church during the time of the Antichrist can be explained as applying to the Church and any just man during any time of great persecution. And so as to avoid increasing the length of this commentary, and because the moral explanation easily stands plain, and can be elicited from the prior exposition, therefore I omit it. Nevertheless, let it be plainly said to everyone who entrusts himself to belong to Christ that he should not in any manner concern himself with those things which now have been recounted of the Antichrist. Let him see to himself that he not be found to be proud, and an oppressor of the poor, or a derider of the simple, or a despiser of the sick. Let him see that he not desire to praise the desires of the vicious, nor those applauding and flattering themselves in the delights of evil; but [let him see] that he reflects always upon the presence of God, and, in the consideration of all his deeds, he everywhere thinks, "Christ is judge."

Let it not appear to apply to him that which is expounded about the Antichrist, **9[26]{10[5]}** *God is not before his eyes*, and, *your judgments are removed from his sight*. Let him not be slanderous, an intimidator, bitter, deceitful, but let such a person busy himself to imitate the way of the Lord Jesus Christ, in order that in the last day he may be found worthy to be separated from the Antichrist and his unhappy colleagues, and to triumph eternally with the most high Christ in the heavens.

## PRAYER

GOD, REFUGE OF YOUR POOR, WHO, IN seeking their necessities from you, you do not forsake: do not despise us who in tribulation cry out to you; but raise us out of the gates of death, so that here and in eternity we may exult in your praises.

*Refugium pauperum tuorum, Deus, qui in necessitatibus suis te quaerentes non derelinquis, ad te nos in tribulatione clamantes non despicias; sed exalta nos de deportis mortis: ut hic et in aeternum exsultemus in laudibus tuis.*

# Psalm 10

## ARTICLE XXIX

### LITERAL EXPOSITION OF THE TENTH PSALM:
### *IN DOMINO CONFIDO.*
### *IN THE LORD I PUT MY TRUST.*

**10{11}[1]**   *Unto the end. A Psalm for David.*

   *In finem. Psalmus David.*

**N**OW, THE TITLE OF THIS PSALM IS:   **10{11}[1]** *In finem, psalmus David, unto the end, a Psalm for David*: that is, this Psalm directs us to Christ or God, and it is David himself, who speaks here in the person of one putting his trust in the Lord. But it should be noted that as the Catholic teachers do with respect to the Scriptures of the Old Testament, which they fittingly apply to any particular member of the faithful and also the entire congregation of the faithful, they explain this Psalm literally as dealing with the Church or any particular true Christian; so the Hebrew teachers of the Scriptures explain this Psalm as literally referring to the Synagogue and any particular real Jew or Israelite. Whence, in the manner that our teachers explain the Song of Songs as pertaining to Christ and to the Church, so the teachers of the Jews explain it of the Messiah king and the Synagogue. And so this Psalm, as the preceding, literally is able to be interpreted as referring to David and the Synagogue, and to the heretics of the old Law, in the manner that the Sadducees were, and others of that kind: and so the Psalm will be explained tropologically of the Church and any one of its members, and allegorically as dealing with Christ.

-----

**10{11}[2]**   *In the Lord I put my trust: how then do you say to my soul: Get you away from hence to the mountain like a sparrow?*

   *In Domino confido; quomodo dicitis animae meae: Transmigra in montem sicut passer?*

   Briefly, therefore, touching upon the first exposition, David, in his person, and as any one of the Jews, or the Synagogue spiritually understood, says   10{11}[2] *In Domino confido, in the Lord I put my trust,* that is, I put the hope of my salvation in the Incarnate Son of God, in the future Messiah king, because by faith in him I expect to be saved. And because this is so, *quomodo, how then,* O Jews (understanding the Law in a carnal way), *dicitis animae meae, Transmigra in montem sicut passer, do you say to my soul, Get you away from hence to the mountain like a sparrow,* that is, ascend and flock together to the law given by the Godhead, and first received upon Mount Sinai,[1] placing your trust upon it? As if without faith in and the grace of Christ you are able to be saved, that is, only by the observation of the law: in the manner that the many Jews imagined. Of whom the Apostle writes: *They, not knowing the justice of God* (namely, that the *just man lives by faith*),[2] and wanting to establish their own (trusting in their own strength and in the external observation of the law), *have not submitted themselves to the justice of God.*[3]

---

10{11}[3]   *For, lo, the wicked have bent their bow; they have prepared their arrows in the quiver; to shoot in the dark the upright of heart.*

*Quoniam ecce peccatores intenderunt arcum; paraverunt sagittas suas in pharetra, ut sagittent in obscuro rectos corde.*

10{11}[4]   *For they have destroyed the things which you have made: but what has the just man done?*

*Quoniam quae perfecisti destruxerunt; iustus autem quid fecit?*

10{11}[3] *Quoniam ecce peccatores, for, lo, the wicked,* that is, the carnal and heretical Jews, *intenderunt arcum, have bent their bow,* that is, they have received through their error the Law according to its literal understanding: of which the Apostle says, *the letter kills;*[4] *paraverunt sagittas suas, they have prepared their arrows,* that is, certain assertions written in the Law, which they are seen to use to make their error apparent, *in pharetra, in the quiver,* that is in their mouth, from which they bring forth these spears of death; *ut sagittent, to shoot,* that is, they may perversely instruct, *in obscuro, in the dark,* that is, in those who have difficulty as to what they ought to understand, *rectos corde, the upright of heart,* that is, the just and the simple, to whom they explain

---

1  Ex. chp. 20.
2  Rom. 1:17b.
3  Rom. 10:3.
4  2 Cor. 3:6b.

such obscurities as a result confirming them in their error.    10{11}[4] *Quoniam quae perfecisti, For those things which you have made,* that is, the sacred laws and Scriptures of the Prophets perfectly and purely inspired by you, *destruxerunt, they have destroyed,* by their forced explanations. *Iustus autem, but the just man,* that is, the true Jew not believing in their assertions, *quid fecit, what has he done?* And he responds:

---

10{11}[5]   *The Lord is in his holy temple, the Lord's throne is in heaven. His eyes look on the poor man: his eyelids examine the sons of men.*

*Dominus in templo sancto suo; Dominus in caelo sedes eius. Oculi eius in pauperem respiciunt, palpebrae eius interrogant filios hominum.*

 10{11}[5] *Dominus in templo sancto suo, the Lord in his holy temple,* that is, God by faith and grace lives in the just man, who is called the temple of God.[5] And, therefore, if it is asked what the just man seeks, he will respond that he hopes in the Lord, because the Lord is in him, as if in a temple, by faith and hope. *Dominus in caelo sedes eius, the Lord's throne is in heaven:* that is, the throne of the Lord is in heaven, that is, in the souls of the just, which is the seat of wisdom; or [we can understand it as] in the empyrean heaven, in which God specially is asserted to be enthroned, because there he acts most excellently, and is seen most clearly. But the incorporeal God has no material throne; for his thrones are the holy souls, in whom he takes rest by faith and grace at the present time, and by a true sight and glory in heaven. And because the rest and dwelling of God by sight and glory is more eminent than the rest and dwelling by faith and grace, therefore God is more properly and more excellently said to dwell and to be enthroned in heaven and in the blessed comprehensors, than on earth and those in the wayfaring state.

The words of this Psalm that follow satisfactorily conform to some degree to this explanation, and they are explained in the same manner; therefore, I defer from their exposition now, and turn to the principle explanation of this Psalm.

---

5  2 Cor. 6:16.

# ARTICLE XXX

## TROPOLOGICAL EXPOSITION OF THE SAME TENTH PSALM IN THE PERSON OF THE CHURCH AND EACH OF THE FAITHFUL WHO IS A TRUE AND LIVE MEMBER OF THE CHURCH.

10{11}[2]    *In the Lord I put my trust: how then do you say to my soul: Get you away from hence to the mountain like a sparrow?*

*In Domino confido; quomodo dicitis animae meae: Transmigra in montem sicut passer?*

HE HOLY PROPHET DAVID, FORESEEING IN the Holy Spirit the fraudulent teachers or heretics of the future time of the Christian law, therefore says in the person of the Church:    10{11}[2] *In Domino confido, in the Lord I put my trust,* that is, in God I place my hope, I believe in the truths of the Sacred Page,[6] I receive the expositions of the holy Fathers and the Catholic Doctors; therefore, O heretics, *quomodo, how then,* that is, by what reason, *dicitis animae meas, Transmigra in montem, do you say to my soul: Get you away from hence to the mountain,* that is, ascend by your own reason, believe in your own personal sense, trust in your own genius, and understand sacred Scripture according to our exposition, which on account of our subtle genius, we call mountains?[7] In what manner, I say, *do you say to my soul, get you away from hence,* from the secure and humble simplicity to the perilous heights and to the prohibited explorations of majesty, *sicut passer, like a sparrow,* that is, quickly and flying high, walking *in wonderful things* above you,[8] flying over those boundaries constituted by the fathers? Vain is this your persuasion: because Solomon says, *He that walks sincerely, walks confidently;*[9] and again, God protects *them that walk in simplicity.*[10] But *he that is a searcher of majesty, shall be overwhelmed by glory.*[11]

---

6   E. N. The words *Sacra Pagina,* literally "Sacred Page," referred to the whole Scripture; they are therefore a synonym for Holy Writ or Sacred Scripture.

7   E. N. In the manner of Kant's *sapere aude!* the heretic is encouraging the soul to exercise his private judgment and to follow him in leaving the Tradition. "It should be noted that all heresies have sprung from the desire to interpret Holy Scripture according to the private judgment of individuals." *A Dogmatic Catechism from the Italian of Frassinetti* (London: R. Washbourne 1827) (6th ed.), 15. The shift from second person singular to third person plural is in the original.

8   Ps. 130:1b.

9   Prov. 10:9a.

10   Prov.2:7b.

11   Prov. 25:27b.

10{11}[3]   *For, lo, the wicked have bent their bow; they have prepared their arrows in the quiver; to shoot in the dark the upright of heart.*

*Quoniam ecce peccatores intenderunt arcum; paraverunt sagittas suas in pharetra, ut sagittent in obscuro rectos corde.*

10{11}[4]   *For they have destroyed the things which you have made: but what has the just man done?*

*Quoniam quae perfecisti destruxerunt; iustus autem quid fecit?*

Consequently, the Prophet [David] shows that these heretics irrationally say,   10{11}[3] *Quoniam ecce peccatores, for, lo, the wicked,* in this instance the heretics, *intenderunt arcum, have bent their bow,* that is, they have placed their genius toward evil teachings, arming them with the authority of divine Scripture, which they understand in a perverse manner; *paraverunt sagittas suas in pharetra, they have prepared their arrows in the quiver,* that is, with ease they hold counterfeit and false words in their heart and tongue, which appear to be reasonable and righteous to the simple: and so under the guise of good they deceive, especially since they fortify themselves with the authority of Scripture; *ut sagittent, to shoot,* that is, they corrupt their doctrine, *in obscuro, in the dark,* that is hiddenly and insidiously, *rectos corde, to the upright of heart,* that is, to the faith and works of Christians.[12] And in this they sin gravely, O Lord,   10{11} [4] *quoniam quae perfecisti, that which you have made,* that is the divine Scriptures, the decrees and ordinances of the Fathers, *destruxerunt, they have destroyed,* that is, they have subverted, introducing new and vain doctrines. *Iustus autem quid fecit? But what has the just man done?* That is, in what manner are these heretics to be resisted? And he responds:

----

10{11}[5]   *The Lord is in his holy temple, the Lord's throne is in heaven. His eyes look on the poor man: his eyelids examine the sons of men.*

*Dominus in templo sancto suo; Dominus in caelo sedes eius. Oculi eius in pauperem respiciunt, palpebrae eius interrogant filios hominum.*

10{11}[5] *Dominus in templo sancto suo, the Lord is in his holy temple,* that is, the Lord remains in the heart of the just, so to protect him from

----

12  *E. N.* "For heresies would not be born and certain perversions of dogma, ensnaring souls and casting them headlong into the deep, unless the good Scriptures are not rightly understood; and that which is in them is not well understood is temerariously and audaciously asserted." St. Augustine, *In Evang. Ioan.,* XVIII, 1, PL 35, 1536.

the fraud of perverse men, and to preserve him in the true faith. It is as if he says: "The just man indeed will not give assent, but will resist, the heretics," not however as a result of his own power, but the Lord dwelling in him by grace gives the efficacious means of resisting, in the manner that the Apostle says: Pray to the Lord, that *we may be delivered from importunate and evil men.*[13] Or [the Psalm can be interpreted thus], *The Lord is in his holy temple,* that is, he dwells in the congregation of his elect, so that might defend them from the depravity of the heretics. *Dominus in caelo sedes eius, the Lord's throne is in heaven.* This is satisfactorily explained in the explanation of the prior verse.

---

## ANOTHER EXPLANATION OF PART OF THE PSALM

10{11}[2]   *In the Lord I put my trust: how then do you say to my soul: Get you away from hence to the mountain like a sparrow?*

*In Domino confido; quomodo dicitis animae meae: Transmigra in montem sicut passer?*

10{11}[3]   *For, lo, the wicked have bent their bow; they have prepared their arrows in the quiver; to shoot in the dark the upright of heart.*

*Quoniam ecce peccatores intenderunt arcum; paraverunt sagittas suas in pharetra, ut sagittent in obscuro rectos corde.*

10{11}[4]   *For they have destroyed the things which you have made: but what has the just man done?*

*Quoniam quae perfecisti destruxerunt; iustus autem quid fecit?*

This part of the Psalm may additionally be explained as relating to the individual faithful, tempted by the spirit of self-exaltation and vainglory. The truly humble man—who glories not in himself, but in the Lord,[14] and does not desire to be put in front of anyone or to be waited upon—says:   10{11}[2] *In Domino confido, in the Lord I put my trust,* from whom comes all the good that I have. *Quomodo, how then,* therefore, O tempter, O devil, or foolish man, or my own thoughts: *how then,* I say, *dicitis animae meae, do you say to my soul,* suggesting interiorly or speaking exteriorly, or providing an occasion of pride, *Transmigra in montem, get you away from hence to the mountain,* that is, extol yourself,

---

13   Cf. 2 Thess. 3:1; 2 Thess. 3:2. *E. N.* 2 Thess. 3:2 continues *for all men have not the faith.*
14   Cf. 2 Cor. 10:17.

reputing yourself to be something when you are in fact nothing,[15] and this, *sicut passer, as a sparrow?* Not that these[16] say this clearly to the soul, so that it may elevate itself to the heights as a sparrow: for if they were to say this [clearly], their persuasive force would not be apparent, nor would it entrap the soul, because the sparrow is a petulant, restless, and trifling animal. Indeed, they say: "Well done, well done, what good have you accomplished, how praiseworthily you have lived! With merit have men regarded you as great and holy." But because this sort of suggestion tends towards this [self-exaltation], wherein a man vainly may be gloried and extolled, as a result of this he may be compared to a flighty sparrow. Consequently, the just and humble man considers not the words of these seducers, but reality: [a reality] in which he makes a point to himself to call attention to their[17] cunning, not willing to give them consent. And therefore, the Psalm adds:    10{11}[3] *Quoniam ecce peccatores, for, lo, the wicked*, namely, the previously mentioned deceitful persuaders, *intenderunt arcum, they have bent their bow*, that is, they have thought noxious counsels, from which, as if from a bow, proceed both words and acts, which deceive others; *paraverunt sagittas suas in pharetra, they have prepared their arrows in the quiver*, that is, they have arranged the adulatory words in their mouth, or the deceptive works in their life, scandalizing, tempting, corrupting others. For the life of sinners, sitting in the seat of pestilence,[18] is called a quiver, because by it the soul of his neighbor is injured. *Ut sagittent, to shoot*, inducing to sin, *in obscuro, in the dark*, setting forth evil and falsity under the form of good and truth. For the Apostle attests to this, *Satan himself transforms himself into an angel of light*: similarly also his ministers transform themselves into ministers of justice.[19] *Rectos corde, the upright of heart*, that is, the innocent and the simple. For such persons are easily corrupted by the dissimulator and the deceitful, because they appraise such to be such as they themselves are: for which reason it is written, *The innocent believes every word*,[20] because Wisdom says: *He that is hasty to give credit, is light of heart, and shall be lessened.*[21] Whence, the innocent and simple lack discretion and caution; and they are in need of the good instruction of experienced men:

---

15  *Cf.* Gal. 6:3.
16  E. N. The devil, the foolish man, or one's own thoughts.
17  E. N. Again, the cunning of the devil, the flatterer, or one's own deceptive thoughts.
18  E. N. *Cf.* Ps. 1:1.
19  *See and cf.* 2 Cor. 11:14–15.
20  Prov. 14:15a.
21  Ecclus. 19:4a.

indeed, unless God, who protects *them that walk in simplicity,*[22] were to protect them, it would be rare or never that they would avoid the snares of the seducers.    10{11}[4] *Quoniam quae perfecisti, for the things you have made,* that is the true and immaculate justice of the divine precepts and counsels which you, O Lord, have commanded, counseled, and implemented by works, which you, who did not come to destroy the law with respect to its precepts but to fulfil it,[23] *began to do and to teach;*[24] *destruxerunt, they have destroyed,* [they meaning] the aforementioned sinners, who, acting against the charity of God and neighbor, endeavor to bring others to ruin.

---

10{11}[5]    *The Lord is in his holy temple, the Lord's throne is in heaven. His eyes look on the poor man: his eyelids examine the sons of men.*

*Dominus in templo sancto suo; Dominus in caelo sedes eius. Oculi eius in pauperem respiciunt, palpebrae eius interrogant filios hominum.*

10{11}[5] *Oculi eius, his eyes,* that is, the mercy and the providence of God, *in pauperem, on the poor man,* that is, the humble man or he who disdains the things of this earth and voluntarily accepts poverty, *respiciunt, they look upon,* hearing their prayers, and preserving them from evil. *Palpebrae eius, his eyelids,*[25] that is the patience and long-sufferance of God, which overlooks the sins of men,[26] delaying punishment; which also delays in bestowing mercy to the just; *interrogant, they examine,* that is, weigh, *filios hominum, the sons of men,* searching into and testing, whether sinners may appear utterly obstinate, or whether just men are truly just; namely, from that wherein God differs in judgment, for he makes known whether evil men wish to be evil in their innermost self, persevering in vice; and also whether the just constantly are just, enduring with equanimity all things. For which reason in Ecclesiastes it states: *because sentence is not speedily pronounced against the evil, the children of men commit evils without any fear.*[27] And again the most wise Solomon says: *This is a very great evil among all things that are done under*

---

22  Prov. 2:7b.

23  *Cf.* Matt. 5:17.

24  Acts 1:1b.

25  *E. N. Quid ergo palpebras Dei, nisi eius iudicia accipimus?* "What else, therefore, do we understand by the eyelids of God except his judgments?" Pope St. Gregory the Great, *Mor. in Iob,* III, 6, 28, 4, 13, PL 76, 454.

26  *Cf.* Wis. 11:24. *E. N.* the verse continues: *for the sake of repentance.*

27  Eccl. 8:11.

*the sun, that the same things happen to all men: whereby also the hearts of the children of men are filled with evil, and with contempt.*[28] We are also fittingly able to understand by the eyelids of God his long-suffering and his patience: for eyelids are the protection and the covering of the eyes or one's vision. But God, from the fact that he appears so long-suffering and patient, appears as if he does not consider or know the deeds of men, but acts according to that which Habakkuk, both impatient and marveling, says to the Lord: *Your eyes are too pure to behold evil, and you cannot not look on iniquity: why do you not look upon them that do unjust things, and hold your peace when the wicked devours the man that is more just than himself?*[29] For God is said not to have regard for the iniquitous because he does not immediately punish them. And from the fact that God permits the just to be afflicted in various ways and he does not reward them in the present, hearts of the inconstant are, during such times, inclined to be troubled, and, as it were, to entertain doubts on the providence of God and to fall way from a virtuous way of life. Of such persons, it is written: *Your words have been unsufferable to me, says the Lord.... You have said: He labors in vain that serves God, and what profit is it that we have kept his ordinances, and that we have walked sorrowful before the Lord?*[30] But of these errors, David in contradiction [to the words of Malachi just quoted], adds:

10{11}[6]   *The Lord tries the just and the wicked: but he that loves iniquity hates his own soul.*

*Dominus interrogat iustum et impium; qui autem diligit iniquitatem, odit animam suam.*

10{11}[6] *Dominus interrogat iustum et impium,* the Lord tries the just and the wicked, that is, in the way just mentioned he tests, tempts, and scatters men, namely through tribulations and heresies and adversities, so that it may become evident who truly may belong to God. For which reason, Moses said: *You shall remember all the way through which the Lord your God ... to afflict you and to prove you, and that the things that were in your heart might be made known, whether you would*

---

28  Eccl. 9:3a. E. N. The verse continues: *while they live, and afterwards they shall be brought down to hell.*
29  Hab. 1:13. E. N. Denis varies the second part of verse Hab. 1:13 and makes it negative, changing the tenor of the verse from a sense of impatience to a sense of inquisitiveness.
30  Mal. 3:13–14.

keep his commandments or not.[31] *Qui autem diligit iniquitatem, but he that loves iniquity*, that is, he who delights in evil, and has an appetite for that which is not lawful, *odit animam suam, hates his own soul*, that is, himself. For just as to love is nothing other than to wish good to another, so to hate is nothing other than to wish evil to another. He who therefore desires that which is repugnant to the salvation of his soul truly hates himself.

---

10{11}[7]    *He shall rain snares upon sinners: fire and brimstone and storms of winds shall be the portion of their cup.*

*Pluet super peccatores laqueos; ignis et sulphur, et spiritus procellarum, pars calicis eorum.*

10{11}[7]    *Pluet, he shall rain*, namely the Lord [shall rain], *super peccatores laqueos, snares upon the sinners.* By this punishment is placed, namely, upon those loving iniquity. For the Lord rains, that is, pours out upon them, snares in the present life, in death, in the future judgment, and in hell. For in the present he constrains with the fetters of vice, so that they are able to do nothing meritorious, nor are they able to raise their mind through charity to God; but they serve the devil, *by whom*, according to the Apostle, *they are held captive at his will.*[32] For this reason, Solomon asserts: *His own iniquities catch the wicked, and he is fast bound with the ropes of his own sins.*[33] Also, in death the Lord rains snares upon sinners, because after death no one is able to repent to the Lord, as the evil angels are not able to after their fall: because as the Damascene[34] says, what the fall is to angels, death is to man. For in the manner that the wicked angels are averse to God without the ability to convert, and remain eternally in that disposition in which they were when upon sinning were cast down, so the souls dying in mortal sin are averse to God without the ability of conversion, and they remain eternally in that disposition of mind and affection in which they were when they separated from the body. And in the future judgment, God *shall rain* snares upon the sinners, for he will hand them over to eternal damnation, which they will have no power to evade, but they will be bound in hell; for they will cast, hands and feet bound, into the exterior

---

31   Deut. 8:2.
32   2 Tim. 2:26b.
33   Prov. 5:22.
34   E. N. This particular reference is to St. John of Damascus's *De Fide Orthodoxa*, II, 4, PG 94, 878.

darkness.[35] And in hell, they will be *ignis, fire* inextinguishable, *sulfur,
brimstone,* that is a horrible stench, *et spiritus procellarum, and storms of
winds,* that is the din of intolerable cries, and the howling of the miserable, a dismally dark atmosphere, and an oppressive clamor of the torture,
*pars calicis eorum, the portion of their cup,* that is their punishments. For
such is the their punishment that to contemplate is not possible, nor is
it able to be thought about fully and entirely: for there are many kinds
of torments, which are not enumerated here, indeed known to no man,
except those who will be and are in hell.

----

10{11}[8]   *For the Lord is just, and has loved justice: his countenance has
beheld righteousness.*

*Quoniam iustus Dominus, et iustitias dilexit: aequitatem vidit
vultus eius.*

Then is stated the cause of such condemnations of the evil.   10{11}
[8] *Quoniam iustus Dominus et iustitias dilexit, for the Lord is just, and
has loved justice:* God certainly is naturally and substantially just. And
as the divine intellect is the measure and source of all truth, so the
divine will is the measure, cause, and fountain of all justice. Whence it
is written: *For so much then as you are just, you order all things justly....
For your power is the beginning of justice.*[36] Whoever, therefore, is seen
to be just by God, and whatever proceeds from him, by the very fact
that he is seen by him to be just, or is caused by him [to be just], is
just. And therefore certain precepts to men by God can be singled out
which, at other times, would not have been just, nor would they have
been commanded by God: such as he commanded Abram to kill his
innocent son;[37] or that which we find in Hosea: *The beginning of the
Lord's speaking by Hosea: and the Lord said to Hosea: Go, take you a wife
of fornications, and have of her children of fornications.*[38] But similar is the
ground of love *(causa dilectionis)*:[39] and therefore God who is just, loves
justice, that is, [loves] just deeds on account of themselves, but [loves]
the doers of justice because of justice. *Aequitatem vidit vultus eius, his*

----

35   Matt. 22:13.
36   Wis. 12, 15a, 16a.
37   Gen. 22:2.
38   Hos. 1:2.
39   E. N. The statement that similarity was the cause or ground of love was a commonplace among Scholastic theologians. Often, reference was made to Ecclus.
13:9: *Every beast loves its like: so also every man him that is nearest to himself.*

*countenance has beheld righteousness*, that is, the equality of retribution which, approved by the divine intellect, is rendered to individuals in accordance to how worthy they are.

It is clear from what has been said above, how full of meaning and medicinal and morally beneficial this Psalm is. And you ought, O brother, when you read this Psalm, to direct all its words to the formation of your character, however much you may be accustomed, and however many times you are tempted by vainglory or the spirit of self-exaltation, and to say within yourself: *In the Lord I put my trust*, etc. Also, while you bring to mind the sins of the ungodly, attend to yourself, that that which you condemn in others may not occur to you. So when you say, *His eyes look upon the poor man*, etc. pay attention to the providence of God, and think — before the eyes of the Judge and carefully sifting through all things — in what fashion you may have walked. Finally, when you say, *He shall rain snares upon sinners*, etc. you ought to conceive a great and holy fear of the strict vengeance of God, and of the punishments of hell. And he who is accustomed to read the Psalms, will discover in such psalmody marvelous fruit and relish.

# ARTICLE XXXI

## ALLEGORICAL EXPOSITION OF
## THE SAME TENTH PSALM OF CHRIST.

10{11}[2]    *In the Lord I put my trust: how then do you say to my soul: Get you away from hence to the mountain like a sparrow?*

*In Domino confido; quomodo dicitis animae meae: Transmigra in montem sicut passer?*

HE HOLY PROPHET [DAVID], SPEAKING IN the person of Christ,    10{11}[2] *In Domino*, in the Lord, he says, *confido*, I put my trust: in the same manner as in a later Psalm he says, *O Lord, my hope from my youth*.[40] *Quomodo*, how then, therefore, O Scribe and Pharisee, *dicitis animae meae, Transmigra in montem*, do you say to my soul: *Get you away from hence to the mountain*, that is, glory vainly, mollified with praise and adulation, and seek to please men, and withdraw from true humility, and say that which pleases men, though it be false?

---

40  Ps. 70:5.

**10{11}[3]**  *For, lo, the wicked have bent their bow; they have prepared their arrows in the quiver; to shoot in the dark the upright of heart.*

*Quoniam ecce peccatores intenderunt arcum; paraverunt sagittas suas in pharetra, ut sagittent in obscuro rectos corde.*

**10{11}[4]**  *For they have destroyed the things which you have made: but what has the just man done?*

*Quoniam quae perfecisti destruxerunt; iustus autem quid fecit?*

**10{11}[3]** *Quoniam ecce peccatores,* for, lo, the wicked, that is the previously-mentioned Jews, *intenderunt arcum,* have bent their bow, that is, snares, *paraverunt sagittas suas,* they have prepared their arrows, that is, their deceitful words, *in pharetra,* in the quiver, that is, in the heart and tongue, *ut sagittent in obscuro rectos corde,* to shoot in the dark the upright of heart, that is Christ and his disciples, of whom they said, *Why does your master eat and drink with publicans and sinners?*[41] And seeking to flatter Christ, they said: *We know that you are a true speaker, and teach the way of God in truth, neither care you for any man.*[42] See the manner they endeavored to transfer him *to the mountain as a sparrow,* the vain enticement with this extent of praise, that he might respond in accordance with their will.   **10{11}[4]** *Quoniam quae perfecisti,* for the things you have made, O Christ, *destruxerunt,* they have destroyed, that is, seeking to nullify by detraction and blasphemies your most perfect life and most morally good doctrine. *Iutus autem,* but the just man, that is Jesus Christ, who is the form of the just and the Saint of Saints, *quid fecit,* what has he done to these? And he responds:

---

**10{11}[5]**  *The Lord is in his holy temple, the Lord's throne is in heaven. His eyes look on the poor man: his eyelids examine the sons of men.*

*Dominus in templo sancto suo; Dominus in caelo sedes eius. Oculi eius in pauperem respiciunt, palpebrae eius interrogant filios hominum.*

**10{11}[5]** *Dominus,* the Lord, that is the Word of God, assuming human nature, *in templo sancto suo,* in his holy temple, that is, in the human nature of Christ, as if in a most holy temple, was and remained, preserving and protecting it everywhere and always. Whence Christ called his body a

---

41  Mark 2:16b.
42  Matt. 22:16b.

temple: *Destroy this temple*, he said, *and in three days I will raise it up.*[43] *But he spoke of the temple of his body.*[44] However, this may not be understood as meaning that the union of the word with the human nature in Christ was only accidental or by means of the indwelling of grace (as the enemy of God, Nestorius, who was the bishop of Constantinople, supposed), and is not able [to be understood] as a personal and the immediate union of the two natures.[45] Christ, therefore, according to the assumed humanity, is said to be the temple in a most excellent way of the Word, and of the entire blessed Trinity, because he was full of all charity and grace, and was never at any time separated from God. *Dominus in caelo, the Lord . . . in heaven,* that is, in the soul of Christ, *sedes eius, his throne,* because in it [his soul] he inseparably rests from the first moment of its creation, much more excellently than in the celestial Thrones,[46] which are said to be in a special way the thrones of God. *Oculi eius, his eyes,* that is to say of the Lord, *in pauperum respiciunt, look upon the poor man,* that is in Christ, who since he was rich, for us he became poor.[47] The rest of the words of this Psalm have been satisfactorily explained [in prior articles].

# PRAYER

YOU WHO ARE THE ETERNAL GOD, BE merciful to us who put our trust in you: grant us your gift to be dissimilar to the swallow; make us able by your power to extinguish the arrows of the wicked, and to live in the righteousness of your grace, which you give to us to be pleasing to you in eternity.

*Qui es Deus aeternus, esto nobis propitius in te confidentibus:*
*tribue nos tuo munere passeribus esse dissimiles; fac nos*
*tua virtute sagittas maligni exstinguere, aequitate*
*gratiae tuae vivere, qua nobis dones tibi in*
*sempiternum complacere.*

43  John 2:19b.

44  John 2:21.

45  The union was made in the [one] person. *E. N.* Denis here rejects the Monophysite heresy, where there is a union of natures in Christ, the divine and the human, thus rejecting a *tertium quid* Christology, and positioning himself squarely with the orthodox doctrine of Christ defined by the Council of Chalcedon.

46  *E. N.* Referring to that choir of angels known as the Thrones. *See* footnote 9-12.

47  *Cf.* 2 Cor. 8:9.

# Psalm 11

## ARTICLE XXXII

### LITERAL EXPOSITION OF THE ELEVENTH PSALM:
### *SALVUM ME FAC, DOMINE, QUONIAM, &c.*
### *SAVE ME, O LORD, FOR THERE, &c.*

**11{12}[1]** *Unto the end; for the octave, a Psalm for David.*

*In finem, pro octava. Psalmus David.*

HE TITLE OF THIS CURRENT PSALM IS: **11{12}[1]** *In finem, pro octava. Psalmus David, unto the end, for the octave, a Psalm for David*: that is, this Psalm directs us to the end, that is, Christ; David, who is speaking here in the person of the perfect man, *for the octave*, that is, at the advent of the future judgment, whose day he desires on account of the multiplication of evil men whom he desires to destroy. For the of judgment is called *the octave* because it will come after the seven ages of the world.[1]

---

**11{12}[2]** *Save me, O Lord, for there is now no saint: truths are decayed from among the children of men.*

*Salvum me fac, Domine, quoniam defecit sanctus, quoniam diminutae sunt veritates a filiis hominum.*

Speaking, therefore, in the person of the just, of one zealous for God, of one having compassion for the world, he says:   **11{12}[2]** *Salvum me fac, Domine, save me, O Lord*, from the company of sinners, from the danger of vice, from all past, present, and future evil, *quoniam defecit sanctus, for there is now no saint*, that is, because there is none who keeps

---

1 E. N. The "seven ages of the world," *septem aetates mundi*, is a reference to St. Augustine's philosophy of history found in his *De catechizandis rudibus* (*On the Catechizing of the Uninstructed*) (XXII, 39), his *De civitate Dei* (*On the City of God*) (X, 14; XVI, 43.3, XXII, 30, 5), his *De Genesi contra Manichaeos* (*On Genesis against the Manichees*) (I, 23), as well as *Enarrationes in Psalmos* (*Narration on the Psalms*) (127, 15); *De divers. quaest. oct. tribus* (*On Diverse Questions*) (58, 2; 64, 2), and his letters (*Epist.* 213). It is based upon an analogy with the seven days of the week. On the evening of the sixth age, Jesus, the Son of Man, is to return, ushering in the seventh age.

your law: and therefore great dangers threaten me, since it is dangerous
to live among the ungodly; nor will I find help in advancing in the world,
because all draw me to sin by their example: consequently, I plead to
be saved by you, that evil may not alter my heart[2] or falsehood ensnare
my soul. *Quoniam diminutae sunt veritates a filiis hominum, for truths
are decayed among the children of men.* For the truths of life are decayed,
since the perversity of morals grows stronger, and the truth of doctrine
shrinks smaller, and this because the examples of error are multiplied.
Diminished is the truth of justice, for all seek that which is their own,
and none seek that which is of Jesus Christ.[3] The just man therefore
says, *Save me, O Lord, for there is now no saint*; not that he regards no
one to be holy in this world other than himself, but because so few
are the saints in comparison to the evil, so that it appears as if they
have thoroughly disappeared. For that which is but little is regarded
as being nothing. And so does Elijah say to the Lord: *They have slain
your prophets with the sword,* [4] *and I alone am left.*[5] For which he also
says, *Take away my soul,*[6] as if saying, *Save me, O Lord, for there is now
no saint.* And compatible with this understanding the Apostle says: *For
all seek the things that are their own; none those that are of Jesus Christ.*[7]

---

11{12}[3]   *They have spoken vain things everyone to his neighbor: with
deceitful lips, and with a double heart have they spoken.*

*Vana locuti sunt unusquisque ad proximum suum; labia dolosa,
in corde et corde locuti sunt.*

Consequently, he declares the manner in which trust is diminished
among the sons of men.   11{12}[3] *Vana, vain things,* he says, *locuti sunt
unusquisque cum proximo suo, they have spoken every one to his neighbor*:
that is, it is as if by speaking false and frivolous things to each other
they are all deceiving, corrupting, and contaminating each other: and
so one draws another to death, since, by his example and his word, the
failings of one man draws another to his manner of life. Therefore *they*

---

2  *Cf.* Wis. 4:11.

3  Phil. 2:21.

4  1 King. 19:10b.

5  1 Kings 19:14b. *E. N.* Denis has *relictus sum ego solus* instead of *derelictus sum
ego solus.*

6  1 King. 19:4b.

7  Phil. 2:21. *E. N.* Denis has *nemo quae Iesu Christi,* "no one those things of Jesus
Christ," in lieu of *non quae sunt Iesu Christi,* "not the things that are of Jesus
Christ."

*have spoken vain things,* because their *labia,* their *lips,* are *dolosa in corde, deceitful in heart,* because they express one thing by their mouths, and another thing they hold in their heart, and so they are double-tongued,[8] dissimulators and cunning. Whence, the Psalm follows with: *et corde locuti sunt, and with [that] heart they have spoken,* that is, they have spoken with a vain and false intention.[9] For such sort of speech is vicious, as is written in Ecclesiasticus: *He that speaks sophistically, is hateful: he shall be destitute of everything. Grace is not given him from the Lord: for he is deprived of all wisdom.*[10] And again Scripture says: *An evil mark of disgrace is upon the double tongued.*[11] And holy Job: *Dissemblers and crafty men prove the wrath of God.*[12] Let us flee, therefore, his most grave vice, because as the Psalm continues:

11{12}[4]   *May the Lord destroy all deceitful lips, and the tongue that speaks proud things.*

*Disperdat Dominus universa labia dolosa, et linguam magniloquam.*

11{12}[5]   *Who have said: We will magnify our tongue; our lips are our own; who is Lord over us?*

*Qui dixerunt: Linguam nostram magnificabimus; labia nostra a nobis sunt. Quis noster dominus est?*

11{12}[4] *Disperdat Dominus universa labia dolosa, may the Lord destroy all deceitful lips,* that is, that he may do away with or take away all the deceitful from the congregation of the faithful, *et linguam magniloquam, and the tongue that speaks proud things,* that is, men that are presumptuous. And may God disperse these kinds of men,   11{12}[5] *qui dixerunt: linguam nostrum magnificabimus, who have said: we will magnify our tongue,* that is, we will speak great and presumptuous and marvelous things about ourselves, seeing that we may be honored among men; *labia nostra, our lips,* that is, our eloquence and our subtle words, *a nobis sunt, are our own,* that is, are ascribed only to ourselves; and for this reason, we are praised. *Quis noster Dominus est? Who is Lord over us?*

---

8  E. N. While Denis calls the deceitful double-tongued (*bilengues*), the translator of the Douay-Rheims has called them "double-hearted."

9  Here, the Douay-Rheim's translation departs slightly from Denis's understanding of the verse: *Labia dolosa, in corde et corde locuti sunt.* Denis understands it as saying, "with lips deceitful in heart, and with such a heart they have spoken."

10  Ecclus. 37:23–24.

11  Ecclus. 5:17.

12  Job. 36:13a.

This either they say openly or, if they do not say so with their mouth, yet they say so with their pride-inflated heart, as if the Lord did not exist: in the manner that Ezechiel said to Pharaoh: *Pharaoh, king of Egypt, you great dragon that lies in the midst of your rivers, and say: The river is mine, and I made myself.*[13] But this which is written, *may the Lord destroy all deceitful lips,* etc. is able to be understood in two ways. The first, in the manner of a prayer, namely, that God might give the deceitful the grace of conversation and amendment: and so they might be destroyed to the extent of their fault, but not insofar as their salvation, that is, that they no longer be as they were, but that they might be converted and live spiritually. The second understanding is in the manner of a prophetic denunciation, as a disclosure of that they may be eternally destroyed by the Lord, and perish, unless they repent.

---

11{12}[6]   *By reason of the misery of the needy, and the groans of the poor, now will I arise, says the Lord. I will set him in safety; I will deal confidently in his regard.*

*Propter miseriam inopum, et gemitum pauperum, nunc exsurgam, dicit Dominus. Ponam in salutari; fiducialiter agam in eo.*

11{12}[7]   *The words of the Lord are pure words: as silver tried by the fire, purged from the earth refined seven times.*

*Eloquia Domini, eloquia casta; argentum igne examinatum, probatum terrae, purgatum septuplum.*

Thence, the Lord reveals himself to have heard the prayer of the perfect man, who says: *Save me, O Lord,* etc. For he says:   11{12}[6] *Propter miseriam inopum, by reason of the misery of the needy,* that is, in order to deliver the needy from their misery, that is, from the imperfections of the present life, from all those dangers and all the daily punishments of this daily life, *et propter gemitum pauperum, and because of the groans of the poor,* that is, because the frequent sighs and heartfelt prayers of the poor in spirit, namely, the humble, *nunc exsurgam, now will I arise,* that is, I will come to the rescue and I will do that which has been prayed for, *dicit Dominus, says the Lord. Ponam in salutari, I will set him in safety,* that is, the needy and the poor I will place under the protection of my grace, or I will establish them in the state of salvation; *fiducialiter agam in eo, I will deal confidently in his*

---

13  Ez. 29:3b.

*regard*, that is, faithfully I will defend them in such protection, and I will not permit them to be perverted by the perverse. And do not doubt, O needy ones, the truth of the promises of the Lord, because    **11{12}** [7] *Eloquia Domini, eloquia casta, the words of the Lord are pure words*, that is, pure with no admixture of falsehood, namely [they are] Sacred Scripture; *argentum igne examinatum, as silver tried by fire*: that is, the words of the Lord might be compared to silver proved by fire, because as such silver is splendid and sweetly-sounding, so is sacred Scripture lucid, and sweet and tasteful to a devout mind. And the words of the Lord are silver, *probatum terrae, purged from the earth*, that is purified from all earthly dregs, *purgatum septuplum, purged seven times*, that is, clean in every possible way. For the word seven designates the whole entirety of something. Therefore the words of the Lord are compared to silver so proven and so purged because they make men unearthly and not carnal, but they will lead them to a heavenly and angelic life during their time on earth; and those men who obey those words, will be filled with the seven gifts of the Holy Spirit.

This part of the Psalm is can be fittingly explained in another way, as in this sense: *By reason of the misery of the needy*, that is for the saving of the misery of the pagans, who were full of all sorts of misery, for they had neither faith, nor the grace of God; *and the groans of the poor*, that is, for the consolation of the sorrow of the faithful of the Old Testament desiring the coming of the Messiah King; *now will I arise*, sending my Son into the world, so that he might deliver them, *says the Lord* God, the Father. *I will set* help and the salvation of the world, *in safety*, that is in my Incarnate Son, by whom all the elect are saved: and of whom Simeon says: *Because my eyes have seen your salvation*;[14] *I will deal confidently in his regard*, this is, efficaciously and infallibly I will operate through him the redemption of the world. *The words of the Lord*, that is, Christian doctrine, *are pure words*, that is, pure and most true: because it is more possible to transcend heaven and earth than it is for the smallest word of the evangelical law to perish.

---

**11{12}[8]**   *You, O Lord, will preserve us: and keep us from this generation forever.*

*Tu, Domine, servabis nos, et custodies nos a generatione hac in aeternum.*

---

14  Luke 2:30.

11{12}[8] *Tu, Domine, You, O Lord,* omnipotent Creator, *servabis nos, will preserve us,* from evil, *et custodies nos, and will keep us* in the good, *a generatione hac, from this generation:* of which it has already been spoken in the words, *May the Lord destroy all deceitful lips,* that we might not partake communion in their evil deeds; *in aeternum, forever:* that is, in the present that you might keep us from their fault, and in the future from their punishment. And this is the word of good hope and is implicitly a certain kind prayer. For the sense of it is: "You, O Lord, will protect us, that is, out of the love and great trust that I place in you, O Lord, I hope that you will protect us: indeed, I pray this intently."

---

11{12}[9]   *The wicked walk round about: according to your highness, you have multiplied the children of men.*

*In circuitu impii ambulant: secundum altitudinem tuam multiplicasti filios hominum.*

11{12}[9] *In circuitu impii ambulant, the wicked walk round about,* that is, they do not direct themselves by the straight and narrow path which leads to life,[15] but they wander about everywhere seeking vain things. *Secundum altitudinem, according to your highness,* that is, according to the majesty and magnitude of your power, *multiplicatis filios hominum, you have multiplied the children of men,* that is, the posterity of our first parents, multiplying the individuals of the human species, within which there are such innumerable persons (*supposita*), so that out of such multitude it might be made manifest how great the power of the Creator is. Or [another possible interpretation:] *according to your highness,* that is, according to that which is becoming for you, sublime and highest Lord, *you have multiplied the children of men,* not only in number, but in merit; not only in exterior goods, but in grace, faith, the gifts of the Holy Spirit, and all manner of virtues: which in the time of the new law especially has been fulfilled, from which the grace of the Holy Spirit is most bountifully poured out.

Finally, this Psalm morally teaches us to completely abhor the vices of the tongue, in the manner that is written: *he that refrains his lips is most wise.*[16]

---

15  Matt. 7:14.
16  Prov. 10:19b.

# PRAYER

OU, O LORD, DEFENDER OF THE FAITHFUL, conserve and defend us from the generation of the perverse, and unite us to the generation of the just who keep your pure words, so that we may also always abide in your love, and, with the help of your protection, we may enjoy to be confirmed in salvation in eternity.

*Tu, Domine, fidelium custos, conserva et custodi nos a generatione pravorum in aeternum, et coniunge nos generationi iustorum eloquia tua casta custodientium: ut et in dilectione tua semper maneamus, et tuae protectionis auxilio, perpeti salute gaudeamus.*

# *Psalm* 12

## ARTICLE XXXIII

### ELUCIDATION OF THE TWELFTH PSALM:
### *USQUEQUO, DOMINE, OBLIVISCERIS, &c.*
### HOW LONG, O LORD, WILL YOU FORGET, *&c.*

12{13}[1]   *Unto the end, a Psalm for David. How long, O Lord, will you forget
me unto the end? How long do you turn away your face from me?*

*In finem. Psalmus David. Usquequo, Domine, oblivisceris me
in finem? Usquequo avertis faciem tuam a me?*

HIS PSALM HAS THIS TITLE:  12{13}[1] *IN
finem, psalmus David, unto the end, a Psalm for David:* that is,
this Psalm leads us to Christ, written by the holy David speaking here
in the person of the faithful vehemently desiring the presence of Christ.
And this Psalm is a poem of a most ardent lover, the words containing
an ardency and a fullness of affection; in the manner of true devotion,
this Psalm consists of a heartfelt song of praise.

The Psalm is able literally to expounded about the Synagogue or of an
individual saint of the Old Testament, before the advent of Christ, namely
before the Incarnation of the Son of God, desiring with the whole heart. In
these persons, the Prophet [David] says: *Usquequo, Domine, oblivisceris me
in finem? How long, O Lord will you forget me unto the end?* That is, how long,
O Son of God, O Word of the eternal Father, coeternal with God the Father,
do you so keep yourself from me, as if even you might have entirely forgotten
of me, namely, by delaying so long your advent? *Usquequo avertis faciem tuam
a me? How long do you turn your face from me?* That is, how long do you keep
aloof from me and withdraw from me your presence, not only the divine
presence by which you always are everywhere, but also your bodily presence,
which in the end of this age you will assume? Surely, the ancient saints most
ardently desired this bodily presence of Christ, as expressed in the manner
found in the beginning of the song of love where Solomon, speaking in the
person of the Synagogue or of the ancient fathers, plaintively expresses:
*Let him kiss me with the kiss of his mouth,*[1] that is, let the Only-Begotten of

---

1  Songs 1:1.

God join himself immediately to my nature in an unmediated and personal union. And Isaiah: *O that you would rend the heavens and would come down.*[2] Habakkuk also says: *How long, O Lord, shall I cry, and you will not hear? shall I cry out to you suffering violence, and you will not save?*[3]

---

12{13}[2]  *How long shall I take counsels in my soul, sorrow in my heart all the day?*

Quamdiu ponam consilia in anima mea, dolorem in corde meo per diem?

12{13}[2] *Quamdiu ponam consilia, how long shall I take counsels,* that is, dubious questionings, *in anima mea, in my soul?* For a man who vehemently desires to obtain something thinks many counsels and many ways by which he might obtain that which he desires. So the saints of old reflected and questioned in multiple ways which sorts of rites of pleading might be efficacious to procure the mercy of God, namely the coming of Christ into the world. And how long, I might say, *dolorem, sorrow,* that is, sadness because of the postponement and delay of the advent of Christ, *in corde meo per diem, in my heart all the day,* that is, incessantly and every day? For *hope that is deferred afflicts the soul.*[4]

---

12{13}[3]  *How long shall my enemy be exalted over me?*

Usquequo exaltabitur inimicus meus super me?

12{13}[3] *Usquequo exaltabitur inimicus meus super me? How long shall my enemy be exalted over me?* That is, how long will the devil and the tinder *(fomes)* of sin and the offense of original sin prevail against me? For without the advent of Christ none of the Saints would be able to enter into the Kingdom of Heaven; they all descended into the infernal limbo.[5] Also, the power of the devil and the fomes of sin, was much greater and stronger before Christ's Incarnation and death, than it was afterwards: and so the enemy then was more exalted over the saints. But Christ bound the strong, armed man, that is, the devil, weakening his power; and robbed him of his possessions,[6] making a temple of God for himself out of men, who before existed as the household of the devil.

---

2  Is. 64:1.
3  Hab. 1:2.
4  Prov. 13:12.
5  *See* footnote 543.
6  *Cf.* Mark 3:27.

**12{13}[4]**   *Consider, and hear me, O Lord my God. Enlighten my eyes that I never sleep in death.*

*Respice, et exaudi me, Domine Deus meus. Illumina oculos meos, ne umquam obdormiam in morte.*

**12{13}[5]**   *Lest at any time my enemy say: I have prevailed against him. They that trouble me will rejoice when I am moved.*

*Nequando dicat inimicus meus: Praevalui adversus eum. Qui tribulant me exsultabunt si motus fuero.*

**12{13}[6]**   *But I have trusted in your mercy. My heart shall rejoice in your salvation: I will sing to the Lord, who gives me good things: yea I will sing to the name of the Lord the most high.*

*Ego autem in misericordia tua speravi. Exsultabit cor meum in salutari tuo. Cantabo Domino qui bona tribuit mihi; et psallam nomini Domini altissimi.*

And so that the enemy no longer greatly might exalt himself over me,   **12{13}[4]** *respice et exaudi me, Domine Deus meus; consider and hear me, O Lord my God*, assuming human nature, and redeeming me from the hand of all who hate me. *Illumina oculos meos, enlighten my eyes*, that is, with faith, grace, and the illumination of the Holy Spirit teach my intellect, both the speculative intellect, so that it might rightly know, as well as the practical intellect, so that it might justly live. Or [one might understand it this way,] illumine my intellect by your Incarnation appearing and living among men and teaching the perfection of the evangelical law: for you are the true light *which enlightens every man that comes into this world.*[7] And this, O Son of God, therefore do, *ne unquam, that I never*, that is, so that I not ever,[8] *obdormiam in mortem, sleep in death*, that is, that I never at any time fall into mortal sin: falling into which, I sleep and spiritually I die, because I fall short from the charity and grace of God;   **12{13}[5]** *nequando, lest at any time*, that is, at no time, *dicat inimicus meus, my enemy say*, he who is opposing the salvation of my soul, *praevalui adversus eum, I have prevailed against him*, leading him to consent to sin, or into eternal damnation.

*Qui tribulant me, they that trouble me*, tempting and attempting to do so that they might turn me from you, *exsultabunt si motus fuero,*

---

7  John 1:9.
8  *E. N.* This is actually reversed since the Douay Rheims already changes *ne unquam,* "I not ever," to *nunquam,* "I never."

*will rejoice when I am moved*, that is, they will rejoice if I will assent to their perversity and fall from your highest and immutable good by inconstancy.    **12{13}[6]** *Ego autem in misericordia tua speravi, but I have trusted in your mercy*, that is, I took a hold of the hope of victory, not from my own strength, but by confiding in the grace of Christ to be saved and to prevail, and to be purged from all sin, from which by the Law I am not able to be cleansed. Whence, in the Act of the Apostles, Paul says to the Jews: By Jesus *the forgiveness of sins is preached to you, . . . from all things from which you could not be justified by the law of Moses.*[9]

*Exsultabit cor meum, My heart shall rejoice* with spiritual joy *in salutari tuo, in your salvation*, that is in the Incarnation of your Son, O eternal Father, who is the Savior and the salvation of all men. In this life indeed I will exalt in him, contemplating him by faith, and expecting him in hope. But in the future age I will exult in him in the form of seeing him, that is, *face to face*: because I will see him as he is, and I *shall know him even as I am known.*[10] *Cantabo Domino qui bona tribuit, I will sing to the Lord, who gives me good things*, that is, I offer praise and give thanks, and I will always be thankful to the Son of God, my Savior, who bestowed upon me such great benefits: *et psallam nomini Domini alitissimi, and I will sing to the name of the Lord the most high*, that is, not only by word, but by word and deed together I will praise the most high God, one and three.

# ARTICLE XXXIV

## TROPOLOGICAL EXPOSITION OF
## THE SAME TWELFTH PSALM

**12{13}[1]**    *Unto the end, a psalm for David. How long, O Lord, will you forget me unto the end? How long do you turn away your face from me?*

*In finem. Psalmus David. Usquequo, Domine, oblivisceris me in finem? Usquequo avertis faciem tuam a me?*

**B**UT EXPOUNDING THIS PSALM MORALLY, THE Prophet [David]—in the person of any holy man or [in the person] of the Church desiring the advent of Christ, in the present by grace and

---

9  Acts. 13:38.
10  1 Cor. 13:12.

in the future by glory—says:   12{13}[1] *Usquequo, Domine, How long, O Lord*, almighty God, whose property is always to have mercy and always to spare,[11] *oblivisceris me, will you forget me*, your servant and pauper, *in finem, unto the end*, that is, for so long a time, not giving the desire for the perfection of life and grace in the current circumstances? For I desire to serve you in holiness and justice. And I pray to you daily that you might grant me the means to curb all my passions, to extirpate vices, to the point that I might tranquilly, with pure and steadfast mind, attend to you; but I do not obtain this grace from you in accordance with my desire. To be sure, O Lord, this is not from a deficiency in your goodness, but because of the unworthiness of my manner of life, because I place a barrier [between me and your grace], and make myself incapable of receiving your grace. But, O Lord, from you is all good: and therefore in whatever that you see in me to be deficient, in that very deficiency deign to help me out of your kindness. *How long*, therefore, *will you forget me unto the end*, not hearing the affections of my heart? *Usquequo avertis faciem tuam a me? How long do you turn away your face from me?* That is, how long will you suspend the gracious mercy of your presence and most sweet consolation of your graces from me—who am desolate and unfruitful, distressed and arid, for I do not taste how sweet is the Lord, nor do I make any progress as I desire and strive for? For sometimes God—for a time—suspends from good men the consolation of his grace, not in fact depriving them of habitual grace, but of devotional activity and experience, and of desired ardor: and this generally happens from a divine dispensation on account of our negligence. But whenever it happens from the divine dispensation, specifically, when we do not glory in inane things or self-exaltation, then grace smiles and is at hand; and this happens so that we may become accustomed to invoke God ardently, frequently, and confidently.

Now this verse may also be explained as for the man who is in love who, with St. Paul, desires to be dissolved, and *to be with Christ*.[12] Such a man says: *How long, O Lord, will you forget me unto the end*, not delivering me from this body of death,[13] from the sojourn of the present miserable exile? *How long do you turn away your face from me?* This is, how long do you deny me the beatific vision of your essence, not transferring me from faith to sight, and from the wayfaring state to the heavenly homeland (*de via ad patriam*)?

---

11  E. N. This phrase—*cui proprium est miserere semper et parcere*—is drawn from
an ancient collect.

12  Phil. 1:23.

13  *Cf.* Rom. 7:24.

**12{13}[2]**  *How long shall I take counsels in my soul, sorrow in my heart all the day?*

*Quamdiu ponam consilia in anima mea, dolorem in corde meo per diem?*

**12{13}[2]** *Quamdiu ponam consilia in anima mea, how long shall I take counsels in my soul,* inquiring and anxiously reflecting in what manner I might perfectly adhere to you, and I might always be perfectly pleasing to you, in the manner so that I might at the end of it all arrive to the enjoyment of your blessed goodness? *Dolorem in corde meo per diem, sorrow in my heart all day,* that is, how long will I be disheartened with myself, in my soul every day, because of the multitude of my imperfections and because of the absence of your grace or of your glory?

---

**12{13}[3]**  *How long shall my enemy be exalted over me?*

*Usquequo exaltabitur inimicus meus super me?*

**12{13}[3]** *Usquequo exaltabitur inimicus meus super me? How long shall my enemy be exalted over me?* That is, how long will I be subject to the temptations of the devil, the flesh, and the world, at the instigation of which I often fall, and show myself to be a servant of sin? And even if I do not sin mortally, yet — how sorrowfully unfortunate! — [14] I sin often venially, because a just man falls seven times a day;[15] and so often this occurs, my enemy is exalted and prevails over me. For I have an enemy within (*domesticum inimicum*):[16] of which the Apostle says, *I see another law in my members, fighting against the law of my mind.*[17] Whence Peter in his first epistle says: *I beseech you as strangers and pilgrims, to refrain yourselves from carnal desires which war against the soul.*[18] And Paul: *They,* he says, *who are in the flesh, cannot please God.*[19]

---

**12{13}[4]**  *Consider, and hear me, O Lord my God. Enlighten my eyes that I never sleep in death.*

---

14  L. *Proh dolor! Alas, the sorrow!*
15  Cf. Prov. 24:16.
16  E. N. This is a marvelous image used by Denis to describe the *fomes peccati*, the fomes or tinder of sin, the concupiscence that lingers even in a man redeemed and justified by habitual grace: *inimicus domesticus* literally means a domestic enemy, a household enemy, a traitor within.
17  Rom. 7:23.
18  1 Pet. 2:11.
19  Rom. 8:8.

*Respice, et exaudi me, Domine Deus meus. Illumina oculos meos,
ne umquam obdormiam in morte.*

12{13}[5]   Lest at any time my enemy say: I have prevailed against him.
They that trouble me will rejoice when I am moved.

*Nequando dicat inimicus meus: Praevalui adversus eum. Qui
tribulant me exsultabunt si motus fuero.*

So that I might efficaciously resist these enemies,   12{13}[4] *Respice,
et exaudi me, Domine Deus meus,* consider and hear me, O Lord my God:
consider me in mercy, which considers all things by knowledge. *Illumina
oculos meos,* enlighten my eyes, that is, teach and direct my intellect and my
memory, so that I may know and fulfill that which pleases you, *ne umquam
obdormiam in mortem, that I never sleep in death,* this meaning, that I might
not ever die in soul, distancing myself from you, fountain of happiness and
of life, that I might not sin mortally; and if I do perchance sin mortally,
that I at least do not remain in it or not end dying in it;   12{13}[5]
*Nequando dicat inimicus meus: Praevalui adversus eum, Lest at any time the
enemy say: I have prevailed against him,* separating him from God.

*Qui tribulant me, they that trouble me,* that is, the demons and their
ministers, *exsultabunt, si motus fuero, will rejoice when I am moved.* As
we have seen, this and the verses which follow have already been satisfactorily explained.

# PRAYER

ALMIGHTY AND ETERNAL GOD, ILLUMINE
the eyes of our hearts with the light of your Spirit, that we
might never sleep in evil acts; but with the aid of your grace, we might
continually keep watch in his precepts: so that, arriving at Christ,
we might cross over to obtain the reward of our supernatural calling.

*Omnipotens sempiterne Deus, illumine oculos cordis nostri lumine
Spiritus tui, ne unquam in perversis actibus dormitemus:
sed tua gratia opitulante, in praeceptis eius iugiter
vigilemus: ut ad praemium supernae vocatio-
nis, Christo adveniente, transeamus.*

# Psalm 13

## ARTICLE XXXV

### LITERAL EXPOSITION OF THE THIRTEENTH PSALM:
### *DIXIT INSIPIENS IN CORDE SUO, &c.*
### *THE FOOL HAS SAID IN HIS HEART, &c.*

**13{14}[1]** *Unto the end, a Psalm for David. The fool has said in his heart: There is no God. They are corrupt, and are become abominable in their ways: there is none that does good, no not one.*

*In finem. Psalmus David. Dixit insipiens in corde suo: Non est Deus. Corrupti sunt, et abominabiles facti sunt in studiis suis; non est qui faciat bonum, non est usque ad unum.*

HIS TITLE OF THIS PSALM IS: **13{14}[1]** *IN finem, Psalmus David, in the end, a Psalm for David,* that is, this Psalm which directs us to Christ, is a Psalm of holy David.

Exposited literally, this Psalm is of the obdurate and false Jews, especially those who disdained to believe Christ while bodily in the world living among men and performing miracles. Therefore, it says: *Dixit insipiens in corde suo, the fool has said in his heart,* that is, the unfaithful Jew despising the teaching of Christ (who is the eternal *Wisdom of God*),[1] who thought about and within himself affirmed, and adjudged: *Non est Deus, there is no God*: that is, this Jesus of Nazareth, whose mother and brothers are with us,[2] who eats with sinners,[3] and does not keep the Sabbath,[4] is neither God, nor is he the Son of God consubstantial and coeternal with God the Father, but rather is a sinner and blasphemer. That these things would be asserted of Christ by the Jews we know from the prophet Jeremiah, where we read this: *For the house of Israel, and the house of Judah have greatly transgressed against me, says the Lord; they have denied the Lord, and said, It is not he.*[5]

---

1 1 Cor. 1:24.
2 Matt. 13:55–56.
3 Mark 2:16.
4 John 9:16.
5 Jer. 5:11–12.

*Corrupti sunt, they are corrupt* with the festering of vices and criminal customs; the unbelieving Jews lost the integrity of mind because of their aversion to the highest, one and true God, Jesus Christ; *et abominabiles facti sunt in studiis suis, and they are become abominable in their ways,* that is, the aforementioned Jews have become contemptible to God and man in their deeds, words, and thoughts: because they have scorned the doctrine and the faith of the celestial Teacher, and have adhered to temporal things. For they were proud and avaricious and were uncircumcised of heart. *Non est qui faciat bonum. There is none that does good.* He does not say simply none are doers of good; but he says *There is none that does good* by reason of them being so detestable and corrupt [of soul] that none of them can do good or meritorious works because the just live by faith:[6] and accordingly he adds, *non est usque ad unum, no not one,* that is, so truly is it there is none who does good from those [*i.e.,* those not in grace and by faith], so that not one is to be found among them who does good: and so the word "one" (*unum*) is written down in an inclusive sense.[7] Whence in this fashion, Christ says of the unbelieving Jews: *how can you speak good things, whereas you are evil?*[8] Of which Jeremiah said: *they have made their faces harder than the rock, and they have refused to return,* and you have *refused* to take *discipline.*[9]

---

**13{14}[2]**   *The Lord has looked down from heaven upon the children of men, to see if there be any that understand and seek God.*

*Dominus de caelo prospexit super filios hominum, ut videat si est intelligens, aut requirens Deum.*

**13{14}[2]** *Dominus, the Lord,* that is, Christ the Word of God and God, *de caelo, from heaven,* that is, from his assumed humanity, in which his divinity lived as it did in heaven, *prospexit super filios hominum, looked down upon the children of men,* that is, attended to and considered the Jews: to whom he was especially sent, in accordance to that which he said,

---

6   Hab. 3:4; Gal. 3:11. E. N. In other words, none is supernaturally enlivened by habitual or sanctifying grace. As St. Thomas Aquinas makes clear, habitual or sanctifying grace "serves as the principle of meritorious works." *ST,* IaIIae, q. 109, art. 6, co. "Without me you can do nothing." John 15:5.

7   E. N. Not only inclusive in the sense of including all possible actors, but inclusive in the sense of including the interior disposition of the actor in reference to the external acts.

8   Matt. 13:34.

9   Jer. 5:3.

*I was not sent but to the sheep that are lost of the house of Israel;*[10] *ut videat si est intelligens aut requirens Deum,* to see if there be any that understand and seek God, that is, whether there is any one [among them] who by faith recognizes God the Father, and he whom he sent, Jesus Christ.[11]

---

**13{14}[3]** *They are all gone aside, they are become unprofitable together: there is none that does good, no not one. Their throat is an open sepulcher: with their tongues they acted deceitfully; the poison of asps is under their lips. Their mouth is full of cursing and bitterness; their feet are swift to shed blood. Destruction and unhappiness in their ways: and the way of peace they have not known: there is no fear of God before their eyes.*

*Omnes declinaverunt, simul inutiles facti sunt. Non est qui faciat bonum, non est usque ad unum. Sepulchrum patens est guttur eorum; linguis suis dolose agebant. Venenum aspidum sub labiis eorum. Quorum os maledictione et amaritudine plenum est; veloces pedes eorum ad effundendum sanguinem. Contritio et infelicitas in viis eorum, et viam pacis non cognoverunt; non est timor Dei ante oculos eorum.*

**13{14}[3]** *Omnes declinaverunt, they are all gone aside,* that is, he came upon none of such persons free from their corruption; but *they are all gone aside,* that is, through their disbelief they have withdrawn from Christ; *simul inutiles facti sunt, they are become unprofitable together:* because they are not able to save themselves, and they are not worthy to praise God. *Non est qui faciat bonum, there is none that does good,* that is, absolutely there is none of them that is doing good. But if this that is said — *there is none that does good* and *they are all gone aside,* etc. — is said of the Jews, it may also be interpreted simply and absolutely to be said of all men, in which case it is then understood as a synecdoche, and by comparison:[12] because manifestly the greater part of the Jews remained unbelievers, indeed, so many of them remained unbelievers, that in a

---

10 Matt. 15:24.
11 *Cf.* John 17:3.
12 E. N. Denis is saying that though the Psalm is referring to the Jews literally, the Jews synecdochally are understood as including all men, being a part of the whole. The synecdoche is a figure of comparison, where a part is used to describe the whole. When Denis says "by comparison" (*per comparationem*), he is using a more generic term [a figure of comparison] following the use of the more specific figure of comparison, that is, the synecdoche. In other words, he is using the two synonymously.

comparison of them with [the number of] others who believed, it is as
if they appeared to be none.[13]

*Sepulchrum patens est guttur eorum, their throat is an open sepulcher,*
that is, it is similar to an open grave: because in the manner that from
such [an open] grave flows out a certain deadly stench and corruption,
so from the hearts of the Jews, through their throat, tongue, and mouth
proceeded out blasphemous and fetid words with death-like breath. *Linguis suis dolose agebant, with their tongues they acted deceitfully.* For they
often tempted Christ, that they might entrap him with words, and they
might have cause against him.[14] For their princes and scribes seduced
others, steering them away from Christ, for in the Passion they also
persuaded the people to plead that they be given Barabbas, so that in
actuality they might have Jesus killed.[15] *Venenum aspidum, the poison
of asps,* that is, infectious words that also kill souls, *sub labiis eorum, is
under their lips,* that is, in the mouths of the faithless Jews, who denied,
defamed, and killed the Author of life and the Savior of the world.
*Quorum os maledictione, for their mouth . . . cursing,* that is, blasphemies
against Christ, *et amaritudine, and bitterness,* that is condemnatory, of
Christ to death, *plenum est, is full of,* for they proclaimed, *He is guilty
of death.*[16] *Veloces pedes eorum ad effundendum sanguinem, their feet are
swift to shed blood.* For with their minds and bodies they were ready
and prompt, so that they might kill Christ; and so, out of the envy of
heart, they also hurried with their bodily feet, running toward Christ
to put him to death.

*Contritio, destruction,* that is, the pulverization of spiritual being, the
destruction of charity, the extinction of grace, *et infelicitas, and unhappiness,* that is, the deprivation of all beatitude, and the turning away
from the highest good, is *in viis eorum, in their ways,* that is, is in their
manner of life and in the endeavor of the perverse Jews. Because they
persecuted the principle of life, the fountain of grace, even God their
salvation; consequently, all spiritual existence of gratifying grace (*gratiae
gratificantis*)[17] is pulverized, destroyed, and shattered, on which account

---

13  E. N. In other words, the number of Jews that accepted Jesus, when compared
    to the number of Jews who rejected him or compared to the number of the
    Gentiles who accepted Jesus, their number pales to virtually nothing.
14  Matt. 22:15.
15  Matt. 27:20.
16  Matt. 26:66b.
17  E. N. Denis uses the term *gratia gratificans,* gratifying grace as a synonym for
    sanctifying, justifying, or habitual grace, the grace which makes one pleasing or
    gratifying to God.

their works unhappily exist, and lead to infernal misery. *Et viam pacis, and the way of peace,* that is, the doctrine of Christ, by which one comes to eternal peace, *non congnoverunt, they have not known,* by its approval or imitation, but rather they have spurned it. Or [one might understand this verse as follows], *the way of peace,* that is, repentance, *they have not known,* but they have become hardened of heart; in the manner that Isaias predicted,[18] *For the heart of this people is grown gross.*[19] *Non est timor Dei ante oculos eorum, there is no fear of God before their eyes:* because they did not fear Christ, nor did they pay heed to this admonitions, nor did they regard the miracles ascribed to his testimony; but blinded by hate, they followed the measure of their fathers,[20] for as these killed the Prophets, so did they kill Christ, the King and the Lord of the Prophets.

---

**13{14}[4]**  *Shall not all they know that work iniquity, who devour my people as they eat bread?*

*Nonne cognoscent omnes qui operantur iniquitatem, qui devorant plebem meam sicut escam panis?*

**13{14}[4]** *Nonne cognoscent omnes qui operantur iniquitatem, shall not all they know that work iniquity,* that is, the evildoing men just discussed above, *qui devorant plebem meam, who devour my people,* that is, they killed Christ and his disciples at the beginning of the nascent Church, *sicut escam panis, as they eat bread? Shall not,* I say, *they know* the truth, namely, that they err? It is as if saying, "No,"[21] because in the present age they do not know, but they remain obstinate, in the manner that a later Psalm says, *Let their eyes be darkened that they see not.*[22] And Isaiah predicts: *Who is blind, but my servant,* that is, the Jewish people?[23] Or thus [as an alternative interpretation]: *Shall not all they know,* etc.? It is as if saying, "Indeed": because in the day of judgment when they shall see *him whom they have pierced,*[24] then they will know by the experience of punishment the truth.

---

18  Isaiah 6:10. *E. N.* Isaiah 6:10 reads: *Blind the heart of this people, and make their ears heavy, and shut their eyes: lest they see with their eyes, and hear with their ears, and understand with their heart, and be converted and I heal them.*

19  Matt. 13:15.

20  *Cf.* Matt. 23:32.

21  *E. N.* In other words, we have a negative rhetorical question.

22  Ps. 68:24a.

23  Is. 42:19a.

24  John 19:37.

**13{14}[5]**  *They have not called upon the Lord: there have they trembled for fear, where there was no fear.*

*Dominum non invocaverunt; illic trepidaverunt timore, ubi non erat timor.*

**13{14}[5]** *Dominum,* the Lord, that is, God the Father and his only-begotten Son, *non invocaverunt, they have not called upon,* that is, that have not prayed with their mind by charity and faith and an internal affection. *Illic trepidaverunt timore, ubi non erat timor, there they have trembled for fear, where there was no fear,* that is, where as a result of merit they should not have fear. For they feared men more than they did God; and they feared temporal punishments more than they did spiritual loss or the loss of the Kingdom of God. Whence they said: *What do we, for this man* (namely, Jesus) *does many miracles? If we let him alone so, all will believe in him; and the Romans will come, and take away our place and nation.*[25] But with respect to those men that adhered to Christ, they ought not to have feared to suffer pain, nor to fear persecution for the sake of justice: the reason for which the Prophet gives:

---

**13{14}[6]**  *For the Lord is in the just generation: you have confounded the counsel of the poor man, but the Lord is his hope.*

*Quoniam Dominus in generatione iusta est, consilium inopis confudistis, quoniam Dominus spes eius est.*

**13{14}[6]** *Quoniam Dominus in generatione iusta est, for the Lord is in the just generation:* that is, almighty God abides in the community of the faithful and in the congregation of those adhering to Christ, and he is in it by charity and by grace. And so he was in the multitude of them who followed Christ, who first came from the Jews, just as the Apostles, and other disciples, and some of the religious women.[26] But, O you unbelieving Jews, *consilium inopis confudistis, you have confounded the counsel of the poor man,* that is, evangelical counsels of Christ you have found contemptible, not willing to relinquish worldly things, and to strive after heavenly things with the whole heart. For this reason, as the Evangelists testified to, since Christ inveighed against avarice, you, standing against him, said: *He is mad: why hear you him?*[27] But Christ summons the poor, for as the Apostle says: because *being rich*

---

25  John 11:47b–48.
26  Luke 8:2; 23:5.
27  John 10:20.

*he became poor, for your sakes.*[28] And why did he do this except so that his temporal and bodily poverty might be for us spiritual abundance, and eternal wealth? Of this poverty Zacharias said regarding Christ: *Shout for joy, O daughter of Jerusalem: Behold your King will come to you, the just and Savior: he is poor, and riding upon an ass.*[29] Therefore, you have *confounded the counsel of the poor man, quoniam Dominus spes eius est, but the Lord is his hope,* that is, because he taught to have hope in God alone, not *in the uncertainty of riches,*[30] nor in the abundance of temporal things.

---

**13{14}[7]** *Who shall give out of Sion the salvation of Israel? When the Lord shall have turned away the captivity of his people, Jacob shall rejoice and Israel shall be glad.*

*Quis dabit ex Sion salutare Israel? Cum averterit Dominus captivitatem plebis suae, exsultabit Iacob, et laetabitur Israel.*

Finally, the holy David prophecies of the final conversion of the Jews,   **13{14}[7]** *Quis,* who, he asks, *dabit ex Sion,* shall give out of Sion, that is, who proceeding and being born from the people of the Synagogue, or the Jewish stock, *salutare,* salvation, that is, redemption, *Israel,* to Israel, this being the Israelite people? It is as if he is saying, "Who will save them?" And he responds: *Cum avertit Dominus captivitate plebis suae, when the Lord shall have turned away the captivity of his people,* that is, when Christ will have expelled from the hearts of the Jews the malice that blinds them, and the devil who reigns over them and who holds them fast in the captivity of perfidy and bound in sin; then *exultabit Iacob, Jacob shall rejoice,* that is, the people that stem from Jacob, the supplanter of power,[31] will rejoice, *et laetabitur Israel, and Israel shall be glad,* namely the people contemplating God: for then they will be glad, for they will recognize the true Messiah, and they will believe in him, and will serve him with a jocund heart, and will do so with a most thankful soul. That this conversion of theirs will occur at the end of time is taken from the preaching of Elijah, of whom Malachi said: *Behold I will send you Elijah the prophet, before the coming of the great and dreadful day of the Lord. And he shall turn the heart of the fathers to the children, and the heart of*

---

28  2 Cor. 8:9.

29  Zach. 9:9.

30  1 Tim. 6:17a.

31  E. N. The reference is to Jacob's supplanting the birthright of Esau, an incident narrated in Chapter 27 of the Book of Genesis.

*the children to their fathers.*[32] Through this — that he will make the Jews receive the true Christ, and most devoutly to worship him [Christ] — the deceased holy fathers, who were adverse to Jews because of their [the Jews'] disbelief, will turn to them and will love them; similarly, the sons who during the time of their infidelity were opposed to the holy fathers, by the faith of Christ will be converted to them. For which reason, the Savior says in the Gospel: Elijah when he will come, *he will restore all things.*[33] That this scripture, namely the final verse of this Psalm, is appropriately explained as referring to the future conversion of the Jews, is clear from this fact: that the Apostle brought out this scripture to the Romans to prove the future conversion of the Jews.[34]

# ARTICLE XXXVI

## MORAL EXPOSITION OF
## THIS SAME THIRTEENTH PSALM

13{14}[1]    *Unto the end, a Psalm for David. The fool has said in his heart: There is no God. They are corrupt, and are become abominable in their ways: there is none that does good, no not one.*

*In finem. Psalmus David. Dixit insipiens in corde suo : Non est Deus. Corrupti sunt, et abominabiles facti sunt in studiis suis; non est qui faciat bonum, non est usque ad unum.*

13{14}[1]    *Insipiens, the fool,* that is, one having no knowledge of God and not following Christ (who is the Wisdom of God), says, *in corde suo: Non est Deus, in his heart: There is no God,* that is, there is not someone who is the Judge and Lord of all, having providential care of the acts of men. For however few or none they may be who might consider God absolutely not to exist, there are yet many who regard God not to exist in the manner that the Catholic faith affirms him to be, namely, the provider, judge, and rewarder of all.

It is possible here to introduce certain difficulties, that is, the manner in which some are able to say in their heart, *There is no God,* when we

---

32  Mal. 4:5–6a.

33  Matt. 17:11.

34  Rom. 11:26. E. N. St. Paul cites to Psalm 13:7 in support of his statement that "all Israel should be saved," confirming Denis's understanding of the meaning of this verse.

regard God's existence as self-evident, as Anselm[35] proposed, and with which the Damascene[36] agrees, who in his first book says, in all men there is naturally inserted the knowledge of the existence of God.[37] Yet Thomas [Aquinas] and [Duns] Scotus reached the opposite result.[38] But I omit [discussion] of these difficulties, because I addressed them diligently in in the book *On the Divine Nature;*[39] and I held [therein] more probably with Anselm, that God's existence is especially known *per se* [*i.e.*, is self-evident], even more than the first principles.[40] It matters not that *the fool has said in his heart* that God does not exist because some of the philosophers denied the first principles [of reason], which nevertheless are known *per se* [*i.e.*, are self-evident] (*per se nota*)].[41] However, now I briefly say that all who dishonor and disregard God and persist in vice say in their heart *There is no God.* For just as he who in his heart does not affirm, or he who does with the mouth proclaim, that God does not exist, so also he who so lives as if he regards God not to exist does. For this reason, the Apostle says: They say *that they know God: but in their works they deny him.*[42] Of whom the Prophet [David] adds:

---

35  E. N. St. Anselm of Bec, Benedictine monk and later Archbishop of Canterbury (*ca.* 1033–1109) and Doctor of the Church (*Doctor Magnificus*), famous for his ontological argument for the existence of God found especially in the various versions of his *Proslogion*, which argue for God's existence based upon the idea of God (something than which nothing greater can be conceived), going from the idea of God to God's existence. This *a priori* argument is rejected by St. Thomas, who denies that God's existence is self-evident, and relies on *a posteriori* proofs founded upon sense perception and contingent being and causality. St. Anselm is frequently touted as the Father of Scholasticism.

36  E. N. St. John of Damascus (676–749), monk and priest, known for his theological writings in defense of the orthodox faith, in particular his zealous defense of icons. He was declared a Doctor of the Church by Leo XIII in 1890.

37  E. N. The reference is to St. John of Damascus's *De Fide Orthodoxa*, 1.1. Cf. PG 94, 790. For St. John of Damascus, *see* footnote P-80.

38  E. N. Both the Dominican St. Thomas Aquinas (1225–1274) and the Franciscan John Duns Scotus (*ca.* 1266–1308) rejected the notion that God's existence was self-evident.

39  Denis refers to his own *De Natura Aeterni et Veri Dei* (*On the Nature of the Eternal and True God*). *See* Doctoris Ecstatici D. Dionysii Cartusiani, *Opera Omnia* (*Opera Minora*, Vol. 2) (Tournai: 1907).

40  E. N. Denis is referring to the self-evident first principles of reason, *e.g.*, the principle of non-contradiction (a thing cannot both be and not be in the same sense and circumstances), the law of excluded middle (for any proposition, either that proposition is true or its negation is true), the principle of identity (each thing is identical to itself).

41  E. N. In other words, the fact that philosophers have held such foolish opinions does not absolve or excuse the less learned from holding the same opinions or those who in their life are practical atheists.

42  Tit. 1:16a.

*Corrupti sunt et abominabiles facti sunt in studiis suis; they are corrupt, and are become abominable in their ways.* They are corrupt and they oppose purity, and they are not at home with anything except in things dealing with their own body; but in things of the spirit, they seek replacements or substitutes. In the manner, therefore, that integrity of the mind comes from having it turned perfectly to God, so the corruption of mind comes from its aversion to God. And so, sinners are corrupt, that is, with a mind averse to God, and wounded with vice; and *they are become abominable in their ways,* that is, in the internal and external preoccupations, because, abandoned and scorned by the Creator, they are occupied with transitory, vain, and unsightly things, seeking to be rich, to obtain pleasure, or to dominate. *Non est qui faciat bonum, there is none that does good* among these, but from the most insignificant even to the most mighty, they are all of them zealous towards illicit things; *non est usque ad unum, no not one,* that is, none of them live well. Or it is possible [to understand], *no not one,* in an exclusive sense, and where it says, *there is none that does good,* can be understood in an absolute sense, so that its sense is as follows:[43] *There is none that does good,* that is, no man from his own strength lives well, for *it is not of him that wills, nor of him that runs,* according to the Apostle, *but of God that shows mercy.*[44] And in Hosea we read: *Destruction is your own, O Israel: your help is only in me.*[45] So, therefore, *there is none that does good, no not one,* that is, all but one: because there is one who of his own virtue does well, and from his natural qualities is holy and just, namely, Christ. And therefore the Apostle says: *For God has concluded all in unbelief, that he may have mercy on all.*[46]

---

**13{14}[2]**  *The Lord has looked down from heaven upon the children of men, to see if there be any that understand and seek God.*

*Dominus de caelo prospexit super filios hominum, ut videat si est intelligens, aut requirens Deum.*

**13{14}[2]** *Dominus de caelo, the Lord from heaven,* that is, he who dwells in heaven, according to the manner previously stated, *prospexit super filios hominum, looked down upon the children of men,* that is, he has

---

43  E. N. By interpreting "no not one" exclusively, and "there is none that does good" absolutely, Denis is able to read this verse as saying: "There is none that does good, except for one."

44  Rom. 9:16.

45  Hosea 13:9.

46  Rom. 11:32.

considered the thoughts, words, and deeds of every single man, *est intelligens aut requirens Deum,* to see if there be any that *unde seek God,* that is, if there is any understanding God, not, to be ill-formed or deprived understanding, but with a formed understanding, and extending itself to holy deeds; or [an understanding] requiring him to be occupied with penance, with fervent prayers, and with an earnest way of life. This is what was expressed in Jeremiah: *O most mighty, great, and powerful, the Lord of hosts is your name. Great in counsel and incomprehensible in thought: whose eyes are open upon all the ways of the children of Adam, to render unto every one according to his ways.*[47] For God is said to gaze from heaven so that he may see, not that his knowledge depends upon some extrinsic cause, but Scripture here speaks about God in a human manner of speaking. Or when it says, *to see,* it can be understood as, "so that he may cause others to see," because in the day of the universal judgment he will expose to view who has done well or has done ill. According to this understanding, it is written: *The Lord said . . . to the children of Israel* (when, namely, they adored the golden calf): *Now presently lay aside your ornaments, that I may know what to do with you,*[48] that is, to know what I will do, inflicting the due punishment for fault.

---

13{14}[3]  *They are all gone aside, they are become unprofitable together: there is none that does good, no not one. Their throat is an open sepulcher: with their tongues they acted deceitfully; the poison of asps is under their lips. Their mouth is full of cursing and bitterness; their feet are swift to shed blood. Destruction and unhappiness in their ways: and the way of peace they have not known: there is no fear of God before their eyes.*

*Omnes declinaverunt, simul inutiles facti sunt. Non est qui faciat bonum, non est usque ad unum. Sepulchrum patens est guttur eorum; linguis suis dolose agebant. Venenum aspidum sub labiis eorum. Quorum os maledictione et amaritudine plenum est; veloces pedes eorum ad effundendum sanguinem. Contritio et infelicitas in viis eorum, et viam pacis non cognoverunt; non est timor Dei ante oculos eorum.*

13{14}[3] *Omnes,* all, namely those who are corrupt, *declinaverunt,* are all *gone aside* from the law of God, and therefore *simul inutiles facti sunt,* and

---

47  Jer. 32:18b–19. E. N. There are slight, insignificant discrepancies between Denis's text and the Sixto-Clementine Vulgate.

48  Ex. 33:5.

*they are become unprofitable*, that is empty and lost. *Non est, there is none* of them *qui faciat bonum non est usque ad unum, that does good, no not one*: for since they do not have charity, which is the life of the soul, they are able to do nothing which is acceptable to the living and true God. *Sepulcrum patens est guttur eorum; their throat is an open sepulcher*: because by bringing forth pernicious things from their throat, they kill, devour, and as it were bury themselves and defile others along with themselves with the stench of their vicious words. *Linguis suis dolose agebant: with their tongues they acted deceitfully*, beguiling others, indeed deceiving even themselves. For he who deceives another, first seduces himself: for every single perversity first flows in oneself and first harms the one urging rather than the one being urged. *Venenum aspidum, the poison of asps*, that is, the most vile rancor or deceitful words, *sub labiis eorum, is under their lips*, so that when they are able, they vomit it forth, and as if they were an asp they poison their neighbor. *Quorum os maledictione*[49] *plenum est; their mouth is full of cursing*, because they repeat evil words to those who speak evil, and, on the other hand, they speak evil to those who contrariwise speak well or do not harm anyone, *et amaritudine, and bitterness*, this being bitter indignation and zeal against God and neighbor, *et dolo, and deceit*,[50] that is, hidden snares. *Veloces pedes eorum, their feet are swift*, that is, the affection of their heart, and also the feet of the body, *ad effundendum sanguinem, to shed blood*, on account of unjust causes. *Contritio, destruction*, that is, the destruction of being in a state of grace, *et infelicitas in viis eorum, and unhappiness in their ways*, that is, in their works; *et viam pacis, and the way of peace*, that is, the loving manner of life by which one arrives at eternal peace, *non cognoverunt, they have not known* by imitation. *Non est timor Dei ante oculos eorum; there is no fear of God before their eyes*, that is, they do not fear God. For if they were to fear God, they would not do evil, because it is written: *The fear of the Lord drives out sin*.[51] And Solomon says: for *he that fears God, neglects nothing*.[52]

---

**13{14}[4]**   *Shall not all they know that work iniquity, who devour my people as they eat bread?*

*Nonne cognoscent omnes qui operantur iniquitatem, qui devorant plebem meam sicut escam panis?*

---

49   *Cf.* Ps. 10:7 according to the Hebrew.
50   E. N. Denis departs from the Psalm in adding this. The Psalm, at least in the Sixto-Clementine Vulgate, does not speak of deceit.
51   Ecclus. 1:27.
52   Eccl. 7:19.

**13{14}[5]**  *They have not called upon the Lord: there have they trembled for fear, where there was no fear.*

*Dominum non invocaverunt; illic trepidaverunt timore, ubi non erat timor.*

**13{14}[4]** *Nonne cognoscent omnes qui operantur iniquitatem? Shall not all they know that work iniquity?* Indeed, they will know those who did evil: because immediately when their souls exit the body they will come before the tribunal of Christ, so that they might know what they deserve, and that they might recognize by their punishments that for which they already know themselves condemned; *qui devorant plebem meam, who devour my people,* that is, they sadden, oppress, and kill the poor in spirit, the innocent, and the simple, *sicut escam panis, as they eat bread,* that is, like bread which is food. But we come across this judgment beautifully expressed in Hosea: *The Lord,* he says, *shall enter into judgment with the inhabitants of the land: for there is no truth, and there is no mercy, and there is no knowledge of God in the land. Cursing, and lying, and killing, and theft, and adultery have overflowed, and blood has touched blood.*[53]    **13{14}[5]** *Dominum non invocaverunt, they have not called upon the Lord,* regarding these it has already been satisfactorily expounded.

---

**13{14}[6]**  *For the Lord is in the just generation: you have confounded the counsel of the poor man, but the Lord is his hope.*

*Quoniam Dominus in generatione iusta est, consilium inopis confudistis, quoniam Dominus spes eius est.*

**13{14}[6]** *Quoniam Dominus in generatione iusta est; for the Lord is in the just generation,* that is, he dwells within the just by grace. Of whom the eternal Wisdom through Solomon says: *My delights were to be with the children of men;*[54] and in Revelation: *Behold the tabernacle of God with men, and he will dwell with them.*[55] *Consilium inopis confudistis, you have confounded the counsel of the poor,* that is, the rebuking, admonition, and instruction of the lowly, the pious, and the religious men, O you ungodly men, you have disdained, in the manner that is written: *The wicked man when he is come into the depth of sins, contemns.*[56] And hence you spurned them *quoniam Dominus spes eius est, but the Lord is his hope,* that is, because

---

53  Hos. 4:1–2.
54  Prov. 8:31b.
55  Rev. 21:3a.
56  Prov. 13:3a.

he proclaims to place hope in God alone, and all carnal amusements, temporal honors, and worldly vanities to be things that should be despised.

---

13{14}[7]    *Who shall give out of Sion the salvation of Israel? When the Lord shall have turned away the captivity of his people, Jacob shall rejoice and Israel shall be glad.*

*Quis dabit ex Sion salutare Israel? Cum averterit Dominus captivitatem plebis suae, exsultabit Iacob, et laetabitur Israel.*

**13{14}[7]** *Quis dabit ex Sion*, who shall give out of Sion, that is who among the contemplative and holy men, *out of Sion*, that is from the congregation of those who keep their eye on God proceeding like one of those who shall give *salutare*, salvation, that is, true happiness, *Israel*, Israel, that is the gathering of the faithful now seeing God by faith? And he [the psalmist] responds: *Cum averterit Dominus captivitatem plebis suae, when the Lord shall have turned away the captivity of his people*, that is, when Christ shall have freed the Christians from slavery of all sin and the yoke of the devil: for it will not be collectively accomplished except in the day of judgment; then, *exsultabit Iacob, Jacob shall rejoice*, that is, the faithful, by displacing evil, and by efficaciously resisting vices, *et laetabitur Israel, and Israel shall be glad*. This amounts to the same thing as "Jacob shall exalt," and "Israel shall rejoice," for Jacob and Israel are one and the same; and every one of the faithful in the present life is called Jacob so long as he wrestles with vice; but in the future he will truly be called Israel, when he will see God face to face. Indeed, Jacob is interpreted as "supplanter":[57] but Israel is interpreted as "man seeing God." The faithful, therefore, who supplants sin, is Jacob; and this is the same as Israel, to the extent he is contemplating God. In the day of judgment Jacob and Israel, that is, every true faithful will rejoice with the mind, and will exult in body, when he will hear the Judge saying: *Come, you blessed of my Father, possess you the kingdom prepared for you from the foundation of the world.*[58] For then *God shall wipe away all tears* from the eyes of the Saints.[59] And then *when this mortal* will put on *immortality*;[60] and he will fill that which Isaiah prophesied the person of God will say: *Behold my servants shall praise for joyfulness of heart, and you, O ungodly, shall cry for sorrow of heart: because the former distresses*

---

57  See footnote 13-31.
58  Matt. 25:34.
59  Rev. 21:4.
60  1 Cor. 15:53a.

*are forgotten.*[61] Whence Malachi says this of the future glory of the blessed: *You shall go forth, and shall leap like calves of the herd, and you shall tread down the wicked . . . in the day that I do this, says the Lord.*[62]

But attend to yourself, O brother, who sings, hears, and reads this Psalm, that those things that are written in it of the false man do not apply to you. Examine and diligently question your conscience; and if you discover any one of these vices in you, do penance, and be wary of the others. Do not live as if God does not exist, but reverently and with fear walk before God. During choir, with God being present, take stock of yourself and see that you are in all things becoming, holding yourself devoutly and in trembling, always directing with all your heart that which is written: *The Lord has looked down from heaven upon the children of men, to see if there be any that understand and seek God;* and finally: *Cursed be he that does the work of the Lord negligently.*[63]

# PRAYER

VERT FROM YOUR PEOPLE, FATHER GOD, the perpetual captivity in which our man Jacob[64] exults in the flesh; and grant to us, we pray, peace in him who makes two one:[65] until at length Israel may be accomplished in us, and he may be found worthy to see you, God.

*Perpetuam captivitatem, Deus Pater, a populo tuo averte; et*
*pacem in illo, qui facit utraque unum, nobis, rogamus,*
*concede: in qua Iacob homo noster exsultet in carne,*
*donec effectus Israel, mereatur te Deum vivere.*

---

61  Is. 65:14, 16b.
62  Mal. 4:2–3.
63  Jer. 48:10. E. N. Denis quotes Jeremiah replacing the Sixto-Clementine Vulgate's *fraudulenter* (deceitfully) with *negligenter* (negligently). *See also* footnote P-129.
64  Jacob is here the "carnal" man, and is also the man on pilgrimage (*in via*), one who is a symbol of the elect over Esau (Rom. 9:13), yet who must be spiritualized into "Israel," and thus made worthy of the vision of God, and thereby also becoming a *comprehensor.*
65  E. N. A reference to Jesus, who "is our peace," and "who has made both one." Eph. 2:14.

# Psalm 14

## ARTICLE XXXVII

EXPOSITION OF THE FOURTEENTH PSALM:
*DOMINE, QUIS HABITABIT, &c.*
*LORD, WHO SHALL DWELL, &c.*

**14{15}[1]** *A Psalm of David. Lord, who shall dwell in thy tabernacle? Or who shall rest in your holy hill?*

*Psalmus David. Domine, quis habitabit in tabernaculo tuo? Aut quis requiescet in monte sancto tuo?*

HE TITLE OF THIS PSALM IS: 14{15}[1] *PSALMUS David, a Psalm of David*: that is, this is the holy David here speaking.

The Prophet [David], wanting to inform us morally the manner in which we are able to truly belong among the number of the elect in the present time by grace and in the future by glory, questions God: *Domine, quis habitabit in tabernaculo tuo? Lord, who shall dwell in your tabernacle?* That is, who truly perseveres in the Church militant, namely in reality and in name, as a live member of Christ, receiving movement and life from Christ the head (that is the work of grace), as a bodily member from its own head? For many abide in the Church only in name, as do evil Christians and heretics. Of these John says in his epistle: *They went out from us, but they were not of us. For if they had been of us, they would no doubt have remained with us.*[1] *Aut quis*, or who, O Lord, *requiescet in monte sancto suo, shall rest in your holy hill*, that is, after the present laborious exile shall enjoy eternal rest in the empyreal heaven, in whom after this life they will sweetly rest, who now are wearied with pious labors for the love of God?

In addition, the Prophet [David] as one taught by the Lord, who opens to those knocking,[2] responds to this question. He sees this question to have two parts to it, because he first asks who might dwell in the militant Church; secondly, [he asks] who remains or who rests in the triumphant Church. But this question is as it were one or simple. For whoever now truly and perseveringly belongs to the Church militant in

---

1 1 John 2:19a.
2 *Cf.* Luke 11:9.

the future will truly belong to the Church triumphant. Consequently, to both questions is given one and the same response, which is:

————————————

14{15}[2]  *He that walks without blemish, and works justice.*

*Qui ingreditur sine macula, et operatur iustitiam.*

14{15}[3]  *He that speaks truth in his heart, who has not used deceit in his tongue: Nor has done evil to his neighbor: nor taken up a reproach against his neighbors.*

*Qui loquitur veritatem in corde suo; qui non egit dolum in lingua sua; nec fecit proximo suo malum, et opprobrium non accepit adversus proximos suos.*

**14{15}[2]** *Qui ingreditur sine macula,* he who walks without blemish, that is, he who shies away from evil, who does not harm anyone, who is not conversant with any mortal sin. Why the prophet [David] prefers to say, *he who walks in (ingreditur)* rather than "he who walks forth" *(egreditur)*—since both might be able to be said—is answered by the Savior, who says: *By me, if any man enter in (introierit), he shall be saved: and he shall go in (ingredietur), and go out (egredietur).*[3] The Prophet receives, therefore, here a walking in *(ingressum)* by an operation which leads without error to the end, who is God. For there are many who err from the way,[4] and these do not walk in *(non ingrediuntur)* without blemish, but are seduced along the way, walking in difficult ways, and ignorant of the way of the Lord.[5] But because it does not suffice to simply turn away from evil, this is therefore added: *et operator iustitiam, and works justice,* this meaning the act of justice, as justice is said to be a general virtue, and it is virtually all virtues; or also, as justice is a special virtue.[6]    **14{15}[3]** *Qui loquitur veritatem in corde suo, he that speaks truth in his heart,* that is, he that is sincere and true to himself,

————————————

3  John 10:9.
4  *Cf.* Wis. 5:6, 7.
5  E. N. The point is difficult to translate into English, but Denis both makes the point that we have to "walk in" or "come in" *(ingreditur)* grace and that we also have to "walk in" *(ingreditur)* the right path, and that if we "walk outside" or "walk from" *(exgreditur)* grace or "walk outside" or "come out" of *(exgreditur)* the right path, we will not reach our final end, which is God.
6  E. N. See *ST,* IIaIIae, q. 58, arts. 5–8, where, following Aristotle, distinctions are made between general (common) justice, and particular (special) justice, general justice dealing with the common good (the community), special justice dealing with relations between individuals.

and thinks honestly within himself, so that he is not a dissimulator and
a hypocrite; *qui non egit dolum in lingua sua, who has not used deceit
in his tongue,* that is, he does not deceive others with fraudulent and
lying words; *nec fecit proximum suo malum, nor has he done evil to his
neighbor,* that is, he has not harmed any Christian exteriorly, and has
loved his neighbor as he has himself; *et opprobrium non accepit adversus
proximos suos, nor taken up a reproach against his neighbors,* that is, he
has not directed disparaging, scurrilous, or invidious words, nor has he
heard such, but has disapproved them; and he has repulsed detractors
in the manner that Solomon in his Proverbs admonishes: *let detracting
lips be far from you.*[7] And again it is written: Flee from a detractor as
from the face of a serpent.[8] For it is the same impiety to detract or to
applaud the detractor, because both by their nature are mortal sins more
even than theft. And if there were not one who would be willing to hear,
there would not be one willing to detract.

---

14{15}[4]   *In his sight the malignant is brought to nothing: but he glorifies
them that fear the Lord. He that swears to his neighbor, and
deceives not.*

Ad nihilum deductus est in conspectu eius malignus; timentes
autem Dominum glorificat. Qui iurat proximo suo, et non decipit.

14{15}[5]   *He that has not put out his money to usury, nor taken bribes
against the innocent: He that does these things shall not be
moved forever.*

Qui pecuniam suam non dedit ad usuram, et munera super innocentem non accepit. Qui facit haec non movebitur in aeternum.

14{15}[4] *Ad nihilum deductus est in conspectus eius malignus; in his
sight the malignant is brought to nothing:* this means the sinner inasmuch
as he is a sinner is of no consideration to the soul of the just, nor — as
a sinner — is he worthy of honor, since honor is the display of reverence
toward an indication of virtue. Though it is also possible to honor a
wrongdoer, to the extent that he is a superior, or as a result that he is
made in the image of God, in the manner that Peter commands slaves
that they obey their masters, not only the gentle, but also the froward

---

7  Prov. 4:24b.
8  *Cf.* Ecclus. 21:2. E. N. The Sixto-Clementine Vulgate has, *quasi a facie colubri
fuge peccata,* flee from *sins* as from the face of a serpent. It is not limited to the
sin of detraction.

(*dyscolis*) [masters].[9] And according to this understanding, Aristotle[10] says that it is magnanimous to be contemptuous of others [in certain cases]: not that simply one ought to spurn others, but he should give little regard to the vicious, and not to give anybody any honor except those whom virtue makes noble. But however much the just ought to hold in contempt the sinner in general, he ought not thereby judge another in particular, except when it comes to manifest and certain sins; nor should he hold in contempt the nature of anyone, but only the vice. But for the nature [of the sinner, that is, as a human being made in the image of God,] he should offer charitable prayers. *Timentes autem Dominum*, but those who hear the Lord, that is, the virtuous, *glorificat, he glorifies*, that is, he should hold in regard and honor.

*Qui iurat proximo suo, et non decipit*, who swears to his neighbor and deceives not, that is, who swears where, when, and in which, and on account of which something should be sworn to, and by the oath might fulfill and verify [a truth]. Or [one can interpret this as follows], *he who swears*, that is firmly asserts and proposes something, and does not deceive.   **14{15}[5]** *Qui pecuniam suam*, he whose money, that is material goods, *non dedit ad usuram, has not put out . . . to usury*, they have caused to be used in the manner of usurers; *et munera super innocentem non accepit, nor taken bribes against the innocent*, that is, he has accepted no gifts, to the extent that it has oppressed an inferior in judgment or in any other cause. From this verse, therefore, it is clear that usury was not allowed to the Jews, or as a precept was licit; but it was only permissively allowed,[11] inasmuch as it was greater evil to prohibit it,[12] as occurred with respect to the bill of divorce.[13] Whence, Aristotle through the instruction of natural reason affirms that usury is greatly against nature.[14] However, in the Gospel, the Lord says to the unjust servant: It would have behooved you to have given my money to the bankers, and upon returning I would have received it with usury.[15] But here money is

---

9 Cf. 1 Pet. 2:18. The Douay-Rheims uses the now archaic "froward" for *dyscolis*, which might be translated as harsh, severe: a contrarian.

10 E. N. See Nicomachean Ethics 1124a5–9, where Aristotle addresses the magnanimous or "great-souled" man (*megalopsychia*/μεγαλοψυχία).

11 Deut. 15:6; 23:19–20.

12 E. N. Law, like politics, is often the art of the possible. This principle is treated by St. Thomas in ST, IaIIae, q. 96, art. 2, co. & ad 2.

13 Matt. 19:8.

14 Politic. I, c. 3 *in fine*; Ethic. iv, c. 1. E. N. See *Politics*, I, 3: 1258b; *Nicomachean Ethics*, IV, 1: 1121b34.

15 See Matt. 25:27; Luke 19:23.

selected [as a symbol or metaphor] for the talent committed [or given to a man], that is, for grace given, and especially for the knowledge of sacred Scripture, which [from what] one has received, he ought to instruct others. And so usury is the fruit of knowledge, or of graces, or of benefits that have been given. More is expected from those who have received more.[16]

Here, therefore, the Prophet [David] describes a just man, attributing to him ten acts of virtue.[17] And then he appends to this: *Qui facit haec, non movebitur in aeternum; he that does these things shall not be moved forever.* Again, in the present he will adhere to the Lord, and he who will be constant by grace will in the future age will be confirmed in it by eternal beatitude. Indeed, of such men or such persons[18] the Lord says in the Gospel: He will be likened *to a wise man that built his house upon a rock.*[19] But this should not be understood, however, as if it is necessary that the just had never fallen into vice, and always possessed the intent to perform these virtuous acts; but rather that he does not remain in mortal sin — indeed he turns back from it — and work diligently to practice holy deeds, in which, if he complete his life [in such state of grace], he will be eternally saved.

From the contemplation of these virtuous acts and these kinds of good things, pay heed unto yourself, O brother, and be a true member of Christ, a dweller in the Church, and one in a state of salvation. Look inward and see whether you might live without mortal sin or fulfill those precepts that bind you, whether that which you have interiorly in your heart you do externally in word and deed, whether you do nothing that you do not want to do; whether the rich and powerful in the flesh are held in great repute [by you], and those eminent in natural gifts and those who are worldly you regard and honor more than you do the poor, the weak, those chaste of body, those adorned with grace, and the cloistered and religious. Pay heed to whom you love more — with whom you find more pleasing to converse and speak to, and whose life and mores you more eagerly imitate.

---

16  E. N. Cf. Luke 12:48. *To whom much is given, much is required.*

17  E. N. He (1) walks without blemish of sin, (2) works justice, (3) speaks the truth, (4) does not have a deceitful tongue, (5) does no evil to his neighbor, (6) does not defame his neighbor, (7) does not honor sinners, but glorifies those who fear the Lord, (8) does not swear falsely or lie, (9) does not commit usury, and (10) does not take bribes.

18  E. N. Denis uses the words *vir* and *homo*; thus, here the word "man" is not used in a generic sense.

19  Matt. 7:24b.

## ALLEGORICAL EXPOSITION

**14{15}[1]**    *A Psalm of David. Lord, who shall dwell in thy tabernacle? Or who shall rest in your holy hill?*

*Psalmus David. Domine, quis habitabit in tabernaculo tuo? Aut quis requiescet in monte sancto tuo?*

**14{15}[2]**    *He that walks without blemish, and works justice.*

*Qui ingreditur sine macula, et operatur iustitiam.*

Finally, this Psalm is in a particular way able to be expounded to deal with Christ. For the Prophet [David], seeing in the Spirit many things to come which were able to be asserted about Christ, and most especially regarding the distinction of the true Christ, namely Jesus of Nazareth, from the Antichrist, he asked the question:    **14{15}[1]** *Domine, quis habitabit in tabernaculo tuo? Lord, who shall dwell in your tabernacle?* That is, who of all men, of all those who from whom one may represent himself to be the Christ, is to be awaited and will endure in the Church militant, as the principal, the head, the Savior of the faithful? *Aut quis requiescet in monte sancto tuo? Or who shall rest in your holy hill?* That is, who of all men will ascend above all the heavens, even to your right hand, so that he might reign with you without end?    **14{15}[2]** *Qui ingreditur sine macula, he that walks without blemish,* that is, not the Antichrist, not the false prophet, not anyone who exalts himself and simulates himself to be Christ; but Jesus, who is the Lamb without blemish, *who did no sin, neither was guile found in his mouth.*[20]

---

**14{15}[5]**    *He that has not put out his money to usury, nor taken bribes against the innocent: He that does these things shall not be moved forever.*

*Qui pecuniam suam non dedit ad usuram, et munera super innocentem non accepit. Qui facit haec non movebitur in aeternum.*

It is easy to regard the manner in which the acts of virtue that follow [in this verse] fittingly meet altogether in Christ. For Christ fulfilled all justice; and because he did this,    **14{15}[5]** *non movebitur in aeternum, he shall not be moved forever.* For *of his kingdom there shall be no end,*[21] in the manner that Zachariah predicted: *Behold a man, the Orient*

---

20  1 Pet. 2:22.

21  Luke 1:33.

*is his name* (but the translation of the Chaldean has, *Messiah is his name*), . . . *and he shall build a temple to the Lord* (namely, the Church militant), *and he shall bear the glory, and shall sit, and rule upon his throne.*[22]

# PRAYER

E BESEECH YOU, O LORD, VISIT US WHO are apart from you while wayfaring in body, and deign to strengthen us in your holy service, so that, assiduously intent in the work of justice and without sin, we may be found worthy to be dwellers of your eternal tabernacle.

*Visita nos, quaesumus, Domine, abs te peregrinantes in corpore,*
*et in tuo sancto servitio confortare dignare: ut iustitiae*
*operationi assidue intenti, sine macula inhabitatores*
*aeterni mereamur esse tabernaculi.*

22  Zach. 6:12, 13.

# Psalm 15

## ARTICLE XXXVIII

### LITERAL EXPOSITION OF THE FIFTEENTH PSALM:
### *CONSERVA ME, DOMINE, &c.*
### *PRESERVE ME, O LORD, &c.*

15{16}[1]   *The inscription of a title to David himself. Preserve me, O Lord, for I have put my trust in you.*

*Tituli inscriptio, ipsi David. Conserva me, Domine, quoniam speravi in te.*

15{16}[2]   *I have said to the Lord, you are my God, for you have no need of my goods.*

*Dixi Domino: Deus meus es tu, quoniam bonorum meorum non eges.*

SCRIBED TO THIS PSALM IS THIS TITLE: 15{16}[1] *Tituli inscriptio, ipsi David; the inscription of a title to David himself.* But this title is not to be believed as being satisfied by [any historical occurrence in] the Old Testament, but by the Gospel, where it is narrated that, at the crucifixion of Jesus Christ, Pilate caused to be placed that which was written, namely, that title, atop the cross: *Jesus of Nazareth King of the Jews.*[1] For, Esdras knew, by means of the Holy Spirit revealing it, that this was to be in the future. And the sense of this title is this: The triumph and reign indicated by the inscription of this predicted title is attributed to David himself, that is, to Christ. For the title which Pilate affixed upon the cross is a triumphal title, signifying that Christ by his faithful death overcame the world and cast out the devil from it.[2]

Christ, therefore, as man and in a certain manner as a wayfarer, said to the Father: *Conserva me, preserve me,* that is, may your will be done in me, deliver me from danger, and *glorify me . . . with the glory which I had,*

---

1   Matt. 27:37; John 19:19.
2   E. N. Denis interprets this Psalm literally in a Christological sense, so much so that the majority of the commentary is written in first person, as if it is Christ's own prayer.

*before the world was,*[3] *Domine, O Lord,* eternal Father. But Christ, because he had full knowledge of God (*comprehensor erat*) and was confirmed in good, did not pray to preserve himself from fault; rather this is to be understood as referring to his Mystical Body, which is the Church, in this sense: "Preserve me, O Lord, that is, take custody of those believing in me, and avert from all evil those predestined, and preserve them in good."[4] And it is fitting, O Father, that you hear me, *quoniam speravi in te, for I have put my trust in you,* that is, I have ascribed all good to you, and I expect from you that all my prayers will be fulfilled. I, Christ, **15{16}** [2] *dixi, have said,* insofar as I am man, *Domino, to the Lord,* to God three-in-one: *Deus meus es tu, you are my God,* in a most singular way, on account of my highest possible reverence and love for you, as it frequently is expressed. And so, you are my God, *quoniam bonorum meorum non eges, for you have no need of my goods:* for although my humanity is united with the Word so that by it the world might be saved, and this was done not because of any need on your part, but for the benefit of man. For your perfection, O Lord, does not increase in any way from the honor and glory that is given to you by your creatures.

---

**15{16}[3]**   *To the saints, who are in his land, he has made wonderful all my desires in them.*

*Sanctis, qui sunt in terra eius, mirificavit omnes voluntates meas in eis.*

After this, Christ changing persons, speaking as the Church of the benefits of God the Father,   **15{16}[3]** *sanctis, to the saints,* says, *qui sunt in terra eius, who are in his land,* that is, the holy Apostles and chosen men who literally were in the land of promise, which is in a special way called the land of God; or [one can understand it in this way], *who are in his land,* that is, those whose *conversation is in heaven,*[5] which is the land of the living, the life of the blessed: this, I say, *to the saints, mirificavit, he has made wonderful,* that is, God has marvelously and most copiously fulfilled, *omnes voluntates meas in eis, all my desires*

---

3  John 17:5.
4  E. N. This verse (15:1) is an instance of the application of Tyconius's first rule of interpretation, where a verse meaning one thing can be applied to Christ, the Head, and meaning something else to Christ's Mystical Body, the Church. The same rule is applicable in 15:3 below; however, there, the verse is applicable only to the Mystical Body. *See* Article IV.
5  Phil. 3:20a.

*in them*, that is, all that I desired, and all my prayers, namely, of Christ, his Son. For often the will is accepted as referring to an act or an effect of the will. But Christ, as man, desired many things from the Father on behalf of his members, namely, the faithful: as occurs in these instances, *I have prayed for you*, Peter, *that your faith fail not.*[6] And elsewhere: *I will ask the Father, and he shall give you another Paraclete.*[7] And *Father, I will*, that *where I am, there also shall by my minister.*[8] For in all these and similar situations Christ *was heard* by the Father *for his reverence.*[9] And the Father sent the Holy Spirit, which gave to the Apostles all those things which Christ prayed for them; therefore, Christ—declaring his prayers where he asked for his members, *preserve me, O Lord* to be heard—says: *to the saints who are in his land*, that is, [to those] who are in the land of the living, whether in reality or by hope, *he has made wonderful my desires in them.*

---

**15{16}[4]** *Their infirmities were multiplied: afterwards they made haste. I will not gather together their meetings for blood offerings: nor will I be mindful of their names by my lips.*

*Multiplicatae sunt infirmitates eorum, postea acceleraverunt. Non congregabo conventicula eorum de sanguinibus; nec memor ero nominum eorum per labia mea.*

**15{16}[4]** *Multiplicatae sunt infirmitates eorum; their infirmities were multiplied*: that is, the sins and other defects of those who have been made saints by faith and grace were many before converting to Christ. *Postea acceleraverunt; afterwards they made haste*: that is, after they recognized through divine inspiration and by holy preaching, the infirmities of which they had been admonished, they then quickly turned to the Lord, and to the grace of baptism, by which all sins are taken away. And that this relates to the conversion of the Gentiles—who before they were converted, sat in darkness and the shadow of death,[10] serving idols—is especially true and clear: over which sin all nature groaned.[11]

I, Christ, *non congregabo, will not gather together* either by myself or through the Apostles *conventicula eorum de sanguinibus, their meetings*

---

6  Luke 22:32.
7  John 14:16.
8  John 17:24; 12:26.
9  Heb. 5:7b.
10  E. N. A reference to the *Magnificat*. See Luke 1:79.
11  *Cf.* Rom. 8:22.

*for blood offerings*, that is, the gatherings or meetings of those who are *for blood offerings*: that is, men of blood or iniquitous men I will not gather together into the Church of the elect: not that I absolutely will not gather them together, since I came to *save that which was lost*;[12] but I will not gather them together according to their malice, and to the extent they are evil: it is clear to see that such will remain [lost] as they were. But I will convert the impious; and they who were evil, will be good; and they who were carnal and diabolical, will be divine and holy. For which reason, it follows: *nec memor ero nominum eorum per labia mea; nor will be mindful of their names by my lips*: that is, I will not call those kind with the name by which they were called before: pagans, blind, unbelievers, unlearned, cast away; after their conversion to me, they will be called Christians, enlightened, faithful, teachers of the Gentiles, and chief of the peoples. This is what the Lord said by Ezechiel: At whatever hour the sinner will bemoan his sin, I will most no longer remember all of his sins.[13] And this is *the change of the right hand of the most High*,[14] of which the Lord speaks through Hosea: I will call those not my people, my people.[15] And Isaiah: *Behold*, he says, *you shall call a nation, which you knew not.*[16] And again: *he will call his servants by another name.*[17]

---

**15{16}[5]**  *The Lord is the portion of my inheritance and of my cup: it is you that will restore my inheritance to me.*

*Dominus pars hereditatem meae, et calicis mei: tu es qui restitues hereditatem meam mihi.*

**15{16}[5]** *Dominum pars hereditatem meae et calicis mei; the Lord is the portion of my inheritance and of my cup*: that is, God is the portion of him who believes in me, who places heavenly things before earthly things, and elects to put God before creation; and this *Lord is the portion . . . of my cup*, that is, God is the end and the reward of my Passion, because I suffered for that reason: so that I might unite men in a blessed union to their last end, namely God, and they receive, as a reward of their labor and my Passion, the reward of his vision. Or

---

12  Luke 19:10.
13  *Cf.* Ez. 18:21–22.
14  Ps. 76:11.
15  *Cf.* Hosea 2:24.
16  Is. 55:5a.
17  Is. 65:15b.

[it can be understood] thus: *The Lord is the portion of my inheritance,*
that is, God is that God, that I, Christ, as man, chose, loved, held, and
possessed before all created good as the portion of my inheritance, as
he first chose and loved me. In this way God through Moses said of
the Levites: You will not give them possession or inheritance among
the children of Israel, for I am their possession and inheritance.[18] But
the Levites prefigure the clergy of the New Testament. And, therefore,
when they [the clerics] are first tonsured, they say this verse, since
they are specially deputed to the divine worship and God is made their
inheritance. For God is said to be our inheritance because we serve him
by venerating him, and we possess him by loving him or enjoying him.
And we call ourselves the inheritance of God because he cares for and
nourishes us by perfecting us and he possesses us by reigning in us.
And so Christ continues saying:

Tu es, *you are*, O Father God, *qui restitues hereditatem meam mihi,*
*who will restore my inheritance to me*, that is, that by your grace will be
drawn to me all those whom you have predestined for me, and all the
elect who are my inheritance you will lead back to me through the merits
of my Passion and death. And these who before they were redeemed
by me were in captivity to the devil and under the guilt of original sin,
for which reason none of them were able to enter into the kingdom of
eternal blessedness. It is these, therefore, that you will restore to me,
in the manner that the Gospel states: No one comes to me *except the*
*Father who has sent me draws him.*[19] And again: *All that the Father gives*
*to me shall come to me.*[20] And so also the Apostle says: *he chose us in*
*him before the foundation of the world;*[21] and again: *he has graced us in*
*his beloved Son.*[22] This is not to be understood as if something is the
cause of predestination, as if it were in God, but [rather] because God
established the effect of predestination for us to be based upon the
merits of his Son. At any rate, God restores this inheritance through
Christ, when that which Luke testifies to in the Acts of the Apostles is
fulfilled: *as many as were ordained to life everlasting, believed.*[23] Indeed,
every day he restores them to himself, either when sinners convert by
grace, or when the just enter upon glory.

---

18  *Cf.* Num. 18:20; Deut. 10:9; 18:1, 2; Joshua 13:33.
19  John 6:44.
20  John 6:37a.
21  Eph.1:4a.
22  Eph. 1:6b.
23  Acts 13:48b.

**15{16}[6]**   *The lines are fallen unto me in goodly places: for my inheritance is goodly to me.*

*Funes ceciderunt mihi in praeclaris; etenim hereditas mea praeclara est mihi.*

**15{16}[7]**   *I will bless the Lord, who has given me understanding: moreover my reins also have corrected me even till night.*

*Benedicam Dominum qui tribuit mihi intellectum; insuper et usque ad noctem increpuerunt me renes mei.*

**15{16}[8]**   *I set the Lord always in my sight: for he is at my right hand, that I be not moved.*

*Providebam Dominum in conspectu meo semper, quoniam a dextris est mihi, ne commovear.*

**15{16}[6]** *Funes ceciderunt mihi in praeclaris; the lines are fallen unto me in goodly places:* that is, given the differences, to which God mercifully calls some people and justly forsakes others, it has fallen to my lot to be among the forechosen and precious, and among those men beloved by God. For since *many are called and few are chosen,*[24] my choice falls upon the elect, so that they are my portion, in which I will eternally reign as if they were my inheritance, now indeed by grace, but in the future by glory. For they are the *blessed of my Father,* for whom is prepared the heavenly kingdom *from the foundation of the world.*[25] Now, it is spoken of "lines"[26] metaphorically. For "lines" are said to be the measures or boundaries by which earthly inheritance is divided. *Etenim hereditas mea; for my inheritance,* that is, the multitude of the predestined from eternity, of whom it is written about in Luke: *Fear not, little flock, for it has pleased your Father to give you a kingdom.*[27] This heredity, I say, *praeclara, is goodly,* that is much beloved, noble, and precious, *est mihi, to me,* Christ, for *I lay down my life* for it; and so it *is goodly to me,* as it is my spouse that I have redeemed with my own blood.

In addition, Christ as man, giving thanks to God for all the wisdom gathered in his soul from the first moment of its creation, which also is united to the Word of God, and was made a contemplator of the Godhead by sight, says:   **15{16}[7]** *Benedicam Dominum qui tribuit*

---

24  Matt. 22:16; 22:14.
25  Matt. 25:34.
26  L. *funes,* lines, ropes, or cords.
27  Luke 12:32.

*mihi intellectum; I will bless the Lord who has given me understanding,* that is, intellectual knowledge of all that which has been previously said.

And notwithstanding that this will be so, yet *insuper, moreover,* that is, beyond this, *et usque ad noctem, even till night,* that is, even to the end of my life or the setting of death, *increpuerunt me, they have corrected me,* that is, they have censured, blasphemed, have had me persecuted, *renes mei, my reins,*[28] that is, the Jews and also the tribe of Juda, of which by flesh and blood I was made incarnate and was born. But they in vain have endeavored to ruin me, because I am the Christ    **15{16}[8]** *Providebam Dominum in conspectu meo semper; I will set the Lord always in my sight:* that is, in both prosperity and adversity, in all situations, places, and times I have set God before the eyes of my heart, and I have always actually beheld him; *quoniam a dextris est mihi; for he is at my right hand,* that is, he is immediately (*immediate*)[29] bound to me, and always stands next to me. For my humanity is unified to the Word through a personal union; but it is united to the Trinity, which is the one, true, and simple God, in one in beatific enjoyment. Thus from the Lord *at my right, ne commovear, I not be moved,* that is, I will not deviate in any manner from the means of virtue, or from right reason, or from the will of God; I will not in prosperity advance, or in adversity retreat, but I will always walk steadily along the royal way.

------

**15{16}[9]**    *Therefore my heart has been glad, and my tongue has rejoiced: moreover my flesh also shall rest in hope.*

*Propter hoc laetatum est cor meum, et exsultavit lingua mea; insuper et caro mea requiescet in spe.*

**15{16}[9]** *Propter hoc laetatum est cor meum; therefore my heart has been glad,* that is the intellect and the affections of my soul, giving thanks for such great benefits, were spiritually delighted in God. Whence, in the Gospel it says: Jesus *rejoiced in the Holy Ghost, and said: I confess to you, O Father, Lord of heaven and earth.*[30] *Et exultavit lingua mea; and my tongue has rejoiced:* that is, from the great interior exuberance of my joy, so also my bodily tongue is moved to the rejoicing praise of

------

28  L. *renes. See* footnote 7-10.

29  L. *immediate,* immediately in the sense that there is nothing mediating or inter-posing the connection between Christ's human nature and the divine nature of God, the human nature intimately, and immediately, joined (without confusion, change, division, or separation) to the divine nature through the intimacy of the hypostatic or personal union.

30  Luke 10:21.

God, and the delightful recollection of his benefits. *Insuper et caro mea; moreover my flesh*, that is, my body, during the three days of death it was separated from the soul (though not indeed from the divinity of the Word), *requiescet in spe, shall rest in hope*, that is, it will lie in the sepulcher in such a hope that it would rise on the third day; but this hope was subjective in the soul of Christ,[31] and so it continues:

---

**15{16}[10]** *Because you will not leave my soul in hell; nor will you give your holy one to see corruption.*

*Quoniam non derelinques animam meam in inferno, nec dabis sanctum tuum videre corruptionem.*

**15{16}[10]** *Quoniam non derelinques animam meam in inferno; because you will not leave my soul in hell.* Here it is as if he said: My flesh rests in the hope of the foretold resurrection that is so close to happening, *because you will not leave*, that is, you will not permit my soul to remain long in hell, that is, in the limbo of the Fathers. For the soul of Christ did not remain there except until the time of his Resurrection which occurred on the third day: indeed, immediately when Christ gave up his spirit on the Cross, the soul of Christ descended to the limbo of the Fathers, and the souls of the saints in that place were glorified with the beatific vision of God, for then, the guilt of original sin, for which alone they suffered delay of the divine vision, was satisfied; but he did not remain there except until the third day. *Nec dabis sanctum tuum videre corruptionem; nor will you give your holy one to see corruption*, that is, you will not allow the body of your most holy Son, who is the Saint of Saints,[32] to undergo corruption, to be reduced to dust, to putrefy, but you will quickly resuscitate it from the tomb.

---

**15{16}[11]** *You have made known to me the ways of life, you shall fill me with joy with your countenance: at your right hand are delights even to the end.*

*Notas mihi fecisti vias vitae; adimplebis me laetitia cum vultu tuo: delectationes in dextera tua usque in finem.*

---

31  E. N. That is, Christ's soul hoped for its reunion with his body; this was not the theological virtue of hope common to all other men. For as Denis makes clear, Jesus did not have the virtue of either faith or hope in the strict sense since he enjoyed the beatific vision of God from the first moment of his human existence.

32  On "Saint of Saints" as a name for Christ, *see* footnote 3-26.

**15{16}[11]** *Notas mihi fecisti vias vitae; you have made know to me the ways of life,* that is, you have given me the saving knowledge by which I might fulfil the acts of virtue, which are the ways of life, and teach others [to do the same]. Or [one might interpret it in this manner], *you have made known to me the ways of life,* that is, you have made known to me experientially, and you have extended to me in a sensory way, the Resurrection which was effected upon me on the third day, and the Ascension completed on the fortieth day. For by the Resurrection and Ascension I attained immortal life. *Adimplebis me laetitia; you shall fill me with joy,* that is, since by the Ascension I will have obtained the perpetual concession of being with you at your right hand, then you will give to me the fullness of beatitude, so that I might be happy not only in soul, which never, in essence, advanced in prerogative, but only that I might be glorified in body, which rose again in glory; but also that I might be exalted *above all the heavens,*[33] above all creatures, above all angelic spirits, so that I fulfill all things, so that *in the name of Jesus every knee should bow:*[34] and so accidentally in prerogative *cum vultu tuo, with your countenance,* that is, I am perfectly fulfilled in the presence of your majesty, which is most excellently considered in heaven. *Delectationes, delights,* that is, various and ineffable joys, *in dextera tua usque in finem, at your right hand even to the end,* that is, favorable in your presence, as if he might be saying: these things which are enjoyed by you being there, which you are present by glory, which you stand by the favor of charity, possessing the multiple delights of both essential as well as accidental rewards: *for eye has not seen, nor ear heard, neither has it entered into the heart of man, what things God has prepared for them that love him* until the end.[35] Or [we might construe it] thus: the *delights,* you furnish are to me Christ, *at your right,* that is, by the fact that I am placed at your right hand.

Finally, that this Psalm should be understood literally as applying to Christ, is here clear in that the most glorious prince of the apostolic band, the most blessed Peter, in the book of Acts, introduces this Psalm where it says, *I set the Lord always in my sight* to prove that Christ rose from the dead.[36]

---

33 Eph. 4:10b.
34 Phil. 2:10a.
35 1 Cor. 22:9; *Cf.* Is. 64:4.
36 Acts 2:25–28.

# ARTICLE XXXIX

## TROPOLOGICAL OR MORAL EXPOSITION
## OF THIS FIFTEENTH PSALM:

15{16}[1]  *The inscription of a title to David himself. Preserve me, O Lord, for I have put my trust in you.*

*Tituli inscriptio, ipsi David. Conserva me, Domine, quoniam speravi in te.*

15{16}[2]  *I have said to the Lord, you are my God, for you have no need of my goods.*

*Dixi Domino: Deus meus es tu, quoniam bonorum meorum non eges.*

NY MEMBER OF THE FAITHFUL IS ABLE TO recite this Psalm in his own person toward his own formation to the glory of God, so that he says:   15{16}[1] *Conserva me, Domine; preserve me, O Lord,* that I not fall into vices, that I not lose grace, but that in all circumstances I will steadfastly persevere in you; *quoniam speravi in te; for I have put my trust in you,* not in my perfections or my strengths.   15{16}[2] *Dixi Domino; I have said to the Lord* all things by means of general causality and providence: *Deus meus es tu; you are my God:* that is, because of the special kindness directed to me by you, and the worship which I bestow uppermost and uniquely to you, you are in a particular way my God, in whom I place every and all of my good, outside of whom I require nothing, and to whose will I completely offer and subject myself; *quoniam bonorum meorum non eges; for you have no need of my goods.* For in you is the perfect and immense perfection of all good and all beautiful and desirable things: and hence deservedly I hope in you, and I submit myself to you, God alone, for you are sufficient to yourself in yourself and by yourself, and you, who in no manner are in need of me, alone are able to save me.

---

15{16}[3]  *To the saints, who are in his land, he has made wonderful all my desires in them.*

*Sanctis, qui sunt in terra eius, mirificavit omnes voluntates meas in eis.*

**15{16}[4]**   *Their infirmities were multiplied: afterwards they made haste.*
*I will not gather together their meetings for blood offerings: nor*
*will I be mindful of their names by my lips.*

*Multiplicatae sunt infirmitates eorum, postea acceleraverunt.*
*Non congregabo conventicula eorum de sanguinibus; nec memor*
*ero nominum eorum per labia mea.*

Inflamed with the love of God, man vehemently desires in all things
to some extent to increase the honor and glory of God: and so the
Psalm adds,   **15{16}[3]** *sanctis qui sunt in terra eius; to the saints who*
*are in his land,* that is, the elect, who either are in the Church militant
still on their pilgrimage to the Lord,[37] or in the Church triumphant
already enjoying the face of the Godhead, *mirificavit omnes voluntates*
*meas in eis; he has made wonderful all my desires in them,* that is, in a
marvelous manner he has filled in them whatever I desired for them:
because he bestows many and abundant gifts of grace to the wayfaring
saints; but only preserves them for the saints who are in heaven who
are not able to desire greater essential rewards.[38]   **[15{16}[4]** *Multi-*
*plicatae sunt infirmitates eorum, postea acceleraverunt; their infirmities*
*were multiplied: afterwards they made haste.* This verse is sufficiently
clear from the prior exposition. *Non congregabo conventicula eorum de*
*sanguinibus; I will not gather together their meetings for blood offerings,*
that is, I will not gather them to be among the number of the blessed,
nor will I place them with the former fathers, since they come from
the assembly of evil men, and are vicious by blood, namely according
to their infirmities they are multiplied; *nec,* nor therefore *memor ero*
*nominum eorum per labia mea; will I be mindful of their names by my*
*lips,* so that I might count them, according to how they are, to belong
to the lot of the saints;[39] but according to how *they afterwards made*
*haste,* that is, according to how frequently they turned to the Lord, I
will esteem them to behold the fellowship of the blessed. This is the
manner that is stated in Zachariah, *Turn you to me, . . . and I will turn*
*to you, says the Lord.*[40]

---

37  Cf. 2 Cor. 5:6.
38  E. N. The time for merit ceases at death. *The night comes, when no man can work.*
John 9:4. So the merits of those in heaven is fixed.
39  E. N. Cf. Col. 1:12: *Giving thanks to God the Father, who hath made us worthy to*
*be partakers of the lot of the saints in light.*
40  Zach. 1:3.

**15{16}[5]**    *The Lord is the portion of my inheritance and of my cup: it is you that will restore my inheritance to me.*

*Dominus pars hereditatis meae, et calicis mei: tu es qui restitues hereditatem meam mihi.*

**15{16}[5]** *Dominus pars hereditatis meae; the Lord is the portion of my inheritance:* not that I may wish to possess something more than God and that he is not the entirety of my good, but only a portion of my good and my inheritance; but *the Lord is the portion of my inheritance,* that is, he is my inheritance, which I loved out of all things and before all things: in the manner that is said in a later Psalm, *you are the God of my heart, and the God that is my portion forever;*[41] *et calicis mei, and of my cup,* that is, the Lord is that good for which I freely endure all adversities, persecutions, and penitential works; for whom I am put to death all day,[42] and walk *through fire and water.*[43] *Tu es qui restitutes hereditatem meam mihi; it is you that will restore my inheritance to me.* Before the Lord is said to be an inheritance; but now the Lord is said himself to be the restoration of his inheritance. What does *it is you that will restore my inheritance to me* mean, therefore, other than, "you will restore yourself to me"? For by sinning we have dismissed God, and we are not able to reacquire him condignly,[44] and only if he anticipates us (*praeveniat nos*) by his mercy, pouring out grace, and we accepting it, do we attain to God. Or [the verse can be construed], thus: *It is you, O Christ, that will restore my inheritance to me,* that is, who by the merits of your Passion, will restore to me eternal life, which we also are able to call our inheritance.

---

**15{16}[6]**    *The lines are fallen unto me in goodly places: for my inheritance is goodly to me.*

*Funes ceciderunt mihi in praeclaris; etenim hereditas mea praeclara est mihi.*

**15{16}[6]** *Funes, the lines,*[45] that is, the partitions, separations, or lots

---

41  Ps. 72:26b.
42  Cf. Rom 8:36; Ps. 43:22. Rom. 8:36: *As it is written: For your sake we are put to death all the day long. We are accounted as sheep for the slaughter.*
43  Ps. 65:12.
44  E. N. Latin *de condigno,* condignly, that is, arising out of a relationship of strict justice. Given the infinite offense against God by our sin, it is impossible for finite man to make amends and repair the rift, the infinite abyss, between God and man after that relationship was severed.
45  L. On *funes,* lines, see footnote 15-26.

of the goods of the Lord, who gives earthly goods only to some, but to others gives heavenly and divine goods; *ceciderunt mihi in praeclaris; are fallen unto me in goodly places*, that is, it has befallen to me [to be vested] in eternal and invisible goods, which are prepared for me in heaven: so that the Lord might hand these excellent goods over to me as part of my inheritance. And consequently this I hope, *etenim, for*, that is, because, *hereditatis mea, my inheritance*, that is, eternal life, *praeclara est mihi, is goodly to me*, that is, it is dear and precious above all other goods. For it is for love of them [the heavenly goods that are the Lord's inheritance] that I spurn all temporal goods and this bodily life. But no one without a special revelation of God is able to know whether he will arrive to this heavenly inheritance: but if and while he perceives himself to desire before all things these [heavenly] goods, and on their account to serve faithfully God, then he is able to have confidence that the Lord has chosen him for this inheritance, and he may with great trust proclaim this verse, *The lines are fallen unto me*,[46] etc. As Jerome[46] said, *Nothing is more happy than a Christian, who is promised the kingdom of heaven.* Truly, to him who works more for temporal goods than in acquiring eternal goods, does not have nor is able to acquire this *goodly inheritance*.

---

**15{16}[7]**   *I will bless the Lord, who has given me understanding: moreover my reins also have corrected me even till night.*

*Benedicam Dominum qui tribuit mihi intellectum; insuper et usque ad noctem increpuerunt me renes mei.*

**15{16}[7]** *Benedicam Dominum qui tribuit mihi intellectum; I will bless the Lord who has given me understanding*, so that I might know about all these things and his other benefits, and so that I might turn to him, and I might attend to give him thanks: *for he has not done in like manner to every nation.*[47]

*Insuper et usque ad noctem; moreover . . . even till night*, that is, even from the consent to sin, which darkens the soul, *increpuerunt me renes mei, my reins*[48] *also have corrected me*, that is, concupiscence and the pas-

---

46   E. N. St. Jerome (*ca.* 347–420) was a priest, theologian, and translator of the Scriptures. He is considered a Doctor of the Church, along with Sts. Gregory, Ambrose, and Augustine, one of the four great Latin Fathers of the Church. The quote (which Denis slightly misquotes) is from one of St. Jerome's epistles to the monk Rusticus. See *Epist.* 125, 1: *Nihil Christiano felicius, cui promittitur regnum coelorum.*

47   Ps. 147:9.

48   L. *renes*. See footnote 7-10.

sions of the sensitive parts have resisted and set themselves in opposition
to the judgment of reason. That is why the Apostle says: *I see another
law in my members, fighting against the law of my mind.*[49] And why [the
Apostle] James says: *From whence are wars and contentions among you?
Are they not . . . from your concupiscences?*[50]

---

**15{16}[8]**  *I set the Lord always in my sight: for he is at my right hand,
that I be not moved.*

*Providebam Dominum in conspectu meo semper, quoniam a
dextris est mihi, ne commovear.*

**15{16}[8]** *Providebam Dominum in conspectu meo semper; I set the Lord
always in my sight,* that is, I consider God as my judge: and consequently
I do not accede to the movements of the sensitive appetites, but I remain
steadfast in the judgment of reason. And so *I set the Lord [in my sight
always], quoniam, because* [of this reason] *a dextris est mihi, for he is at
my right hand,* that is, he assists me by his favorable and desirable grace,
*ne commovear, that I be not moved,* that is, that I may not abdicate from
the use of reason, that I may not become inconstant and withdraw from
God, and that I may not yield to vices.

---

**15{16}[9]**  *Therefore my heart has been glad, and my tongue has rejoiced:
moreover my flesh also shall rest in hope.*

*Propter hoc laetatum est cor meum, et exsultavit lingua mea;
insuper et caro mea requiescet in spe.*

**15{16}[9]** *Propter hoc, therefore,* that is, because of the large amount
of mercy and grace of God over me, *laetatum est cor meum; my heart has
been glad,* not in itself, but in the Lord, *et exsultavit lingua mea; and my
tongue has rejoiced,* giving thanks to him. *Insuper et caro mea; moreover
my flesh also,* that is, this corruptible body, *requiescet, shall rest,* that is,
shall stably be subjected to the judgment of reason, and will govern the
soul with tranquil repose, mitigating the movements of its flesh. So truly
it shall rest *in spe, in hope,* that is, in the expectation of future felicity;
because if one subjects in this way [the flesh] to the soul in allegiance
to God, it will thereafter be glorified with the soul in the kingdom of
heaven. Or [it can be understood] thus: *moreover my flesh also shall rest*

---

49  Rom. 7:23.
50  James 4:1.

*in hope*, after its separation from the soul in the grave, in the hope of
the resurrection of the blessed, in the manner that the wise man says,
The *bodies* of the saints *are buried in peace.*[51]

---

**15{16}[10]** *Because you will not leave my soul in hell; nor will you give
your holy one to see corruption.*

*Quoniam non derelinques animam meam in inferno, nec dabis
sanctum tuum videre corruptionem.*

**15{16}[11]** *You have made known to me the ways of life, you shall fill me
with joy with your countenance: at your right hand are delights
even to the end.*

*Notas mihi fecisti vias vitae; adimplebis me laetitia cum vultu
tuo: delectationes in dextera tua usque in finem.*

**15{16}[10]** *Quoniam non derelinques animam meam in inferno; because
you will not leave my soul in hell,* that is, you will not permit me to
die in mortal sin, nor will you condemn me eternally; but if because I
undertook insufficient satisfaction in this life,[52] I will descend in "hell,"
that is, in purgatory,[53] *you will not leave* me in that state: for the debt
of punishment once accomplished, immediately you will lead my soul to
the kingdom of heaven. For in Scripture, there are times where the word
hell is understood as referring to purgatory. Whence also the Church
sings: *Lord Jesus Christ, deliver the souls of the faithful departed from the
pains of hell,*[54] that is, of purgatory. *Nec dabis sanctum tuum; nor will you
give your holy one,* that is your faithful servant, *videre corruptionem, to see
corruption,* that is, to experience eternal death, which is the irrecoverable
and perfect corruption of all spiritual and blessed being.

---

51  Ecclus. 44:14a.
52  E. N. That is, because, though I died in a state of grace and not in mortal sin,
    I did not in this life satisfy the temporal punishments associated with my sins.
53  E. N. The term "hell" is used loosely here, and interpreted to mean Purgatory,
    which is similar to hell in terms of the fact that temporal punishments (are
    temporarily) suffered there. "In Purgatory," says the *Summa*, "there are two pun-
    ishments; one will be of loss (*damni*), to the extent the divine vision is delayed,
    and second, of sense (*sensus*), namely being punished by corporeal fire. And in
    regard to both punishments, the least pain of Purgatory exceeds the greatest
    punishment of this life." ST, IIIae (Supp.App.), q. 1, art. 3, co.
54  E. N. *Domine Iesu Christe, libera animas fidelium defunctorum de poenis
    inferni*... This is an excerpt from the Offertory of the Requiem Mass, the Mass
    for the Dead, and is a perfect instance of the principle *lex orandi, lex credendi* (the
    law of prayer is the law of belief), here applied in the context of Biblical exegesis.

All these are words of good hope, and thus implicitly are the words to be used by all persons praying. And so, O Lord, I hope that all these things may be fulfilled in me, because    **15{16}[11]** *Notas mihi fecisti vias vitae; you have made known to me the ways of life*, that is, the life and the moral teachings of Christ: whose doctrine and way of life, if I but imitate it, I will rightly walk toward eternal life. Which, if I do so perseveringly, *adimplebis me laetitia cum vultu tuo; you shall fill me with the joy with your countenance*, giving me the most happy vision of your countenance, which — once acquired — I will be able to desire nothing else any more. *Delectationes, delights* both pure and intellectual, *in dextera tua, at your right*, that is, in you, the greatest possible good, *usque in finem; even to the end* consummated, and being consumed, without end, that is to say, eternally.[55] It is as if he is saying: delights are those which are attached to your right hand, that is, in your heavenly and invisible goods, which are the dowries of the soul, namely, possession, vision, and fruition,[56] of which is said in a later Psalm: *We shall be filled with the good things of your house.*[57] In any event, in light of the fact that God cannot be circumscribed or be subject to any boundaries, one is not to understand the word "at your right" in a bodily way.

Finally, blessed the man who lives his life in the way that this Psalm allows to be sung as pertaining to one's own person, who so purges his affections from earthly and trifling things, so that he might truthfully say, *the Lord is the portion of my inheritance*; who with such frequency[58] desires to be dissolved,[59] and to possess the heavenly kingdom, so that he is able to say, *for my inheritance is goodly to me*, that is, that it belongs to him, who is able to say with the Apostle, *I count* all things *but as dung, that I may gain Christ.*[60] Blessed is he who in this life always keeps

---

55  E. N. *Consummantem, et sine fine consumente.* This play on words is a reference on the end of the world, *e.g.*, Matt. 28:20 (*usque ad consummationem saeculi*, "even to the consummation of the word") and the consuming nature of God's glory, *i.e.*, Heb. 12:29 (*Deus noster ignis consumens est*, "our God is a consuming fire"). Though there is an end to history, there is no end to our glory.

56  E. N. Denis identifies the "three dowries" of the soul as *tentio, visio,* and *fruitio.* In the Supplement to the *Summa Theologiae*, some of the various formulations of the schoolmen are given: *visio, dilectio,* and *fruitio* (vision, love, and fruition); *visio, comprehensio,* and *fruitio* (vision, comprehension, and fruition); *visio, delectatio,* and *comprehensio* (vision, delight, and comprehension). *ST*, IIIae (*Supp.*), q. 95, art. 5, co.

57  Ps. 64:5b.

58  E. N. The editor suggests another reading, namely *ferventer*, fervently, instead of *frequenter*, frequently.

59  E. N. *Cf.* Phil. 1:23.

60  Phil. 3:8b.

the Lord before him, so that with the most blessed Elijah and Elisha he can truthfully confess: *As the Lord lives the God of Israel, in whose sight I stand.*[61] For such a person, the Lord is at his right hand, and he shall not be moved: because he will not permit him to be tempted beyond that which he is able, but he causes that temptation to yield a happy harvest.[62]

# PRAYER

MOST CLEMENT GOD, KEEP US WHO hope in you safe in your protection; you make known to us the ways of life which, constantly walking until the end with you as our leader, we might delight to be filled with eternal joy and to be fully content before your countenance.

*Sperantes in te, clementissime Deus, tua protection conserva;*
*notas nobis fac vias vitae, quas te duce usque in finem*
*constanter incedentes, aeterna laetitia adimpleri, et*
*vultu tuo delectemur satiari.*

---

61  1 Kings 3:1b; 2 Kings 3:14a.
62  *Cf.* 1 Cor. 10:13.

# Psalm 16

## ARTICLE XL

### EXPOSITION OF THE SIXTEENTH PSALM:
### *EXAUDI, DOMINE, IUSTITIAM MEAM, &c.*
### HEAR, O LORD, MY JUSTICE, &c.

**16{17}[1]**   *The prayer of David. Hear, O Lord, my justice: attend to my supplication. Give ear unto my prayer, which proceeds not from deceitful lips.*

*Oratio David. Exaudi, Domine, iustitiam meam; intende deprecationem meam. Auribus percipe orationem meam, non in labiis dolosis.*

HE TITLE TO THIS PSALM IS:   16{17}[1] *ORATIO David, the prayer of David.* And however much this Psalm may be explained literally as referring to this David, in accordance with the subsequent explanation, it is to be construed with reference to the Church, one of whose preeminent members is David, and also to any one of the perfect, of which David was not the least; nevertheless, so as to avoid prolixity and tedium, I omit this exposition, especially since it can be known most easily from the explanation that follows. Therefore, expositing on this Psalm with reference to Christ, the sense of the title is: *the prayer of David,* that is, the prayer fittingly said by Christ signified by David.

Christ by reason of his assumption of humanity, says to the Father, or to the whole Trinity: *Exaudi, Domine, iustitiam meam; hear, O Lord, my justice,* that is, make it be [that I be heard] on account that I have lived justly, and never have I receded from true justice, but I was obedient even unto death.[1] For Christ accomplished all justice during his life, not to obtain his own personal blessedness, nor in order to augment his essential reward because he was always before the sight of God (*semper comprehensor fuit*);[2] but he did all things so as to obtain for us happiness,

---

1   Cf. Phil. 2:8.
2   E. N. For the difference between a *comprehensor,* and how it differs from someone not enjoying the sight of God (*viator*), see footnotes P-41 and 1-46 and Article IX (Psalm 1:3); for the distinction between essential beatitude and reward and accidental beatitude and reward, see footnote 1-48.

and any one act of his life merited for us, in a most excellent way, eternal life. This is so because whatever he did derived from the most ardent love of God and neighbor. What else, therefore, does Christ pray for when he says, *Hear, O Lord, my justice*, other than, "Give to the world salvation, grant to men grace, save all the elect, since it is for this reason that I did justice?" And Christ also did his justice for his own accidental reward, in which he made progress, namely because of the glory of the resurrection, ascension, and of judicial power.[3] Consequently he prays that his justice be heard also for this cause, namely, that his resurrection and ascension may be hastened. *Intende deprecationem meam; attend to my supplication*, that is, take notice of that which I pray interiorly and diligently. *Auribus, with your ear* of your mercy *percipe orationem meam; perceive my prayer*: not that God perceives something anew, but rather in this sense, *perceive*, that is, knowingly carry out. Often [Christ] repeats the same sentence to express the feeling of his ardor for the salvation of the world. *Perceive*, I say,[4] *my prayer non in labiis dolosis effusam, which proceeds not from deceitful lips*. This is said in the manner that Isaiah writes, *This people honors me with their lips: but their heart is far from me*.[5] For he, whose vocal prayer does not proceed from the affection of his mind prays with deceitful lips; or [also] if he prays for that which is not expedient for his salvation: for such a person deceives himself from the very first.

---

**16{17}[2]**  *Let my judgment come forth from your countenance: let your eyes behold the things that are equitable.*

> *De vultu tuo iudicium meum prodeat; oculi tui videant aequitates.*

**16{17}[2]** *De vultu tuo iudicium meum prodeat; let my judgment come forth from your countenance*, that is, all that is manifested in what I am is from you. For I did not live in this manner so that I might be bashful to know [the truth]: *for he that does truth, comes to the light, that his works may be made manifest, because they are done in God*.[6] Christ therefore says to the Father: *from your countenance*, that is, from the manifestation of your justice, *my judgment*, that is the knowledge of all things that I

---

3   *E. N. Cf.* John 5:22 (*the Father has given all judgment to the Son*) and Matt. 28:19 (*All power is given to me in heaven and upon earth*).

4   *E. N.* Here and elsewhere in this Psalm's explanation, Denis is supposing this to be Christ's prayer; hence the use of the first person.

5   Matt. 15:8; *cf.* Is. 29:13.

6   John 3:21.

assumed, did, and carried out for the redemption of the human race, *come forth*, that is, that it might be made public by the Apostles and other teachers of all men, so that all men might know how unjustly I have been judged and have suffered. *Oculi tui, your eyes,* O Lord Father, *videant aequitatem, let ... behold the things that are equitable,* that is, may your intellect consider my justice, and accordingly give me recompense of bodily glory, and hear my prayers for all others.

---

16{17}[3]   *You have proved my heart, and visited it by night, you have tried me by fire: and iniquity has not been found in me.*

*Probasti cor meum, et visitasti nocte; igne me examinasti, et non est inventa in me iniquitas.*

16{17}[4]   *That my mouth may not speak the works of men: for the sake of the words of your lips, I have kept hard ways.*

*Ut non loquatur os meum opera hominum: propter verba labiorum tuorum, ego custodivi vias duras.*

16{17}[5]   *Perfect you my goings in your paths: that my footsteps be not moved.*

*Perfice gressus meos in semitis tuis, ut non moveantur vestigia mea.*

16{17}[3] *Probasti cor meum; you have proved my heart,* with that temptation of troubles by which men are proved just: *you have proved,* I say, *my heart,* that is, by the many adversities most patiently endured you have found it to be proved good and upright before you; *et visitasti, and you have visited* me *nocte, by night,* that is, you have visited me through adversity, permitting me to suffer evil from the perverse Jews; *igne me examinasti; you have tried me with fire,* that is, you have examined me by the punishment of death, in the manner Job said: *the Lord has tried me as gold that passes through the fire.*[7] Christ also says he is being proved and examined by the Father, not as if the Father had been ignorant of his Son being without sin, but because by [Christ] showing himself out as one proved or one examined, while he [the Father] permitted his only begotten Son to suffer so often and so much, it might stand as an example to all of how great the perfection and the obedience of Christ was. And so the Psalm continues: *et non est inventa in me iniquitas; and iniquity has not been found in me:* for Christ (as is testified in Isaiah) did

---

7 Job 23:10.

not do any iniquity.[8] And this which I say about my perfection I said and say, O Lord, I say without boasting or vainglory:   **16{17}[4]** *Ut non loquatur os meum opera hominum; that my mouth may not speak the works of* men: that is, I have said and I say, that *my mouth may not speak the works of men*, that is pride, presumption, ingratitude, and any other works that are common in the sons of men that might be ascribed to me.

*Propter verba labiorum tuorum; for the sake of the words of your lips*, that is, for the sake of the law and the divinely-inspired prophecies, so that I might have fulfilled, *ego custodivi vias duras; I have kept hard ways*, receiving circumcision, suffering hunger, thirst, and weariness, and even dying on the Cross.   **16{17}[5]** *Perfice gressus meos; perfect you my goings*, that is, that which I began to do and to suffer for the salvation of the world, leading to final happiness, so that by my Passion I might save the human race; *in semitis tuis; in your paths*, that is, so *perfect the goings* of my works, that they might remain in your paths; *ut non moveantur vestigia eius; that my footsteps be not moved*, that is, so that my deeds may not detract from the merit of the hastening of the resurrection and glorious ascension.

---

**16{17}[6]** *I have cried to you, for you, O God, have heard me: O incline your ear unto me, and hear my words.*

*Ego clamavi, quoniam exaudisti me, Deus; inclina aurem tuam mihi, et exaudi verba mea.*

**16{17}[6]** *Ego*, I, Christ, *clamavi*, have *cried* to you, fervently praying, *quoniam exaudisti me, Deus; for you, O God, have heard me*: that is, crying out, I here affirmed my trust, that I experienced myself always to be heard by you; so also do now that which you to this point have always done, namely, *inclina aurem tuam mihi; incline your ear unto me*, that is, direct to me your mercy, *et exaudi verba mea; and hear my words*: which follow.

---

**16{17}[7]** *Show forth your wonderful mercies; you who wave them that trust in you.*

*Mirifica misericordias tuas, qui salvos facis sperantes in te.*

**16{17}[8]** *From them that resist your right hand keep me, as the apple of your eye. Protect me under the shadow of your wings.*

*A resistentibus dexterae tuae custodi me, ut pupillam oculi. Sub umbra alarum tuarum protege me.*

---

8 Is. 53:9.

**16{17}[9]** *From the face of the wicked who have afflicted me. My enemies have surrounded my soul.*

*A facie impiorum qui me afflixerunt. Inimici mei animam meam circumdederunt.*

**16{17}[10]** *They have shut up their fat: their mouth has spoken proudly.*

*Adipem suum concluserunt; os eorum locutum est superbiam.*

**16{17}[11]** *They have cast me forth and now they have surrounded me: they have set their eyes bowing down to the earth.*

*Proiicientes me nunc circumdederunt me; oculos suos statuerunt declinare in terram.*

**16{17}[12]** *They have taken me, as a lion prepared for the prey; and as a young lion dwelling in secret places.*

*Susceperunt me sicut leo paratus ad praedam, et sicut catulus leonis habitans in abditis.*

**16{17}[7]** *Mirifica, wonderfully show forth,* that is, to declare to be marvelous, *misericordias tuas, your mercies* abundantly giving to me that which I ask for, and reconciling the world to yourself through me, and displaying your graces so abundantly and marvelously during the time of the evangelical law. *Qui salvos facis sperantes in te; who save them that trust in you,* **16{17}[8]** *a resistentibus dexterae tuae; from them that resist your right hand,* that is, from the hardened and rebellious Jews who ascribed to the devil the gracious and miraculous works done by me for you[9] and who spurned all my doctrine, *custodi me; keep me,* either so that they are unable to kill me before the preordained time, or that I might not be held in the grave beyond the third day: and so diligently *keep me, ut pupillam oculi, as the apple of your eye,* which is carefully guarded. And Christ says to the Father, *from them that resist your right hand:* for he who resists the Son, resists also the Father; and *he who honors not the Son, honors not the Father who has sent him.*[10] *Sub umbra alarum tuarum; under the shadow of your wings,* that is, under the defenses of your omnipotence and your clemency, *protege me, protect me,* according to the manner that has been stated before, **16{17}[9]** *a facie, from the face,* that is, from the hard presence and the invidious bearing, *impiorum qui me afflixerunt; of the wicked who have afflicted me:* namely, of the Jews and the others who have persecuted me.

9 Matt. 12:24.
10 John 5:23b.

*Inimici mei animam meam; my enemies . . . my soul,* that is, my very self, *circumdederunt, have surrounded,* that is, by tempting, being put to the test, laying hands upon, binding, and killing me;    **16{17}[10]** *adipem suum concluserunt; they have shut up their fat,* that is, they have withdrawn the internal organs of piety from me, neither expressing sympathy or exercising forbearance toward me; *os eorum locutum est superbiam; their mouth has spoken proudly,* against me saying, *He has blasphemed;*[11] *he is guilty of death;*[12] and *we know that this man is a sinner.*[13]    **16{17}[11]** *Proiicientes me nunc circumdederunt me; they have cast me forth and now they have surrounded me:* in the manner that we read in the Gospel, that they thrust him out of the synagogue, and led him *to the brow of the hill, . . . that they might cast him down headlong;*[14] *oculos suos statuerunt declinare in terra; they have set their eyes bowing down to the earth,* that is, they have averted their intellect from the divine truth, and they have followed their passions, looking contemptibly downwards and not upwards, and not willing to believe the signs which the Father brought forward as testimony of his Son.    **16{17}[12]** *Susceperunt me sicut leo paratus ad praedam, et sicut catulus leonis habitans in abditis ; they have taken me as a lion prepared for the prey, and as a young lion dwelling in secret places,* when they saw that the cohort and tribunes and ministers of the Jews had approached and laid hands on Jesus, and bound him and led him to Caiaphas.[15] This Jeremiah prophesied of Christ: *I have given* (he said) *my dear soul into the land of her enemies; my inheritance* (that is the Jewish people) *is become to me as a lion in the wood; it has cried out against me, therefore have I hated it.*[16]

---

**16{17}[13]**    *Arise, O Lord, disappoint him and supplant him; deliver my soul from the wicked one: your sword.*

*Exsurge, Domine: praeveni eum, et supplanta eum; eripe animam meam ab impio.*

**16{17}[14]**    *From the enemies of your hand. O Lord, divide them from the few of the earth in their life: their belly is filled from your*

---

11  Matt. 26:65a.
12  Matt. 26:66b.
13  John 9:24b.
14  Luke 4:29. E. N. Luke speaks of the Jews throwing Jesus out of the city, not necessarily the synagogue where the Jews were first angered at Christ's teaching. Cf. Luke 4:28–29. Denis is implying he was also forcibly thrown out of the synagogue.
15  Matt. 26:50, 57; John 18:12, 24.
16  Jer. 12:7b–8.

*hidden stores. They are full of children: and they have left to their little ones the rest of their substance.*

*Frameam tuam ab inimicis manus tuae. Domine, a paucis de terra divide eos in vita eorum; de absconditis tuis adimpletus est venter eorum. Saturati sunt filiis, et dimiserunt reliquias suas parvulis suis.*

**16{17}[13]** *Exsurge, Domine; arise, O Lord,* for the purpose of rendering aid; *praeveni eum; disappoint him,* so that you might first come to me in rendering help, and you might smite those who are blind at heart and those having power to kill me. Whence, we read in the Gospel, that, as the Passion loomed imminent, an angel from heaven appeared to Christ to comfort him.[17] *Et supplanta eum; and supplant him,* that is, deprive these Jewish people who are persecuting me, so that they might lose the kingdom and the priesthood. *Eripe animam meam ab impio; deliver my soul from the wicked one, this people,* not forsaking it [my soul] as long as it is with this evil generation, but reuniting it on the third day with an impassible[18] body. *Frameam tuam, your sword,* that is, from the power or the sword which you bestowed upon those who were against me, deliver me **16{17}[14]** *ab inimicis manus tuae, from the enemies of your hand,* that is, from my persecutors and crucifiers, who would not otherwise have been able to put me to death. For Christ told Pilate: *You would not have any power against me, unless it were given you from above.*[19] And to the Jews: *This is your hour, and the power of darkness.*[20] Christ prayed that this be removed from the Jews, a long enough time so that they would not be able to persecute him prior to the time fixed by God. It is for this reason that at the instance of the Passion, he said to the Apostles: *For the things concerning me have an end.*[21] Or [this verse may be understood] thus: *Your sword,* that is, my soul, which is called a sword (*framea*), that is, your power and your sword (*gladius*) because by it you have overcome the prince of this world, and you have put to death death, you restored (*reparasti*)

---

17 Luke 22:43.

18 L. *impassibili,* impassible; that is, after his Resurrection, Christ's glorified body enjoyed the four gifts of glorified bodies: impassibility (the inability to suffer), subtlety, agility, and clarity (or brightness). *See* Catechism of the Council of Trent, Part I, art. XI. 90–91.

19 John 19:11a.

20 Luke 22:53b.

21 Luke 22:37b.

the fall of the angels and you repaired (*reparasti*),[22] the whole world and placed it under your rule (*imperio*): this sword [meaning the soul] deliver *from the enemies of your hand*, that is, from the powers of the Jews, reuniting it with the immortal body.

Consequently, Christ prays for the general ejection of the Jews, which he desires to the extent it conforms to the divine will and righteousness. *Domine, a paucis de terra divide eos in vita eorum; O Lord, divide them from the few of the earth in their life*. It is as if he says: "O Lord Father, divide them from the earth, that is, expel them from the holy lands, and disperse them in diverse places; and destroy them by the sword, hunger, and captivity, and distinguish from them the few, that is [separate out of them] the faithful elect, which, in comparison to the reprobate, are few. And those few, do not divide them, but collect them in the unity of the Church by faith, hope, and charity; but divide those in their lives, in the manner predicted, in the manner fulfilled by Vespasian and Titus."[23]

*De absconditis tuis; from your hidden stores*, that is, from your most excellent and highest bodily and earthly goods, *adimpletus est venter eorum; their belly is filled*, that is, they have been made satisfied and rich. For the land of all the most excellent lands, flowing with milk and honey, you gave them; but they were ungrateful to you, and they killed me, your only Son. Or thus [it might be understood]: *From your hidden stores*, that is, from sins and disordered desires of those disregarding you with your approbation, *their belly is filled*, that is, the affections of their flesh which they satisfied, because they were avaricious, lustful, and ambitious. *Saturati sunt filiis; they are full of children* because you have given to them the fertility of carnal propagation, multiplying them as the stars of heaven; *et dimiserunt reliquias suas; and they have left*, that is, those things in which they overflowed, *parvulis suis*, to their

---

22  E. N. It is odd for Denis to have two similar verbs, using *reparasti*, "you repaired," for both the angels and the world in general; and so this may be an error in the text. I have translated the former use of *reparasti* as "you restored," since fallen angels cannot be redeemed, but it is a common (speculative) teaching that the loss of the number of fallen angels is to be made up by the souls of men in heaven. It is mentioned, for example, in the *Summa Theologiae*, Ia, q. 23, art. 7, co. ("Concerning the number of all the predestined, some say that so many men will be saved as angels fell; some, so many as there were angels left; others, as many as the number of angels created by God. It is, however, better to say that, 'to God alone is known the number for whom is reserved eternal happiness.'").

23  *See* Arts. XII (Psalm 2:5) XXIV (Psalm 7:13) and footnote 2-23.

*little ones*, that is, their successors. For [in this verse] Christ recollects all the benefits of God gathered together, so that the aggravation of their sin may be more amply shown. Or [it might be viewed] thus: *They are full of children*, that is, evil deeds. Indeed, deeds are called the children of their doers, because for all things that are done, the character of the agent is reflected in his deeds. And so a deed, according to this rule of similitude, proceeds from the agent; yet [the essence of] filiation consists in similitude. The Jews have scattered forth the remnants of disbelief,[24] namely, infidelity, malediction, and vices, *their little ones*, that is, their posterity. For the wrath of God has come over them even up to the end, according to the Apostle. And it is fulfilled in them that which they exclaimed before Pilate of Christ: *His blood be upon us and our children.*[25]

---

**16{17}[15]**   *But as for me, I will appear before your sight in justice: I shall be satisfied when your glory shall appear.*

*Ego autem in iustitia apparebo conspectui tuo; satiabor cum apparuerit gloria tua.*

Therefore, so it is that they will be lost from you;   **16{17}[15]** *Ego autem in iustitia apparebo conspectui tuo; but as for me, I will appear before your sight in justice*, that is, I will always walk justly and with holiness before you, and the mystery of human redemption accomplished, after the Ascension I will appear with you in glory, sitting at your right hand, and interceding on behalf of the elect. *Satiabor, I shall be satisfied* with all the joy of accidental rewards,[26] *cum apparuerit gloria tua; when your glory shall appear*, that is, when your glory, which you gave to me, and which I merited through my Passion while in the world, will be made manifest to all the saints in heaven and on earth. For then I will be satisfied,[27] seeing your honor restored by me, and the walls of the heavenly Jerusalem rebuilt by me.

---

24  *Cf.* 1 Thess. 2:16.
25  Matt. 27:25b.
26  For the difference between essential rewards and accidental rewards, *see* Arts. XII (Psalm 2:5) XXIV (Psalm 7:13) and footnote 2-23.
27  *Cf.* John 19:28. E. N. Denis's reference to John is to one of Christ's seven last words on the Cross: *I thirst, Sitio.* The image intended by Denis, then, is that Christ's thirst will be satisfied, his thirst for the restoration of the divine order, the new Jerusalem, so that *God may be all in all.* 1 Cor. 15:28. For the reference to the walls of the heavenly Jerusalem, *see* Rev. 21:9-14; 17-18.

# ARTICLE XLI

## EXPLANATION OF THIS SIXTEENTH PSALM OF THE
## CHURCH AND OF ANY PERFECT AND FAITHFUL MAN

16{17}[1]  *The prayer of David. Hear, O Lord, my justice: attend to my
supplication. Give ear unto my prayer, which proceeds not from
deceitful lips.*

*Oratio David. Exaudi, Domine, iustitiam meam; intende depre-
cationem meam. Auribus percipe orationem meam, non in labiis
dolosis.*

OW ACCORDING TO THE MORAL SENSE,
that which is said, namely: *Exaudi, Domine, iustitiam meam; hear,
O Lord, my justice,* can be the prayer of any perfect man, who trusts, not
only in the mercy of God, but in his own merits, for, with respect to
these merits of his, he knows them to be the gifts of God, a concession
to him from the divine mercy. So it is in this sense [that the verse should
be understood in the moral sense]:  16{17}[1] *Exaudi, Domine, hear, O
Lord*, not only my vocal prayer, but *iustitiam meam, my justice,* so that all
the good and meritorious works that I do might be pleasing to you, and
that you might grant to me, for the justice of my life, that which I long for.
For prayer is a good and meritorious work before God; and he who does
not cease to live in a praiseworthy manner, does not cease to pray. But
blessed is he who with a secure and humble conscience is able to assert
before God the perfection of his life and individual merit. Hezekiah, of
whom Isaiah speaks, plainly was such a person: *Hezekiah wept with great
weeping, and said, I beseech you, O Lord, remember how I have walked before
you in truth, and with a perfect heart, and have done that which is good in
your sight.*[28] The efficaciousness of that prayer came from the fact that
not only did God fulfill the prayer of Hezekiah, adding to the life that he
had formerly lived, and which was naturally at its end, fifteen years; but
on top of this and at his instance the sun was reversed ten lines [degrees],
by the degrees by which it had descended in the sun dial of Achaz.[29]

This verse, *Hear, O Lord, my justice,* may also be understood to be
the prayer of the imperfect man, who is so humbly aware of his own

---

28  Is. 38:3. E. N. Denis flips the verse so that the second sentence of the verse in
the Scripture is the first, and the first the second.
29  Is. 38:5, 8. E. N. Achaz is sometimes spelled Ahaz.

imperfection that he says: *Hear*, that is, hold it to be acceptable, *O Lord, my justice*, not despising it because of the imperfections annexed to it: *for I know to be true that which Isaiah holds, all our justices as the rag of a menstruous woman;*[30] but add, O Lord, your merciful kindness (*pietas*) to that in which it is deficient as a result of my weakness, and hear *my justice*, which is not worthy in any absolute sense to be called justice, but perhaps better should be called injustice.

*Intende deprecationem meam; attend to my supplication*, I ask that all my evil be overlooked as to me. *Auribus percipe orationem meam; give ear unto my prayer*, I plead that the virtues and grace be always granted to me. *Prayer*, I say, done *non in labiis dolosis, not from deceitful lips*, that is, with wandering or timorous mind, and not poured forth with the intent of remaining in sin.

---

**16{17}[2]**  *Let my judgment come forth from your countenance: let your eyes behold the things that are equitable.*

*De vultu tuo iudicium meum prodeat; oculi tui videant aequitates.*

**16{17}[2]** *De vultu tuo iudicium meum prodeat; let my judgment come forth from your countenance*, that is, let all that I judge with respect to myself or with respect to others come from your countenance, that is, let it all be directed according to your divine truth, so that I might judge neither temerariously or fallaciously, nor condemn someone on the grounds of suspicion alone, nor presume to judge another against the evangelical wisdom.[31] Or [it might be understood] so: *From your countenance*, that is, from your mercifully kind aspect, *my judgment*, which will be judged by you, *come forth*, not that I might justly be condemned,

---

30 Is. 64:6a.

31 E. N. Needless to say, the "evangelical wisdom" regarding judgment is broader than a mindless, absolutist, and exceptionless application of one of its restrictive boundaries, *Judge not, that you not be judged.* Matt. 7:1. It includes — as part of its boundaries along with a legion of other guidance which urge us to judge charitably and not rashly — the affirmative obligation *to* judge, though *not according to the appearance, but judge just judgment.* John 7:24. "To avoid rash judgment, everyone should be careful to interpret insofar as possible his neighbor's thoughts, words, and deeds in a favorable way: 'Every good Christian ought to be more ready to give a favorable interpretation to another's statement than to condemn it. But if he cannot do so, let him ask how the other understands it. And if the latter understands it badly, let the former correct him with love. If that does not suffice, let the Christian try all suitable ways to bring the other to a correct interpretation so that he may be saved.'" CCC § 2478 (quoting St. Ignatius of Loyola, *Spiritual Exercises*, 22).

but that I might mercifully be saved. *Oculi tui videant; let your eyes behold,* that is, let them benignly regard, and with regard bring about, *aequitatem, that which is equitable,*[32] that is, the righteousness of my interaction with others.

---

16{17}[3]  *You have proved my heart, and visited it by night, you have tried me by fire: and iniquity has not been found in me.*

*Probasti cor meum, et visitasti nocte; igne me examinasti, et non est inventa in me iniquitas.*

16{17}[4]  *That my mouth may not speak the works of men: for the sake of the words of your lips, I have kept hard ways.*

*Ut non loquatur os meum opera hominum: propter verba labiorum tuorum, ego custodivi vias duras.*

16{17}[3] *Probasti cor meum; you have proved my heart* by both prosperity and adversity, tempting and experiencing whether I remained in all things faithful to you; *et visitasti nocte, and visited by night,* that is, through scourges you have come to me, applying paternal chastisement, in the manner that is attested to in Revelation: *Such as I love, I rebuke and chastise.*[33] *Igne me examinasti; you have tried me by fire,* that is, through forceful and most difficult tribulations you have examined me, proving whether I would persist constant even unto death; *et non est inventa in me iniquitas; and iniquity has not been found in me.* This is said of the Church or of the just man, either because he has not sinned mortally (something which is believed to be true of many saints), or because he has repented of sin, or because — if he has sinned — so also through trials, visitations,[34] and examinations he has been purged of his sins, as we have in Job: *Blessed is the man whom God corrects.*[35]  16{17}[4] *Ut non loquatur os meum opera hominum; that my mouth may not speak the words of men,* that is, that I may not say these things because of vainglory, for just as fashions are vain to men, so are they who praise the works of men and not God.

---

32  The Sixto-Clementine Vulgate has the plural *aequitates,* which Denis has as singular *aequitatem.*

33  Rev. 3:19.

34  L. *visitationes,* visitations. This word has the connotation both of coming to investigate, examine, but also the sense of visiting affliction, chastisement, or punishment, *e.g.,* Hosea 12:2. Both senses are fair in this context.

35  Job 5:17a. E. N. The scripture verse continues: *refuse not therefore the chastising of the Lord.*

*Propter verba labiorum tuorum; for the sake of the words of your lips,* that is, due the fulfilling words of sacred Scripture, *ego custodivi vias duras; I have kept hard ways,* that is, I have kept custody of my heart, of which there is nothing more difficult to do, and I have done acts of virtue, which are *hard ways:* because according to the Philosopher,[36] art and virtue are concerned with difficult things.[37] And this, to the extent it is applied to beginners — for whom it is akin to punishment to renounce the old life, to abstain from all illicit desires, and to enter through the narrow gate[38] — is most especially true. But in regard to the proficient, it is in some ways seen also to be true. But with respect to the perfect, that which the Savior says is true: *For my yoke is sweet and my burden light.*[39] And in Ecclesiasticus: *There is nothing sweeter,* it says, *than to have regard to the commandments of the Lord.*[40] This is so since no informing principle operates as promptly and as sweetly as love. Thus, the more we are proficient in divine love, the more all the difficult things we do are easier and sweeter, *for love is strong as death.*[41] Therefore, the Church of the perfect, who not only keeps the commandments of God, but also fulfills the counsels of Christ,[42] most truly says to the Lord: *For the sake of the words of your lips,* with which, O Christ, you said of those who will fulfill your counsels, will receive a hundredfold, and shall possess life everlasting,[43] *I have kept hard ways,* that is, the precepts and the counsels, which at least to begin with were difficult for me, and things of nature are difficult unless your grace be present.

---

**16{17}[5]**  *Perfect you my goings in your paths: that my footsteps be not moved.*

*Perfice gressus meos in semitis tuis, ut non moveantur vestigia mea.*

But because no one is in this life so perfect and so clean that he cannot be more and more perfect, especially since the Apostle says, *I do not count myself to have apprehended,* but those things which are behind are forgotten, and I reach out to those things before me.[44] Consequently, he

---

36  Like St. Thomas Aquinas, Denis refers to Aristotle as "the Philosopher."
37  Ethc. II, c. 3 *in fine. E. N. Nicomachean Ethics,* 1105a1.
38  Matt. 7:13.
39  Matt. 11:30.
40  Ecclus. 23:37.
41  Songs 8:6.
42  E. N. For the distinction between the divine precepts and the evangelical counsels, *see* CCC §§ 1965–1974.
43  *Cf.* Matt. 19:29.
44  Phil. 3:13.

adds to this,   **16{17}[5]** *Perfice gressus meus; perfect you my goings,* that is, all my affections and all my works, wherein I tend to the end,[45] *in semitis tuis; in your paths,* that is by the observation of your commandments and counsels, *ut non moveantur; that they be not moved,* that is, that they do not recede from your law, *vestigia mea, my footsteps,* that is, the works by which I advance towards you.

---

**16{17}[6]**   *I have cried to you, for you, O God, have heard me: O incline your ear unto me, and hear my words.*

*Ego clamavi, quoniam exaudisti me, Deus; inclina aurem tuam mihi, et exaudi verba mea.*

**16{17}[6]** *Ego clamavi, I have cried* with my voice, *quoniam exaudisti me, Deus; for you, O God, have heard me,* that is, because you heard my mental prayer in which I requested you to inspire prayers that were saving to me and pleasing to you, making it so that I had interiorly that which I prayed with my mouth. For you hear that prayer which you yourself inspire. Or [the verse might be understood] thus: *I have cried,* now praying to you, *for you, O God have heard me,* while I have prayed before or at other times; and so from this hearing on your part, I take up the courage now to pray to you. *Inclina aurem tuam mihi; incline your ear unto me,* that is, approach me with your benign favor, *et exaudi verba mea; and hear my words,* which are the outward signs of my interior affections.

---

**16{17}[7]**   *Show forth your wonderful mercies; you who save them that trust in you.*

*Mirifica misericordias tuas, qui salvos facis sperantes in te.*

**16{17}[8]**   *From them that resist your right hand keep me, as the apple of your eye. Protect me under the shadow of your wings.*

*A resistentibus dexterae tuae custodi me, ut pupillam oculi. Sub umbra alarum tuarum protege me.*

**16{17}[9]**   *From the face of the wicked who have afflicted me. My enemies have surrounded my soul.*

*A facie impiorum qui me afflixerunt. Inimici mei animam meam circumdederunt.*

---

45  E. N. *Deus igitur maxime est omnium rerum finis:* "God above all things therefore is the end of all things." *Summa Contra Gentiles,* b. 3 cap. 17 n. 3.

**16{17}[10]**   *They have shut up their fat: their mouth has spoken proudly.*

*Adipem suum concluserunt; os eorum locutum est superbiam.*

**16{17}[11]**   *They have cast me forth and now they have surrounded me: they have set their eyes bowing down to the earth.*

*Proiicientes me nunc circumdederunt me; oculos suos statuerunt declinare in terram.*

**16{17}[12]**   *They have taken me, as a lion prepared for the prey; and as a young lion dwelling in secret places.*

*Susceperunt me sicut leo paratus ad praedam, et sicut catulus leonis habitans in abditis.*

**16{17}[7]** *Mirifica misericordias tuas; show forth your wonderful mercies,* that is, the more you see me more miserable, more unworthy, and more in need, come to my aid more generously in all things in which I need the aid of your merciful kindness, as your mercy is to be magnified, that is, it is marvelous that it has acknowledged me; indeed how much more amply it has magnified me, the worse and more vile I am. And so, O Lord, *show forth your wonderful mercies,* that is, display in me the manifold kindness of your grace, so that I might be with the holy Apostle a *vessel of election,*[46] a *vessel of mercy* in honor, and not a *vessel of wrath* in reproach.[47]   **16{17}[8]** *A resistentibus dexterae tua; from them that resist your right hand,* that is, from the temptations of demons, from the vanity of worldly men, and from every vice of the proud, resistant to the extent of their powers, *of your right hand,* that is, of your justice and your most straightly right will. Or [we might see it this way], *Your right hand,* that is, the law of Christ and of grace, by which one arrives at to his right hand in heaven; *custodi me; keep me,* that I not agree with them, that I not will to resist you by disobedience; and that not in that fashion, but diligently — in all circumstances, places, and times — *keep me ut pupillam oculi, as the apple of your eye,* which is most diligently kept. *Sub umbra alarum tuarum protege me; protect me under the shadow of your wings.* This speaks transumptively of God,[48] as has been satisfactorily clarified in the explanation of this verse in the preceding exposition.[49] *Under the shadow of your wings* it says, that is, under the breadth of

---

46  Acts. 9:15.
47  *Cf.* Rom. 9:21–23.
48  L. *transumptive.* On transumptively, see footnote 5-14.
49  Article XL (Ps. 16:8).

goodness and the multitude of your mercy protect me   16{17}[9] *a facie impiorum; from the face of the wicked*, that is, from the invasion of the world, the flesh, and the devil, *qui me afflixerunt; who have afflicted me*, by tempting, persecuting, causing disorder. For the disordered soul is itself its own affliction.[50]

*Inimici mei, my enemies*, who endeavor to divert me from God, *animam meam, my soul*, which is placed in the middle of snares, *circumdederunt, they have surrounded*. For the demons surround it, suggesting vices; the disordered desires of the flesh, stimulate it; the world, attracts it to illicit things.   16{17}[10] *Adipem suum concluserunt; they have shut up their fat*, that is, the carnal blandishments they have hidden between themselves, so that they can, by proposing delectable things, draw me towards evil under the guise of good. *Os eorum locutum est superbiam; their mouth has spoken proudly*, for they begin to seek to make me rebel from God, and they dare to propose to me and to praise that which is prohibited by the divine law.   16{17}[11] *Proiicientes me nunc; they cast me forth and now*, these enemies of mine already mentioned, from divine contemplation toward inane curiosities, from stability in God to the wandering of the heart in the world, from the love of God to an inordinate affection for creatures, *circumdederunt me; they have surrounded me* with evil counsel and various deceits; *oculos suos statuerunt declinare in terram; they have set their eyes bowing down to earth*, because they have diverted their considerations from heavenly and divine goods, and they are beholden to the love of temporal and fleeting things, and they labor to incline others and me to such things.   16{17}[12] *Susceperunt me, they have taken me*, when I have sinned, and they have bound me to the slavery and the chains of vices, that I might not immediately return to my Creator and my Judge. *They have taken*, I say, *me sicut leo paratus ad praedam; as a lion prepared for the prey*, as placed under their dominion, they have brought me back, and they have spiritually devoured and destroyed me; *et sicut catulus leonis habitans in abditis; and as a young lion dwelling in secret places*, that is, in hidden places. Whence Peter says: *Your adversary the devil, as a roaring lion, goes about seeking whom he may devour.*[51]

---

50  E. N. This is a veiled reference to St. Augustine's *Confessions*, I, 12. *Iussisti, Domine, et sic est, ut poena sua sibi sit omnis animus inordinatus.* "You have commanded, O Lord, and so it is, that every disordered soul be its own punishment for itself."

51  1 Pet. 5:8.

**16{17}[13]** *Arise, O Lord, disappoint him and supplant him; deliver my soul from the wicked one: your sword.*

*Exsurge, Domine: praeveni eum, et supplanta eum; eripe animam meam ab impio.*

**16{17}[14]** *From the enemies of your hand. O Lord, divide them from the few of the earth in their life: their belly is filled from your hidden stores. They are full of children: and they have left to their little ones the rest of their substance.*

*Frameam tuam ab inimicis manus tuae. Domine, a paucis de terra divide eos in vita eorum; de absconditis tuis adimpletus est venter eorum. Saturati sunt filiis, et dimiserunt reliquias suas parvulis suis.*

　　**16{17}[13]** *Exsurge, Domine; arise, O Lord,* so as to help me; *praeveni eum, disappoint him,* that is, before any adversary of my salvation is able to kill my soul, you come, and grant you grace, and manifest your victory; *et supplanta eum, and supplant him,* so that through your aid I might prevail over them, namely, the devil, the world, and all sin. *Eripe anima meam ab impio; deliver my soul from the wicked one,* that is from all the aforesaid enemies. *Frameam tuam, your sword,* that is the power of persecuting, killing, deceiving, that the enemies have gathered from you: *for there is no power but from God,*[52] also that which the impious abuse: *deliver this sword* **16{17}** **[14]** *ab inimicis manus tuae; from the enemies of your hand,* that is, from the demons, the world, and the flesh, that the adversaries relying on your powers, neither prevail against me in a public way, nor deceive me in a hidden way. And powers conceded to the demons they are not able to be used as they please, but only insofar as permitted by God, who restrains them through the holy angels, [and so] they are not able to harm me as much as they might wish or might be otherwise able. The faithful man prays, therefore, for the restraining of the power of the devil, when he says; *Your sword,* etc.

　　*Domine, a paucis de terra; Lord, from the few of the earth,* that is from the elect who are formed from the earth insofar as their body, *divide eos, divide them,* that is the earlier-mentioned enemies, separate them from the just, *in vita eorum, in their life,* that is, now by the judgment discretion, and thereafter by the judgment of retribution.[53] Or [it can be understood] thus: *Lord, from the few of the earth,* that is, separate

---

52  Rom. 13:1.

53  For the difference between the judgment of discretion and the final judgment or judgment of retribution, see footnote 1-39.

them from Church militant, which is on earth in the manner of a pilgrim: separate, he says, the enemies and the reprobate *from the few*, that is, the elect, in their, that is to say, their enemies' life, that is, now. For God separates now the evil from the good by promise and merit; but hereafter he will separate them by place and reward, when *these shall go into everlasting punishment: but the just, into life everlasting.*[54]

*De absconditis tuis, from your hidden stores*, that is, from those by their sins unknown to you by approbation, *adimpletus est venter eorum, their belly is filled*, that is, their unclean appetite, in which—as if in a stomach in the belly—there is amassed filth of vices, the stench of disordered desires, and the overabundance of all evil: for which reason also they are hateful to you, and are regarded as fetid, vain, and miserable by you. *Saturati sunt filiis, they are full of children*, because they generate many and innumerable children through the imitation of sin. For how many children does the Devil—he who is most vile, who is *king over all the sons of pride*[55]—have? And the foolish, who do not find response in the eternal Wisdom, namely Christ, are seemingly endless in number: and all these are the children, namely, of the devil, the flesh, and the world: for which reason *of children* it is said *they are full*. Or, as it has [otherwise] been explained, *they are full of children*, that is, the workers of evil who are begotten from the vicious habits hidden within them, which have been previously mentioned regarding the verse *from your hidden stores their belly is filled. Et dimiserunt reliquias suas parvulis suis; and they have left to their little ones the rest of their substance*, that is, those whom the devils and worldly men by themselves were unable to deceive, they abandoned, deceiving their posterity. Or, *they have left the rest of their substance*, that is, the evil memories of their perversities or bad examples, and other things that they obtained from their vices, *to their little ones*, that is, to the sons following the sins of their fathers.

---

**16{17}[15]**    *But as for me, I will appear before your sight in justice: I shall be satisfied when your glory shall appear.*

*Ego autem in iustitia apparebo conspectui tuo; satiabor cum apparuerit gloria tua.*

**16{17}[15]** *Ego autem, but as for me*, who by your grace, O Lord, do not belong to this sort, but I attend fervently to your service, *in iustitia*,

---

54  Matt. 25:46.
55  Job 41:25b.

*in justice,* that I have done, *apparebo conspectui tuo; I will appear before your sight,* when I will be presented before your tribunal: for the works of every single person follow them.[56] And, as the Apostle says, *For we must all be manifested before the judgment seat of Christ.*[57] *Satiabor, I shall be satisfied,* that is, I will be filled with all good and will be enriched with such happiness, that I will not be able to desire any increase, *cum apparuerit gloria tua; when your glory shall appear,* that is, when you shall manifest yourself to me as you are,[58] so that I may see you by sight, you, who I now perceive by faith. For nothing is able to satisfy the rational appetite except for infinite good; no other thing is able to fulfil the intellect, except for eternal truth. Therefore, then shall the desire of the just be satisfied, when it shall attain to the clear vision of the divine truth and the blessed enjoyment of the immense divine goodness. Nevertheless, the souls of the blessed in heaven anticipate and desire the bodily glory and the future resurrection: so, accordingly, in what way can we say that they are now satisfied? Certainly, they are satisfied now insofar as the essential reward, which is the vision of God, for they will see God ever-so-clearly, and they will sweetly enjoy him who they desired. But after that day of judgment they shall be satisfied insofar as it concerns an accidental reward,[59] though it is such a small reward in comparison with the essential reward so that it is as if one might regard it as nothing. And so now also one is able to say that all the blessed in heaven are satisfied with all good. For as the Philosopher has attested, that which is small, is regarded as nothing.[60]

Oh, how great is the virtue of this Psalm! Oh, how burning and fervid are the prayers contained within it, prayers whose ardor he who sings this Psalm with a pure heart can sweetly taste! But especially is this true of three of its verses, namely, beginning with *Show forth your wonderful mercies,* and the two following verses [*i.e.,* Psalm **16**:**7-9**], which are most full with the fire of the Holy Spirit and all holy affection: of which it is fitting first for the beginner, second for the proficient, and third for

---

56  *Cf.* Rev. 14:13b.

57  2 Cor. 5:10a. E. N. The verse continues, *that everyone may receive the proper things of the body, according as he has done, whether it be good or evil.*

58  *Cf.* 1 John 3:2.

59  E. N. On the distinction between the essential reward of the beatific vision (the vision of God) and the accidental rewards (here, the reunification of the soul with its glorified body), *see* footnote 1-48.

60  Physic. II, c. 5 in fine. E. N. A reference to Aristotle. *See, e.g., ST,* IaIIae, q. 65, art. 1, ad 1; IIaIIae, q. 62, art 2, ad. 4; q. 66, art. 6, ad 3; q. 158, art. 3, co., where St. Thomas applies the same principle.

the perfect. However often, therefore, O brother, you are oppressed by
your miseries, however often you are wearied by temptations, however
often you are disturbed by the pricks of vices, cry out to the Lord: *Show
forth your wonderful mercies* in me, you who make hale those who hope
in you. Therefore, let us dedicate ourselves to stripping our souls always,
but especially during the time of prayer, of such useless phantasms, so
that we might be able to sing this Psalm intently and enjoying its full
savor, and to draw from it copiously the effect of its prayers.

# PRAYER

HOW FORTH, O GOD, YOUR WONDERFUL
mercies, and protect us under the shadow of your wings, as
you keep the apple of your eye: that perfecting our goings in your
paths, we might appear before you in justice and be satisfied when
your glory shall appear.

*Mirifica, Deus, misericordias tuas, ut sub umbra alarum
tuarum nos protegas, ut pupillam oculi custodias:
quo perfectis gressibus nostris in semitis tuis, in
iustitia tibi appareamus, et satiemur cum
apparuerit gloria tua.*

# Psalm 17

## ARTICLE XLII

### EXPOSITION OF THE SEVENTEENTH PSALM:
### *DILIGAM ET, DOMINE, &c.*
### *I WILL LOVE YOU, O LORD, &c.*

17{18}[1]   *Unto the end, for David the servant of the Lord, who spoke to the Lord the words of this canticle, in the day that the Lord delivered him from the hands of all his enemies, and from the hand of Saul.*

*In finem. Puero Domini David, qui locutus est Domino verba cantici huius, in die qua eripuit eum Dominus de manu omnium inimicorum eius, et de manu Saul, et dixit.*

THIS PSALM BEARS THE TITLE:   17{18}[1] *IN finem. Puero Domini David, qui locutus est Domino verba cantici huius, in die qua eripuit eum Dominus de manu omnium inimicorum eius, et de manu Saul. Unto the end, for David the servant of the Lord, who spoke to the Lord the words of this canticle, in the day that the Lord delivered him from the hands of all his enemies, and from the hand of Saul.* In the books of Samuel and Chronicles[1] we find written the way in which David sang to the Lord this Psalm in thanksgiving of God's benefits after the various victories he enjoyed by divine concession, and after the death of Saul. Since this Psalm here literally intends to be about David, there is little need to explain this title. But because this Psalm is also able to be expounded as treating of the whole Christ, that is, of Christ and his Mystical Body, that is, the Church which embraces all the elect from Adam even unto the end of the world, so therefore is the [meaning of the] title clear. The sense of the title, therefore, is: *the words of this canticle* directing us *unto the end,* namely Christ, are becoming to *David, the servant of the Lord,* that is, Christ, the Son of God: which words Christ *spoke to the Lord,* that is, to the glory of the Father for himself and for his faithful, *in the day that the Lord delivered him from the hands of his enemies,* that is, in the day of the Resurrection, when he rose again from the dead, was delivered from the powers of the Jews, and when he delivered the Church from being

---

1   2 Sam. 22:1 *et seq.*

in the thrall of the devil, *and from the hand of Saul,* that is, the power of death. For *Christ rising again from the dead, dies now no more.*[2]

---

**17{18}[2]**   *I will love you, O Lord, my strength.*

  *Diligam te, Domine, fortitudo mea.*

**17{18}[3]**   *The Lord is my firmament, my refuge, and my deliverer. My God is my helper, and in him will I put my trust. My protector and the horn of my salvation, and my support.*

  *Dominus firmamentum meum, et refugium meum, et liberator meus. Deus meus adiutor meus, et sperabo in eum; protector meus, et cornu salutis meae, et susceptor meus.*

Giving thanks to God in this manner for this spiritual liberation, Christ says:   **17{18}[2]** *Diligam te, Domine; I will love you, O Lord.* And the beginning of this Psalm is something fittingly applied to Christ as man, and to the Church, and indeed to any true member of the faithful. Therefore he says: *I will love you, O Lord,* that is, I shall always love you, sometimes because of your immense goodness, for which you are loveable beyond any measure; sometimes because of the benefits that you have conveyed to me; sometimes because of the promises you have prepared for me. Indeed, love is the first and greatest gift, and in it all gifts are given gratuitously. Consequently, we are not able to repay God for his benefits — indeed we are unable to repay any benefactor whatsoever — with anything greater or more dignified than love. For Christ as God, loves the Father with a love simply infinite; but as man, he loves God with a greater love than all the elect put together. But every single one of us is obligated more ardently to love God the more benefits he has received from him. And this verse can be understood as a kind of prayer, in this sense: *I will love you, O Lord,* that is, grant that I may love you, O Lord. *Fortitudo mea, my strength,* that is, cause of all my fortitude, without whom I am able to do nothing.   **17{18}[3]** *Dominus, the Lord* is *firmamentum meum, my firmament,* that is, my stable support, and the cause of my stability. For Christ throughout all of his Passion remained constant and unyielding, in no fashion were acts of reason or operations of virtue impeded or disordered in him: for his stability was firmly supernatural. *Et refugium meum, and my refuge.* For Christ, immediately before his Passion, found refuge with the Father saying, *My*

---

2  Rom. 6:9a.

*Father, if it be possible, let this chalice pass from me.*[3] *Et liberator meus, and my deliverer*, from the tempter, the devil, and from the persecution of the Jews, who frequently endeavored to put me to death when my time had not yet come;[4] or [we might understand alternatively this way], *My deliverer*, for you raised me up again to life impassible.[5]

*Deus meus, my God* is *adiutor meus, my helper*, insofar as I am man. For Christ performed miracles, not as a result of human or natural [powers], but from divine power. *Et sperabo in eum; and in him will I put my trust*, that is, I will expect all good from him that I do not yet have. For the manner in which it was fitting for Christ to hope in God is frequently mentioned [in this Commentary]. *Protector meus, my protector*, that is, God is the defender of my humanity, defending it from all the evil of fault; *et cornu, and the horn*, that is, the superior and eminent cause, *salutis meae, of my salvation*, that is, of the happiness both of the body as well as my soul, beatifying me immediately in my soul, when you created it, and in the body when you raised me up again from the dead;[6] *et susceptor meus, and my support*, that is, God, the Son of God, assumed my humanity unto its personal subsistence.

---

17{18}[4]   *Praising I will call upon the Lord: and I shall be saved from my enemies.*

*Laudans invocabo Dominum, et ab inimicis meis salvus ero.*

17{18}[4] *Laudans invocabo Dominio; praising, I will call upon the Lord.* Frequently in the Gospels, we read Christ invoking the Father with praise and thanksgiving, as with John: *Father*, he said, *I give you thanks that you have heard me.*[7] *Et ab inimicis meis, and from my enemies*, namely, the Jews, *salvus ero, I shall be saved*, by the resurrection from the dead. For also Christ by praying merited that he might quickly be raised from the dead, as from all causes he was due a quick resurrection, but especially because of the union of his humanity with the Word.[8]

---

3   Matt. 26:39.
4   John 7:30; 8:20.
5   E. N. Denis uses the perfect indicative tense, *resuscitavit me*, though it would seem that since the prayer is at the Garden of Gethsemane that it should be in the future, *resuscitaverit*. As to the word impassible, *see* footnote 3-22.
6   E. N. Denis again uses the perfect indicative tense, *sucscitavit*.
7   John 11:41b.
8   E. N. As St. Thomas Aquinas states, Christ had a two-fold grace, the grace of union — which was infinite — and the fullness of sanctifying or habitual grace. Whereas the former is infinite *simpliciter*, the latter is infinite as to its specific

**17{18}[5]**    *The sorrows of death surrounded me: and the torrents of iniquity troubled me.*

> Circumdederunt me dolores mortis, et torrentes iniquitatis conturbaverunt me.

**17{18}[5]** *Circumdederunt me dolores mortis; the sorrows of death surrounded me,* that is, the punishments and the sadness of death: because the Gospel says, Jesus *began to fear, to be heavy,*[9] *and to be sad.*[10] On the Cross, moreover, when he entirely fulfilled the satisfaction [for sins], and the pains of death encompassed him about, he said, *It is consummated; and bowing his head, he gave up the ghost.*[11] *Et torrentes iniquitatis, and the torrents of iniquity,* that is, the many iniquities, namely, the unjust persecutions from the Jews against me, abundantly brought against me at the time of the Passion, *conturbaverunt me, troubled me,* that is, they insulted the inferior part of my soul and bodily nature from their natural disposition because of the harshness of the inflicted punishment: but they did not however disturb or cause disorder to the act of reason in Christ. But there is a certain disturbance willingly assumed which is good, such as the kind which John speaks of when he says, that Jesus was troubled, groaned in the spirit, and wept.[12]

---

**17{18}[6]**    *The sorrows of hell encompassed me: and the snares of death prevented me.*

> Dolores inferni circumdederunt me, praeoccupaverunt me laquei mortis.

**17{18}[6]** *Dolores inferni, the sorrows of hell,* that is, the sorrows arising from the consideration of the damnation of men in hell, *circumdederunt me, encompassed me.* For while Christ hung upon the Cross, he said, *I thirst,*[13] which signifies he thirsted for the deliverance of men: and at that

---

nature, but finite as a being since it resides in all its fullness in the human soul of Christ as a subject, and the human soul of Christ — being a part of creation — is necessarily limited. *See ST,* IIIa, q. 7, art. 11, co. The fulness of sanctifying grace, Christ's lack of sin, his perfect love of God, and all other merits of Christ in his human nature warranted a quick resurrection, but it was the grace of union in particular that warranted a quick resurrection.

9   Mark 14:33b.
10   Matt. 26:37b.
11   John 19:30.
12   John 11, 33, 35.
13   John 19:28. *E. N.* "Grow in that intimate love, and you will understand not only 'I thirst,' but everything. Humanly speaking we cannot understand 'love one another as I have loved you' [or] 'Be ye holy as I am holy.' But it all comes under 'I thirst.'

hour he was tormented with a most vehement pain of the heart, because he considered that so many would be destined to enjoy no profit in his Passion and because of their ingratitude they were destined to descend into hell. And for this reason it says: *The sorrows of hell encompassed me,* that is, they have invaded my soul. *Praeoccupaverunt me, prevented me,* that is, have come before me, *laquei mortis, the snares of death,* that is, the snares leading to death. Not that Christ in any way unexpectedly touched any such trap or even was able to be ensnared, but because the unfaithful Jews regarded him to be ignorant of the plan by which they handled how they might deceitfully seize him and kill him, [14] and, he being ignorant [they thought], they did not anticipate he might flee. For it is a practice of Scripture to recount something as it is [held to be] in the opinion of many.

-------

17{18}[7]   *In my affliction I called upon the Lord, and I cried to my God: And he heard my voice from his holy temple: and my cry before him came into his ears.*

*In tribulatione mea invocavi Dominum, et ad Deum meum clamavi: et exaudivit de templo sancto suo vocem meam; et clamor meus in conspectu eius introivit in aures eius.*

17{18}[7] *In tribulatione mea, in my affliction,* namely, at the inception of the Passion, *invocavi Dominum, I called upon the Lord*: because, as it is written, Jesus falling upon his face, prayed a long time, and his sweat flowed to earth in drops of blood; [15] *et ad Deum meum clamavi, and I cried to my God*: because the Apostle [Paul] attests, Christ prayed with strong cries and tears [16] *Et exaudivit, and he heard* the Lord *de templo sancto suo, from his holy temple*, that is, from the high heaven, or from my heart, in which as in choicest temple he dwelled not only by grace, but also by the supposital union, [17] understanding by the word heart the soul itself, *vocem meam, my voice*, that is, the prayer which I poured out; *et clamor meus,*

-------

The fruit of faith is the understanding of 'I thirst.' . . . Get rid of sin quickly so we can hear Jesus say, 'I thirst for your love.' The most important thing is that we must encounter the thirst of Jesus, but the encounter with Jesus' thirst is a grace." St. Theresa of Calcutta, *Where There is Love, There is God* (New York: Doubleday 2010), 52.

14   Matt. 26:4.

15   Matt. 26:39; Luke 22:43–44.

16   Heb. 5:7. As to the Pauline attribution by Denis, see footnote 8-34.

17   E. N. Denis uses the Latin *suppositalem unionem*, suppositional union. Since a *suppositum* may be both rational or nonrational, this is a more general, looser way of expressing the grace of union in Christ, that is, the personal or hypostatic union, a union occurring in the *suppositum* where the *suppositum* is a rational nature.

*and my cry*, that is, the fervent affections of my heart, *in conspectus eius*, *before him*, that is, before his presence, *introivit in aures eius, came into his ears*, that is, [my voice] pleased the ears of his mercy, so that it was heard.

---

17{18}[8]   *The earth shook and trembled: the foundations of the mountains were troubled and were moved, because he was angry with them.*

*Commota est, et contremuit terra, fundamenta montium contur-bata sunt, et commota sunt, quoniam iratus est eis.*

17{18}[8] *Commota est et contremuit terra; the earth shook and trembled.* This was literally fulfilled in Christ when suspended on the Cross, for it was then [upon his death] that the earth quaked.[18] In a similar way, on the day of the Resurrection, when the angel descended to the sepulcher of Christ, there was a great shaking of the earth.[19] *Fundamenta montium conturbata sunt et commota sunt; the foundations of the mountains were troubled and were moved*: because during the time of the Passion, the Holy Land which is said to be mountainous, was strongly moved, so that even rocks were split asunder, according to the witness of the evangelist;[20] *quoniam iratus est eis; because he was angry with them*, namely, the Lord: that is, the Lord grew angry, as men struck and killed his beloved Son, and he showed this in the earthly elements, disturbing and moving inanimate objects: so that, as the inanimate things sufficiently perceived him suspended on the cross so as to feel sorrow, even rational creatures might pay attention to their error.

Or this [understanding is possible], and better: *was shook*, through wonder, *and trembled*, though fear, *the earth*, that is, the inhabitants of the earth, namely, the Jews and the Gentiles — especially those in the Holy Land — when they saw Christ dying, the sun supernaturally eclipsing, the earth moving, and Jesus in a loud voice crying out while giving up his spirit. Whence in the Gospel it is written: *Now the centurion and they that were with him*, seeing the *things that were done*, and because Jesus gave up his spirit crying out in this fashion, *they were sore afraid.*[21] And the centurion glorified God, and also said: *Indeed this was a just man.* And all the multitude of them, who had come to that sight, *and saw the things that were done, returned striking their breasts*[22] *The foundations of the mountains were troubled*: that is, the chiefs of the proud,

---

18   Matt. 27:51.
19   Matt. 28:2.
20   Matt. 27:41.
21   Matt. 27:54.
22   Luke 23:47, 48.

namely, the chief priests, Pilate, and Herod, *were troubled and were moved*: because seeing these marvels that have been mentioned, the most high chief priests surely at the time quaked with great fear when they saw the veil of the temple rent,[23] and the guards of the sepulcher reported back those things that had happened at the tomb by the angel;[24] most possibly also when the dead who together with Christ rose from the dead, appeared to them (as it is believed).[25] And so they were *troubled and moved, because he was angry with them*, that is to say, the Lord [was angry with them]. The anger of God is the vengeance of divine justice. But this vengeance — with regard to the impenitent — begins here [in the present time], and in the future lasts eternally. Now, the previously mentioned things were done by God in revenge of the sins of those who murdered Christ and who did not repent of it: because those who saw these things and who were not converted more grievously are condemned. Consequently, because the Lord is angry with them, abandoning them is most just, for they were troubled and they were moved, not to repentance and faith, but to astonishment and obstinacy. Or [yet another interpretation is this], *the foundations of the mountains*, that is, the teachers of the philosophers, *were troubled and were moved*, that is, were made to marvel and were stupefied with Christ suffering, saying this because of the most marvelous eclipse of the sun: Either God underwent suffering in nature, or the stars lied, or the frame of the world will perish. Of which things Dionysius writes about in his letter to Polycarp.[26]

---

**17{18}[9]**  *There went up a smoke in his wrath: and a fire flamed from his face: coals were kindled by it.*

*Ascendit fumus in ira eius, et ignis a facie eius exarsit; carbones succensi sunt ab eo.*

Consequently, it describes the punishments of those persecuting Christ, namely, of the obstinate Jews, who were not converted by these or the miracles done by the Apostles, and Stephen, and the other saints of the early Church, while it continues:    **17{18}[9]** *Ascendit fumus; there went*

---

23  Matt. 27:51.
24  Matt. 28:11.
25  Matt. 27:52, 53.
26  E. N. The reference is to the Pseudo-Areopagite, and the (now known to be) fictional Epistle 7 to the hierarch (bishop) Polycarp (PG 3, 1081) which addresses the supposed arguments of the Greek sophist Apollophanes against Pseudo-Dionysius's conversion to Christianity.

*up smoke*, that is, the vapor of fire by which Titus burned up Jerusalem and the other neighboring cities, *in ira eius, in his wrath*, that is, in the revenge with which God the Father vindicated the injury inflicted upon Christ by the Jews; *et ignis, and a fire* of the fire just referred to, *a facie eius, from his face*, that is, from the face of divine justice most justly judging all things, *exarsit, flamed from*, quickly consuming all things. *Carbones, coals*, that is the perverse Jews, darkened by the blindness of infidelity and black with vice, *succensi sunt ab eo; were kindled by it*, that is, by God, in their burning up. Or [an alternative understanding], *coals*, that is, the combustible matter, *were kindled by it*, because the rulers of the Romans, ordained and instigated by God, set on fire the homes of the Jews.

---

**17{18}[10]** *He bowed the heavens, and came down: and darkness was under his feet.*

   *Inclinavit caelos, et descendit; et caligo sub pedibus eius.*

   **17{18}[10]** *Inclinavit caelos, he bowed the heavens*, [the heavens meaning] Christ himself, that is, [Christ] living in heaven, himself plainly descending from his royal throne to the womb of the most sweet Virgin: for *he emptied himself, taking the form of a servant;*[27] *et descendit, and he came down* into the *lower parts of the earth,*[28] according to the Apostle. *Et caligo, and darkness*, that is all the obscurity of dark baseness and vice, *sub pedibus eius, under his feet*, that is, far from there: because he was light itself, *and in him there is no darkness,*[29] according to John. Or [it could be understood this way], *darkness*, that is, the devil darkening the hearts of men, *under his feet*: because Christ trampled upon and utterly defeated the devil. Whence John in the first part of his epistle says: *For this purpose, the Son of God appeared, that he might destroy the works of the devil.*[30]

---

**17{18}[11]** *And he ascended upon the cherubim, and he flew; he flew upon the wings of the winds.*

   *Et ascendit super cherubim, et volavit; volavit super pennas ventorum.*

   **17{18}[11]** *Et ascendit, and he ascended*, namely Christ [ascended], *super cherubim, upon the cherubim*, that is, above that order of angels in

---

27  Phil. 2:7.
28  Eph. 4:9b.
29  1 John 1:5b.
30  1 John 3:8b.

the day of his Ascension, *et volavit, and he flew* even to the right hand
of the Father. Or [this verse can be understood this way], *upon the
cherubim,* that is, above all the plenitude of created knowledge, because
Christ transcended all the capacity of intellectual creatures. *Volavit super
pennas ventorum; he flew upon the wings of the winds,* that is, above all
speculations of rational animals. Without doubt, contemplation is the
feather of the soul;[31] and the soul is called the wind, according to Isaiah:
*breathings I will make,* that is, souls [I will make]. For the soul, having
the likeness of wind, is speedily movable.

---

**17{18}[12]** *And he made darkness his covert, his tabernacle round about
him: dark waters in the clouds of the air.*

> *Et posuit tenebras latibulum suum; in circuitu eius tabernaculum
> eius, tenebrosa aqua in nubibus aeris.*

**17{18}[12]** *Et posuit tenebras; and he made darkness,* that is, the
incomprehensible fullness of his own light, *latibulum suum, his covert,*
that is, his hidden dwelling. For God is hidden from us because of the
immensity of his perfections and light. Whence according to the Apostle,
he *inhabits light inaccessible;*[32] and, according to that most sacred prince
of the theologians, Dionysius[33] in the epistle to the monk Gaius, the
invisible plenitude of divine light is called divine obscurity or darkness.
God makes this obscurity or darkness his hiding place (*latibulum*) since
he is incomprehensible because of it. Therefore, Dionysius states: *The
divine darkness, he says, wholly covers all light, and is hidden from all vision,
because of the boundless and superlatively most full brightness of its unique*

---

31  E. N. Contemplation is called by Denis the "feather or wing of the soul," *penna
animae,* which appears to me a novel expression unique to him. St. Ephraim of
Syria referred to chastity, continence, humility, and obedience as "feathers of the
soul." In *De beatudine animae,* II. St. Gregory Nazianzus called the Old and
New Scriptures the "feathers of the soul." In his *De rerum naturis,* II, 6, Rabanus
Maurus speaks of the "feathers of the soul of the saints" as their virtue. Famously,
Boethius refers to the feathers of the mind (*pennae mentis*) in the context of
philosophical contemplation. But as far as I have been able to determine, the
only person to call contemplation the feather of the soul is Denis the Carthusian.

32  1 Tim. 6:16a.

33  For Dionysius the Areopagite is a reference to Pseudo-Dionysius (Pseudo-Denis),
*see* footnote P-36. For Denis, who here describes him as *sacratissimum principem
theologorum,* the most sacred prince of theologians, Pseudo-Dionysius was of
the highest authority. Denis refers here to Pseudo-Dionysius's first letter to
Gaius Therapeutes.

*splendor.*[34] Or [another way of understanding this is], *he made darkness,* that is, the sacramental forms, *his covert,* because beneath them in the Sacrament of the Altar, Christ is ineffably hidden; or [again an alternative interpretation], *darkness,* that is, the mortal flesh which he assumed, for the divinity in it was marvelously concealed. *In circuitu eius, round about him,* that is, those who from every quarter draw near him, that is to say in all of the saints in heaven and on earth, *tabernaculum eius, his tabernacle,* because God dwells in those who draw near him; and in the saints on earth is *his tabernacle* that is called the Church militant; but in the saints in heaven is *his tabernacle* that is called the Church triumphant.

*Tenebrosa aqua, dark waters,* that is, obscure knowledge, is *in nubibus aeris, in the clouds of the air,* that is, in the holy Prophets and Apostles, of whom Isaiah says, *Who are these, that fly as clouds, and as doves to their windows?*[35] For all the knowledge of the wayfarer is obscure, as the Apostle testifies to: *We know now,* he says, *through a glass in a dark manner,* and *Now I know in part.*[36] The Apostles and Prophets are called *the clouds of the air* because above all other men they received the most superior and most full illuminations of divine light, and through contemplation of these they flew most highly. And [the phrase] *the clouds of the air* is also said from the differences of the angels which are called the clouds of heaven, according to Dionysius in his last chapter of his book *On the Celestial Hierarchy.* Not, of course, that they [the Prophets] flew so high while they were pilgrims and strangers on earth[37] as the holy angels who received divine illuminations by an excellent, clear, and immediate reception; for men receive such illuminations in a secondary, symbolic, and mediated way, since they are brought down to them by the angels, according to the Theologian.[38]

Moreover, these words of the Psalmist can be especially referred to the Apostles before the Passion of Christ, when, as a result of their ignorance, they deserved to hear from Christ: *Are you also yet without understanding?*[39] And also before the Ascension because John says of himself that during a particular time, he did not know the Scripture, namely

---

34  E. N. The "vision" here referred to is mental vision or knowledge.
35  Is. 60:8.
36  1 Cor. 13:12. E. N. Denis departs from the Sixto-Clementine Vulgate's "We *see* (*videmus*) now through a glass . . . ." with "We *know* (*cognoscimus*) now . . . ."
37  E. N. This is an implied reference to Heb. 11:13.
38  E. N. This is Denis's honorific for Pseudo-Dionysius, as "the Philosopher" is for Aristotle. For Dionysius the Areopagite, *see* footnote P-36.
39  Matt. 15:16.

that Christ had to rise again from the dead,[40] even though, before his Passion, Christ had nevertheless frequently and clearly predicted this.[41] Thereby we see that the Apostles were remarkably ignorant[42] until the sending of the Holy Spirit; by which of course the Christian's faith is unalterably strengthened, as is evident by the fact that idolatry [among the pagan Gentiles] was extirpated by so few and so unpolished[43] and simple men, and such supernatural a faith was spread throughout the whole world. For this would not have been possible but for the fact that after Christ's Passion they were supernaturally illumined and taught in the manner that Christ before his Passion had promised them.

---

**17{18}[13]** *At the brightness that was before him the clouds passed, hail and coals of fire.*

> *Prae fulgore in conspectu eius nubes transierunt, grando et carbones ignis.*

**17{18}[13]** *Prae fulgore, at the brightness,* that is, before the clearness of doctrine, and on account of the illumination of Christ which was entrusted to the Apostles, *in conspectus eius, in his sight,*[44] that is, in the good graces and in the merciful presence of the gaze of the Lord and Savior, *nubes, clouds,* that is, the holy Apostles, *transierunt, passed* throughout the whole world to preach the Gospel to every creature.[45] It is as if it said: At the clarity of wisdom, and because of the bright illumination which Christ would infuse into the Apostles on the day of Pentecost,[46] these same Apostles were given all that they comprehended in the sight of the Lord, and they, who before were huddled together in a locked room for fear of the Jews, departed boldly and securely.[47] For it is the practice of Scripture that something is said to be before the Lord *(coram Domino),* or in the sight of the Lord *(in conspectum Domini)* when it is agreeable to the Lord, as for instance when it is said that Jesse begot David, who walked before the Lord. So, therefore, the Apostles

---

40 John 20:9.
41 Matt. 16:21; 17:9, 22; 20:19; 26:32, 27:63.
42 L. *simplices,* literally, simple, as in ignorant, unlearned, uninstructed.
43 L. *rudes,* literally, rude, rough, ignorant, uncultivated.
44 E. N. The Sixto-Clementine Vulgate might appropriately be translated as "in his sight," rather than "that was before him" as the Douay-Rheims has translated it, and it more adequately follows Denis's argument.
45 Mark 16:15.
46 Acts 2:4.
47 John 20:19.

*passed in the sight* of the Lord, for their passing through pleased the Lord.[48] Or [we might look at it] thus: *At the brightness before his sight the clouds passed*, because while Christ was abiding among his disciples in the world, he sent them two-by-two to every place where he himself was to go.[49] Or thus [it might be understood] as well: *At the brightness*, that is, because of the excellence of the perfection, clarity, and wisdom of Christ, *before his sight*, that is, in comparison to them, *clouds*, that is, all the Saints *passed over*, that is, fell short, and in a certain way vanished, because however holy and learned they were, yet in comparison with Christ it is as if they were nothing, and this so much so that the Evangelist affirms of that great giant of a man, John the Baptist, that *He was not the light*.[50] Whence, Origen[51] says that, in comparison to Christ, Peter and Paul are darkness. In addition, one is able to say that when *at the brightness (prae fulgore)* is said, this is one word *(dictio)*, so that it has this sense: *gleaming (praefulgorae)*,[52] that is, *very bright (praefulgidae)*,[53] *clouds in his sight*, etc. But it is more fitting, I suggest, that it should be said with two words.

And so, *at the brightness before his sight the clouds passed*, that is, the Apostles, who not only are clouds, but also *grando, hail*, being threatened with the storms of the ungodly, forcefully resisting falseness, and striking blows at the hearts of those hearing by their rebukes; *et, and*, they are *carbones ignis, coals of fire*, illuminating the world, and igniting the minds of believers with divine love; or [alternatively], *coals of fire*, that is, consumed with fire of tribulations, like ignited coals.

---

48    E. N. There is a play on words here that is not fully seen in the English translation. The Latin *transierunt* has connotations of "passing over," or "going through," such as passing over a bridge or going through a tunnel, but it also bespeaks of a change, a transition, a conversion. So here Denis states: *Apostoli transierunt in conspectu Domini, quia placuit Domino transitus ille.* "The Apostles passed or travelled through *(transierunt)* in the sight of the Lord, for that change *(transitus ille)* found favor with the Lord."

49    Luke 10:1.

50    John 1:8a.

51    E. N. Origen of Alexandria (ca. 184–ca. 253), an early Greek-speaking Christian and brilliant Scriptural exegete recognized as a Church Father, though because of some moral (*e.g.*, his self-castration if the ecclesiastical chronicler Eusebius is believed) and doctrinal aberrations (*e.g.*, his teachings on the pre-existence of souls and universalism in salvation, the so-called apokatastasis), he is considered neither a Saint nor a Doctor.

52    As Cassiodorus puts it in his commentary on the Psalms, *praefulgorae* is a nominative plural adjective corresponding to the noun "clouds."

53    This is an adjective declined as nominative plural, apparently considered by Denis as a synonym for *praefulgorae*.

**17{18}[14]** *And the Lord thundered from heaven, and the highest gave his voice: hail and coals of fire.*

> *Et intonuit de caelo Dominus, et Altissimus dedit vocem suam: grando et carbones ignis.*

**17{18}[14]** *Et intonuit de caelo Dominus; and the Lord thundered from heaven*: this obviously refers to Christ in the day of Pentecost, when *suddenly there came a sound from heaven, as of a mighty wind coming, . . . and it sat upon every one of them;*[54] *et Altissimus, and the Highest*, that is, Christ, *dedit vocem suam, gave his voice*, for on that day he fulfilled that which a short to prior he had solemnly promised the Apostles: *I will give you a mouth and wisdom, which all your adversaries shall not be able to resist and gainsay.*[55] Then, therefore, he gave them their voice, when he spoke through them, as he had told them earlier: *It is not you that speak, but the Spirit of your Father that speaks in you.*[56] For the voice of God is sacred Scripture: and because he gave knowledge of the Scriptures to the disciples, so it is that he gave them his voice. Or [an alternative explanation would be], *the Highest gave his voice*, for Christ after the Resurrection by his personal presence spoke to his Apostles. And Christ's voice is *grando et carbones ignis, hail and coals of fire*, for the reasons hereinbefore given.

---

**17{18}[15]** *And he sent forth his arrows, and he scattered them: he multiplied lightnings, and troubled them.*

> *Et misit sagittas suas, et dissipavit eos; fulgura multiplicavit, et conturbavit eos.*

**17{18}[15]** *Et misit, and he sent forth*, namely Christ [sent forth], *sagittas suas, his arrows*, that is, the most acute words, speaking through mouth of the Apostles. *For the word of God is living and effectual, and more piercing than any two-edged sword; and reaching unto the division of the soul and the spirit.*[57] *Et dissipavit eos, and he scattered them*, separating the elect from the reprobate, the faithful from the unfaithful, the good from the evil: such as he did in the day of Pentecost, with Peter speaking the acute and fiery words whereby three thousand of the Jews were converted.[58] *Fulgura, lightnings*, that is, excellent signs and great

---

54 Acts 2:2a, 3b.
55 Luke 21:15.
56 Matt. 10:20.
57 Heb. 4:12.
58 Acts 2:41.

miracles, *multiplicavit, he multiplied*, by his faithful and his saints, in the manner that he predicted: *He that believes in me, the works that I do, he also shall do; and greater than these shall he do;*[59] *et conturbavit eos, and troubled them*, namely [he troubled] those who heard and those who observed, some to repentance, some to astonishment, but some to fear.

---

**17{18}[16]** *Then the fountains of waters appeared, and the foundations of the world were discovered: At your rebuke, O Lord, at the blast of the spirit of your wrath.*

*Et apparuerunt fontes aquarum, et revelata sunt fundamenta orbis terrarum, ab increpatione tua, Domine, ab inspiratione spiritus irae tuae.*

**17{18}[16]** *Et apparuerunt, there appeared*, by the illumination of Christ and the preaching of the Apostles, *fontes aquarum, the fountains of waters*, that is, streams of wisdom *springing up into life everlasting.*[60] These *fountains*, that is, of sacred doctrine, *appeared*, that is, were made manifest in the hearts of men, as the Savior discussed:[61] *He that believes in me, . . . out of his belly shall flow rivers of living water.*[62] *Et revelata sunt fundamenta orbis terrarum; and the foundations of the world were discovered*: that is, the holy Prophets who were the foundations of the world, that is, of the militant Church spread throughout the whole world, were understood and truly ascertained by Christ and his disciples. For before Christ's advent, the words of the Prophets were obscure, but through the sending forth of the Apostles by the illumination of the Holy Spirit these were most clearly understood and explained to the people. Christ also manifested in himself the truth of the Prophets, fulfilling in himself those things that had been prophesized about him. For which reason John said: *The law was given by Moses; grace and truth came by Jesus Christ.*[63]

This has been accomplished *ab increpatione tua, Domine; at your rebuke, O Lord*, in that you yourself or your holy preachers rebuked men in order that they might repent, and so they might suitably turn to the reception of the appearances that have been previously mentioned,[64] and the revelations of sacred Scripture. And these things have been done *ab*

---

59  John 14:12.
60  John 4:14b.
61  L. *disseruit*: can also mean sowed, scattered, or planted.
62  John 7:38.
63  John 1:17.
64  E. N. Immediately above, in discussing Ps. 17:16.

*inspiratione spiritus irae tuae, at the blast of the spirit of your wrath*, that is, by the incitement of the Holy Spirit, terrifying intimately the hearts of sinners. For the Holy Spirit first salubriously is angry with the elect in the present, punishing upon them temporal punishments through penance, that he might not be angry with them in the future, punishing them with eternal punishment through condemnation. Consequently, the Holy Spirit fills the minds of the penitent with consolation, he shows the truth, and he fills them with light, so that the *fountains of water* may appear to them. [This expression is fitting] since at first, he cleanses; secondly, he illuminates; and thirdly, he perfects.

---

**17{18}[17]** *He sent from on high, and took me: and received me out of many waters.*

> *Misit de summo, et accepit me; et assumpsit me de aquis multis.*

**17{18}[18]** *He delivered me from my strongest enemies, and from them that hated me: for they were too strong for me.*

> *Eripuit me de inimicis meis fortissimis, et ab his qui oderunt me. Quoniam confortati sunt super me.*

**17{18}[19]** *They prevented me in the day of my affliction: and the Lord became my protector.*

> *Praevenerunt me in die afflictionis meae; et factus est Dominus protector meus.*

Then Christ through the voice of his assumed [human] nature speaking to the Father, says: **17{18}[17]** *Misit, he sent*, meaning God the Father [sent], *de summo, from on high*, that is, from his bosom, his eternal Word; *et, and* his Word *accepit me, took me*, uniting into his divine and uncreated personality my humanity; and God the Father *assumpsit me de aquis multis; received me out of many waters*, that is, he sustained me during various tribulations in the day of the Resurrection and of the Ascension, when—from all possibility of suffering[65] and from having to dwell with the enemy—he took me up unto himself. **17{18}[18]** *Eripuit me de inimicis meis fortissimis; he delivered me from my strongest enemies*, that is, from the chief priests, *et ab his qui oderunt me; and from them that hated me*, that is, from my other persecutors; *quoniam confortati sunt super me; for they were too strong for me*, that is, because they were granted permission for a time to prevail against my passible nature,

---

65  L. *passibilitate*, the property of susceptibility to suffering or change.

against which they struck and put to death.    **17{18}[19]** *Praevenerunt me; they prevented me*[66] many accusations and deceitful questions, so that they would have reasons against me to put me to death, *in die afflictionis meae, in the day of my affliction,* namely in the day of my Passion; *et factus est Dominus protector meus; and the Lord became my protector,* that they might not harm my soul.

---

**17{18}[20]** *And he brought me forth into a large place: he saved me, because he was well pleased with me.*

Et eduxit me in latitudinem; salvum me fecit, quoniam voluit me.

**17{18}[21]** *And the Lord will reward me according to my justice; and will repay me according to the cleanness of my hands.*

Et retribuet mihi Dominus secundum iustitiam meam, et secundum puritatem manuum mearum retribuet mihi.

**17{18}[20]** *Et eduxit me,* and *he brought me forth* from the narrow sepulcher, *in latitudinem, into a large place* of paradise; or [we might understand it as follows], *he led me forth* from the straitness of death *into a large place* of joys. *Salvum me fecit, he saved me* from death by the Resurrection, *quoniam voluit me; because he was well pleased with me,* that is, because he loved me. *This is my beloved Son,* he said, *in whom I am well pleased.*[67]    **17{18}[21]** *Et retribuet mihi Dominus; and the Lord will reward me* with an accidental reward in which I could increase, namely a quick resurrection, a bodily glorification, and blessed ascension; *secundum iustitiam meam; according to my justice,* that is, according to the exigencies of my merits. For God will reward everyone in accordance with that which he merits. *Et secundum puritatem manuum mearum; and according to the cleanness of my hands,* that is, according to the perfection of my words, *retribuit mihi, he will repay me,* in the day of my Resurrection, as it has all been fulfilled.

---

**17{18}[22]** *Because I have kept the ways of the Lord; and have not done wickedly against my God.*

Quia custodivi vias Domini, nec impie gessi a Deo meo.

---

66  The English word prevent (from Latin *prae-venire,* to come before) as used by the Douay-Rheims here means to go before someone or something. Such a sense is still found, for example, in the notion of prevenient grace, or a preventative remedy.

67  Matt. 3:17; 17:5.

**17{18}[23]** *For till his judgments are in my sight: and his justices I have not put away from me.*

*Quoniam omnia iudicia eius in conspectu meo, et iustitias eius non repuli a me.*

**17{18}[22]** *Quia custodivi vias Domini; because I have kept the ways of the Lord,* that is, I fulfilled all acts of virtue, especially the love of God and neighbor; *nec impie fessi, and have not done wickedly,* acting against the divine law or undertaking any act of renunciation *a Deo me, against my God.* And so I have not walked away from him,    **17{18}[23]** *quoniam omnia iudicia eius, for all his judgments,* that is, all that he has dictated to be good or evil, *in conspectu meo, in my sight,* that is, are in the consideration of my soul, so that they might be observed; *et iustitias eius, and his justices,* that is, the observation of his commandments, *non repuli a me; I have not put away from me,* by disobedience, negligence, or contempt. Whence Christ in the Gospel says: *as the Father has given me commandment, so do I.*[68] And again: *I do always the things that please him.*[69]

---

**17{18}[24]** *And I shall be spotless with him: and shall keep myself from my iniquity.*

*Et ero immaculatus cum eo; et observabo me ab iniquitate mea.*

**17{18}[25]** *And the Lord will reward me according to my justice; and according to the cleanness of my hands before his eyes.*

*Et retribuet mihi Dominus secundum iustitiam meam, et secundum puritatem manuum mearum in conspectu oculorum eius.*

Because I therefore lived so justly, as a consequence    **17{18}[24]** *Et ero immaculatus, and I shall be spotless* from all sin, *cum eo, with him,* that is, firmly adhering to him; or [an alternate reading is], *with him,* that is, as he himself is spotless: just like that which is written, *You will be holy, as also I am holy: I am the Lord your God.*[70] *Et observabo me ab iniquitate mea; and I shall keep myself from my iniquity.* Christ neither did nor had iniquity: in what manner, therefore, does it say, *and I shall keep myself from iniquity?* [This cannot be understood] unless it is explained in this way, *I shall keep myself from iniquity* which I may have had except that the Lord had preserved me from it. For if you take away grace from the man Christ,

---

68  John 14:31.
69  John 8:29b.
70  Lev. 11:45; 19:2; 20:26. Denis blends these verses together.

there is in him nothing that would differ him from others, according to Augustine.[71]    **17{18}[25]** *Et retribuet mihi Dominus secundum iustitiam meam; and the Lord will reward me according to my justice,* in the day of the final judgment, when through the merit of my Passion I will beatify all the elect: from which beatification there will be adjoined a certain accidental reward to me, for I will rejoice with my spouse, which is the Church of the elect. *Et secundum puritatem manuum mearum; and according to the cleanness of my hands,* namely, the hands I had, *in conspectus oculorum eius, before his eyes,* that is, before him who perceives all things, from which you should imply he will restore [all things] to me.

# ARTICLE XLIII

## CONTINUATION OF THE EXPOSITION OF THE SEVENTEENTH PSALM ON CHRIST.

**17{18}[26]** *With the holy, you will be holy; and with the innocent man you will be innocent.*

> *Cum sancto sanctus eris, et cum viro innocente innocens eris.*

**17{18}[27]** *And with the elect you will be elect: and with the perverse you will be perverted.*

> *Eet cum electo electus eris, et cum perverso perverteris.*

**17{18}[26]** *Cum sancto sanctus eris, et cum viro innocente innocens eris; with the holy, you will be holy; and with the innocent man you will be innocent. With the holy,* it says, that is, with Christ, who is the Saint of Saints,[72] and who is naturally and completely holy, *you will be holy,* O any member of the faithful, if you constantly adhere to him, and if you never withdraw from his paths; and *with the innocent man,* that is, with Christ, who as far as he himself is concerned, did not do anything hurtful, but he did good in all things in the highest and most complete manner, *you will be innocent,* if you would but imitate him.    **17{18}[27]** *Et cum electo, and with the elect,* that is, with Christ who by reason of the assumed nature he is called the elect: because according to the

---

71  E. N. This is a reference to St. Augustine's Sermon: *Tolle gratiam istam, quid Christus, nisi homo? Quid nisi quod tu?* "Take away this grace, what then is Christ except a man? What else is he other than you?" *Sermo* 67.4.7, PL 48, 436.

72  On "Saints of Saints" as a name for Christ, *see* footnote 3-26.

Apostle, he *was predestinated the Son of God in power, according to the spirit of sanctification.*[73] And in Isaiah: Behold, he says, my son whom I have elected; *my soul delights in him:*[74] As pertaining to Christ it is said literally, as the words which follow show. With this elect, therefore, if you will perseveringly serve him, *electus eris, you will be elect*: not that someone is newly made elect, because all the elect have been elect from eternity; but *you will be elect*, that is, you will obtain the beatitude of the elect. According to this sense, Augustine says: "If you are not predestined, so act that you become predestined,"[75] that is, if you suspect yourself not to be predestined, do not on that account cease from doing good works, but so live that you might be worthy of the glory of the predestined. *Et cum perverso, and with the perverse,* that is, with him who does not follow Christ, *perverteris, you will be perverted,* if you follow his manner of life.

---

17{18}[28] *For you will save the humble people; but will bring down the eyes of the proud.*

> *Quoniam tu populum humilem salvum facies, et oculos super-borum humiliabis.*

And this therefore is certain to be true: 17{18}[28] *Quoniam tu, for you,* O Lord, *populum humilem salvum facies; will save the humble people,* in the present maintaining themselves living in grace, and in the future by glory, as it says in the Gospel: *Blessed are the poor in spirit,* that is, the humble, *for theirs is the kingdom of heaven.*[76] And again: *he that humbles himself, shall be exalted; and he who exalts himself shall be humbled.*[77] *Et oculos superborum, and the eyes of the proud,* that is, the presumptions and the self-estimation of those who are large in their eyes you will condemn, and such proud persons *humiliabis, you will bring down* even to the depths of hell. And to all the saints you will show, especially in the day of judgment, how abominable and how condemned all the proud are. Whence also it is written: *Pride is hateful before God and men.*[78]

---

73 Rom. 1:4.

74 Is. 42:1a. Isaiah 42:1a reads: *Behold my servant, I will uphold him: my elect, my soul delights in him.*

75 This saying — *Si non es praedestinatus, fac ut praedestineris* — is popularly ascribed to St. Augustine, but it is not found in his works.

76 Matt.5:3.

77 Luke 14:11; 18:14. Denis reverses the order of the verses cited, putting the humble man before him who exalts himself. For example, Luke 18:14 reads: *every one that exalts himself, shall be humbled: and he that humbles himself, shall be exalted.*

78 Ecclus. 10:7a.

**17{18}[29]** *For you light my lamp, O Lord: O my God enlighten my darkness.*

> *Quoniam tu illuminas lucernam meam, Domine; Deus meus, illumina tenebras meas.*

**17{18}[29]** *Quoniam tu illuminas lucernam meam; for you light my lamp,* that is, [you light] my reason, which is the ruler and lord of all my acts, for reason directs the will and the other powers; *Domine, O Lord,* Jesus Christ, who is *the true light,* enlightening *every man that comes into this world.*[79] And he enlightens me not only with a natural light, but also the light of grace. And because this is so, *Deus meus, illumine tenebras meas; O my God, enlighten my darkness,* that is, all of the darkness in the recesses of my interior, which, because of their great imperfection and the obscurity of vices in them are called darkness, in the manner that very virtuous and erudite men are called light. And so, O Lord Christ, *enlighten my darkness,* that is, expel from my soul the blindness of ignorance, the overshadowing of passions, and the stains of all sins: since it is fitting for me, for *when I sit in darkness, the Lord is my light. . . . he will bring me forth into the light, I shall behold his justice.*[80]

---

**17{18}[30]** *For by you I shall be delivered from temptation; and through my God I shall go over a wall.*

> *Quoniam in te eripiar a tentatione; et in Deo meo transgrediar murum.*

**17{18}[30]** *Quoniam, for* O Lord, *in te, by you,* that is, by your virtue and your grace, *eripiar a tentatione, I shall be delivered from temptation,* that is, from all the attacks of the devil and of the Jews persecuting me; *et in Deo meo, and through my God,* that is, in the power and with the help of my God, *transgrediar murum, I shall go over a wall,* that is, I will overcome every obstacle that endeavors to divert me from God. Or [one may look at this verse] historically, *I shall go over a wall:* because Christ rose from the enclosure of the sepulcher, and he entered to his disciples behind locked doors,[81] so he was able to travel past the stone tomb and through the locked door of the room [of the apostles], which can be given the name of a wall.

---

79  John 1:9.
80  Micah 7, 8b, 9b.
81  Matt. 27:66; John 20:19, 26.

**17{18}[31]** *As for my God, his way is undefiled: the words of the Lord are fire tried: he is the protector of all that trust in him.*

*Deus meus, impolluta via eius; eloquia Domini igne examinata; protector est omnium sperantium in se.*

**17{18}[32]** *For who is God but the Lord? Or who is God but our God?*

*Quoniam quis Deus praeter Dominum? Aut quis Deus praeter Deum nostrum?*

**17{18}[31]** *Deus meus*, my God, who is the holy Trinity and single Godhead, *impolluta via eius, his way is undefiled*, that is, the immaculate law by which he is led to God; in the manner that Solomon says, *The Lord's ways are beautiful ways, and all his paths are peaceable;*[82] *eloquia Domini, the words of the* Lord, namely, the precepts, counsels, testimony — indeed all of Sacred Scripture — *igne examinata, are fire tried*, that is, purified by the brightness of the Holy Spirit, and so beautiful, as if they were clarified with fire; *protector est, he is the protector*, the Lord, *omnium sperantium in se, of all that trust in him*. Consequently, it is true: **[32]** *Quoniam quis Deus praeter Dominum; For who is God but the Lord?* That is, who is the true God, able to save those who place their trust in him, and to defend them from all danger, unless it be the Lord who is the creator, provider, and ruler of all the universe? It is as if he were saying, "No one."[83] *Aut quis*, or who is the true *Deus praeter Deum nostrum, God but our God*, that is, the God of the Christians, who is one in essence and three in persons, who said in Deuteronomy: *See you that I alone am, and there is no other God besides me.*[84] And again, Moses said: *There is no other God like the God of the rightest . . . By his magnificence the clouds run here and there. His dwelling is above, and underneath are the everlasting arms.*[85]

---

**17{18}[33]** *God who has girt me with strength; and made my way blameless.*

*Deus qui praecinxit me virtute, et posuit immaculatam viam meam.*

**17{18}[33]** *Deus qui praecinxit me, the God who has girt me* Christ, insofar as I am man, *virtute, with strength*, that is, with the power of the Holy Spirit, in the quick-running life, and in the carrying out and in the most

---

82  Prov. 3:17. E. N. Denis changes the subject from Wisdom (*sapientia*) to the Lord's ways (*viae Domini*), slightly adapting the text.

83  E. N. Denis is saying that this question is negatively rhetorical, implying a negative answer.

84  Deut. 32:39a.

85  Deut. 33:26–27a.

victorious and most ready suffering, all of which relates to the mystery of human redemption, and at the defeat of the powers of the air.[86] For the soul of Christ was most perfectly full of the gifts of the Holy Spirit and all virtues.[87] *Et posuit immaculatam viam meam; and made my way blameless,* that is, my whole manner of life and all my deeds which I performed in the world. For Christ in no manner at all was stained by any sin.

---

**17{18}[34]** *Who has made my feet like the feet of harts: and who sets me upon high places.*

*Qui perfecit pedes meos tamquam cervorum, et super excelsa statuens me.*

**17{18}[35]** *Who teaches my hands to war: and you have made my arms like a brazen bow.*

*Qui docet manus meas ad praelium; et posuisti, ut arcum aereum, brachia mea.*

**17{18}[36]** *And you given me the protection of your salvation: and your right hand has held me up: And your discipline has corrected me unto the end: and your discipline, the same shall teach me.*

*Et dedisti mihi protectionem salutis tuae, et dextera tua suscepit me; et disciplina tua correxit me in finem, et disciplina tua ipsa me docebit.*

**17{18}[34]** *Qui perfecit pedes meos, who has made my feet,* that is, my paths and my deeds, *tanquam cervorum, like the feet of harts:*[88] namely, so that they might operate most quickly and most efficaciously, and to suffer in the world all that which pleases the will of the Father; and so I kept thirsting for the salvation of men during all my life, in the manner that a weary deer desires flowing waters.[89] *Et super excelsa, and upon high places,* that is, in the hearts of contemplative men who through hope are confident of heaven, *statuens me, set me,* that is, causing me by grace to inhabit the hearts of such kind of men, as the Apostle says: *I bow my knees to the Father of our Lord Jesus Christ, of whom all paternity in*

---

86  E. N. For "powers of the air," *see* footnote 3-29.

87  Is. 11:2–3. E. N. wisdom, understanding, counsel, fortitude, knowledge, piety, and fear of the Lord. The virtues would include the cardinal virtues — justice, prudence, fortitude, and temperance — and the theological virtue of charity, and — to a very limited extent — hope.

88  E. N. Harts: adult male deer, after their crown antlers are formed; stags.

89  *Cf.* Ps. 41:2.

*heaven and earth is named, that he would grant you, according to the riches of his glory, to be strengthened by his Spirit with might unto the inward man, that Christ may dwell by faith in your hearts.*[90] Or [we might see it this way], *upon high places,* that is, above the heights of all the heavens, at his right hand, *you set me* in the day of the Ascension. Or [alternatively], *upon high places,* that is, at the height of all virtues *you set me,* creating all the perfect virtues of my soul.    **17{18}[35]** *Qui docet manus meas, who teaches my hands,* that is, my practical intellect and my will, which are the two principal operative powers, *ad praelium, to war* against the devils and the Jews and all the adversaries of human salvation.

Then Christ changes person, and says to the Father: *Et posuisti ut arcum aereum brachia mea; and you have made my arms like a brazen bow,*[91] that is, my virtues by which I conquered the world and the devil. For in the manner that a brazen bow forcefully injures and quickly and powerfully shoots forth arrows, so the virtues of Christ speedily killed death, in the manner said [by Hosea, which words can be ascribed to Christ]: *O death, I will be your death!* [Christ's virtues also] wounded and diminished the devil, as the same [prophet] testified, *O hell, I will be your bite!*[92] And [Christ's virtues], like arrows, incessantly produced the most optimal works.    **17{18} [36]** *Et dedisti mihi, and you have given me,* O Father, *protectionem salutis tuae, the protection of your salvation,* that is, you have protected me with the protection of salvation, by which I am saved in respect to the Resurrection and the glorification of my body.[93] But the world was saved by him from eternal death, and the elect will receive on the day of judgment, eternal beatitude of mind and body. *Et dextera tua, and your right hand,* that is, your gracious and happy presence, *suscepit me, has held me up,* hearing my prayers and rescuing the human nature that I assumed from all the temporal evil of that wicked age and of that evil generation.[94]

---

90  Eph. 3:14-17.

91  *E. N.* Brazen means made of brass.

92  Hosea 13:14a.

93  *E. N.* Christ, as man and as our Redeemer and Head, did not need redemption or salvation. *See, e.g.,* Thomas Aquinas, *Super Sent.,* lib. 3 d. 3 q. 1 a. 1 qc. 2 co. *Christus enim hoc singulariter in humano genere habet ut redemptione non egeat, quia caput nostrum est, sed omnibus convenit redimi per ipsum* ("For Christ possessed the human race in a singular way, so that he did not need redemption, because he is our head, but it behooved all to be redeemed by him."). The only "saving" needed in Christ's life as man, pertained to his rising from the dead, his ascension into heaven, and the glorification of his body, which were also the limited objects of Christ's hope.

94  *E. N.* For "wicked generation," *see* Luke 11:29. That generation that witnessed the historical Jesus.

*Et disciplina tua,* and your discipline, that is, the paternal and merciful chastisement, *correxit,* has corrected, that is, punished, *me in finem, me unto the end,* that is, even unto the obtaining of eternal life of the elect. For he *corrected* and punished me not because of my own fault, but so as to take away the sins of the world, in the manner that is written in Scripture: *the chastisement of our peace was upon him,* by whose *bruises we are healed;*[95] and so his wounds were because of our sins. Whence, the Apostle: He was made, he says, *a curse for us,* so that he might free us from the curse.[96] *Et disciplina tua,* and your discipline, that is, the Passion that you, O Lord, O Father, willed for me to undergo, *ipsa me docebit, the same shall teach me* by the experience of compassion,[97] as the Apostle testifies to: It behooved him, he says, to assimilate[98] himself in all things with his brothers, so that he might be merciful.[99] And again: *We have not,* he says, *a high priest, who cannot have compassion on our infirmities.*[100]

---

**17{18}[37]** *You have enlarged my steps under me; and my feet are not weakened.*

*Dilatasti gressus meos subtus me; et non sunt infirmata vestigia mea.*

**17{18}[37]** *Dilatasti, you have enlarged,* that is, through charity you made wide, abundant, and many, *gressus meos [subtus me], my steps under me,* that is, the acts of my soul, by which I honored you and by which I saved the world: because from the very instant of my maternal conception even until the last moment of my life, I never ceased from the actual exercise of virtuous works; *et non sunt infirmata vestigia mea; and my feet are not weakened,* that is, my works which are a sign and indication of my internal love and disposition: because I did not do things sluggishly, nor did I shy from undertaking to work, even while I hung on the Cross, when I said, *It is finished.*[101]

---

95  Is. 53:5.
96  Gal. 3:13.
97  L. *compati,* present infinitive passive of *compatior,* to suffer with and to have compassion or pity towards another.
98  E. N. That is, to make himself similar in all things to us, namely, by assuming passible human nature.
99  *Cf.* Heb. 2:17. Denis attributes the epistle of Hebrews to St. Paul. *See* footnote 8-34.
100  Heb. 4:15.
101  John 19:30.

**17{18}[38]** *I will pursue after my enemies, and overtake them: and I will not turn again till they are consumed.*

> *Persequar inimicos meos, et comprehendam illos; et non convertar donec deficiant.*

**17{18}[39]** *I will break them, and they shall not be able to stand: they shall fall under my feet.*

> *Confringam illos, nec poterunt stare; cadent subtus pedes meos.*

**17{18}[38]** *Persequar inimicos meos, I will pursue after my enemies*, that is, the devils, expelling them from the hearts of sinners and from the temples of idolaters. Hence in the Gospel we read that they cried out to Christ: *What have we to do with you, Jesus of Nazareth? Are you come here to torment us before the time?*[102] This persecution is to the devil something all the more painful the greater his envy is against men. *Et comprehendam eos, and I will overtake them*, defeating them and binding them; *et non convertar, and I will not turn*, that is, I will not turn back nor will I cease from the prosecution of demons, *donec deficient, until they are consumed*, that is, until that day of judgment, when they will be thoroughly separated [from the elect] and condemned. For Christ constantly through his holy angels and virtuous men persecutes, torments, and defeats devils.    **17{18}[39]** *Confringam illos, I will break them*, that is, those whose will exerts itself to seduce the elect, *nec poterunt stare, they shall not be able to stand*, resisting my power; but *cadent, they shall fall* vanquished *subtus pedes meos, under my feet*, that is, they will be fully and in all things oppressed and overthrown by me. For the demons are utterly subject to the power of the Savior.

Or thus [we might interpret these verses]: *I will pursue after my enemies*, this being the unbelieving Jews through the coming of the military leader of the Romans, on account of the fear of which all fled from Jerusalem; *and will overtake them*, that is, within Jerusalem I caused that they be seized, as it in fact occurred; *and I will not turn again* from my anger, *until they are consumed*, that is, until they are destroyed, sold, or dispersed, and deprived of all their prior power and glory. But *I will break them*, because of obstinate perfidy; *and they shall not be able to stand*: as it is set forth. And this is what the Lord says: *For the children of Israel shall sit many days without king, and without prince, and without sacrifice, and without altar, and without ephod, and without theraphim.*[103]

---

102  Mark 1:24; Matt. 8:29. E. N. Denis combines the verses taking the first question from Mark, but the second question from Matthew.

103  Hosea 3:4. E. N. *Theraphim* comes from the Greek θεραφίν (*theraphin*), which

And in Daniel there is the same clear prediction: *And after sixty-two weeks, he says, Christ shall be slain: and the people that shall deny him shall not be his. And a people with their leader that shall come, shall destroy the city and the sanctuary: and the end thereof shall be waste, . . . and the desolation shall continue even . . . to the end.*[104] And although all this in a short time[105] was fulfilled, nevertheless the most blind Jews persisted in their disbelief, just as the prophets who had predicted this, and in which we find them [the prophets] to be true.

-----

17{18}[40] *And you have girded me with strength unto battle; and have subdued under me them that rose up against me.*

> *Et praecinxisti me virtute ad bellum, et supplantasti insurgentes in me subtus me.*

17{18}[40] *Et praecinxisti me virtute ad bellum,*[106] *and you have girded me with the strength unto battle.* This has already been mentioned and has been explained. *Et supplantasti, and have subdued,* that is, you have cast down, *insurgentes in me, them that rose up against me,* that is my persecutors, *subtus me, under me,* that is under my power: because Christ is appointed as judge of those who judged him.

-----

17{18}[41] *And you have made my enemies turn their back upon me, and have destroyed them that hated me.*

> *Et inimicos meos dedisti mihi dorsum, et odientes me disperdidisti.*

17{18}[41] *Et inimicos meos dedisti mihi dorsum; and you have made my enemies turn their back upon me,* that is, you have made them to flee as if vanquished. For he who flees from another, turns away his face from him, and turns his back towards him: and so the Lord says the following about sinners speaking through the prophet: *They have turned their back to me,*

-----

itself is a transliteration of the Hebrew מיפרת, a word which is generally believed to mean household idols.

104  Dan. 9:26.

105  E. N. That is a short time after Christ's death, resurrection, and ascension when Rome finally destroyed Jerusalem and its temple in 70 A. D., during the Siege of Jerusalem, where the Romans were led by the future emperor Titus.

106  E. N. The Carthusian editor notes here that the word *bellum*, war, and not the word *proelium*, combat or battle, should have been used by Denis, though one notes that the English translators of the Douay-Rheims chose the narrower term battle, and not the broader term war in translating *bellum*.

*and not their face.*[107] Then, therefore, the enemies of Christ (that is, the unbelievers) turn their backs to Christ when they flee from the face of Christians: this is something often fulfilled. And this may be explained best in this way: *My enemies,* that is, the Jews, who at one time had persecuted me, *you have made them turn their back upon me,* that is, you have made them subject to me, so that they would take my yoke upon them, and would learn from me that I am meek and humble of heart,[108] and they would bear the weight of the day and its heats[109] upon the backs of their hearts and their bodies: as did the eight thousand converted through Peter,[110] and manifested in Paul himself who beyond all measure (as he painfully admits) persecuted the Church.[111] For such persons Christ before the Passion told the Jews: *When you shall have lifted up the Son of man, then shall you know, that I am he.*[112] However, the first explanation agrees more with that which follows: *et odientes me, them that hated me,* that is, the Jews about which the Savior said in the Gospel: *But now they have both seen and hated both me and my Father . . . without cause.*[113] These, therefore, O Lord, O Father, *disperdisti, you have destroyed,* in the persecution of Titus, and thereafter by the whole world, handing them over to this heavy captivity even until the end of the world. Or [we can say], *you have destroyed,* that is, in diverse ways you have destroyed them, depriving them in the present of grace, and, after this life, of glory, and oppressing them with other calamities as until now they have been oppressed, for they have neither any princes, nor territory, nor inheritance, but they are subjected to the dominion of their enemies.

---

**17{18}[42]** *They cried, but there was none to save them, to the Lord: but he heard them not.*

*Clamaverunt, nec erat qui salvos faceret; ad Dominum, nec exaudivit eos.*

**17{18}[42]** *Clamaverunt, they cried,* [that is,] the Jews spoken about before when they were devastated by Titus [cried], because, as Josephus

---

107  Jer. 2:27; 32:33.
108  Matt. 11:29.
109  Matt. 20:12. E. N. The reference is to the Parable of the Laborers in the Vineyard.
110  Acts 2:41; 4:4. E. N. 3,000 are said to have been baptized in one instance, and 2,000 more later, to make the total number 5,000.
111  Gal. 1:13.
112  John 8:28a.
113  John 15:24b, 25b.

reports,[114] many prayers and sacrifices were offered to the Lord for their liberation; *nec erat qui salvos faceret eos, but there was none to save them* from their danger, because the Lord *has despised them.*[115] They also cried out, not to false gods, in the manner that their fathers frequently had done, but *ad Dominum, to the Lord,* who is the true God; *nec exaudivit eos, but he heard them not,* because they had killed his Son; indeed even in the present day he does not hear them, since there has already run from the year of the Lord one thousand four hundred thirty four years.[116] This sort of thing would not be possible unless they were guilty of some very great sin, and the sin of their fathers must be so great as this captivity of them is greater and more serious than all the captivity of their fathers. But such a sin cannot be anything other than the killing of Christ. Whence, they clearly show themselves to have distressed Christ: for if one examines that the holy prophets predicted that they would be forsaken in perpetuity for their sin in a manner that is clearly apparent, and clearly (if the Lord grants us to see) this is so apparent.

---

17{18}[43] *And I shall beat them as small as the dust before the wind; I shall bring them to naught, like the dirt in the streets.*

> *Et comminuam eos ut pulverem ante faciem venti; ut lutum platearum delebo eos.*

17{18}[43] *Et comminuam eos,* and I shall beat them small, namely, my enemies earlier spoken about, *ut pulverem ante faciem venti; as the dust before the wind,* depriving them of all spiritual being, so they would spiritually die. And also by the sword and with hunger killing them in body, and dispersing in the manner of *dust before the wind* to all the ends of the world, that is, dispersed by the presence of wind. *Ut lutum platearum, like dirt in the streets,* that is removed from another place, *delebo eos, I will bring them to nothing* from the land of their fathers.

---

114  E. N. A reference to the Romano-Jewish historian Titus Flavius Josephus (A. D. 37–ca. 100), known for his two most important and popular works, *Antiquities of the Jews* and *The Jewish War.*

115  Ps. 52:6b.

116  Which is the number of years from the birth of Christ to when this author wrote this.

**17{18}[44]** *You will deliver me from the contradictions of the people: you will make me head of the Gentiles.*

*Eripies me de contradictionibus populi; constitues me in caput gentium.*

Thereafter Christ says to the Father:    **17{18}[44]** *Eripies me de contradictionibus populi; you will deliver me from the contradictions of the people* of the Jews, who were asked by Pilate, *Shall I crucify your king?* To which they responded, *We have no king but Caesar.*[117] From this contradicting people, Christ by his Resurrection was delivered. *Constitues me, you will make me,* O Father, *in caput gentium, head of the Gentiles,* that is, leader and prince of the Gentiles converted to the Catholic Faith, as you said through Isaiah: *Behold I have given him for a witness to the people, for a leader and a master to the Gentiles.*[118] For Christ is the head and the law-giver of the Church militant,[119] principally collected from the Gentiles.

---

**17{18}[45]** *A people, which I knew not, has served me: at the hearing of the ear they have obeyed me.*

*Populus, quem non cognovi, servivit mihi; in auditu auris obedivit mihi.*

**17{18}[45]** *Populus quem non cognovit; a people, which I knew not,* that is, the Gentiles whom I did not know by approbation[120] during the time of their infidelity and their vices, *servivit mihi, have served me,* faithfully, after they were converted to the Faith; *in auditu auris, at the hearing of the ear,* that is, promptly and steadily since they had heard my words, *obedivit mihi,* fulfilling all the divine commandments. This is what Isaiah cries out to the Lord: *Behold you shall call a nation, which you knew not: and the nations that knew you not shall run to you.*[121] Or [alternatively] thus: *A people which I knew not,* that is, sinners that were counted among the Jews, in the manner that the publicans and the Samaritans were devoted to me: because of them Christ said, *For I am not come to call the just, but sinners;*[122] and again, *For the Son of man is come to seek and to save that which was lost.*[123] And among such as

---

117 John 19:15.
118 Is. 55:4.
119 Eph. 1:22; 5:23 *and elsewhere.*
120 For God's knowledge by approbation and what it means, *see footnote* 5-11.
121 Is. 55:5a.
122 Matt. 9:13b.
123 Luke 19:10.

these there was Matthew, Zacchaeus, and Mary Magdalen: who also *at the hearing of the ear* were obedient to Christ, as the Gospels attest.[124]

---

**17{18}[46]** *The children that are strangers have lied to me, strange children have faded away, and have halted from their paths.*

> *Filii alieni mentiti sunt mihi, filii alieni inveterati sunt, et claudicaverunt a semitis suis.*

**17{18}[46]** *Filii alieni, the children that are strangers,* that is, that were children only in name, as were the Pharisees and the Scribes, and the unbelieving Jews, of whom Christ asserted: *But the children of the kingdom shall be cast out into the exterior darkness;*[125] of whom also openly said, *That the publicans and the harlots shall go into the kingdom of* heaven *before you.*[126] These children, therefore, *mentiti sunt mihi, have lied to me,* telling themselves to expect the Messiah king, and willing to believe in him, but refusing the Messiah king and the true Christ that appeared in their presence. These *have lied* and they have done so *to me,* mixing feigning and adulatory words, so that they might try to trip me up. And *filii alieni inveterate sunt; strange children have faded away* in vices and obdurate in evil, for they did not hear this, *Break up anew your fallow ground, and sow not upon thorns;*[127] *et claudicaverunt a semitis suis, and have halted from their paths,* that is, they have not walked in the precepts of God that were given them.

---

**17{18}[47]** *The Lord lives! And blessed be my God! And let the God of my salvation be exalted!*

> *Vivit Dominus! Et benedictus Deus meus! Et exaltetur Deus salutis meae!*

With respect to the conversion of the Gentiles and the other benefits already spoken about, Christ, as man, giving thanks to God said:    **17{18} [47]** *Vivit Dominus! the Lord lives!* three and one, who is the fountain of life, and is by nature that pure and most blessed life, fully and superessentially[128] living. And so of this immense blessedness of life of God,

---

124  Luke 5:27, 28; 19:5-8; 7:27 *et seq.*

124  Luke 5:27, 28; 19:5-8; 7:27 *et seq.*
125  Matt. 8:12a.
126  Mat. 21:31b. *E. N.* Denis substitutes "kingdom of heaven" for "kingdom of God."
127  Jer. 4:3b.
128  *E. N.* Denis frequently uses superlatives and even super-superlatives to refer to God, in this particular instance the superlative *superessentialiter.* In his

Christ manifesting thankful joy (*congratulans*) says: *The Lord who works all these things, lives! Et benedictus Deus meus! and blessed be my God!* that is, he is in himself holy, and worthy of all praise, and the most liberal giver of all blessings, who is my God according to the form of a servant which I have received.[129] *Et exaltetur Deus salutis meae! And let the God of my salvation be exalted!* That is, that in all things I recognize him, love him, and honor him with all reverence and all obedience. For this applies to the true love of God and neighbor, so that we opt with all our affections to exalt God in all things, since this is the honor due God and our happiness: of which the first requirement [of charity] is the love of God, but the second is love of neighbor.

---

**17{18}[48]** *O God, who avenges me, and subdues the people under me, my deliverer from my enemies.*

> *Deus qui das vindictas mihi, et subdis populos sub me; liberator meus de inimicis meis iracundis.*

**17{18}[49]** *And you will lift me up above them that rise up against me: from the unjust man you will deliver me.*

> *Et ab insurgentibus in me exaltabis me; a viro iniquo eripies me.*

**17{18}[48]** *Deus qui das vindictas,* O God, who avenges me, that is, the previously mentioned just vengeances and victories, *mihi, et subdis populos sub me; me, and subdues the people under me,* giving to them faith and grace

---

commentary of Psalm 26 [Article LIX (Psalm 26:8)], for example, Denis uses the super-superlative *superbeatissimam*. There is an intrinsic difficulty in translating these words because, as St. Thomas says in his commentary on the *Divine Names* of Pseudo-Dionysius, the naming of God brings us to a two-fold excess (*excessus autem est duplex*): "the first is excess within a genus, and it is signified by the comparative or the superlative; the second is excess outside a genus, and is signified by the addition of this preposition: *super.*" In commenting on this passage of St. Thomas, Jean-Louis Chrétien in his *The Ark of Speech* asks: "So should we say that God is *pulcherrimus,* 'that which is most beautiful,' or that he is *superpulchrum, huperkalon,* 'beyond the beautiful?' Can beauty name God in himself or only in his gifts? And does the path of beauty lead to a supreme beauty or altogether beyond beauty?" Jean-Louis Chrétien (Andrew Brown, trans.), *The Ark of Speech* (New York: Routledge 2004), 82. In short, do we understand these terms of Denis cataphatically or apophatically? As implying the genus *eminently* or as implying something *beyond* the genus. Or, in some cases, perhaps we might understand them as implying both?

129 Phil. 2:7. E. N. Denis means with respect to Christ's human nature, by which the eternal Word "emptied himself, taken the form of a servant, being made in the likeness of men, and in habit found as man."

with which they might convert to me, and to serve me, *liberator meus de inimici meis iracundis; my deliverer from my enemies*, that is, the Jews who acted with fury against me, whom you drove away.    17{18}[49] *Et ab insurgentibus in me exaltabis me; and you will lift me up above them that rise up against me*, that is, from the unfaithful, and the tyrant, and most of all from the Antichrist: of whom these words follow, *a viro iniquo eripies me; from the unjust man, you will deliver me*, because he is *the man of sin, the son of perdition*.[130] From this, I say, you will exalt me, destroying their depravity, and increasing my justice. But especially in the day of judgment you will exalt me by this, because then you will make me justly to exercise judgment over all of them. And then that which is said will be fulfilled, *They shall come to him* (namely, Christ), *and all that resist him shall be confounded*.[131]

---

17{18}[50] *Therefore will I give glory to you, O Lord, among the nations, and I will sing a Psalm to your name.*

> *Propterea confitebor tibi in nationibus, Domine, et nomini tuo Psalmum dicam.*

17{18}[51] *Giving great deliverance to his king, and showing mercy to David his anointed: and to his seed forever.*

> *Magnificans salutes regis eius, et faciens misericordiam christo suo David, et semini eius usque in saeculum.*

And because this is so,    17{18}[50] *Propterea confitebor tibi in nationibus, Domine; therefore will I give glory to you, O Lord, among the nations*, that is, by myself and through the Apostles and all my disciples I will praise you before the Gentiles and the Jews, in such a manner that all is fulfilled; *et nomini tuo, and to your name*, that is, to you alone, *Psalmum dicam, I will sing a Psalm*, that is, by mouth and deed I will openly offer you all that is praiseworthy. And I will do this with merit, because he is    17{18}[51] *Magnificans salutes, great deliverance*, that is, given great happiness of soul and body, *regis eius, to his king*, that is Christ, his Son; *et faciens misericordiam Christo suo David; and showing mercy to David his anointed*, that is, Jesus the Nazarene, whose human nature only by merciful goodness was assumed by the Word, and filled with all grace, and raised again on the third day. It is customary among the holy prophets to understand the name David as Christ, in the manner that the Lord speaks through Ezechiel: *I will save my flock . . . and I will set up one*

---

130  2 Thess. 2:3.
131  Is. 45:25b.

*shepherd over them, and he shall feed them, even my servant David,* that is the Christ; *and my servant David the prince* of them.[132] And Jeremiah: *But they,* he says, *shall serve . . . David their king,*[133] that is, the Messiah according to all commentators. And not only is the Lord *showing mercy to David his anointed,* but *et semini eius, but to his seed,* that is, the Christian people, reborn spiritually in Christ, *usque in saeculum, forever,* that is, in eternity. Whence, according to the magnitude of the mercy of God over the Christian people, the time of the law of the Gospel is called the time of the new law, that is, the time of grace. This is beautifully intimated in Zachariah, where it is said: *He that has offended among them in that day shall be as David: and the house of David, as that of God, as an angel of the Lord in their sight;*[134] that is, as David after his great sin was able to obtain mercy, so he who offends among them, that is among the Christian people, in that day, that is, in the time of grace, is able to obtain mercy. Because of this it is said that the philosophers know the majesty of God, the Jews his justice, but the Christians his mercy. Of this *seed* it is written: *If he shall lay down his life for sin, he shall see a long-lived seed.*[135]

# ARTICLE XLIV

## ALLEGORICAL EXPOSITION OF THE
## SAME SEVENTEENTH PSALM

17{18}[1]   *Unto the end, for David the servant of the Lord, who spoke to the Lord the words of this canticle, in the day that the Lord delivered him from the hands of all his enemies, and from the hand of Saul.*

*In finem. Puero Domini David, qui locutus est Domino verba cantici huius, in die qua eripuit eum Dominus de manu omnium inimicorum eius, et de manu Saul, et dixit.*

FURTHER, ACCORDING TO THE ALLEGORICAL explanation of this Psalm, by David is to be understood the Church, and any member of the faithful. And so the sense of previously introduced title is this:   17{18}[1] *Verba cantici huius, the words of this canticle,* that is, [the words of] this Psalm directing us *in finem,*

132   Ez. 34:22–24.
133   Jer. 30:9a.
134   Zach. 12:8.
135   Is. 53:10.

*unto the end,* that is, unto Christ, are appropriate *David puero Domino,* *for David the servant of the Lord,* that is, for the Church or for the individual faithful who is the son of God by the grace of adoption: which words any member of the faithful *locutus est Domino, was spoken to the Lord,* that is, unto his praise, *in die qua eripuit eum Dominus de manu inimicorum suorum; in the day that the Lord delivered him from the hands of all his enemies,* that is, from all the vexation of temptation *et de manu Saul, and from the hand of Saul,* that is, the empire of death.

---

**17{18}[2]**  *I will love you, O Lord, my strength.*

*Diligam te, Domine, fortitudo mea.*

**17{18}[3]**  *The Lord is my firmament, my refuge, and my deliverer. My God is my helper, and in him will I put my trust. My protector and the horn of my salvation, and my support.*

*Dominus firmamentum meum, et refugium meum, et liberator meus. Deus meus adiutor meus, et sperabo in eum; protector meus, et cornu salutis meae, et susceptor meus.*

Any member of the faithful, therefore, reflecting upon the benefits of God shown him, considering his redemption by Christ, and paying heed to his invitation to the good of future happiness, most thankfully, most joyfully, and most ardently will say to the Lord in his heart:    **17{18}[2]** *Diligam te, Domine; I will love you, O Lord,* adhering to him before all things,[136] and not because of receiving any created good from him, for he is *fortitudo mea, my strength.*    **17{18}[3]** *Dominus firmamentum meum, the Lord is my firmament*: this has already been satisfactorily expounded upon; *et refugium meum, and my refuge,* to which I run back to confidently in every necessity, as to a most faithful beloved, a most invincible helper, and the most benignant Savior, who everywhere and always has open wide the arms of mercy so as to embrace the one taking refuge in him; *et liberator meus, and my deliverer*: because the Father sent his Son to deliver me, and the Son with his own Blood redeemed me.[137]

*Deus meus, my God,* whom I most affectionately devote myself to, is *adiutor meus, my helper,* working within me by his grace; *et, and therefore sperabo in eum, in him I will put my trust,* and not in any mere creature; and I will put by trust in him alone without despairing, but, doing what I

---

136  Cf. Ps. 72:28a. *But it is good for me to adhere to my God, to put my hope in the Lord God.*

137  Cf. John 3:16; Rom. 8:32, 34.

am able,[138] I will put my trust in him faithfully: not, however, principally in my own merits, but in him, *I will put my trust*, for without his help we are unable to persevere in any good.[139] And this Lord is *protector meus, my protector* from the snares of the devil, the lies of men, and at the occurrence of any dangers, *et cornu, and the horn*, that is, the one who reveals or introduces, *salutis meae, my salvation*. For we recognize through the very one revealing in whom our true salvation consists.[140] And thus God is said to be a *horn* on account of a resemblance. For a horn is an instrument whose sound customarily is used to introduce something to others. Because, therefore, by natural reason man is not able to know in what true beatitude or salvation might consist in, but it becomes known to him by divine revelation, so God is said to be *the horn* of our salvation. But other explanations of these words also find support.[141] *Et susceptor meus, and my support*, that is, the hearer of my prayers, and he who embraces me by mercy.

There is here put forth many names, really all signifying the same thing or one including another, since man, totally inflamed with love, affectionately expresses himself to God by using such a variety of names; and always knowing that [the use] of the names that follow thus produces such affections in his soul, so that the affection [caused by the use] of the prior names is strengthened, renewed, and ignited. Hence, this is a most devout and most efficacious way of praying to and praising God, using many loving names which mutually include each other to proffer to and ascribe to God, as is now is done. Consequently, there is added:

---

138  E. N. Denis does not advocate any sort of spiritual fatalism, lethargy, or any kind of quietism, nor certainly is he advocating any sort of Pelagianism, but he insists that we must do what we can — *age quod agis* — and hope in the Lord's promise to furnish us the prevenient, cooperating, and subsequent graces we need.

139  Cf. John 15:5. *I am the vine: you the branches: he that abides in me, and I in him, the same bears much fruit: for without me you can do nothing.*

140  Cf. John 17:3. *Now this is eternal life: That they may know you, the only true God, and Jesus Christ, whom you have sent.*

141  E. N. In the Scriptures, the word "horn" (In Hebrew קֶרֶן, [ke'ren], in Greek κέρας [keras], and in Latin *cornu*) has a variety of meanings, including trumpets, drinking vessels, flasks, hill summits or peaks, the horns of an animal, and even rays of light. The metaphorical or symbolic use of horns is similarly broad, including strength, honor, defense, authority, wisdom. The intrinsic problematic of the word horn is reflected in St. Jerome's translation of Exodus 34:29–35, where Moses, when he came down from Mount Sinai, states *ignorabat quod cornuta esset facies sua*, "he was unaware that he bore horns on his head," giving rise to the "horned" Moses, most famously in Michelangelo's masterpiece, whose face only should have been as if it projected rays of light, and not literally horned. In light of this hornet's nest of meanings of the word horn Denis — perhaps wisely — foregoes other interpretations.

**17{18}[4]**  *Praising I will call upon the Lord: and I shall be saved from my enemies.*

>   *Laudans invocabo Dominum, et ab inimicis meis salvus ero.*

**17{18}[4]**  *Laudans invocabo Domino; praising, I will call upon the Lord,* that is, I will attribute to God the many commendatory prayers discussed above, and I will mix with these supplicatory words,[142] saying: O eternal God, omnipotent, immense, superglorious, by nature good, receive me, take possession of me, perfect me always and save me. For since to pray and to praise are two noble acts of worship (*latriae*), and although to praise God is more noble than to pray [to God in petitionary prayer, seeking to obtain a good or to avoid an evil], it is a fact that the acts are often mixed with each other, and this is most noble: praising to pray to God, or praying to praise God; and this act is a strong remedy against all temptations, adversities, and sorrows. For this reason, the following is added [to the Psalm], *et ab inimicis meis salvus ero; and I shall be saved from my enemies,* that is, I will be delivered from temptations; nothing will wound my soul, however much it might afflict the flesh. Here it is written: *Is any of you sad? Let him pray. Is he cheerful in mind? Let him sing.*[143]

---

**17{18}[5]**  *The sorrows of death surrounded me: and the torrents of iniquity troubled me.*

>   *Circumdederunt me dolores mortis, et torrentes iniquitatis conturbaverunt me.*

**17{18}[6]**  *The sorrows of hell encompassed me: and the snares of death prevented me.*

>   *Dolores inferni circumdederunt me, praeoccupaverunt me laquei mortis.*

---

142  E. N. Denis distinguishes commendatory language (*commendatoria*) with deprecatory language (*deprecatoria*). Modernly, the word deprecatory has the connotation of wishing evil on someone; however, that is not the principal meaning in Latin, nor was it always so in English. For example, "deprecate" is defined as "to pray for the removal of," "to regret deeply"; and a "deprecatory" prayer would be understood as a prayer "serving to avert evil" from oneself or others. *See* James Douglas, *English Etymology* (Edinburgh: Oliver and Boyd 1872) (s.v. "precor"), 92–93. Because of the negative connotations modernly associated with that word, however, I have translated *verba deprecatoria* as "supplicatory words" to avoid the negative connotation that has crept into the word deprecatory in English.

143  James 5:13.

And with merit I say, *I shall be saved from my enemies*, because    **17**{**18**}[**5**]
*Circumdederunt me, they have surrounded me*, that is, they are entrenched
everywhere around me, and they are determined against me, *dolores mortis*,
*the sorrows of death*, that is, inordinate affections and penal passions[144]
like anger, envy, sadness that might be afflicting the soul and bringing it
to perpetual death. Or [another way of looking at it], *the sorrows of death*,
that is, the punishment following from original sin, namely, the distresses
of the body and the loss of powers of the soul.[145] *Torrentes iniquitatis, the*
*torrents of iniquity*, that is, the capital vices,[146] from which as if from a
fountain all others are derived, *conturbaverunt me, troubled me*, that is, they
disquieted me, battling against me or striving to bring me to consent to
them. Or [another manner of understanding this is as follows], *the torrents*
*of iniquity*, that is, the iniquity of temptations and of those persecuting me,
which can be imagined as many and large torrents of water, *troubled me*, by
reviving and alluring or [troubling me] in some similar fashion.    **17**{**18**}
[**6**] *Dolores inferni, the sorrows of hell*, that is, the diabolic evil, or afflictions
so grave, that they appear able to be compared to the sorrows of hell, that
is, the pains of hell, *circumdederunt me, encompassed me* the misery of such
evil that one confronts in the valley of tears;[147] *praeoccupaverunt, they*
*prevented*,[148] that is, they possessed me even before the other evil invaded
me, [that is, before] the *laquei mortis, the snares of death*, that is, original sin,
which is something that may said to be one thing formally, namely, with
respect to the privation of original justice due to nature, yet according to
Anselm,[149] it is also many things materially, because of its effects or the

---

144  E. N. Denis refers to *passiones poenales*, and not to passions in general. Scholastics distinguished between penal or culpable passions (*passiones poenales/culpa-
biles*) which are sins in and of themselves (*e.g.*, envy, pride) and so have no parvity
of matter, and those passions that are not sinful *qua* passions, but may be as a
result of a disordering (by excess or defect) of that passion (*e.g.*, anger, sorrow).

145  E. N. The punishments suffered by mankind as a result of original sin include
punishments to the body and punishments of the soul. Sanctifying grace was
lost, as was integrity, infused knowledge, and immortality.

146  E. N. The seven capital vices (also referred to as the seven deadly sins or the
cardinal sins) are lust (*luxuria*), gluttony (*gula*), greed (*avaritia*), sloth (*acedia*),
wrath (*ira*), envy (*invidia*), and pride (*superbia*). See CCC § 1866.

147  E. N. Denis uses the term *in hac valle lacrimarum* as a description of the life
*in via*, an implied reference to Psalm 83:7 (*In valle lacrimarum, in loco quem*
*posuit* or *in the vale of tears, in the place which he has set*), a phrase also found
in both the *Salve Regina* and the *Dies Irae*.

148  For the use of "prevented" *see* footnote 17-66.

149  E. N. For Anselm, *see* footnote 13-35. This appears to be a reference to St.
Anselm's treatise on the *Virginal Conception and Original Sin*, where he sees
original sin (and its punishment) as being the privation of the original justice

four wounds of the soul, by which are infected its powers, as has previously been stated.[150] Therefore, this sin is called plurally, *the snares of death*: for it took captive the soul by means of its guilt, and it made us to be conceived as *children of wrath*;[151] and we were on that account condemned before we were conceived.[152] Hence, this very thing is written about in a much later Psalm: *For behold I was conceived in iniquities.*[153]

---

**17{18}[7]**   *In my affliction I called upon the Lord, and I cried to my God: And he heard my voice from his holy temple: and my cry before him came into his ears.*

*In tribulatione mea invocavi Dominum, et ad Deum meum clamavi: et exaudivit de templo sancto suo vocem meam; et clamor meus in conspectu eius introivit in aures eius.*

**17{18}[7]** *In tribulatione mea, in my affliction,* that is, during the time of temptation and difficulty, *invocavi, I called upon,* that is, with an internal affection I called upon, *Dominum, the Lord* to come to my help; *et ad Deum meum, and to my God,* in whom I place all my trust, *clamavi, I have cried,* by vocal exclamation born from the flowing out of the interior fervor. And you, O brother, therefore in all your trials and necessities, accustom yourself to call upon the Lord, because as the book of Chronicles puts it, *Since we know not what to do, we can only turn our eyes to the Lord.*[154] And such an invocation cannot be in vain, for [to the Psalm] is added: *Et exaudivit* (scilicet Dominus) *de templo sancto suo; and he heard* (namely, the Lord heard) *from his holy temple,* that is, from the place of his dwelling, *vocem meam, my voice.* In the same manner that it is said that God is in a temple, or in a place, or any particular creature,[155] so he is said to go to, and to be heard from, that

---

due human nature. See *De Conceptu Virginali et de Originali Peccato,* chp. 27.

150   E. N. See Article XXV (Ps. 7:7). The wounds are concupiscence, weakness, ignorance, and malice.

151   See Eph. 2:3

152   E. N. Denis says *prius damnati, quam nati,* we are condemned to die before we are conceived or born. This is a saying frequently attributed to St. Bernard. In his second sermon for Pentecost Sunday, St. Bernard says something quite close to it: *Erraveramus ab utero, in utero damnati antequam nati: quia de peccato et in peccato concepti.* "We are lost from the womb, in the womb we are condemned before we are born; for we are conceived from and in sin." PL 183, 327.

153   Ps. 50:7a. E. N. The Psalm verse continues: *And in sins did my mother conceive me.*

154   2 Chr. 20:12b.

155   E. N. See, *e.g.,* Article XX (Psalm 5:6).

temple, or that place, or that creature. *Et clamor meus in conspectus eius introivit in aures eius; and my cry before him came into his ears*: because as Ecclesiasticus says, *The prayer of the just man shall pierce the clouds* (or as another version says, *The prayer of him that humbles himself shall pierce the clouds*).[156] Hence Moses says: *When you shall seek there the Lord your God, you shall find him: yet so, if you seek him with all your heart, and all the affliction of your soul.*[157]

---

**17{18}[8]**   *The earth shook and trembled: the foundations of the mountains were troubled and were moved, because he was angry with them.*

*Commota est, et contremuit terra, fundamenta montium conturbata sunt, et commota sunt, quoniam iratus est eis.*

**17{18}[8]** *Commota est et contremuit terra; the earth shook and trembled*: that is, the residents of the earth, the men of the world, who heard the preaching of Christ and of his apostles and of the other faithful, and whose souls were moved to repentance, and they feared greatly to make satisfaction with the body. *Fundamenta montium, the foundations were moved*, that is, the tyrants and princes of the proud, *conturbata sunt, were troubled*, because of the great prodigies that they saw being done by the saints and the martyrs, *et commota sunt, and they were moved*, not towards the emendation [of their life], but to the hardening [of their hearts], saying that those miracles were being done by the magic arts; and this was so, *quoniam iratus est eis, because he was angry with them*, that is, because the Lord justly withdraws grace from them, delivering them over *to a reprobate sense.*[158]

---

**17{18}[9]**   *There went up a smoke in his wrath: and a fire flamed from his face: coals were kindled by it.*

*Ascendit fumus in ira eius, et ignis a facie eius exarsit; carbones succensi sunt ab eo.*

**17{18}[9]** *Ascendit fumus, there went up a smoke*, that being a tearful prayer (*lacrimosa oratio*), *in ira eius, in his wrath*, that is, from the fear of the wrath of God or the vengeance due sin: because sinners, hearing the preaching of the Gospel that [informed the hearer that] the ungodly

---

156 Ecclus. 35:21a. E. N. The latter version quoted by Denis is what is found in the Sixto-Clementine Vulgate.

157 Deut. 4:29.

158 Rom. 1:28.

will go to the eternal flames,[159] became sorrowful of heart, and with tears pleaded for pardon. *Et ignis a facie eius exarsit; and a fire flamed from his face*, that is, the divine love in the hearts of those who preached repentance was enkindled in those who received pardon as a result of their pleading; *from his face*, that is, from the countenance and the mercy of the divine kindness. For after the tearful repentance of sins, the goodly Lord is accustomed to infuse sweet and fervent desires for the attainment of eternal joy, as the Scripture attests to: *After a storm you make a calm*.[160] *Carbones, coals*, that is, Ethiopians of soul and body, formerly black, and all sinners blackened with vice,[161] *succensi sunt ab eo, were kindled by it*, that is, they are filled with divine love by God. For where iniquity abounded, grace also did more abound.[162]

---

**17{18}[10]** *He bowed the heavens, and came down: and darkness was under his feet.*

*Inclinavit caelos, et descendit; et caligo sub pedibus eius.*

**17{18}[10]** *Inclinavit caelos, he bowed the heavens*, that is, God sent holy angels, who are all ministering spirits for the purpose of guarding men,[163] so that they might prepare the way of his entry into the hearts of men: which, once it was so prepared, *et, and*, he himself *descendit, came down*, that is, he infused the great goodness of his grace, and by the faith and the charity in the souls of the elect, he constituted it as a dwelling for himself, as is held by the prophet Zachariah: *Behold I come, and I will dwell in the midst of you: says the Lord*.[164] Not, of course, that God descends in the manner of moving from one place to another, but as being made worthy by his clemency.

---

159  Matt. 25:41. *Depart from me, you cursed, into everlasting fire which was prepared for the devil and his angels.*

160  Tobit 3:22b. The verse continues: *and after tears and weeping you pour in joyfulness.*

161  E. N. Ethiopians were understood as symbolic of the soul darkened by sin, a soul in a state of mortal sin understood as being black (*nigris*), and sin being something that blackens (*denigrare*) the soul. For an example of this, we might turn to Origen in one of his homilies on Jeremiah: "At first we are likened to the Ethiopians in our souls, then we are cleansed in order that we might become whiter." Origen, *Hom. Ierem.* 11.6 (quoted in Aaron P. Johnson, "The Blackness of Ethiopians: Classical Ethnography and Eusebius's Commentary on the Psalms," *The Harvard Theological Review*, 99:2 (April 2006), pp. 172–73 & n. 57).

162  Cf. Rom. 5:20.

163  Cf. Heb. 1:14.

164  Zach. 2:10b.

**17{18}[14]**[165] *And the Lord thundered from heaven, and the highest gave his voice: hail and coals of fire.*

> *Et intonuit de caelo Dominus, et Altissimus dedit vocem suam: grando et carbones ignis.*

**17{18}[14]** *Et intonuit de caelo Dominus; and the Lord thundered from heaven,* this is, God the Father, through his incarnate Son, has spoken to the world, in a forceful and uncommon and marvelous manner — in such a manner that the Jews who were sent by their chiefs to Christ, when they returned back to them stated, *Never did man speak like this man.*[166] Or [we may understand it] thus: *and the Lord thundered from heaven,* that is, from the mouths of the Apostles, who are referred to as coming from heaven, have spoken very forceful words, alike even to thunder. For also Christ called John and James sons of thunder, as the evangelist Mark describes.[167]

---

**17{18}[17]** *He sent from on high, and took me: and received me out of many waters.*

> *Misit de summo, et accepit me; et assumpsit me de aquis multis.*

Then the Church says:[168]   **17{18}[17]** *Misit de summo, he sent from on high,* that is, God the Father from the throne of glory sent his Only-Begotten, *et accepit me, and took me* as a glorious spouse, not having wrinkle or spot,[169] giving my members, that is, the faithful, powers to become sons of God.[170] Or [alternatively], *he took me,* that is, the Son of God sent to me assumed the nature of my likeness. *Et assumpsit me de aquis multis; and received me out of many waters,* that is, he redeemed me from eternal death, from an abundance of sorrows.

---

**17{18}[18]** *He delivered me from my strongest enemies, and from them that hated me: for they were too strong for me.*

> *Eripuit me de inimicis meis fortissimis, et ab his qui oderunt me. Quoniam confortati sunt super me.*

---

165  Denis skips Ps. 17:11–13.
166  John 7:46.
167  Mark 3:17.
168  E. N. Denis skips over the remainder of verse 14, and skips entirely verses 15 and 16, without explanation.
169  Cf. Eph. 5:27.
170  John 1:12.

**17{18}[19]** *They prevented me in the day of my affliction: and the Lord became my protector.*

> *Praevenerunt me in die afflictionis meae; et factus est Dominus protector meus.*

**17{18}[20]** *And he brought me forth into a large place: he saved me, because he was well pleased with me.*

> *Et eduxit me in latitudinem; salvum me fecit, quoniam voluit me.*

**17{18}[18]** *Eripuit me de inimicis meis fortissimis, et ab his qui oderunt me; he delivered me from my strongest enemies, and from that hated me,* that is, from the power and servitude of the devil which, unless it is rescued by the grace of God, human weakness is not able to resist. Accordingly, there follows: *quoniam confortati sunt super me; for they were too strong for me,* that is, they were stronger than my natural powers, since they may be invisible, most astute, and indefatigable. **17{18}[19]** *Praevenerunt me, they prevented me,*[171] that is, at first they invaded me, asserting for themselves a claim to a certain kind of law in me, *in die afflictionis meae, in the day of my affliction,* that being in the day that I was conceived in the womb or the day I departed from the womb. Because we are conceived in original sin and are born with it, the demons injure us from the first instant of the beginning of our being, because at the suggestion of the devil it came to be that our first parents infected nature with such sin.[172] By the term *in the day of my affliction* we can also properly understand the day of our birth, because through pain and labor we are born to so many miseries. But from guilt of this sin, and from all other evils, Christ delivers us. Therefore is added [to the Psalm]: *et factus est Dominus protector meus; and the Lord became my protector.* **17{18}[20]** *Et eduxit me; and he brought me forth* from the bonds of sin, *in latitudinem, in a large place* of charity. For also in Baptism, where the original sin is taken away, faith, hope, charity, and the other virtues are infused [into us], so it is that the soul is expanded in order that it may receive God within itself. *Salvum me fecit, he saved me,* not because of any merits of mine, but *quoniam voluit me, because he was well-pleased with me,* that is, because it was pleasing to him, and because he chose me, as we read with respect to Ezechiel, *It is not for your sake that I will do this,* says the Lord, *let it be known to you, but for my holy name's sake.*[173]

---

171  E. N. For the use of the word "prevented," *see* footnote 17-66.

172  Gen. 3:1–6.

173  Ez. 36:22, 32. Denis quotes this with significant editing, quoting some from verse 22, some from verse 32, and then closing with some from verse 22.

**17{18}[21]** *And the Lord will reward me according to my justice; and will repay me according to the cleanness of my hands.*

> *Et retribuet mihi Dominus secundum iustitiam meam, et secundum puritatem manuum mearum retribuet mihi.*

**17{18}[22]** *Because I have kept the ways of the Lord; and have not done wickedly against my God.*

> *Quia custodivi vias Domini, nec impie gessi a Deo meo.*

Thereafter, the prophet [David] in the person of a virtuous man, says: **17{18}[21]** *Et retribuet mihi Dominus, and the Lord will reward me,* [referring to] Christ *the just judge,*[174] *secundum iustitiam meam, according to my justice,* that is, in relation to my good manner of living; *et secundum puritatem manuum mearum, and according to the cleanness of my hands,* that is, according to the cleanness of heart and of my deeds, *retribuet mihi, he will repay me,* in the present with grace, in the future with glory. So it is also written in Revelation, *Behold, I come quickly; and my reward is with me, to render to every man according to his works.*[175]     **17{18}[22]** *Quoniam custodivi vias Domini, [nec impie gessi a Deo meo]; because I have kept the way of the Lord, [and have not done wickedly against my God],* this refers to the commandments or the counsels of one walking by the narrow path.[176]

---

**17{18}[26]** *With the holy, you will be holy; and with the innocent man you will be innocent.*

> *Cum sancto sanctus eris, et cum viro innocente innocens eris.*

**17{18}[27]** *And with the elect you will be elect: and with the perverse you will be perverted.*

> *Et cum electo electus eris, et cum perverso perverteris.*

**17{18}[26]** *Cum sancto sanctus eris; with the holy, you will be holy,* because their good example aroused you to the imitation [of them]; *et cum viro innocente, and with the innocent man,* that is, the man doing no evil, *innocens eris, you will be innocent,* following in his innocence.     **17{18}[27]** *Et cum electo electus eris, and with the elect you will be elect,* that is, you will acquire the glory of the elect by following their mores and their life; *et*

---

174  2 Tim. 4:8.
175  Rev. 22:12.
176  Without discussion, Denis foregoes commentary on the remainder of verse 22, and skips over verses 23–25.

*cum perverso perverteris; and with the perverse you will be perverted.* Here, it is obvious that evil associations may injure just as good associations prove useful. Therefore, men desirous of advancing to God are to avoid — whether in the form of association, or, especially, in the form of familiarity — him who is not sincere, fearful, and solicitous in his service of God; because, as Scripture says, *He that touches pitch, shall be defiled with it.*[177] And the Apostle: *Go out,* he says, *from among them, and be you separate . . and touch not the unclean thing.*[178] In short, to be associated with, or familiar with, a virtuous man greatly confers a desire to grow spiritually. For this reason, it is written: *But be continually with a holy man, whomsoever you shall know to observe the fear of God, whose soul is according to your own soul.*[179]

---

**17{18}[33]** God who has girt me with strength; and made my way blameless.

 *Deus qui praecinxit me virtute, et posuit immaculatam viam meam.*

**17{18}[34]** Who has made my feet like the feet of harts: and who sets me upon high places.

 *Qui perfecit pedes meos tamquam cervorum, et super excelsa statuens me.*

**17{18}[33]**[180] *Deus qui praecinxit me virtute ; God who has girt me with strength,* that is, he arms with spiritual fortitude my soul, for whatever virtue there is in me is given to me by him; *et posuit immaculatam viam meam; and made by way blameless,* that is, he has made my manner of living free from servitude of mortal sin; or if such [sin] does strike and find its way in, by penance he will purge me of it.    **17{18}[34]** *Qui perfecit pedes meos, who has made my feet,* that is, the pathways of my soul, namely, my affections by which I accede to God, *tanquam cervorum, like the feet of harts,*[181] that is, with the quality of the feet of harts, so that like a hart runs quickly and ascends to the heights, so my soul, with fervent affection and a most responsive heart will keep and fulfill whatever it knows to be pleasing to God, keeping the commandments, or — better — running the way of the commandments,[182] that is, observing the

---

177  Ecclus. 13:1. The verse continues: *and he that has fellowship with the proud, shall put on pride.*

178  2 Cor. 6:17. E. N. St. Paul appears to be referring to Is. 52:11.

179  Ecclus. 37:15-16a.

180  Denis skips over verses 27-32.

181  On the meaning of "harts," see footnote 17-88

182  Cf. Ps. 118:32. *I have run the way of your commandments, when you did enlarge my heart.*

counsels that allow men to keep the commandments in an unencumbered manner. But all that he might do will be for the glory of God and eternal happiness, and not because it is temporally expedient or for human praise. And by this, he will aspire like a hart towards its high mountain, that is, towards the heavenly mansion. For this reason, [the Psalm] adds, *et super excelsa statuens me, and who sets me upon the high places*, that is, by the contemplation in and the hope in the heavenly things placed in me, giving me [the ability] to lead the angelic life in the flesh, as the Apostle says, *Our conversation is in heaven.*[183] This accords with him who fulfills this: *serve the Lord with a perfect and most sincere heart.*[184]

---

**17{18}[35]** *Who teaches my hands to war: and you have made my arms like a brazen bow.*

> *Qui docet manus meas ad praelium; et posuisti, ut arcum aereum, brachia mea.*

**17{18}[36]** *And you given me the protection of your salvation: and your right hand has held me up: And your discipline has corrected me unto the end: and your discipline, the same shall teach me.*

> *Et dedisti mihi protectionem salutis tuae, et dextera tua suscepit me; et disciplina tua correxit me in finem, et disciplina tua ipsa me docebit.*

**17{18}[35]** *Qui docet manus meas ad praelium, who teaches my hands to war*, that is, who gives me spiritual discretion and instructs me how particular vices are resisted, and how it is necessary to oppose the demons, how the world, how the flesh, and how to extirpate particular passions, and how I have the duty to defeat all indolence. *Who teaches my hands to war*, that is, my actions, *to war*, that is, so that on account no attack of an adversary I might cease doing good, that I might slacken neither for love nor partiality, that I might not break down for fear, that I might not be dejected for sorrow or with lack of courage; but that, in the manner of Judas Maccabaeus, I might be so instructed for spiritual battle, whose words point out the form of all spiritual battle, and prescribe the knowledge of fighting. Of whom one reads: *But Maccabaeus ever trusted with all hope that God would help them, and he exhorted his people not to fear, but ... to hope for victory from the Almighty. And speaking to them*

---

183  Phil. 3:20a. The verse continues: *from whence also we look for the Savior, our Lord Jesus Christ.*

184  Joshua 24:14a.

*out of the law, and the prophets.... He armed every one of them, not with defense of shield and spear, but with very good speeches.*[185] And again: *But Judas, and they that were with him ... fought with their hands, but with their hearts they called upon the Lord.*[186] So also it behooves us to do this against tempters, with hands (that is with good works) fighting against the malicious, and to call upon the Lord with our hearts for triumph, in the matter that is stated by Isaiah: *Who has walked in darkness and has no light? Let him hope in the name of the Lord and lean upon his God.*[187] Nevertheless, we must always do what is in us.[188]

Then in the person of the perfect man the prophet [David] says: *Et posuisti, you have made, O Lord, ut arcum aereum brachia mea, my arms like a brazen bow,*[189] that is my virtues and works, stabilizing me in all virtue and holy life, by which I overcome the ·devil, the flesh, and the world, as through *a brazen bow* the enemy might be more easily wounded and killed.   **17{18}[36]** *Et dedisti mihi protectionem salutis tuae; and you have given me the protection of your salvation*, that is, you protected me in the adversities and the temptations of the salvation of my soul, which is your salvation, for it is received from you; *et dextera tua, and your right hand*, that is, the goodness of your grace and your merciful presence, *suscepit me, has held me up*, taking refuge with you.

*Et disciplina tua, and your discipline*, that is, the merciful vengeance by which you in the present chastise your elect, so that you may not later punish them more heavily,[190] *correxit me, have corrected me*, that is, so that I might be distressed about and make amendment for my sins, *in finem, unto the end*, that is, for this reason: that I might attain eternal happiness, which is our end, in manner that you say: *Such as I love, I rebuke and chastise.*[191] For since sins are not able to be persevered in without satisfaction, it is a great mercy of God, and an excellent indication

---

185  2 Mac. 15: 7–9, 11.

186  2 Mac. 15: 26, 27.

187  Is. 50:10b.

188  *See* footnote 17-138. We might also turn to CCC § 2834: "'Pray and work.' 'Pray as if everything depended on God and work as if everything depended on you.'" The first quote is from the Rule of St. Benedict 20, 48. The second quote is generally attributed to St. Ignatius of Loyola. Joseph de Guibert, SJ, *The Jesuits: Their Spiritual Doctrine and Practice*, (Chicago: Loyola University Press, 1964), 148, n. 55.

189  For "brazen" *see* footnote 17-91.

190  E. N. These merciful chastisements may result in less sin in the future, and hence less temporal punishments associated with those sins that have been avoided through the current chastisement.

191  Rev. 3:19.

of divine love, when God at the present time scourges the sinner. For which reason, the Apostle [Paul] says: *But if you be without chastisement, whereof all are made partakers, then are you bastards, and not sons.*[192] Patiently, therefore, ought we endure whatever adversities befall us, and to ask the Lord that such passing punishments might be ascribed to us for our sins, so that such being purged, we might rendered more open in this life to his graces, and we may more exuberantly share in his glory in heaven. For as the Apostle says, *That which is at present momentary and light of our tribulation, works for us above measure exceedingly an eternal weight of glory.*[193] Or [we might comprehend it] thus: *Your discipline,* that is, the instruction of your discipline and the illumination of salvation, *have corrected me,* that is, has made me repent of my sins, and has made me willingly to assume punishments in satisfaction [of my sins], and to do all this because of eternal life: therefore it adds, *unto the end.*

*Et disciplina tua,* and *your discipline,* that is, the punishment inflicted in mercy, *ipsa me docebit, the same shall teach me* henceforth to be way of sin, to humble myself, and to be able to obtain counsel from others. Or [an additional insight is], *your discipline,* that is, your instructions, these will teach me, so that I might know myself and that I might walk before you with all mindfulness.[194] Indeed, the discipline of God makes us experienced, approved, and well-practiced.[195] For it is written: *What does he know, that has not been tried?* And again: *A man that has much experience, shall think of many things.*[196]

---

**17{18}[37]** *You have enlarged my steps under me; and my feet are not weakened.*

*Dilatasti gressus meos subtus me; et non sunt infirmata vestigia mea.*

**17{18}[37]** *Dilatasti gressus meos subtus me; you have enlarged my steps under me,* that is, by the fervor of charity and the increase of grace, you have made my acts that are under the empire of reason more ample, and more abundant or more in number, so as to abound in good works,[197]

---

192  Heb. 12:8. On the Pauline authorship of Hebrews which Denis accepts, *see* footnote 8-34.

193  2 Cor. 4:17.

194  *Cf.* Micah 6:8b.

195  L. *expertos nos facit, probatos et exercitatos.*

196  Ecclus. 34:9a.

197  *Cf.* 2 Cor. 9:8: *And God is able to make all grace abound in you; that you always, having all sufficiency in all things, may abound to every good work.*

and [you have caused] that the passions and movements or affections of the senses might be under the dominion of reason. Consequently, it adds: *et non sunt infirmata vestigia mea; and my feet are not weakened,* that is, my virtuous works, with which I followed you and by which I proceeded to your blessedness, were not found wanting.

---

**17{18}[38]** *I will pursue after my enemies, and overtake them: and I will not turn again till they are consumed.*

> *Persequar inimicos meos, et comprehendam illos; et non convertar donec deficiant.*

**17{18}[39]** *I will break them, and they shall not be able to stand: they shall fall under my feet.*

> *Confringam illos, nec poterunt stare; cadent subtus pedes meos.*

Because, O Lord, you have conveyed to me so much grace, so I confidently say:  **17{18}[38]** *Persequar inimicos meos, I will pursue after my enemies,* which endeavor to hinder me from the observance of the divine law: these I will fight against with devout prayer, with the tears of penance, by means of good and holy affections. For by these things demons are greatly afflicted, and their servants, namely, depraved men, are greatly dejected. *Et comprehendam eos, and I will overtake them,* that is, I will vanquish their temptations; *et non convertar, and I will not turn again,* from this resolution, *donec deficient, until they are consumed,* defeated by me.  **17{18}[39]** *Confringam illos, I will break them,* that is, I will begin to see the effects of their evil toppling in me, *nec poterunt stare, and they shall not be able to stand,* that is, to resist me. *Cadent subtus pedes meos, they shall fall under my feet,* that is, defeated from rendering my works deficient.

---

**17{18}[40]** *And you have girded me with strength unto battle; and have subdued under me them that rose up against me.*

> *Et praecinxisti me virtute ad bellum, et supplantasti insurgentes in me subtus me.*

**17{18}[42]** *They cried, but there was none to save them, to the Lord: but he heard them not.*

> *Clamaverunt, nec erat qui salvos faceret; ad Dominum, nec exaudivit eos.*

**17{18}[43]** *And I shall beat them as small as the dust before the wind; I shall bring them to naught, like the dirt in the streets.*

> *Et comminuam eos ut pulverem ante faciem venti; ut lutum platearum delebo eos.*

**17{18}[40]** *Et praecinxisti me virtute; and you have girded me with strength,* that is, with spiritual weapons, *ad bellum, unto battle* against all temptations; *et supplantasti insurgentes in me subtus me, and you have subdued under me them that rose up against me,* because I will attribute all my victory to you. **17{18}[42]**[198] *Clamaverunt, they cried,* my enemies [cried], namely, wicked men at the time of their anguish for help, *nec erat qui salvos faceret eos; but there was none to save* them from the vengeance of divine justice, which often in the present time begins to wreak vengeance on the sins of the reprobate who in the future will be eternally punished. And because no one will be able to render aid, so they cry out together *ad Dominum: nec exaudivit eos; to the Lord: but he heard them not:* because the cry of their prayer does not come from a heartfelt repentance, nor out of divine love, but from the anguish of punishment, and from servile fear, which is deserving of nothing, as in the manner that is written about Antiochus:[199] *This wicked man prayed to the Lord, of whom he was not like to obtain mercy.*[200]   **17{18}[43]** *Et comminuam eos ut pulverem ante faciem venti; and I shall beat them as small as the dust before the wind,* that means that which has already been said: *I will break them, and they shall not be able to stand. I shall beat,* it says, *them,* not their nature, but I will oppose their perversity. Therefore, *ut lutum platearum delebo eos; I shall bring them to naught, like the dirt in the streets,* that is, I will repel and will cast off those from my [will's] consent.

---

**17{18}[44]** *You will deliver me from the contradictions of the people: you will make me head of the Gentiles.*

> *Eripies me de contradictionibus populi; constitues me in caput gentium.*

---

198 Denis skips verse 41.
199 Antiochus IV Epiphanes (ca. 215 B.C.–164 B.C.) was the king of the Seleucid Empire from 175 B.C. until his death. His harsh rule over the Jews in Judea resulted in the Maccabean revolt. The wretched end of Antiochus, as related by 2 Macc. 9:5–12, certainly is symbolic of his fall from grace, and his prayers came too late and are based upon improper motive and so were not heard by God. 2 Mac. 9:12–13. There are times, St. Jean Vianney noted, when between the bridge and the water, an act of sorrow for sins may be heard. But there are times—alas for the soul of Antiochus if Denis is right—when they are not.
200 2 Mac. 9:13.

**17{18}[45]** *A people, which I knew not, has served me: at the hearing of the ear they have obeyed me.*

> *Populus, quem non cognovi, servivit mihi; in auditu auris obedivit mihi.*

**17{18}[46]** *The children that are strangers have lied to me, strange children have faded away, and have halted from their paths.*

> *Filii alieni mentiti sunt mihi, filii alieni inveterati sunt, et claudicaverunt a semitis suis.*

In addition, the Church says this to Christ:    **17{18}[44]** *Eripies me de contradictionibus populi; you will deliver me from the contradictions of the people,* that is, the perfidy and the attack of heretics, of schismatics, and of all those who are detracting to me. For God does not abandon his elect forever, but ultimately he will deliver them. *Constitues me in caput gentium; you will make me head of the Gentiles,* that is, you will make me to have power over all peoples. For of all peoples, the Christian people is the most worthy and is superior to all other Gentiles: to whom the prince of the Apostles thus says, *But you are a chosen generation, a kingly priesthood, a holy nation, a purchased people.*[201] Or [this verse can be understood] thus: *you will make me head,* that is, the prelates and priests of the Church, *head of the Gentiles,* that is, to be in rule and in power over the rest.    **17{18}[45]** *Populus quem non cognovi; a people, which I knew not,* that is, hardened and unbelieving sinners, *servivit mihi, has served me,* that is, after they were converted by repentance and belief; and then *in auditu auris obedivit mihi; at the hearing of the ear, they have obeyed me,* that is, [they have obeyed] the precepts of the Church.    **17{18}[46]** *Filii alieni, children that are strangers,* that is, the Christians in name only, the dissimulators, the contumacious, the hypocrites, the false religious, *mentiti sunt mihi, have lied to me:* because they say one thing, but they do another; they exhibit one thing in appearance, and another thing in real life. *They come . . . in the clothing of sheep,* but within *they are ravening wolves.*[202] *Filii alieni inveterate sunt; strange children have faded away,* that is, they are obdurate in vice. For they did not pay heed to the Apostle exhorting to the Colossians: Strip yourselves *of the old man with his deeds,* and put on *the new, . . . who is renewed unto knowledge of God.*[203] And elsewhere: *Be renewed in the spirit of your mind, . . . and be you kind one*

---

201  1 Pet. 2:9.
202  Matt. 7:15.
203  Col. 3:9b–10a.

to another; merciful, forgiving one another, even as God has forgiven you
in Christ.[204] *Et claudicaverunt a semitis suis; and have halted from their
paths*, that is, they have strayed from the doctrine and the law of God
that had been set forth to them.

---

**17{18}[47]** *The Lord lives! And blessed be my God! And let the God of
my salvation be exalted!*

> *Vivit Dominus! Et benedictus Deus meus! Et exaltetur Deus
> salutis meae!*

**17{18}[48]** *O God, who avenges me, and subdues the people under me, my
deliverer from my enemies.*

> *Deus qui das vindictas mihi, et subdis populos sub me; liberator
> meus de inimicis meis iracundis.*

**17{18}[49]** *And you will lift me up above them that rise up against me:
from the unjust man you will deliver me.*

> *Et ab insurgentibus in me exaltabis me; a viro iniquo eripies me.*

Finally, the Church, giving thanks to God for the benefits already
called to mind, says:   **17{18}[47]** *Vivit Dominus! et benedictus Deus
meus! et exaltetur Deus salutis meae! The Lord lives, and blessed be my
God, and let the God of my salvation be exalted!* Which verse is sufficiently explained in the preceding [Article].   **17{18}[48]** *Deus qui das
vindictas mihi; God who avenges me*, punishing the persecutors of the
just and of the Church: in the manner that is written: *Vengeance is
mine, I will repay, says the Lord;*[205] *et subdis populos sub me; and you
subdue the people under me*, converting sinners to the bosom of mother
Church, and to holy obedience, or, subduing the unbelievers with the
power of faith; *liberator meus de inimicis meis iracundis; my deliverer
from my enemies*, as, for example, the demons: in which (according to
Dionysius[206]) there is an irrational fury, a mad desire, and a shameless
imagination.[207] However, this [notion of Dionysius] must be sagaciously

---

204  Eph. 4:23, 32.

205  Rom. 12:19. *E. N. See also* Heb. 10:30; Ez. 25:14

206  For Dionysius the Areopagite, *see* footnote P-36.

207  *E. N. furor irrationalis, amens concupiscentia, et phantasia proterva.* The text
      reads *phantasma protervum.* The Carthusian editor, however, suggests (rightly)
      that Denis intended *phantasia proterva* (a reckless, impudent, wanton, shame-
      less imagination or fantasy, one that is vehement, violent, pressing), a sort of
      shameless or evil *idée fixe.* The trinity of defects comes from Pseudo-Dionysius's

understood [as being metaphorical or analogical], since demons, as they are incorporeal beings, do not have material passions. And not only *my deliverer from my enemies*— O Lord — of demons, but also of irascible, perverse, and reprobate men.   **17{18}[49]** *Et ab insurgentibus in me, and from those that rise up against me*, namely from the adversaries who rise up against me, so long as I live in this present state of exile, as Augustine says: *Persevere unto the end, because temptation perseveres unto the end.*[208] From this, therefore, *exaltabis me, you will lift me up*, giving me victory in the present, and the crown of glory in the future; *a viro iniquo, from the unjust man*, that is, from any pestiferous man, *eripies me, you will deliver me*, that I will not be infected by him.

---

**17{18}[50]** *Therefore will I give glory to you, O Lord, among the nations, and I will sing a psalm to your name.*

> *Propterea confitebor tibi in nationibus, Domine, et nomini tuo psalmum dicam.*

**17{18}[51]** *Giving great deliverance to his king, and showing mercy to David his anointed: and to his seed forever.*

> *Magnificans salutes regis eius, et faciens misericordiam christo suo David, et semini eius usque in saeculum.*

**17{18}[50]** *Propterea, therefore*, that is, because of your great benefits, *confitebor tibi in nationibus, Domine; I will glory to you, O Lord, among the nations*, preaching and gloriously praising your name before the people, and joyfully and with great affection making known to them your

---

*The Divine Names*. See *De Div. Nom.* IV, 23. The term *phantasia proterva* is consistent with St. Thomas's numerous quotations of Dionysius in the *Summa Theologiae*, Ia, q. 54, art. 5, and elsewhere, e.g., *In II Sent.*, d. 7, q. 2 art. 1 et ad 1; *De Potentia*, q. 6 art. 6 ad 3; *De Malo*, q. 16 art.1 ad 3; *Quest. disp. De Anima*, q. 19 ad 8. *Phantasia proterva* is difficult to translate and a quick internet search reveals such options as "arbitrary fantasy," "reckless fantasy," "evil imagination," "shameless imagination," "perverse imagination," "headlong fancy," and "headstrong fancy." Not only is it difficult to translate; as Denis makes clear, it must be understood with sagacity since it imputes passions to demons, which — being spirits — are dispassionate.

208  E. N. *Persevera usque in finem, quia tentatio perseverat usque in finem.* This is a popular misquotation from St. Augustine's Tractate on the Gospel of John. See *In Ev. Ioan.*, 45, 13. The real quote is: *Tentatio accidit, persevera usque in finem: quia tentatio non perseverat usque in finem.* "Temptation can strike anytime: persevere unto the end, because temptation does not persevere unto the end."

benefits and your mercy. This the Church does daily through preachers of the divine word. *Et nomini tuo, and to your name,* O Lord, *Psalmum dicam, I will sing a Psalm,* praising you by mouth and by deeds. This everyone is able to do and ought to do of themselves, because the Lord is   **17{18}[51]** *magnificans salutes, giving great deliverance,* that is, [giving the] greatly esteemed and highly appreciated redemption and happiness or the double robe [of happiness of soul and body],[209] *regis eius, to his king,* that is, to any one of the Christians or his elect; for these are called kings because they have dominion over the devil and over their own souls, and thus are stronger than a king assaulting cities and fortresses. Indeed, so high a value and so great an estimation did God place upon our salvation, that is, the glorification of our body and our soul, that in order to restore them, he sent his Only-Begotten to the world.[210] He did not give such a kind and so great a gift for little reason. And you, therefore, magnify and greatly esteem this salvation of yours; do not be willing to neglect it because of bodily delights, because of sensory comforts, or because of temporal honors; but put on a manly and noble soul, and esteem little and spurn all transitory, vain, or vile things in the purchase of eternal and invisible goods. *Et, and* the Lord *faciens misericordiam Christo suo David; showing mercy to David his anointed,* that is, any perfect man, one excellently anointed with the anointment of the Holy Spirit, *et semini eius, and his seed,* that is, to them whom he spiritually generates in Christ, teaching them by word and deed: in the manner that the Apostle said of some: *My little children, of whom I am in labor again, until Christ be formed in you;*[211] *usque in saeculum, forever.*

That which in the preceding two expositions[212] has been declared is here omitted.

Finally, how blessed is he who can recite this Psalm about these great gifts of God and sublime perfections as applying to himself and can sing to glory of the Lord! But he who has not yet arrived at such perfection so that he is able to recite this Psalm as applying to his own person, can learn from it how far away he is from true perfection, how much he has to strive, and that which is demanded from him by the

---

209  *E. N. duplicem stolam.* The notion of a "double robe" (*stola duplici*) refers to the double "robe" or "stole" of happiness of soul and happiness of body.

210  *Cf.* John 3:16: *For God so loved the world, as to give his only begotten Son; that whosoever believes in him, may not perish, but may have life everlasting.*

211  Gal. 4:19.

212  *See* Articles XLII–XLIII.

Lord; and he should apply to order his life in such a fashion, and to acquire such perfection, so that he may be able to sing with a ready and grateful heart, as applicable to himself, all that which has been stated to the honor of God.

# PRAYER

REMOVE FROM US, O LORD, THE DARKNESS of our sins, and enlighten our hearts with the lamp of your consubstantial Word: gird us, we beseech you, with his virtue, and show us the unsullied life in him.

*Amove a nobis, Domine, peccatorum nostrorum obscura, et*
*illumina corda nostra consubstantialis Verbi tui lucerna:*
*eius nos, quaesumus, virtute praecinge, et viam*
*nobis in eo immaculatam ostende.*

# Psalm 18

## ARTICLE XLV

**EXPOSITION OF THE EIGHTEENTH PSALM:**
*CAELI ENARRANT GLORIAM DEI, &c.*
THE HEAVENS SHOW FORTH THE GLORY OF GOD, *&c.*

**18{19}[1]**   *Unto the end. A Psalm for David.*

*In finem. Psalmus David.*

**18{19}[2]**   *The heavens show forth the glory of God, and the firmament declares the work of his hands.*

*Caeli enarrant gloriam Dei, et opera manuum eius annuntiat firmamentum.*

**18{19}[3]**   *Day to day utters speech, and night to night shows knowledge.*

*Dies diei eructat verbum, et nox nocti indicat scientiam.*

BEFORE THIS PSALM IS AGAIN WRITTEN THIS title:   **18{19}[1]** *In finem, Psalmus David; unto the end, a Psalm for David:* that is, this Psalm is written by David, have regard *unto the end,* that is, unto Christ. For here it speaks of the first advent of Christ, who was made in the end of ages[1] and the fullness of time.[2] And it speaks of the preaching of the evangelical law, and of the purity of the Christian law, and says:   **18{19}[2]** *Caeli enarrant gloriam Dei; the heavens show forth the glory of God.* This can be understood in three ways. The first is thus: *Caeli,* that is, the holy Evangelists and Apostles, *enarrant gloriam Dei, show forth the glory of God,* that is, they preached the kingdom and the excellence of Christ. *Et opera manuum eius, the work of his hands,* that is, the marvelous works of Christ, namely his miraculous works, which are *the works of his hands,* that is, the divine and human powers. For the miracles of Christ were principally done by divine power, but instrumentally through the human power. Hence, the humanity of Christ

---

1  E. N. Christ came at the last age (*in fine saeculorum*), the sixth age, the final age prior to the consummation of the world. For the "seven ages" of history, *see* footnote 11-1.

2  Gal. 4:14. *But when the fullness of the time was come, God sent his Son, made of a woman, made under the law.*

was united to his divine nature as an instrument is joined and moved by its artist. *Annuntiat firmamentum, the firmament declares,* that is, the Church, in which perfect men are confirmed, as the stars in heaven are affixed;³ and the Church is firmly established on the firm rock which is Christ. The Apostles and the Evangelists may be understood as *the heavens* because their heavenly manner of life and because of the divine dwelling [through sanctifying grace], and because of their eminence of graces; and so also all spiritual men are called *the heavens,* in the manner that Moses says: *Hear, O you heavens, the things I speak, let the earth give ear to the words of my mouth.*⁴ And Isaiah: *Hear, O you heavens, and give ear, O earth.*⁵ Indeed, quite rightly are spiritual men called *the heavens,* to whom the Apostle speaks: *But you are not in the flesh, but in the spirit.*⁶   **18{19}[3]** *Dies diei eructat verbum, day to day utters speech:* that is, those illuminated by the divinity and wise men utter, or with a full heart announce, *day to day,* that is, to spiritual and learned men, *speech (verbum),* that is, Christ, inasmuch as he is God, as the Apostle says, *Howbeit we speak wisdom among the perfect;*⁷ and also, *And if we have known Christ according to the flesh; but now we know him so no longer.*⁸ *Et nox nocti indicat scientiam; and night to night shows knowledge:* that is, men of little knowledge, or those previously discussed perfect men receiving a person from those who are imperfect (in the manner the Apostle asserts, *I became all things to all men... To the weak I became weak, that I might gain the weak),*⁹ so that they might teach men who

---

3  E. N. Such confirmation, of course, refers to the Church triumphant in heaven, and the suffering souls in the Church suffering; it does not apply in the same manner to the Church militant, where, without the grace of final perseverance, the fall from sanctifying grace through mortal sin is possible since grace, unless it is finally efficacious, is frustratable. This is also implied since the firmament or the heavens is symbolic of the Church in heaven. Denis could also mean the ordained priesthood when he refers to the "perfect men" that are "confirmed."

4  Deut. 32:1. E. N. This is the beginning of the Canticle of Moses, and is addressed to the Hebrews, whom he calls "you heavens."

5  Is. 1:2a.

6  Rom. 8:9a.

7  1 Cor. 2:6a.

8  2 Cor. 5:16b.

9  1 Cor. 9:22. E. N. Denis edits this verse for his purposes, placing the latter part first, the first part later, and editing out a portion. This sort of commendable Pauline "accompaniment" with the sinner, the weak, or the ignorant and uninstructed allows for an accommodation to the imperfect to the extent that virtue or the requirements of morality or doctrine permit; however, as St. Augustine points out in his letters to St. Jerome, St. Paul became all to all *compassione misericordia, non simulatione fallaciae* and *non mentientis astu, sed compatientis*

are still carnal and unformed, *knowledge,* that is, knowledge pertaining
to the created nature of Christ, namely, the mystery of his humanity,
in a manner so that they might eagerly pursue it: as the Apostle says
elsewhere: *I, brethren, could not speak to you as unto spiritual, but as unto
carnal. As unto little ones in Christ. I gave you milk to drink, not meat.*[10]

This part of the Psalm can be explained in a second manner thus:
*Caeli, the heavens,* that is, the celestial orbs, *enarrant gloriam Dei, show
forth the glory of God,* that is, they display his majesty and his power.
For *the heavens* are said to show forth *the glory of God,* as they are said
to bless God or to praise him, namely, because they supply to those
who wonder at them an occasion and the matter for contemplating the
power, the wisdom, and the perfection of the Creator.[11] For this reason,
it is written: *Lift up your eyes on high, and see who has created these
things.*[12] *Et, and* in a similar manner, *opera manuum eius, the work of his
hands,* that is, the creatures of divine power, *annuntiat firmamentum, the
firmament declares,* that is, the eighth sphere[13] — in which the stars are
fixed — certainly *declares* in a material way the works of God, because it
is an object the contemplation of which shows how powerful and glorious are all the things that have been created by God. *Dies diei eructat
verbum, et nox nocti indicate scientiam; day to day utters speech, and night
to night shows knowledge.* For time is used to express that which is made
in time,[14] and thus day and night are said to utter *speech* also to indicate
*knowledge,* because such works are made through an interval of time;
and from day to day and from night to night the knowledge of God or
the preaching of Christ increased. This way of reading is according to
the first book of the Maccabees: *Jonathan saw that the time served him.*[15]

---

*affectu,* "with the compassion of mercy, not by the donning of error," and "not by
the adroitness of lying, but with the affection of compassion." *Eps.* 40, 4, 4, PL 33,
155; 82, 3, 26, PL 33, 237.

10  1 Cor. 3:1–2a.

11  E. N. "Wonder is the feeling of a philosopher, and philosophy begins in wonder."
Plato, *Theaetetus* 155c–d (tr. Jowett); "For men were first led to study philosophy,
as indeed they are today, by wonder." Aristotle, *Metaphysics* 982B (tr. A. E. Taylor).

12  Is. 40:26a.

13  E. N. This is a reference to the geocentric medieval cosmology which was based
upon the ideas of Ptolemy (*fl.* 150 B. C.). The earth — fixed and motionless — was
at the center of the cosmos, and there were various revolving concentric spheres
named after the planets. The outermost, or eighth, sphere was that of the fixed
stars (the firmament), which is what Denis is referring to. Outside that eighth
sphere was the Prime Mover (*Primum Mobile*).

14  E. N. *Dicitur tempus facere id quod fit in tempore.* In other words, the word "day" or
"night" — words expressive of time — are used to express things occurring in time.

15  1 Mach. 12:1a.

The third explanation of this passage is anagogical, so that it is [to be understood] in this sense: *Caeli, the heavens,* that is, the angelic spirits and all the blessed, *enarrant gloriam Dei, show forth the glory of God,* because they unceasingly praise God; *et opera manuum eius, and the work of his hands,* that is, the effects of divine power, *annuntiat firmamentum, the firmament declares,* that is, Christ, who is the head and the strength of all the saints, and he illumines all those enjoying the vision of God (*comprehensores*) in heaven by reason of his divine effect. *Dies diei eructat verbum; day to day utters speech,* that is, the superior angels infuse the inferior angels out of the fullness of their knowledge, cleansing, illuminating, and perfecting them, according to Dionysius [the Areopagite].[16] *Et nox nocti indicat scientiam; and night to night shows knowledge,* because demons often reveal certain secrets to perverse men.

Although the second interpretation is seen to be more literal, the first, however, if truth be told, is literal from the intention of the prophet [David], and is more fitting and more consistent with the [parts of the Psalm] that follow.

---

**18{19}[4]**   *There are no speeches nor languages, where their voices are not heard.*

*Non sunt loquelae, neque sermones, quorum non audiantur voces eorum.*

**18{19}[5]**   *Their sound has gone forth into all the earth: and their words unto the ends of the world.*

*In omnem terram exivit sonus eorum, et in fines orbis terrae verba eorum.*

**18{19}[4]** *Non sunt loquelae, neque sermones, there are no speeches nor languages,* that is, there is no kind of language or words, *quorum non audiantur voces eorum, where their voices are not heard,* that is, from them, namely from the *heaven* we have just mentioned and of the Apostles. For the Apostles spoke all languages.[17] And Paul said: *I thank my God that I speak in tongues for all of you.*[18]   **18{19}[5]** *In omnem terram exivit sonus eorum, their sound has gone forth into all the earth,* that is, [the sound] of the Apostles; *et in fines orbis terrae verba eorum, and their words unto the ends of the world:* because the Apostles made a division

---

16   E. N. on Dionysius the Areopagite (Pseudo-Dionysius) *see* footnote P-36.
17   Acts 2:4, 6, 8, 11.
18   1 Cor. 14:18.

within themselves,[19] wherein they themselves or their disciples would preach the Gospel of Christ in the four quarters of the earth and in the principle parts of the world.[20] And this is what is predicted by Isaiah: *From the ends of the earth we have heard the praises and the glory of the Just One.*[21] And again through Isaiah the Lord openly says: *I will send some of those who will have been saved to the Gentiles in the sea, to Africa, and to those who draw the bow in Lydia, to Italy and Greece, to islands far away, and.... And they will announce my glory to the Gentiles.*[22] Finally, with respect to that which is written — *their sound has gone forth into all the earth: and their words unto the ends of the world* — the Apostles were sent to declare openly [the Gospel], for *faith comes from hearing*[23] and from the preaching of the Apostles. Hence, it follows that this Psalm speaks of Christ and the Apostles and the preaching of the evangelical law.

---

18{19}[6]   *He has set his tabernacle in the sun: and he, as a bridegroom coming out of his bride chamber, has rejoiced as a giant to run the way.*

*In sole posuit tabernaculum suum; et ipse tamquam sponsus procedens de thalamo suo, exsultavit ut gigas ad currendam viam.*

18{19}[7]   *His going out is from the end of heaven, and his circuit even to the end thereof: and there is no one that can hide himself from his heat.*

*A summo caelo egressio eius. Et occursus eius usque ad summum eius; nec est qui se abscondat a calore eius.*

Thereafter is added matters relating to the incarnation of Christ: 18{19}[6] *In sole, in the sun,* that is, in the inferior world, under the sun, namely before the eyes of men, *posuit, he has set,* the Son of God *tabernaculum suum, his tabernacle,* that is, the assumed [human] body which is called the temple of the invisible Godhead: because, as is said by the Prophet [Baruch], *He was seen on earth and he conversed with men;*[24] since he who before was hidden in the bosom of God the Father, would

---

19  This is a reference to the so-called *divisio Apostolorum* where the Apostles divided up the known world among themselves, assigning parts of the world to certain apostles, traditionally allotting, for example, Spain (Hispania) to St. James the Greater.

20  Mark 16:20.

21  Is. 24:16.

22  Is. 66:19.

23  Rom. 10:17.

24  Baruch 3:38.

appear in the form of assumed flesh; and he who before dwelled in light inaccessible, now through his incarnation would show himself visible to the eye, and palpable to the hands, as John witnessed: *He whom we have seen with our own eyes, he whom we have heard, . . . and whom our hands have certainly touched: he is the Word of Life.*[25] Finally, we know that this incarnation of God was foretold by Zachariah, where it says thus: *Sing praise and rejoice, daughter of Zion, for behold, I approach, and I will dwell in your midst, says the Lord.*[26] And the Lord through Isaiah says: *I myself that spoke, behold I am here.*[27] And again: *The first, that is, eternal God, shall say to Zion, behold I am here.*[28] Or [we might look at it] thus: *In the sun,* that is, in the blessed virgin Mary, *he has set* Christ *his tabernacle,* that is, his Body, dwelling in her womb for nine months, in the manner that Jeremiah says: *The Lord has created a new thing upon the earth; a woman shall compass a man.*[29] For the most happy virgin Mary is called the sun because of the most excellent splendor of divine grace in her. Of which [excellent splendor of grace] the Song of Songs says: *You are all fair, O my love.*[30] And again: *fair as the moon, bright as the sun.*[31] *Et ipse,* and he, Christ *tamquam sponsus procedens de thalamo suo; as a bridegroom coming out of his bride chamber,* that is, from the virginal womb, in which, putting on flesh, he espoused the Church to himself, as before he had for a long time and frequently promised through the Prophets.

*Exsultavit ut gigas ad currendam viam; he has rejoiced as a giant to run the way,* that is, Christ joyfully came, and cheerfully descended into the womb of his most beloved Daughter, the most loveable Virgin, *to run the way,* that is, quickly pursuing the mystery of human redemption; or [alternatively], *to run the way,* that is, to abide in this world, he whose life is the way to the blessed life [in heaven].    **18{19}[7]** *A summo caelo egressio eius; his going out is from the end of heaven.* For Christ descended from the bosom of the Father to the womb of the Virgin; he descended from the intellectual heaven to the sensible world. For he said: *And no man has ascended into heaven, but he that descended from heaven, the Son of man who is in heaven.*[32] But he descended, not by a change of place,

---

25  1 John 1:1. E. N. Denis reverses the order (heard, seen, etc.) to (seen, heard, etc.).
26  Zach. 2:10.
27  Is. 52:6.
28  Is. 41:27a. E. N. Denis changes this verse by changing *Ecce adsunt* ("Behold, they are here") to *Ecce adsum* ("Behold, I am here").
29  Jer. 31:22b.
30  Songs. 4:7. The verse continues: *and there is not a spot in you.*
31  Songs 6:9b.
32  John 3:13.

but by newly appearing, not by means of essence, but [by means] of effect (*effectus*). For he is the one who testified through Jeremiah: *I fill heaven and earth.*[33] *Et occursus eius, and his circuit,* that is, Christ's return or his Ascension,[34] *usque ad summum eius, even to the end thereof,* that is, even unto that same place from where he left, namely, from the right hand of the Father, as he said: *I came forth from the Father, and am come into the world; again I leave the world, and I go to the Father.*[35]

*Nec est qui se abscondat a calore eius; and there is no one that can hide himself from his heat,* that is, nobody is able to excuse himself from the love of Christ, because these benefits are so openly many and so great that ignorance excuses no one. Consequently, all are obliged to love Christ above all things. Or [we can understand this verse] thus: *there is no one that can hide himself from his heat,* that is, from the operations or examinations of the Holy Spirit, who is the most ardent love of the Father and the Son. For Christ foretold of the Holy Spirit when he said: *when he,* the Spirit of truth, *is come, he will convict the world of sin, and of justice, and of judgment.*[36] For he convicts men of the sins committed, of justice omitted, and [he spurs them] to consider in advance and with fear the judgment by which they might be condemned. Or because *there is no one that can hide himself from his heat* is what is said, therefore what is meant is [something along these lines:] because so great is the liberality of grace of the Holy Spirit during the time of the new law, no one ought to hide from its merit and receiving it.

---

18{19}[8]  *The law of the Lord is unspotted, converting souls: the testimony of the Lord is faithful, giving wisdom to little ones.*

*Lex Domini immaculata, convertens animas; testimonium Domini fidele, sapientiam praestans parvulis.*

18{19}[8]  *Lex Domini, the law of the Lord,* that is, the Christian religion and the tradition of Christ, *immaculata, is unspotted,* having no vice or impurity mixed in with it, *convertens animas, converting souls,*

---

33  Jer. 23:24b. E. N. Denis adapts the verse from an interrogative to declarative statement.
34  E. N. The Latin *occursus* is the sense of a course or a circuit, implying a sort of circular *exitus/reditus*, a coming forth and a returning back, which is a thought that Denis seizes upon by referring to Christ's summary of his mission in John 16:28.
35  John 16:28.
36  John 16:8.

that is, men (for it states a part for the whole),[37] because he draws back those who obey him from unlawful and fleeting things to holy words, and to the highest and unchangeable good. *Testimonium Domini fidele, the testimony of the Lord is faithful*: that is, the articles of the Christian faith are true, and are not false; *sapientiam praestans parvulis, giving wisdom to little ones*, that is, the knowledge of divine things furnished to the humble, who submit their intellect to the faith, and who confirm what they believe with deeds. Hence Isaiah says: *Unless you believe, you will not understand*.[38] And the Savior: *I confess to you*, he says, *O Father, Lord of heaven and earth, because you have hidden these things from the wise and prudent, and have revealed them to little ones*,[39] that is, the faith and manner of life of the humble. But *the testimony* properly pertains to those things that must be believed (*credenda*) just as it does the [moral or religious] precepts that need to be done (*agenda*).

---

37  E. N. That is the word "souls" is used synecdochally to refer to men. *See* footnote 13-12.

38  Is. 7:9 *according to* LXX. E. N. Denis quotes the Latin translation of the Septuagint Greek: *Nisi credideritis, non intelligetis* (ἐὰν μὴ πιστεύσητε οὐδὲ μὴ συνῆτε). The Sixto-Clementine Vulgate reads *Si non credideritis, non permanebitis*, "if you will not believe, you shall not continue." In his encyclical letter *Lumen Fidei*, Pope Francis comments on this issue: "Unless you believe, you will not understand (*cf.* Is 7:9). The Greek version of the Hebrew Bible, the Septuagint translation produced in Alexandria, gives the above rendering of the words spoken by the prophet Isaiah to King Ahaz. In this way, the issue of the knowledge of truth became central to faith. The Hebrew text, though, reads differently; the prophet says to the king: 'If you will not believe, you shall not be established.' Here there is a play on words, based on two forms of the verb *'amān*: 'you will believe' (*ta'amînû*) and 'you shall be established' (*tē'āmēnû*). Terrified by the might of his enemies, the king seeks the security that an alliance with the great Assyrian empire can offer. The prophet tells him instead to trust completely in the solid and steadfast rock which is the God of Israel. Because God is trustworthy, it is reasonable to have faith in him, to stand fast on his word. He is the same God that Isaiah will later call, twice in one verse, the God who is Amen, 'the God of truth' (*cf.* Is 65:16), the enduring foundation of covenant fidelity. It might seem," Pope Francis continues, "that the Greek version of the Bible, by translating 'be established' as 'understand,' profoundly altered the meaning of the text by moving away from the biblical notion of trust in God towards a Greek notion of intellectual understanding. Yet this translation, while certainly reflecting a dialogue with Hellenistic culture, is not alien to the underlying spirit of the Hebrew text. The firm foundation that Isaiah promises to the king is indeed grounded in an understanding of God's activity and the unity which he gives to human life and to the history of his people. The prophet challenges the king, and us, to understand the Lord's ways, seeing in God's faithfulness the wise plan which governs the ages." *LF*, No. 23.

39  Luke 10:21.

**18{19}[9]** *The justices of the Lord are right, rejoicing hearts: the commandment of the Lord is lightsome, enlightening the eyes.*

*Iustitiae Domini rectae, laetificantes corda; praeceptum Domini lucidum, illuminans oculos.*

**18{19}[9]** *Iustitiae Domini, the justices of the Lord,* that is, the divine precepts, *rectae, are right* and just, and leading without error to beatitude, *laetificantes corda, rejoicing hearts* of them who observe them in charity. For it is naturally pleasing to live virtuously and to obey God in all things. For this reason (according to the Philosopher)[40] a sign of virtue is the delight in the connected works [flowing from virtue]. *Praeceptum Domini lucidum, the commandment of the Lord is lightsome,* that is, brilliant and splendid like a ray of divine justice and eternal light, *illuminans oculis, enlightening the eyes* of the heart, namely the intellect and the memory, so that it may not sink into the darkness of vices, but remain in God.

---

**18{19}[10]** *The fear of the Lord is holy, enduring for ever and ever: the judgments of the Lord are true, justified in themselves.*

*Timor Domini sanctus, permanens in saeculum saeculi; iudicia Domini vera, iustificata in semetipsa.*

**18{19}[11]** *More to be desired than gold and many precious stones: and sweeter than honey and the honeycomb.*

*Desiderabilia super aurum et lapidem pretiosum multum; et dulciora super mel et favum.*

**18{19}[10]** *Timor Domini sanctus, the fear of the Lord is holy,* that is, filial fear, amicable and chaste, not servile or of man, *permanens in saeculum saeculi, is enduring for ever and ever:* [this is so] because it begins here and it perseveres in heaven as a habit,[41] and also as any particular act performed under [the habit of filial fear] subsists in heaven insofar as reverential submission [to God would require it]. But it does not remain in heaven as from a fear that arises from aversion (*ad fugam*): for the blessed know that they are not able to turn away from God,

---

40  *E. N.* A reference to Aristotle. *See* footnote 16-36.

41  *E. N.* By "habit" Denis understands a stable quality in a person by which one acts easily and pleasantly, in this case, an infused grace by God that confirms us in obedience to the Lord. *See ST,* IaIIae, q. 49, arts. 1‑4. In Latin, the word *habitus* can mean either "dress" or "nature," and so a habit might be seen as something with which we are draped or bedecked which affects our nature.

consequently they do not fear an evil future, but they remain subject to God with reverential fear.[42]

*Iudicia Domini, the judgments of the Lord*, that is, all the dictates and all the judgments of divine Wisdom are, *vera, true*, and are *iustificata in semetipsa, justified in themselves*: because from the very fact that they are judgments of God it is necessary that they will be just and holy; there is no other reason required or no other higher authority to be invoked, because God is the measure (*mensura*) and the ground (*ratio*) of all truth and justice.   18{19}[11] *Desiderabilia super aurum et lapidem pretiosum multum; More to be desired than gold and many precious stones.* For nothing of bodily or sensible goods can be so loveable and also so desirable as the divine judgment, that is, the precepts and the testimonies of the divine law, which are given and approved by God and lead to eternal happiness. Hence, it is said in a later Psalm: *The law of your mouth is good to me, above thousands of gold and silver.*[43] *Et dulciora super mel et favum, and sweeter than honey and the honeycomb*, that is, in observing the divine judgments and precepts one obtains greater sweetness than in any other carnal or sensible thing. For the spiritual delights by their nature are greater than the delights of the body, although at times from our perspective it may seem the opposite because of our imperfections and our being prone to evil. But to the perfect man, how sweet it is to experience the Lord,[44] sweeter are divine things than any carnal thing; indeed, the more they partake in divine things, the more they will see as foolish the things of the senses.

---

18{19}[12] *For your servant keeps them, and in keeping them there is a great reward.*

*Etenim servus tuus custodit ea; in custodiendis illis retributio multa.*

---

42   E. N. According to St. Thomas, there is no servile fear in heaven because there is no fear of evil or fear of punishment, for when charity is perfected, there is no fear of the loss of everlasting blessedness. On the other hand, filial fear increases with charity. See *ST,* IIaIIae, q. 19, art. 11. Quoting St. Augustine, St. Thomas states that this filial or reverential fear is a fear "that has possession in a good," namely God, "which we cannot lose." *Id.* co. (quoting *De Civ. Dei*, XIV). He excludes from the blessed "the fear that denotes solicitude, and anxiety about evil, but not secure fear," that is, fear that one can have in secure circumstances, namely reverential fear. *Id.* ad 1.

43   Ps. 118:72.

44   Cf. Ps. 33:9a. *O taste, and see that the Lord is sweet.* 1 Pet. 2:3. *You have tasted that the Lord is sweet.*

**18{19}[12]** *Etenim servus tuus custodit ea, for your servant keeps them,* not only having them in mind, but also through charity and obedience as he fulfills and performs them. Not uselessly, because *in custodiendis illis retributio multa, in keeping them there is a great reward,* that is the eternal life that will be bestowed as a recompense to him who has kept the divine judgments or precepts. This is what Christ in the Gospel promised to those who imitated him: He who has *left . . . father or mother, [or wife, or children, or lands for my name's sake,] shall receive a hundredfold, and shall possess life everlasting.*[45] For a hundred fold he [already] receives in the present, for this where his reward begins; for he receives grace, God loves him, he tramples upon[46] the world and the flesh, he shines with virtues, and he acquires spiritual delights.

---

**18{19}[13]** *Who can understand sins? From my secret ones cleanse me, O Lord.*

*Delicta quis intelligit? Ab occultis meis munda me.*

**18{19}[14]** *And from those of others spare your servant. If they shall have no dominion over me, then shall I be without spot: and I shall be cleansed from the greatest sin.*

*Et ab alienis parce servo tuo. Si mei non fuerint dominati, tunc immaculatus ero, et emundabor a delicto maximo.*

**18{19}[13]** *Delicta quis intelligit? Who can understand sins?* That is, who is able to oppose himself to any single sin, whatever it may be? It is as if [he were] saying, "No one." *For the just man falls seven times a day;*[47] and so great is our fragility that we are by no means individually able to know, deplore, and avoid daily failures. For which reason in the book of Job we find: man will not be justified *compared with God; if he will contend with him, he cannot answer him one for a thousand.*[48] Therefore, because it is so, I pray, O Lord, *ab occultis meis, from my secret ones,* that is, from this hidden sins, unknown to me, *munda me, cleanse me,* giving to me the memory of them to the extent it is becoming or

---

45  Matt. 19:29. E. N. I have put in brackets that part of the verse Denis appears to have included in his "etc."
46  L. *suppeditat* could mean either amply supply or furnish, or walk upon and trample (*sub-peditat* = *suppeditat*). One could opt with the former on the basis of Matt. 16:3, or the latter based upon Luke 10:19. I have chosen the latter as more likely an understanding given Denis's and the Carthusians' asceticism.
47  Prov. 24:16a.
48  John 9:2, 3.

advantageous, or imparting on me a penance generally sufficient,[49] or henceforth giving me, to the extent possible, to be protected against them. **18{19}[14]** *Et ab alienis, and from those of others*, that is, from the devil and all the adversaries of my salvation, *parce servo tuo, spare your servant*, not permitting them to prevail over me through nefarious temptations, as we pray for in the Lord's Prayer daily: *And lead us not into temptation*,[50] that is, into the consent of anything unlawful, or into a temptation so strong that we are not able to fight against it, but make it be that *with temptation there will also be provided the way of escape [that you may be able to bear it.]*[51]

*Si mei non fuerint dominati; if they shall have no dominion over me*, that is, if the enemies mentioned before do not prevail against me by reason of having overcome them, *tunc immaculatus ero, then shall be without spot*, that is, free from the stain of sin from those desires to which they would want to lead me to. For a temptation to which there is no consent given is not a sin, but is an exercise of virtue and merit, and is an occasion of celebrating a triumph. *Et emundabor a delicto maximo, and I shall be cleansed from the greatest sin*, that is, from an evil practice or a vicious habit.[52] For from the fact that we often succumb to those things that tempt us, it generates in us an evil manner of living or a depraved habit: from which we are cleansed, when we perseveringly resist those things that tempt us; and that done, that which follows [in the Psalm] is fulfilled [in us]:

---

49  E. N. Because some of the sins are unknown or their extent not fully known, Denis prays for a penance that would be considered commonly or generally sufficient to satisfy the temporal punishments associated with these hidden sins.

50  Matt. 6:13.

51  1 Cor. 10:13. E. N. The parts in brackets were left off by Denis or the editor, it would appear in error. Also, I have here departed from the Douay-Rheims and used the Revised Standard Version (Catholic Edition) for reasons of increased clarity. There are perhaps just a handful of persons in the world which can understand what the Douay Rheims's "but will make also with temptation issue, that you may be able to bear it" means.

52  E. N. In Sermon 151, 4, St. Augustine says that where customary evil approaches, any customary good dies, and the fight for virtue ceases. Perhaps no better psychological understanding of customary sin — "living in sin" — would be that found expressed by July in Evelyn Waugh's *Brideshead Revisited*: "'Living in sin'; not just doing wrong . . . doing wrong, knowing it is wrong, stopping doing it, forgetting. . . . '*Living in sin*, with sin, by sin, for sin, every hour, every day, year in, year out. Waking up with sin in the morning, seeing the curtains drawn on sin, bathing it, dressing it, clipping diamonds to it, feeding it, showing it round, giving it a good time, putting it to sleep at night with a tablet of Dial [a barbiturate] if it's fretful." Evelyn Waugh, *Brideshead Revisited* (Boston: Little Brown 1945), 278.

**18{19}[15]** *And the words of my mouth shall be such as may please: and the meditation of my heart always in your sight. O Lord, my helper, and my redeemer.*

> *Et erunt ut complaceant eloquia oris mei, et meditatio cordis mei in conspectu tuo semper. Domine, adiutor meus, et redemptor meus.*

**18{19}[15]** *Et erunt ut complaceant eloquia oris mei; and the words of my mouth shall be such as may please*: that is, if such was my manner of life, so that I might be clean from hidden sins, and I might prevail over my enemies, then *the words of my mouth shall be such as may please* you, that is, then do my words please you. For the word of him whose life is virtuous is pleasing to you. *But to the sinner God has said: Why do you declare my justices?*[53] *Et meditatio cordis mei in conspectu tuo semper; and the meditation of my heart is always in your sight*: that is, if I have the life that has been here just described, then my thought will be *always in your sight*, that is, you will perceive all things with the approval and pleasure of your Wisdom, and you will approve all good. Or [it could be understood] thus: *and the meditation of my heart is always before your sight*, that is, all my thought, whether it is good or whether it is evil, is known to you, who know all things, and who search the reins and the heart.[54] [You do this] in the manner that Elijah says: *As the Lord lives ... in whose sight I stand.*[55] And Job speaking to the Lord said: *You indeed have numbered my steps.*[56] For how blind is he, therefore, and how unhappy, is he who lives without concern, and does not walk with fear before the Lord! Certainly, he who neglected in the present life to honor the countenance of the divine presence which sees all things, will, after this life, come in horror to the hands of the living God.[57]

*Domine, O Lord*, you are, or [, if not, then] be, I pray, *adiutor meus, my helper*, working together in me with your grace, *et redemptor meus, and my redeemer*, you who delivered me from all danger with your own blood.

O with what joyful and devout spirit should this Psalm, in which the foundations of the Christian faith are set forth, be sung by any Christian: [the verses of this Psalm] marvelously comprehend the preaching of the Apostles, the Incarnation of the Word, the recommendation

---

53  Ps. 49:16a.
54  Cf. Ps. 7:10. *The wickedness of sinners shall be brought to nothing: and you shall direct the just: the searcher of hearts and reins is God.* For "reins," *see* footnote 7-10.
55  1 Kings 17:1.
56  Job 14:16.
57  Heb. 10:31. *It is a fearful thing to fall into the hands of the living God.*

of the Evangelical Law, but also the recognition of our own fragility and the imploration of the divine mercy! The more (if I do not err) any member of the faithful will sweetly descant, and will heartfully and chastely sing concordantly [this Psalm], the more he will more ardently love the common good that is the Catholic Faith and the Incarnation of Christ.

# PRAYER

**L** ORD, OUR HELPER AND REDEEMER, MAY our hearts rejoice in your right justice: with the grace of your Word, cleanse us of our hidden sins, that, expiated from our great faults, the meditation of our hearts and the words of our mouths might be pleasing in your sight.

*Domine, adiutor noster et redemptor, iustitiae tuae rectae*
*laetificent corda nostra, occulta nostra verbi tui gratia*
*emunda: quo nobis a delictis maximis expiatis,*
*placeat in conspectu tuo meditatio cordis,*
*et eloquia oris nostris.*

# Psalm 19

## ARTICLE XLVI

EXPOSITION OF THE NINETEENTH PSALM:
*EXAUDIAT TE DOMINUS, &c.*
THE HEAVENS SHOW FORTH THE GLORY OF GOD, *&c.*

**19{20}[1]** *Unto the end. A Psalm for David.*

*In finem. Psalmus David.*

HE [MEANING OF THE] TITLE OF THIS PRES-
ent Psalm, namely, **19{20}[1]** *In finem, Psalmus David; unto the
end, a Psalm of David* is satisfactorily evident from that which has been
said before.[1] For in many Psalms this title has already been explained.

---

**19{20}[2]** *May the Lord hear you in the day of tribulation: may the name
of the God of Jacob protect you.*

*Exaudiat te Dominus in die tribulationis; protegat te nomen
Dei Iacob.*

**19{20}[3]** *May he send you help from the sanctuary: and defend you out of Sion.*

*Mittat tibi auxilium de sancto, et de Sion tueatur te.*

But first, [this Psalm] can be explained as pertaining to Christ, to
whom the prophet [David] prays to give him from God the Father, that
which the revealing Holy Spirit knew would be gifted to him. And so he
says: **19{20}[2]** *Exaudiat te Dominus, may the Lord hear you,* that is, may
*the Lord,* the almighty God, *hear you* O Christ, *in die tribulationis, in the
day of tribulation,* that is, during the time of your pilgrimage on this earth,
in which the entire course of your life was full of tribulation, and often you
prayed for the salvation of the world. Or [it can be thought of this way], *in
the day of tribulation,* that is in the day of Passion, when you pled on behalf
of those who had transgressed against you, saying: *Father, forgive them, for
they know not what they do.*[2] *Protegat te nomen Dei Iacob; may the name*

---

1 *See* Article XVIII (Psalm 4:1).
2 Luke 22:34. E. N. Denis's text here departs slightly from the Sixto-Clementine
Vulgate, but not with any change in meaning.

*of the God of Jacob protect you*, that is, [may] the true God [protect you], not from an evil of fault, because you were not able to sin in any way, but from the evil of punishment, which the Jews often prepared for you before [the appointed] time.[3]   **19{20}[3]** *Mittat tibi auxilium; may he send you help*: not because of your indigence or out of necessity, but for reasons of dispensation, in the manner that the angel of heaven appeared to you,[4] to strengthen you; *de sancto, from the sanctuary*, that is, from him himself. Or [one might see it] thus: *May he send you help*, that is, may he confer upon you the assistance and grace of your assumed [human] nature for the liberation of the human race; *from the sanctuary*, that is, from you yourself, as you are God. For whatever powers were in the human nature of Christ, they overflowed from the divinity of the Word. *Et de Sion; and out of Sion*, that is from the heavens, *tueatur te, defend you* from those opposed to you, as has already been said.

---

**19{20}[4]**   *May he be mindful of all your sacrifices: and may your whole burnt offering be made fat.*

*Memor sit omnis sacrificii tui, et holocaustum tuum pingue fiat.*

**19{20}[5]**   *May he give you according to your own heart; and confirm all your counsels.*

*Tribuat tibi secundum cor tuum, et omne consilium tuum confirmet.*

**19{20}[4]** *Memor sit omnis sacrificii tui; may he be mindful of all your sacrifices*, that is all of the labors which you offered to him for the salvation of men in preaching, praying, laboring, fasting; *et holocaustum tuum, and your burnt offering*, that is, your human nature, which, consumed in the fire of your Passion, you fully immolated to the Father on the Cross, *pingue fiat, may be made fat*, that is, efficacious and abundant to all those you sought to give succor to. The prophet [David] prayed: not that the sacrifice and holocaust of Christ were able to be unacceptable to the eternal Father—since he is the *Lamb without blemish*,[5] and the beloved Son, in whom the Father was pleased[6]—but so that God through the merits of the sacrifice and the holocaust of Christ might relieve and spare the world and that he might save it.   **19{20}[5]** *Tribuat tibi, may he give*

---

3  E. N. Jesus frequently spoke about his time (or hour) not having come. *E.g.,* John 2:4; 7:6, 8, 30; John 8:20, and then that his time had come or was at hand. *E.g.,* John 13:1.; 17:1; Matt. 26:18. Denis is making reference to this.
4  Luke 22:43.
5  Ex. 12:5.
6  Matt. 3:17; 17:5.

*you*, O Christ, O God, *secundum cor tuum*, *according to your own heart*, that is, whatever it is you might desire; *et omne consilium tuum*, *and all your counsels*, which you decreed to redeem the world, *confirmet, confirm*, that is, that it might lead to the salutary effect, namely, that the world may acquire happiness in the manner that you prayed for in the Gospel: I will, O Father, that where I am, they may be and minister to me.[7]

---

**19{20}[6]**  *We will rejoice in your salvation; and in the name of our God we shall be exalted.*

> *Laetabimur in salutari tuo; et in nomine Dei nostri magnificabimur.*

Which having completed,  **19{20}[6]** *Laetabimur, we will rejoice*, O heavenly Father, *in salutari tuo, in your salvation*, that is in Christ, your Son, our Savior, who is called *your salvation* because it is through him that you have saved us. *Et in nomine Dei nostri, and in the name of our God*, that is, by the power of, and the faith in, the Holy Trinity, *magnificabimur, we shall be exalted* with the spiritual dignity so that we might be sons of God and joint heirs with Christ.[8]

---

**19{20}[7]**  *The Lord fulfill all your petitions: now have I known that the Lord has saved his anointed. He will hear him from his holy heaven: the salvation of his right hand is in powers.*

> *Impleat Dominus omnes petitiones tuas; nunc cognovi quoniam salvum fecit Dominus christum suum. Exaudiet illum de caelo sancto suo, in potentatibus salus dexterae eius.*

**19{20}[7]** *Impleat Dominus omnes petitiones tuas; the Lord fulfill all your petitions*, O Christ, including those poured out for the glorification of your own body,[9] as well as those which you presented for others, as well as those also which even now you, seated at the right hand of the Father, intercede for us,[10] showing the Father your side and your wounds.

> *Nunc, now* I, David, by the Spirit *cognovit quoniam salvum fecit Dominus Christum suum*, have I known that the Lord has saved his anointed [*his Christ*],

---

7  *Cf.* John 17:24a: *Father, I will that where I am, they also whom you have given me may be with me; that they may see my glory which you have given me.* John 12:26: *If any man minister to me, let him follow me; and where I am, there also shall my minister be. If any man minister to me, him will my Father honor.*
8  *Cf.* Rom. 8:17a: *And if sons, heirs also; heirs indeed of God, and joint heirs with Christ.*
9  John 17.
10  *Cf.* Rom. 8:34.

resurrecting him from the dead. And he [David] speaks of the future by words in the present tense because of the certitude of the prophecy. *Exaudiet illum, he will hear him*, namely, God the Father [will hear] Christ, *de caelo sancto suo, from his holy heaven*, that is, the throne of glory, or the empyrean heaven: from where God is said to hear because it is in it that he is specially to be and is considered to inhabit.[11] *In potentatibus, in powers*, that is, with the assistance of the great powers or strength of God, he stands firm and is *salus dexterae eius, the salvation of his right hand*, that is, the beatification or redemption of men, proceeding from his right hand, that is, the assistance from the bounteous favor of God or from his mercy. For our salvation is given to us by the mercy of God, and it consists in acts of preeminent virtues which strengthen and confirm the soul in God.

---

**19{20}[8]** *Some trust in chariots, and some in horses: but we will call upon the name of the Lord our God.*

*Hi in curribus, et hi in equis; nos autem in nomine Domini Dei nostri invocabimus.*

**19{20}[9]**[12] *They are bound, and have fallen; but we are risen, and are set upright. O Lord, save the king: and hear us in the day that we shall call upon you.*

*Ipsi obligati sunt, et ceciderunt, nos autem surreximus, et erecti sumus. Domine, salvum fac regem, et exaudi nos in die qua invocaverimus te.*

**19{20}[8]** *Hi in curribus, some in chariots*, that is, some in this world place their trust in transitory and fleeting goods of this world; *et hi in equis, and some in horses*, that is, some of them place their hope in vanities, pomps, honors, and their own powers; *nos autem, but we*, who truly are connected through charity and faith to Christ, *in nomine Domine Dei nostri, in the name of the Lord our God*, that is, through Christ, the Son of God, *invocabimus, we call upon* the Father, in the manner that he teaches in the Gospel, *If you ask the Father anything in my name, he will give it*

---

11  E. N. The empyrean heaven was the highest level of heaven in Medieval cosmology and theology. It is the "place" God inhabits in some special way, where the throne of majesty, glory, and grace is found; it is equivalent to the "third heaven" (*tertium caelum*) mentioned by St. Paul in 2 Cor. 12:2. In his *Summa*, St. Thomas Aquinas mentions that the gloss on 2 Cor. 12:2 "says that the 'third heaven,'" which he equates with the empyrean heaven, "is a spiritual heaven, where the angels and the holy souls enjoy the contemplation of God." *ST* IIaIIae, q. 175, art. 3, ad. 4.

12  Denis has this verse split into two. I have maintained it as one, as in the Douay Rheims.

*you.*[13]  **19{20}[9]** *Ipsi*, they, trusting in chariots and horses, *obligati sunt*, are bound to vices and to the guilt of being addicted to the doing of various sins, *et ceciderunt*, and they have fallen through the repentance of sin, *et erecti sumus*, and we are set upright by the contemplation of God.

*Domine*, O Lord, Father, *salvum fac regem*, save the king, that is Christ, placing upon him a quick end to his distresses, and raising him to immortal status; *et exaudi nos*, and hear us through Christ, namely, through his merit hear us who wish for these things, *in die qua invocaverimus te*, in the day that we shall call upon you, that is, in whatever hour we might be praying for help, for always while we call upon you, you spiritually are "day" to us because Christ, who is the intellectual day and sun of justice, enlightens through faith and the clarity of grace in our hearts, especially since prayer is nothing other than the ascent of the mind to God.[14]

# ARTICLE XLVII

## EXPOSITION OF THE SAME NINETEENTH PSALM OF THE CHURCH AND ANY MEMBER OF THE FAITHFUL

**19{20}[2]**   *May the Lord hear you in the day of tribulation: may the name of the God of Jacob protect you.*

*Exaudiat te Dominus in die tribulationis; protegat te nomen Dei Iacob.*

**19{20}[3]**   *May he send you help from the sanctuary: and defend you out of Sion.*

*Mittat tibi auxilium de sancto, et de Sion tueatur te.*

**B**ECAUSE THE LOVE (*CARITAS*) OF GOD BRINGS together all the elect, and makes them one in the Lord, so the Acts of the Apostles states that *the multitude of believers had but one heart and one soul.*[15] Consequently, the holy Prophet [David] pressed forward by

---

13  John 16:23; *cf.* John 14:13.

14  E. N. Prayer as the *ascensus mentis in Deum*, the raising of the mind to God, is the classic definition of prayer by St. John of Damascus. *Oratio est ascensus mentis in Deum: aut eorum quae consentanea sunt postulatio a Deo.* "Prayer is the uplifting of the mind to God or a petitioning of God for what is fitting." *De Fid. Orth.*, III, 24, PG 94, 1089-90. *See also* CCC § 2559.

15  Acts 4:32a.

charity,[16] prays for the whole Church and for any one of its members and says:    19{20}[2] *Exaudiat te, may he hear you,* O Church of God and any one of the faithful, *in die tribulationis, in the day of tribulation,* that is, in the hour of temptation, of necessity, or adversity, *protegat te nomen Dei Iacob, may the name of the God of Jacob protect you,* namely, [the God] of the holy Patriarch, so you may not succumb, so that you may not be placed in danger.    19{20}[3] *Mittat tibi auxilium, may he send you help,* by that consolation and victory which you obtain, *de sancto, from the sanctuary,* that is, from the most holy liberality of his immense kindness, by which (James as a witness) *he gives to all men abundantly and does not upbraid.*[17] *Et de Sion, and out of Sion,* that is, from the triumphant Church, which he beheld through a vision, *tueatur te,* [may the God of Jacob] *defend you,* against that which is adverse, sending, namely, holy angels to the end of guarding, protecting, and delivering you.

---

**19{20}[4]**    *May he be mindful of all your sacrifices: and may your whole burnt offering be made fat.*

*Memor sit omnis sacrificii tui, et holocaustum tuum pingue fiat.*

**19{20}[4]** *Memor sit omnis sacrificii tui; may he be mindful of all your sacrifices,* that is, all the services that you have rendered him, kindly receiving back from him, and in exchange rewarding you for it with beatitude. *Et holocaustum tuum, and your whole burnt offering,* that is, that internal and charity-driven sacrifice, which you yourself offer to the Lord and by which you worship him, as is said in a later Psalm, *Because for your sake we are killed all the day long;*[18] *pingue fiat, may it be made fat,* that is, may it be adorned with good works, and may it fill you and enrich you with his copious mercy. Indeed, in the Old Testament, holocaust was the name given to those things that were entirely consumed by fire in God's honor. So they who totally deny themselves and carry before them the cross of Christ offer themselves as a holocaust to the Lord. And so by the word "holocaust" we can understand one's will or one's soul, which is "made fat" when it is fattened with the love of Christ, and is enlarged by divine consolations.[19]

---

16   *Caritate urgente.* E. N. Cf. St. Paul's statement in 2 Cor. 5:14: *Caritas enim Christi urget nos. For the charity of Christ presses us.* Denis uses the same words harkening back to St. Paul.

17   James 1:5b.

18   Ps. 43:22b. The verse continues: *we are counted as sheep for the slaughter.*

19   E. N. The enlargement of divine consolation referred to by Denis is, of course, sanctifying grace, the *gratia sanans,* the grace which heals nature, the *gratia*

Or [we can understand it] thus: *May he*—the Lord—*be mindful*, O Church, *of your sacrifice*, that is, the Sacrament of the Altar, which is the sacrifice of the new law, which the Prophet [David] entreated the Lord to remember, not because it was possible that this sacrifice would displease him, but rather that God not be offended by the sins of the person offering it and so that the effect of this sacrifice may not be given to the faithful. For, as the Apostle [Paul] said, *Whosoever shall eat this bread, or drink the chalice of the Lord unworthily, shall be guilty of the body and of the blood of the Lord.*[20] Hence, also, the priest in the Mass prays that the Sacrament of the Body and the Blood of Christ be acceptable to God, saying: *Supra quae propitio ac sereno vultu,* etc. *Deign to look upon these offering with a favorable and serene countenance,* etc.[21] *Et holocaustum tuum, and your holocaust,* O Church, that is, that same sacrifice which is called a holocaust, because Christ offered himself in a perfect and complete manner *for an odor of sweetness,*[22] as the Apostle [Paul] said. This—I say—holocaust *pingue fiat, may be made fat,* that is, that it may bring about that the persons receiving and offering become spiritually fat, giving them the sacramental effects.

---

**19{20}[5]**   *May he give you according to your own heart; and confirm all your counsels.*

*Tribuat tibi secundum cor tuum, et omne consilium tuum confirmet.*

**19{20}[5]**   *Tribuat tibi, may he give you,* O God, *secundum cor tuum, according to your own heart,* that is, according to the reasonable desires of your heart;[23] *et omne consilium tuum confirmet, and confirm all your counsels,*

---

*sanctificatonis* or *habitualis*, the sanctifying and habitual grace by which our acts are rendered supernaturally meritorious — which necessarily implies a *fides formata caritate*, a faith informed by charity (*see* Gal. 5:6) in the offeror — and so is a prerequisite to an acceptable holocaust. For, as St. Paul says, *If I should deliver my body to be burned, and have not charity, it profits me nothing.* 1 Cor. 13:3b.

20  1 Cor. 11:27.

21  *Supra quae propitio ac sereno vultu respicere digneris: et accepta habere, sicuti accepta habere dignatus es munera pueri tui iusti Abel, et sacrificium Patriarchae nostri Abrahae, et quod tibi obtulit summus sacerdos tuus Melchisedech, sanctum sacrificium, immaculatam hostiam.* "Deign to look upon them with a favorable and serene countenance, and to accept them as you did accept the offerings of your just child Abel, and the sacrifice of our Patriarch Abraham, and that which your high priest Melchisedech offered up to you, a Holy Sacrifice, an Immaculate Victim."

22  Eph. 5:2b. *Christ . . . has delivered himself for us, an oblation and a sacrifice to God for an odor of sweetness.*

23  E. N. Rom. 12:1: *I beseech you therefore, brethren, by the mercy of God, that you present your bodies a living sacrifice, holy, pleasing unto God, your reasonable service.*

to the extent the counsels in you may remain in him and may be inspired, directed, and perfected by him.[24] Because it is by this that God gives the gift of counsel to the soul, by which it is made effectively pliable to the Holy Spirit in all matters requiring counsel. And we ought always to call upon the Lord for the gift of counsel, in the manner that the Lord said with Isaiah: *Woe to you, apostate children, ... that you would take counsel, and not of me: and would begin a web, and not by my Spirit.*[25] For we are in need of this gift so that we are not ensnared by the counsels based upon the fluctuation of human concerns and the variety of circumstances and events, all of which are not able to consider[26] unless we are moved in counsel by the Holy Spirit, because it is written: *For the thoughts of mortal men are fearful, and our counsels uncertain.*[27] With merit does the Prophet [David] pray, *And confirm all your counsels.*

---

**19{20}[7]**  *The Lord fulfill all your petitions: now have I known that the Lord has saved his anointed. He will hear him from his holy heaven: the salvation of his right hand is in powers.*

*Impleat Dominus omnes petitiones tuas; nunc cognovi quoniam salvum fecit Dominus christum suum. Exaudiet illum de caelo sancto suo, in potentatibus salus dexterae eius.*

**19{20}[7]**[28] *Nunc cognovit quoniam salvum fecit Dominus,* now I have known that the Lord has saved, [that is, that] Jesus Christ [has saved], *christum suum,* his anointed, that is, any member of the faithful anointed in his interior by the anointment of the Holy Spirit, as John says: *But you have the anointment from the Holy One, and know all things.*[29] *Exaudiet,* He will hear, Christ [that is, will hear] *illum,* him thus anointed *de caelo sancto suo, from his holy heaven,* in which he lives, reigns, and abides with the Father and the Holy Spirit.[30]

---

24  Cf. Tobit 4:20: *Bless God at all times: and desire of him to direct your ways, and that all your counsels may abide in him.*

25  Is. 30:1.

26  E. N. Denis is saying that there is no way that we can know all human concerns and all circumstances so as to exercise human prudence with certainty. At best, human reason is based upon moral certainty, and there is always the possibility of having missed or misjudged something.

27  Wis. 9:14.

28  Denis skips Ps. 19:6 and skips the first part of Ps. 19:7.

29  1 John 2:20. I have changed the Douay-Rheims "unction" to the synonymous "anointment" to fit better with Denis's commentary before it.

30  E. N. Denis does not address the last phrase of Ps. 19:7.

**19{20}[9]**[31] *They are bound, and have fallen; but we are risen, and upright. O Lord, save the king: and hear us in the day* ⸬ *shall call upon you.*

> *Ipsi obligati sunt, et ceciderunt, nos autem surreximus, et erecti sumus. Domine, salvum fac regem, et exaudi nos in die qua invocaverimus te.*

**19{20}[9]**[32] *Domine, salvum fac regem, O Lord, save the king,* that is, any one of the teachers, rulers, or prelates of the Christians. Or [we could understand it thus], *king,* that is, anyone who governs himself in accordance with reason and is lord over his own soul. The rest [of the Psalm] is satisfactorily clarified by prior discussion.[33]

Finally, anyone is able to say this Psalm praying it for himself, that is to say, directing the words as applying to his own soul, and so [for example] a priest about to celebrate Mass may fittingly say it as if speaking of himself. But especially three verses contained within it, namely, *May he send you help from the sanctuary,* along with the two following verses;[34] and they are particularly fitting and may be said by those standing about the priest, when he turns during the Mass to the people, asking them to pray for him.

# PRAYER

**L**OOK UPON US, WE BESEECH YOU, O LORD, in the day of our tribulations, and protect us from all evil, so that arising and standing erect, with our enemies prostrate before us, we may always exult in you, the Lord our God.

> *Exaudi nos, quaesumus, Domine, in die tribulationis, et protege nos ab omnibus malis: ut surgentes et erecti stantes, prostratis hostibus, in te Domino Deo nostro semper exsultemus.*

---

31 Denis splits this verse into two. I have maintained it as one, as in the Douay Rheims.

32 E. N. Denis skips over Ps.19:8, and the first Part of Ps. 19:9.

33 E. N. Denis thus does not address the last part of Ps. 19:9.

34 E. N. That is, Ps. 19:3–5.

# Psalm 20

## ARTICLE XLVIII

### EXPOSITION OF THE TWENTIETH PSALM:
### DOMINE, IN VIRTUTE TUA, &c.
### IN YOUR STRENGTH, O LORD, &c.

20{21}[1]   *Unto the end. A Psalm for David.*

*In finem. Psalmus David.*

GAIN, THE PSALM NOW BEING EXPOUNDED has this as a title:   **20{21}[1]** *In finem, Psalmus David; unto the end, a Psalm of David:* that is, this Psalm is attributed to David, directing his mind so as to consider it in Christ: of whom and of whose reign, this Psalm literally expounds.

---

20{21}[2]   *In your strength, O Lord, the king shall joy; and in your salvation he shall rejoice exceedingly.*

*Domine, in virtute tua laetabitur rex, et super salutare tuum exsultabit vehementer.*

But first the glorious Prophet [David] expresses the benefits to the humanity of Christ that are obtained from his divinity, and says:   **20{21} [2]** *Domine,* O Lord Father, *of whom* (according to the Apostle [Paul]) *all paternity in heaven and earth is named,*[1] *in virtute tua, in your strength,* that is, in the omnipotence of your majesty as the object, *laetabitur rex, the king shall joy,* that is, the Lord Jesus, who is the *king of kings,*[2] and the *prince of the kings of the earth.*[3] For Christ as man was glorified by the divine perfection and power through which he performed miracles; and insofar as he was man, he did not rejoice in himself, but in God. *Et super salutare tuum, and in your salvation,* that is, of the salvation of his Body through the Resurrection, and of all the blessedness in him given by you, especially of the personal union of his humanity with the Word, *exsultabit vehementer, he shall rejoice exceedingly:* because Christ as man,

---

1 Eph. 3:15.
2 Rev. 17:14.
3 Rev. 1:5a; Rev. 19:16.

exceedingly rejoiced in God to that extent that he discerned himself more
chosen by God, and [discerned] the many salutary gifts received from him.

---

20{21}[3]  *You have given him his heart's desire: and have not withheld
from him the will of his lips.*

*Desiderium cordis eius tribuisti ei, et voluntate labiorum eius
non fraudasti eum.*

20{21}[3] *Desiderium cordis eius tribuisti ei; you have given him his
heart's desire,* hearing him in all things, and beatifying his soul from the
beginning of its creation; *et voluntate labiorum eius, and the will of his
lips,* that is, the effect of prayers, instruction, and the other words of his,
*non fraudasti eum, you have not withheld from him,* but you heard him,
and you have made his doctrine to bear fruit unto eternal life in the
hearts of the elect; and you subjected the unclean spirits to the power
of his mouth, for demons we cast out at the command of Christ, in the
manner that is attested to by the Evangelists.[4]

---

20{21}[4]  *For you have prevented him with blessings of sweetness: you
have set on his head a crown of precious stones.*

*Quoniam praevenisti eum in benedictionibus dulcedinis; posuisti
in capite eius coronam de lapide pretioso.*

20{21}[5]  *He asked life of you: and you have given him length of days
for ever and ever.*

*Vitam petiit a te, et tribuisti ei longitudinem dierum in saeculum,
et in saeculum saeculi.*

20{21}[6]  *His glory is great in your salvation: glory and great beauty shall
you lay upon him.*

*Magna est gloria eius in salutari tuo; gloriam et magnum
decorem impones super eum.*

Therefore, men may suitably say regarding Christ,   20{21}[4] *Quoniam praevenisti eum in benedictionibus dulcedinis; for you have prevented[5]
him with blessings of sweetness:* for with all grace you most excellently
adorned the soul of Christ from the instant of its creation, preserving
it immune from all original and actual sin, filling it with all the most

---

4  Matt. 4:24; 8:16, 32; *and elsewhere.*
5  For the word "prevented" as here used, *see* footnote 17-66.

sweet gifts of the Holy Spirit, and — that [gift to his humanity outside of the grace of union] which is above all these — you graced it with your beatific vision; and all this you did without his antecedent [or foreseen] merits.[6] Truly, the blessing of God is called the collective bestowal of his grace.[7] Therefore, the soul of Christ was prevented with the blessings of delight, with the gratuitous gifts of the divine collective bestowal [of graces] without foreseen merits (*sine praeviis meritis*).

*Posuisti, you have set,* O Lord Father, *in capite eius, on his head,* that is, in the superior part of the soul of Christ, in which the image of the Trinity is found, namely, in his intellect, *coronam, a crown,* a triumphant, saving, and victorious [crown], *de lapide pretioso, of precious stones,* that is, a combination (*compactam*) of perfect and most firm charity. This is because the beatitude of the intellect is perfected, confirmed, and rendered immobile (*immobilitatur*)[8] by the act of charity. **20{21}[5]** *Vitam, life,* that is, the resurrection coming quickly after death, namely so that he might rise again on the third day, *petit, he asked,* Christ [asked] *a te, from you,* Lord Father, *et tribuisti ei, and you have given him,* by resurrecting him on the third day: not only did you give him life, but also a life impassible and eternal (in the manner that the Apostle [Paul] says, *Christ rising again from the dead, dies now no more*).[9] Therefore there is appended [to the verse], *longitudinem dierum in saeculum et in saeculum saeculi; the length of days for ever and ever,* that is, you have given him eternal life, whose duration includes all time.[10] And therefore **20{21}[6]** *Magna est gloria eius, great is his glory,* that is, his delight, *in salutari tuo, in your salvation,*

---

6  E. N. This was true for Christ's grace of union and his other graces and gifts. Cf. *ST*, IIIa, q. 24, art. 3, co. (the human nature in Christ was united to the Son of God without any antecedent merits).

7  E. N. *collatio gratiae,* which suggests a bestowal of a number of graces brought together into one sort of collection or group.

8  E. N. *immobilitatur,* rendered or made immobile or unfluctuating. According to one scholar, this was a neologism coined by John of St. Thomas (John of Poinsot) to characterize the immutability of divine charity in the Christian soul. Krzysztof Olaf Charamsa, *L'Immutabilità di Dio: L'insegnamento di San Tommaso d'Aquino nei suoi sviluppi presso i commentatori scolastici* (Roma: Editrice Pontificia Università Gregorian 2004), 215. But this is impossible, since John of St. Thomas lived between 1589 and 1644, and Denis lived between 1402 and 1471. Accordingly, it would appear that — at least with respect to between John of St. Thomas and Denis the Carthusian, Denis's use of this neologism predates John of St. Thomas's use by about a century.

9  Rom. 6:9.

10  E. N. In other words, the human life, both body and soul, of Christ is aeviternal, not eternal, since it had a beginning in time, but will last forever. Denis is not speaking of the Word in his divine nature, without beginning or end, and which, of course is eternal and outside of time altogether.

that is, in the saving quality that is adjoined to you. For the glory of Christ the man is his blessed union with God, and so much greater is this glory as it is nearer to the union with God.[11] *Gloriam, glory,* that is the joyfulness of the soul for the salvation of the elect, and for the restoration of the heavenly Jerusalem, *et magnum decorum, and great beauty,* that is, the most splendid glorification of the body, *impones super eum, you shall lay upon him,* namely, upon Christ, as in the day of the Resurrection and the Ascension that has already occurred. Or [we might look at it] thus: *Glory,* that is clear knowledge, *and great beauty,* that is, a brilliant ornament, *you shall lay upon him,* that is, joining the immaculate Church to him, praiseworthily having clear knowledge of her Bridegroom, honoring and rejoicing in him, as a bride honors and rejoices in her bridegroom.

---

20{21}[7]   *For you shall give him to be a blessing for ever and ever: you shall make him joyful in gladness with your countenance.*

*Quoniam dabis eum in benedictionem in saeculum saeculi; laetificabis eum in gaudio cum vultu tuo.*

Therefore, you do these things, O God, the Father,   20{21}[7] *Quoniam dabis eum,* for you shall give him, namely Christ, *in benedictionem in saeculum saeculi; to be a blessing for ever and ever:* so that not only might he be in himself eternally blessed, but also that he might bless otherwise through him: as a later Psalm says, *And in him shall all the tribes of the earth be blessed.*[12] *Laetificabis eum in gaudio, you shall make him joyful in gladness,* that is, you will fill Christ with all joy, *cum vultu tuo, with your countenance,* that is, from the seeing of your countenance, in which the beatific vision consists, so that Christ now being present to you, rejoices not only of his own personal happiness, but also for all of those saved with his salvation.

---

20{21}[8]   *For the king hopes in the Lord: and through the mercy of the most High he shall not be moved.*

*Quoniam rex sperat in Domino; et in misericordia Altissimi non commovebitur.*

---

11   *E. N.* Obviously, since the grace of union is one of perfect union, it follows that this grace is infinite, as infinite as God. So does St. Thomas Aquinas conclude that the grace of union is infinite since the person of God is infinite. *ST,* IIIa, q. 7, art. II, co. *(gratia unionis .... constat esse infinitam, secundum quod ipsa persona verbi est infinita).*

12   Ps. 71:17b.

But such accidental rewards and glories are owed to Christ [8] *Quoniam rex, for the king*, that is, Christ, *sperat in Domin the Lord*, that is, any good not yet achieved is expected from him, a... attributed to him; and no created power is judged to suffice to achieve happiness, but he places all trust in God; *et in misericordia Altissimi non commovebitur; and through the mercy of the most High he shall not be moved*, that is, hoping in the mercy of God, he does not forsake, nor does he separate himself from, the Lord. For Christ [as man] never moved away from or separated from the Lord.[13]

---

20{21}[9]  *Let your hand be found by all your enemies: let your right hand find out all them that hate you.*

*Inveniatur manus tua omnibus inimicis tuis; dextera tua inveniat omnes qui te oderunt.*

20{21}[10]  *You shall make them as an oven of fire, in the time of your anger: the Lord shall trouble them in his wrath, and fire shall devour them.*

*Pones eos ut clibanum ignis in tempore vultus tui: Dominus in ira sua conturbabit eos et devorabit eos ignis.*

20{21}[11]  *Their fruit shall you destroy from the earth: and their seed from among the children of men.*

*Fructum eorum de terra perdes, et semen eorum a filiis hominum.*

Consequently, the Prophet [David] moves on to the address the reprehension of the enemies of Christ, and says:   20{21}[9] *Inveniatur, let it be found*, O Christ the Judge, *manus tua, your hand*, that is, your power of punishing sins, *omnibus inimicis tuis, by all your enemies*, namely, heretics, schismatics, and the impenitent, so that they who did not want during this earthly pilgrimage (*in via*) to obtain your clemency might

---

13  E. N. This insistence by Denis—that the human nature (both body and soul) of Christ never moved from, much less ever separated itself from, the grace of union (or the beatific vision) in any manner is expressed by a prayer from the Ethiopic Liturgy: *Credo, credo, credo quod divisa non fuerit divinitas eius ab humanitate eius, ne hora quidem una, aut nictu oculi* [=*non in ictu oculi*]. Charles Edward Hammond, ed. *Liturgies Eastern and Western* (Oxford: Clarendon 1878), 261. "I believe, I believe, I believe that his [Christ's] divinity was not divided from his humanity, for no time whatsoever, for not even the blink of an eye." This will be particularly important in Denis's explanation of Psalm 21 and the cry of dereliction of Jesus on the Cross and his descent into "hell," the limbo of the Fathers.

experience your justice in punishment. *Dextera tua, your right hand,* that is, your most righteous and strict justice, *inveniat, may find out,* through examination and the infliction of punishments, *omnes qui ti oderant, all them that hate you,* that is, the perverse and incredulous Jews, who killed you through their envy.[14] These have the greater punishment, because they sinned more gravely. And so it was, for    20{21}[10] *pones eos in clibanum ignis, you shall make them as an oven of fire,* setting them afire in the body with the fire of sense, and in the soul with the power of pain and the worm of conscience, *in tempore vultus tui, in the time of your anger,* that is, in the day of your just judgment, when you will examine by retribution that which by means of longsuffering patience you let pass unnoticed.[15] *Dominus, the Lord* Christ *in ira sua, in his wrath,* that is, in the vengeance of his justice, *conturbabit eos, shall trouble them,* casting them into exterior darkness, *where the shadow of death, and no order, but everlasting horror dwells;*[16] *et devorabit eos ignis, and fire shall devour them,* an infernal [fire], not so they might die by being consumed in flames, but so that they might be enfolded in misery and eternally tormented, as we read in the book of Judith: *The Lord almighty will take revenge on them, in the day of judgment he will visit them. For he will give fire, and worms into their flesh, that they may burn, and may feel forever.*[17]    20{21}[11] *Fructum eorum, their fruit,* that is, their carnal and foul delights, *de terra perdes, you shall destroy from the earth,* that is, you will separate from the region of the living, that they who now take delight in illicit things in the world might not take pleasure in heaven with God; *et semen eorum, and their seed,* that is, their works, you will destroy *a filiis hominum, from among the children of men,* that is, from the blessed society of those who lived humanely and piously in the world in accord with reason, in the manner that is written: let us do away with the wicked, that they may not see the glory of God.[18]

All of this judgment, which distinguishes between the good and the evil, is also beautifully signified by Malachi: *You shall return,* he says, *and shall see the difference between the just and the wicked: and between him that serves God, and him that serves him not.*[19] *Behold, the day shall*

---

14  Matt. 27:18: *For he knew that for envy they had delivered him.*
15  *Cf.* Matt. 25:41.
16  Job. 10:22.
17  Jud. 16:20b–21.
18  *Cf.* Is. 26:10. *Let us have pity on the wicked, but he will not learn justice: in the land of the saints he has done wicked things, and he shall not see the glory of the Lord.* E. N. Here, Denis appears to be pushing the limits of the text.
19  Mal. 3:18.

*come kindled as a furnace: and all the proud, and all that do wickedly shall be stubble: and the day that comes shall set them on fire, says the Lord of hosts, it shall not leave them root [nor branch].*[20]

Moreover, this in a special and fitting way—indeed, also in a literal way—can be explained as referring to the oppression, massacre, and burning of the Jews by the Roman rulers, so [it can be understood] in this sense: *Let your hand be found, O Christ, by all your enemies*, that is, let all the unfaithful Jews experience your power and your just vengeance. *You shall make them as an oven of fire*, supplying great and various calamities, *in the time of your anger*, that is, in the day of judgment, which by Titus and his followers you looked at to vindicate the death that was inflicted upon you. *The Lord shall trouble them in his wrath* with fear and with sorrow; *and fire shall devour them*, that is, a great and forceful punishment will consume them, as in fact occurred. *Their fruit you shall destroy from the earth [and their seed from among the children of men].* For in the persecution [of the Jews] mentioned a little while ago, they and their children were expulsed from their lands even until the present day.

---

**20{21}[12]** *For they have intended evils against you: they have devised counsels which they have not been able to establish.*

> *Quoniam declinaverunt in te mala; cogitaverunt consilia quae non potuerunt stabilire.*

**20{21}[13]** *For you shall make them turn their back: in your remnants you shall prepare their face.*

> *Quoniam pones eos dorsum; in reliquiis tuis praeparabis vultum eorum.*

That which follows is also very well expounded of the aforementioned Jews. For the following [verses] provide the cause of such oppression, and say: **20{21}[12]** *Quoniam declinaverunt*, for they have intended, O Christ, *in te mala*, evils against you, imposing upon you a great reproach. For before Pilate they exclaimed: *If he were not a malefactor, we would not have delivered him up to you;*[21] and again: *Away with him; away with him; crucify him.*[22] *Cogitaverunt consilia quae non potuerunt stabilire;* they have devised counsels which they have not been able to establish. For

---

20  Mal. 4:1. Denis left off the end of the verse "nor branch" which I have added in brackets.

21  John 18:30.

22  John 19:15; *Cf.* Luke 23:18, 21.

frequently, the Jews devised counsels by which they had certain occasion to find themselves against Christ; but they were not able to make firm that counsel because they were unable to discover reasonable cause, nor were they able to prove or verify their accusations.    **20{21}[13]** *Quoniam pones eos dorsum, for you shall make them turn their back,* that is, you will permit them to be blind, to be hardened, and to be completely adverse to you, so that they might flee from your law and your faith,[23] turning against you the back, and not the face, of the mind.[24] *In reliquitis tuis, in your remnants,* that is in the few that you have elected from them for yourself, of whom the Apostle [Paul] said to the Romans: *A remnant shall be saved,*[25] *praeparabis, you will prepare,* that is, you will rightly dispose and ordain, *vultum eorum, their face,* that is, the knowledge of the Law and the Prophets, which they understood badly and carnally; and they boastfully believed themselves to be wise with respect to [the knowledge of the Law and the Prophets], but it was not so. Truly, Christ through the Holy Spirit, conveyed to his remnant the true and sound knowledge of the Law and the Prophets, and so he prepared beforehand (*praeparavit*), or perfectly prepared (*paravit*), the elect of his remnant, the *face* or the knowledge of the carnal Jews.

20{21}[14] Be exalted, O Lord, in your own strength: we will sing and praise your power.

> *Exaltare, Domine, in virtute tua; cantabimus et psallemus virtutes tuas.*

**20{21}[14]** *Exaltare, Domine, Be exalted, O Lord* Christ, *in virtute tua, in your own strength,* that is, rise again, ascend by your own power, and declare yourself to the world through the doctrine and the miracles of the Apostles, cast out the prince of this world,[26] reign in the hearts of the faithful, and subdue the whole world to your empire. Which when done, *cantabimus, we will sing* with voice *et psallemus, and praise* with our life and in our manner of living *virtutes tuas, your power,* that is, the sanctity and the perfection of your manner of life, the miracles, and the

---

23    E. N. The "faith" here intended not as a subjective genitive (Christ's fidelity or belief), but as an objective genitive, meaning *faith in Christ.*
24    Jer. 32:33: *And they have turned their backs to me, and not their faces: when I taught them early in the morning, and instructed them, and they would not hearken to receive instruction.*
25    Rom. 9:27b.
26    John 12:31.

other things that redound to the honor and glory of your name. For immediately after the Ascension of Christ and the sending of the Holy Spirit, the Church began publicly and with secure mind to sing and praise, to preach and to write about, the power of its Savior.

# ARTICLE XLIX

## ANAGOGICAL EXPOSITION OF THIS TWENTIETH PSALM

20{21}[2]  *In your strength, O Lord, the king shall joy; and in your salvation he shall rejoice exceedingly.*

*Domine, in virtute tua laetabitur rex, et super salutare tuum exsultabit vehementer.*

**B**RIEFLY, ACCORDING TO THE ANAGOGICAL understanding, this Psalm is explained as being about any one of the blessed in heaven. For the Church, in its celebration of the martyrs, adopts in its song [*i.e.*, its liturgy] a large part from this present Psalm. Therefore the Psalm says:   20{21}[2] *Domine, O Lord* one and three, who are the fountain of all holy joy, *in virtute tua, in your strength,* that is, in you yourself, you who are your own strength; or [alternatively], *in your strength,* that is, in Christ your Son, who (as attested by the Apostle [Paul]) is your power and wisdom;[27] *laetabitur rex, the king shall joy,* that is, anyone in the vision of God in heaven (*comprehensor in patria*): because in your vision and that of our Son consists eternal beatitude, as your Only-Begotten testified: *Now this is eternal life,* he said, *that they may know you, the only true God, and Jesus Christ, whom you have sent.*[28] For all the blessed in heaven, with merit are called kings, since they are the forechosen and perfect sons of the eternal King in the manner that is written in Revelation: *And they shall see his face.... and they shall reign for ever and ever.*[29] *Et super salutare tuum, and in your salvation,* that is, the knowledge of your salvation, or the clear vision of your essence, *exsultabit vehementer, he shall rejoice exceedingly,* indeed, ineffably and incomprehensibly to any wayfarer (*viatori*): as the Lord says through his prophet: *Unto you that fear my name, the Sun of justice shall arise, and health in his wings .... And you shall leap like calves of the herd, and you shall tread down*

27  *Cf.* 1 Cor. 1:24.
28  John 17:3.
29  Rev. 22:4–5.

*the wicked.*[30] And the most sacred prince of the Apostles [Peter] in his epistle: Seeing, he says, Jesus, *you shall rejoice with joy unspeakable and glorified, receiving the end of your faith, even the salvation of your souls.*[31] And Paul: *The sufferings of this time,* he says, *are not worthy to be compared with the glory to come, that shall be revealed in us.*[32]

---

**20{21}[3]** *You have given him his heart's desire: and have not withheld from him the will of his lips.*

> *Desiderium cordis eius tribuisti ei, et voluntate labiorum eius non fraudasti eum.*

**20{21}[4]** *For you have prevented him with blessings of sweetness: you have set on his head a crown of precious stones.*

> *Quoniam praevenisti eum in benedictionibus dulcedinis; posuisti in capite eius coronam de lapide pretioso.*

Therefore, O Lord, *I will rejoice exceedingly* without end, because **20{21}[3]** *desiderium cordis eius,* his heart's desire, that is, his heart's desired good, *tribuisti ei,* you have given him, giving to him yourself as a reward. Or [alternatively], *you have given him his heart's desire,* that is, the affection which he desires to see you at present, you have led into actualization, showing yourself and that evangelical truth to him saying: *Well done, good and faithful servant, because you have been faithful over a few things, I will place you over many things: enter into the joy of your Lord.*[33] But properly summarizing the desire for the enjoyment of future good, the Saints in heaven do not have desire with respect to the essential reward in this manner, but only love, because love is a present good; but they do have a desire with respect to accidental reward. Nevertheless, Peter speaking of Christ, said that the angels have in them a desire to see [Christ],[34] in which of course the prospective essential reward consists. But there the desire [for love] is exchanged for a love excluding a sense of surfeit (*fastidium*).[35] *Et voluntate labiorum eius,* and

---

30 Mal. 4:2–3.
31 1 Pet. 1:8–9.
32 Rom. 8:18.
33 Matt. 25:21, 23.
34 1 Pet. 1:12.
35 E. N. Denis, distinguishing between essential and accidental beatitude and reward, makes the further point that the only desire that relates to the essential reward of the beatific vision is the love of God. Here is the problem with this. If there remains a desire to love in heaven, then there is no fulfilment, and such suggests

*the will of his lips*, that is, the desire of the prayer of his lips, with which, while on pilgrimage (*in via*), always prays that one may come to heaven (*ad patriam*), *non fraudasti eum, you have not withheld from him*. And this therefore,   **20{21}[4]** *quoniam praevenisti eum in benedictionibus dulcedinis, for you have prevented him with the blessings of sweetness*, that is, because from eternity you have chosen him to this blessed and most sweet glory. As he says through the Apostle [John]: *You have not chosen me: but I have chosen you.*[36] Or [another way], *for you have prevented him with the blessings of sweetness*, that is, the theological virtues, namely faith, hope, and charity, by which we are blessed and are adjoined to God, you have infused in him while on pilgrimage (*in via*) without foreseen merit (*sine praevio merito*). For these virtues no one merits with strict justice (*de condigno*), nor [does one strictly merit] the new habit of grace;[37] but God mercifully prevents[38] us according to the order of eternal predestination, providing to us all those things necessary to attain eternal life.

*Posuisti in capite eius, you have set on his head*, that is, in his intellect, which is the supreme power of the soul according to Thomas [Aquinas],[39] *coronam, a crown*, that is the essential reward, which theologians

---

a happiness frustrated. However, if the desire of love is satiated, that satiation (like the desire for food after hunger is satiated) causes that love to lose its charm, and may even lead to surfeit, *ennui*, boredom, even nausea, disgust, and hatred (the word Denis uses is *fastidium*). But, unlike the earthly loves we know, the love of God in heaven is not subject to these limitations. The traditional (paradoxical) formula is that, when it comes to charity — the love of God in heaven that the blessed enjoy — there is desire with satisfaction, and satisfaction with desire (*desiderium cum satietate, et satietas cum desiderio*). St. Augustine, for example, addresses this issue in his third Tractate on the Gospel of John: *Noli timere ne fastidio deficias: talis erit illa delectatio pulchritudinis, ut semper tibi praesens sit, et nunquam satieris; imo semper satieris, et nunquam satieris. Si enim dixero quia non satiaberis, fames erit; si dixero quia satiaberis, fastidium timeo: ubi nec fastidium erit, nec fames, quid dicam nescio.* "Do not fear [that your delight in contemplating God in heaven] may be lost by surfeit (*fastidio*): such will that delight of beauty be that it will be present to you always and you will never be satisfied; indeed, you will always be satisfied, and never satisfied. For if I were to say that you will not be satisfied, it will mean you hunger; and if I were to say you will be satisfied, I fear surfeit (*fastidium*): where there is neither surfeit (*fastidium*) nor famine."

36  John 15:16a.

37  By "new habit of grace" (*habitum gratiae novum*), Denis means sanctifying, justifying, habitual grace, the grace known as *gratia gratum faciens*. For condign or strict justice (*de condigno*), see footnote 15-44.

38  For this specific meaning of prevent, see footnote 17-66.

39  E. N. See *ST*, Ia, q. 82, art. 3, co. *Simpliciter tamen intellectus est nobilior quam voluntas.* "Strictly speaking, the intellect is nobler than the will."

call the crown, namely, the vision of the divine essence;[40] and this crown *you have set on his head* is *de lapide pretioso, of precious stones*, that is, eternal of object or caused by the supreme good, because it is from the union of the intellect with God that this happiness is caused in him. And so the crown of the saints [in heaven] is *of precious stones*, not from any material cause, but from a final or efficient cause; for the sublime and blessed God is both the one who effects and who is the end of all the happiness of creatures. With this crown one is not crowned, *except he strive lawfully*[41] and he serve God with a pure heart. For this crown makes us similar to the perfect God, or it makes us deiform, in that way that we read with John: *Dearly beloved, we are now the sons of God; and it has not yet appeared what we shall be. We know, that, when he shall appear, we shall be like to him: because we shall see him as he is.*[42]

---

20{21}[5] *He asked life of you: and you have given him length of days for ever and ever.*

> *Vitam petiit a te, et tribuisti ei longitudinem dierum in saeculum, et in saeculum saeculi.*

20{21}[6] *His glory is great in your salvation: glory and great beauty shall you lay upon him.*

> *Magna est gloria eius in salutari tuo; gloriam et magnum decorem impones super eum.*

20{21}[5] *Vitam, life* eternal and celestial *petiit a te, he asked of you*, while he still was wayfaring in this world, which life is better called death than it is life, according to Gregory;[43] *et tribuisti ei, and you have given him* that which he asked for, namely, *longitudinem dierum in saeculum et in saeculum saeculi, the length of days for ever and ever*, that is, an eternal day that is not caused by a sensible sun, but from divine clarity, as John

---

40  *E.g., ST*, IIIa (Supp.) q. 96, art. 1, co. "Man's essential reward, which is his beatitude, consists in the perfect union of the soul with God, inasmuch as it enjoys God perfectly as seen and loved perfectly. Now this reward is called a 'crown' or 'aurea' metaphorically."

41  2 Tim. 2:5.

42  1 John 3:2.

43  E. N. Pope St. Gregory the Great (*ca.* 540–604 A. D.). This is a reference to Pope St. Gregory's Homily 37, 1 on the Gospels. In comparing life here on earth with the life of the blessed in heaven, Gregory says: *Temporalis vita aeternae vitae comparata, mors est potius dicenda, quam vita.* "Life here on earth, compared to eternal life, might better be called death, than life." PL 76, 1275.

gives testimony to: *And the city has no need of the sun, nor of the moon, to shine in it. For the glory of God has enlightened it, and the Lamb is the lamp thereof.*[44]    **20{21}[6]** *Magna est gloria eius,* his glory is great, namely, of any one of those enjoying the beatific vision, *in salutari tuo, in your salvation,* that is, in the contemplation of the eternal Word: for the beatific vision is reposited in Christ. *Gloriam et magnum decorum, the glory and great beauty,* that is, the double robe,[45] namely the happiness of the soul and the clarity of the body, *impones super eum, you shall lay upon him,* in the resurrection of the dead, when *this mortal has put on immortality,*[46] and when *the just shine as the sun, in the kingdom of their Father.*[47] Or [alternatively] thus: *the glory,* that is, the three dowries of the soul,[48] namely, the vision which follows faith, the possession which follows hope, and the fruition which follows charity, *and great beauty,* that is, the four dowries of the body, namely, clarity, impassibility, agility, and subtility, *you shall lay upon him.*

---

**20{21}[7]**    *For you shall give him to be a blessing for ever and ever: you shall make him joyful in gladness with your countenance.*

*Quoniam dabis eum in benedictionem in saeculum saeculi; laetificabis eum in gaudio cum vultu tuo.*

**20{21}[7]** *Quoniam dabis eum in benedictionem, for you shall give him to be a blessing,* that is, you will make him to adhere to your blessing, namely, he will be blessed *in saeculum saeculi, for ever and ever,* that is, without end: for every one of the blessed in heaven is confirmed in good; *laetificabis eum in gaudio cum vulto tuo, you shall make him joyful in gladness with your countenance,* that is, from the clear and immediate seeing of your face, as it is said in an earlier Psalm, *You shall fill me with joy with your countenance.*[49]

---

**20{21}[8]**    *For the king hopes in the Lord: and through the mercy of the most High he shall not be moved.*

*Quoniam rex sperat in Domino; et in misericordia Altissimi non commovebitur.*

---

44  Rev. 21:23.
45  E. N. *Duplicem stolam,* the double robe or double stole. See footnote 17-209.
46  1 Cor. 15:54a.
47  Matt. 13:42a.
48  For the three "dowries" of the soul, see footnote 15-56.
49  Ps. 15:11a.

The blessed person in heaven has all of the goods mentioned earlier, for in this life he hoped in the divine goodness. So the Psalm follows with:    20{21}[8] *Quoniam rex sperat in Domino, for the king hopes in the Lord*, not when in heaven, but while in the wayfaring state. For in heaven faith and hope no longer remain because faith includes the obscurity of knowledge and hope the absence of the desired good: neither of which remain in heaven. *Et in misericordia Altissimi non commovebitur; and through the mercy of the most High, he shall not be moved*, that is, trusting in the Lord, and leaning upon his graces and mercies, he does not fall, nor is he condemned. Therefore Solomon says: *The name of the Lord is a strong tower: the just run to it, and shall be exalted.*[50] And Isaiah: *But they that hope in the Lord shall renew their strength, they shall take wings as eagles, they shall run and not be weary, they shall walk and not faint.*[51]

---

20{21}[14] *Be exalted, O Lord, in your own strength: we will sing and praise your power.*

    *Exaltare, Domine, in virtute tua; cantabimus et psallemus virtutes tuas.*

Finally, the Church triumphant says to the Lord, not requesting, but giving thanks: 20{21}[14][52] *Exaltare, Domine, in virtute tua, be exalted, O Lord, in your own strength*, condemning and casting away your adversaries, namely, all the reprobate, as is contained in Revelation: Under the altar of God, the Saints cried out, *How long, O Lord . . . do you not judge and revenge our blood?*[53] That done, *cantibus et psallemus virtutes tuas, we will sing and praise your power*, praising your justice and your power. Hence it is written: *Rejoice over her, heaven, and you holy apostles and prophets; for God has judged your judgment.*[54] The remaining verses[55] are discussed in the preceding explanation.

Behold, we have heard from the exposition of the present Psalm the blessedness of the elect and the horrible punishments of the wicked. Let everyone for himself, therefore, choose with whom he desires to be placed and which reward to receive after this brief and fleeting life; and let him busy himself now to imitate the works of those with whom he

---

50  Prov. 18:10.
51  Is. 40:31.
52  Denis skips verses 9 through 13, and starts up again with verse 14.
53  Rev. 6:10.
54  Rev. 18:20.
55  *E. N.* Presumably Ps. 20:9–13.

wants to rest. For if we wish to reign with the blessed in heaven, let us occupy ourselves with them to suffer with Christ, to despise the world, immoderate passions, and to abhor vice; and with an ordered, pure, and constant mind to serve the almighty Lord.

# PRAYER

ITH THE MERITS OF YOUR STRENGTH by which we devoutly sing and praise your powers, grant us, O Lord, to obtain your perpetual benediction, and to rejoice with joy forever in the presence of your desirable countenance.

*Virtutum meritis, Domine, nos exalta, quibus devote cantemus*
*et psallamus virtutes tuas: da nobis benedictionem*
*perpetuam consequi, et gaudio per aevum cum*
*vultu tuo desiderabili laetificari.*

# Psalm 21

## ARTICLE L

### LITERAL EXPOSITION OF THE TWENTY-FIRST PSALM:
### *DEUS, DEUS MEUS, RESPICE, &c.*
### GOD, MY GOD, LOOK UPON ME, *&c.*

**21{22}[1]**  *Unto the end, for the morning protection, a Psalm for David.*
*In finem, pro susceptione matutina. Psalmus David.*

TOP OF THIS PSALM IS THIS TITLE:  **21{22}[1]**
*In finem, pro susceptione matutina. Psalmus David; Unto the end, for the morning protection, a Psalm for David:* that is, the end this Psalm directs us to is David, that is, to Christ as figured by David, *for the morning assumption or protection,*[1] that is, for his Resurrection, which occurred in the morning and is prayed for in this Psalm; or [alternatively, we can understand it in this manner], for the morning deer,[2] that is, for the human nature of Christ, which is compared to a deer, because it is similar to a deer that always ascends to the heights by contemplation and leaps across the earth.

That this Psalm literally expounds of Christ is consistent with that which the most blessed Evangelist asserts with respect to the words of this Psalm during the Passion of Christ, as will be made clear. And Jerome[3] and many others say that Christ on the Cross uttered the entirety of this Psalm together with the subsequent Psalms until that verse, *In manus tuas commendo spiritum meus, into your hands I commend my spirit,*[4] which is sufficiently probable. For Matthew and Mark testify that Christ on the Cross uttered the beginning of this Psalm, namely, *God, my God, why have you forsaken me?*[5] But Luke is mindful that he said that verse, *Into your hands I commend my spirit.*[6] Whence, one looks

---

1  E. N. Denis relies on alternative readings for the first verse *pro susceptione matutina* (for the morning undertaking) and *pro assumptione matutina* (for the morning assumption or receiving).
2  E. N. Denis relies on yet another alternative reading of the title, *pro cerva matutina* (for the morning deer).
3  For St. Jerome, *see* footnote 15-46.
4  Ps. 30:6.
5  Matt. 27:46; Mark 15:34.
6  Luke 23:46 (Ps. 30:6).

at what the intermediate verses said. For in Hebrew, this Psalm begins in this fashion: *Eli, Eli, lamma sabachthani?* But that which we find in our translation, *Respice in me, look upon me,* is not in the Hebrew, nor in the translation from the Hebrew by Jerome, but it is believed to be an interpretative addition from the Septuagint.[7]

Further, this Psalm is intensely most beautiful, and most full with every devotion; and it is sung of Christ with faith and pious compassion. And he who recites it without affection, I do not know if he is thankful to Christ or whether he even loves him. For there is no other Psalm which so evidently, determinately, and properly describes the Passion of Christ as does this Psalm; so much so that this Psalm can be seen more as history than as prophecy. Nor do I recall in all of the Old Testament such an extended and clear description of the Passion of Christ as is found in this place, even in the fifty-third chapter of Isaiah.[8] For although Daniel very openly says that the Christ would die,[9] he did not describe it so in such an ample and determinate manner and [did not describe] the bitterness of this death in the manner that David and Isaiah did in the places mentioned above. With great care, therefore, and with great affection, with as much as the Lord deigns to give, the expounding of this Psalm is most sweet, and a wonder full with power, whose singular words are little torches, as it were, of the fire of divine love, which is the Holy Spirit. Oh how clear and full of grief the most holy David saw in the Spirit the bitterness, the horror, and all the steps of the Lord's Passion, and [all] that Christ patiently suffered when he wrote this Psalm together with him![10] And how the power of the principle cause of this Psalm, namely, the power of the Holy Spirit, resounds and is contained in this its effect, namely, in the present Psalm!

---

7  E. N. The Septuagint (from the Latin word for seventy, *septuaginta,* often indicated by the Roman numeral for seventh LXX) is a Greek translation of the Hebrew Scriptures. The translations pre-dated the birth of Christ. The title Septuagint comes from the tradition that 70 scholars translated the Hebrew Scriptures into Greek. The Septuagint is frequently quoted verbatim in the New Testament, indicating its wide-spread use by Jews during the time of Christ and the Apostles.

8  Is. 53. E. N. This famous chapter speaks of the "Suffering Servant," that *despised, and the most abject of men, a man of sorrows, and acquainted with infirmity,* who was *wounded for our iniquities, bruised for our sins,* and yet *by his bruises we are healed.* Is. 53:3, 5.

9  Dan. 9:26a: *And after sixty-two weeks Christ shall be slain: and the people that shall deny him shall not be his.*

10  E. N. Christ, acting through the Holy Spirit, wrote this Psalm together with David, the inspired human author.

**21{22}[2]**   *O God my God, look upon me: why have you forsaken me?*
*Far from my salvation are the words of my sins.*

*Deus, Deus meus, respice in me: quare me dereliquisti? Longe*
*a salute mea verba delictorum meorum.*

And so, therefore, the Prophet [David] in the person of Christ or, better, Christ's very self by reason of his assumed human nature:   **21{22}**
**[2]** *Deus, Deus meus,* God, my God. The repetition of the word "God," is
an indication of fervent desires. And so, *Deus,* God of the universe, *Deus
meus, my God,* in a most particular way, as is frequently expounded [in
this Commentary]. Whence, after the Resurrection, Christ said to Mary
Magdalene: *I ascend to my Father and to your Father, to my God and
your God.*[11] In this he designates that as God is especially his Father by
reason of the divine nature, which he received by [eternal] generation
from the Father, so in a special manner is he his God by reason of his
assumed humanity, [the assumed humanity] which the Father loved more
than the entirety of the universe; and he [Christ as man] also loved God
more than he loved the entire universe: as is pointed out.

And so the only and the most beloved Son of God, hanging on the gibbet of the Cross, and surrounded by unthinkable punishment says: *Deus,
Deus meus, respice in me,* O God, my God, look upon me, that is, attend
and see that which I endure for your honor and the salvation of the world.
In what manner do you so turn away, or, better, do you seem so to turn
away *your face from your servant*[12] of whom you often asserted, *This is my
beloved Son?*[13] *Look upon me,* that is, show sympathy to me, who always
respected you with all reverence doing that which was pleasing to you.[14]

*Quare me dereliquisti? Why have you forsaken me?* That is, why do you
so hold yourself towards me as if I do not belong (*pertinerem*) to you at all,
but as if I am displeasing to you and am relegated to oblivion, as those of
which Scripture says, *I know you not?*[15] *Why have you forsaken me* into
the hands of the ungodly? *Why have you forsaken me,* withdrawing from
the passible nature and the inferior powers [of my human nature] the
accustomed sweetness of divine consolation, or the usual overabundance
of joy from the superior powers of the soul to its inferior powers? For in

---

11  John 20:17b.
12  Ps. 68:18a. *And turn not away thy face from your servant: for I am in trouble,
    hear me speedily.*
13  Matt. 3:17; 17:5.
14  Cf. John 8:29.
15  Matt. 25:12; Luke 13:25, 27.

the hour of the Passion, there was not any overabundance of happiness in his inferior powers which Christ had in the higher powers of his soul, by relation of them to the Word; but so great did he suffer punishment in the body, and so great was he afflicted with sorrow in soul, [it was] as if he seemed forsaken by God. Not, however, that he was strictly speaking (*simpliciter*) forsaken, for neither the personal union with the Word, nor the beatific enjoyment of the [human] soul (*mentis*) in God was lost. Indeed, the intellect and the will of the soul of Christ during the time of the Passion were together and at the same time in the maximum joy of the beatific enjoyment and in the [state of] maximum suffering in relation to his human nature which was undergoing complete affliction while it was redeeming all of human nature.[16] Here also it is approved [as commonly held by theologians] that no other martyr endured a more bitter death than Christ. For martyrs in their passions have marvelous consolations, to such an extent that many of them in some fashion do not feel the tortures externally applied to them.[17] In order to allow in, therefore, the most bitter pains of his Passion, and so as also to rouse in you [the faithful] a pious and Christian compassion, Christ said: *Why have you forsaken me* so that I might seem to be wholly contemptible to you? This is what we read with Isaiah: *We have thought him as it were a leper, and as one struck by God and afflicted.*[18]

In fact, that which follows, *longe a salute mea, far from my salvation,* can refer to that which precedes it, namely, *Why have you forsaken me?* So as to have this sense: "Why from soundness of body or corporal health have you forsaken me, exposing me to such misery?" Following this, we have the cause of this kind of forsakenness, as it says: *verba delictorum meorum, are the words of my sins,* that is, the tumult of vice sounding evil in the ears of God, which vices are mine, that is, of the

---

16 E. N. "Our Lord Jesus Christ is the chief and most glorious of Martyrs, . . . but we do not call him a Martyr, as being much more than a Martyr. True it is, he died for the Truth; but that was not the chief purpose of his death. He died to save us sinners from the wrath of God. He was not only a Martyr; he was an Atoning Sacrifice." St. John Henry Newman, "Martyrdom," Sermon 4, *Parochial and Plain Sermons* (London: Scriber, Welford & Co. 1868), 42.

17 One example, of many that could be cited, is the *Assatum est iam, versa!* "I'm done, turn me over" of St. Lawrence. In Jacob de Voragine's *Golden Legend*, we are told that three internal fires overcame the sufferings of the external fires: the magnitude of Lawrence's faith, the ardency of his love, and the true knowledge of God (*fidei magntitudo, ardens dilectio, vera Dei cognitio*). A biblical example of this phenomenon would be the instance of Shadrach, Meshach, and Abednego in the fiery furnace. *See* Dan. 3:6.

18 Is. 53:4b.

men being delivered by me. These words are the cause of my Passion: in the manner that Isaiah testified: *But he was wounded for our iniquities, he was bruised for our sins.*[19] And so *sins (dilectorum),* and *my (meorum)* are to be construed separately. Though they can also be construed together, so that because of the unity of Christ and the Church, or the head and the members, Christ states that our sins are his transgressions.[20]

We are also able to refer that which is said—*far from my salvation*—as referring to that which follows, namely, *the words of my sins,* so that it is understood in this sense: "The word of my sins that are far from my salvation because they force asunder and divide God and man[21] and they are the cause for which I am so forsaken and I suffer; as Jeremiah prophesied, *The breath of our mouth, Christ the Lord, is taken in our sins.*[22] For Christ suffered so as to carry away the sins of the world according to the Apostle: *With Christ I am nailed to the cross, . . . and he delivered himself up for me.*[23] Whence in Daniel it is most clearly written: [The angel] Gabriel said to Daniel: *Seventy weeks are shortened upon your people, . . . iniquity may be abolished, and everlasting justice may be brought, and vision and prophecy may be fulfilled; and the Saint of Saints may be anointed.*[24]

---

**21{22}[3]**　*O my God, I shall cry by day, and you will not hear: and by night, and it shall not be reputed as folly in me.*

*Deus meus, clamabo per diem, et non exaudies; et nocte, et non ad insipientiam mihi.*

**21{22}[3]** *Deus meus, clamabo per diem,* O my God, I shall cry by day: for Christ in the day of Passover around the ninth hour cried out: *Eli, Eli, lama sabachthani?*[25] as we have already attended to. *Et non exaudies,*

---

19　Is. 54:5a.

20　A good discussion of the "cry of dereliction" from a traditional point of view and critical of some of the novel modern theories to explain it, is Bruce D. Marshall, "The Dereliction of Christ and the Impassibility of God," *Divine Impassibility and the Mystery of Human Suffering* (Grand Rapids, MI: Wm. B. Eerdmans Publishing 2009), 246–98. Here again Denis invokes the first rule of interpretation of Tyconius, where the "cry of dereliction" can be referred to both Christ (in one way) and to his Mystical Body (in another way).

21　Is. 59:2. *But your iniquities have divided between you and your God, and your sins have hid his face from you that he should not hear.*

22　Lam. 4:20a.

23　Gal. 2:19b, 20b.

24　Dan. 9:22, 24.

25　Matt. 27:46.

*and you will not hear*, by diminishing the suffering of my body and the sorrow of my soul, but you will permit me to be killed by a most bitter and most repulsive death. *Et nocte, and by night* I shall cry out, that is, before the day of the Passion, when three times I prayed those words and said, *My Father, if you will, remove this chalice from me.*[26] But now *you will not hear*: not, however, that my prayer was unbecoming or reprehensible. For this reason there follows: *et non ad insipientiam mihi, and it shall not be reputed as folly in me*, that is, neither you nor anyone else can impute any foolishness or indiscretion to me from the fact that that which I prayed for I was not heard.[27]

However, there is [in this matter an altogether] not small difficulty. For in John's Gospel, we have Christ saying: *Father, I give you thanks that you have heard me. And I knew that you hear me always.*[28] How, therefore, does he now say, *O my God, I shall cry out by day, and you will not hear?* Moreover, in his epistle to the Hebrews, the Apostle [Paul] also very clearly says that Christ, *in the days of his flesh, with a strong cry and tears, offering up prayers and supplications to him that was able to save him from death, was heard for his reverence.*[29]

Therefore, in reply, as the Damascene[30] affirms, prayer is the petition of something becoming from God; and according to Augustine, it is licit to pray for that which it is licit to desire.[31] But Christ never prayed to God anything that was unbecoming or illicit. Therefore, anything whatsoever he prayed for absolutely, that is, he always obtained whatever through his deliberate will he asked for. But the prior requests [by Christ in Gethsemane and referred to in this Psalm], wherein Christ asserts that he is not being heard, were not prayers poured out strictly speaking (*simpliciter*), but were [prayers] with a certain condition; and they proceeded more from

---

26  Mark 14:36; Luke 22:42.

27  E. N. Christ's prayer that the chalice be removed from his *appears* unanswered, from which no negative inference can be made as to Christ. Denis proceeds to explain the difference between a human longing, which is not strictly a prayer, and a prayer strictly so called arising out of human reason and the deliberate intellectual will.

28  John 11:41b–42a.

29  Heb. 5:7. As to the authorship of the epistle to the Hebrews ascribed to St. Paul by Denis, *see* footnote 8-34.

30  E. N. John of Damascus; *see* footnote P-80; for St. John of Damascus's definition of prayer, *see* footnote 19-14.

31  E. N. *ea licet orare quae licet desiderare.* This definition of prayer adapted by Denis — *hoc licet orare, quod licet desiderare* — is derived (by free paraphrase) from St. Augustine's Epistle 1130 to Probam, PL 33, 502. In his *Summa*, St. Thomas quotes it as paraphrased. *E.g.*, ST IIaIIae, q. 83, art. 6, co.

the feeling of pain and movement of the sensitive part than from the full judgment of reason, though they were for all that not against the order of reason. Christ willed to pour forth these prayers, which he knew would not be heard [by the Father for two reasons]. First, so that he could exhibit that he truly was incarnate and passible, so as to confound heretics with opposite opinions. Second, for our instruction, namely, that we might not tire, we might not despair, when we are not heard by God immediately or as we might have wished; but, by the example of Christ, we may place ourselves under and commit ourselves to the good pleasure of the Creator, certain [of his good will towards us] because he takes care of us.[32]

That these prior prayers that were said were not strictly and absolutely prayers is evident from this fact, that while Christ said, *Father, remove this chalice from me*, he immediately added, *but not what I will, but what you will*,[33] not, however, that Christ's human will was contrary to the divine will, but in this Christ subjected all his longing, even his sensitive longing, to the divine will. And so absolutely speaking, he was heard because of his reverence, but he was not heard as it related to the nature of his human longing, according his own consideration, because naturally [the human longing] abhors death. But nevertheless, as far as this his longing [is concerned, Christ] was heard in relation to the superior reason and the divine will [which are above this longing], because he finally and absolutely wished to die for the salvation of the world. For this reason, after the three prayers [in the Garden of Gethsemane] he proceeded quickly and undaunted to meet the Jews, saying: *Whom do you seek?*[34] Had he acted otherwise, we would have seen him not personally fulfilling that which he taught others: *Fear you not them that kill the body, and are not able to kill the soul: but rather fear him that can destroy both soul and body in hell.*[35]

----

21{22}[4]   *But you dwell in the holy place, the praise of Israel.*

*Tu autem in sancto habitas, laus Israel.*

21{22}[4] *Tu autem in sancto habitas*, but you dwell in the holy place. It is as if Christ said: With merit I said, *and it will not be reputed as folly in me* that I am not heard, because from this it does not follow I am in any manner to be adverse to you; but you, O Lord Father, *in the*

----

32 1 Pet. 5:7: *Casting all your care upon him, for he has care of you.*
33 Mark 14:26; Luke 22:42.
34 John 18:4b.
35 Matt. 10:28.

*holy place*, that is, in me, your Son, your most favored and holy, *you dwell*, and you are always in me and remain there. Whence, the Savior says: *You, Father, in me, and I in you ... because you have loved me before the creation of the world.*[36] And elsewhere: *The words*, he says, *that I speak to you, I speak not of myself. But the Father who abides in me, he does the works.*[37] You, therefore, *dwell in the holy place*, [you,] *laus Israel, the praise of Israel*, that is, the object of my praise, [abide in me] who am a true Israelite, *in whom there is no guile*,[38] and who saw your face always by sight, and never once ceased from the contemplation of you.

---

21{22}[5]   *In you have our fathers hoped: they have hoped, and you have delivered them.*

*In te speraverunt patres nostri; speraverunt, et liberasti eos.*

21{22}[6]   *They cried to you, and they were saved: they trusted in you, and were not confounded.*

*Ad te clamaverunt, et salvi facti sunt; in te speraverunt, et non sunt confusi.*

21{22}[5] *In te, in you*, that is, in your most beneficent goodness, *speraverunt patris nostri, our fathers have hoped*, namely, the Patriarchs, the Prophets, and other just ones; *speraverunt, they have hoped*, not without cause, because *et liberasti eos, and you have delivered them*. For this reason, other Scripture says: You *must remember how our father Abraham was tempted, and being proved by many tribulations, was made the friend of God. So Isaac, so Jacob, so Moses, and all that have pleased God, passed through many tribulations, remaining faithful. But they that did not receive the trials in the fear of the Lord, and in patience, ... were destroyed.*[39]   21{22}[6] *Ad te clamaverunt, they cried to you*, in the time of necessity and distress, *et salvi facti sunt, and they were saved*, as to their soul, although sometimes it was permitted to be severely whipped or wounded in body, or killed. *In te speraverunt, et non sunt confusi; they trusted in you, and were not confounded*: because that which they desired to obtain from you, namely the blessed life and eternal rest, they received after they were dealt these temporal afflictions, and they were not frustrated in their hope. This is

---

36   John 17:21a, 24b.
37   John 14:10b.
38   John 1:47b. *E. N.* The statement is said to Nathanael by Jesus, but if true of Nathanael, it is *a fortiori* true for our Lord.
39   Judith 8:22–25a.

what the venerable Mattathias[40] recalled: *Was not Abraham found faithful in temptation, and it was reputed to him unto justice?*[41] *Joseph in the time of his distress kept the commandment, and he was made lord of Egypt.*[42] *Daniel in his innocence was delivered out of the mouth of the lions.*[43]*....* and *none that trust in him fail in strength.*[44]

---

**21{22}[7]**  But I am a worm, and no man: the reproach of men, and the
outcast of the people.

Ego autem sum vermis, et non homo; opprobrium hominum,
et abiectio plebis.

**21{22}[7]** *Ego autem sum vermis, et non homo; but I am a worm, and no man*: that is, I was so horribly lacerated, treated with contempt, and tortured in my such lamentable Passion that I might have appeared to have been a worm, rather than a man; indeed, so much did my perse-cutors scorn me it is as if they were irrational brutes: just as is prophe-sized by Isaiah: *there is no beauty in him, nor comeliness ... whereupon we esteemed him not.*[45] And Luke says: *the men that held Jesus, mocked him, and struck him, and they blindfolded him, and smote his face,*[46] and *began to spit on him,*[47] and spat on his face. Behold how much contempt, behold that which the Lord endured to his majesty, so that his mingling of such punishments would achieve for us eternal honor and heavenly beatitude. *Opprobium hominum, the reproach of men*, that is, he was made the reproach of the Jews, before Pilate saying: *We have found this man perverting our nation.*[48] And again: *Write not, The King of the Jews; but that he said, I am the King of the Jews.*[49] *Et abiecto plebis, and the outcast of the people*, so that he would appear more vile to all men: in the manner that is narrated in the Gospel, where it reads thus: *Then therefore, Pilate took Jesus, and scourged him; and the soldiers* (lending aid) *platting a crown of thorns, put it upon his head; and they put on him a purple garment, and*

---

40  E. N. Mattathias (†165 B. C.), son of John, the son of Simeon, father of Judas Maccabeus and his brothers.

41  Gen. 22:2–10.

42  Gen. 39:12; 41:41.

43  Dan. 6:22; 14:30–40.

44  1 Mach. 2:52–53, 60, 61b.

45  Is. 53:2–3.

46  Luke 22:63, 64.

47  Mark 14:65.

48  Luke 23:2a.

49  John 19:21.

*they came to him, and said: Hail, king of the Jews; and they gave him blows,*
*and so forth.*[50] *Jesus therefore came forth, bearing the crown of thorns and*
*the purple garment. And he said to them: Behold the Man. When the chief*
*priests, therefore, and the servants, had seen him, they cried out, saying:*
*Crucify him, crucify him.*[51] Behold, O Christian, consider with a faithful
heart what Christ, the king of glory, deigned to suffer for you. Imprint
this spectacle unceasingly in your soul in the manner that Christ exhorts
in the Song of Songs: *Put me as a seal upon your heart.*[52]

---

**21{22}[8]**    *All they that saw me have laughed me to scorn: they have spoken*
*with the lips, and wagged the head.*

*Omnes videntes me deriserunt me; locuti sunt labiis, et moverunt*
*caput.*

**21{22}[9]**    *He hoped in the Lord, let him deliver him: let him save him,*
*seeing he delights in him.*

*Speravit in Domino, eripiat eum: salvum faciat eum, quoniam*
*vult eum.*

**21{22}[8]** *Omnes videntes me, deriserunt me; all they that saw me have*
*laughed me to scorn:* not strictly speaking all, for Nicodemus, Joseph of
Arimathea, and many others did not laugh him to scorn;[53] but all those
previously described by which *I was made . . . the reproach of men, and the*
*outcast of the people,* namely, all perverse men. Or [it might be thought
of in this manner], *All* strictly speaking, however the word is applied to
the genus of each individual, but not to the individual of each genus.[54]
Or [alternatively], *All,* that is, so many that, in comparison with all those

---

50  John 19:1–3.
51  John 19:5–6.
52  Songs 8:6a.
53  John 19:38, 39; Luke 23: 50, 51.
54  E. N. *Distributio pro generibus singulorum* — when a noun is understood as referring
to the genus (or species or kind) of the individual — as distinguished from *distributio*
*pro singulis generum* — when a noun is understood as referring to individuals of the
genus (or species or kind). In short, the distinction is whether we are dealing with
the individuals of a kind or the kinds of individuals. So when Ps. 21:8 says *all men*
*derided me,* the "all men" is to be understood as saying some of all the kinds of men
(Jews, Gentiles, Roman soldiers, thieves) around Christ derided him, and not that
all men did. This distinction is particularly important in understanding 1 Tim. 2:4
("God wills all men to be saved"), which, as St. Thomas Aquinas clarifies, is to be
understood as referring to some men of all classes and conditions of men, but not
all men of every class and condition. *See* ST, Ia, q. 19, art. 6, ad. 2.

who were present and who did not laugh me to scorn, it seems as if there were none. Therefore, *all they that saw me have laughed me to scorn.* And so then all these laughed to scorn the Son of God and the Wisdom of the eternal Father:[55] when Herod with his army mocked Christ, and amused themselves (as it says in the Gospel of Luke) by dressing him in white; [56] and when *Pilate gave sentence that it should be as they required,*[57] delivering Jesus after he had been scourged over to their will *to be crucified*; and when *bearing his own cross, he went forth*; and when *they crucified him,* with thieves *one on each side, and Jesus in the midst.*[58] For these reasons, it was predicted: *so shall his visage be inglorious among men.*[59] And Jeremiah said: *I am made a derision to all my people, their song all the day long.*[60] Whence, just as the holy prophet Ezechiel as a figure of Christ is so often called the son of man,[61] so in the figure of Christ it is said to him by the Lord: I gave you as *a sign of things to come to the house of Israel.* This say to the sons of Israel: *I am a sign of things to come.*[62] And again: *Ezechiel shall be unto you for a sign of things to come.*[63]

*Locut sunt labiis, they have spoken with the lips* many blasphemies against me; *et moverunt caput, and wagged the head,* rejoicing in my miseries, and detesting and sneering at me as a false prophet. But that which they said [with their lips] is added:   **21{22}[9]** *Speravit in Domino, he hoped in the Lord.* This is asserted in a derisory way, as if they might be saying: "He claims to hope in the Lord." And therefore *eripiat eum, let him deliver him* from this torture, *salvum faciat eum, let him save him* from this most repulsive death, *quoniam vult eum, seeing he delights in him,* that is, because he claims himself to be the chosen one of God and the Son of God. For as the most sacred evangelists affirm, the chief [priests] and the Pharisees with all the rest ridiculed the Lord Jesus hanging on the Cross, and said: *He trusted in God; let him now deliver him if he will have him; for he said: I am the Son of God.*[64] Oh what a marvelous agreement of the Gospel history with the prophetic announcement!

---

55  1 Cor. 1:24b: *Christ the power of God, and the wisdom of God.*
56  Luke 23:11.
57  Luke 23:24.
58  John 19:16, 17, 18.
59  Is. 52:14.
60  Lam. 3:14.
61  E. N. The term "son of man," *fili hominis,* a translation of *ben-'adam* (בן אדם), which appears in Ezechiel 93 times. Ezechiel is a figure of Christ.
62  Ez. 12:6, 11.
63  Ez. 24:24.
64  Matt. 27:43; see Matt. 27:42; Luke 23:35.

**21{22}[10]** *For you are he that has drawn me out of the womb: my hope from the breasts of my mother.*

> *Quoniam tu es qui extraxisti me de ventre, spes mea ab uberibus matris meae.*

**21{22}[11]** *I was cast upon you from the womb. From my mother's womb you are my God.*

> *In te proiectus sum ex utero; de ventre matris meae Deus meus es tu.*

**21{22}[12]** *Depart not from me. For tribulation is very near: for there is none to help me.*

> *Ne discesseris a me, quoniam tribulatio proxima est, quoniam non est qui adiuvet.*

But because these things were fitting for Christ since he took up the form of a servant for us,[65] therefore is added:  **21{22}[10]** *Quoniam tu, for you,* O Lord Father, *es qui extraxisti me, are he who have drawn me out,* in a supernatural and ineffable manner, according to this, *Who shall declare his generation?*[66] *De ventre, out of the womb,* that is, of the incorrupt and enclosed and virginal womb of Mary, my going forth *(exitui)* from the Virgin's womb, notwithstanding dimensions of bodies;[67] *spes mea, my*

---

65  Phil. 2:7. *But emptied himself, taking the form of a servant, being made in the likeness of men, and in habit found as a man.*

66  Is. 53:8. E. N. The term "generation" is interpreted in the manner of Christ's being (eternally) generated, not as meaning generation in the sense of those people born and living at roughly the same time as Christ. The "supernatural and ineffable" manner of Christ's generation and birth, of course, is not only a reference to the virginal conception of Christ, but also the virginal and miraculous birth of Christ and the perpetual virginity of Mary — Mary as ἀειπάρθενος (*aeipárthenos*), ever-virgin — so that Mary remained a virgin *ante partum, in partu,* and *post partum. See* CCC § 499. This is clear from the commentary which follows.

67  E. N. This is a reference to the miraculous birth of Christ, where the infant Jesus, like he did when he visited the disciples through shut doors after the Resurrection (John 20:19–26), "passed through" the Virgin's body without damaging in any manner its virginal integrity. The *Summa Theologiae* addresses the issue of whether by a miracle it is possible for two bodies to be in the same place in *Summa Theologiae,* IIIa (Supp.), q. 83, art. 3. The *sed contra,* which is proved in the *respondeo,* notes that *Beata Virgo filium suum miraculose peperit. Sed in illo partu oportuit duo corpora esse simul in eodem loco: quia corpus pueri exiens claustra pudoris non fregit. Ergo potest miraculose fieri quod duo corpora sint in eodem loco.* "The Blessed Virgin Mary gave birth miraculously to her son. But in this birth, it was required that two bodies be in the same place at the same time, because the body of the child exiting the gate of chastity *(claustra pudoris)* did not break. Therefore, it is possible by a miracle that two bodies can be in the same place." The term *claustra pudoris,* whose image

*hope,* insofar as I am man, *ab uberibus matris meae, from the breasts of my mother*: because Christ as man from the very beginning of the incarnation hoped in the Lord, not by the hope that is a theological virtue, but by the expectation, or that certain kind of trust, through which he expected the future good from God, and whatever goods he had, he attributed to him, as has often been already explained.[68]   21{22}[11] *In te, by you,* O Father, *proiectus sum, I was cast off,*[69] a casting off of loving adhesion and of filial trust, *ex utero, from the womb*: because from the instant that Christ was born from the Virgin, he adhered to the eternal Father, and he was confirmed in him in the manner that is stated in a later Psalm: *the Lord my hope . . . from my youth, by you have I been confirmed from the womb.*[70]

*De ventre matris meae Deus meus es tu, from my mother's womb you are my God*: whom I worship unceasingly, honor most highly, love most ardently, behold unceasingly: and so   21{22}[12] *ne discesseris a me, depart not from me,* forsaking me completely. And this I pray, *quoniam tribulatio proxima est, for tribulation is very near,* that is, because my Passion is so imminent, *et non est qui adiuvet, and there is none to help me,* delivering me from the cruelty of those who want to crucify me. This is what Christ said through Isaiah: *I looked about, and there was none to help: I sought, and there was none to give aid.*[71] And elsewhere: *Awake, O sword, against my shepherd, and against the man that cleaves to me, says the Lord . . . strike the shepherd, and the sheep shall be scattered.*[72] The evangelist Matthew makes known that this is said about Christ.[73]

---

21{22}[13] *Many calves have surrounded me: fat bulls have besieged me.*

*Circumdederunt me vituli multi; tauri pingues obsederunt me.*

21{22}[14] *They have opened their mouths against me, as a lion ravening and roaring.*

*Aperuerunt super me os suum, sicut leo rapiens et rugiens.*

---

so delicately and tastefully refers to the Virgin Mary's anatomy, is taken from the Advent hymn *Veni Redemptor Gentium* written by St. Ambrose.

68  See Article XIX (Psalm 4:10) and Article XXIV (Psalm 7:2).

69  The Douay-Rheims has "cast upon," which I have changed to "cast off," since it is encompassed by the Latin *proiectus* and is more consonant with the discussion of Denis.

70  Ps. 70:5, 6.

71  Is. 63:5a.

72  Zach. 13:7a.

73  Matt. 26:31: *Then Jesus said to them: All you shall be scandalized in me this night. For it is written: I will strike the shepherd, and the sheep of the flock shall be dispersed.*

21{22}[13] *Circumdederunt me vituli multi, many calves have surrounded me,* that is the Jewish persecutors, men with the likeness of bull-calves wild and lascivious; *tauri pingues, fat bulls,* that is, their teachers and their chiefs, and also the gentiles and those in service to Pilate, men with the likeness of proud and hardened bulls. Whence, in Ecclesiasticus it is said: *Extol not yourself in the thoughts of your soul like a bull.*[74] They, therefore, *obsederunt me, have besieged me.* For as the evangelist attests, when Christ told the Jews, *You are come out as it were to a robber with swords and clubs to apprehend me;*[75] *then the band and the tribune, and the servants of the Jews, took Jesus, and bound him.*[76] Also, being as it was the morning on the day of Passover, they led him to their council, saying: *If you be the Christ, tell us* in our presence.[77]   21{22}[14] *Aperuerunt super me os suum, sicut leo rapiens et rugiens; they have opened their mouths against me, as a lion, ravening and roaring.* When else did this occur except before Pilate, when they cried out, *Crucify him! Crucify him!* And the more he labored to persuade them, the more loudly they cried out, *Away with him! Away with him!* And *If you release this man, you are not Caesar's friend.*[78] And their voices grew more powerful. But since Pilate sent Jesus to Herod, the chiefs of the priests stood by (as Luke bears witness) *constantly accusing him.*[79] But he did not respond with one word, in order to fulfill that which was set by the prophet [Isaiah]: *As a sheep to the slaughter, and shall be dumb as a lamb before his shearer, and he shall not open his mouth.*[80] And elsewhere: *And I was as a meek lamb, that is carried to be a victim.*[81]

---

21{22}[15] *I am poured out like water; and all my bones are scattered. My heart is become like wax melting in the midst of my bowels.*

*Sicut aqua effusus sum; et dispersa sunt omnia ossa mea. Factum est cor meum tamquam cera liquescens in medio ventris mei.*

21{22}[15] *Sicut aqua effusus sum, I am poured out like water,* that is, with all my body I am exhausted of blood, because the frequency of the

---

74  Ecclus 6:2a.
75  Matt. 26:55.
76  John 18:12.
77  Luke 22:66b.
78  John 19:6, 12, 15; Matt. 27:23.
79  Luke 23:23, 7, 10, 9.
80  Is. 53:7b.
81  Jer. 11:19a.

effusion of my blood in the day of Passover, namely, with the relentless scourging of the body, with the crowning of my head with thorns, especially when they struck my head with a cane, and pierced my feet and my arms; *et dispersa sunt omnia ossa mea, and all my bones are scattered*, that is, they are disjoined from each other, and disunited from their natural joints because of the most violent bodily overextension on the Cross.

*Factum est cor meum tamquam cera liquescens, my heart is become like wax melting.* On occasion in Scripture by the word heart is understood the mind or will, in the manner that Christ said: *Blessed are the pure of heart.*[82] But sometimes by the word heart is understood the bodily organ of the sensitive part [of an animal]: as when the Philosopher [Aristotle] says that the heart of an animal is the first thing to live and the last thing to die.[83] Using the first way of understanding the meaning of the word heart, then, [the verse is understood] in this sense: *My heart is become like wax*, that is, my mind is spiritually loosened, softened, and is in a way spilling itself out confronted with so great an affection of divine honor and of human salvation, and also confronted with the violence of suffering nature, and confronted with the sadness arising from the ungratefulness of the reprobate in the way that the spouse says in the Song of Songs: *My soul melted when he spoke.*[84] And so as to provide a sign of his vehement affection and ardor, Christ in the Last Supper said to his disciples: *With desire I have desired to eat this pasch with you, before I suffer.*[85] But if we understand the word heart in the second way, then the sense [of the verse] is this, that as wax dissolves or liquefies with the heat of fire, so the heart of Christ is transformed, and liquified before the great sorrow and affliction of suffering nature and of all the powers of the soul. For the passions or affections of the sensitive part [of man] come with a bodily transformation. And from the great affection of the upper appetite, namely, the will, there always follows some transformation in the inferior appetite or the heart. So the heart of Christ has the appearance of liquified wax during the time of the Passion when through the overflowing of the affection of the will transferred into the sensible pains of the inferior appetites. Yet it seems

---

82  Matt. 5:8.

83  E. N. This is probably a reference to Aristotle's *De motu animalium* 10 (603a30ff) which states that the heart lives first and dies last. This view acknowledged by St. Albert the Great. *See Albert the Great, Questions Concerning Aristotle's on Animals* (Catholic University of America: Washington D. C. 2008) (trans. Irven M. Resnick and Kenneth F. Kitchell, Jr.), 382.

84  Songs 5:6b.

85  Luke 22:15.

that in this place the word heart is understood in the second way because of what follows: *in medio ventris mei, in the midst of my bowels,*[86] that is, in the middle of my deep interior parts.

---

**21{22}[16]** *My strength is dried up like a potsherd, and my tongue has cleaved to my jaws: and you have brought me down into the dust of death.*

*Aruit tamquam testa virtus mea, et lingua mea adhaesit faucibus meis, et in pulverem mortis deduxisti me.*

**21{22}[16]** *Aruit tanquam testa virtus mea, my strength is dried up as a potsherd*: that is, in the way a broken piece of a pot is dried up with fire and withers up, so does my strength fail and dry up because of the dissolution of natural harmony, the pouring out of blood, and the loss of vital humors;[87] *et lingua mea adhaesit faucibus meis, and my tongue has cleaved to my jaws*, confronted with the dryness and bodily thirst; *et in pulverem mortis, and into the dust of death*, that is, in the dissolution of bodily life, *deduxisti me, you have brought me down*, O Lord Father, that is, you have permitted me to be lead into them. For then the bodily life of Christ was brought down as if to nothing, when his soul was separating from the body.

---

**21{22}[17]** *For many dogs have encompassed me: the council of the malignant has besieged me. They have dug my hands and feet.*

*Quoniam circumdederunt me canes multi; concilium malignantium obsedit me. Foderunt manus meas et pedes meos.*

**21{22}[18]** *They have numbered all my bones. And they have looked and stared upon me.*

*Dinumeraverunt omnia ossa mea. Ipsi vero consideraverunt et inspexerunt me.*

**21{22}[19]** *They parted my garments amongst them; and upon my vesture they cast lots.*

*Diviserunt sibi vestimenta mea, et super vestem meam miserunt sortem.*

---

86  E. N. The word "bowels" here being used in the sense of the deepest interior core or depths of one's person.

87  Based upon Hippocratean medical theory, vital humors were seen as four: blood, phlegm, black bile, and yellow bile. Good health required that they be in balance.

**21{22}[17]** *Quoniam circumdederunt me, for they have encompassed me* while hanging on the Cross, [they as] *canes multi, many dogs,* that is, men raving and furious men against me, thirsting for my blood, and all round about me biting me with blasphemous words, hateful scorn, and painful blows; *consilium*[88] *malignantium obsedit me, the council of the malignant has besieged me,* that is, the evil counselors, the Pharisees and others, thinking with what choice tortures or shameful death they might kill me,[89] so they might satisfy themselves with my pains.[90] These sorts fortify themselves around me. *Foderunt manus meas et pedes meos, they have dug my hands and feet,* that is, with large, thick, and dull nails they have pierced and affixed to the Cross my hands and feet. O good Jesus, O innocent Lamb, O holy Son of God, how many things did you endure for me![91] Truly, as the Apostle [Paul] said, the heavenly Father *spared not even his own Son,*[92] for he exposed you to such a horrendous death, one most full of punishments. And this piercing of the feet and the hands of Christ, was one of the most oppressive of all his punishments. For death by crucifixion is a very oppressive death, because the manner by which one is fastened, the manner of the restraining, is also one of greatest sensitivity and pain. **21{22}[18]** *Dinumeraverunt omnia ossa mea, they have numbered all my bones,* that is, they were able to count [my bones] because, from the violent stretching of my members the joints of my bones appeared, especially since Christ is believed to have been suspended naked, as Adam sinned when naked.[93] Also, this stretching out of the most sacred body of Christ was most tormenting by any estimation.

*Ispsi vero, and they,* my persecutors and enemies, *consideraverunt et inspexerunt me, have looked and stared upon me,* blaspheming, deriding, with exulting all the more heartily the more seriously they saw me suffer. **21{22}[19]** *Diviserunt sibi vestimenta mea, they have divided my garments among them,* [they,] the four crucifying soldiers, *et super vestem mea, and upon my vesture,* that is, over my seamless tunic, *miserunt sortes, they cast lots,* as to whose it might be totally, because they did not want

---

88  Others [reading] *Concilium.*

89  *Cf.* Wisdom 2:19, 20: *Let us condemn him to a most shameful death.... These things they thought.*

90  *Cf.* Job 16:11. *They have opened their mouths upon me, and reproaching me they have struck me on the cheek, they are filled [may be satisfied] with my pains*

91  E. N. *O bone Iesu, O innocens Agne, O sancte Fili Dei, quanta sustinuisti pro me!*

92  Rom. 8:32a.

93  Gen. 3:10. E. N. In a sort of opposite Dantean *contrapasso,* since Adam sinned naked, it was fitting that Jesus redeemed that sin naked.

to divide it [among themselves]. Truly, this scripture was fulfilled in Christ as asserted by the evangelist John.[94]

Further these things which now were raised of Christ's Passion, conform with those things that are read about [in the life] of holy Job:

> Now my sorrow has oppressed me, and all my limbs are brought to nothing. My wrinkles bear witness against me, and a false speaker rises up against my face, contradicting me. He has gathered together his fury against me, and threatening me he has gnashed with his teeth upon me: my enemy has beheld me with terrible eyes. They have opened their mouths upon me, and reproaching me they have struck me on the cheek, they are filled with my pains. God has shut me up with the unjust man, and has delivered me into the hands of the wicked. . . . He has taken me by my neck, he has broken me, and has set me up to be his mark. He has torn me with wound upon wound, he has rushed in upon me like a giant. My face is swollen with weeping, and my eyelids are dim. These things have I suffered without the iniquity of my hand.[95]

Also, the Wise man wrote beautifully and notably of the Passion of Christ and the counsel of the Jews:

> They have said, reasoning with themselves, . . . let us therefore lie in wait for the just [man] . . . because he is contrary to our doings, and upbraids us with transgressions of the law. . . . He boasts that he has the knowledge of God, and he calls himself the Son of God. . . . He is grievous unto us, even to behold: for his life is not like other men's. . . . We are esteemed by him as triflers . . . and he glories that he has God for his father. Let us see then if his words be true. . . . For if he be the true son of God, he will defend him, and will deliver him from the hands of his enemies. Let us examine him by outrages and tortures, that we may know his meekness and

---

94  John 19, 23–24.
95  Job 16:8–13, 15, 17, 18a. Job as a figure or type of Christ was famously handled by Pope St. Gregory the Great's masterpiece *Moralia in Job*. St. Gregory saw in Job not only a great prophet of the Incarnation and the Resurrection, but also a prophet (and sign or type) of Christ's suffering. In the preface of that work, St. Gregory states: *[B]eatus Iob, qui tanta incarnationis eius mysteria conversatione signaret . . . tantoque verius passionis illius sacramenta praediceret, quanto haec non loquendo tantummodo, set etiam patiendo prophetaret. Mor. In Iob.*, praef. 14, PL 75, 524–25. "Blessed Job, who by his conversation so greatly pointed out the mystery of his [Christ's] Incarnation . . . and more greatly predicted the mysteries of his [Christ's] Passion, and these he prophesied not so much by speaking, but rather by his suffering."

*try his patience. Let us condemn him to a most shameful death: for there shall be respect had unto him by his words.*[96]

This they thought, and in this they erred: for he blinded them for their malice.

Finally, from this and many other testimonies of sacred Scripture the blindness of the Jews is clearly shown. [These Jews] supposed Christ in his first coming to be a coming with so great majesty and glory so as to subject the whole world to himself, and that with a bodily sword to subdue all the rulers of the Jewish people, and to summon all to serve him. But this is discordant with the true understanding of the Prophets. For the holy Prophets speak of a double coming, of which the first is in humility and poverty, so that he may be judged, and die; and the second [coming] of which is in majesty and glory, since he is to judge and to reign.

Of the first coming we read in Zechariah: *Rejoice greatly, O daughter of Sion, . . . behold your king will come to you, the just and Savior: he is poor, and riding upon an ass, and upon a colt the foal of an ass.*[97] And Jeremiah says: *Why will you be a stranger in the land, and as a wayfaring man turning in to lodge? Why will you be as a wandering man, as a mighty man that cannot save?*[98]

Oh how notable and how beautiful are these words of the most blessed Jeremiah! For from this is clearly demonstrated that Christ is to be truly God and man. For that this is said of God, who through the Incarnation would come as a poor man or a stranger into the world, is evidenced from that which was discussed a short while ago: *We have sinned against you, O expectation of Israel, the Savior in time of trouble.* And immediately there is placed thereunder, *Why will you be a stranger [in the land, and as a wayfaring man turning in to lodge]?*[99] Which prophecies agreed with that which Christ testifies to in the Gospel about himself: *The birds of the air have nests and foxes have holes: but the Son of man has nowhere to lay his head.*[100] And the blessed Apostle [Paul] speaking of Christ: *For our sakes,* he said, *he being rich became poor, so that through his poverty, we might be rich.*[101]

---

96  Wis. 2:1, 12, 13, 15–21.
97  Zach. 9:9.
98  Jer. 14:8b–9a.
99  Jer. 14:7b–8a.
100  Matt. 8:20; Luke 9:58. E. N. Denis reverses the order of the foxes and birds.
101  Cf. 2 Cor. 8:9.

Let us, therefore, brothers firmly imprint the image of Jesus crucified upon our hearts, let us fasten indelibly his singular torments in our minds, so that we individually may have the strength to say with the Apostle: *With Christ I am nailed to the cross. And I live, now not I; but Christ lives in me.*[102] And again: *From henceforth let no man be troublesome to me; for I bear the marks of the Lord Jesus in my body.*[103] For there is no more efficacious memory for the overcoming of all temptations, nor is there a more advantageous way to acquire all virtues, than continually to contemplate, with great affection to think, and diligently to attend to Christ suspended on the Cross. For how is he who does not cease to recall the most bitter punishments suffered by Christ for him able to take delight in anything carnal? And how can he not love God or how can he be ungrateful to Christ who considers that God did not spare his only Son[104] and moreover that the Son obeyed even unto death, [105] and did so for him?

# ARTICLE LI

## CONTINUATION OF THE EXPOSITION
## OF THIS TWENTY-FIRST PSALM

21{22}[20] *But you, O Lord, remove not your help to a distance from me; look towards my defense.*

> *Tu autem, Domine, ne elongaveris auxilium tuum a me; ad defensionem meam conspice.*

21{22}[21] *Deliver, O God, my soul from the sword: my only one from the hand of the dog.*

> *Erue a framea, Deus, animam meam, et de manu canis unicam meam.*

21{22}[22] *Save me from the lion's mouth; and my lowness from the horns of the unicorns.*

> *Salva me ex ore leonis, et a cornibus unicornium humilitatem meam.*

FTER CHRIST BROUGHT TO MIND THAT which he suffered, praying for the glory of the Resurrection, and prescribing for us a form of prayer, he adds:   21{22}[20] *Tu autem,*

---

102  Gal. 2:19b–20a.
103  Gal. 6:17.
104  *Cf.* Rom. 8:32.
105  *Cf.* Phil. 2:8.

*Domine;* but you, O Lord, eternal Father, *ne elongaveris, remove not to a distance from me,* that is, do not delay long, *auxilium tuum a me, your help from me,* but immediately, namely on the third day, raise me up again; *ad defensionem meam conspice, look towards my defense,* that is, look towards me to defend me, not that I do not die, but that I am not detained in death, and that my enemies do not long deride me after death, saying: Behold the manner that seducer rose from the dead.[106]   **21{22}[21]** *Erue a framea, deliver from the sword,* that is, from death or a sword, that is, from all injury, *animam meam, my soul:* not that the essence of the soul in itself can be wounded or can die, indeed I know and believe it to be immaterial and perpetual; but that it remain not long separated from its body; *et de manu canis, and from the hand of the dog,* that is, from the power of the furious and rabid people of the Jews that are against me in the manner of barking of a barking dog, deliver *unicam meam, my only one,* that is, my soul, loved supremely by you, which alone was not in need of a Redeemer, and which has no equal.   **21{22}[22]** *Salva me ex ore leonis, save me from the lion's mouth,* that is, from the devouring of the pride of the people who want to destroy me completely and who want to brand me eternally as a false prophet; *et cornibus unicornium, and from the horns of the unicorns,* that is, from the presumptions and the pride of the evildoers, *humilitatem meam, my lowness,* that is, me among men as a pauper, humble and abject: from these, I say, save me, exalting my humility, and humiliating the proud. And unicorn is a good word to designate the presumptuous, because the unicorn is a most haughty animal; it (so it is said) dies with indignation if it is forced to do something against its desire.

---

**21{22}[23]** *I will declare your name to my brethren: in the midst of the church will I praise you.*

*Narrabo nomen tuum fratribus meis; in medio ecclesiae laudabo te.*

**21{22}[23]** *Narrabo nomen tuum, I will declare,* Lord Father almighty, *fratribus meis, to my brethren,* namely, the holy Apostles and the other disciples. For after the Resurrection Christ frequently appeared to these, and taught them of the divinity of the Father and the Son, and the glory of the entire Trinity, in the manner that the Gospels recount.[107]

---

106  Cf. Matt. 7:63–64.
107  Matt. 28:18–20; Mark 16:12–19; Luke 24:13 *et seq.* John chps. 20, 21.

*In medio Ecclesiae, in the midst of the Church,* that is, among the faithful, *laudabo te, I will praise you* and through me also others.[108] For Christ by himself praised the Father before his Ascension, standing in the midst of his disciples; and after the sending of the Paraclete, he praised him throughout all the world by the preaching of the Apostles and the other faithful. But here the Apostle asserts that the verse foretells of Christ, where he says: *He is not ashamed to call them brethren, saying: I will declare your name to my brethren; in the midst of the church will I praise you.*[109] Whence Christ told Mary Magdalen as it is written: *But go to my brethren, and say to them: I ascend to my Father.*[110]

---

**21{22}[24]** *You that fear the Lord, praise him: all you the seed of Jacob, glorify him.*

> *Qui timetis Dominum, laudate eum; universum semen Iacob, glorificate eum.*

**21{22}[25]** *Let all the seed of Israel fear him: because he has not slighted nor despised the supplication of the poor man. Neither has he turned away his face from me: and when I cried to him he heard me.*

> *Timeat eum omne semen Israel, quoniam non sprevit, neque despexit deprecationem pauperis; nec avertit faciem suam a me: et cum clamarem ad eum exaudivit me.*

And so Christ said to the Father: *In the midst of the Church I will praise you.* But if I praise you in this manner and so praising I shall pronounce    **21{22}[24]** *Qui timetis Dominum, You that fear the Lord,* with a chaste and holy fear, *laudate eum, praise him,* ascribing to him all goods as if coming from a fountain, and doing all things to his praise and for his glory.[111] *Universum semen Iacob, all you the seed of Jacob,* that is all who truly are the children of the patriarch Jacob, whose name is interpreted to mean supplanter;[112] *glorificate eum, glorify him,* that is

---

108  E. N. A reference to the grace of Christ, the grace of union, the *gratia unionis,* and the grace of being the head of all mankind and the Church, the *gratia capitis. For there is one God, and one mediator of God and men, the man Christ Jesus.* 1 Tim. 2:5.

109  Heb. 2:11b–12 (which references Ps. 21:23).

110  John 20:17b.

111  1 Cor. 10:31: *Therefore, whether you eat or drink, or whatsoever else you do, do all to the glory of God.*

112  Gen. 25:25; 27:36. E. N. Jacob, the son of Isaac and Rebecca, is said to be a "holder of the heel" or "supplanter" because he twice deprived his twin brother Esau of the latter's birthright.

give the glory to his name, and not to yourselves, because the Apostle [Paul] also says: *only to God be honor and glory.*[113] And the Lord says through Isaiah: *I the Lord, this is my name: I will not give my glory to another.*[114]   **21{22}[25]** *Timeat eum omne semen Israel,* let all the seed of Israel fear him, that is, all the children of Jacob, who is called Israel because he saw God. Therefore, I beheld all men, namely, the pure of heart and the simple, and those reposed in love are the *seed of Israel,* that is, imitators of the life and contemplation of holy Jacob, insofar as he is called Israel. For in Genesis we read: *Esau became a skillful hunter, and a husbandman, but Jacob a plain man dwelt in tents;*[115] Therefore, *all the seed of Israel* feared God with reverential and filial fear, lest they be ungrateful of the benefits of Christ and as a consequence to the entire human race aggregately. For it continues: *quoniam non sprevit, because he has not slighted,* with inner displeasure, *neque despexit, nor despised,* with external repulsion, *deprecationem pauperis, the supplication of the poor man,* namely to me, his Son, who lived as a pauper in the world. *Nec avertit faciem suam, neither has he turned away his face,* that is, the respect of his kindness, *a me, from me; et cum clamarem ad eum, exaudivit me, and when I cried to him he heard me.* This appears contrary from that said above[116]— *My God, I shall cry by day, and you will not hear.* But because it is shown there that it is allowed to say Christ is not heard by the Father with respect to a particular issue, yet — strictly speaking — he is nevertheless heard; consequently what is now said [that I cried out I was heard] is consistent with the prior verse, and corroborates it.

---

**21{22}[26]** *With you is my praise in a great Church: I will pay my vows in the sight of them that fear him.*

> *Apud te laus mea in ecclesia magna; vota mea reddam in conspectu timentium eum.*

Thereafter Christ says to the Father:   **21{22}[26]** *Apud te laus mea in Ecclesia magna; with you is my praise in a great Church:* that is, the praise that I praise, and I exhort to praise you, is with you, that is, pleases you, and is referred by you *in a great Church,* that is, in the Christian Church, which is diffused far and wide throughout the terrestrial globe: for God the Father and his Son are praised by all Catholic peoples. For which

---

113  1 Tim. 1:17b.
114  Is. 42:8a.
115  Gen. 25:27.
116  Article L (Psalm 21:3).

reason, the Lord says: *For from the rising of the sun even to the going down, my name is great among the Gentiles.*[117] And again: *Sing you to the Lord a new song, his praise is from the ends of the earth.*[118] *Vota mea, my vows,* that is, the Sacrifice of the New Law, namely the Sacrifice of my Body and Blood, *reddam, I will pay,* that is, I will cause to be offered through my priests to the Lord, *in conspectus timentium, in the sight of them that fear him,* that is, [in the sight of] the present and foreseen Christian peoples. And also Christ accomplished his vows, that is, his desires, to God the Father *in the sight of them that fear him,* when after the Supper and at the approach of his Passion he prayed, and praying he expressed his desires: for the glorification of the Father, his own glorification, and the salvation of all the disciples and of the elect. Whence it says in John: *Father, the hour is come, glorify your Son, that your Son may glorify you.*[119] And again: *Holy Father, keep them in your name whom you have given me.*[120]

---

**21{22}[27]** *The poor shall eat and shall be filled: and they shall praise the Lord that seek him: their hearts shall live for ever and ever.*

*Edent pauperes, et saturabuntur; et laudabunt Dominum qui requirunt eum; vivent corda eorum in saeculum saeculi.*

**21{22}[27]** *Edent pauperes, the poor shall eat,* that is, the humble will eat the Sacrament of the Altar, not only sacramentally, but also spiritually; consequently *et saturabuntur, and they shall be filled,* that is, they will be mentally fattened with charity, grace, consolations, and the gifts of the Holy Spirit; *et laudabunt Dominum, and they shall praise the Lord* Jesus Christ, who in the Sacrament is both the giver and the gift, *qui requirunt eum, to they that seek him,* with affection, faith, and deeds, following his footsteps; *vivent corda eorum, their hearts shall live,* the spiritual life, *in saeculum saeculi, for ever and ever,* that is, without end. For now they live by faith and charity; and, at the consummation of the course of the present exile, they will live by contemplation and glory. For they will live because they will worthily receive the fountain of life, namely Christ, as he himself testified: *I am the living bread which came down from heaven. If any man eat of this bread, he shall live forever.*[121]

---

117 Mal. 1:11a.
118 Is. 42:10a.
119 John 1:1b.
120 John 1:11b.
121 John 6:51–52a.

**21{22}[28]** *All the ends of the earth shall remember, and shall be converted to the Lord: And all the kindreds of the Gentiles shall adore in his sight.*

*Reminiscentur et convertentur ad Dominum universi fines terrae; et adorabunt in conspectu eius universae familiae gentium.*

**21{22}[29]** *For the kingdom is the Lord's; and he shall have dominion over the nations.*

*Quoniam Domini est regnum, et ipse dominabitur gentium.*

Moreover, holy David foreannounces the conversion of the whole world to Christ, saying:   **21{22}[28]** *Reminiscentur, they shall remember,* that is, they shall recall all of their sins and all of the divine benefits which they had not thought about, *et convertentur ad Dominum, and shall be converted to the Lord* the Savior by *universi fines terrae, all the ends of the earth,* hearing the preaching of the truth of the Gospel. See here how the conversion of the Gentiles is most openly announced. This also Daniel predicted under these words: *Lo, one like the Son of Man came with the clouds of heaven, and he came even to the Ancient of Days. . . . And he gave him power, and glory, and a kingdom: and all peoples, tribes and tongues shall serve him.*[122] And Isaiah said: *The Lord has prepared his holy arm in the sight of all the Gentiles: and all the ends of the earth shall see the salvation of our God.*[123]   **21{22}[29]** *Quoniam Domini, For the Lord's* the Savior's *est regnum, is the kingdom,* of which there shall be no end.[124] For this is the kingdom of the Church militant and triumphant, just as Jeremiah predicted: *A king shall reign, and he shall be wise.*[125] *Et ipse, and he* the Lord *dominabitur gentium, shall have dominion* of all the nations being obedient by faith. Whence in Zachariah we have the following said about Christ: *He shall speak peace to the Gentiles, and his power shall be from sea to sea, and from the rivers even to the end of the earth.*[126]

---

**21{22}[30]** *All the fat ones of the earth have eaten and have adored: all they that go down to the earth shall fall before him.*

*Manducaverunt et adoraverunt omnes pingues terrae; in conspectu eius cadent omnes qui descendunt in terram.*

---

122  Dan. 7:13–14a.
123  Is. 52:10.
124  Luke 1:33b.
125  Jer. 23:5b.
126  Zach. 9:10b.

**21{22}[31]** *And to him my soul shall live: and my seed shall serve him.*

*Et anima mea illi vivet; et semen meum serviet ipsi.*

**21{22}[30]** *Manducaverunt, they have eaten* the Body and the Blood of Christ sacramentally and spiritually, *et adoraverunt, and have adored,* that Sacrament, namely Christ contained in the Sacrament, *omnes pingues terrae, all the fat ones of the earth,* that is, all in the grace of God and the divine virtues, of whom the Lord says through Isaiah: *Your soul shall be delighted in fatness;*[127] and in the Songs, *Eat, O friends, and drink, and be inebriated, my dearly beloved.*[128] *In conspectus eius cadent; they shall fall before him,* that is, they will devoutly worship and will humbly adore Christ, *omnes qui descendunt in terram, all they that go down to the earth,* that is, all those born and inhabiting the world, according to that which Abraham said: *And in your seed,* namely Christ, *shall all the nations of the earth be blessed.*[129] But these distributions are to be understood of the genus of each individual, and not of the individual of each genus.[130]   **21{22}[31]** *Et anima mea illi vivet, and to him my soul shall live:* that is, the whole of his life shall be consecrated to the service of God to his honor and glory; *et semen meum, my seed,* that is, they who are converted to the Lord by my example, *serviet ipsi, shall serve him.* This can [also] be said literally of David because his soul was faithful to God and many of his children were most devoted to God.

---

**21{22}[32]** *There shall be declared to the Lord a generation to come: and the heavens shall show forth his justice to a people that shall be born, which the Lord has made.*

*Annuntiabitur Domino generatio ventura; et annuntiabunt caeli iustitiam eius, populo qui nascetur, quem fecit Dominus.*

**21{22}[32]** *Annuntiabitur Domino generatio ventura, there shall be declared to the Lord a generation to come,* that is, the Christian people said to belong to Christ and by the pronouncement of preachers converted to

---

127  Is. 55:2b.
128  Songs 5:1b.
129  Gen. 22:18a.
130  E. N. For the distinction between a distribution of the genus of each individual (*distributio de generibus singulorum*) and a distribution of the individual of each genus (*distributio de singulis generum*), see footnote 21-54. Denis's point here is that when Gen. 22:18 says "all nations of the earth shall be blessed" it is to be understood as meaning at least some of every nation on earth shall be blessed, but not all of every nation.

Christ; *et annuntiabunt caeli iusitiam eius, and the heavens shall show forth his justice*, that is, the Apostles and others living on earth in heavenly conformity, preached the evangelical law, *populo qui nascetur, to a people that shall be born*, that is, the people believing in Christ, *quem fecit Dominus, which the Lord has made*, that is, which are reborn by water and the Holy Spirit.[131] This connection is seen as marvelous, for the verb of future time, namely, *shall be born (nascetur)*, is joined to a verb of past time, namely *has made (fecit)*. For the holy Prophet [David] saw the future as temporal succession, he saw as already done according to eternal predestination; and so he knew the future in a most certain way and as if it had already occurred.

# ARTICLE LII

## MORAL EXPOSITION OF THIS TWENTY-FIRST PSALM

**21{22}[2]**  *O God my God, look upon me: why have you forsaken me? Far from my salvation are the words of my sins.*

*Deus, Deus meus, respice in me: quare me dereliquisti? Longe a salute mea verba delictorum meorum.*

ULTIMATELY, THE HOLY CHURCH, OR ANY member of the faithful, conforming to its Head, and cruciformly following the footsteps of Christ, and gravely troubled with diverse tribulations can cry out with Christ to the Lord:   21{22}[2] *Deus, Deus meus; O God, my God*, that is, O my Creator, whom alone I love, to whom I commit myself completely, in whom I most fully hope, *respice me, look upon me* miserable and afflicted, not with the eyes of vengeful justice, but with the eyes of your paternal love, of your infinite kindness, of your most bountiful goodness. *Quare me dereliquisti, why have you forsaken me* to fall in this manner, to be tempted so strongly, to be afflicted so dreadfully, to be vexed with such aridity and desolation of mind, so that it appears to be *longe a salute mea, far from my salvation*, that is, from an interior union with you, my God and Lord? But yet I say this not as supposing that it arises without a rational cause or without being permitted by you. Whence, I weigh carefully the cause of this my dereliction to be my sins: in the manner that we read in Isaiah: *Behold the hand of the Lord is not shortened that it cannot save, neither is his ear*

131  John 3:5.

*heavy that it cannot hear. But your iniquities have divided between you and your God.*[132] Whence Jeremiah says: *We have done wickedly, and provoked you to wrath: therefore you are inexorable.*[133] Consequently, the believer is told the designated cause of his dereliction: *Verba delictorum meorum, the words of my sins,* that is, the insolence or clamor of my vices, this is what expels [God]: as also it is elsewhere written: *Is it a great matter that God should comfort you? But* your sins *hinder this.*[134]

---

**21{22}[3]**    *O my God, I shall cry by day, and you will not hear: and by night, and it shall not be reputed as folly in me.*

*Deus meus, clamabo per diem, et non exaudies; et nocte, et non ad insipientiam mihi.*

**21{22}[3]** *Deus meus, clamabo; O my God, I shall cry* with heart and mouth *per diem, by day,* that is every day — indeed, unceasingly — as the Apostle [Paul] says: *Pray without ceasing;*[135] *et non exaudies, and you will not hear* my wishes or according to my desires, according to that which James says, *You ask, and receive not; because you ask amiss.*[136] For that which is not asked in the name of the Savior, that is, that which is not favorable to true beatitude, is evil to ask for. And *I shall cry* to you in the manner of a sick man, who because of the pain of his malady he often asks that he be cured, but what he asks for is opposed [to the cure]; but you, O Lord, in the manner of a most kind and most expert physician do not hear [my errant prayers] because you love me. Therefore, you do not hear that for which I ask because it is not profitable to my soul; but if I persistently knock,[137] you hear [prayers that are profitable] to salvation; for you will give to me that which you know to be beneficial to the beatitude of my soul. In like manner the most indulgent father denies to the foolish son that which he asks for, and gives to him that which he does not ask for or even that which he does not want. *Et nocte, et non ad insipientiam mihi; and by night, and it shall not be reputed as folly in me,* that is, by night I cry out to you, you who will not hear; but

---

132  Is. 59:1–2a. The rest of 59:2 reads: *and your sins have hid his face from you that he should not hear.*
133  Lam. 3:42.
134  Job. 15:11. The Sixto-Clementine Vulgate has *sed verba tua prava hoc prohibent,* but your wicked words hinder this. But in this context the meaning is the same.
135  1 Thess. 5:17.
136  James 4:3.
137  Luke 11:5–13.

my crying out will not be reputed as folly in me, so long as my intention is good. For we are not always able to know that which is good for us.[138]

In this place we are instructed, therefore, that we not abandon our duties, that we not pusillanimously quit praying when we are not heard according to our desires; but we should ascribe the delay and the fact that we are not heard due to our sins and sometimes due also [from the fact] that it is useful to us or is according to the divine disposition; and let us believe most firmly in the words of Christ, of the Prophets, and of the Apostles, because whatever we ask from God, if we ask as it ought to be asked for, namely, perseveringly, salubriously, and for ourselves, then without any uncertainty we will receive from God that which we pray for. For Christ, who is not able to lie, says: *Everyone who asks, receives: and he that seeks, finds: and to him that knocks, it shall be opened.*[139]

---

**21{22}[4]** *But you dwell in the holy place, the praise of Israel.*

*Tu autem in sancto habitas, laus Israel.*

And so, O Lord, *you will not hear,* but *it shall not be reputed as folly in me,* because of that which follows: **21{22}[4]** *Tu autem in sancto habitas,* but *you dwell in the holy place,* that is, in those who obey your precepts, who with the Prophet [David] are able to say: *Preserve my soul, for I am holy.*[140] Because it is written: *For thus says the High and the Eminent that inhabits eternity: and his name is Holy, who dwells in the high and holy place, and with a contrite and humble spirit, to revive the spirit of the humble, and to revive the heart of the contrite.*[141] *Tu,* you therefore *in sancto,* in the holy place, that is in the pure heart, *habitas,* dwell by charity, faith, and grace, *laus Israel, the praise of Israel,* that is, he whom every Israelite or the contemplative man praises, who has overthrown vices, he whose *conversation* — like the Apostle — is in heaven,[142] *beholding the glory of the Lord with open face.*[143]

---

138  E. N. "Lord, I know not what I should ask of you.... O Father! Give your child that for which he does not know how to ask.... Behold my needs which I do not know.... Teach me to pray; pray you yourself in me." *Seigneur, je ne sais ce que je dois vous demander.... Ô Père! donnez à votre enfant ce qu'il ne sait pas lui même demander.... Voyez mes besoins que je ne connois pas.... Apprenez-moi à prier; priez vous même en moi.* François de Salignac de la Mothe Fénelon, Méditation XVIII, Oeuvres, Vol. 7, 546.

139  Matt. 7:8; Luke 11:10.

140  Ps. 85:2a.

141  Is. 57:15.

142  Phil. 3:20a.

143  2 Cor. 3:18a.

**21{22}[5]** *In you have our fathers hoped: they have hoped, and you have delivered them.*

> *In te speraverunt patres nostri; speraverunt, et liberasti eos.*

**21{22}[6]** *They cried to you, and they were saved: they trusted in you, and were not confounded.*

> *Ad te clamaverunt, et salvi facti sunt; in te speraverunt, et non sunt confusi.*

**21{22}[5]** *In te speraverunt patres nostri, in you have our fathers hoped,* the holy Apostles, martyrs, anchorites, hermits, and all adult Christian men; *speraverunt, et liberasti eos; they have hoped, and you have delivered them,* from the present misery and from eternal damnation, and from anything contrary to the salvation of souls.    **21{22}[6]** *Ad te clamaverunt, they have cried to you* with certain, persevering, and unshaken trust, as if saying along with Job: *Although he should kill me, I will trust in him.*[144] And so *salvi facti sunt, and they were saved,* as much as have attained eternal happiness. *In te speraverunt, et non sunt confusi; they trusted in you, and were not confounded:* this in the manner that is read in Ecclesiasticus: *My children behold the generations of men: and know you that no one has hoped in the Lord, and has been confounded. . . . Or who has called upon him, and he despised him?*[145]

---

**21{22}[7]** *But I am a worm, and no man: the reproach of men, and the outcast of the people.*

> *Ego autem sum vermis, et non homo; opprobrium hominum, et abiectio plebis.*

**21{22}[8]** *All they that saw me have laughed me to scorn: they have spoken with the lips, and wagged the head.*

> *Omnes videntes me deriserunt me; locuti sunt labiis, et moverunt caput.*

**21{22}[9]** *He hoped in the Lord, let him deliver him: let him save him, seeing he delights in him.*

> *Speravit in Domino, eripiat eum: salvum faciat eum, quoniam vult eum.*

**21{22}[7]** *Ego autem sum vermis, et non homo; but I am a worm, and*

---

144  Job 13:15a.
145  Ecclus. 2:11–12.

*no man.* This anyone is able to say either due to the evil of punishment (*mala poena*), or due to the evil of fault (*mala culpae*).[146] Whence, he who is suffering from various punishments of body or soul, in order to summon the mercy of the Lord can cry out to him: *I am a worm* because he is trampled upon by punishments and the suffering *and no man*, that is, not similar to other men, but more miserable than them.[147] Consequently I am *opprobrium hominum et abiecto plebis, the reproach of men, and the outcast of the people.* For all despise, revile, and desert me. And so it continues: **21{22}[8]** *Omnes videntes me, deriserunt me; locuti sunt labiis; all they that saw me have laughed at me to scorn: they have spoken with the lips* against me, *et moverunt caput, and wagged the head,* deriding and mocking me. And so deriding me they say: **21{22} [9]** *Speravit in Domino, eripiat eum; he hoped in the Lord, let him deliver him.* Carnal men say this when they see the just being afflicted, not understanding that God in the present life purifies (*expurgat*) his elect, so that, to the extent they have atoned [for the temporal punishments due their sin], he receives them immediately after death.[148] Here indeed is read: *The just stand with great constancy against those that have afflicted them.*[149] And with respect to the ungodly, it adds: *These seeing it, shall be troubled with terrible fear . . . saying . . . These are they whom we had some time in derision, and for a parable of reproach. We fools esteemed their life madness, and their end without honor.*[150] Whence also Christ said to his disciples: *And you shall be hated by all men for my name's sake.*[151]

---

146 Denis here distinguishes between the evil of punishment or evil of penalty (*mala poenae*) and the evil of fault (*mala culpae*), a very important distinction often overlooked or not understood by Catholics. These may be viewed, respectively, as natural, physical, or temporal evil, on the one hand, and moral evil, on the other hand. It is a distinction central to understanding the Catholic doctrines of justification, indulgences, and Purgatory. In the wake of every sin, there is the evil of fault and the evil of punishment associated with that evil of fault. Because of this distinction, we can be forgiven for the evil of fault (*i.e.*, the sin) without being forgiven of the temporal punishment associated with that sin (though we can also be forgiven of that, or obtain indulgence for that, or make atonement for that by suffering or doing good works in a state of grace in this life, and by passive suffering in Purgatory).

147 E. N. This sentiment is quite Pauline: *A faithful saying, and worthy of all acceptation, that Christ Jesus came into this world to save sinners, of whom I am the chief.* 1 Tim. 1:15.

148 E. N. So that they avoid the need to be cleansed or purified and the need to suffer temporal punishments after death in Purgatory.

149 Wis. 5:1a.

150 Wis. 5:2–4.

151 Matt. 10:22a.

Finally that which is said — *but I am a worm* — can be explained as referring to a man because of the evil of fault (*mala culpae*), so [it may be read] in this sense: *But I am a worm and no man*, that is, I have lived so irrationally, I am subject to so many sins, and I am oppressed by so much fault, that I am not worthy to be called a man, but rather a worm.[152] *All they that saw me*, that is, the devils, *have laughed at me to scorn*. For the devils will laugh at us at the time when we are seduced by them, when we depart from the way of God, and when we consent to their suggestions. So also those with worldly minds laugh at me, as also Job said, *The just man is laughed to scorn*.[153]

---

**21{22}[10]** *For you are he that has drawn me out of the womb: my hope from the breasts of my mother.*

*Quoniam tu es qui extraxisti me de ventre, spes mea ab uberibus matris meae.*

**21{22}[10]** *Quoniam tu*, for you, O Lord, *es qui extraxisti me de ventre, are he who has drawn me out of the womb*, that is, reborn in Christ by sacred Baptism, you have led me by your ministers. For the Church is our Mother whose womb we might say is sacred Baptism by which we are spiritually regenerated.[154] By this, God draws out the baptized, because he draws those out adorned with grace and with [theological and infused] virtues. And you, O Lord, are *spes mea*, my hope, that is,

---

152  E. N. With all our emphasis on human dignity, we have forgotten the difference between what J. Brian Benestad in his book *Church, State, and Society: An Introduction to Catholic Social Doctrine* (Washington, DC: Catholic University of America, 2011) calls "ontological dignity," which all men share, and "developmental dignity," which can be increased with virtuous act (which make us "more human") and decreased by virtuous act (which make us "less human"). It is this developmental dignity, for example, which is behind Pope Pius XII's statement regarding the death penalty: "When it is a question of the execution of a condemned man, the State does not dispose of the individual's right to life. In this case it is reserved to the public power to deprive the condemned person of the enjoyment of life in expiation of his crime *when, by his crime, he has already disposed himself of his right to live*." Pius XII, *Address to the participants in the First International Congress on Histopathology of the Nervous System*, September 14, 1952, 33. It is this developmental dignity that Denis is referring to. By sin we "undignify" ourselves.

153  Job. 12:4b.

154  E. N. The word regenerated is derived from the Latin *re-generare*, to be created again, or to be born again. *If then any be in Christ a new creature, the old things are passed away, behold all things are made new.* 2 Cor. 5:17. *Wonder not, that I said to you, you must be born again.* John 3:7.

the object, cause, and end of my hope, *ab uberibus matris meae, from the breasts of my mother*, that is from the breasts of our holy Mother Church. For the breasts of the Church are wisdom and charity. Therefore the faithful man says to God: *My hope from the breasts of my mother*, that is, I had trust in you from that time that I was molded by the Church with the instruction of saving wisdom, and have viscerally experienced your charity around me. This corresponds to them who may have kept unstained the clothes of the innocence received in Baptism. The Song of Songs writes about these breasts: *Your breasts are better than wine, smelling sweet of the best ointments.*[155] And elsewhere: *Rejoice for joy with her, all you that mourn for her, that you may suck, and be filled with the breasts of her consolations.*[156] Finally, the most excellent arch-apostle [Peter] in his first epistle exhorts us to suck from these breasts, saying: *As newborn babes, desire the rational milk without guile, that thereby you may grow unto salvation.*[157]

---

**21{22}[11]** *I was cast upon you from the womb. From my mother's womb you are my God.*

> *In te proiectus sum ex utero; de ventre matris meae Deus meus es tu.*

This just man, therefore, whose hope is God from the breasts of his mother, is able to say that which follows:　**21{22}[11]** *In te proiectus sum ex utero; I was cast upon you from the womb*, that is, from the fountain of Baptism I have been joined to you by faith, hope, and charity. For in Baptism not only are we rid of sin, but we are also infused with grace, the virtues, and the divine gifts. *De ventre matris meae, from my mother's womb* I have already spoken about, namely, from that Baptism of the Church, *Deus meus es tu, you are my God*, by worship, because during that time with faith and works I have worshipped only you as God.

When, O sinner,[158] you say or hear these things, groan with compunction of your heart that you have lost the clothes of your innocence, that you have again returned to the vomit,[159] that you are unable to

---

155　Songs 1:1b, 2a.
156　Is. 66:10b–11a.
157　1 Pet. 2:2.
158　E. N. A "sinner" in the sense of one who has lost sanctifying grace, one in mortal sin.
159　Cf. 2 Pet. 2:22a: *For, that of the true proverb has happened to them: The dog is returned to his vomit.*

say these words about yourself; and busy yourself so as to recuperate the lost grace, and take care that you do not lose that which you have recuperated, but that you may make progress incessantly in it.

---

21{22}[12] *Depart not from me. For tribulation is very near: for there is none to help me.*

> *Ne discesseris a me, quoniam tribulatio proxima est, quoniam non est qui adiuvet.*

21{22}[13] *Many calves have surrounded me: fat bulls have besieged me.*

> *Circumdederunt me vituli multi; tauri pingues obsederunt me.*

21{22}[14] *They have opened their mouths against me, as a lion ravening and roaring.*

> *Aperuerunt super me os suum, sicut leo rapiens et rugiens.*

21{22}[12] *Ne discesseris a me, depart not from me,* removing grace, or not hearing me; *quoniam tribulatio, for tribulation,* that is, the manifold temptation of the world, the flesh, and the devil, *proxima est, is very near* to me, who in the midst of dangers I hesitate and vacillate. And so *depart not from me, quoniam non est qui adiuvet, for there is none to help me,* that is, [there is none that] is able to help me, except for you. For if someone else were to help me, this is still done through your strength, as is attested: *I am the Lord, and there is no other; a just God and a savior there is none besides me.*[160]    21{22}[13] *Circumdederunt me vituli multi; many calves have surrounded me,* that is lustful, petulant, unstable men who put pressure upon me to incline to vices, and with which they are soiled; *tauri pingues, fat bulls,* that is, the proud filled with vices, *obsederunt me, have besieged me,* to the degree they with either smooth talk or flattery turn me away from your service.    21{22}[14] *Aperuerunt super me os suum, they have opened their mouths,* calumniating and persecuting me, *sicut leo rapiens et rugiens, like a lion ravening and roaring,* because they are conniving to rob my soul of its spiritual life.

---

21{22}[15] *I am poured out like water; and all my bones are scattered. My heart is become like wax melting in the midst of my bowels.*

> *Sicut aqua effusus sum; et dispersa sunt omnia ossa mea. Factum est cor meum tamquam cera liquescens in medio ventris mei.*

---

160  Is. 45:18b, 21b.

**21{22}[16]** *My strength is dried up like a potsherd, and my tongue has cleaved to my jaws: and you have brought me down into the dust of death.*

> *Aruit tamquam testa virtus mea, et lingua mea adhaesit faucibus meis, et in pulverem mortis deduxisti me.*

**21{22}[15]** *Sicut aqua effusus sum, I am poured out like water,* that is, I am wearied of spirit, and exhausted of strength and vanquished, I have lost virtues and grace, and by this *I am poured out,* that is, with an emptied soul; *et dispersa sunt omnia ossa mea, and all my bones are scattered,* that is, the virtues of my sick soul are weakened because of the continually arising adversities. But these words can plainly be understood as applying to the holy martyrs, who have shed their blood for Christ and are tortured in body. *Factum est cor meum tanquam cera liquescens, my heart is become like wax melting in the midst of my bowels,* that is, before the desire of future good my heart is weakening in you, and before the fear and the pain of various evils, it is softening as if wax, *in medio ventris mei, in the midst of my bowels,*[161] that is, [in the midst] of my body.   **21{22}[16]** *Aruit tanquam testa virtus mea, my strength is dried up like a potsherd,* that is, the fortitude of my soul is shattering into pieces, and it is failing as with tedium or sloth (*acedia*), when it sees your graces and the internal consolations that you are withdrawing or suspending from me; *et lingua mea adhaesit faucibus meis, and my tongue has cleaved to my jaws,* because on account of sterility of soul and the lack of grace I do not have in [my] mouth a word of consolation or information, so that I might be able to do something else profitable. For when the Holy Spirit is not acting inwardly, the tongue of the mouth immediately fails. For which reason the Lord says through Ezechiel: *I will make thy tongue stick fast to the roof of your mouth, and you shall be dumb, and not as a man that reproves.*[162] Against which it is said through Isaiah: *The Lord has given me a learned tongue, that I should know how to uphold my word.*[163] Oh how great a gift this is, and above all things especially necessary! *Et in pulverem mortis deduxisti me, and you have brought me down into the dust of death,* that is, you permitted charity, which is the life of the soul, to be extinguished or be reduced in me, as demanded as a result of my fault. Also, this can be understood as applying bodily to martyrs, during the time of their suffering, on account that the pouring out of blood dries out bodily strength, as is shown by Christ.

---

161  As to "bowels," see footnote 21-86.

162  Ez. 3:26.

163  Is. 50:4a.

**21{22}[17]** *For many dogs have encompassed me: the council of the malignant has besieged me. They have dug my hands and feet.*

> Quoniam circumdederunt me canes multi; concilium malignantium obsedit me. Foderunt manus meas et pedes meos.

**21{22}[18]** *They have numbered all my bones. And they have looked and stared upon me.*

> Dinumeraverunt omnia ossa mea. Ipsi vero consideraverunt et inspexerunt me.

**21{22}[19]** *They parted my garments amongst them; and upon my vesture they cast lots.*

> Diviserunt sibi vestimenta mea, et super vestem meam miserunt sortem.

**21{22}[17]** *Quoniam circumdederunt me canes multi, for many dogs have encompassed me,* that is, detractors, angry and furious, who either by flattering or by deterring endeavor to bite my soul, that is, to divert it from meekness, humility, and tranquility, and to conform to their dog-like activities. Of which, the Apostle [Paul] says to the Philippians: *Beware of dogs, beware of evil workers, beware of the concision.*[164] *Consilium*[165]*malignantium obsedit me, the council of the malignant has besieged me,* that is, men in the sitting in the *chair of pestilence,*[166] namely, lacking in word or deed, have built a wall around me, so as to entrap me. *Foderunt manus meas et pedes meos, they have dug my hands and feet,* that is, that have wounded, they have corrupted, they have impeded my deeds and the paths of my soul. For frequently the perverse impede the good from some of their good works, and then their hands and feet are as if pierced, bound, and rendered immobile.    **21{22}[18]** *Dinumeraverunt omnia ossa mea, they have numbered all my bones,* that is, they have closely inspected all my more virtuous and steadfast works, not so that they might imitate them, but so that they might interpret them evilly or so that they might scrutinize them as an occasion for calumny.

*Ipsi vero, and they,* the evil men just mentioned, *consideraverunt, have looked* with their mind, *et inspexerunt, and stared* with bodily eyes *me, upon me* out of envy so as to harm me.    **21{22}[19]** *Diviserunt sibi vestimenta*

---

164  Phil. 3:2. E. N. Concision (*concisionem*) is a translation of the Greek κατατομήν (*katatomēn*) which has been translated as "mutilators of the flesh," or "false circumcision."

165  Others [reading] *Concilium*.

166  Ps. 1:1b.

*mea, they have parted my garments among them*, that is, they have taken external goods from me, or the virtues of soul, with which it is spiritually adorned, they have corrupted in me to the extent they were able; *et super vestem meam, and upon my vesture*, that is, upon the charity which is the wedding garment of those chosen to eat at the eternal banquet,[167] *miserunt sortem, they cast lots*, taking counsel among themselves, which of them might be so wily, that he might be able to kill the charity in me, and by this to be utterly lost. For often, worldly men, when they see someone strongly adhering to God, or someone leaving all behind and entering into a monastery, they diligently seek after a subtle seducer and wolf covered in sheep's clothing[168] so that he might tear off the clothing of conversion, that is, so that he might kill the fervor of charity in him, and [with such charity then] cooled, he might be led back to his former way of life.

---

**21{22}[20]** *But you, O Lord, remove not your help to a distance from me; look towards my defense.*

> *Tu autem, Domine, ne elongaveris auxilium tuum a me; ad defensionem meam conspice.*

**21{22}[21]** *Deliver, O God, my soul from the sword: my only one from the hand of the dog.*

> *Erue a framea, Deus, animam meam, et de manu canis unicam meam.*

**21{22}[22]** *Save me from the lion's mouth; and my lowness from the horns of the unicorns.*

> *Salva me ex ore leonis, et a cornibus unicornium humilitatem meam.*

**21{22}[20]** *Tu autem, Domine, ne elongaveris auxilium tuum a me; but you, O Lord, remove not your help to a distance from me*, when placed in so many tribulations; *ad defensionem meam conspice, look towards my defense*, that is, see which helps I am in need of, and as I am in need of them, so always come to my aid. **21{22}[21]** *Erue a framea, deliver from the sword*, that is, from mortal sin, which is the sword and the death of the rational creatures, *animam meam, my soul* pardoning my punishment and fault; *et de manu canis, and from the hand of the dog*, that is, from their power and from their harm of those we have spoken of, deliver *unicam meam, by only one*, that is, my soul of which there is

---

167   Cf. Matt. 22:11.
168   Cf. Matt. 7:15.

but one in me, which is contrary to those who place many substantial forms in one individual.[169] Or [we might understand it this way], *my only one*, that is, my soul, which alone before all other created things I am obliged to keep, to save, and to love. *For what does it profit a man, if he gain the whole world, and suffer the loss of his own soul?*[170]    **21{22}** [22] *Salva me ex ore leonis, save me from the lion's mouth*, that is, from the devouring of the devil, who goes about as *a roaring lion . . . seeking whom he may devour.*[171] Of whom it is written: *Behold, he will drink up a river*, that is, worldly souls, *and not wonder: and he trusts that the Jordan*, that is, religious souls, *may run into his mouth.*[172] *Et, and* save *a cornibus unicornium, from the horns of the unicorns*, that is, from the ruin and the ostentation of the proud, *humilitatem mea, my lowness*, that is, my poverty and my worthlessness, seeing myself as vile and as a pauper. Indeed, the humble man desires not to be called humble, but vile. Whence, while a pious man may call himself humble, he does not intend to ascribe to himself the virtue of humility, but he desires all to know of his vileness and abjection, in the manner that David says: *But I am a poor man, and of small ability.*[173] And elsewhere: *I will both play and make myself meaner than I have done: and I will be little* (that is, vile) *in my own eyes.*[174]

---

**21{22}[23]** *I will declare your name to my brethren: in the midst of the church will I praise you.*

*Narrabo nomen tuum fratribus meis; in medio ecclesiae laudabo te.*

**21{22}[23]** *Narrabo, I will declare* O Lord, *nomen tuum fratribus meis, your name to my brethren*, that is, I will declare to others your praise; *in medio Ecclesiae, in the midst of the Church*, that is among the faithful, *laudabo te, I will praise you*, not ashamed of your name before men, but

---

169  The human soul is the substantial form of the human body. However, some, including Plato, claimed that there were multiple souls in man, such as a sensitive soul and a nutritive soul, in addition to his intellectual soul. Denis rejects this notion as did St. Thomas Aquinas, maintaining that individuals can only have one substantial form, and so man has only one substantial form, his soul, which is the form of his body. See *ST*, Ia, q. 76, arts. 3, 4.

170  Luke 9:25; Matt. 16:26.

171  1 Pet. 5:8b.

172  Job 40:18.

173  1 Sam. 18:23b.

174  2 Sam. 6:22a.

in their presence I will confess you with my mind, mouth, and works.[175]
Someone declares, praises, or preaches God with their mouth, and not
their works, where they not do what they teach; and from the very fact
that they so teach in this manner, they sin mortally, because they empty,
to the extent it is in them to do so, the truth of Scripture and the
intention of the Holy Spirit (who is the principal author of Scripture).
Others, like monks, may teach merely by life and reputation, and these
do well sufficiently well, even though they do not reach out with vocal
proclamation; these others may be understood in the words of Isaiah:
*dumb dogs not able to bark.*[176] Others may teach with their mouth and
words; of whom it is said, *But they that are learned shall shine as the
brightness of the firmament: and they that instruct many to justice, as stars
for all eternity.*[177]

---

**21{22}[26]** *With you is my praise in a great Church: I will pay my vows
in the sight of them that fear him.*

> *Apud te laus mea in ecclesia magna; vota mea reddam in
> conspectu timentium eum.*

**21{22}[27]** *The poor shall eat and shall be filled: and they shall praise the
Lord that seek him: their hearts shall live for ever and ever.*

> *Edent pauperes, et saturabuntur; et laudabunt Dominum qui
> requirunt eum; vivent corda eorum in saeculum saeculi.*

**21{22}[26]**[178] *Apud te,* with you, Lord God, *laus mea in Ecclesia magna,*
is my praise in a great Church, that is, the praise which I bestow to you
in the Christian Church, is *with you,* that is, in your presence, you who
see all things, and is pleasing to you. *Vota mea,* my vows, that is desires
and prayers and sacrifices, *reddam,* I will pay, that is, I will offer to the
divine Majesty, *in conspectus timentium eum, in the sight of them that fear
him,* publicly doing good and sacrificing to God in the manner that the
Savior admonishes in the Gospel: *So let your light shine before men, that
they may see your good works, and glorify your Father who is in heaven.*[179]
Now let it be understood of these goods, to which we are obligated by

---

175  Luke 12:8, 9: *And I say to you, Whosoever shall confess me before men, him shall
the Son of man also confess before the angels of God. But he that shall deny me
before men, shall be denied before the angels of God.*
176  Is. 56:10a. "Dumb" in the sense of lacking the faculty of speech.
177  Dan. 12:3.
178  Denis skips verses 24 and 25 without comment.
179  Matt. 5:16.

debt,[180] that they ought not contain marks of idiosyncrasy or simulation.    **21{22}[27]** *Edent pauperes, the poor shall eat*, that is, they will be spiritually fed by the Lord, in the manner that is written: *With the bread of life and understanding, he shall feed him;*[181] *et saturabuntur, and shall be filled*, with divine piety and eternal consolations in the presence inchoatively, and in the future completely. The rest [of this Psalm] is satisfactorily elucidated from what has been written before.

# PRAYER

GOD, ALMIGHTY FATHER, WHO SENT your Son, our Lord Jesus Christ into the world to his Passion, and willed to call back men, seduced by the taste of the forbidden tree, and driven out from the happiness of Paradise, to the heavenly Kingdom: look upon us who cry out to you, deliver us from the words of sins, and save those who hope in you in eternity.

*Deus Pater omnipotens, qui Filium tuum Dominum nostrum Iesum*
*Christum ad passionem in mundum mittere, et hominem*
*ligni vetiti gustu seductum, et a paradisi felicitate*
*eiectum, ad caelestia regna revocare voluisti:*
*respice nos ad te clamantes, libera nos*
*a verbis delictorum, et salvos*
*facias in te sperantes*
*in aeternum.*

---

180  E. N. "So you also, when you shall have done all these things that are commanded you, say: We are unprofitable servants; we have done that which we ought to do." Luke 17:10.

181  Ecclus. 15:3. I have changed the personal pronoun in the Douay-Rheims from "she" (referring in the context to Wisdom, *Sapientia*, a noun of female gender) to "he," since Denis is using the verse to refer to the Lord. In Latin the verb *cibabit* is genderless.

# Psalm 22

## ARTICLE LIII

22{23}[1]  *A Psalm for David. The Lord rules me: and I shall want nothing.*
*Psalmus David. Dominus regit me, et nihil mihi deerit.*

HE TITLE ASCRIBED TO THE PRESENT PSALM
is such:   22{23}[1] *Psalmus David, a Psalm for David*: that is, this
Psalm relates to David and he who is signified by him, namely, Christ
and the Church, and any one member of the true faithful.

Expounding upon this Psalm first as it relates to the Church and to
any one of the faithful, it says thus: *Dominus, the Lord*, who has the care
of all,[1] *regit me, rules me* in the exile of pilgrimage: *he rules me*, that is,
he directs me unto eternal beatitude, by necessity both of soul as well as
body, he will provide to me, and he will take away from me all the those
impediments to reaching it; *he rules me*, because he makes me submissive
to his law and faith, and he defends me from the dominion of the Devil
and the slavery of sin. Because he so rules me, therefore *et nihil mihi deerit,
and I shall want nothing*: in the way that it is stated in a later Psalm, *Fear
the Lord, all you his saints: for there is no want to them that fear him*:[2] not
that, strictly speaking (*simpliciter*), nothing is wanting them. Some being
perfectly blessed [in heaven] do not prefer another life. But [in this verse,
as to all men that are wayfarers, this lack of want is to be understood
thus:] nothing is wanting them of those things that are necessary for
salvation, or of those things which they request from God. Whence the
Lord says in the Gospel: *Seek you therefore first the kingdom of God, and
his justice, and all these things shall be added unto you.*[3] And also nothing
is wanting to him whom God rules by special providence: because a
future good which is not possessed in reality is possessed in hope and
by approaching disposition; indeed already he has one foot in heaven.

1  Wis. 12:13a.
2  Ps. 33:10.
3  Matt. 6:33.

415

**22{23}[2]**   *He has set me in a place of pasture. He has brought me up, on the water of refreshment.*

*In loco pascuae ibi me collocavit. Super aquam refectionis educavit me.*

And so nothing is wanting to me, but where? The verse continues, **22{23}[2]** *in loco pascuae, in a place of pasture,* that is, in the house of the Church militant, in which are the most saving sacraments, the divine Scriptures, and diverse virtues; *ibi me collocavit; he has set me there,* making me a faithful and obedient member of the Church, so that standing and persevering in ecclesiastical unity, I may be able to enjoy the mentioned pastures of the Church in which faithful souls are spiritually fattened. This, therefore, is the first benefit of the grace of God: that God put man in the unity of the Church, which in sacred Scripture frequently is called the Kingdom of God. For which reason the Apostle [Paul] says: *We give thanks to God, and the Father of our Lord Jesus Christ . . . who has translated us into the kingdom of the Son of his love.*[4] And Peter: *You may declare his virtues, who has called you out of darkness into his marvelous light.*[5]

Then is recalled the second benefit of God. *Super aquam refectionis educavit me, he has brought me up on the water of refreshment,* that is, he has nourished me with the instruction of salvation, so that I am able to discern between good and evil in virtues, and I can come by spiritual increase to perfection. The *water of refreshment* is the divine doctrine consoling to the soul, comforting and nourishing, as it stated in Ecclesiasticus: *The water of saving wisdom he will drink there.*[6] And [in St. Paul's epistle] to the Romans: *For whatever things were written, were written for our learning: that through patience and the comfort of the scriptures, we might have hope.*[7] Upon such water, therefore, a man is educated by God when, illuminated by the Holy Spirit, he understands — either as a result of his own study or, alternatively, from a teacher — those things to attend to for inner perfection. This is as the Apostle advises: *Teaching and admonishing one another in psalms, hymns, and spiritual canticles, singing in grace in your hearts* to the Lord always.[8] And Isaiah says: *You*

---

4   1 Col. 1:3b, 13b.
5   1 Pet. 2:9.
6   Ecclus. 15:3a. I have departed from the Douay Rheims which translates this as she [Wisdom] shall *give him the water of wholesome wisdom to drink.*
7   Rom. 15:4.
8   Col. 3:16; Cf. Eph. 5:19.

*shall draw waters with joy out of the Savior's fountains,*[9] that is, from the Gospels or the teachings of Christ.

———————

**22{23}[3]**  *He has converted my soul. He has led me on the paths of justice, for his own name's sake.*

*Animam meam convertit. Deduxit me super semitas iustitiae, propter nomen suum.*

Then is given the third benefit of God.  **22{23}[3]** *Animam meam convertit, he has converted my soul,* that is, through saving instruction he has lit up my soul with divine love which unites the created mind with its own Creator, which loving union is called the conversion of the mind to God. And so, he has *converted my soul* from many things to one, from disturbance to rest, from created and fleeting things to the uncreated and unchanging Good.

After this is attached a fourth benefit. *Deduxit me super semitas ius-titiae, he has led me on the paths of justice. The paths of justice* are the words of the divine teacher (*preceptor*). And so, *he has led me on the paths of justice,* that is, with his helping grace and with his leadership he makes me to serve the divine precepts, to fulfil the commandments of the love (*caritatis*) of God and neighbor: and this he brings about in me not because of my merits, but *propter nomen suum, for his own name's sake,* that is, because of his own goodness and charity to the glory of his name. [He does this] in the manner that Solomon says: *The Lord has made all things for himself.*[10] Whence through Hosea, the Lord says: *Destruction is your own, Israel,*[11] outside of you; in me only because of your grace [is there no destruction]. No one, therefore, is to rejoice in himself, no one is to glory in himself for his justice; but as the Apostle [Paul] says, *He that glories, let him glory in the Lord.*[12]

But pay attention to the most beautiful order: first, the soul is led over the refreshing waters; second, it is converted; third, it is led on the paths of justice. For the first is needed to illumine the soul so that it may know; thereafter, the knowledge of the truth to inflame to the love of the good; third, out of love to strive to rectitude in one's exterior way of life.

But we are able also to explain this especially of the people of the new law, so that it reads in this sense: *on the water of refreshment,* that

———————

9  Is. 12:3.
10  Prov. 16:4a.
11  Hos. 13:9a.
12  2 Cor. 10:17.

is in the fountain of Baptism regenerating men spiritually, reforming[13] them by grace, *he leads me*, that is, he transports my soul from an imperfect childlike state to the state of perfection. *He has led me on the paths of justice*, that is, he has given me the evangelical counsels[14] to fulfil: and in this *he leads me*, for he first fulfilled these, since I follow in his footsteps.

------

22{23}[4]   *For though I should walk in the midst of the shadow of death, I will fear no evils, for you are with me. Your rod and your staff, they have comforted me.*

*Nam, etsi ambulavero in medio umbrae mortis, non timebo mala, quoniam tu mecum es. Virga tua, et baculus tuus, ipsa me consolata sunt.*

In addition, a fifth benefit is set down, which is as it were a sign of the previous benefits.   22{23}[4] *Nam, et si ambulavero in medio umbrae mortis; for, though I should walk in the midst of the shadow of death*, that is, if I were in great dangers which are closely near death, as the gloom of darkness, *non timebo mala, I will fear no evils*, that is, I will not fear to fall into the evil of fault, nor will I fear perpetual evil of punishment,[15] because the trust of the mind and the fortitude of soul which you have given me. Whence, the verse follows: *quoniam tu mecum est, for you are with me*, namely, by grace. The Apostle [Paul] was like this: *I am sure that neither death, nor life, nor angels, [nor principalities, nor powers, nor things present, nor things to come, nor might, Nor height, nor depth,] nor any other creature, shall be able to separate us from the love of God.*[16] This is what is said by Jeremiah: *The Lord is with me as a strong warrior: therefore they that persecute me shall fall, and shall be weak.*[17] *Virga tua,*

------

13   Others [read] refresh (*refoventis*).
14   E. N. Denis, of course, has a monastic audience in mind, and so he speaks of the evangelical counsels. "The life consecrated to God is characterized by the public profession of the evangelical counsels of poverty, chastity, and obedience, in a stable state of life recognized by the Church." CCC § 944. The spirit of the evangelical counsels, however, apply to all the Christian faithful. "Christ proposes the evangelical counsels, in their great variety, to every disciple." CCC § 914.
15   E. N. When Denis refers to perpetual evil of punishment (*perpeti mala poenae*), he refers to the Hell of the damned, because the evil of punishment suffered passively in Purgatory and actively here on earth is not perpetual. For the difference between evil of punishment and evil of fault, *see* footnote 21-146.
16   Rom. 8:38–39. E. N. The matter in brackets supplant the "*etc.*" of Denis.
17   Jer. 20:11a.

*your rod*, that is, your paternal correction, *et baculus tuus, and your staff*, that is, your kindly assistance, *ipsa me consolata sunt, they have comforted me*: because by such vicissitude of your visitations[18] I have conceived trust in you, believing myself to belong to the number of your children, who in the present life you correct from faults through the *rod* of current tribulations and you support by the *staff* of pious consolations. Also such vicissitudes make me to recognize my own weakness and to experience your mercy. Let us therefore rejoice when we are shaken with adversity: because as Job said: *Blessed is the man whom the Lord corrects;*[19] and in Revelations, the Lord: *Such as I love*, he says, *I rebuke and chastise.*[20] And this is the sixth benefit of God.

---

22{23}[5]  *You have prepared a table before me against them that afflict me. You have anointed my head with oil; and my chalice which inebriates me, how goodly is it!*

*Parasti in conspectu meo mensam, adversus eos qui tribulant me; impinguasti in oleo caput meum; et calix meus inebrians quam praeclarus est!*

22{23}[6]  *And your mercy will follow me all the days of my life. And that I may dwell in the house of the Lord unto length of days.*

*Et misericordia tua subsequetur me omnibus diebus vitae meae; et ut inhabitem in domo Domini, in longitudinem dierum.*

22{23}[5] *Parasti in conspectus meo mensam, you have prepared a table before me*, that is, the Communion of the Body and Blood of Christ, *adversus eos qui tribulant me, against them that afflict me*, that is, against all temptations of the enemies of my soul. Or [we can understand it thus], *table*, that is, the divine Scriptures, in which there are as many salutary senses contained in them as there might be meal courses [on a table during dinner]. And this is the seventh benefit of God.

*Impinguasti in oleo caput meum, you have anointed my head with oil*, that is, you have filled my soul with spiritual joy: and that is the eighth benefit. *Et calix meus inebrians, and my chalice which inebriates me*, that

---

18  E. N. I have translated *visitationum tuarum* as your visitations. The word "visitation" can have the meaning (as used herein) of a temporal punishment or chastisement (the "shadow of death") visited upon us by God. It is used, then, in the sense used in Jer. 44:13. *And I will visit them that dwell in the land of Egypt, as I have visited Jerusalem by the sword, and by famine, and by pestilence.*

19  Job. 5:17a. Denis replaced "God" in the verse with "the Lord."

20  Rev. 3:19a.

is, the Blood of Christ contained in the chalice of benediction inflaming the mind with divine love and making it be as if one is drunk. [It does this] because it makes the soul heedless of lower things and thirstful for divine things. *Quam praeclarus est! How goodly is it!* That is, it is clear, holy, and noble in a manifold manner; indeed, much more than is able to be said or be believed. And finally the ninth benefit is stated.    22{23}

[6] *Et misericordia tua subsequetur me monibus diebus vitae meae, and your mercy will follow me all the days of my life,* that is, your grace, which in your goodness preceded me,[21] will remain in me; and that I never move away from you until I will arrive before you, the beatifying sovereign Good: and this is the word of good hope.

All these stated [blessings], O Lord, you have set forth before me for the sake of what follows: *Et ut inhabitem in domo Domini, and that I may dwell in the house of the Lord,* that is, so that after the delay of the present misery I may be found worthy in the kingdom of heaven, which is your house: of which is written in the Gospel: *In my Father's house there are many mansions.*[22] And this, indeed, is the end to which all gifts and all deeds of the present life should be referred to. That, I say, I might dwell in your home, not for a small time or for a finite time, but *in longitudinem dierum, unto length of days,* that is, in eternity.

# ARTICLE LIV

## ANAGOGICAL EXPOSITION OF THE SAME TWENTY-SECOND PSALM, OF CHRIST AND OF THE BLESSED OR COMPREHENSORS

22{23}[1]    *A psalm for David. The Lord rules me: and I shall want nothing. Psalmus David. Dominus regit me, et nihil mihi deerit.*

---

21   E. N. Here again is the notion of prevenient grace, *gratia tua quae me pie praevenit.* We might turn to Canon 5 of the Second Synod of Orange, which summarizes St. Augustine, the Doctor of Grace: "If anyone says that the increase as well as the beginning of faith and the very desire of faith — by which we believe in him who justifies the sinner and by which we come to the regeneration of holy baptism — proceeds from our nature and not from a gift of grace . . . reveals himself in contradiction with the apostolic doctrine." DS 375 *Enchirdion Symbolorum* (Ignatius Press: San Francisco 2012) (43rd ed.) (eds. Peter Hünermann, Robert Fastiggi and Anne Englund Nash), 135.

22   John 14:2a.

**22{23}[2]**  *He has set me in a place of pasture. He has brought me up, on the water of refreshment.*

*In loco pascuae ibi me collocavit. Super aquam refectionis educavit me.*

**22{23}[3]**  *He has converted my soul. He has led me on the paths of justice, for his own name's sake.*

*Animam meam convertit. Deduxit me super semitas iustitiae, propter nomen suum.*

**22{23}[4]**  *For though I should walk in the midst of the shadow of death, I will fear no evils, for you are with me. Your rod and your staff, they have comforted me.*

*Nam, etsi ambulavero in medio umbrae mortis, non timebo mala, quoniam tu mecum es. Virga tua, et baculus tuus, ipsa me consolata sunt.*

AYFARERS ON THE WAY TO GOD (*VIATORES*) are ruled one way, and those enjoying the beatific vision (*comprehensores*) another way. For wayfarers are ruled by this: that they direct themselves toward the beatitude or the end which is still distant from them and which they have not yet attained. Christ, therefore, as a man or as one enjoying the beatific vision (*comprehensor*) and any one of the blessed can say in heaven, recalling the goodness of God and the glory of the Creator:   22{23}[1] *Dominus regit me, the Lord rules me,* for in no manner am I in a condition to go astray, *et nihil mihi deerit, and I shall want for nothing,* because I am eternally content in God;   22{23}[2] *in loco pascuae, in a place of pasture,* that is, the supercelestial Paradise of most blessed desire, *ibi me collocavit, he has set me up,* that is, among the angelic choirs. Or [alternatively], *in a place of pasture,* that is, in an abundance of heavenly delights.

*Super aquam refectionis educavit me, he has brought me up on the water of refreshment,* that is, he fed me with the clear vision by the sight or the beatific knowledge of the divine essence. Of which vision, a later Psalm says: *you shall make them drink of the torrent of your pleasure.*[23] For this is the vision of God, the refreshment of all the blessed [in heaven], [a refreshment] containing the fullness of all joy: and with this vision the soul of Christ from the first moment of his Incarnation was most excellently full.   22{23}[3] *Animam meam convertit,* that is,

---

23  Ps. 35:9b.

inavertibly²⁴ unites [my soul] to himself, confirming it in his love, so that it is not able to desire anything inordinately. *Deduxit me super semitas iustitiae propter nomen suum, he has led me on the paths of justice, for his name's sake.* The blessed in heaven attribute to God the fact that they are saved, and they return thanks to him for their salvation, saying among themselves: *he has led me on the paths of justice* when I was still undergoing pilgrimage in the world, and he did not forsake me and allow me to fall: but *for his name's sake* he led me by a right track of life to heaven (*ad patriam*).    **22{23}[4]** *Nam et si ambulavero in medio umbrae mortis, non timebo mala, quoniam tu mecum es; for though I should walk in the midst of the shadow of death, I will fear no evil, for you are with me.* This verse is certain to apply to the blessed [in heaven], because it is not possible for them to fear the punishment of evil of fault or the evil of punishment.²⁵ For although the gift of fear remains in them, it does not arise from their acts of fleeing evil, but from their acts of revering God.²⁶

*Virga tua et baculus tuus, your rod and your staff,* with which you visited me while in a wayfaring state (*in via*),²⁷ *ipsa me consolata sunt, they have comforted me,* that is, they conducted me to this heavenly consolation. For the scourges inflicted for sins, which are signified by the word "rod," purify the soul, so that it be made able to be united with the divine light; but the divine consolation in this life mercifully infused by God to alight the soul to desire the perfect sweetness of heaven. The blessed in heaven, therefore, returning thanks to God that he so paternally corrected them, and that he so sweetly sustained them, in this life, say: *Your rod and your staff they have comforted me.* But it would seem that this is not possibly fitting for the Blessed, namely that they might be mindful in heaven of those things that they suffered while in the wayfaring state, because in Isaiah we have the following: *The former distresses are forgotten, . . . and the former things shall not be in remembrance.*²⁸ In response, the saints in heaven are mindful of the evils that they suffered while they were wayfarers, since such memory is a matter of joy; [but they are not mindful] to the extent any memory of any evil or punishment is an occasion for

---

24  L. *inavertibiliter.* For the meaning of "inavertibly," *see* footnote 1-93.

25  For the distinction between evil of fault (*mala culpae*) and evil of punishment (*mala poenae*), *see* footnote 21-146.

26  E. N. In other words, there is no fear of evil, servile or filial, but only a filial reverential fear. *See* Denis's discussion of this in Article XLV (Psalm 18:10) and footnote 18-42.

27  For "visited," *see* footnote 22-18.

28  Is. 65:16b–17a.

any sadness. For also Christ himself in his most glorious body retains marks of his five wounds, not only so that in the day of judgment he may exhibit to the ungrateful that which he suffered for them, but so that in eternity holy men in heaven may see that which he endured for their salvation, and from that they may be inestimably made aflame with love and the giving of thanks.

---

22{23}[5]   *You have prepared a table before me against them that afflict me. You have anointed my head with oil; and my chalice which inebriates me, how goodly is it!*

*Parasti in conspectu meo mensam, adversus eos qui tribulant me; impinguasti in oleo caput meum; et calix meus inebrians quam praeclarus est!*

22{23}[6]   *And your mercy will follow me all the days of my life. And that I may dwell in the house of the Lord unto length of days.*

*Et misericordia tua subsequetur me omnibus diebus vitae meae; et ut inhabitem in domo Domini, in longitudinem dierum.*

22{23}[5] *Parasti in conspectus meo mensam adversus eos qui tribulant me,* you have prepared a table before me against them that afflict me. This does not apply to the blessed [in heaven], because nothing afflicts them; but it can be explained as relating to Christ, according to that which he experienced on earth and he was passible just like any wayfarer (*viator*).[29] Therefore, Christ said to God: *You have prepared a table before me,* that is with that bread that you feed to me always, of which is written in the Gospels: *Blessed is he that shall eat bread in the kingdom of God.*[30] For that table, which is prepared for the blessed in heaven, of which the Savior says, *And I dispose to you . . . a kingdom, that you may eat and drink at my table, in my kingdom.*[31] This table, was always prepared for the soul of Christ, because he always saw God face to face (*per speciem*), as do the blessed [in heaven]. But this *table* can be understood as that happiness in the way that all sorts of delightful foods are put upon a table. Because as Boethius[32] states, Happiness is the state made

---

29  E. N. Since Jesus was both a *comprehensor* and a *viator* — a unique circumstance, *sui generis* — he is the only person with a human nature that suffered on earth while he saw God in heaven, enjoying the beatific vision.

30  Luke 14:15.

31  Luke 22:29–30a.

32  E. N. Boethius (*ca.* 477–524 A. D.) was a Roman senator, consul, Master of Offices (*magister officiorum*), and philosopher eventually exiled and executed on

perfect by the aggregation of all good.[33] So of this *table* Christ says to the Father: *Parasti in conspectu meo mensam, you have prepared a table before me,* that is, you have shown and granted me perfect happiness in my soul, *adversus eos qui tribulant me, against them that afflict me,* namely, the Jews. This indeed is a *table* inasmuch as it strengthened and rendered immobile[34] the soul of Christ so it did not fear his adversaries.

*Impinguasti in oleo caput meum, you have anointed my head with oil,* that is, with perfect sweetness and most sweet happiness you have given joy to my mind. This applies to all the blessed in heaven (*comprehensoribus*). *Et calix meum inebrians, and my chalice which inebriates me,* that is, the fountain of life drank to my satiety, or the taste of the fully refreshed fountain of eternity, *quam praeclarus est! how goodly is it!* That is, how incomparably it exceeds all sensible delights! Since no one knows or has experienced it.    22{23}[6] *Et misericordia tua subsequetur me omnibus diebus vitae meae, and your mercy will follow me all the days of my life,* that is, the light of glory, which is grace consummated, and the heavenly beatitude, which is eternal life, bestowed to me mercifully, that is, way beyond anything strictly merited (*ultra condignum*),[35] in order that I will persevere without end, so that I might be secure of my eternal beatitude. *Et ut inhabitem in domo Domini, and that I may dwell in the house of the Lord,* that is, in the empyrean heaven,[36] which is the place of blessed contemplation; *in longitudinem dierum, unto length of days,* that is, for an infinite time, or aeviternally,[37] which is the measure of time of the blessed [in heaven], as if they were infinite days all possessed at once.

See in this Psalm the deiform Prophet, in few a words, but with not a few virtues, commemorates the many and great and special benefits of God. So this Psalm teaches us to sing more cordially, more joyfully, and with greater devoutness, for such a great benefactor we are obligated to love more ardently, and diligently to consider, and greatly to esteem,

---

conspiracy charges by the Ostrogothic King Theoderic the Great. While in exile Boethius wrote his famous *The Consolation of Philosophy*. He wrote a number of philosophical books as well as some theological tractates, including a work on the blessed Trinity entitled *De Trinitate*.

33  *Felicitas est status omnium bonorum aggregatione perfectus.* Denis appears to cite to *On the Consolation of Philosophy*, III, 2. The actual quote is: *Liquet igitur esse beatitudinem statum bonorum omnium congregatione perfectum.* "It is clear, therefore, beatitude is the perfect state achieved by the union of all goods."

34  L. *immobilitavit*, rendered immobile or unfluctuating. *See* footnote 20-8.

35  E. N. On the notion of strict (condign) justice, *see* footnote 15-44.

36  On the empyrean heaven, *see* footnote 19-11.

37  E. N. For "aeviternal" *see* footnote 1-94.

and to love his most kind and most bounteous gifts. And, of course, he who attentively utters this Psalm expressing it with great eagerness is able to grow warm in the love of God.

# PRAYER

OR YOUR NAME'S SAKE, O LORD, LEAD us in the paths of justice: let your mercy follow us so that we may dwell in your home for eternity.

*Propter nomen tuum, Domine, deduc nos super semitas iustitiae:
subsequatur nos misericordia tua, ut in sempiternum
habitemus in domo tua.*

# Psalm 23

## ARTICLE LV

### EXPOSITION OF THE TWENTY-THIRD PSALM:
### *DOMINI EST TERRA, &c.*
### THE EARTH IS THE LORD'S, *&c.*

23{24}[1]  *On the first day of the week, a Psalm for David. The earth is the Lord's and the fulness thereof: the world, and all they that dwell therein.*

*Prima sabbati. Psalmus David. Domini est terra, et plenitudo eius; orbis terrarum, et universi qui habitant in eo.*

RIEFLY, THE TITLE TO THIS PSALM IS:    23{24} [1] *Prima sabbati. Psalmus David,* On the first day of the week, a Psalm for David. The first day of the week is the Lord's day, when the Lord rose again from the dead. In reverence of the Sabbath, the Jews numbered all days of the week from the Sabbath. For the day immediately following the day of the Sabbath then called the first day after the Sabbath (*primam sabbati*); the second day that followed, the second day after the Sabbath (*secundam sabbati*), and so on for the others. But the Gentiles called the days by the names of the planets, saying the Day of the Sun, the Day of the Moon, *etc.* But the Christians called days holidays (*ferias*) because one is always to take holidays from sin. And this, therefore is the sense of this title: *Psalmus David, a Psalm for David,* that is, this Psalm is written by David, for the glory of the Resurrection of Christ, which occurred *prima sabbati, on the first day of the week* very early in the morning.[1]

And so it says: *Domini, the Lord's,* to whose will all things submit, *est terra et plenitudo eius, is the earth and the fullness thereof,* that is, its elements and all that is contained in it, namely, men, those things born of the earth, and brute beasts; this is more clearly expounded in the clause that follows. *Orbis terrarum, the world,* that is, all the surrounding parts of the earth, *et universi qui habitant in eo, and all they that dwell therein.* All these are *the Lord's* as creator, governor, and conserver, in the manner that the book of Job refers to God: *What other has he appointed over the earth? Or*

---

1  Mark 16:2, 9.

*whom has he set over the world which he made?*[2] About this, the Manichaean heresy[3] and Valentinus[4] were confusedly mistaken in declaring that this inferior [world] was not created by the God of light.

---

**23{24}[2]**   *For he has founded it upon the seas; and has prepared it upon the rivers.*

> *Quia ipse super maria fundavit eum, et super flumina prae-paravit eum.*

This sign, namely that *the Lord's is the earth and the fullness thereof,* is that which follows:   **23{24}[2]** *Quia ipse, for he* the Lord *super maria, upon the seas,* that is, upon the arms of the oceanic seas which encompass and surround the earth, *fundavit, he has founded,* that is, firmly placed, *eum, it,* that is, the orb of the earth—not that the earth simply is floating above the water, because the earth is the mid-point of the universe: whence it is necessary for it itself be the mid-point of world, and, as a consequence, it is encompassed by water and in large part it is located amidst it.[5] Therefore, it is said that the earth is founded upon the sea because the divine power fashioned it so that the earth is not entirely covered by water, nor may the sea cover it by surging out over it. But part of it is above the sea; and, as to the parts of land next to the sea, it is [founded] in such a way such that animals are able to dwell upon it. Therefore, the verse continues: *et super flumina praepara-vit eum, and has prepared it upon the rivers,* that is, he made the orb of the earth, with respect to certain places, to have banks higher than the river waters, preparing it for the inhabitation of living creatures. And in

---

2  Job 34:13.

3  E. N. The Manichean heresy, founded by the Persian pseudoprophet Mani (*ca.* 216–274 A. D.), proposed conflict between the spiritual world and the material world, the former which they viewed as good, but latter evil. In trying to resolve the problem of evil, Mani resorted to an extreme dualism in cosmogony, deny-ing the omnipotence of God, and proposing two opposing powers: a good god who created the spiritual reality, and an evil god that created matter. According to the Manichaeans, this greater cosmological battle between spirit and matter, between the good god and the evil god, found a battle ground within man, in a cosmological battle writ small.

4  E. N. Valentinus (*ca.* 100–*ca.* 160 A. D.) was a Gnostic who adopted a dualistic theology, thereby placing a rift between the ideal forms in the mind of God and the lower material world.

5  E. N. The point being that the earth (in a geocentric universe) has to be the mid-point, and so the earth is not floating upon the seas (since that would make the water, and not the earth, the mid-point).

this there appears ineffable wisdom, and the omnipotent power of the Creator in the manner that the Lord speaking through Jeremiah says: *Hear, O foolish people, and without understanding.... Will not you then fear me ... I have set the sand a bound for the sea, an everlasting ordinance, which it shall not pass over: and the waves thereof shall toss themselves, and shall not prevail: they shall swell, and shall not pass over it.*[6] And blessed Job also: *Who shut up the sea with doors, when it broke forth as issuing out of the womb? I set my bounds around it, and made it bars and doors. And I said: Hitherto you shall come, and shall go no further, and here you shall break your swelling waves.*[7]

But this part of the Psalm can be better explained in a spiritual sense, so that it reads in this sense: *The Lord's is the earth*, that is, the Church militant in a pilgrim state on earth, and the bountiful fruits of the goods of the earth and image of its producing of a holy manner of life, *and the fullness thereof*, that is, all the virtues, grace, and the perfection of the faithful, which is ascribed to the Lord, as the giver who gives, and the end for which all things ought to be done. *The world*, that is, the Church itself diffused throughout the whole world, or the peoples collected from all the ends of the earth, *and all they that dwell therein*, that is, all the Christian faithful in ecclesiastical unity, firmly founded with faith and works, are the Lord Jesus Christ's, who by his own Blood acquired the same, according to the Apostle.[8] For this reason, there is added to the verse: *For he ... upon the seas*, that is, upon worldly men who seem as if they were the sea, fluctuating from vanity to vanity, and never stable in the Lord; or [another possibility], *upon the sea*, that is, upon the tribulations and the bitternesses and fluxes of the world. *He founded it*, that is, he strengthened the Church; not that the things mentioned previously are the foundation of the Church; but because Christ established the Church in opposition to the things that were mentioned, lest it be overwhelmed or utterly overcome by them;[9] and he made the Church more firm and more sublime than

---

6 Jer. 5:21-22.

7 Job 38:8, 10-11.

8 Acts 20:28: *Take heed to yourselves, and to the whole flock, wherein the Holy Ghost has placed you bishops, to rule the Church of God, which he has purchased with his own blood.* Eph. 5:25-27. *Husbands, love your wives, as Christ also loved the Church, and delivered himself up for it: That he might sanctify it, cleansing it by the laver of water in the word of life: That he might present it to himself a glorious Church, not having spot or wrinkle, or any such thing; but that it should be holy, and without blemish.*

9 E. N. This is a reference to the Church's indefectibility, which, as the First Vatican Council defined it, means that the Church possesses "an invincible stability,"

these things upon which it is asserted [in the Psalm] it is founded. For this reason, there is added: *and...upon the rivers*, that is, above the vices which are like the flow of a river, such as [for example] lust (*luxuria*) and avarice (*cupiditas*), which run in a disordered manner and without rest in delightful and useful goods, never satisfying, but always arousing. And so above these *rivers he has prepared it*, that is, the Church or the congregation of the faithful, disposing it for war against these vices, in the manner that the Apostle [Paul] says: *For though we walk in the flesh, we do not war according to the flesh. For the weapons of our warfare are not carnal, but mighty to God.*[10]

---

23{24}[3]  *Who shall ascend into the mountain of the Lord? Or who shall stand in his holy place?*

*Quis ascendet in montem Domini? Aut quis stabit in loco sancto eius?*

After the Prophet has testified that all things are the Lord's, now he inquires into and declares how such great majesty can pertain to the Lord, and he says:    23{24}[3] *Quis ascendet in montem Domini? Who shall ascend into the mountain of the Lord?* That is, who by nature shall be able to come to the summit of grace? Who from this worthless world will enter into holy religion? Who from the slavery of sin will climb so as to be obedient to Mother Church? Who from imperfection will ascend unto perfection? Who from this valley of tears will ascend to the Kingdom of Heaven? *Aut quis stabit in loco sancto eius? Or who shall stand in his holy place?* That is, who will persevere until the end in *the mountain of the Lord* just spoken of and explained? For the reprobate ascend for a while, yet none *stand* but the elect. All of these questions appear to be re-asked and all are resolved by the following response. For the Prophet [David] responds:

---

23{24}[4]  *The innocent in hands, and clean of heart, who has not taken his soul in vain, nor sworn deceitfully to his neighbor.*

*Innocens manibus et mundo corde, qui non accepit in vano animam suam, nec iuravit in dolo proximo suo.*

---

and is a "standard lifted upon among the nations," which "rests on solid ground." DS 3013, 3014.

10  2 Cor. 10:3–4a.

**23{24}[5]**  *He shall receive a blessing from the Lord, and mercy from God his Savior.*

> Hic accipiet benedictionem a Domino, et misericordiam a Deo salutari suo.

**23{24}[4]** *Innocens manibus, the innocent in hands*, that is, he who does not inflict injury upon others by his deeds, *et mundo corde, and clean of heart*, that is, cleaned from the sordidness of sins, *qui non accepti in vano animam suam, who has not taken his soul in vain*, that is, who does not neglect to fill it with that for which his soul was made and infused within the body. For the soul is created in conjunction with the body that it might be adorned with virtues, that it might strive to attain saving knowledge, that it may serve the Lord with full obedience. He, therefore, who acquires and fulfills these things has not *taken his soul in vain*. *Nec iuravit in dolo proximo suo, nor has he sworn deceitfully to his neighbor*, that is, he has not promised that which he has not fulfilled, he has not firmly affirmed that which he is unable to verify, he has not asserted under oath so that he might defraud another.   **23{24}[5]** *Hic, he*, who observes these things, *accipiet benedictionem, shall receive a blessing from the Lord*, that is, the gift of grace and the multiplication thereof, *a Domino, et misericordiam, from the Lord, and mercy*, that is, indulgence and all that which he asks for, *a Deo salutari suo, from God his Savior*, that is from God in whom his salvation consists, or from Christ, the Savior.

---

**23{24}[6]**  *This is the generation of them that seek him, of them that seek the face of the God of Jacob.*

> Haec est generatio quaerentium eum, quaerentium faciem Dei Iacob.

Finally, though it has said this in a singular sense, it applies in justice to all.   **23{24}[6]** *Haec, this*, that is, those who live in this manner, *est generatio quaerentium eum, is the generation of them that seek him*: because these are reborn in the Lord, they belong to the number of those regenerated in Christ,[11] and they seek the Lord by faith and by holy desire and by good works. They do not seek the Lord only by faith; but these are (it says) *the generation quaerentium faciem Dei Iacob, of them that seek the face of the God of Jacob*, that is, desirous to see God in heaven

---

11  E. N. On "regenerated" see footnote 21-154.

clearly and face-to-face, who at present seek him, wanting to contemplate him now as they now are able, but in the future they desire to know him as they are known.[12] For if you seek God, therefore, to see him, if you desire to join yourself to him, do to your neighbor that which you would want done to yourself.[13] Show such things to your brothers which you wish that God should show you. Purify the attention of your mind from all vanity, and all vile occupations, and malice, because God approaches none but he who has the most pure mind; and no stain, not even a minor stain, is able to be in the soul which is joined in immediate union with the divine light, because we are as distant from God in the same proportion as we are attached to vices.

---

**23{24}[7]**   *Lift up your gates, O princes, and be lifted up, O eternal gates: and the King of Glory shall enter in.*

> *Attollite portas, principes, vestras, et elevamini, portae aeternales, et introibit rex gloriae.*

**23{24}[7]** *Attollite portas, principes, vestras; lift up your gates, O you princes.* This is the voice of the holy angels, they who descended with Christ to hell,[14] and foreannounced him as servants of the Lord, and so did they speak to the demons: *Lift up,* that is, open, O princes of darkness, *your gates,* that is, the entrance of hell, or the power and right that up to now you had over the souls of the elect on account of the guilt of original sin, and on account of which they were impeded from entry into the kingdom of heaven. *Et elevamini, portae eternales, and be you lifted up, O eternal gates,* that is, let these just mentioned gates open up, which from the origin of the world were entirely shut, and without end you will remain shut to the reprobate as to their liberation. Or [an alternative interpretation is] *and be you lifted up, O eternal gates,* that is, lift yourselves up to the contemplation of Christ, O souls of the elect, whom Christ in a way enters into, and will remain so in you for eternity, through the beatific vision. For which reason, the Psalm continues: *et introibit rex gloriae, and the King of Glory shall enter in*: which refers to

---

12  *Cf.* 1 Cor. 13:12.

13  Tob. 4:16: *See you never do to another what you would hate to have done to you by another.*

14  E. N. This is not the Hell of the damned, but the hell referred to in the Creed, to which the human soul of Jesus (still, along with his dead body though separated from it, hypostatically united to the Word) after his death and before his Resurrection, the so-called limbo of the fathers (*limbus patrum*).

either of the two just-mentioned interpretations. For Christ entered hell (that is, the limbo of the fathers) and also the minds of the souls there held captive. For immediately as the soul of Christ was separated from his most glorious body, it entered hell, and beatified all the souls of the saints with a clear vision of the Godhead, for he more than amply satisfied for original [sin], for which guilt the holy souls were been delayed from the beatific vision.

———————

**23{24}[8]**   *Who is this King of Glory? The Lord who is strong and mighty: the Lord mighty in battle.*

*Quis est iste rex gloriae? Dominus fortis et potens, Dominus potens in praelio.*

At this voice, the astonished demons said:   **23{24}[8]** *Quis est iste rex gloria? Who is this King of Glory?* Who so unusually, who so gloriously, and who so fearlessly descends among us? To which the holy angels respond: *Dominus fortis, the Lord who is strong,* by reason of his divinity, *et potens, and mighty,* by reason of his humanity, by whose Passion and death he overcame the devils; *Dominus potens in proelio, the Lord mighty in battle,* that is, in the Passion through which he bound the prince of this world, cast him outside, and rifled his goods.[15] This, therefore, is the *King of Glory.* Finally, by the fact that in this verse Christ is called the *King of Glory,* and then *the Lord who is strong* it manifestly shows that he is the true God. For no mere creature is able to be called the *King of Glory,* or *the Lord who is strong* because he [the creature] does not have the regal or dominical authority within himself.[16]

———————

**23{24}[9]**   *Lift up your gates, O princes, and be lifted up, O eternal gates: and the King of Glory shall enter in.*

*Attollite portas, principes, vestras, et elevamini, portae aeternales, et introibit rex gloriae.*

**23{24}[9]** *Attollite portas, principes, vestras;* lift up your gates, O you princes. This is the voice of the holy angels, preceding Christ in the

15  Matt. 12:29. *Or how can anyone enter into the house of the strong, and rifle his goods, unless he first bind the strong? and then he will rifle his house.*

16  E. N. In other words, creatures have been *delegated* regal and dominical authority. As Christ told Pilate: *You would not have any power against me, unless it were given you from above.* John 19:11. So anyone claiming regal or dominical power as a matter of right (*in se*) would have to be God.

Ascension, and crying out to the heavenly citizens and princes: *Lift up your gates, O you princes,* that is, angelic powers, *your gates:* that is, unlock the entryway to the Kingdom of Heaven, prepare for the entry of the Son of God and those who are coming with him, so they may be received with due reverence. *Et elevamini, portae aeternales; and be you lifted up, O eternal gates,* that is, throw open you, the gates of eternal life. These gates are not to be understood in a corporal sense; but the gates of the heavens are the faculty, power, or right of entry to eternal life. *Et introibit rex gloria, and the King of Glory shall enter in:* as the Apostle [Paul] said: *For Jesus is not entered into the holies made with hands, the patterns of the true: but into heaven itself, that he may appear now in the presence of God for us.*[17]

---

**23{24}[10]** *Who is this King of Glory? The Lord of hosts, he is the King of Glory.*

> *Quis est iste rex gloriae? Dominus virtutum ipse est rex gloriae.*

While hearing this proclamation and seeing Christ ascending so gloriously, the angels question those angels superior to them:    **23{24}[10]** *Quis est iste rex gloriae? Who is this King of Glory?* [They do so] as if desiring to be taught by those more learned than them. To which the angels coming with Christ respond: *Dominum virtutum, the Lord of hosts,* that is, God himself, the Only-Begotten of God the Father, who is the *Lord of Hosts,* that is, the armies and all the powers of heaven, *ipse est rex gloriae, he is the King of Glory,* that is, the Prince of joy, the Fountain of felicity eternal, the King of highest excellence, and, insofar as he is man, he is given *all power in heaven and on earth.*[18]

It ought to be observed here that according to the divine doctrine of the great Dionysius, in the seventh chapter of the *Divine Hierarchy,*[19] the angels were given three questions at the ascension of Christ. [The first was:] *Who is this King of Glory?* For they did not so perfectly know the mysteries of Christ as did the superior angels, although, according to Augustine, all holy angels knew from the beginning of the world, at least generally, the mystery of Christ, namely, the Incarnation of the Son of God. The second question the first level of angels and the highest in the hierarchy asked among themselves: *Who is this that comes*

---

17  Heb. 9:24. Denis believes St. Paul to be the author of *Hebrews. See* footnote 8-34.
18  Matt. 28:18.
19  *E. N.* On Dionysius (Pseudo-Dionysius) *see* footnote P-36.

*from Edom, with dyed garments from Bosra?*[20] Edom is interpreted as
"bloody"; but Bosra as "armed." So therefore [it is understood] in this
sense: "Who is this, so brilliant and shining white, who comes from
the world so bloodied by sin, and armed against God through malice?"
But the highest angels ask themselves this question, not as wanting by
it to teach each other, because all of them are immediately illuminated
by God; but they seek by discussing among themselves that they may
exhibit themselves in a condition of longing for that the holy knowledge,
not daring to anticipate the divine processive instruction to them[21]
or overleaping the predetermined boundaries [of their knowledge]. [It
is] as if they deliberate first among themselves so that they may make
themselves suitable for the divine illumination. Whence also Christ
himself replies to them: *I, that speak justice, and am a defender to
save.*[22] The third question is that which the highest angels ask Christ
saying: *Why then is your apparel red, and your garments like theirs that
tread in the winepress?*[23] For the clothing of Christ is his Body, which
was the temple and the hiding-place of his divinity. And so [it is to be
understood] in this sense: "Why was your Body reddened with blood,
as your scars testify to, if you are not only so just, but also Savior?"
To which Christ responds: *I have trodden the winepress alone, and of
the Gentiles there is not a man with me,*[24] that is, the devil, sin, and
the world I alone have overcome, and have undergone the Passion for
all; there is not anyone else who suffered with me for the sins of the
world. These are the questions the highest angels ask, for they are not
by themselves able to penetrate the profundity of the Incarnation and
of the other mysteries of the Savior, the Lord.

See this light-streaming Psalm briefly teaches us to contemplate
the divine majesty, to whose rule all things submit, in order that it
might excite us to reverence and to the holy fear of the most high
Creator. It also teaches how he who desires to belong to the Lord
must necessarily be, since it exhorts us to be clean of heart. Finally, it
teaches us about the most happy Ascension of Christ since it raises

---

20  Is. 63:1a.
21  E. N. *Processivam instructionem.* The word *processive* suggests the sort of pro-
    cession of the Holy Spirit from the Father and the Son, suggesting that this
    knowledge or instruction (*instructio processiva*) proceeds immediately from God,
    as the angels are immediately illuminated by God. It is distinguished from *reflex-
    ive instruction* or a *mediate instruction.*
22  Is. 63:1b.
23  Is. 63:2.
24  Is. 63:3a.

our hearts toward that which is above: in the manner that the Apostle [Paul] says: *Seek the things that are above; where Christ is sitting at the right hand of God; mind the things that are above, not the things that are upon the earth.*[25]

# PRAYER

ORD OF HOSTS AND KING OF GLORY, purify our conscience so that always proceeding innocent of hand and clean of heart we may obtain from you eternal blessing and mercy.

*Domine virtutum et Rex gloriae, purifica conscientiam nostram: ut inocentes manibus et mundi corde semper exsistentes, bendictionem et misericordiam aeternam a te percipiamus.*

---

25  Col. 1b–2.

# Psalm 24

## ARTICLE LVI

### EXPOSITION OF THE TWENTY-FOURTH PSALM:
#### AD TE DOMINE, LEVAVI, &c.
#### TO YOU, O LORD, HAVE I LIFTED UP, &c.

24{25}[1]  *Unto the end, a Psalm for David. To you, O Lord, have I lifted up my soul.*

> *In finem. Psalmus David. Ad te, Domine, levavi animam meam.*

24{25}[2]  *In you, O my God, I put my trust; let me not be ashamed.*

> *Deus meus, in te confido; non erubescam.*

24{25}[3]  *Neither let my enemies laugh at me: for none of them that wait on you shall be confounded.*

> *Neque irrideant me inimici mei : etenim universi, qui sustinent te, non confundentur.*

HE TITLE OF THIS PSALM IS:  24{25}[1] *IN finem, Psalmus David; unto the end, a Psalm for David*: that is, this Psalm directs us to the end which perfects and is our consummation, that is, Christ, and David is speaking this in person of the penitent man corrected by scourges. For this Psalm is the prayer of the Church or any person truly contrite, one seeking consolation and help against the evil of fault and of punishment.[1]

And so it says: *Ad te, to you*, God, the whole of my salvation and sovereign good of my heart, *Domine, levavi animam meam; to you, O Lord, have I lifted up my soul*, contemplating you by a most firm faith, leaving all things of the flesh and of the senses, and most affectionately affixing with the apex of the mind my gaze at you, the highest of all things: in the manner that Isaiah admonishes: *Shake yourself from the dust, arise, sit up.*[2]  24{25}[2] *Deus meus, O my God*, whom most supremely and

---

1  E. N. On the difference between evil of fault (*mala culpae*) and evil of punishment (*mala poena*), see footnote 21-146.

2  Is. 52:2a.

alone I worship and love,[3] *in te confido, in you I put my trust*, not in fleeting things: consequently, *non erubescam, let me not be ashamed*, that is, grant to me that I might do nothing worthy of shame, namely, that I may not sin. For shame is the fear of something filthy. But nothing can be more filthy than sin. Or [we can understand it] thus: *let me not be ashamed*, that is, let me not fear to confess my sins, but let me fulfill this: *My son, give glory to the Lord God of Israel, and confess, and tell me what you have done.*[4] Or [alternatively], *let me not be ashamed* of good works: of which the imperfect are often ashamed because of various consequences, namely, because of punishment or the ridicule of others. And so, *let me not be ashamed*, let it not pertain to me what you, O Lord Jesus, say in the Gospel: *He that shall be ashamed of me and of my words, of him the Son of man shall be ashamed, when he shall come* into his kingdom.[5] But there is a certain kind of shame which is good, of which the Philosopher [Aristotle] says that it is a good passion.[6] For it is the fear of something dishonest.[7] Of this [sort of shame] the Prophet [David] is not speaking; indeed we ought to pray to the Lord that we may be fully ashamed when with commit something sinful, lest we hear him say to us: *You had a harlot's forehead, you would not blush.*[8] For they who have become accustomed to evil are not ashamed.

Or [we might understand the verse this way]: *let me not be ashamed*, that is, that I might not be confounded by you, in the day of my particular judgment, when my soul exits my body and stands to be judged

---

3  E. N. This appears to suggest the classic tri-partite distinction, wherein only God is given the supreme worship, latreiutic worship (the cult of *latreia*), the adoration due only God. There are lesser forms of veneration give to "God in his angels and his saints," *Deus in Angelis suis, et in Sanctis suis*, of dulia, and — reserved for the Blessed Virgin Mary alone — *hyperdulia*. For the distinctions between *latria*, *hyperdulia*, and *dulia*, see ST, IIaIIae, q. 84, art. 1; q. 103, arts. 1-4.

4  Joshua 7:19a.

5  Luke 9:26. Instead of *cum venerit in maiestate tua* (*when he shall come in his majesty*), Denis has *cum venerit in regno suo* (*when he shall come into his kingdom*).

6  E. N. Aristotle, *Nicomachean Ethics*, IV, 9, 1128b10-12.

7  E. N. The Latin word *inhonesto*, dishonest, is used by Denis in a moral sense that is more general than simply not saying the truth. An honest good (*bonum honestum*) is an object that is morally good to choose. Its opposite is something dishonest (*inhonestum*). In Pope Paul VI's encyclical *Humanae Vitae*, No. 14, for example, the use of artificial contraception with the direct intent to prevent conception was called *intrinsece inhonestum*, intrinsically dishonest, or intrinsically morally wrong. As to Denis's point regarding shame: "Where is yet shame," Samuel Johnson wrote, "there may in time be virtue." *Journey to the Western Islands of Scotland*, The Works of Samuel Johnson (New York: George Dearborn 1837), Vol. II, 619.

8  Jer. 3:3b.

by you, nor in the day of the universal judgment.[9] Whence it continues:   **24{25}[3]** *Neque irrideant me inimici mei, neither let my enemies
laugh at me,* namely, the demons, who in a hidden way laugh at those who
serve them, but in the day of each man's judgment, and most especially
also in the date of final judgment, they will openly laugh. *Etenim universi
qui sustinent te, for none of them that wait on you,* that is, they who now
do all that pertains to them with equanimity, and commit to you the
punishment and judgment, in the manner that is written: *Vengeance is
mine, I will repay, says the Lord.*[10] These persons *non confundentur, shall
not be confounded* in the time of their judgment; but they will hear the
words that convey so much honor and sweetness, *Come, you blessed of
my Father, possess you the kingdom [prepared for you from the foundation
of the world].*[11]

---

**24{25}[4]**   *Let all them be confounded that act unjust things without cause.
Show, O Lord, your ways to me, and teach me your paths.*

*Confundantur omnes iniqua agentes supervacue. Vias tuas,
Domine, demonstra mihi, et semitas tuas edoce me.*

**24{25}[5]**   *Direct me in your truth, and teach me; for your are God my
Savior; and on you have I waited all the day long.*

*Dirige me in veritate tua, et doce me, quia tu es Deus salvator
meus, et te sustinui tota die.*

**24{25}[4]** *Confundantur omnes iniqua agentes supervacue, let all them be
confounded that act unjust things without cause:* that is, *let all sinners* who
perpetrate evil uselessly and vainly, *be confounded* in the present life toward
saving repentance so that they may not be eternally confounded, in the
manner that is written: *be confounded, and ashamed at your own ways,* says
the Lord.[12] And this way of understanding *let all them be confounded* is
the preferable explanation. Or [another explanation is] thus: *let all those
doing needless evil be confounded,* that is, that they might be censured by
you, and that they might perish in eternity, as you have forewarned: *I will
bring an everlasting reproach upon you, and a perpetual shame which shall*

---

9  E. N. There is a particular judgment immediately after death. "Each man receives
   his eternal retribution in his immortal soul at the very moment of his death."
   CCC § 1022. This is distinct from the Last Judgment. "The Last Judgment will
   come when Christ returns in glory." CCC § 1040.
10 Rom. 12:19; Hebr. 10:30.
11 Matt. 25:34. The words in brackets supplant Denis's "etc."
12 Ez. 36:32b.

*never be forgotten.*[13] And so when it says *let them be confounded* we should understand it in a prophetic sense, and not in a optative sense, [in other words,] only that the Prophet [David] says this of those who remain obstinate or [says this] conforming his state of mind to the divine justice.[14]

*Vias tuas, your ways,* that is, your commandments, *Domine, demonstra mihi, O Lord show [them] to me,* that is, fill me up with the light of your grace, so that I might actually ponder and I might diligently observe your precepts. *Et semitas tuas edoce me, and teach me your paths.* Nothing more needs to be said about this but what has already been said; but what is said, is a restatement of what was said, [and this repetition is done] because of his [the Prophet's] feeling of fervor, and so that our hearts might be inflamed.[15] Or [alternatively], *your ways,* that is, the perfect ways, which are the evangelical counsels, teach me, and not only so that I might be informed about them by knowing about them, which [knowledge] a reprobate can also have, but so that I might carry them out by deed and in truth.[16]    **24{25}[5]** *Dirige me, direct me* to you yourself and to eternal beatitude, so that I might do all things to your honor; *in veritate tua, in your truth,* that is, in the divine law, since according to its rectitude and doctrine it disposes and orders all my deeds toward the ultimate end; *et doce me, and teach me,* so that *I may know what is acceptable* before you at all times,[17] and I may know (as the Apostle urged) *what is the good, and the acceptable, and the perfect will of God.*[18] And so I pray that I may learn from you, *quia tu es Deus salvator meus, for you are God my savior,* who put down your life for me,[19] and you redeemed me from sin, from the yoke of the devil, and from eternal

---

13  Jer. 23:40.

14  E. N. With respect to these and other maledictory verses, they may be understood in a prophetic sense, that is, either (1) the prophet is warning what will happen if the sinner persists in his sin, or (2) the prophet is conforming his thoughts to the reality of the divine judgment. They are not to be understood in an optative sense, that is, in the sense that the prophet is wishing that the sinner be confounded or suffer eternal punishment.

15  E. N. In other words "your paths" (*semitas tuas*) is the same "your ways" (*vias tuas*) in the prior verse, and so further elaboration is not required. The same thing is repeated either because of David's fervor or because of the desire to inspire fervor in us. *See* discussion of this characteristic in Scripture by Denis in Article XII (Psalm 2:4) and Article XX (Psalm 5:3).

16  For the evangelical counsels, *see* footnote 22-14.

17  Wis. 9:10b.

18  Rom. 12:2b.

19  *Cf.* John 10:15: *As the Father knows me, and I know the Father: and I lay down my life for my sheep.*

damnation. *Et te sustinui tota die*: that is, all the time that I live under the sun, I expect your clemency, and I commit to your goodness myself and all things which happen to me. Consequently:

---

**24{25}[6]**   *Remember, O Lord, your bowels of compassion; and your mercies that are from the beginning of the world.*

*Reminiscere miserationum tuarum, Domine, et misericordiarum tuarum quae a saeculo sunt.*

**24{25}[6]** *Reminiscere miserationum tuarum, Domine, et misericor-diarum tuarum quae a saeculo sunt; Remember, O Lord, your bowels of compassion; and your mercies that are from the beginning of the world.* Remembering and forgetting is not something that properly befalls to the incommutable[20] God; but it is said transumptively[21] that God remembers, when he hears, spares, or rescues; but to forget is to be understood in the opposite manner. So the attribute of mercy (*misericordia*), according as it is considered to be in God, is nothing but his most kindly goodness. But an act of mercy (*miseratio*) of God is the effect of his mercy (*misericordiae*). Therefore, many can be the acts of mercy of God (*miserationes*), because many are the works of divine kindness; but the attribute of mercy (*misericordia*), which is the divine essence, is but one. Why else, therefore, is *your mercies* (*misercordiarum tuarum*) said in a plural manner, except that the divine mercy (*misericordia*), which is in itself one and simple, is said in a plural sense because of the diversities of its effects?[22] Therefore, O Lord, *remember your acts of mercy*, that is, consider how much kindness and grace you gave to prior saints; and in the same manner do to me what you did to them, having mercy upon me always and in all things. And *remember your mercies that are from the beginning of the world*, that is, that you might recall your eternal kindness, which from the origin of the world was in you, and pour out the effects of your great kindness upon me; extend to me eternally the abyss of your clemency and the ocean of your so great a mercy (*misericordiae*).

---

20   L. *incommutabili*, incommutable, not capable of being changed; immutable.
21   E. N. On the word transumptively, see footnote 5-14.
22   The Douay-Rheims's translation does not reflect Denis's argument; indeed, it appears to suggest the opposite of the argument that Denis makes. If *misericordia* is thought of as referring to the attribute of God, and *miseratio* to refer to the specific acts of mercy, then Psalm 24:6 would something along the lines of: "Remember, O Lord, your acts of mercy; and your mercies that are from the beginning of the world."

24{25}[7]  *The sins of my youth and my ignorances do not remember. According to your mercy remember me: for your goodness' sake, O Lord.*

*Delicta iuventutis meae, et ignorantias meas ne memineris. Secundum misericordiam tuam memento mei tu, propter bonitatem tuam, Domine.*

24{25}[7] *Delicta iuventutis meae, the sins of my youth,* that is the sins of commission occurring in youth, *et ignorantias meas, and my ignorances,* that is, the sins of omissions,[23] *ne memineris, do not remember* reserving for me eternal punishment for them; but in the present grant to me that I might efface them. Or [understood another way]: *the sins,* that is, sins done from malice or perpetrated by evil choice, and *ignorances,* that is, sins performed as a result of weakness, *do not remember.* For all who sin either sin out of passion, and these [sins] are most easily amended, for when the passion ceases, the sin ceases; or a person sins due to sinful habit, namely, out of a certain malice, and this kind is more difficult to correct because it is difficult to extirpate a habit. But theologians say sin proceeds either from weakness, which is a sin against the Father, to whom is appropriated power; or ignorance, which is a sin against the Son, to whom is appropriated wisdom; or out of a certain malice, which is a sin against the Holy Spirit, to whom is appropriated goodness.[24] But these

---

23  "Sins... can be divided ... as sins in thought, word, deed, or omission." CCC § 1853. For sins of omission — often overlooked — refer to Jacques Debout, *My Sins of Omission: An Average Catholic's Examination of Conscience* (Herder: St. Louis 1930) (trans. J. F. Scanlan).

24  In his *Quodlibet Questions,* St. Thomas mentions this opinion, which he attributes to "modern teachers." *Doctores vero moderni dixerunt, quod quia patri attribuitur potentia, filio sapientia, spiritui sancto bonitas; peccatum ex infirmitate est peccatum in patrem, peccatum ex ignorantia est peccatum in filium, peccatum ex certa malitia est peccatum in spiritum sanctum. Quia ergo ignorantia vel infirmitas excusat peccatum vel in toto vel in parte, dicunt, quod peccatum in patrem vel in filium remittitur quia vel totaliter culpa caret, vel culpa diminuitur; malitia vero non excusat peccatum, sed aggravat: et ideo peccatum in spiritum sanctum non remittitur neque in toto neque in parte, quia non habet in se aliquam rationem veniae, per quam diminuatur culpa.* "But modern teachers said that because power is attributed to the Father, wisdom to the Son, and goodness to the Holy Spirit, sin out of weakness is a sin against the Father, sin out of ignorance is sin against the Son, and sin out of certain malice is a sin against the Holy Spirit. Because, therefore, ignorance or weakness may excuse sin either completely or in part, they say that the sin against the Father or the Son may be remitted because it lacks total fault, and the fault may be diminished. But the malice does not excuse sin, but aggravates it; and so sin against the

three [kinds of sin] can be reduced to the two [categories] previously mentioned. *Secundum misericordiam tuam memento mei tu; according to your mercy remember me*: that is, [remember me] not according to my sin, not according to the rigor of your justice, but act against me *according to your mercy*, forgetting the sins, infusing grace, and keeping me in all good: and this do *propter bonitatem tuam, Domine; for your goodness' sake, O Lord*, that is, for you yourself and for the honor of your name. This is what Nehemiah says: *Remember me, O my God, unto good; and wipe not out your kindnesses from me.*[25]

---

**24{25}[8]**   *The Lord is sweet and righteous: therefore he will give a law to sinners in the way.*

*Dulcis et rectus Dominus; propter hoc legem dabit delinquentibus in via.*

**24{25}[8]** *Dulcis et rectus Dominus, the Lord is sweet and righteous*, that is, *sweet* in himself and kind to others; he is also *righteous*, that is, is just: indeed he, whose sweetness in himself truly exists in an immeasurable and simple way, is the fountain-like cause of all sweetness. *Propter hoc legem dabit delinquentibus in via; therefore he will give a law to sinners in the way*, that is, to men who often do wrong in this present life, which is a pilgrimage along the way to eternal life. God has bestowed to men a three-fold law, namely the natural law, the written law, and the law of the Gospel; and all these laws are given to men so that they may live justly. And God on account of his sweetness and equity has presented them to men because it was good and just that the Creator set before the law by which rational creatures ought to live. For which reason, Ecclesiasticus says: *God showed to men both good and evil; and the law of life for an inheritance. He showed them his justice and judgments; and he said to them: Beware of all iniquity.*[26] But that he says here, *the Lord is sweet and righteous*, fittingly is directed to Christ, who gave the evangelical law on the mount, where he declared the eight beatitudes to his disciples.[27]

---

Holy Spirt is not remitted either in whole or in part, because it does not of its nature the quality of being lessened, by which it might be diminished of fault. *Quodlibet* II, q. 8 a. 1 co.

25   2 Esdras 31b, 14a. Denis replaces the personal pronoun in the last verse, changing "my kindnesses" (*miserationes meas*) with "your kindnesses" (*miserationes tuas*).

26   Ecclus. 17:6b, 9b, 10b, 11b.

27   Matt. 5:1 *et seq.*

**24{25}[9]**    *He will guide the mild in judgment: he will teach the meek his ways.*

*Diriget mansuetos in iudicio; docebit mites vias suas.*

**24{25}[9]** *Diriget, he will guide* the Lord himself [will guide] by the inspiration and the grace of the Holy Spirit, *mansuetos, the mild,* that is, those who are patient, *in iudicio, in judgment* of discretion,[28] that they might truly scrutinize, judge, and amend themselves. *He will guide* without doubt those [the mild], because they lack impatience, which in a significant way deprives judgment of reason. And because of this [mildness or patience] they are capable and are worthy to be directed by the Lord through the gifts of the Holy Spirit. For it is by the gift of wisdom that we judge about things that are divine; and by the gift of knowledge, [we judge] of the things of creation; by the gift of counsel, of human acts. *Docebit mites vias suas; he will teach the meek his ways,* that is, the Lord will inform men, who overcome the movements of anger, with salvific and holy acts because he will direct them to all good. It is generally accepted that mildness (*mansuetudo*) and meekness (*mititas*) ought to be considered the same thing; but because the Prophet [David] has spoken of them as distinct, consequently mildness (*mansuetudo*) is taken to mean patience, which is the moral virtue checking the passion of sorrow, as also meekness (*mititas*) [is the moral virtue which] constrains anger.

---

**24{25}[10]** *All the ways of the Lord are mercy and truth, to them that seek after his covenant and his testimonies.*

*Universae viae Domini, misericordia et veritas, requirentibus testamentum eius et testimonia eius.*

**24{25}[10]** *Universae viae Domini, all the ways of the Lord,* that is, all the works of God, are *misericordia et veritas, mercy and truth*: that is, the mercy of God and his justice appear and are aglow in all the effects of God. But in some, as in the elect, the mercy of God clearly appears; and in some justice appears more manifest, as in the reprobate. But because the reprobate are forsaken in this life and tormented in hell less than they in strict justice (*citra condignum*) deserve by God, thus the mercy of God appears in them. But the elect are rewarded more than they in strict justice deserve (*ultra condignum*), and so mercy has a place in them. And because this is true, it corresponds *requirentibus testamentum eius et testimonia eius, to them that seek after his covenant*

---

28  For the notion of a judgment of discretion, *see* footnote 1-39.

*and his testimonies*, that is, men who in this life strove after the divine law and devoted themselves to the truths which are to be believed from it. Many are able there to say in what fashion in all the works of the Creator they received mercy and truth. Anselm[29] in his *Prologion* most beautifully addressed this matter, showing it to be just in a certain way on the part of God that he extends mercy to the evildoer: for God is so good that he is just even in doing good to the evildoer. But there is a kind of justice on the part of God also to us, since he benefits the doer of good. But why God justly elects to be merciful to one evildoer rather than another is something the reason for which we cannot discover. Indeed, as Augustine said, *This do not investigate if you don't want to err.*[30] But I will pass over this material, and I will refer those who wish to study this issue to Anselm.

---

**24{25}[11]** *For your name's sake, O Lord, you will pardon my sin: for it is great.*

*Propter nomen tuum, Domine, propitiaberis peccato meo; multum est enim.*

**24{25}[11]** *Propter nomen tuum, [Domine]; for your name's sake, [O Lord]*, that is, for you yourself, and so that you show your riches of mercy in me, *propitiaberis peccato meo, you will pardon my sin*, so I hope; *multum est enim, for it is great*: not that the multitude of sin is the meritorious cause of the indulgence of God, but because the remission (*remissio*) of sin can be meant by propitiation (*propitiatio*) [of sin].[31] But

---

29  E. N. For Anselm, *see* footnote 13-35. Denis is referring to chapters 9–11 of St. Anselm's *Proslogion*, where, during the course of his ontological argument for the existence of God, St. Anselm addresses the relationship between God's mercy and justice. The reflection begins with the question: *Verum malis quomodo parcis, se es totus iustus et summe iustus?* "But how do you spare the evil, if you are all just and supremely just?" PL 158, 251 *ff*.

30  E. N. *Hoc noli investigare, si non vis errare.* The reference is to St. Augustine's commentary on John 6:44: *Quem trahat et quem non trahat, quare illum trahat et illum non trahat, noli velle iudicare, si non vis errare.* "Whom he draws to himself and whom he does not draw to himself: why he draws to himself and why he does not draw to himself, do not will to adjudge if you do not wish to err." *In. Ioann. Evang.*, XXVII, 2, PL 35, 1607.

31  E. N. To understand what Denis is getting at here, one must understand the difference between remission (*remissio*) of sins, and propitiation (*propitiatio*) for sins. We might take a look at St. Paul's letter to the Romans here, where Paul speaks of Christ's redemption, for Jesus "whom God has proposed to be a propitiation (*propitiationem*) through faith in his Blood, to the showing of his

here a singular is placed for a plural when it says *you will pardon my sin* (*peccato meo*): because the sense of this is: *you will pardon all of my sins* (*omnibus peccatis meis*). For one mortal sin cannot be remitted without all the others in one who has multiple mortal sins; but one venial sin is able to be remitted without other [venial sins].[32]

24{25}[12] *Who is the man that fears the Lord? He has appointed him a law in the way he has chosen.*

> *Quis est homo qui timet Dominum? Legem statuit ei in via quam elegit.*

24{25}[13] *His soul shall dwell in good things: and his seed shall inherit the land.*

> *Anima eius in bonis demorabitur; et semen eius haereditabit terram.*

24{25}[14] *The Lord is a firmament to them that fear him: and his covenant shall be made manifest to them.*

> *Firmamentum est Dominus timentibus eum; et testamentum ipsius ut manifestetur illis.*

At this time the Prophet [David] changes person, and adds:    24{25} [12] *Quis est homo qui timet Dominum*, who is the man who fears the Lord with a chaste and filial fear? Because the Lord *legem statuit ei*, has appointed him a law, that is, he has proposed to him a divine law, *in via quam elegit, in the way he has chosen*, that is, in that holy manner of life

---

justice, for the remission (*remissionem*) of former sins." (Rom. 3:25) Propitiation is the act of making reconciliation between two parties, in this case between God and mankind, accomplished by the Passion, Death, and Resurrection of Christ (his "Blood"). Remission is the removal or the taking away of the guilt of sins or the temporal punishment associated with those sins; in short, remission is the application of the propitiation. When Ps. 24:11 says "you will *propitiate* my sin" (translated in the Douay Rheims as "pardon" to avoid the problem noted by Denis) it suggests that the sin is its own propitiation (the meritorious cause of God's mercy). This, of course, is false. What Denis is saying here is that when the word *propitiaberis* (you will propitiate) is used in this instance in Ps. 24:11, it can be fairly construed as a synonym for *remiseris* (you will remit).

32  E. N. This principle is succinctly summarized in a sermon by Fr. Franz Hunolt: "[A]ccording to the present arrangement of divine Providence, one mortal sin cannot be remitted without the others, and none without true sorrow; all must be forgiven together, or else none at all." Franz Hunolt, *The Penitent Christian* (New York: Benziger Brothers 1889) Vol. 1, 293 (trans. J. Allen).

which he willingly assumes, spurning an evil manner of life. **24{25}[13]**
*Anima eius, his soul* who thus fears the Lord *in bonis demorabitur, shall
dwell in good things,* that is, he will persevere in grace and in virtue in
the present life, and in the future he will remain eternally in glory with
the elect: and he will be among the riches of Christ. *Et semen eius, and
his seed,* that is, his fruitful life, *hereditabit terram, shall inherit the land,*
that is, in this age he will have his body subject to reason, and in the
future age he will possess the Kingdom of Heaven, which is the region
of those living (*regio vivorum*) or the land of the living (*terra viventium*).[33]
And of both [of these expressions], this *land* [or region] can be explained
according to what has been stated before: that Christ in the Gospel
says: *Blessed are the meek: for they shall possess the land.*[34] **24{25}[14]**
*Firmamentum, a firmament,* that is the cause of all stability and perfection,
*est Dominus timentibus eum, is the Lord to them that fear him*: in the
manner that the Apostle [Paul says]: *For it is best,* he says, *that the heart
be established with grace.*[35] *Et testamentum ipsius, and his covenant,* that is,
the law of God given for this purpose, *ut manifestetur illis, shall be made
manifest to them,* that is, so that it may be known and fulfilled by them.

---

**24{25}[15]** *My eyes are ever towards the Lord: for he shall pluck my feet
out of the snare.*

*Oculi mei semper ad Dominum, quoniam ipse evellet de laqueo
pedes meos.*

Now follows a verse that is most sweet and most salubrious: **24{25}**
**[15]** *Oculi mei semper ad Dominum, my eyes are ever towards the Lord,*
that is, the intention and the contemplation of my heart is always raised
up to God, that is, at all times bound, or always in act or in habit.[36]

---

33  E. N. Denis here refers to alternative expressions in the Psalms for the kingdom
of heaven as entailing the place of eternal life. *Regio vivorum* is taken from
Psalm 114:9 (*I will please the Lord in the land [region] of the living (in regione
vivorum)*). The term *terra viventium* is taken from Psalm 26:13 (*I believe to see
the good things of the Lord in the land of the living (in terra viventium)*). Some
commentators appear to have suggested that *regione vivorum* meant the world
here below and *terra viventium* meant the world above; others held them to be
synonyms. Denis appears to opt for the latter view.

34  Matt. 5:4.

35  Heb. 13:9b.

36  E. N. Only in heaven is the contemplation of God fully in act, and not in habit,
for "in heaven, where the rational creature with his whole heart loves God in
act (*actu*), and loves nothing except by referring it actually (*actualiter*) to God,
charity is possessed inamissibly [in a manner that it cannot be lost]; but in

This agrees with that which the Apostle Paul could say: *But we all beholding the glory of the Lord with open face, are transformed into the same image from glory to glory.*[37] Whence Jeremiah says: *Let us lift up our hearts with our hands to the Lord in the heavens.*[38] And therefore, *my eyes are ever towards the Lord, quoniam ipse evellet de laqueo, for he shall pluck my feet out,* that is, he will deliver me from the snares of the enemy, from all temptation and vice which take captive the soul, *pedes meo, my feet,* that is, during my pilgrimage, or in the acts of my life in this exile so full of snares.

-------

24{25}[16] *Look upon me, and have mercy on me; for I am alone and poor.*

   *Respice in me, et miserere mei; quia unicus et pauper sum ego.*

24{25}[17] *The troubles of my heart are multiplied: deliver me from my necessities.*

   *Tribulationes cordis mei multiplicatae sunt; de necessitatibus meis erue me.*

24{25}[16] *Respice in me, look upon me,* filling within my heart affections for good things, *et miserere mei, quoniam unicus; and have mercy on me, for I am alone,* that is by myself, not having any helper or anyone who can grant mercy except for you, *et pauper, and poor,* that is, lacking your grace, and not having power within me to do good, *sum ego, am I.* In this manner the most holy Esther was alone and poor as she said to the Lord: *Help me a desolate woman, and who have no other helper but you.*[39]   24{25}[17] *Tribulationes cordis mei multiplicatae sunt,* the troubles

-------

the wayfaring state charity does not perfect all of the potentialities of the soul, which is not always moving to God actually (*actualiter*), referring with actual intention (*actuali intentione*) all things to him." Thomas Aquinas, *De virtutibus,* q. 2 a. 12 co. Because it is not possible to contemplate God in act at all times on this side of heaven (*e.g.,* during sleep or when occupied with a task that requires concentration), we must do so at least in in habit. As Archbishop Ullathorne put it: "These desires of charity ought to be continual, if not in act, at least in habit and virtually; for this virtual desire abides in all that we do from the love of God. It is in this sense that our prayer should be continual and never ceasing." William Bernard Ullathorne, *Christian Patience: The Strength and Discipline of the Soul* (London: Burn & Oates 1886) (6th ed.), 196.

37  2 Cor. 3:18.
38  Lam. 3:41.
39  Esther 14:3b. E. N. The Douay Rheims has "desolate" for *solitariam.* The word desolate comes from Latin *de-solus,* thoroughly alone.

*of my heart are multiplied*: because I am afflicted by the committed sins, I am afflicted because of the defects in perfection, I am afflicted by the fear of punishment and the desire of joy. For *hope that is deferred afflicts the soul*.[40] I am afflicted by the annoyance of temptations and the sufferings of my neighbor. Because I am oppressed by so many evils now, therefore I pray, *de necessitatibus meis erue me, deliver me from my necessities*, that is from the needs of this body — from the needs of food, drinks, sleep, dress, and other similar needs — deliver me, so that they do not so frequently hamper the soul from divine contemplation, but that I may make use only with that amount that is fitting; not being solicitous about tomorrow, but that I might first seek the kingdom of God, and by this all these things shall be added unto me.[41]

---

**24{25}[18]** *See my abjection and my labor; and forgive me all my sins.*

> *Vide humilitatem meam et laborem meum, et dimitte universa delicta mea.*

**24{25}[19]** *Consider my enemies for they are multiplied, and have hated me with an unjust hatred.*

> *Respice inimicos meos, quoniam multiplicati sunt, et odio iniquo oderunt me.*

**24{25}[18]** *Vide humilitatem meam, see my abjection*, that is, consider in a benign fashion by lowness and my sorrow by which I disdain myself, *et laborem meum, and my labor*, that is, the satisfaction from my faults, the efforts I undertake that are done by me so as to obtain additional grace; *et dimitte universa delicta mea, and forgive me all my sins*, both as to their penalty and fault.[42]    **24{25}[19]** *Respice inimicos meos, consider my enemies*, that is, restrain demons, convert evil men, and defend me from them, *quoniam multiplicati sunt, for they are multiplied*: that is, because I am unable to resist these by my own strength, therefore I take refuge in your kindness; *et odio iniquo oderunt me, and they have hated me with an unjust hatred*, for they endeavor to remove from me spiritual goods and they desire to separate me from you, my God; and this is a most wicked hate, that is called envy of a brother's grace, and is a sin against the Holy Spirit.[43]

---

40  Prov. 13:12a.

41  *Cf.* Matt. 6:33, 34.

42  E. N. For the distinction between fault and penalty, see footnote 21-146.

43  E. N. Some authorities identified six kinds of sin against the Holy Spirit, namely, despair (*desperatio*), presumption (*praesumptio*), impenitence (*impoenitentia*),

**24{25}[20]** *Keep my soul, and deliver me: I shall not be ashamed, for I have hoped in you.*

> *Custodi animam meam, et erue me; non erubescam, quoniam speravi in te.*

**24{25}[20]** *Custodi animam meam, keep my soul* in making progress in virtue and in all manner of good. For I know that Scripture usefully admonishes: *With all watchfulness keep your heart, because life issues out from it.*[44] But because I am inadequate by my own virtue to fulfil this, for (as Jeremiah said) *the way of a man is not his;*[45] so, O Lord, keep you my soul by your continual grace and angelic aid, that it never withdraw from you. *Et erue me, and deliver me,* from all evils — past, present, and future. *Non erubescam, quoniam speravi in te; I will not be ashamed, for I have hoped in you.* This has been sufficiently explained in the first verse of this Psalm.

---

**24{25}[21]** *The innocent and the upright have adhered to me: because I have waited on you.*

> *Innocentes et recti adhaeserunt mihi, quia sustinui te.*

**24{25}[22]** *Deliver Israel, O God, from all his tribulations.*

> *Libera, Deus, Israel ex omnibus tribulationibus suis.*

Finally, he brings to mind all the many benefits obtained by him from the Lord, or the fruits of hoping in God, and he says to the glory of the Creator:    **24{25}[21]** *Innocentes et recti, the innocent and the upright,* that is, the simple, those not guilty of harming anyone but turning away from evil, and those justly doing good, *adhaeserunt mihi, have adhered to me* with the consent of their hearts, approving my works, and applying themselves to my pursuits, *quia sustinui te, because I have waited on you,* that is, patiently and faithfully I have seen you in all circumstances. For each person applauds those similar to him, because similarity is a cause of love.[46] Therefore the good adhere to the good: and this alone is the true and holy love, one that is founded upon a similarity of virtue or an

---

obstinacy (*obstinatio*), resisting acknowledged truth (*impugnatio veritatis agnitae*), and envy of the spiritual good of one's brother (*invidentia fraternae gratiae*). It is the last of these to which Denis refers here.

44  Prov. 4:23.

45  Jer. 10:23a.

46  E. N. *See ST*, IaIIae, q. 26, art. 3, co. *Similitudo, proprie loquendo, est causa amoris.* "Similarity, properly speaking, is a cause of love."

honest good.[47]    **24{25}[22]** *Libera, Deus, Israel, Deliver Israel, O God,* that is, the people contemplating you faithfully, *ex omnibus tribulationibus suis, from all his tribulations,* giving eternal life and rest to him, after this time of penal pilgrimage.

See how most affectionately and efficaciously the prayers that are contained in this Psalm are; and how sweetly and clearly it praises God both as to him himself as well as in the order of his effects. Let us therefore study this most noble Psalm to sing it with heartfelt contrition, with mental relish, with divine charity, with the delight of a divine public crier, and with the ardent affection of progress so that we might be found worthy to share in the effect of devout prayer and the fruit of divine praise.

# PRAYER

**R**EMEMBER US, O LORD, ACCORDING TO your mercy and your goodness, and pluck us out from the snares of our enemies, so that they who at any time lived in a manner inclined to run toward evil, may ultimately grasp the ways and paths of justice you teach, and not cease to advance in them constantly and perseveringly.

*Memento nostri, Domine, secundum misericordiam et bonitatem*
*tuam, et pedes nostros de laqueo inimicorum evelle: ut*
*qui aliquando ad mala currendo proni exsistebant,*
*vias et semitas iustitiae tandem te docente*
*apprehendant, easque constanter*
*et perseveranter incedere*
*non desistant.*

---

47  E. N. On the meaning of "honest good," *bonum honestum,* see footnote 24-7.

# Psalm 25

## ARTICLE LVII

### EXPOSITION OF CHRIST OF THE TWENTY-FIFTH PSALM
### IUDICA ME, DOMINE, &c.
### JUDGE ME, O LORD, &c.

25{26}[1]   *Unto the end, a Psalm for David. Judge me, O Lord, for I have walked in my innocence: and I have put my trust in the Lord, and shall not be weakened.*

*In finem. Psalmus David. Iudica me, Domine, quoniam ego in innocentia mea ingressus sum, et in Domino sperans non infirmabor.*

HE TITLE TO THIS PSALM IS BRIEF, NAMELY: 25{26}[1] *Psalmus David, a Psalm for David.*[1] And some who have expounded upon this Psalm say that in this place by David we are not to understand Christ, but [rather] any perfect man. But whatever may be said about that, it seems [to me] that all this Psalm can be expounded of Christ, even more aptly that it can of any other person.

Therefore, Christ, as man, says to God: *Iudica me, Domine; Judge me, O Lord*, that is, distinguish and separate me from evil men, and according to my justice reward me with accidental rewards.[2] For Christ desired to separate from evil men, to return to the Father, and to be beatified in body. Whence in the Gospel it says: *O unbelieving and perverse generation, how long shall I be with you? How long shall I suffer you?*[3] And again: *Father, glorify me . . . with the glory which I had, before the world was, with you.*[4] God also judged Christ the man with the judgment of discretion and remuneration.[5] Therefore, I also pray to judge, O Lord, *quoniam ego in innocentia mea ingressus sum, for I have walked in my innocence*, that is, innocently in

---

1   E. N. According to the Douay Rheims, this has the addition of *unto the end.*

2   E. N. For the difference between essential rewards and accidental rewards, *see* Arts. XII (Psalm 2:5) XXIV (Psalm 7:13) and footnote 2-23.

3   Matt. 17:16; Mark 9:18. Denis varies slightly from the Latin Sixto-Clementine Vulgate.

4   John 17:5.

5   For the difference between the judgment of discretion and the final judgment or judgment of retribution, see footnote 1-39.

all the course of my life, *et in Domino sperans, non infirmabor; and I have put my trust, and shall not be weakened* in my mind, though I allow that I will suffer in my body: for my spirit will be stable and fixed upon the Lord. For through a perfect fortitude of mind, Christ never was found wanting [in innocence] however much with a willing dispensation he assumed some passions of the soul. Indeed, these passions [that he willingly assumed] did not impede any act of reason in him. For no passion of the sensitive appetite came in front of [and impeded] the reason in Christ, but that [passion or suffering] that he willed, he voluntarily allowed.[6]

---

25{26}[2]    *Prove me, O Lord, and try me; burn my reins and my heart.*

*Proba me, Domine, et tenta me; ure renes meos et cor meum.*

**25{26}[2]** *Proba me, Domine; prove me, O Lord,* permit me to suffer adversely and severely for the salvation of the world, so that all may know me to be proved and accepted by you. And so, *prove me,* that is, prove my obedience through punishment, not so you need to learn something new [that you do not already know about me], but so that you might show others my probation and my approbation.[7] *Et tenta me, and try me,* that is, I am from without by Satan and the Pharisees and the Scribes[8] so that my temptations may be the cause of others overcoming temptations, and my resistance and victory [over them] be to others a model of resisting temptations and overcoming them. *Ure, burn,* with the fire of the Passion, *renes meos et cor meum, my reins and my heart,*[9] that is, the sensitive nature and its appetite. For the whole corporeal nature of Christ was made to suffer with vehement pain; also an interior pain and fear and sorrow, as they are passions of the soul, afflicted the heart, that is, the sensitive appetite, of the soul of Christ. Or [alternatively] thus: *burn,* with the fire of the Holy

---

6  E. N. Jesus suffered from no disordered passions whatsoever. Never were his passions not under the control of his reason; or, phrased differently, never was his reason overcome by his passions. For this reason, to distinguish the unique condition of the passions in Christ relative to other men, theologians call Christ's incipient passions which never overcame the order of reason *propassions (in Latin, propassiones).* St. Thomas Aquinas addresses this issue in the *Summa Theologiae,* IIIa, q. 15, art. 4, co.

7  E. N. *probationem ac approbationem.* Probation is the period of time that a person is being tested or proved. Approbation is the act of approval or accepting the passing of the test or period of probation.

8  E. N. Christ was free from internal disorder, and so could not be tempted from within through concupiscence or disordered passions the way we are. All his temptation was external to him or came from extrinsic sources.

9  For "reins" *see* footnote 7-10.

Spirit, *my reins and my heart*, namely, so that the fervor of charity existing in the will flows into the inferior parts of the soul and makes the sensitive appetite ardently prepared to endure the ignominy of death for the world. This was all fulfilled in Christ. For, after he rose up from prayer, he went undaunted to meet the Jews, and said: *Whom do you seek?*[10] So that at that time the inferior nature [of Christ] most promptly and without dread followed the intellectual appetite and reason.

Moreover, that this [verse] is applicable to Christ is clear from that which the Apostle [Paul] said: *For we have not a high priest, who cannot have compassion on our infirmities: but one tempted in all things like as we are, without sin.*[11] And again speaking of Christ he says: *It behooved him, he says, in all things to be made like unto his brethren . . . for in that, wherein he himself has suffered and been tempted, he is able to succor them also that are tempted.*[12] Therefore Christ prays to be tested, to be tempted and to be burned, because otherwise he would not be able to enter into his glory and to save the world in the way that he himself asserted: *Ought not Christ to have suffered these things, and so to enter into his glory?*[13]

---

**25{26}[3]**   *For your mercy is before my eyes; and I am well pleased with your truth.*

*Quoniam misericordia tua ante oculos meos est, et complacui in veritate tua.*

Consequently, he gives a reason why he is so untroubled in this desire, and he says to God:   **25{26}[3]** *Quoniam misericordia tua ante oculos meos est, for your mercy is before my eyes*, that is, because I incessantly trust in you, and I am confirmed in your grace which you so mercifully furnished me, and of which I am certain that I am not able to lose; *et complacui in veritate tua, and I am well pleased with your truth*, that is, in your justice and according to the demands or the dictates of your divine justice I have pleased you, in that I neither contracted nor did even one sin whatsoever.[14] This is what the Evangelists testify the Father told Christ: *You are my beloved Son; in you I am well pleased.*[15]

---

10  John 18:4b, 7a.
11  Heb. 4:15. On Denis's attribution of the epistle to the Hebrews to the apostle Paul, *see* footnote 8-34.
12  Heb. 2:17–18.
13  Luke 24:26.
14  E. N. Being impeccable, Jesus never contracted either original sin or any actual sin.
15  Matt. 3:17; Mark 1:11.

**25{26}[4]**  *I have not sat with the council of vanity: neither will I go in with the doers of unjust things.*

*Non sedi cum concilio vanitatis, et cum iniqua gerentibus non introibo.*

**25{26}[5]**  *I have hated the assembly of the malignant; and with the wicked I will not sit.*

*Odivi ecclesiam malignantium, et cum impiis non sedebo.*

**25{26}[4]** *Non sedi cum concilio vanitatis, I have not sat with the counsel of vanity*, that is, I have not spent time with vain counselors seeking vain and evil things, availing myself of their counsel, or providing them counsel; *et cum iniqua gerentibus non introibo, neither will I go with the doers in unjust ways*, doing those things that they do, or sharing in their unfruitful works: and this I do because **25{26}[5]** *Odivi ecclesiam malignantium, I have hated the assembly of the malignant*, that is, the congregation of those who by design insist in sinning: these I hate, to the degree they are malignant, though not insofar as they are men. The hate I have of them is not as to their nature, but to their fault: indeed, Christ loves, instructs, converts, redeems sinners, for *the Son of man is come to seek and to save that which was lost.*[16] *Et cum impiis, and with the wicked* who sin against God, *non sedebo, I will not sit*, approving what they do with my mind. Christ however (as is written in the Gospel) sometimes ate, drank, and sat with publicans and sinners,[17] but not for any reason of course except that he might lead them out of their error, knowing that the sick are in need of a physician.[18]

---

**25{26}[6]**  *I will wash my hands among the innocent; and will compass your altar, O Lord.*

*Lavabo inter innocentes manus meas, et circumdabo altare tuum, Domine.*

**25{26}[7]**  *That I may hear the voice of your praise: and tell of all your wondrous work.*

*Ut audiam vocem laudis, et enarrem universa mirabilia tua.*

**25{26}[6]** *Lavabo inter innocentes manus meas, I will wash my hands among the innocent*, that is, I will exhibit my pure deeds; or I will defend myself before you, O Lord, in a truthful fashion, from any sin the Jews

---

16  Luke 19:10.
17  Matt. 9:10–11.
18  Matt. 9:12.

imputed to me, just as all the innocent who are falsely accused are able to do. *Et circumdabo altare tuum, Domine; and I will compass your altar, O Lord*: that is, the charity with which I love you and neighbor everywhere I adorn by holy works, doing and enduring whatever charity may require. To call charity the altar of God is well said, because it is necessary that all things be offered and all things be done in charity. Whence in Leviticus we find: *This is the perpetual fire which shall never go out on the altar.*[19] For charity, which is always demanded to burn in the altar of the heart, is designated by this fire.    **25{26}[7]** *Ut audiam vocem laudis, that I may hear the voice of your praise*: that is, I because I encompass your altar so that I may hear the voice of praise, namely, that I may direct myself with my mind to that which God of his majesty and by means of praise reveals to me; [and this] in the manner that a Psalm below provides, *I will hear what the Lord God will speak in me.*[20] And with Isaiah we read about Christ: *The Lord God has opened my ear, and I do not resist: I have not gone back.*[21] For this reason there is appended: *et enarrem mirabilia tua, and tell of your wondrous works.* For Christ in preaching made known the wondrous works of God to men, according to that which the Apostle [John] said: *whatsoever I have heard of my Father, I have made known to you.*[22] For Christ has made known all those things which God inspired the soul of Christ to make manifest to men. Not, however, that he in a strict sense (*simpliciter*) made known all the wonderous works of God, for the world is not able to contain it.[23]

---

**25{26}[8]** *I have loved, O Lord, the beauty of your house; and the place where your glory dwells.*

> *Domine, dilexi decorem domus tuae, et locum habitationis gloriae tuae.*

**25{26}[8]** *Domine, dilexi decorum domus tuae; I have loved, O Lord, the beauty of your house*, that is, the interior ornament of the soul or purity of heart, for this I taught by word and by deed. The soul is called the house of God, because the soul of the just man is the seat of wisdom;[24] and

---

19  Lev. 6:13.

20  Ps. 84:9a.

21  Is. 50:5.

22  John 15:15b.

23  John 21:25: *But there are also many other things which Jesus did; which, if they were written every one, the world itself, I think, would not be able to contain the books that should be written.*

24  Cf. Prov. 14:33: *In the heart of the prudent rests wisdom, and it shall instruct all the ignorant.*

God by faith inhabits in our hearts, as the Apostle [Paul] attests.[25] Or [it could be understood] thus: *I have loved, O Lord the beauty of your house,* that is, that your decorous house, namely the Church militant, which I have chosen as my spouse, *not having spot or wrinkle:*[26] I love it because for its salvation I shed blood. And I also loved *locum habitationis gloriae tuae, the place where your glory dwells,* that is, the Church triumphant, because I descended into the world and endured death so that it would be rebuilt from its ruin, but also because with great affection I ascended to that heavenly place.[27] This is what the Apostle [Paul] says: *For it became him, for whom are all things, and by whom are all things, who had brought many children into glory, to perfect the author of their salvation, by his Passion.*[28]

---

**25{26}[9]**    *Take not away my soul, O God, with the wicked: nor my life with bloody men.*

*Ne perdas cum impiis, Deus, animam meam, et cum viris sanguinum vitam meam.*

**25{26}[10]**    *In whose hands are iniquities: their right hand is filled with gifts.*

*In quorum manibus iniquitates sunt, dextera eorum repleta est muneribus.*

**25{26}[9]** *Ne perdas cum impiis, Deus, animam meam;* take not away my soul, O God, with the wicked, sending it for a long time to hell,[29] but only until the third day, as it was often predicted. *Et,* and do not lose *cum viris sanguinum,* with bloody men, that is, sinners, *vitam meam,* my life, my bodily [life], delaying my Resurrection beyond three days.    **25{26}[10]** *In quorum,* in whose, the sinner's *manibus,* hands, that is, [their] works, *iniquitates sunt,* are iniquities: because their words are vicious. *Dextera eorum,* their right hand, that is, their action which appears just, *repleta est muneribus,* is filled with gifts: because they fall off from the

---

25  *Cf.* Eph. 3:17a.
26  Eph. 5:27a.
27  The Church triumphant is in heaven and is described here as "that heavenly place." As the Catechism of the Council of Trent puts it: "The Church triumphant is that assemblage of blessed spirits most glorious and most happy, . . . who have triumphed over the world, the flesh, and the most iniquitous Satan, and are now delivered from the troubles of this life and enjoy complete everlasting beatitude . . . and now in the possession of its heavenly country (*patria*)." *Catechismus Concilii Tridentini* (Paris: Gauthier Fratres 1831) (arts. VIII, IX), 76.
28  Heb. 2:10.
29  This is the limbo of the fathers, not the Hell of the damned. *See* footnote 7-27.

right way. For there is a gift from the tongue, namely, praise, or human favor; a gift from the hand, either money or earthly things; a gift from allegiance, as the devotion of a servant. Because these gifts of many are with the right hand, that is, appearing with justice, justice is tied up and corrupted. As Scripture attests, *Presents and gifts blind the eyes of judges.*[30]

---

**25{26}[11]** *But as for me, I have walked in my innocence: redeem me, and have mercy on me.*

> *Ego autem in innocentia mea ingressus sum; redime me, et miserere mei.*

**25{26}[12]** *My foot has stood in the direct way: in the churches I will bless you, O Lord.*

> *Pes meus stetit in directo; in ecclesiis benedicam te, Domine.*

**25{26}[11]** *Ego autem,* but as for me, Christ, your Son *in innocentia mea ingressus sum,* I have walked in my innocence: because I lived without guile and injustice; *redime me,* redeem me from the evils of the present age, *et miserere mei,* and have mercy on me, accelerating the resurrection of my body.    **25{26}[12]** *Pes meus,* my foot, that is the paths of all my course of life, *stetit in directo,* stood in the direct way, that is, it remained and was stable in the straight and right way[31] which leads to life: in the manner that is written, *that I love the Father: and as the Father has given me commandment, so do I.*[32] [*In ecclesiis bendicam te, Domine;* in the Church I will bless you, O Lord.][33]

---

## A LITERAL EXPLANATION OF CHRIST

**25{26}[4]** *I have not sat with the council of vanity: neither will I go in with the doers of unjust things.*

> *Non sedi cum concilio vanitatis, et cum iniqua gerentibus non introibo.*

---

30  Ecclus. 20:31a; Denis also cites to Ex. 23:8: *Neither shall you take bribes, which even blind the wise, and pervert the words of the just.*

31  *Cf.* Matt. 7:14: *How narrow is the gate, and strait is the way that leads to life: and few there are that find it!*

32  John 14:31.

33  E. N. The editor appears to have added this to the text to complete the verse. There is no commentary attached to it.

**25{26}[5]**  *I have hated the assembly of the malignant; and with the wicked I will not sit.*

*Odivi ecclesiam malignantium, et cum impiis non sedebo*

Finally, this place can be explained as referring literally to Christ: so that it befits to briefly touch on it. So Christ says:    **25{26}[4]** *Non sedi cum concilio vanitatis, I have not sat with the counsel of vanity,* namely, of the Jews, of whose counsel I never took part, or consented to; *et cum iniqua gerentibus, and with the doers of unjust things,* that is, with the Scribes and the Pharisees, who understood the law of Moses in a carnal way and ill-served it, *non introibo, I will not go in,* lest I be a participant in their perversity.    **25{26}[5]** *Odivi ecclesiam malignantium, I have hated the assembly of the malignant,* namely, of the previously mentioned Jews, who were rather of the synagogue of Satan than of God,[34] *et cum impiis, and with the wicked,* with these, *non sedebo, I will not sit* in the *chair of pestilence,*[35] teaching that which I do not do, in the manner that they did. But in using these words, Christ touched the reason why the Jews were afire with envy against him and killed him. For because he censured their life and sought to withdraw himself from it, therefore they hated him, in the way that is written in another place: *His life is not like other men's, and his ways are very different, and we are esteemed by him as triflers, and he abstains from our ways as from filthiness, and he prefers the latter end of the just, and glories that he has God for his father.*[36] *Therefore, let us try his patience, and let us condemn him to a most shameful death.*[37]

---

**25{26}[6]**  *I will wash my hands among the innocent; and will compass your altar, O Lord.*

*Lavabo inter innocentes manus meas, et circumdabo altare tuum, Domine.*

**25{26}[7]**  *That I may hear the voice of your praise: and tell of all your wondrous work.*

*Ut audiam vocem laudis, et enarrem universa mirabilia tua.*

---

34  Rev. 2:9b: *You are blasphemed by them that say they are Jews and are not, but are the synagogue of Satan.*
35  Ps. 1:1b.
36  Wis. 2:15b–16.
37  Wis. 2:19b–21a.

**25{26}[8]**  *I have loved, O Lord, the beauty of your house; and the place where your glory dwells.*

*Domine, dilexi decorem domus tuae, et locum habitationis gloriae tuae.*

**25{26}[6]** *Lavabo inter innocentes manus meas, I will wash my hands among the innocent,* that is, among the Apostles and the other of my disciples, I will live an immaculate life, and I will converse with them irreprehensibly; *et circumdabo altare tuum, Domine, and will compass your altar, O Lord,* that is the altar of the temple, which was in Jerusalem, in which Christ often entered and taught.[38] Or [alternatively], *the altar,* that is, that table in which Christ first celebrated the first Mass in the day of the Last Supper.[39] This altar Christ encompassed when he extended out to every single Apostle his Body and Blood.[40]  **25{26}[7]** *Ut audiam vocem laudis, that I may hear the voice of your praise:* for in both of the altars there were some good men and women praising God whose voices Christ readily heard; *et enarrem universa mirabilia tua, and tell of all your wondrous works.* For so did Christ encompass the altar of the temple and the altar of the cenacle, since he taught and proclaimed the *wondrous works* of God, as is written: *The Lord, whom you seek, ... shall come to his temple. . . . and he shall sit refining and cleansing the silver, and he shall purify the sons of Levi.*[41]  **25{26}[8]** *Domine, dilexi decorum domus tuae; I have loved, O Lord, the beauty of your house,* namely, the temple in Jerusalem, for which reason he cast out from it all the merchants and the money changers, and said: Make not the house of my Father a house of merchant traffic.[42] *Et, and he loved locum habitationis gloriae tuae, the place where your glory dwells,* because God declared that he wished to live in that temple.

---

38  Matt. 21:12, 23.

39  Matt. 26:26–28.

40  E. N. This is a lovely thought on Christ's sacramentally circumscribing the table (altar) at the Last Supper. The Church teaches that the "Eucharistic presence of Christ begins at the moment of the consecration and endures as long as the Eucharistic species subsist. Christ is present whole and entire in each of the species and whole and entire in each of their parts, in such a way that the breaking of the bread [or the sharing of the chalice of the precious Blood] does not divide Christ." CCC § 1377. This image is also captured by St. Thomas in his hymn *Sacris Solemnis (Panis Angelicus)* (English translation by John David Chambers):

| | |
|---|---|
| Corpus Dominicum | the Lord unto the Twelve |
| datum discipulis, | his Body gave to eat; |
| sic totum omnibus, | the whole to all, no less |
| quod totum singulis. | the whole to each did mete. |

41  Mal. 3:1, 3.

42  John 2:15b; *see also* Matt. 21:12; Mark 11:15; John 2:16.

**25{26}[9]**  *Take not away my soul, O God, with the wicked: nor my life with bloody men.*

*Ne perdas cum impiis, Deus, animam meam, et cum viris sanguinum vitam meam.*

**25{26}[10]**  *In whose hands are iniquities: their right hand is filled with gifts.*

*In quorum manibus iniquitates sunt, dextera eorum repleta est muneribus.*

**25{26}[9]** *Ne perdas cum impiis,* do not lose with the wicked Jews, *Deus, animam meam,* O God, my soul, abandoning me to their hands; *et cum viris sanguinum,* nor with bloody men, who killed the Prophets,[43] and who want to kill me, do not lose *vitam meam,* my life, my bodily life. **25{26}[10]**[44] *Dextera eorum repleta est muneribus, their right hand is filled with gifts,* because with money to my disciple they procured that he would betray me,[45] as it is written: *If it be good in your eyes, bring here my wages: and if not, be quiet. And they weighed for my wages thirty pieces of silver. And the Lord said to me: Cast it to the statuary, a handsome price, that I was prized at by them.*[46] The rest has already been satisfactorily expounded.

# ARTICLE LVIII

## TROPOLOGICAL EXPOSITION OF THE
## SAME TWENTY-FIFTH PSALM, OF
## EACH PERFECT MAN

**25{26}[1]**  *Unto the end, a Psalm for David. Judge me, O Lord, for I have walked in my innocence: and I have put my trust in the Lord, and shall not be weakened.*

*In finem. Psalmus David. Iudica me, Domine, quoniam ego in innocentia mea ingressus sum, et in Domino sperans non infirmabor.*

**25{26}[2]**  *Prove me, O Lord, and try me; burn my reins and my heart.*

*Proba me, Domine, et tenta me; ure renes meos et cor meum.*

---

43  Matt. 23:34.
44  E. N. Denis does not quote the beginning of this verse, *in quorum manibus iniquitates sunt, in whose hands are iniquities.*
45  Matt. 26:15.
46  Zach. 11:12b–13a.

HE PROPHET [DAVID] AGAIN SPEAKING IN
the person of a virtuous man says:    25{26}[1] *Iudica me, Domine,
Judge me, O Lord.* Since the Apostle [Paul] says, *It is a fearful thing to
fall into the hands of the living God;*[47] and Solomon, *Man knows not
whether he be worthy of love, or hatred: But all things are kept uncertain
for the time to come,*[48] it seems incautious and presumptuous to say
to the Lord, *Judge me, O Lord.* This is true inasmuch as according to
common consent it is so held that no man knows without a special
inspiration or revelation whether he is pleasing to God;[49] yet if someone has a share in true perfection, so that as to be able to say with
the Apostle [Paul], *I wish to be dissolved;*[50] and again: *Who then shall
separate us.... from the love of God, which is in Christ Jesus, our Lord?*[51]
And again, *For the Spirit himself gives testimony to our spirit, that we are
the sons of God:*[52] such a person can safely say, *Judge me, O Lord,* that
is, do to me according to my justice, and separate me now according to
merit from evil, and in the future separate me from it by recompense
or reward. Therefore, the holy man says *Judge me* not presuming on his
own merits, but from the testimony of his conscience, and from the
divine charity, because he desires to adhere to the Lord alone, and to
have no communion with evil.

And so, *Judge me, O Lord,* now with the judgment of discretion,[53] do
not make me to be like the ungodly to whom you do not give grace but you

---

47  Heb. 10:31. E. N. On Denis's attribution of Hebrews to St. Paul, *see* footnote 8-34.

48  Eccl. 9:1b–2a. E. N. Verse 2 continues to describe the inscrutability of Provi-
    dence: *because all things equally happen to the just and to the wicked, to the good
    and to the evil, to the clean and to the unclean, to him that offers victims, and to
    him that despises sacrifices. As the good is, so also is the sinner: as the perjured, so
    he also that swears truth.*

49  E. N. As is made clear by the Council of Trent, it is a dogma of the Faith that
    without a special inspiration or revelation no one can know with certainty that
    he is in a state of sanctifying grace or belongs to the number of the elect and is
    saved. DS 1534, 1540, 1565, 1566. That this is so does not impugn the theological
    virtue of hope.

50  Cf. Phil. 1:23: *But I am straitened between two: having a desire to be dissolved
    [desiderium habens dissolvi] and to be with Christ, a thing by far the better.* Denis
    states *cupio dissolvi,* a foreshortened or compressed statement of St. Paul's desire
    to be "dissolved and to be with Christ." It is sometimes rendered *cupio solvi.* In his
    controversial *Biathanatos,* John Donne refers to this desire to be dissolved with
    Christ as the greatest perfection of charity, a perfection — in a phraseology redo-
    lent of St. Anselm's ontological argument — "that than which none can be greater."

51  Rom. 8:35a, 39b.

52  Rom. 8:16.

53  On the meaning of "judgment of discretion" *see* footnote 1-39.

abandon; but give to me an increase of graces and deliver me from those things deserving of evil. This private judgment is what Job complained of, with respect to the fact that he sustained the evil of punishment: *The Lord lives who has taken away my judgment.*[54] And this is what the most pious Ezechiel desired, who said: *I beseech you, O Lord, remember how I have walked before you in truth, and with a perfect heart.*[55] For this reason, the Prophet [David] added why he dared to implore judgment: *Quoniam ego in innocentia mea ingressus sum,* for I have walked in my innocence by the paths of your commandments, and by a manner of life giving no offense or doing no harm to others. Because, therefore, I know that I will be measured by that measure I mete out,[56] and I am not conscious of any injustice against God or neighbor, therefore I do not fear to be judged. And so the good man confesses his perfection, not by inanely boasting about himself or preferring himself to others, but in humbly giving thanks to God.[57] For this is what we often read that holy men did, as Job says: *Until I die I will not depart from my innocence.*[58] And Jeremiah: *I have not desired the day of man, you know.*[59] In what, therefore, did the Pharisee who said, *I give you thanks that I am not as the rest of men,*[60] sin? Of course, it is immediately evident from his words that he slighted others and he did not sincerely attribute to God his good. For this reason, he exalted himself and esteemed himself above others. This is directly contrary to what is written: *The greater you are, the more humble yourself in all things.*[61]

Again, that a perfect man does not say this out of any vanity or self-exaltation, or confident in his own virtue is apparent from that which follows: *et in Domino sperans non infirmabor,* and I have put my trust in the Lord, and I shall not be weakened: that is, I desire to be judged, therefore, because I trust in God; and, trusting in him, that I will not become weakened in soul, that is, I will not be vanquished by any temptation or

---

54  Job 27:2a.
55  2 Kings 20:3a.
56  *Cf.* Matt. 7:2: *For with what judgment you judge, you shall be judged: and with what measure you mete, it shall be measured to you again.*
57  E. N. He will know, in the words of St. Augustine: "God crowns his own merits, not your merits, at least if they are of yourself, and they are not from him. For if these are such, they are evil, which God does not crown; but if they are good, they are the gifts of God." (*Dona sua coronat Deus, non merita tua, si tibi a te ipso, non ab illo sunt merita tua. Haec enim si talia sunt, mala sunt; quae non coronat Deus: si autem bona sunt, Dei dona sunt.*) *De grat. et lib. arb.,* 6, 15, PL 44, 890.
58  Job 27:5b.
59  Jer. 17:16.
60  Luke 18:11.
61  Ecclus. 3:20a.

dejected by any adversity, but day by day I will be strengthened in and make headway in all grace. Hence, I still dare to say:    **25{26}[2]** *Proba me, Domine, Prove me, O Lord*, in adversity and prosperity, and through your paternal reproofs, examine me — not as if you do not know me, but so that you show me proved and you may crown me — just like you proved holy Job, who said: The Lord *tried me as gold that passes through the fire.*[62] Thus it is that I want to be proved, because I know *all that will live godly in Christ Jesus, shall suffer persecution.*[63] And, as the Apostle [Paul] says in the Acts of the Apostles, *through many tribulations we must enter into the kingdom of heaven.*[64] Therefore, *prove me, O Lord*, so that I might belong to their company, of which it is said: *As gold in the furnace he has proved them, and as a victim of a holocaust he has received them.*[65] And so now is added:

*Et tenta me, and try me.* The word "to try"[66] means to enter upon the experience of something. But God knows all things, and therefore it is not necessary for God on his own behalf to tempt. It is for this reason that James in his epistle says: *Let no man, when he is tempted, say that he is tempted by God. For God is not a tempter of evils, and he tempts no man.*[67] But we ought to be aware that there are diverse ends to temptation. For sometimes one person tempts another so that he may be harmed or he may fall; but sometimes, so that he might know; and yet sometimes so that he might be instructed or aided. The devil and the world tempt the first way: and of this kind of temptation that is understood when, in the Lord's Prayer, we say, *And lead us not unto temptation.*[68] The man who does not know tests in the second way, to certify (*certificari*) something desiring to know what sort of thing it is.[69] God tempts in the third way, in the manner that is reflected in Genesis: *God tempted Abraham.*[70] Now whether someone ought to desire temptations of the devil or the world, of this different persons think different things; but it would seem that the perfect can desire them without danger, because they rejoice in adversity. Yet they desire

---

62  Job 23:10b.

63  2 Tim. 3:12.

64  Acts 14:21b. E. N. Denis replaces "kingdom of God" with "kingdom of heaven."

65  Wis. 3:6a.

66  E. N. The Latin *tentare* (to tempt, try, test) and *tentatio* (temptation, trial, proof) is used throughout. It is variously translated as try, tempt, test depending upon context.

67  James 1:13.

68  Matt. 6:13.

69  E. N. The Latin word *certificari* is derived from *certus* (fixed, sure, certain) plus the root of *facere* (to make, to do); thus, to be certain of the truth of something, to vouch, or confirm.

70  Gen. 22:1a.

them under the direction and with the presupposition of divine aid.[71]

*Ure renes meos, burn my reins,*[72] that is, by the labor of abstinence and by the affliction of penance restrain and extinguish in me carnal delights and carnal faults: thus *stet cor meum, my heart,* that is, the inordinate affections and the thoughts and spiritual vices. Or [it might be understood] thus: *Burn* with the fire of divine love and ignite with the flame of charity *my reins,* that is my sensitive appetite, which is divided into concupiscible and irascible parts[73] *and my heart,* that is, the intellectual appetite or the will, so that the fire of the Holy Spirit may so vehemently ignite the will that love or this fire might flow into this lower appetite, and subject it all to reason and a holy will. Or [yet again] thus: *Burn,* with the fire of tribulation in the present, *my reins and my heart,* that is, my body and soul in order that in this way I might be cleansed (*expurger*) from vice in this age, so that I might not be forced to endure other punishments (*poenam*) in Purgatory, and so that I might suffer with (*compatiar*), and conform to, Christ in mind and body, as is becoming a servant to suffer with, and to conform to, his Lord.

---

25{26}[3] *For your mercy is before my eyes; and I am well pleased with your truth.*

    *Quoniam misericordia tua ante oculos meos est, et complacui in veritate tua.*

25{26}[4] *I have not sat with the council of vanity: neither will I go in with the doers of unjust things.*

    *Non sedi cum concilio vanitatis, et cum iniqua gerentibus non introibo.*

Therefore, O Lord, all this I trustingly ask of you,  25{26}[3] *Quoniam misericordia tua ante oculos meos est, for your mercy is before my eyes,* that is, because I know your kindliness, I always take it into consideration, and I never want to depart from this trust; *et complacui in veritate tua, and I am well pleased with your truth,* that is, in the true justice of your justice. For the innocent and the just are very pleasing to you. And for this reason, I please you because  25{26}[4] *Non sedi cum*

---

71  Other versions read presumption [instead of presupposition].

72  E. N. For "reins" see footnote 7-10.

73  E. N. In the sensitive part of man, there are two appetitive powers, the concupiscible and the irascible. The concupiscible power is that by which one is inclined to seek what is a suitable sensible good and to flee from what is hurtful. The irascible power is that power by which one resists any attacks which hinder obtaining what is suitable and which threaten harm. See *ST,* Ia, q. 81, art. 2.

*consilio vanitatis, I have not sat with the council of vanity*, that is, I have not sought to obtain the agreement of, nor have I provided assistance to, vain counselors: therefore I am blessed, for as an earlier Psalm says it: *Blessed is the man who has not walked in the counsel of the ungodly.*[74]

---

**25{26}[6]**  *I will wash my hands among the innocent; and will compass your altar, O Lord.*

*Lavabo inter innocentes manus meas, et circumdabo altare tuum, Domine.*

**25{26}[7]**  *That I may hear the voice of your praise: and tell of all your wondrous work.*

*Ut audiam vocem laudis, et enarrem universa mirabilia tua.*

**25{26}[6]**[75] *Et circumdabo altare tuum, Domine; and I will compass your altar, O Lord.* According to Ambrose[76] the altar of God is Christ as man:[77] for in him and by him ought all our works and sacrifices be offered and done. What is therefore, *I will compass your altar, O Lord*, other than, I will adhere to your Son, Jesus Christ, and I will approach him, I will follow him, and by contemplation I will encompass him? And also the altar of God is a devout man in which is offered to God *an afflicted spirit.*[78] And so *I will compass your altar, O Lord*, that is, I will return into myself, I will scrutinize my mind, and I will adorn it with holy affections.  **25{26}[7]** *Ut audiam, that I may hear*, with the ears of the heart, of which the Gospel says, *He that has ears to hear, let him hear;*[79] *vocem laudis, the voice of praise*, that is, the doctrine of Christ and sacred

---

74  Ps. 1:1a.

75  E. N. Denis skips the rest of verse 4, the entirety of verse 5, and the first part of verse 6 in this discussion, skipping directly to this part of verse 6.

76  E. N. St. Ambrose (A. D. *ca.* 340–397) was Bishop of Milan. St. Ambrose is a Doctor of the Church and was instrumental in the conversion of St. Augustine to Catholic Christianity from the Manichaean heresy. St. Ambrose was a notable opponent of the Arian heresy, and he wrote a number of books on both theological and moral topics, including Scriptural commentaries, homilies, and hymns.

77  *Altare Dei est Christus ut homo.* St. Ambrose, in the second chapter of his work on the Sacraments, states: *Introibo ad altare Dei. . . . Forma corporis altare est, et corpus Christi est in altari.* "I will enter unto the altar of God. . . . The altar is a type of the body, and the body of Christ is on the altar." *De Sacramentis*, IV, 7, PL 16, 437. And also later where St. Ambrose asks rhetorically: *Quid est enim altare Christi nisi forma corporis Christi?* "For what else is the altar of Christ but the type of the body of Christ?" *Ibid.*, V, 7, PL 16, 447.

78  Ps. 50:19a.

79  Luke 8:8b.

Scripture: as it is written, *He that is of God, hears the words of God;*[80] and again, *Blessed are they who hear the word of God, and keep it.*[81] *Et enarrem universa mirabilia tua, and tell of all your wondrous works,* that is, so that which I hear and learn regarding the divine praise and the sacred Scripture I will announce to others, or at the very least repeat it over and over again in my own mouth, praising and blessing the Lord, who has done so many wondrous things for men, as the divine Scriptures attest.

---

**25{26}[8]**  *I have loved, O Lord, the beauty of your house; and the place where your glory dwells.*

*Domine, dilexi decorem domus tuae, et locum habitationis gloriae tuae.*

**25{26}[8]** *Domine, dilexi decorum domus tuae; I have loved, O Lord, the beauty of your house,* that is, the prosperous condition, the making of progress, and the perfection of the faithful,[82] the congregation of which is the *house* of God, which is called the Church. For we ought to desire, to pray for, and to love most eagerly the common good, and the spiritual progress of the whole Church, so that it may become for us that which Jeremiah said: *This is a lover of his brethren, and of the people of Israel: this is he that prays much for the people, and for all the holy city.*[83] Or [we can look at it this way], *I have loved the beauty of your house,* that is, the interior splendor and holiness of my soul, desiring to show you a heart that is an immaculate and pleasing dwelling place, as I have been counseled: *Be prepared to meet your God, O Israel.*[84] And I have loved *et locum habitationis gloriae tuae, and the place where your glory dwells,* that is, the celestial mansion and the kingdom of heaven. Of which, the Apostle [Paul] says: *For we know, if our earthly house of this habitation be dissolved, that we have a building of God, a house not made with hands,*

---

80  John 8:47a.
81  Luke 11:28.
82  E. N. The three verbs are *prosperitatem, profectum,* and *perfectionem. Prosperitas* can be translated by prosperity, good fortune, or even a desirable state or condition of health. I have opted for "prosperous condition" since it seems to suggest the state of sanctifying grace, the first step in the three stages or ages or ways of the spiritual life: the purgative, illuminative, and unitive, or the three "classes" of Christians, beginners, proficient, and the perfect, or the three kinds of prayer, vocal, mental, and contemplation. It is this sort of progressive spiritual dynamism that Denis seems to want to express.
83  2 Mac. 15:14.
84  Amos 4:12b.

*eternal in heaven.*[85] And the Savior himself: *I go to prepare a place for you.... I will come again, and will take you to myself; that where I am, you also may be.*[86] This place, O Lord, I love, not for the sake of place, but because of you, the occupant and the Lord of that place, so that I might see you with my eyes, *the King* of glory *in his beauty.*[87]

---

### SPECIALLY APPLICABLE TO PRIESTS

25{26}[6]    *I will wash my hands among the innocent; and will compass your altar, O Lord.*

    *Lavabo inter innocentes manus meas, et circumdabo altare tuum, Domine.*

25{26}[7]    *That I may hear the voice of your praise: and tell of all your wondrous work.*

    *Ut audiam vocem laudis, et enarrem universa mirabilia tua.*

25{26}[8]    *I have loved, O Lord, the beauty of your house; and the place where your glory dwells.*

    *Domine, dilexi decorem domus tuae, et locum habitationis gloriae tuae.*

Further all of this Psalm can be especially applied to priests, in particular from that part that says,   25{26}[6] *Lavabo inter innocentes manus meas, I will wash my hands among the innocent,*[88] The priest of Christ therefore says this devoutly and with dignity: *Lavabo, I will wash,* when I

---

85  2 Cor. 5:1.

86  John 14:2b–3.

87  Is. 33:17a.

88  This, of course, the Church recognizes in her liturgy. In the Latin rite, the priest washes his hands at the so-called "Lavabo," named precisely after the first word of the recitation of Psalm 25:6-12, which the priest prays during the ritual washing of his hands. In his *Summa Theologiae,* St Thomas Aquinas observes: "The washing of the hands is done in the celebration of Mass out of reverence for this sacrament; and this for two reasons: first, because we are not wont to handle precious objects except the hands be washed; hence it seems indecent for anyone to approach so great a sacrament with hands that are, even literally, unclean. Secondly, on account of its signification, because, as Dionysius says (*Eccl. Hier.* iii), the washing of the extremities of the limbs denotes cleansing from even the smallest sins, according to John 13:10: 'He that is washed needeth not but to wash his feet.' And such cleansing is required of him who approaches this sacrament ... hence it is said in Psalm 25:6: 'I will wash my hands among the innocent.'" ST, IIIa, q. 83, art. 5 ad 1. (trans. Fathers of English Dominican Province).

draw near to the celebration of Mass, *inter innocentes, among the innocents,* that is, with the saints and the true priests of the New Law, which is to harm no one, but by word and example to benefit all; *manus meas, my hands,* not only bodily with which I will handle the Sacraments of Christ, but also my affections, thoughts, and works: these I wash in confession, because as Scripture attests, *all is washed in confession.*[89] But also the priest before he approaches to the celebration of Mass, he washes his fingers — or better, washes the tips of his fingers. [He does this] first, to show reverence for the Sacrament; second, as a sign of spiritual washing by which it behooves the soul to be cleansed from the stain of sins. For the washing of the tips of the fingers, according to Dionysius,[90] signifies the wiping away of venial fault. For the priest standing before God ought not only to abhor, confess, and flee mortal or grave sins, but he also ought to seek to avoid small sins, so that he may be fully clean and collected of soul, and fervent and steadfast in affection, having Christ and his Passion and all other benefits of God firmly impressed in his heart.

*Et circumdabo altare tuum, Domine; and I will compass your altar, O Lord,* namely the material altar of the church, between which opposite corners I will stand when I celebrate Mass. **25{26}[7]** *Ut audiam vocem laudis, that I may hear the voice of your praise,* that is, the song of the Church, and the response of the choir, or at least [the responses] of my ministers, who jointly praise God, and worthily participate in the mystery of such a great Sacrament. *Et ennarem, and I will tell* at the Mass, *universa mirabilita tua, of all your wondrous works,* that is, all the wondrous mysteries of Christ, namely, the Incarnation, the Passion, the Resurrection, and the Ascension, which are recalled in the office of the Mass. **25{26} [8]** *Domine, dilexi decorum domus tuae; I have loved, O Lord, the beauty of your house,* that is, the devotion of the minister of the altar and the people who do not unworthily celebrate Mass or take Communion, lest we bring it about that we be *guilty of the Body and of the Blood* of Christ.[91]

---

89   *Omnia in confessione lavantur.* It is not in Scripture *in haec verba,* but it is a common summarization of the Scriptural teaching of confession, and was used, among others, by St. Francis of Assisi, St. Bernard of Clairvaux, and Peter Cellensis. Denis's text cites to Ps. 31:5 and Prov. 28:13 for scriptural support. Ps. 31:5: *I have acknowledged my sin to you, and my injustice I have not concealed. I said I will confess against myself my injustice to the Lord: and you have forgiven the wickedness of my sin.* Prov. 28:13: *He that hides his sins, shall not prosper: but he that shall confess, and forsake them, shall obtain mercy.*

90   For Dionysius (Pseudo-Dionysius), *see* footnote P-36. The reference is *Ecclesiastical Hierarchies,* III, 9.

91   1 Cor. 11:27.

*Et locum habitationis gloriae tuae, and the place where your glory dwells,*
because I desire now in the Church militant to handle Christ under the
sacramental veils so reverently and faithfully, so that afterwards I may
be found worthy in the Church triumphant also to see clearly all those
for whom I pray and celebrate: as he promised to the worthy minister:
*I will manifest myself to him.*[92]

---

**25{26}[9]** *Take not away my soul, O God, with the wicked: nor my life*
*with bloody men.*

*Ne perdas cum impiis, Deus, animam meam, et cum viris san-*
*guinum vitam meam.*

**25{26}[9]** *Ne perdas cum ipiis, take not away . . . with the wicked,* that
is, the evil priests and ungrateful men, *Deus, animam meam, my soul, O*
*God,* deserting it in the presence of grace, and repelling it in the future
of glory; *et cum viris sanguinibus, and with bloody men,* who eat the
Body of Christ and drink his Blood unworthily,[93] or entirely abstain
from sacred Communion out of hate of Christ, or from their negligence,
*take not away vitam meam, my life,* abandoning me to live viciously and
dishonorably, and afterwards damning me in Hell.

---

**25{26}[11]** *But as for me, I have walked in my innocence: redeem me, and*
*have mercy on me.*

*Ego autem in innocentia mea ingressus sum; redime me, et*
*miserere mei.*

**25{26}[12]** *My foot has stood in the direct way: in the churches I will bless*
*you, O Lord.*

*Pes meus stetit in directo; in ecclesiis benedicam te, Domine.*

**25{26}[11]**[94] *Ego autem in innocentia mea ingressus sum; but as for me,*
*I have walked in innocence,* walking about in this world by faith, hope, and
charity. And so, O Lord, *redime me, redeem me,* so I do not fall into fault,
and I lose innocence I have thus far managed to preserve. For I ought
not rest secure during this life of exile, but rather I should *walk solicitous*
*with the Lord.*[95] *Et miserere mei, and have mercy on me,* overlooking the

---

92  John 14:21b.
93  *Cf.* 1 Cor. 11:29.
94  Denis skips verse 10, which is curious since it is part of the priest's *Lavabo* ritual.
95  Mal. 6:8b.

imperfections of my justice, which are *as the rag of a menstruous woman*,[96] if it is compared to the perfection of divine justice, and to the sanctity of the eternal Mind, substantially, totally, and unboundedly holy.   **25{26}** [**12**] *Pes meus, my foot,* that is, the manner of life which tends towards you, *stetit in directo, stood in the direct way,* that is, in the observance of your precepts. *In ecclesiis, in the churches,* that is among the faithful, *benedicam te, Domine, I will bless you, O Lord,* praising the benefits you have conceded to me, and glorifying your blessed name eternally. And the rest omitted [of this Psalm] is seen sufficiently explained in the preceding exposition.

See how from this compact and splendid Psalm we hear that which pertains to the perfect Christian. If therefore at whatever hour we come upon it,[97] we should return thanks to God and resolve toward perfection. But if the mentioned perfections of perfect men are far from us, let us groan, let us amend ourselves, and in accordance with the word of the glorious Apostle [Paul], *with fear and trembling* we should *work out* our salvation.[98]

# PRAYER

OD, AUTHOR OF THE INNOCENT AND sanctifier of righteous souls, burn our reins and our heart, putting into us the peace of a pure life, that we may not sit with the council of vanity, and so that standing with our feet standing in the direct way, we may be worthy to bless your name in the Church.

*Deus innocentiae auctor, et rectarum mentium sanctificator, ure renes nostros et cor nostrum, castimoniae pacem nobis inserendo; non sedeamus cum consilio vanitatis: ut stantibus pedibus nostris in directo, digne in ecclesiis nomen tuum benedicamus.*

## *Finis*

VOLUME I

---

96  Is. 64:6a.
97  E. N. Whenever this Psalm is encountered in the monastic hours of the Divine Office.
98  Phil. 2:12b.

## ABOUT THE TRANSLATOR

NDREW M. GREENWELL IS A MAR-
ried Catholic layman, with three children and four
grandchildren. He is a civil trial and appellate lawyer based
in Corpus Christi, Texas, who has written articles for Catholic Online and for a number of years wrote a blog on the
natural moral law called *Lex Christianorum*. He has translated
works from German, Latin, French, and Italian into English.
He is a member of the Latin Mass Community at St. John
the Baptist Church in Corpus Christi, Texas. Angelico Press
is publishing his translations of all of Denis the Carthusian's
works on the Mass and the Eucharist.

CPSIA information can be obtained
at www.ICGtesting.com
Printed in the USA
LVHW020912170321
681674LV00004B/28